Alexander Cunningham

Archeological Survey of India Volume I.

Alexander Cunningham

Archeological Survey of India Volume I.

ISBN/EAN: 9783741170331

Manufactured in Europe, USA, Canada, Australia, Japa

Cover: Foto ©ninafisch / pixelio.de

Manufactured and distributed by brebook publishing software (www.brebook.com)

Alexander Cunningham

Archeological Survey of India Volume I.

ARCHÆOLOGICAL SURVEY
OF
INDIA.

FOUR REPORTS
MADE DURING THE YEARS
1862-63-64-65,

BY

ALEXANDER CUNNINGHAM, C. S. I.,
MAJOR-GENERAL, ROYAL ENGINEERS (BENGAL RETIRED);
DIRECTOR GENERAL OF THE ARCHÆOLOGICAL SURVEY OF INDIA;
MEMBER, ROYAL ASIATIC SOCIETY; HON. MEMBER, BENGAL ASIATIC SOCIETY;
MEMBER, ANTHROPOLOGICAL INSTITUTE;
MEMBER, NUMISMATIC SOCIETY.

VOLUME I.

"What is aimed at is an accurate description, illustrated by plans, measurements, drawings or photographs, and by copies of inscriptions, of such remains as most deserve notice, with the history of them so far as it may be traceable, and a record of the traditions that are preserved regarding them." —— LORD CANNING.

"What the learned world demand of us in India is to be quite certain of our data, to place the monumental record before them exactly as it now exists, and to interpret it faithfully and literally." —— JAMES PRINSEP.

Bengal Asiatic Society's Journal, 1838, p. 227.

SIMLA:
PRINTED AT THE GOVERNMENT CENTRAL PRESS.
1871.

PREFACE.

THE matter contained in these two volumes is the result of the archæological survey which I conducted during four consecutive years from 1862 to 1865. The object of this survey cannot be better stated than in the memorandum which I laid before Lord Canning in November 1861, and which led to my immediate appointment as Archæological Surveyor to the Government of India, as notified in the following minute:

Minute by the Right Hon'ble the GOVERNOR GENERAL OF INDIA in Council on the Antiquities of Upper India,—dated 22nd January 1862.

"IN November last, when at Allahabad, I had some communications with Colonel A. Cunningham, then the Chief Engineer of the North-Western Provinces, regarding an investigation of the archæological remains of Upper India.

"It is impossible to pass through that part,—or indeed, so far as my experience goes, any part—of the British territories in India without being struck by the neglect with which the greater portion of the architectural remains, and of the traces of by-gone civilization have been treated, though many of these, and some which have had least notice, are full of beauty and interest.

"By 'neglect' I do not mean only the omission to restore them, or even to arrest their decay; for this would be a task which, in many cases, would require an expenditure of labour and money far greater than any Government of India could reasonably bestow upon it.

"But so far as the Government is concerned, there has been neglect of a much cheaper duty,—that of investigating and placing on record, for the instruction of future generations, many particulars that might still be rescued from oblivion, and throw light upon the early history of England's great dependency; a history which, as time moves on, as the country becomes more easily accessible and traversable, and as Englishmen are led to give more thought to India than such as barely suffices to hold it and govern it, will assuredly occupy, more and more, the attention of the intelligent and enquiring classes in European countries.

"It will not be to our credit, as an enlightened ruling power, if we continue to allow such fields of investigation, as the remains of the old Buddhist capital in Behar, the vast ruins of Kanouj, the plains round Delhi, studded with ruins more thickly than even the Campagna of Rome, and many others, to remain without more examination than they have hitherto received. Every thing that has hitherto been done in this way has been done by private persons, imperfectly and without system. It is impossible not to feel that there are European Governments, which, if they had held our rule in India, would not have allowed this to be said.

"It is true that in 1844, on a representation from the Royal Asiatic Society, and in 1847, in accordance with detailed suggestions from Lord Hardinge, the Court of Directors gave a liberal sanction to certain arrangements for examining, delineating, and recording some of the chief antiquities of India. But for one reason or another, mainly perhaps owing to the officer entrusted with the task having other work to do, and owing to his early death, very little seems to have resulted from this endeavour. A few drawings of antiquities, and some remains, were transmitted to the India House, and some 15 or 20 papers were contributed by Major Kittoe and Major Cunningham to the Journals of the Asiatic Society; but, so far as the Government is concerned, the scheme appears to have been lost sight of within two or three years of its adoption.

"I enclose a memorandum drawn up by Colonel Cunningham, who has, more than any other officer on this side of India, made the antiquities of the country his study, and who has here sketched the course of proceeding which a more complete and systematic archæological investigation should, in his opinion, take.

"I think it good,—and none the worse for being a beginning on a moderate scale. It will certainly cost very little in itself, and will commit the Government to no future or unforeseen expense. For it does not contemplate the spending of any money upon repairs and preservation. This, when done at all, should be done upon a separate and full consideration of any case which may seem to claim it. What is aimed at is an accurate description,—illustrated by plans, measurements, drawings or photographs, and by copies of inscriptions,—of such remains as most deserve notice, with the history of them so far as it may be traceable, and a record of the traditions that are retained regarding them.

"I propose that the work be entrusted to Colonel Cunningham, with the understanding that it continue during the present and the following cold season, by which time a fair judgment of its utility and interest may be formed. It may then be persevered in, and expanded, or otherwise dealt with as may seem good at the time.

"Colonel Cunningham should receive Rs. 450 a month, with Rs. 250 when in the field to defray the cost of making surveys and measurements, and of other mechanical assistance. If something more should be necessary to obtain the services of a native subordinate of the Medical or Public Works Department, competent to take photographic views, it should be given.

"It would be premature to determine how the results of Colonel Cunningham's labours should be dealt with; but whilst the Government would of course retain a proprietary right in them for its own purposes, I recommend that the interests of Colonel Cunningham should be considered in the terms upon which they may be furnished to the Public."

Memorandum by COLONEL A. CUNNINGHAM, of Engineers, regarding a proposed investigation of the archæological remains of Upper India.

"DURING the one hundred years of British dominion in India, the Government has done little or nothing towards the preservation of its ancient monuments, which, in the almost total absence of any written history, form the only reliable sources of information as to the early condition of the country. Some of these monuments have already endured for ages, and are likely to last for ages still to come; but there are many others which are daily suffering from the effects of time, and which must soon disappear altogether, unless preserved by the accurate drawings and faithful descriptions of the archæologist.

"All that has hitherto been done towards the illustration of ancient Indian history has been due to the unaided efforts of private individuals. These researches consequently have always been desultory and unconnected and frequently incomplete, owing partly to the short stay which individual officers usually make at any particular place, and partly to the limited leisure which could be devoted to such pursuits.

"Hitherto the Government has been chiefly occupied with the extension and consolidation of empire, but the establishment of the Trigonometrical Survey shows that it has not been unmindful of the claims of science. It would redound equally to the honor of the British Government to institute a careful and systematic investigation of all the existing monuments of ancient India.

"In describing the ancient geography of India, the elder Pliny, for the sake of clearness, follows the footsteps of Alexander the Great. For a similar reason, in the present proposed investigation, I would follow the footsteps of the Chinese pilgrim Hwen Thsang, who, in the seventh century of our era, traversed India from west to east and back again for the purpose of visiting all the famous sites of Buddhist history and tradition. In the account of his travels, although the Buddhist remains are described in most detail with all their attendant legends and traditions, yet the numbers and appearance of the Brahmanical temples are also noted, and the travels of the Chinese pilgrim thus hold the same place in the history of India, which those of Pausanias hold in the history of Greece.

"In the North-Western Provinces and Bihár the principal places to be visited and examined are the following, which are also shown in the accompanying sketch map:

"1. *Khálsi*, on the Jumna, where the river leaves the hills.—At this place there still exists a large boulder stone, covered with one of Asoka's inscriptions, in which the names of Antiochus, Ptolemy, Antigonus, Magas, and Alexander are all recorded. This portion of the inscription, which on the rock of Kapurdigiri (in the Yusufzai plain), and of Dhauli (in Cuttack) is much mutilated and abraded, is here in perfect preservation. A copy of this inscription and an account of the ruins would therefore be valuable.

"II. *Haridwár*, on the Ganges, with the opposite city Mayurpoora.

"III. *Manddwar, Sambhal,* and *Sahaswán,* in Rohilkhand.

"IV. *Karsána* near Khásganj.

"V. *Sankissa,* between Mainpuri and Fattehgarh, where it is known that many remains of Buddhism still exist. This was one of the sacred places amongst the Buddhists.

"VI. *Mathura.*—In one of the ancient mounds outside the city the remains of a large monastery have been lately discovered. Numerous statues, sculptured pillars, and inscribed bases of columns, have been brought to light. Amongst these inscriptions, some, which are dated in an unknown era, are of special interest and value. They belong most probably to the first century of the Christian era, and one of them records the name of the great King Huvishka, who is presumed to be the same as the Indo-Scythian King Hushka.

"VII. *Delhi.*—The Hindu remains of Delhi are few, but interesting. The stone pillars of Asoka and the iron pillar are well known, but the other remains have not yet been described, although none have been more frequently visited than the magnificent ruined cloisters around the Kutb Minar, which belong to the period of the Great Tuár dynasty.

"VIII. *Kanouj.*—No account of the ruins of this once celebrated capital has yet been published. Several ruins are known to exist, but it may be presumed that many more would be brought to light by a careful survey of the site.

"IX. *Kausámbi.*—On the Jumna 30 miles above Allahabad.—The true position of this once famous city has only lately been ascertained. It has not yet been visited, but it may be confidently expected that its remains would well repay examination.

"X. *Allahabad.*—The only existing relics of antiquity that I am aware of are the well known pillar of Asoka and the holy tree in one of the underground apartments of the fort. Many buildings once existed, but I am afraid that they were all destroyed to furnish materials for the erection of the fort in the reign of Akbar.

"XI. To the south of Allahabad there are the ruins of *Kajráho* and *Mahoba,* the two capitals of the ancient Chándel

Rajas of Bundlekhand. The remains at Kajráho are more numerous and in better preservation than those of any other ancient city that I have seen. Several long and important inscriptions still exist, which give a complete genealogy of the Chándel dynasty for about 400 years.

"XII. *Banáras.*—The magnificent tope of Sárnáth is well known; but no description of the tope, nor of the ruins around it, has yet been published. At a short distance from Banáras is the inscribed pillar of Bhitari, which requires to be re-examined.

"XIII. *Jonpur.*—Although the existing remains at this place are Muhammadan, yet it is well known that the principal buildings were originally Hindu temples, of which the cloisters still remain almost unaltered. These ruins have not yet been described, but from my own success, in the beginning of this year, in discovering a Sanskrit inscription built into one of the arches, I believe that a careful examination would be rewarded with further discoveries of interest illustrative of the great Ráthor dynasty of Kanouj.

"XIV. *Fyzábád.*—The ruins of Ajudhya have not been described. Numerous very ancient coins are found in the site and several ruined mounds are known to exist there; but no account has yet been published. As the birth-place of Ráma and as the scene of one of the early events in Buddha's life, Ajudhya has always been held equally sacred, both by Brahmins and Buddhists, and I feel satisfied that a systematic examination of its ruins would be rewarded by the discovery of many objects of interest.

"XV. *Srávasti.*—Even the site of this once celebrated city is unknown, but it may be looked for between Fyzábád and Gorakhpur.

"XVI. *Kapilavastu*, the birth-place of Buddha, was held in special veneration by his followers, but its site is unknown.

"XVII. *Kusinagara*, the scene of Buddha's death, was one of the most holy places in India in the estimation of Buddhists, but its site is at present unknown. It may, however, confidently be looked for along the line of the Gunduk river. At *Kapila* and *Kusinagara*, the scenes of Buddha's birth and death, numerous topes and stately monasteries once existed to attest the pious munificence of his votaries. The ruins of many of these buildings must still exist, and would no doubt reward a careful search. At *Mathia, Radhia,* and *Bakra,* in Tirhut, stone pillars still remain, and in other places ruined topes were seen by Major Kittoe; but no description of these remains has yet been made known.

"XVIII. *Vaisáli.*—This city was the scene of the second Buddhist synod, and was one of the chief places of note amongst Buddhists. At Bassar, to the north of Patna, one tope is known to exist, but no search has yet been made for other remains. The people of Vaisáli were known to Ptolemy, who calls them Passalæ.

"XIX. *Patna.*—The ancient Palibothra. I am not aware that there are any existing remains at Patna, but numerous coins, gems, and seals are annually found in the bed of the river.

"XX. *Rajagriha,* between Patna and Gaya, was the capital of Magadha in the time of Buddha. Some of the principal scenes of his life occurred in its neighbourhood, and the place was consequently held in very great veneration by all Buddhists. Every hill and every stream had been made holy by Buddha's presence, and the whole country around Rajagriha was covered with buildings to commemorate the principal events of his life. Numerous ruined topes, sculptured friezes, and inscribed pillars still remain scattered over the country as lasting proofs of the high veneration in which this religious capital of Buddhism was held by the people.

"In this rapid sketch of the places that seem worthy of examination, I have confined myself entirely to the North-Western Provinces, and Bihár, as containing most of the cities celebrated in the ancient history of India. But to make this account of Indian archæological remains more complete, it would be necessary to examine the ancient cities of the Panjáb, such as Taxila, Sákala, and Jálandhar on the west, the caves and inscribed rocks of Cuttack and Orissa on the east, and the topes and other remains of Ujain and Bhilsa, with the caves of Dhamnar and Kholvi in Central India.

"I believe that it would be possible to make a careful examination of all the places which I have noted during two cold seasons. The first season might be devoted to a survey of Gaya and Rajagriha, and of all the remains in Tirhut to the eastward of Banáras and Gorakhpur, while the survey of all to the westward of Banáras would occupy the second season.

"I would attach to the description of each place a general survey of the site, showing clearly the positions of all the existing remains, with a ground plan of every building or ruin of special note, accompanied by drawings and sections of all objects of interest. It would be desirable also to have photographic views of many of the remains, both of architecture and of sculpture; but to obtain these it would be necessary to have the services of a photographer. Careful fac-similes of all inscriptions would of course be made, ancient coins would also be collected on each site, and all the local traditions would be noted down and compared. The description of each place with all its accompanying drawings and illustrations would be complete in itself, and the whole, when finished, would furnish a detailed and accurate account of the archæological remains of Upper India."

A perusal of the four reports contained in these volumes will show that I carried out with but little deviation the programme laid down in this memorandum. The report of each season's works was written during the following hot weather and rains, which was too short a period to admit of sufficient reading and reflection for the preparation of a well considered account of all the interesting places visited. Each report was printed immediately after its submission to Government for official circulation. Some of these official copies have been reprinted, but the whole stock was soon exhausted, and, as frequent enquiry is still made for them, the present publication is intended to place within the reach of all who are interested in archæological researches a cheap account of the only systematic, though incomplete, survey that has yet been made of the antiquities of Northern India.

The work has been carefully examined and cleared of all obvious errors; and numerous alterations and additions have been made to the text, which is now supplied with the necessary notes and references that were wanting in the official copies. To make the account as complete as possible, I have added no less than ninety-nine maps, views, plans and other illustrations, all of which have been drawn by my own hand.

SIMLA;   A. CUNNINGHAM.
The 15th October 1871.

CONTENTS.

VOLUME I.

PREFACE
INTRODUCTION

REPORT OF 1861-62

1. Gaya ... ...
2. Buddha-Gaya ... ...
3. Bakror ... ...
4. Pauwa ... ...
5. Kurkihár, or Kukkutapáda-giri ...
6. Giryek, or Indra-sila-guha ...
7. Rájgir, or Rájagriha ...
8. Baragaon or Nálanda ...
9. Bihár ... ...
10. Ghosráwa ... ...
11. Titaráwa ... ...
12. Aphsar ... ...
13. Barábar ... ...
14. Dharáwat ... ...
15. Besárh or Vaisáli ... ...
16. Kesariya ... ...
17. Lauriya Ara-Ráj ... ...
18. Lauriya Navandgarh ...
19. Padaraona, or Páwá ... ...
20. Kasia, or Kusinagara ...
21. Khukhundo, or Kiskkindapura ...
22. Kahaon, or Kakubhagráli ...
23. Nathára-dah ... ...
24. Bhitari ... ...
25. Banáras Sárnáth ... ...

VOLUME I.

REPORT OF 1862-63

			Page.
1.	Delhi	...	131
2.	Mathura	...	231
3.	Khâlsi	...	244
4.	Madâwar, or Madipur	...	248
5.	Kâshipur, or Govisana	...	251
6.	Râmnagar, or Ahichhatra	...	255
7.	Soron, or Surakshetra	...	265
8.	Atranjikhera, or Pilosana	...	268
9.	Sankisa, or Sangkasya	...	271
10.	Kanoj, or Kanyakubja	...	279
11.	Kâkupur, or Ayuto	...	293
12.	Daundiakhera, or Hayamukha	...	296
13.	Allahabad, or Prayâga	...	ib.
14.	Kosam or Kosâmbi	...	301
15.	Sultânpur, or Kusapura	...	313
16.	Dhopâpapura	...	315
17.	Ajudhya, or Sâketa	...	317
18.	Hâtila, or Asokpur	...	327
19.	Sâhet-Mâhet, or Srâvasti	...	330
20.	Tânda	...	348
21.	Nizwar	...	349
22.	Bârikhar	...	351
23.	Dewal	...	352
24.	Parsadu-kot	...	357
25.	Bilal-khera	...	358
26.	Kâhar	...	ib.

DESCRIPTIVE LIST OF PLATES.

VOLUME I.

No.		Page.
I.	Map of the Gangetic Provinces, showing the travels of Fa Hian and Hwen Thsang	1
II.	Map of North-West India, showing Hwen Thsang's Route ...	
III.	Map of Gaya and Bihár	8
IV.	Plan of the Great Temple at Buddha-Gaya, with the *Bodhidrúm*, or Holy Fig tree, and the Buddhist Railing surrounding the Tree and Temple	6
V.	Pedestal of Statue in the Great Temple, with Niches from the exterior ornamentation of the Great Temple, and Temple of Tára Devi	ib.
VI.	Pavement Slabs from the granite floor of the Great Temple, showing worshippers paying their adorations after the manner of the Burmese *Shikoh*	9
VII.	The *Buddha-pad*, or Prints of Buddha's feet, in front of the Great Temple. Inscriptions on Granite Pillars reading *Ayaye Kuragiye dánam*	ib.
VIII.	Corner and middle Pillars of the Sandstone Railings—in the Samádh of Guru Chait Mall, marked D and C in Plate IV.	10
IX.	Sculptured Bas-reliefs on the Buddhist Railings. The letters A. E. F. refer to sandstone Pillars in the Samádh, and the Nos. to Granite Pillars in the Mahant's residence ...	ib.
X.	Ditto ditto ditto ...	ib.
XI.	Ditto ditto ditto ...	ib.
XII.	Maps of Punáwa and Kurkihár	13
XIII.	Inscriptions at Nálanda, Rájgir, Giryek, and Kurkihár. Inscriptions Nos. 1 and 2 contain the name of Nálanda. No. 1 gives the name Gopála, the founder of the Pála dynasty of Bengál in the 1st year of his reign ...	15
XIV.	Map of Rájgir and Giryek, showing the site of the ancient city of Kuságárapura and the positions of its five surrounding hills	16
XV.	View of Jarasandha's Baithak at Giryek	18
XVI.	Map of the ruins of Nálanda	28
XVII.	Bihár Pillar Inscriptions	37
XVIII.	Map of Barábar and Nágárjuni Hills	40
XIX.	Plans and Sections of Barábar and Nagurjuni Caves ...	45
XX.	Inscriptions in ditto ditto ...	47
XXI.	Map of Besárh and Bakra	55
XXII.	Pillars at Bakhra and Lauriya	60
XXIII.	Maps of Kesariya and Lauriya Navandgarh ...	64

CONTENTS.

VOLUME I.

DESCRIPTIVE LIST OF PLATES.

No.		Page.
XXIV.	View of the Kesariya Stupa and Mound ...	65
XXV.	View of the Pillar and Mounds at Lauriya ...	69
XXVI.	Map of Kasia, or Kusinagara ...	76
XXVII.	View of Kasia ...	78
XXVIII.	Maps of Khukhundo and Kahaon ...	85
XXIX.	Kahaon and Bhitari Pillars ...	92
XXX.	Inscriptions on ditto ditto ...	94
XXXI.	Maps of Sárnáth, Banáres ...	104
XXXII.	Major Kittoe's Excavations at Sárnáth ...	116
XXXIII.	Lieutenant Cunningham's ditto ditto ...	120
XXXIV.	Ditto Inscriptions from Sarnáth ...	123
	No. 1 is the Buddhist profession of faith,' found at 10 feet from the top of the Great Stupa.	
	No. 2 gives the characters in use when the Stupa was building.	
	No. 3 records the religious gift (of a statue) of Sákya Bhikshu by Buddha Sena.	
	No. 4 records a gift by Hari Gupta.	
	No. 5, in much later characters, gives the Buddhist profession of faith, and records the religious gift of the Upásika, Thakkur Sri Yajuska?	
XXXV.	Map of the Ruins of Delhi ...	132
XXXVI.	Map of Lálkot, the Hindu Citadel of Delhi ...	152
XXXVII.	Hindu Pillar, and mason's marks on pillars ...	172
XXXVIII.	Plan of the Masjid Kutb ul Islám, or Kutb Masjid	187
XXXIX.	Map of Mathura ...	233
XL.	Female statue from Mathura ...	240
XLI.	Asoka Inscription on Rock at Khálsi ...	247
XLII.	Maps of Madáwar and Káshipur ...	249
XLIII.	Map of Abichhatra ...	257
XLIV.	View of Stupa and Ruins at Ahichhatra ...	259
XLV.	Map of Sankisa and Agahat Sarai ...	271
XLVI.	Elephant Capital of Asoka Pillar at Sankisa ...	274
XLVII.	Map of Kanoj ...	290
XLVIII.	Map of Kosámbi ...	301
XLIX.	Map of Ajudhya ...	317
L.	Map of Srávastí ...	330
LI.	Inscription at Dewal in Rohilkhand ...	355

INTRODUCTION.

THE study of Indian antiquities received its first impulse from SIR WILLIAM JONES, who in 1784 founded the Asiatic Society of Bengal. Amongst the first members were Warren Hastings, the ablest of our Indian rulers, and Charles Wilkins, who was the first Englishman to acquire a knowledge of Sanskrit, and who cut with his own hands the first Devanágari and Bengáli types. During a residence of little more than ten years, Sir William Jones opened the treasury of Sanskrit literature to the world by the translation of Sakuntala and the institutes of Manu. His annual discourses to the Society showed the wide grasp of his mind; and the list of works which he drew up is so comprehensive that the whole of his scheme of translations has not even yet been completed by the separate labours of many successors. His first work was to establish a systematic and uniform system of orthography for the transcription of Oriental languages, which, with a very few modifications, has since been generally adopted. This was followed by several essays—On Musical Modes—On the Origin of the Game of Chess, which he traced to India—and On the Lunar Year of the Hindus and their Chronology. In the last paper he made the identification of Chandra-Gupta with Sandrakottos, which for many years was the sole firm ground in the quicksands of Indian history. At the same time he suggested that Palibothra, or Pátaliputra, the capital of Sandrakottos, must be Patna, as he found that the Sôn River, which joins the Ganges only a few miles above Patna, was also named *Hiranyabáhu*, or the "golden-armed," an appellation which at once re-called the Erranoboas of Arrian.

The early death of Jones in 1794, which seemed at first to threaten the prosperity of the newly established Society, was the immediate cause of bringing forward Colebrooke, so that the mantle of the elder was actually caught as it fell by the younger scholar, who, although he had not yet appeared as an author, volunteered to complete the Digest of Hindu Law, which was left unfinished by Jones.

CHARLES WILKINS, indeed, had preceded him in the translation of several inscriptions in the first and second volumes of the Asiatic Researches, but his communications then ceased, and on Jones' death in 1794 the public looked to Davis, Wilford, and Colebrooke for the materials of the next volume.

SAMUEL DAVIS had already written an excellent paper on Hindu astronomy, and a second on the Indian cycle of Jupiter; but he had no leisure for Sanskrit studies, and his communications to the Asiatic Society now ceased altogether.

FRANCIS WILFORD, an officer of engineers, was of Swiss extraction. He was a good Classical and Sanskrit scholar, and his varied and extensive reading was successfully brought into use for the illustration of ancient Indian geography. But his judgment was not equal to his learning;[*] and his wild speculations on Egypt and on the Sacred Isles of the West, in the 3rd and 9th volumes of the Asiatic Researches, have dragged him down to a lower position than he is justly entitled to both by his abilities and his attainments. His " Essay on the comparative Geography of India," which was left unfinished at his death, and which was only published in 1851 at my earnest recommendation, is entirely free from the speculations of his earlier works, and is a living monument of the better judgment of his latter days.

HENRY COLEBROOKE was the worthy successor of Sir William Jones, and though his acquirements were, perhaps, not so varied as those of the brilliant founder of the Society, yet he possessed a scholarship equally accurate in both the Classical and Sanskrit languages. This soon ripened into a wide knowledge of Sanskrit literature, and his early mathematical bias and training, combined with a singularly

---

[*] H. H. Wilson, in his Hindu Theatre, I, 9, calls Wilford a "learned and laborious, but injudicious writer."

sound judgment, gave him a more complete mastery over the whole range of Sanskrit learning,—its religion, its law and its philosophy, its language and its literature, its algebra and its astronomy,—than any other scholar has since acquired. All Colebrooke's papers may be read both with interest and advantage.

In the first year of this century he gave translations of Visala Deva's inscriptions on the Delhi pillar. These were followed by other translations in the 9th volume of the Researches in 1807, and in the 1st volume of the Royal Asiatic Society's Translations in 1824, which exhibit the same critical scholarship and sound judgment. But a more valuable contribution is his "Essay on the Vedas,"* which first gave to the European world a full and accurate account of the sacred volumes of the Hindus. Other essays followed at intervals,—on the Sanskrit and Prâkrit languages; on the Philosophy of the Hindus; on the Indian and Arabian divisions of the Zodiac; on the notions of Hindu astronomers concerning the Precession; and on the Algebra of Brahma Gupta and Bhâskara. The mere titles of these essays are sufficient to show the wide range of his studies. But the grasp is as firm as the range is wide, and these essays still remain our standard works on the subjects of which they treat.

Colebrooke left India in 1815. For several years after his return to England he continued his studies and gave to the world some of the essays which have already been noticed. But his latter years were clouded by family bereavements and continued ill health, under which he at last sank on the 10th March 1837, in his 72nd year.†

In the year 1800 Dr. BUCHANAN (who afterwards took the name of Hamilton) was deputed by the Marquis of Wellesley to make an agricultural survey of Mysore. This particular duty he performed with much ability; but the value of his work is greatly increased by several interesting notices which he has given of the antiquities of the country, and of the various races of people in Southern India. The best acknowledgment of the value of this work was the

---

* Asiatic Researches, Vol. IX.
† The main facts of this brief sketch are taken from a deeply interesting and instructive memoir written by his son.—New Journal of Royal Asiatic Society, Vol. V.

appointment of Buchanan, in 1807, by the Court of Directors, to make a statistical survey of the Bengal Presidency.

For seven years Buchanan pursued his survey through the provinces of Bihár, Sháhábád, Bhágalpur, Gorakhpur, Dinajpur, Puraniya, Rangpur, and Asaam, when his labours were unfortunately brought to an abrupt close. The results of the survey were transmitted to England in 1810, where they remained unnoticed until 1838, when Mr. Montgomery Martin "obtained permission to examine the manuscripts, which eventually led to their publication." To him we certainly owe the publication of this valuable work; but I must confess that the warmth of my gratitude for this welcome service is absolutely frozen by the coolness of appropriation displayed on the title-page, where the name of Buchanan is entirely omitted, and the districts of Eastern India are stated to have been "surveyed under the orders of the Supreme Government, and collated from the original documents at the East India Office by Montgomery Martin." This singular proceeding has not escaped the notice of M. Vivien de St. Martin, who remarks that the three volumes had been published "sans y mettre le nom de M. Buchanan." It is, however, but fair to say that full credit is given to Buchanan in the introduction, and that the work appears to be satisfactorily edited.

Although the instructions given to Buchanan included neither the history nor the antiquities of the country, yet both were diligently explored by him; and when, after a lapse of upwards of twenty years, a great mass of the matter collected by the survey was found to have become useless, the value of the traditional or recorded history, and of the monuments and relics of antiquity, remained unchanged. All this part of the work has been published by the editor with a fair proportion of plates, from which we learn that Buchanan was amongst the first to perceive the value and importance of detailed plans and exact measurements of remarkable buildings and ancient sites. His notices of the Buddhist remains at Gaya and Baragaon In Bihár, of Kasia and Kahaon in Gorakhpur, and at many other places, are not less creditable to him because, through delay in the publication of his work, they were partly anticipated by James Prinsep. His historical and archæological researches in the districts of Eastern India are specially valuable for their sound judgment and conscientious accuracy. I have myself visited many of the places described by Buchanan, and I can vouch for the meritorious minuteness and strict correctness of his descriptions.

The Indian mantle of Jones, which Colebrooke had worn so worthily for twenty years, was not destined to remain without a claimant. Before Colebrooke left India in 1815 HORACE HAYMAN WILSON had become Secretary of the Asiatic Society, and had published his translation of the *Megha-duta*, or "cloud-messenger" of Kálidása. This was followed in 1819 by his Sanskrit Dictionary, a work of great labour and merit, and in 1827 by his Hindu Theatre, which opened to the European world a novel and interesting variety of the dramatic art. At the same time he contributed many valuable papers to the Quarterly Oriental Magazine, amongst which his translations of stories from Sanskrit and of some episodes from the Mahábhárata, are perhaps the most pleasing, and his review of the first fifteen volumes of the Asiatic Researches the most important. In 1825 he published an essay on the Hindu history of Kashmir, which gives a clear and very interesting account of the early history of the famous valley.

In the beginning of 1833 Wilson returned to England, where he continued his Oriental studies with unabated ardour. The two principal works of his English career were an account of the coins and antiquities of Afghanistan, contained in "Ariana Antiqua," and his translation of the Rig-Veda. The geographical portion of Ariana Antiqua, under the head of "Early Notices of Ariana," is full and valuable; but his account of Masson's collection of coins makes no advance in Indian numismatics, beyond the point which Prinsep had reached at the time of his death. Indeed, Wilson's archæological writings have added little, if anything, to his reputation. His fame rests on his Sanskrit scholarship, and on the many valuable works, both original and translated, which he gave to the world during his long and brilliant career. To the general public, his most popular work is undoubtedly the Hindu Theatre, in which his true poetic taste and feeling enabled him to do full justice to the masterpieces of the Indian drama. This work has just been re-printed, and it is not likely to be soon superseded by any future scholar, as the different qualities required to produce

INTRODUCTION.

an adequate poetic translation are very rarely combined in one person as they were in Horace Hayman Wilson.

In Western India the Kánhari Caves in the Island of Salset were described and illustrated by Salt as early as 1800, although his account was not published until 1819 in the 1st volume of the Bombay Transactions. In the same volume appeared Erskine's admirable account of the elephanta caves, which, however, was written as early as 1813. Like Buchanan in Bengal, Erskine anticipated the period when vague and glowing accounts would give place to accurate descriptions and detailed plans. His essay on the Elephanta Caves has been corrected in a few points by succeeding observers; but it is still the best account that we possess of those interesting Brahmanical excavations.*

In the 3rd volume of the same transactions, Colonel Sykes gave the first description of the Muhammadan city of Bijapur, which has since been amply illustrated by the drawings of Hurt and Cumming, and the photographs of Loch, with text by Meadows Taylor and James Fergusson. To Colonel Sykes also belongs the credit of a good account of Ellora, which had been previously illustrated by the drawings of Wales engraved by the Daniells.

The earliest illustrations of Southern India we owe to Thomas Daniell, who, at the close of the last century, visited Madras and made several admirable drawings of the seven pagodas at Mahâmallaipur, which are not surpassed by the best photographs. About the same time Colonel Colin Mackenzie began his antiquarian career in the South, which his successive positions in the Survey Department enabled him to extend successfully over the greater part of the peninsula. His collection of manuscripts and inscriptions is unrivalled for its extent and importance.† His drawings of antiquities fill ten folio volumes; and to this collection Mr. Fergusson was indebted for several of the most

---

* A new description of the cave temples and other antiquities of Elephanta is shortly about to be published by Mr. J. Burgess, illustrated with plans and other drawings, besides thirteen photographs. As Mr. Burgess has already proved himself a most competent describer of Indian antiquities by his two previous works,—"The Temples of Káthiáwár," illustrated by forty-one photographs, and the "Temples of Satrunjaya," illustrated by forty-five photographs, his new work on Elephanta will, no doubt, be a most valuable and welcome addition to the library of Indian Archæology.

† See Taylor's Catalogue of the Oriental Collection of the Library of the College of Fort St. George, 3 Vols., thick, 8vo.

valuable illustrations of his "tree and serpent worship." Colin Mackenzie was an ardent and successful collector of archæological materials, but he was not an archæologist. He could dig up and make drawings of the splendid sculptures at Dharanikotta, but he could neither restore the building, nor translate the inscriptions. But, although not a writer himself, the splendid collection of antiquities which he left behind him has been the cause of writing in others. To his drawings we partly owe Fergusson's "tree and serpent worship," and to his collection of manuscripts and inscriptions we are indebted for the greater part of what we at present know of the early history of the southern portion of the peninsula.*

When Horace Wilson left India in 1833 the mantle of Sanskrit scholarship fell to Dr. Mill, whose acquaintance with the sacred language of India is acknowledged to have been as profound and as critical as that of his three great predecessors. To him we owe the translation of several important inscriptions; and his early departure from India, in the end of 1837, was looked forward to by James Prinsep as a loss that was not likely to be soon supplied.

But a new era now dawned on Indian archæology, and the thick crust of oblivion, which for so many centuries had covered and concealed the characters and language of the earliest Indian inscriptions, and which the most learned scholars had in vain tried to penetrate, was removed at once and for ever by the penetrating sagacity and intuitive perception of JAMES PRINSEP. During a great part of the years 1836 and 1837, the most active period of his career, I was in almost daily intercourse with him. With our mutual tastes and pursuits this soon ripened into the most intimate friendship. I thus had the privilege of sharing in all his discoveries during their progress. The matured results will be found in the pages of the Bengal Asiatic Society's Journal; but the germs of his discoveries are related in his letters to me, sometimes almost in the same words as he afterwards made use of in the journal, but generally in the more familiar language of friendly correspondence.

* See Professor Dowson's account of the Southern Kingdoms in the Royal Asiatic Society's Journal, VIII., 1; and H. H. Wilson's Historical Sketch of the Kingdom of Pandya in the Royal Asiatic Society's Journal, III., pp. 199 & 387.

VIII   INTRODUCTION.

Prinsep's first great work was the partial decipherment of the Arian Páli legends of the Bactrian Greek coins, and his last and most important achievement was the decipherment of the Indian Páli legends of the coins of Suráshtra, and the consequent decipherment and translation of the still earlier edicts of Asoka on the pillars at Delhi and Allahabad. In both of these achievements the first step towards discovery was made by others, and this was most freely and fully acknowledged by Prinsep himself. Regarding the decipherment of the Arian Páli alphabet, he says—
"Mr. Masson first pointed out in a note addressed to myself through the late Dr. Gerard, the Pehlvi signs which he had found to stand for the words *Menandrou, Apollodotou, Ermaiou, Basileos*, and *Soteros*. When a supply of coins came into my hands, sufficiently legible to pursue the enquiry, I soon verified the accuracy of his observation, found the same signs with slight variation constantly to recur, and extended the series of words thus authenticated to the names of twelve kings, and to six titles or epithets. It immediately struck me that if the genuine Greek names were faithfully expressed in the unknown character, a clue would through them be formed to unravel the value of a portion of the alphabet, which might in its turn be applied to the translated epithets and titles, and thus lead to a knowledge of the language employed. Incompetent as I felt myself to this investigation, it was too seductive not to lead me to a humble attempt at its solution."[*]

The clue pointed out by Masson was eagerly followed up by Prinsep, who successfully recognized no less than sixteen, or just one-half of the thirty-three consonants of the Arian alphabet. He discovered also three out of the five initial vowels, and two of the medials, or just one-half of the vowels. Here his progress was unfortunately stopped by sudden illness; and he was soon after cut off in the very midst of his brilliant discoveries leaving the task to be slowly completed by others.

In the May number of his journal for 1837,[†] Prinsep published his readings of the legends on the small silver coins of Suráshtra. In this case he has also given a brief notice

---
[*] Bengal Asiatic Society's Journal, 1835, p. 329.
[†] Published in June 1837.

of the steps which led to the discovery; but as his letters to me convey a much more vivid and lively account of the untiring perseverance which secured his success, I will give a connected version of the discovery in his own spirited language by extracts from his letters:

11th May 1837.—"Here are two plates addressed to me by Harkness on the part of J. R. Steuart, quarto engravings of 28 Sauráshtra coins, all Chaitya reverses, and very legible inscriptions, which are done in large on the next plate. Oh ! but we *must* decipher them ! I'll warrant they have not touched them at home *yet*. Here to amuse you try your hand on this" (here follows a copy of three of the coin legends, with the letters forming the words *Rajnah* and *Kshatrapasa*, each of which occurs twice, marked, respectively, 1, 2, 3, 4, 5, 6, shewing that he had begun to analyze them the same day).

12th May, 7 *o'clock, a. m.*—" You may save yourself any further trouble. I have made them all out this very moment on first inspection. Take a few examples (here follow both the original legends and the Nágari renderings)

1 to 4—*Raja Krittamasa Rudra Sdhasa Swámi Jahatuma putrasa.*

5 to 8—*Raja Krittamasya Sagadamia Raja Rudra Sáhasa putrasya.*

And thus every one of them gives the name of his father of blessed memory, and we have a train of some eight or ten names to rival the Guptas !! Hurra ! I hope the chaps at home wont seize the prize first. No fear of Wilson at any rate ! I must make out a plate of the names on ours added to Steuart's, and give it immediate insertion. It is marvellously curious that, like the modern Sindhi and Multáni, all the matras, or vowels, are omitted, and the Sanskrit terminations *sya*, &c., *páli* or vernacularized. This confirms the reading which I had printed only a day or two ago, *Vijaya Mitasa* for *Mitrasya*, of Mithra, identifying him and the devise with our Okro bull coin ! Bravo, we shall unravel it yet."

Here we see that, although he had mastered the greater part of these legends almost at first sight, yet the readings of some of the names were still doubtful. But two days later he writes as follows:

Sunday (postmark, May 14, 1837).—" Look into your cabinet and see what names you have of the Saurâshtra series. Steuart's list is as follows:

Rajas *Rudra Sah*, son of *Swâmi Janadâma*.
,, *Atri Dâmâ* ,, *Rudra Sah*.
&c., &c.

"The Sanskrit on these coins is beautiful, being in the genitive case after the Greek fashion. We have *Rajnya* for *Raja*, *Atri-Dâmnah* for *Atri-Dâma*, *Vira-Dâmnah* for *Vira-Dâma*, *Viswa Sâhâsya* for *Viswa Sâha*, which are all confirmed by the real name losing the genitive affix when joined to *putrasya*.

"I have made progress in reading the Peacock Saurashtrans—

Sri bama saga deva jayati
——————— *kramaditya paramesa.*

"Chulao bhai, juldee puhonchoge!"*

In these lively letters we see that the whole process of discovery occupied only three days, from the first receipt of Steuart's plates to the complete reading of all the legends. Nothing can better show the enthusiastic ardour and unwearying perseverance with which he followed up this new pursuit than these interesting records of the daily progress of his discoveries. When I recollect that I was then only a young lad of twenty-three years ago, I feel as much wonder as pride that James Prinsep should have thought me worthy of being made the confidant of all his great discoveries.

But the decipherment of the legends on the Saurâshtran coins was but the precursor of a still more important discovery. Success only seemed to inspire James Prinsep with fresh ardour. No difficulty daunted his enthusiasm, and no labour tired his perseverance. Only a few years previously he had analyzed the characters of Samudra Gupta's inscription on the Allahabad pillar, and had distinguished the

---

* This is the common exclamation of palki bearers to encourage one another—"Go on brother, we shall soon get there!"

attached vowels, *a, e, i,* and *u;* but the long *f* he mistook for *o*. At that time he had despaired of reading these old inscriptions,* from "want of a competent knowledge of the Sanskrit language." But his present success stimulated him to renew his former attempt. Fortunately just at this time he received a number of short inscriptions from the great *stupa* at Sânchi near Bhilsa. These he read almost at a glance with the exception of two or three letters, which, however, soon yielded to his perseverance. He then proceeded to examine the inscriptions on the Delhi pillar, and at once read the opening sentence without any difficulty or hesitation.

Prinsep's final readings of the Saurâshtran coin legends was announced to me on the 14th May, and this later discovery of the still older inscriptions of the Sânchi Stupa and Delhi pillar was completed before breakfast on 23rd May, or only nine days later. His formal account of the discovery is given in the journal; † but his brief announcement to me is very interesting, as it shows that he had *at once* determined to attempt the translation of the whole of Asoka's edicts. I give this letter entire.

23rd May 1837.—" MY DEAR CUNNINGHAM,—Hors du departement de mes études !‡ Sultan Adil, &c. No, but I can read the Delhi No. 1, which is of more importance, the Bhilsa inscriptions have enlightened me. Each line is engraved on a separate pillar or *dhwaja*. Then, thought I, they must be gifts of private individuals, whose names will be recorded. All end in *dânam*—that must mean 'gift, or given,' *dânam*—genitive must be prefixed. Let's see.

Isa-pâlitasa-cha Sâmanasa-cha dânam.

"The gift of Isa-Pâlita (protected of God) and of Sâmana.

Sâmanerasa Abeyakasa Sethinon dânam

"The gift of Sâmanera and Abeyaka Sethi.

---

* See Journal of Bengal Asiatic Society, 1834, p. 117, and compare 1837, p. 152.

† In Bengal Asiatic Society's Journal, 1837, p. 460.

‡ This was an expression by the famous French academician, Raoul Rochette, regarding the Aryan legends of the Bactrian coins. It tickled Prinsep's fancy particularly; and he was frequently quoting it. In the present instance I had sent him a Muhammadan coin and asked if he could read it. Instead of saying no, he quoted Raoul Rochette.

xii   INTRODUCTION.

> *Buddha-pálitasa lichhunon dánam.*
> "The gift of the protected of Buddha, the Lichhunân."*
> *Vijigatasa dánam.*
> "Eh? will not this do? and the pillar inscription
> *Devánam piya piyadasi Raja hevam akd.*
> "The most particularly-beloved-of-the-gods Raja declareth thus.
> "I think with Ratna Pála, whom I shall summon, we shall be able to read the whole of these manifestoes of the right faith—Buddha's bulls. Will send plates after breakfast.
> "Yours,
> "J. P."

The formal announcement of this discovery was made in the June number of the journal which was published in July, by which Prinsep had recognized the true values of all the letters which he had yet found, and the old alphabet was complete with the exception of the very rare letters *gh* and *jh*, and the guttural, palatal, and cerebral *n's*.

To Professor Lassen belongs the honor of having been the first to read any of these unknown characters. In the previous year, 1836, he had read the Indian Páli legend on the square copper coins of Agathokles as *Agathukla Raja.*† James Prinsep was puzzled by finding "that nearly the same characters appear on the coins of Pantaleon." He admitted, however, that "it might be possible to assimilate the word to the Greek on the supposition of the first syllable being wanting," thus forming *tolava*. On referring to the coin indicated I find that the first letter is actually wanting, and that he had read the three letters of the name correctly. So near was he to making the discovery at that time that it would probably have been completed at once had there been a perfect coin of Pantaleon to refer to for the first letter of the name.

---
* This word should be *Bhichhuno*, the mendicant monk, but Prinsep had not then recognized the true form of the *bh*. He took *t* for *bh*, and when he came to the true *t* in *tasa*, he read the word as *Raja*, as in the next instance which he gives from the Delhi Pillar.

† In a letter to James Prinsep referred to in the Journal of Bengal Asiatic Society, 1836, p. 723.

INTRODUCTION.

As mentioned in his letter to me, Prinsep had at once invited Ratna Pâla, the Páli scholar, to assist him in reading the inscription, and with his aid he was able to translate at once several important passages, such as, "in the twenty-seventh year of my reign." So unremitting was his industry and so rapid his intuitive perception, that he had finished his translation by the end of July, and the complete version appeared in the journal for that month, which was published in the middle of August.

Coins and inscriptions now poured in upon him so fast from all parts of India that much of his valuable time was now occupied in private correspondence, and when I left Calcutta towards the end of October 1837, he was working from twelve to sixteen hours daily. Much of his time was, of course, occupied with his public duties as Assay Master of the Calcutta Mint, as he wrote to me, "my whole day is consumed at the scales. What a waste of precious moments!"

A few days after my departure he received copies of the Udayagiri and Khandagiri inscriptions from Kittoe, and faithful impressions of all the inscriptions on the Allahabad pillar from Colonel Smith. With all his wonted industry and enthusiasm he set to work upon these new records, and was able to give a revised translation of Samudra Gupta's inscription in the November number of his journal, and a long and valuable note on the inscriptions from Udayagiri and Khandagiri in the December number. Yet, in spite of all these labours, so little conscious did he feel of exhaustion that he wrote to me on "December 27th, 7 A. M., to get a new Gupta inscription for the January Number!!"

Prinsep now took up the rock-inscriptions of Asoka, and in a postscript to a letter of 12*th February* 1838, he said to me "dont expect me to write again for a long spell. I must set to work on the Girnâri." But on the 3*rd March* I heard from him again that he had "made une découverte epouvantable! no less than the treaty (an article at least) between Antiochus and Sophagasenas. Shall I leave you to guess how, where, and when? No, but keep it secret till I announce it at the Society. I have happily discovered that many of the edicts at Gujarât and Cuttack are verbatim the same. Among them is one announcing the establishment of a medical arrangement for men and animals." This discovery was announced to the Asiatic Society on the 7th March, and published in the February number of the journal.

As Prinsep proceeded with his examination of the rock-inscriptions, he discovered the names of Ptolemy, Antigonus, and Magas, in addition to a second mention of Antiochus. He had previously felt the want of a good impression of the Girnâr inscription, but this brilliant discovery made him still more anxious to obtain a complete and correct copy. After thinking over the matter for some time, it seemed that the surest and quickest way was to address the Governor General on the subject, which was accordingly done at once, as explained in the following letter to me :

28th March 1838.—" In the enthusiasm of the moment I took up my pen and addressed the enclosed bold petition to Lord Auckland, which, on sober reflection, I am afraid of sending, lest I should be thought presumptuous in imagining others care as much about old inscriptions as I do ! I therefore enclose it to you instead that you may act upon it as you may find a fit occasion. The passage in the 14th edict is much mutilated, and I long for a more correct copy. * * It really becomes interesting to find Egypt and Ptolemy known to Asoka ! I must give *you* the real text" (here follows the text in the original Pâli characters, which I give in *italic* letters with Prinsep's interlinear translation):

> *Yona râja paran cha tena Chaptâro*
> Greek King furthermore by whom the *Gypta*
> *Rajâno Tulamayo cha Antigona cha Maga cha*
> Rajas, Ptolemy and Antigonus and Magas and
> * * * *savata Devânampiyasa*
> * * * everywhere beloved's
> *Dhammânusasti anubatate yata pajati*
> Religious precept reaches where goes.

Some doubt about the *Ptâro râjâno*, or *Chaptâro*, which may be read *chatuedro rajâno*, 'the four kings ;' *Ptaro*, the *Pta* or *Ptha* (worshipping) kings, *Guptaro*, or *Chaptaro*, *rajano*, the 'Koptic or Aegyptic kings ;' but the name of Magas is so distinct that I give up the four kings in favor of Egypt.

"I have no time to expatiate hereupon. I shall publish in the next journal, although probably I shall be forced to alter my Antiochus *the Great* theory to the contemporary Antiochus of Ptolemy Philadelphus (247 B. C.), in whose time Magas held part of Egypt (Cyrene), and whose period agrees better with Asoka's reign. Hurrah for inscriptions!"

Prinsep's bold appeal to the head of the Government was of course successful, for Lord Auckland was a liberal patron of both literature and science. The Governor of Bombay was accordingly requested to depute a qualified officer for the purpose of taking a *fac-simile* of the inscriptions.* The new impressions were made with great care, but they did not reach Calcutta until after Prinsep's departure. I was not even aware that they had been sent to Calcutta until last January, when, looking for some of Kittoe's inscriptions, I stumbled on the Girnâr edicts of Asoka.

In the meantime Prinsep continued his labours by publishing a translation of the Junagarh inscription of Rudra Dâma in the April number of the journal; an "examination of the separate edicts at Dhauli in Cuttack" in the May number; translations of some additional short records from the Sânchi Stupâ near Bhilsa in the June number; and the "discovery of the Bactrian alphabet" in the July number; which was published about the middle of August. These were his last contributions to the Journal of the Asiatic Society of Bengal.†

After his revision of the Bactrian alphabet, he naturally turned to the inscriptions which Ventura and Court had extracted from the stupas at Mânikyâla, and which Masson had obtained from the stupas of the Kabul Valley. His attention was also turned to the reading of the later coins "which mark the decadence of Greek dominion and Greek skill. These are the most precious to the student of Indian history. Through their Native legends we may yet hope to throw light on the obscure age of Vikramâditya and the Scythian successors of the Greeks on the north of India."‡ So important did he consider this class of coins that he

---

* See Bengal Asiatic Society's Journal, 1838, p. 365.

† Three different articles will be found in the Journal of the Bengal Asiatic Society for 1838, pp. 364, 484, 562, & 636.

‡ Bengal Asiatic Society's Journal, 1831, p. 685.

specially invited attention to them, and promised to return to their investigation, his text being "those coins on which the Native and Greek legends differ, or record different names."

This subject still occupied his attention when he was overtaken by sickness and obliged to proceed to sea for change of air. He was "off Kedgeree" on the 28*th September* 1838, when he wrote his last letter to me to acknowledge the receipt of the coins which I had selected from Sir Alexander Burnes' new collection for his examination. He was disappointed at not finding any new names, and says "I almost fear the field is exhausted; my only hope is of new *Spalahara* types among the crowd of 'frustes' coins." As the coins of *Spalahara* belong to the class "on which the Native and Greek legends differ, this passage shows that down to the very last his thoughts were engaged on the completion of the Bactrian alphabet, and the translation of the tope inscriptions. I also draw the same conclusion from another paragraph of the same letter where he says, "I told you (did I not?) that Lassen had hit upon the exact key to the Bactrian alphabet I have made use of."

His trip to sea did him no good, as he wrote to me that he "never was so idle, so listless, or so headachey in his life;" and after a long and amusing account of all the surrounding discomforts, he exclaims "Oh! the pleasures of running down to the Sandheads for a week to restore the health!" He longed "to get home to his own desk" in Calcutta, where he hoped to find that Dr. McLeod had arrived safe, that is, with the mass of Burnes' collection of coins.

On his return to Calcutta he gradually became worse and was obliged to leave India in the end of October. He was in a hopeless state when he reached England from softening of the brain, and after lingering for about a year he sank on the 22nd of April 1840, at 40 years of age. Thus died James Prinsep in the very prime of life, and in the very midst of his brilliant discoveries. When we remember that he was only just thirty-nine years old when his career was suddenly arrested by illness, it is impossible to help regretting that he was not spared for a few years longer to complete and perfect what he had already done, and perhaps to add fresh laurels to his fame by further discoveries. But

James Prinsep had done his work; for all his brilliant discoveries, which would have been the labour of ten or a dozen years to most other men, were made during the last three years of his career; and although he was still young in years, he had already done the work of a good old age. The career of James Prinsep has been fitly and eloquently described by his friend Dr. Hugh Falconer, who knew him well. From this able sketch I extract the following appreciative notice of Prinsep's rare talents: "Of his intellectual character the most prominent feature was enthusiasm—one of the prime elements of genius; a burning irrepressible enthusiasm, to which nothing could set bounds, and which communicated itself to whatever came before him. The very strength of his mental constitution in this respect was perhaps opposed to his attaining the excellence of a profound thinker; it led him to be carried away frequently by first impressions, and to apply his powers to a greater range of subjects than any human mind can master or excel in. To this enthusiasm was fortunately united a habitude of order, and power of generalization, which enabled him to grasp and comprehend the greatest variety of details. His powers of perception were impressed with genius—they were clear, vigorous, and instantaneous."[*]

Dr. Falconer formed a true and just estimate of Prinsep's powers of perception, which were equally remarkable for their vigour and their instantaneousness. The quickness of his perception was indeed wonderful, so that many of his discoveries may be said literally to have flashed upon him; or, as he himself describes one of them in a letter to me, "like inspiration, or lightning, or Louisa's eyes, the light at once broke upon me."[†] But the great point in Prinsep's character was his ardent enthusiasm, which charmed and melted all who came in contact with him. Even at this distance of time, when a whole generation has passed away, I feel that his letters still possess the same power of winning my warmest sympathy in all his discoveries, and that his joyous and generous disposition still communicates the same contagious enthusiasm and the same strong desire to assist in further achievements.

---

[*] Extracted from the Colonial Magazine for December 1840, by Mr. E. Thomas in his edition of Prinsep's "Essays on Indian Antiquities."

[†] Letter of 27th January 1838. The name of Louisa is written in Asoka characters as Lu-i-ja.

The powerful impulse given to Indian archæology by James Prinsep was produced quite as much by the enthusiasm which he kindled in every one who came in contact with him, as by his translations of the old inscriptions of Asoka, which gave life to records that had been dead for more than two thousand years, and that now form our chief land-marks in ancient Indian history. The impulse was not lost after his death; but the progress of research, which during his life-time had been conducted as one great voyage of discovery under his sole command, has since been limited to lesser expeditions in various directions. As these were led by many different persons, each acting independently, the amount of progress may, perhaps, seem comparatively little, whereas it has been really great, and only seems little because the work actually done has been very gradually achieved and has never yet been summed up and gathered together.

Of James Prinsep's successors during the last thirty years, the most prominent have been James Fergusson, Markham Kittoe, Mr. Edward Thomas, and myself, in Northern India; Sir Walter Elliot in Southern India; and Colonel Meadows Taylor, Dr. Stevenson, and Dr. Bhau Daji in Western India.

From the foundation of the Asiatic Society by Sir William Jones in 1784 down to 1834, a period of just half a century, our archæological researches had been chiefly literary, and, with a few notable exceptions, had been confined to translations of books and inscriptions, with brief notices of some of the principal buildings at Delhi and Agra and other well known places. The exceptions are several valuable essays by Jones, Wilford,* Colebrooke, and Wilson, on the religion, the geography and the astronomy of the Hindus, which have already been noticed. These early labourers may be called the Closet or Scholastic Archæologists. The travellers of their day gave glowing accounts of the wonders of Ellora, of the massive grandeur of the Kutb Minar, and of the matchless beauty of the Táj Mahal at Agra. But all was vague and indefinite. There were but few measurements and no plans. True history was then but little known, and

---

* I consider Wilford's essays valuable in spite of their wild speculations, as they contain much information and undigested learning, in which important facts and curious classical references will be found imbedded in a mass of crude speculation.

the lying gabble of Brahmans, which connected every place with the wanderings of Ráma or the exile of the five Pándus, was accepted as the real voice of genuine tradition.

But a new era opened for Indian archæology in 1834, when James Prinsep gave to the world the first results of Masson's researches in the Kabul valley, and of Ventura's and Court's explorations in the Panjáb, followed immediately by my own excavation of the stupa at Sárnáth, Banáras, and of the ruins around it. Facts now poured in rapidly, but though many in number, they were still bare and unconnected facts, mere fossil fragments of the great skeleton of lost Indian history. The full skeleton has not yet been set up; but many of its members are now almost complete, and we have acquired a very fair knowledge of the general outline and of the various forms which it has assumed at different periods. For this result we are much indebted to men who are not Sanskrit scholars, and whose success has been achieved by actual measurements and laborious explorations in the field, combined with patient research and studious investigation in the closet. During James Prinsep's life-time, the materials collected by these "field archæologists," or "travelling antiquarians" as he called them, were all made over to him, but since his death, each observer has worked independently in his own line, and has published separately the results of his own labours.

Amongst the foremost and most successful of the later archæologists is my friend JAMES FERGUSSON, whose masterly works on Indian architecture are the result of extensive travels through a great part of India, undertaken for the express purpose of studying this important and interesting subject. It is entirely his own, and I trust that he may shortly be able to fulfil his long-cherished project of publishing an illustrated history of Indian architecture, such as he only can give us.

Mr. Fergusson's first publication was an account of the "rock-cut temples of India, 1845, in which he gives a detailed account of all the groups of caves that were then known, and endeavours to fix their approximate dates by differences of style and other distinctive characteristics. This rule is rigorously true in principle; but to make its results of any value, it is absolutely necessary that we should have at least a few fixed stand-points of known dates for comparison. Thus we may be quite certain that any temple B is an improvement on A, and is less advanced than C ; and we conclude accordingly that it is of intermediate age between A C. But if the dates of A and C are both unknown, our deduction is comparatively of little value; and even if we should know the date of C, any deduction as to the date of B will be liable to at least half the amount of error in the assumed date of A. No one is more fully aware of this than Mr. Fergusson himself, as he admits that his conclusions " have been arrived at almost entirely from a critical survey of the whole series, and a careful comparison of one cave with another, and with the different structural buildings in their neighbourhood, the dates of which are at least *approximately* known."* But I think that he is inclined to overrate the value of these critical deductions, when he says that " inscriptions will not certainly by themselves answer the purpose;" and he gives in proof of this assumption the fact that there is a comparatively modern inscription in the Ganes Gumpha Cave at Udayagiri. But what proof have we that many of the caves were not originally quite plain like those of Barâbar, and that the ornamentation is not the work of a much later age? I differ from Mr. Fergusson on this point, as I consider that inscriptions are, beyond all doubt, the most certain and the most trustworthy authority for determining the dates of Indian monuments, whether buildings or caves. I freely admit the corroborative value of architectural evidence when it is founded on ascertained dates; but when it is unsupported by inscriptions, I look upon it, in the present state of our knowledge, as always more or less uncertain, and, therefore, weak.

The best proof which I can give of the weakness of Mr. Fergusson's argument, in the present state of our knowledge, is to quote the dates which he has deduced for the well-known caves of *Kânhari* in Salset, which he assigns as follows: " First those in the ravine in the fourth or fifth century, those last described, with those on each side of the great cave, probably at least a century later ; then the great cave."† Now the inscriptions in the Kânhari caves are very

---

* Rock-cut Temples of India, p. 2.
† Rock-cut Temples of India, p. 39.

INTRODUCTION.   XXI

numerous; and though there are a few mediæval records, yet
any evidence of late date which they might be supposed to
afford is utterly annihilated by the presence in the same
caves of much older inscriptions of the same style and
character as the mass of the Kánhari records, which are certainly not later than the Gupta inscriptions of Northern
India. In fact, one of them gives the date of 30 of the *Saka-
ditya-kála*, or A. D. 108. I have copied part of the inscription in the great cave with my own hand, and, after comparing my copy with that of Mr. West, I can see no difference of age between the characters used in the great
cave and those in the other caves. I therefore refer the
great mass of the Kánhari inscriptions to the first and second
centuries of the Christian era, so that there is a difference
of at least four centuries between Mr. Fergusson's mean
date and mine.

The Kárle caves Mr. Fergusson is inclined to assign
to the first, or even the second century before Christ.* One
of the caves is certainly older than the Christian era, as it
possesses an inscription of the great Satrap King Nahapána.†
But there are two others of King Pudumayi, the son of
Vásithi, whom I place in the beginning of the second century
of the Christian era, but whom Mr. Fergusson assigns to the
middle of the fourth century, although in his chronology
he admits that Ananda, also a son of Vásithi, and therefore
most probably a brother of Pudumayi, and the founder of one
of the gateways of the Great Sánchi Tope, lived towards the
end of the first century.

I have entered thus fully into the question of the dates
of the Western Caves, partly lest my silence should be
looked upon as acquiescence in Mr. Fergusson's conclusions,‡ and partly out of deference to his deservedly high
name and well-earned reputation as an earnest and able
enquirer into Indian History and Archæology. Mr. Fergusson is well aware that I differ from him on many points

---

* Rock-cut Temples of India, pp. 30-34.
† Journal, Bombay Asiatic Society, V.; Kárli Inscription No. 5, for Nahapana; and Nos. 4 and 18 for Pudumayi.
‡ This, indeed, has already happened, as Mr. C. R. Markham, in his Memoir on the Archæological Survey, p. 181, concludes that Mr. Fergusson's Rock-cut Temples of India "may be considered as having placed the theory of the age and uses of those monuments on a basis of certainty, which has never since been called in question."

of early Indian chronology; and I believe that by thus publicly stating my views on these points, we shall the sooner arrive at the truth, as probably others will now be led to think upon the subject, who would otherwise perhaps have passed it entirely over as a matter that was undisputed, and therefore finally settled.

In his next work, entitled "Picturesque Illustrations of Ancient Architecture in India," Mr. Fergusson makes use of the same principles of characteristic differences and similarities of style to fix the dates of the mediæval temples of the Brahmans and Jains. Here I agree with him throughout; for the process of deduction is now perfectly trustworthy, being founded on actual dates, as there is a sufficient number of structural temples of the Jains and Brahmans of known age to furnish us with data for determining very closely the ages of uninscribed buildings. This is specially noteworthy in the case of the rock-cut Brahmanical temples of Dhamnár, which, from their general style, Mr. Fergusson has assigned to the eighth or ninth century,[*] a date which must be very close to the truth, as I found a statue in one of the smaller temples inscribed with characters which certainly belong to that period. The examples of Indian architecture given by Mr. Fergusson in this work are very fine and choice, especially the rich temple at Chandrávati, which I have seen, and which I agree with him in thinking "the most elegant specimen of columnar architecture in Upper India."

In his "Handbook of Architecture (1855) he has given a classification of all the different Indian styles, both Hindu and Muhammadan, which is considerably enlarged and improved in his later work, the "History of Architecture" (1867). In the latter we have the matured result of a long and critical study of the subject. The classification is complete and comprehensive, and though perhaps exception may be taken to one or two of the names, yet it is difficult to find others that would be better. The limited space at his command has obliged him to treat each different style very briefly, but the distinctions are so broadly and clearly defined in the typical examples selected for illustration, that I cannot help feeling impatient for the appearance

---

[*] Rock-cut Temples of India, p. 44.

of his great work, the "Illustrated History of Indian Architecture," which he originally projected more than a quarter of a century ago, and for which, during the whole of that time, he has been assiduously collecting materials.

Mr. Fergusson's last work, named "Tree and Serpent Worship" is the most sumptuously illustrated work on Indian antiquities that has yet been published. In it he gives a description of the two richly-sculptured Stupas of Sânchi and Amaravati, with a profusion of excellent illustrations from Colonel Maisey's accurate drawings and Captain Waterhouse's photographs of the former, and from Colonel Mackenzie's drawings, and the actual bas-reliefs of the latter which are now in London. Mr. Fergusson has accepted my dates for the Sânchi Tope and its gateways, namely, B. C. 250, during the reign of Asoka for the former, and the first century A. D. for the latter; but the Amaravati Tope he places three hundred years later, in the first half of the fourth century A. D. I understand that he has been led to adopt this difference of age chiefly on account of the difference of style which he has observed in the sculptures of the two monuments. I must confess that this great difference of style is not palpable to me. On the contrary, from the similar dress of the men, and the similar general nakedness of the women, save only the peculiar belt of five rows of beads, the sculptures of the two monuments appear to me to be of much the same age. I draw the same conclusion also from the inscriptions which are undoubtedly of the same age as those of the caves of Kânhari and of the Sânchi Tope Gateways. As I have already pointed out, there are in the Kânhari caves two inscriptions of Pudumayi, the son of Vâsithi, in exactly the same characters as those of Ananda, the son of Vâsithi, on the south gateway of the Sânchi Tope. I conclude, therefore, with some certainty, that Pudumayi and Ananda were brothers; and consequently I refer all the inscriptions of the King Gotamiputra Sâtakarni and his successors Pudumayi and Yâdnya Sri to the first and second centuries A. D. As by far the greater number of the Amaravati inscriptions are in exactly the same characters, it seems almost certain that they must belong to the same period. This conclusion is strengthened by the fact that Buddhist coins of all these three Princes have been found at Amaravati, with types and inscriptions which range them as contemporaries of the Satrap Chiefs of Surashtra. Mr. Fergusson has adopted the statement of the Puránas, that the Andhras ruled over Magadha in succession to the Kanwas; but this position is quite untenable, as we know from Pliny that at this very time the Prasii, that is the people of Palásaka or Magadha, were dominant on the Ganges, and possessed an army six times greater than that of the Andaræ Indi.*

With respect to the title of this last work of Mr. Fergusson,—"Tree and Serpent Worship,"—I submit that it is not borne out by the illustrations; and further, that, as serpent-worship was antagonistic to Buddhism, such a title is not applicable to a description of the religious scenes sculptured on a Buddhist Stupa. I can perceive no serpent-worship in these illustrations. On the contrary, I find that the Nágas are generally doing homage to Buddha, in perfect accordance with all the Buddhist legends, which invariably represent the Nágas as at first the bitter enemies of Buddha. Afterwards, when converted by his preaching, they became his staunchest adherents, and are specially stated to have formed canopies over his head with their hoods to protect him from the sun and rain. The presence of *Nágas* in the Amaravati sculptures is only natural, as the king of the country and his subjects are described in all the legends as Nágas. In the sculptures, therefore, the king and his women are generally represented with serpent hoods; but, as far as I have observed, they are invariably the worshippers of Buddha, and not the objects of worship.

On these two points I am sorry to be obliged to differ from Mr. Fergusson. But neither of them affects the main purpose of the work, which is devoted to the illustration and restoration of the Amaravati Tope. This work he has done most thoroughly, and I accept his restoration as almost certain.

MARKHAM KITTOE was already known for his architectural taste by his design for the little church at Jonpur, and his drawings of Muhammadan buildings, when, towards the close of 1836, the march of his regiment from the Upper Provinces to Medinipur brought him through Calcutta,

---

* James Prinsep saw that these successive dynasties of the Puránas must have been parallel or contemporary.—Journal, Bengal Asiatic Society, 1838, p. 347.

where he first saw James Prinsep. He was then engaged
in the preparation of a work, which apppeared in 1838,
under the title of "Illustrations of Indian Architecture."
The work was chiefly valuable for its illustrations, of which
many have now been superseded by photographs. Kittoe's
antiquarian zeal and architectural knowledge were strong
recommendations to James Prinsep, who induced him to pay
a visit to the Khandagiri rock to examine the inscription in
old Pali characters, of which Stirling had published a poor
and imperfect copy in the Asiatic Researches. The result
was an excellent copy of a very important inscription of
King Aira, and the discovery of one of Asoka's edicts at
Dhauli, with sketches of the more important caves and principal sculptures.

Kittoe's services were warmly acknowledged by James
Prinsep in the Journal of the Asiatic Society, and also in a
letter to me of 4th November 1837, in which he mentions
"a beautifully illustrated journal from poor Kittoe," and
begs me to "keep an eye to his interests, for he would be
an invaluable antiquarian traveller." At this time Kittoe
was temporarily removed from the army for bringing indiscreet charges of oppression against his Commanding Officer,
for which there was but little foundation save in his own
over-sensitive disposition. Through Prinsep's influence he
was appointed Secretary of the Coal Committee, which led
to his extended tour through Orissa, the results of which
were published in the Bengal Asiatic Society's Journal for
1838 and 1839. He was afterwards restored to his position
in the army, and appointed to the charge of one of the
Divisions of the High Road from Calcutta to Bombay, leading through Chutia Nágpur.

For several years he was employed in the uncongenial
work of a Road Officer, and it was not until 1846 that he
had the opportunity of returning to his archæological
researches. In doing so he felt that he was partly carrying
out the wishes of James Prinsep, "who oft expressed a wish
that he should ramble over the district of Bihár, and cater
for him."[a] During 1846 and 1847, he accordingly travelled
over a great part of the districts of Bihár and Sháhábád,
and added much valuable information to our knowledge of

---

[a] Bengal Asiatic Society's Journal, 1847, p. 273.

their antiquities. But his chief aim seems to have been to make a large collection of drawings of choice specimens of sculpture with a view to future publication. In following out this plan much of his valuable time was wasted in making drawings of sculptures and architectural ornaments, of many of which photography has since given us finer and even more detailed copies. But no less praise is due to him for the unwearied industry and patience with which he performed his self-appointed task, the results of which now form a valuable collection of about one hundred and fifty drawings belonging to the library of the East India Museum.

About this time, through the influence of Mr. Thomason, Lieutenant-Governor of the North-Western Provinces, Kittoe was appointed "Archæological Enquirer" to Government, on a salary of Rs. 250 a month. Whilst engaged on this work he was requested to prepare a design for the proposed Sanskrit College at Banâras. His design was approved; and, when the building was fairly begun, Kittoe was obliged to reside altogether at Banâras to superintend its construction. With this work he was fully occupied during the remainder of his career, his only archæological researches being some rather extensive excavations at Sârnâth, where he uncovered a complete monastery, and added considerably to his collection of sculpture drawings. The work at the College was severe, as he had to model most of the mouldings with his own hands. On the 19th May 1852, he wrote to me "Oh how I wish the College were out of hand, that I might set to work and compile my drawings and papers into some shape." When I saw Kittoe at Gwalior in September 1852, he spoke despondingly of himself. His health was evidently much impaired, and he complained of headache and want of appetite.

He was sick of the drudgery of the college work; and in the beginning of 1853 his health completely broke down, and he was compelled to seek for change of air in England. On the 2nd of February he gave a lecture in Calcutta before the Asiatic Society on the antiquities of Sârnâth, and exhibited to the meeting his collection of sculpture drawings. The voyage to England did him no good, and on his arrival he was so ill that he saw no one, and, as one of his friends informed me, "he went straight to his home and died" in

June 1853. Like Prinsep he sank from overwork, and at about the same age.

As a draughtsman Kittoe was painstaking and accurate, and therefore always trustworthy; as an explorer, he was enthusiastic and indefatigable, qualities which generally command success; but as an investigator, he was wanting in scholarship and faulty in judgment. As specimens of his defective judgment, I may cite his continued doubts as to the identity of Asoka and Piyadasi, and his serious suggestion that the Barâbar Cave inscription of Dasaratha, which Prinsep had truly assigned to the historical Dasaratha of Magadha, one of the immediate successors of Asoka, might probably be referred to the half fabulous Dasaratha of Ayodhya, the father of Râma.

Kittoe's chief discoveries were limited to temples, sculptures and inscriptions, and I cannot recal a single locality which he identified, or a single historical doubt which he settled, or a single name of any dynasty which he established. His discoveries were the result of unwearying exploration, and not the fruit of mental reasoning and reflective deduction. Such also, when his career was drawing to a close, was his own modest estimate of himself. On the 10th May 1852 he wrote to me: " Let me not lead you to suppose that I claim knowledge. I am woefully deficient. I am a self-educated man, and no Classic or Sanskrit scholar; I merely claim a searching eye and mind, and a retentive memory of figure and fact, and place or position. Hence my great success in finding inscriptions where many have searched in vain!—Cuttack and Gya to wit." This estimate of himself seems fully to justify my opinion of him, while at the same time it corroborates the prophetic judgment of James Prinsep that Kittoe would make "an invaluable antiquarian traveller."

The principal subject which has engaged the attention of Mr. EDWARD THOMAS is the History of India as illustrated by its coins and inscriptions, and other monuments. His numerous essays, range over the long period of eighteen hundred years, from the establishment of the Bactrian monarchy in B. C. 246 to the final extinction of the Pathân empire of Delhi on the accession of Akbar in A. D. 1554. The following list of his principal essays shows the extent and variety of the contribution which he has made to Indian archæology during the past twenty years.

1. 1848—Journal of Royal Asiatic Society, Vol. IX.,—Coins of the Hindu Kings of Kabul.
2. 1848—Ditto ditto, Vol. IX.,—Coins of the Kings of Ghazni.
3. 1850—Ditto ditto, Vol. XII.,—Coins of the Sah Kings of Saurashtra.
4. 1855—Journal, Bengal Asiatic Society, Vol. XXIV.,—On the Epoch of the Gupta Dynasty.
5. 1855—Ditto ditto, Vol. XXIV.,—On the Coins of the Gupta Dynasty.
6. 1855—Ditto ditto, Vol. XXIV.,—On ancient Indian Numerals.
7. 1858—Prinsep's Indian Antiquities, 2 Vols., thick 8vo; with numerous plates of coins, and many able independent notices, bringing the state of knowledge in each branch up to the date of publication.
8. 1860—Journal, Royal Asiatic Society, Vol. XVII.,—Supplementary Notice of the Coins of the Kings of Ghazni.
9. 1864—Journal, Bengal Asiatic Society, Vol. XXXIV.,—On ancient Indian Weights (continued in the same journal for 1835).
10. 1865—Ditto ditto, Vol. XXXV.,—On the identity of Xandrames and Krananda.
11. 1866—Ditto ditto, Vol. XXXVI.,—The Initial Coinage of Bengal.
12. 1871—Chronicles of the Pathán Kings of Delhi.

On all these different periods and subjects Mr. Thomas has thrown a flood of light by his accurate observations and critical sagacity. But his principal researches have been directed to the Muhammadan History of India, and more especially to the two periods of the Ghaznivide and Pathán dynasties. Here he has had the field entirely to himself; and to his critical sifting of evidence and noteworthy accuracy, we are mainly indebted for the clear and satisfactory settlement of the chronology of the Muhammadan kingdoms of Ghazni and Delhi. He has also initiated the same accurate arrangement of the chronology of the

Pathán kingdom of Bengal, which will eventually be completed as more coins and inscriptions are brought to light and made available.

The greater number of Mr. Thomas's essays have been confessedly limited to the almost technical description and illustration of various important series of oriental coins. But in his notes and independent articles, inserted in his edition of Prinsep's Essays, and more particularly in his last production,—the "Chronicles of the Pathán Kings of Delhi,"—he has made good use of all accessible inscriptions, and of numerous passages of historians and geographers, which bear upon his subject. His "leading object," as he himself states, "has been to collect materials for history, in the form of documents, which it was primarily desirable to retain in their most authentic form." This object he has accomplished in the most complete and satisfactory manner; and the future historian of Muhammadan India will be saved much of the weary and vexatious trouble of weighing the respective values of conflicting evidence, and of balancing the probabilities of opposing dates. All this laborious work has been well and carefully done by Mr. Thomas, whose critical sifting of evidence, and able scrutiny of all available information, have effectually winnowed most of the chaff of doubt and dispute, and left little but the true grains behind.

In Madras SIR WALTER ELLIOT completed what Colonel Mackenzie had left undone. Mackenzie's great collection of 8,070 inscriptions was made chiefly in the Támilian provinces to the south of the Krishna River, while Sir Walter's collection of 595 inscriptions was formed principally in the ancient Karnáta country, amongst the upper branches of the Krishna. His first contribution to Indian archæology was a very valuable and interesting historical sketch,* founded solely on the inscriptions of the principal dynasties which had ruled over the countries between the Narbada and the Krishna for nearly eight centuries. Of these the great Chálukya family was the oldest, the strongest, and the most lasting; and its line has since been traced back to the early part of the fourth century by the discovery of other inscriptions. Its career probably began in A. D. 319. For the

---

* In Royal Asiatic Society's Journal, IV., for 1836, and re-printed with corrections in the Madras Literary Journal, Vol. VII., p. 193.

early history of the northern half of the peninsula, this invaluable essay is our principal, and indeed almost our only, guide.

Sir Walter has also illustrated the history of the Chálukyas and other southern dynasties by their coins, which he was the first to arrange systematically. He thus obtained their trustworthy evidence in support of the more extensive data supplied by the inscriptions. All previous enquiries had been contented to arrange the coins according to their devices, without regard to their age, or to the localities in which they were usually found. Thus, all the coins bearing the type of an elephant were assigned to the *Gajapati* dynasty, which was asserted to have reigned over Orissa; all those with a horse to the *Aswapati* dynasty; those with the figure of a man to the *Narapati* dynasty; and those with an umbrella to the *Chhatrapati* dynasty. These are currently believed to have been the titles of four tributary princes who held the four chief provinces of Southern India under the rule of the one supreme sovereign of Delhi. The single omission of the boar of the Chálukyas is fatal to this neatly-contrived scheme.

In Western India Colonel MEADOWS TAYLOR has chiefly confined his attention to the mysterious cromlechs and cairns, and stone circles, of which he himself made numerous and important discoveries in the Shorapur District.* The origin of these monuments is at present unknown. Colonel Taylor calls them pre-historic remains, and attributes them to the great Turanian or Scythian race which occupied Southern India before the immigration of the Aryas. "Certain it is," he remarks, "that in the purely Aryan and Northern Provinces of India, no such structures have been found."† But this is a mistake, as they have already been found in the hilly parts of the districts of Delhi, Mirzapur, and Orissa, and I conclude that they will hereafter be discovered in many other parts of Northern India. I am inclined also to doubt that these monuments were peculiar to the Turanian races, for I look upon the stone colonnade that surrounds the great Sanchi stupa as only an improved version of the rude stone circle enclosing an earthen

---

* See his able account of this interesting subject in the Journal of the Ethnological Society, Vol. I., p. 157., "On the Pre-historic Archæology of India."

† "Student's Manual of the History of India," p. 10.

INTRODUCTION. xxxi

tumulus; and as the Sanchi monuments is an undoubted Aryan structure, the probabilities seem to be rather in favour of the Aryan origin of its prototype, than that the Aryas borrowed the design from the earlier Turanian settlers. This however is, at present, a matter of opinion which will probably be settled by further researches. In the meantime the public is deeply indebted to Colonel Taylor for the very full and accurate details which he has given of the early stone monuments of Southern India.

In his Student's Manual of Indian History, Colonel Taylor has assigned the building of the second tope at Sânchi to Pushpamitra, the first of the Sunga dynasty of Magadha, whom he affirms to have been Buddhists, and "famous for their religious zeal in the construction of religious edifices and excavation of cave temples."* Now, this is certainly a mistake, as Pushpamitra was a noted persecutor of the Buddhists, and is recorded to have offered a reward of one hundred dinars for the head of every Srâmana.† As Colonel Taylor rarely quotes authorities, it is impossible to trace the source of this error. I can only conjecture that it is founded on a misreading by Dr. Stevenson of one of the cave inscriptions, which will be presently noticed, in which he identifies a petty Buddhist chief, Nâyak, named Agnimitra, with the great Sunga King of Magadha, who would certainly appear to have been a Brâhmanist, as well as his father, Pushpamitra.‡

To the REVEREND J. STEVENSON, D. D., we owe the only series of translations that have yet appeared of the numerous inscriptions in the caves of Western India. These were published in 1857* from copies of the inscriptions prepared by Lieutenant Brett, which, though carefully and laboriously made, are deficient in many places, and are not sufficiently accurate in others to be fully relied upon. For these reasons several passages, and even a few whole inscriptions, were left untranslated by Dr. Stevenson, whilst others were insufficiently or incorrectly rendered by him. Now and much more accurate copies of the inscriptions in the Kânheri and Nâsik caves have since been published by Mr. West, but even

---

* Student's Manual of Indian History, page 64.
† Burnouf "Introduction à l' Histoire du Buddhisme Indien," page 431.
‡ See the drama of Mâlarikâgnimitra in Wilson's Hindu Theatre.

these are only hand copies, carefully reduced, it is true, by squares, but still only hand copies, and not *fac-similes* or impressions. I have myself visited both of those places, and I can state that I have not seen any inscriptions that would yield better impressions than the great Satrap and Andhra records of the Nâsik caves. The most beautiful and perfectly accurate impressions or rubbings of these precious records might have been made by Mr. West in one-tenth of the time which was occupied in making his much less trustworthy hand reductions.

Taking Dr. Stevenson's translations altogether, there is no doubt that he has succeeded in giving the general scope of all the more important inscriptions, and has thereby added a very valuable amount of authentic information to the scanty records of early Indian history. With some of the shorter inscriptions he has been less successful; for instance, he has taken *Dâmilâya* as a masculine name, and identified *Dâmilâ* with the famous Chânakya, the minister of Chandra Gupta Maurya, thus ignoring, not only the feminine possessive termination in *aya*, but also the preceding feminine word *Bhikkuniya*, or "mendicant nun," the inscription, in fact, being the simple record of a gift of the female mendicant *Dâmilâ*.* In a second short inscription, by reading *Maharavisa*, "of the emperor," instead of *Maharathisa*, "of Maharashtra," he identifies the *Nâyak*, or "petty chief," Agnimitra of Mahârâshtra with the great King Agnimitra of Magadha, the son of Pushpamitra, the founder of the Sunga dynasty.† Again, in his anxiety to obtain some name that would help to fix the dates of these inscriptions, he has identified *Sakara* with Vikramâditya by reading *Sakâri*, where the preceding names of Nabhâga, Nahusha, and Janamejaya, as well as the following name of Yayâti, should have shown him that the solar hero *Sagara* was the person really intended.‡

---

* Historical names and facts contained in the Kânheri Inscriptions.—Bombay Journal, V., page 24, No. 14, Inscription from Kânheri.

† Sahyâdri Inscriptions.—Bombay Journal, V., page 152, No. 1, Inscription from Karle.

‡ On the Nâsik cave Inscriptions (Bombay Journal, V., page 43, No. 1 Inscription), Dr. Bhau Dâji has adopted this erroneous identification of Vikramâditya in his Essay on Kâlidâsa. I pointed out Dr. Stevenson's error to Mr. Fergusson, but he refers to it as if a Vikramâditya was mentioned by name.—See his Essay on Indian Chronology, page 82, note 1 ("The Vikramâditya mentioned in Gotamiputra's inscription is evidently, from the company in which he is named, of pre-historic antiquity"). Mr. Fergusson must have remembered imperfectly what I told him, for there is no mention whatever of any Vikramâditya in Gotamiputra's Nâsik inscription.

INTRODUCTION.   XXIII

To Dr. Stevenson we owe the first real progress that was achieved since Prinsep, in reading the numerical figures of these old inscriptions. But he contented himself with noting the more obvious cyphers, and hastily adopted values for others, which in one case led him to make the curious blunder of assigning thirty-two days to a fortnight. This happened from reading the letter *y* as the figure for 30, by which he changed "*batiya 2*" into "*bati 32*."*

Dr. Stevenson also published several papers on the early religion of the Hindus of Southern India,† and a single paper on the *Tithyas* or *Tirthakas* of the Buddhists, whom he identifies with the Gymnosophists of the Greeks, and with the *Digambara* sect of Jains.‡ These papers show much patient research and accurate observation in a new and interesting field of inquiry, and lead us to regret that Dr. Stevenson should have been cut off in the very midst of his career, just when his judgment had become mature, and promised to guide his acknowledged scholarship to useful results.

Since Stevenson's death the study of archæology in Western India has been taken up ably and enthusiastically by a Native gentleman, Dr. BHAU DAJI, whose contributions to the Bombay Journal have thrown much light on the early history of the northern half of the peninsula. As a scholar he very early earned the thanks of all students of Indian literature and history by his essay on the Poet Kâlidâsa, and by his translations of the inscriptions in the Ajanta Caves, and of the inscriptions of Rudra Dâma and Skanda Gupta at Junagarh.§ . His reputation has since been amply maintained by his interesting and valuable notice of the "Inroads of the Scythians into India,"‖ and by his discovery of the values of several of the unknown early numerals which had puzzled Dr. Stevenson.¶

---

* See Journal of Bombay Asiatic Society, Vol. V., No. 18, Inscription from Karle, line 2.

† Royal Asiatic Society's Journal, V., pp. 189, 264, and VI., 239, "On the ante-Brahmanical worship of the Hindus of the Dakhan ;" ditto, VII., 1, "On the intermixture of Buddhism with Brahmanism in the religion of the Hindus of the Dakhan ;" ditto, VII., 64, "On the Buddha-Vaishnavas of the Dakhan."

‡ Bombay Asiatic Society's Journal, Vol. V.

§ Bombay Asiatic Society's Journal, VI., published in 1867, "On the Sanskrit Poet Kâlidâsa ;" ditto, VII., "Ajanta Inscriptions," and "Translations of the Rudra Dâma and Skanda Gupta Inscriptions at Junagarh."

‖ Ditto, IX., p. 189, "The Inroads of the Scythians into India."

¶ Ditto, VIII., p. 225, "The Ancient Sanskrit Numerals in the Cave Inscriptions, and on the Sah Coins."

But Dr. Bhau Daji's judgment has not kept pace with his scholarship, and he has consequently been led to the publication of several very grave errors. He thus rashly announces his condemnation of Dr. Mill's translation of part of the Bhitari Inscription: "I may now warn writers on Indian antiquities against implicitly receiving as correct the names given by Dr. Mill of the female connexions of the Guptas, namely, Lichchhavi and Kumári Devi."* I am happily in a position to settle this point by proving the absolute accuracy of Dr. Mill's translation, by referring Dr. Bhau Dáji to the gold coins of Chandra Gupta bearing two figures, male and female, on the obverse, and a female seated on a lion on the reverse. These precious coins would almost seem to have been designed by Chandra Gupta's mint-master for the special purpose of refuting Dr. Bhau Dáji's assertion, by labelling the two figures on the obverse as "*Chandra Gupta*" and "*Kumári Devi*," and by adding the name of *Lichchhavayah* on the reverse.†

In another place he has seriously proposed the alteration of the Chinese chronology of the pilgrim Hwen Thsang by sixty years to suit the date of Jayendra of Kashmir, simply because Hwen Thsang mentions that, on his arrival at the capital of Kashmir, he was lodged in the *Jayendra Vihára*. But surely one may sleep in a palace of Akbar without becoming a contemporary of that great Mogul. If not, then Hwen Thsang's date is hopelessly dubious, for he had already lodged in the *Hushkara Vihára* opposite Varáhamúla, and must, therefore, have been a contemporary of the Indo-Scythian prince *Hushka* or *Huvishka*, at the latter end of the first century before Christ.

I pass over some wild identifications proposed in Dr. Bhau Dáji's "Brief Survey of Indian Chronolgy," to note the curious error in what he calls a *correct* genealogical table of the Balabhi Kings supported by dates from copper plates. In this genealogy I notice that Dhruva Sena, who is dated in 310, is followed by *six* generations, all of which are made to pass away by 346, so that *seven generations*, including Dhruva

---

* Bombay Asiatic Society's Journal, VII., p. 216.

† I possess two of these coins with the legends quite legible. The names of the King and Queen are written perpendicularly. The reverse legend has hitherto been erroneously read as Panch Chharapah.

Sena, or six without him, are born, marry, and die in 30 years, which allows exactly six years to each generation.*

His last proposal is to read *cha Gilika rájena* in the Khálsi version of the famous passage in Asoka's edicts, which gives the names of the four Kings,—Ptolemy, Antigonus, Magas, and Alexander,—thus making *Gilika* a Pali form of the Latin *Græci*. But this name was not applied to the *Hellénes* until long after Asoka's time, and could not properly have been applied to the Macedonians at any time. Dr. Bhau Dáji says—" I take this opportunity of announcing that the word *Kilakila*, or *Kailakila*, *Yavanas*, which puzzled me before, is only a corruption, or rather a mislection of *Gilika* or Greek."† As I furnished Dr. Bhau Dáji with his copy of this portion of the Khálsi inscription, I am quite familiar with the words which he has thus strangely perverted. I read them as *chatuli*, 4, *rajena*, "the four, 4, Kings," taking the character, which he has made a *k*, to be the numerical symbol for 4, a mere repetition of the written word *chatuli*. The same repetition is found also in the Ariano Pali version of Kapurdigiri, where the word *chaturi* is followed by four upright strokes I I I I, like the well known Roman numeral, which cannot possibly mean anything else but the simple number 4.

But in spite of these errors due to hasty opinions and rash speculations, which will no doubt be modified hereafter by more mature judgment, I feel that Dr. Bhau Dáji is a worthy successor of Dr. Stevenson, and that he has well sustained the cause of Indian archæology in the Bombay Presidency.

Of my own share in the progress of Indian archæology I may be permitted to give a brief statement of what I have written, and of the discoveries which I have been able to make during a long and active career in India. The following is a list of my writings on my Indian antiquities:

1.—1840—Bengal Asiatic Society's Journal, IX., p. 867—Description of some new Bactrian coins.

---

* Bombay Journal, VIII., p. 236, " Brief Survey of Indian Chronology ;"—Genealogy of Balabhi Kings, p. 245.

† Bombay Asiatic Society's Journal, IX., p. CXXIV. I note that both Dr. Bhau Dáji and Babu Rajendra Lál use the barbarous word "mislection." I believe that the *Kilakila Yavanas* are not mentioned until after the Andhras, that is, not until several centuries after the total extinction of the Greek power in North-West India and the Panjáb. They were probably either Indo-Scythians, or Parthians.

2.—1842—Bengal Asiatic Society's Journal, XI., p. 130—Second notice of some new Bactrian coins.

3.—1843—Royal Asiatic Society's Journal—Account of the discovery of the ruins of the Buddhist city of Sankisa.

4.—1843—Numismatic Chronicle—The ancient coinage of Kashmir.

5.—1843—Numismatic Chronicle—Attempt to explain some of the monograms on the Greek coins of Ariana and India.

6.—1845—Bengal Asiatic Society's Journal, XIV., p. 430—Notice of some unpublished coins of the Indo-Scythians.

7.—1854—The Bhilsa Topes, or Buddhist Monuments of Central India, 8vo.

8.—1854—Bengal Asiatic Society's Journal, XXIII.—Coins of Indian Buddhist Satraps with Greek inscriptions.

9.—1863—Bengal Asiatic Society's Journal, XXXII.—Translation of the Bactro-Pali inscription from Taxila.

10.—1865—Bengal Asiatic Society's Journal, XXXIV.—Coins of the nine Nâgas, and of two other dynasties of Narwar and Gwalior.

11.—1867—Numismatic Chronicle—Coin of the Indian Prince Sophytes, a contemporary of Alexander the Great.

12.—1868-1869-1870—Numismatic Chronicle—"Coins of Alexander's successors in the East," Part I.; the Greeks of Bactriana, Ariana, and India.

13.—1870—The ancient Geography of India, Vol. I.; the Buddhist period, 8vo.

In my account of James Prinsep's final labour, I have been able to show from his letters that the anxiety which he publicly expressed to obtain more specimens of the latter coins, "which mark the decadence of Greek dominion and Greek skill," and of "those coins on which the Native and Greek legends differ, or record different names," continued down to the last, when in October 1838 he was compelled by ill health to give up work and to seek for change of air in England. This subject I was able to follow up in 1840, when the acquisition of a large number of coins from Afghanistan put me in possession of new specimens of Gondophares and Abdagases, which I published in the Journal of the Asiatic Society for that year. Several collectors then placed their cabinets at my disposal; and with the purchase of a second collection from Kandahâr and Sistân, I was able to prepare during the years 1840-41-42 no less than fifteen lithographed plates of all the known coins of the Greek and Indo-Scythian Kings of Bactriana, Ariana, and India.

While this work was in progress, I published, in 1842, a second notice of new Bactrian coins, in which I first made known the names of the Greek Kings Straton, Telephus, Hippostratus, Nikias, and Dyonysius, of the Greek Queen Kalliope, and of the Scytho-Parthian Kings Arsakes and Pakores. In these two papers I gave the true symbols of the Arian letters *d*, *g*, and *ph*, from the Native legends of the coins of Gondophares, Abdagases, and Telephus, and the true symbol for the compound letter *st* from the coins of Straton and Hippostratus. These discoveries were followed up by finding the title of *Strategasa*, for the Greek *Stratégos* or General, on the coins of the Aspa Varmma, which bear the name of the great King Azas on the obverse, and that of his Hindu General on the reverse. "These," as Prinsep truly said, "are the most precious to the student of Indian history," for they prove that the military discipline of the Greeks was still in use nearly half a century after their dominion had passed away.

At the same time I found that the reverse legends of the coins of Queen Agathokhia, which had puzzled Prinsep and Lassen, contained only the titles and name of Straton, who must, therefore, have been her husband. Continuing my discoveries, I obtained the true value of the Arian *bh* from the words *bhráta-putrasa*, or "brother's son," which, on the coins of Abdagases are the equivalent of the Greek *Adelphideós*. Following up this clue I next discovered the symbol for *gh* on the coins of the Native King *Amoghabhuti*.

About the same time I assigned one of Prinsep's series of imitations of the Indo-Scythian money to its proper country Kashmir, by identifying the coins of no less than eighteen of the Hindu Rajas, from Toramâna to Jaga Deva, who ruled from about A.D. 500 to 1200. This discovery was published in the Numismatic Chronicle for 1843. A few years later, in 1847, I was able to assign another series of some extent, but of later date and of less interest, to the Hindu Rajas of Kangra.

In 1845, in a notice of some new coins of the Indo-Scythians, I first published the reading of the name of the great *Kushán* tribe of Indo-Scythians on the coins of Kujula, and in the Mánikyála inscription of General Court. At the same time I added a genuine Buddhist type to the known coins of Kanishka.

In January and February 1851, Lieutenant Maisey and myself explored a large number of Buddhist stupas, or topes, in the Bhilsa District. In the same year I submitted a short account of our discoveries to H. H. Wilson, which he published in the Journal of the Royal Asiatic Society. At the same time I prepared a detailed account of all the stupas that we explored, with translations of several hundred short inscriptions. This work, which was completed in 1851, was not published until 1854, under the title of "The Bhilsa Topes." Twenty years have since passed, many of them years of rare experience in archæological investigation, and I see no reason to alter the dates which I then proposed of the third century B. C., for the erection of all the principal topes, and of the first century A. D. for the sculptured gateways of the great stupa.

These dates have been generally accepted; in fact, I am not aware that they have been disputed by any one save H. H. Wilson.* His arguments I will now examine at length, as it seems to me to be very important that there should be no doubt as to the age of these remarkable monuments, whose sculptures are so valuable for the illustration of Indian art. In justice also to myself I think it is absolutely necessary that I should take notice of the objections which have been publicly brought forward in a lecture on Buddha and Buddhism, by so eminent an oriental scholar as Horace Hayman Wilson.

He begins by stating that I make the age of the great Bhilsa tope as old as Asoka, "its being as old as Asoka, depending upon the identification of Gotiputra, the teacher of Mogaliputra, who presided, it is said, at the third council

---

* Royal Asiatic Society's Journal, Vol. XVI., "On Buddha and Buddhism," by H. H. Wilson, pp. 250-261.

In B. C. 241, a statement altogether erroneous, as Mogaliputra, Maudgala, or Maudgalâyana, was one of Sâkya's first disciples three centuries earlier." In this passage it is Wilson's own statement that is "altogether erroneous," and not mine; and I now repeat my former assertion that Mogaliputra *did* preside at the Buddhist synod held in the reign of Asoka. The mistake which Wilson has here made is a strange one for an oriental scholar, as he not only ignores the detailed history of this council given in the Mahawanso,* but stranger still he confounds Mogalâna or Maudgalyâyana, the disciple of Buddha, with one of his descendants, for Mogaliputra bears the same relation to Mogali that Will's-son, or Wilson, does to Will.

A little further on he falls into another error, equally great, and almost as strange as that just noticed. He objects to the date of the Bhilsa topes, which I had inferred from the inscriptions on the relic caskets, because "no legitimate conclusions can be drawn from inscriptions of this class as to the date of the Sânchi monuments," as the presence of relics in any monument is no more a proof of its antiquity, than would the hairs of Buddha, if ever dug up, prove the Shwê-Dagon of Rangoon to have been built in his day." Here the professor has entirely lost sight of the one great fact on which I relied, that the inscriptions on the caskets are *engraved in characters of Asoka's age*. On this fact alone I argued that the stupas which contained these relic caskets must be as old as the reign of Asoka. Having ignored this fact altogether and tilted against an argument which I never used, he then proceeds to say that the topes of Ceylon "*appear to be* of an earlier date, if we may credit the tradition which ascribes the erection of the Ruanvelli mound at Anurâdhapura to King Dutthagâmini, who reigned 161 B. C. to 137 B. C." So that, in the opinion of one of the most eminent Sanskrit scholars, a tradition is of more historical value than a self-evident fact, the truth of which has been admitted by every one except Wilson himself.

Having thus settled to his own satisfaction that the topes of Ceylon, which could not have been built before the

* It seems almost superfluous to refer to the Mahawanso for a fact which is so well known; but as Wilson has publicly asserted that Mogaliputra was a disciple of Buddha himself, and has branded my statement as "altogether erroneous," I refer the reader to the 3rd Chapter of Turnour's Mahawanso for the proceedings of the First Buddhist Synod under Mahakasapo; to the 4th Chapter for the Second Synod; and to the 5th Chapter for the Third Synod, held during the reign of Asoka, under the guidance of Mogaliputra.

conversion of the Ceylonese to Buddhism by Mahindo, the son of Asoka, are older than the great Sânchi stupa, which, as I have pointed out in my Bhilsa topes, almost certainly gave its name to the hill of *Chetiyagiri* which was known by that name before the birth of Mahindo, Wilson continues his remarks as follows : " A somewhat *earlier* period than that of the Indian stupas may be assigned to another important class of Buddhist monuments, the cave temples belonging to that persuasion, but they also, as far as has been yet ascertained, are subsequent to Christianity." Thus, according to Wilson, the cave temples of Western India, in which not a single inscription of Asoka's period has yet been found, are older than the Sânchi stupa, the railings of which are literally covered with inscriptions of Asoka's age.

But although the points to which Wilson so strangely took exception are not inaccurate, there are in my Bhilsa topes several undoubted errors, of which, perhaps, the worst is my making the five Kings of Magadha, whose names are mentioned by Hwen Thsang, form a continuation of the great Gupta dynasty. Their true period would appear to have been seven hundred years prior to Hwen Thsang's visit, or about 60 B. C. Accordingly I look upon these five Kings as the immediate successors of the Sunga dynasty in Magadha, and the predecessors of the Guptas, while the Kanwa Kings of the Purânas were their contemporaries in North-Western India. Following out this view, I now place the building of the great temple at Bodh-Gaya in the first century B. C.

In the same year, 1854, I published a notice of the " Coins of Indian Buddhist Satraps with Greek inscriptions," in which I made known the symbols for the Arian letters *ch* and *chh* and *rm*,* and applied the discovery of the former to prove the Buddhist faith of the Scythian King Kozola Kadaphes, who calls himself on his coins *Sachha dharma thidasa*, the " supporter of the true dharma."† Here, again, I was met by the adverse and erroneous criticism of Wilson,‡ who

---

* *Ch* is found in *aprati-chakra*, "invincible with the discus," *chh* in *chhatrapa* or Satrap, and *rm* in the two Hindu names, Aspavarmma and Indra Varmma.

† I have adopted the reading of *thidasa* from Professor Dowson, in lieu of *pidasa*, which was my original rendering.

‡ London Athenæum, 15th March 1856.

objected that "the legends of these coins had not been satisfactorily read; and he especially objected to the reading of the word *K'shatrapasa* or Satrap, the letters of which were very doubtful, and no other evidence being found to prove that this title had ever been borne by a Hindu prince." The statement that no other evidence had been found is strangely incorrect, as Prinsep had found the title in the Girnar bridge inscription of Rudra Dâma, a Hindu prince, and Wilson's own translation of this inscription, afterwards furnished to Mr. Thomas,[*] contains the title of *Mahakshatrapa* applied to Rudra Dâma. The Satraps whose coins I brought to notice in this paper were Zeionises or Jihoniya, and Raziobalos or Rajubul; and I may add of the legends of their coins, which Wilson declared "had not been satisfactorily read," that every single letter was rightly assigned.

In the same paper I first made known the names of the Scytho-Parthian Kings Orthagnes and Sasi, or Sasan, both of whom claim on their coins to be connexions of the great King Gondophares. I also added my mite towards the identification of Chandra Gupta Maurya with Sandrakoptos by bringing to notice a fragment of Euphorion, the librarian of Antiochus the Great, which makes "the Indian Môrias live in wooden houses," and the statement of Hesychius that "the Môrias were Indian Kings."

In November 1861 I began my explorations as Archæological Surveyor to the Government of India, and the results of my four years' work form the subject of the present volumes, in which are recorded the discovery of many ancient cities, of which the most famous are Taxila and Sangala in the Panjâb, Srughna, Ahichhatra, Kosâmbi, and Srâvasti in the north-west, and Nâlanda in the east.

In 1862 I discovered the names of the Macedonian months, *Artemisios* and *Apellaios*, in two of the Ariano Pali inscriptions from Afghanistan. This discovery was also made independently by Professor Dowson; and, although objected to by Babu Rajendra Lâl, it has since been fully confirmed by the further discovery of the names of *Panemos* and *Daisios* in other inscriptions. The name of Panemos occurs in the well known Taxila inscription of the Satrap

---

[*] Prinsep's Essays on Indian Antiquities, II., 68.

Liako Kujulako, dated in the 78th year of the great King *Moga*, whom I identified with the *Moas* of the coins, a conclusion which is now generally accepted. I also published a partial translation of this inscription, in which I made known the values of the Arian compounds of the letter *r* in the words *purvva*, *sarvva*, and *áchárya*, which were at the same time independently made out in England by Professor Dowson.

In a note on the same inscription, published shortly afterwards in the Journal of the Asiatic Society of Bengal, I gave the true values of the old Indian cyphers for 40, 50, 60, and 70, of which three had not previously been ascertained by Dr. Bhau Dáji in his paper published in the same journal.

In 1865 appeared my essay on the "Coins of the Nine Nágas, and of two other dynasties of Narwar and Gwalior." The coins of the Nága Kings are of considerable importance as they are certainly as old as those of the Gupta dynasty, and comprise as many names. The coins of Pasupati are valuable, as their date is almost certain; Pasupati being the son of Toramána, who ruled over the countries between the Jumna and the Narbada towards the end of the third century A.D. The latest series of coins are also interesting as they are dated and include one Hindu Prince Chábara Deva, who for a long time was the successful opponent of the early Muhammadan Kings of Delhi. In the same paper I successfully identified Narwar with the city of Padmávati of the poet Bhavabhuti, by the names of no less than four streams in its immediate vicinity which are mentioned in the drama of Málati and Mádhava.

During my stay in England from 1866 to 1870, I published first an account of the "Coin of a Indian Prince Sophytes, a contemporary of Alexander," preparatory to a long-contemplated work on the "Coins of Alexander's successors in the East," of which the first part, relating to the Greeks of Bactrina, Ariana, and India, is now nearly complete, nine out of ten portions having already appeared in the Numismatic Chronicle. In this work I have added coins of the new Kings Artemidorus, Epander, Theophilus, Apollophanes, and Straton II. Altogether there are described the coins of no less than thirty Kings with pure Greek names, of whom only seven are mentioned in history. As the coins of several of these princes are found in considerable numbers in the Panjáb and North-Western India, there can be little doubt that their conquests extended far into India, as stated by several Greek writers, and as admitted in a few passages of Sanskrit writers, which have only lately been made accessible. The history of the Eastern Greeks is, therefore, intimately connected with that of India for more than a century after the time of Asoka, when their dominions passed to the Indo-Scythians, whose occupation of Northern India, though equally certain, is barely acknowledged by Hindu writers.

Of my last work, "The Ancient Geography of India," which appeared at the close of 1870, I will say no more than that it is chiefly devoted to the illustration of the campaigns of Alexander and of the pilgrimage of Hwen Thsang.

In closing this review of the progress of Indian archæology, in which the chief share has been achieved by men who were not professed scholars, I beg it to be distinctly understood that we field archæologists make no claim to more than ordinary scholarship, and that if we have been successful in many of our archæological researches, we can truly ascribe our success in great measure to the hitherto difficult path having been smoothed by the labours of our great Sanskrit scholars, whose translations have placed within our reach nearly all the chief works of Indian learning. If we have sometimes been able to perceive what had escaped the notice of our more learned contemporaries, it has been owing to the lift that we have got from them; for, as the old scholiast says, *Pygmæi gigantum humeros, &c.*, "even pygmies on the shoulders of giants can see farther than the giants themselves."

ARCHÆOLOGICAL REPORT.

Report of operations of the Archæological Surveyor to the Government of India, during Season 1861-62.

In the explorations which I have carried out during the past season, I have adhered strictly to the plan of proceedings sketched in the memorandum which I submitted to the Governor General in November 1861. I began work in December at Gaya; and after exploring all the places of antiquarian interest in Bihâr, Tirhut, and Champâran, I visited several ancient sites in Gorakhpur, Azimgarh, and Jonpur, on my way to Banâras, where, on the 3rd April, I closed work for the season. I will now give a brief sketch of my operations at the different places in the order in which I visited them:

I. GAYA.

There are two places of the name of Gaya, one of which is called *Buddha-Gaya*, or Buddhistical Gaya, to distinguish it from the city of Gaya, which is situated six miles to the northward.* In Gaya itself there are no ancient buildings now existing; but most of the present temples have been erected on former sites and with old materials. Statues, both Buddhistical and Brahmanical, are found in all parts of the old city, and more especially about the temples, where they are fixed in the walls, or in small recesses forming separate shrines in the court-yards of the larger temples. I have noted the names and localities of all these statues.

The inscriptions at Gaya are numerous; but, owing to the destruction of the ancient temples, there are but few of them in situ, or attached to the objects which they were originally designed to commemorate. I have taken copies of all the inscriptions, of which the most interesting is a long and perfect one, dated in the era of the *Nirvân*, or death of Buddha. I read the date as follows:

Bhagavati parinirvritte samvat 1819 Karttike badi 1 Budhe,

that is, "in the year 1819 of the emancipation of Bhagavata, on Wednesday, the first day of the waning moon of Kartik."

---

* See Plate III.

If the era here used is the same as that of the Buddhists of Ceylon and Burmah, which began in 543 B.C., the date of this inscription will be 1810—543=A.D. 1270. The style of the letters is in keeping with this date, but is quite incompatible with that derivable from the Chinese date of the era. The Chinese place the death of Buddha upwards of 1,000 years before Christ, so that, according to them, the date of this inscription would be about A.D. 800, a period much too early for the style of character used in the inscription. But as the day of the week is here fortunately added, the date can be verified by calculation. According to my calculation the date of the inscription corresponds with Wednesday, the 17th September, A.D. 1342. This would place the *Nirvâna* of Buddha in 477 B.C., which is the very year that was first proposed by myself as the most probable date of that event. This corrected date has since been adopted by Professor Max Muller.*

Some of the inscriptions, though less interesting, are still valuable for the light which they will throw upon the mediæval period of Indian history. Several Rajas are mentioned in them; and in one of them the date is very minutely detailed in several different eras.

The most noteworthy places at Gaya are the temples of *Vishnu-pad*, or "Vishnu's feet;" of *Gadádhar*, or the "macebearer," a title of Vishnu, and of *Gayeswari Devi*. The figure in this last temple is, however, that of Durgâ slaying the Buffalo, or Maheshâsur; but as the destruction of the Asur Gaya is universally attributed to Vishnu, this temple's must originally have contained a statue of that god as Gayeswara Deva, or the "lord of Gaya." Gaya was an *Asur* or demon. All the gods and goddesses sat upon him, but were unable to keep him down, when Vishnu put his foot upon him and prevailed; and the giant is said to be still lying there under the temple of *Vishnu-pad*. This, however, is the Brahmanical story, for the Buddhists say that the name is derived from Gaya Kasyapa, a fire-worshipper, who on this very spot was overcome by Buddha in argument.

---

* I have since submitted this date to the scrutiny of my learned friend Bapu Deva Sastri, the well known astronomer; according to whose calculation the 1st of *Kartik badi* in A.D. 1270 was a Friday, and in A.D. 1342 a Monday; but in A.D. 1341 it fell on Wednesday the 7th of October N.S., which would place the beginning of the Buddhist era in B.C. 478.

ג.

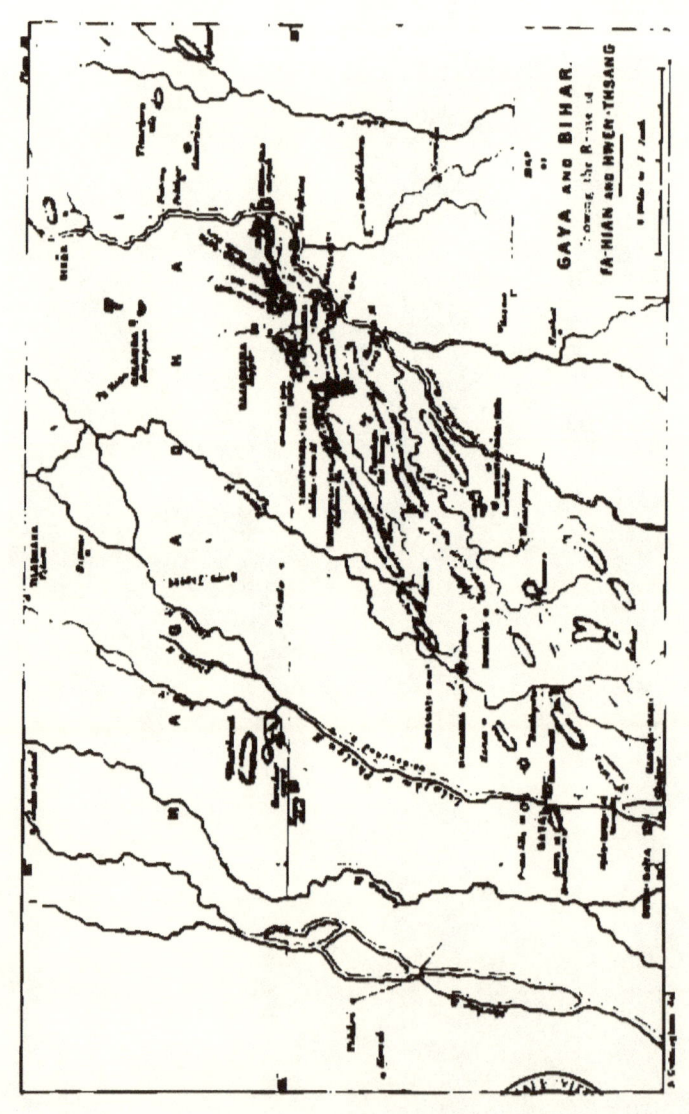

MAP
of
N.W. INDIA
A.D 630

showing HWEN-THSANG'S route

32 Miles to 1 Inch

Several interesting sculptures, and one long and well preserved inscription, are also to be seen at the *Krishna Dwárika* temple.

In the neighbourhood of the Vishnu-pad there is a deep tank called Suraj Kūnd, to the west of which is a temple to *Surya* or the Sun. The vestibule of this temple is formed of two double rows of pillars, all ten feet in height, and all leaning more or less to the north. There are five pillars in each row. The whole temple, both inside and outside, has been repeatedly white-washed, so as almost to conceal the ornaments of the pillars. One long inscription was found inside, and a second was afterwards obtained by scraping off the thick coating of white-wash from a part of the wall pointed out by a good-natured Brahman. This inscription was the valuable one first mentioned as containing a date in the era of the death of Buddha.

The several hills in the immediate neighbourhood are also esteemed holy, and are accordingly crowned with temples. The highest of these, to the south of the town, is called *Brahmjuin*, or *Brahma-yoni*, the temple on its summit being dedicated to the *Sakti*, or female energy of Brahma, whose five-headed statue is enshrined in the temple.* This figure is placed on an old pedestal which is said to have been inscribed with a verse stating the date of erection in V. S. 1690 or A. D. 1633. The destruction of the statue is attributed with much probability to Aurang Shah. On the left hand of this statue there is a small two-armed standing figure with a horse on the pedestal. It is, therefore, most probably a statue of Sambhunáth, the 3rd of the 24 Jain hierarchs, whose cognizance is a horse. Beside this figure there is a group of Siva and Párvati with the Bull Nandi below, and a short imperfect inscription in three lines, of which only one-half now remains. The characters belong to the period of the 10th or 11th century. The hill is 450 feet in height, and very steep on the town side. But the ascent has been rendered easy to pilgrims by the erection of a long flight of steps from the base to the summit by the Mahratta Deva Rao Bhao Saheb, since the accession of the present Maharaja Jáyaji, of Gwalior, that is, within the last 18 years, as recorded on an inscription slab let into the pavement.

---

* See Plate III. for the position of this hill. This statue belongs properly to Siva who has five heads, as Brahma has only four heads.

To the north of the town, the granite hill of *Rámsila* rises to a height of 372 feet. The granite temple on its summit contains a lingam called *Pátáleswara* Mahadeva, as well as small figures of Siva and Párbati. The upper portion of this temple is modern, being constructed of various ancient fragments that do not fit well together, and which are in some instances placed upside down. The lower part of the temple, from eight to ten feet in height, is undoubtedly old; and perhaps the date of 1071 Samvat, or A. D. 1014, found on one of the blocks of the granite pavement may record the actual period of the erection of the temple. The basement mouldings are strikingly bold and effective.

To the north-west of the town, the hill of *Pretsila* bears a small temple erected by Ahalya Bai to pacify the ghost or spirit *(preta)* who is said to dwell in the hill. I could learn nothing of the origin of this spirit, who is held in great awe, from which I infer that he is identical with Yama, the god of death, one of whose titles is *Pretaraja*, or king of ghosts, that is, of departed spirits. The hill is 641 feet in height, and its rocks are believed to contain gold. The shrine is much frequented by pilgrims who seek to appease the dread spirit by their offerings. There is a curious serpentine road leading from the foot of Rámsila to Pretsila. The road has been metalled, and trees have been planted on both sides of it by some wealthy devotees.

Ráma Gaya is a small hill on the eastern bank of the Phalgu River, opposite Brahmjuin. There are some ruins and broken statues scattered about it, but nothing of any interest except one short inscription of *Sri Mahendra Pála Deva*, dated in the eighth year of his own reign, or of some new era.

II. BUDDHA-GAYA.

Buddha-Gaya is famous as the locality of the holy Pipal tree under which Sákya Sinha sat for six years in mental abstraction, until he obtained Buddhahood. The name is usually written Buddha-Gaya; but as it is commonly pronounced Bodh-Gaya, I have little doubt that it was originally called Bodhi-Gaya, after the celebrated Bodhi-drûm or "tree of knowledge." A long and detailed account of this sacred place is given by the Chinese pilgrim Hwen Thsang, who travelled all over India between the years A. D. 629 and

642. He describes minutely all the temples and statues which surrounded the celebrated Pipal tree, known throughout the Buddhist world as the *Bodhi-drūm*. Several of the objects enumerated by the Chinese pilgrim I have been able to identify from their exact correspondence with his description.*

The celebrated Bodhi tree still exists, but is very much decayed; one large stem, with three branches to the westward, is still green, but the other branches are barkless and rotten. The green branch perhaps belongs to some younger tree, as there are numerous stems of apparently different trees clustered together. The tree must have been renewed frequently, as the present Pipal is standing on a terrace at least 30 feet above the level of the surrounding country. It was in full vigour in 1811, when seen by Dr. Buchanan (Hamilton), who describes it as in all probability not exceeding 100 years of age. Hwen Thsang also describes an early renewal by King *Purna Varmma* after its destruction by King *Sasángka*, who dug up the ground on which it had stood, and moistened the earth with sugar-cane juice to prevent its renewal.

Immediately to the east of the Pipal tree there is a massive brick temple, nearly 50 feet square at base and 160 feet in height from the granite floor of the lower story to the top of its broken pinnacle. This is beyond all doubt the *Vihár*, from 160 to 170 feet in height, described by Hwen Thsang as standing to the east of the Bodhi tree. Its base was about 20 paces square. It was built of bluish bricks plastered with lime; it was ornamented with niches in stages, each niche holding a golden statue of Buddha, and was crowned with an *amalaka* fruit in gilt copper. The existing temple, both in size and appearance, corresponds so exactly with this description, that I feel quite satisfied it must be the identical temple that was seen by Hwen Thsang. The ruined temple, as it now stands, is 160 feet in height, with a base of rather less than 50 feet square. It is built entirely of dark red brick of a bluish tinge, and has formerly been plastered all over. Lastly, the walls are ornamented externally

---

* The life and travels of Hwen Thsang have been given to the world by M. Stanislas Julien in three volumes entitled *Voyages des Pélerins Bouddhistes*. This translation, the work of twenty years' persevering labor in the acquisition of Chinese and Sanskrit, combined with an intimate knowledge of Buddhist literature, is a lasting monument of human industry and learning.

with eight tiers, or rows, of niches, many of which still hold figures of Buddha. These figures are made of plastered brick, but they were no doubt formerly gilt, as is done with the plaster statues of the Burmese at the present day. There is, however, no trace of the copper-gilt *amalaka* fruit. I have thus been particular in noting the points of correspondence between the two temples, because there seems to me to be a very strong probability that the existing temple was originally built by the celebrated *Amara Sinha*, the author of the *Amara Kosha*, as I will now proceed to show.

On the site of this temple, according to Hwen Thsang, there was originally a small *Vihár* built by Asoka between 250 and 241 B. C.* Afterwards, a new temple of very great size was built by a Brahman in compliance with the instructions of the god Mahadeva conveyed to him in a vision. Inside the temple was placed a statue of the ascetic Buddha as he appeared when seated in meditation under the Bodhi tree. The statue was 11 feet and 5 inches in height, 8 feet 8 inches in breadth across the knees, and 6 feet 2 inches across the shoulders. The figure was sitting cross-legged facing the east. Now these particulars correspond almost exactly with the arrangements of the present building. Its doorway is towards the east, and consequently the enshrined statue must have faced toward the east. The statue itself has long ago disappeared, but its pedestal still remains in good order. Its dimensions are as follows: length 13 feet 2 inches, breadth 5 feet 8 inches, and height 4 feet ½ inch, which measurements agree most closely with those recorded by Hwen Thsang; namely 12 feet 5 inches in length by 4 feet 2 inches in height. Considering how exactly both the temple and the pedestal of the figure correspond in size and in other respects with the description of Hwen Thsang, I think there can be no reasonable doubt that the present temple is the same that was seen by him in the 7th century of our era.†

Now, in an inscription dated in A. D. 948, which was found at Buddha-Gaya, and translated by Sir Charles Wilkins,‡ the author of the record ascribes the building of this

---
* Julien's Hwen Thsang, II., 465.
† See Plate IV. for a plan of the temple, and Plate V. for the pedestal.
‡ Bengal Asiatic Researches, vol. I.

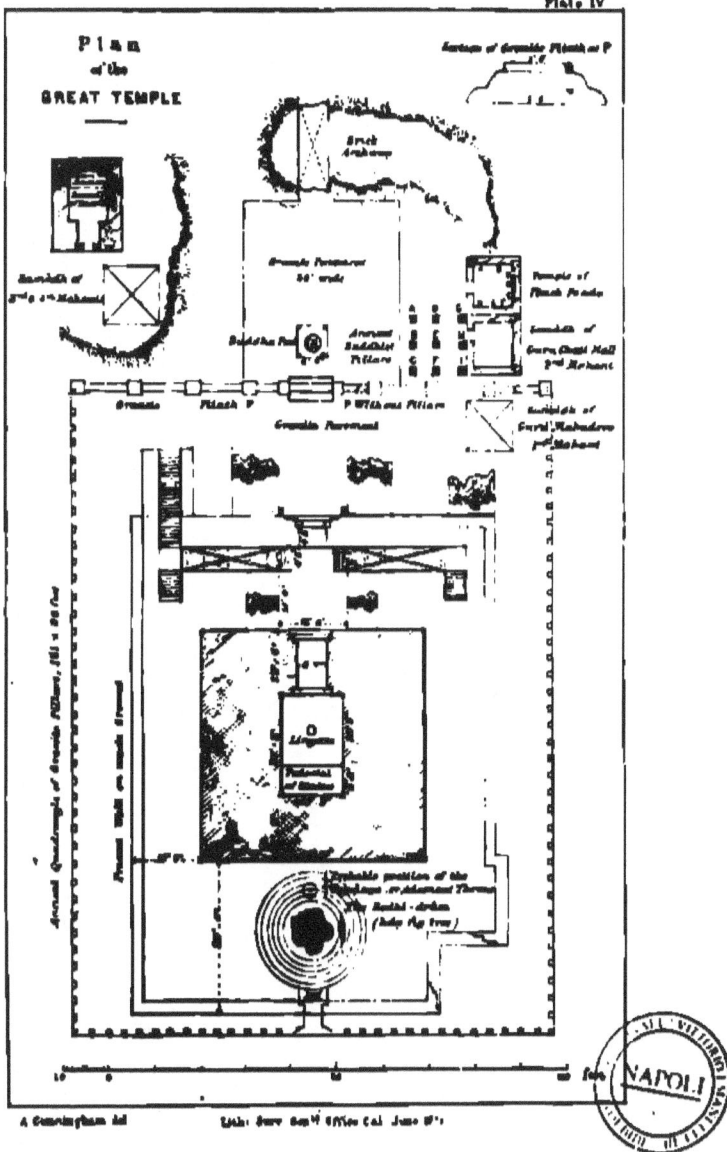

BUDDHA—GAYA.

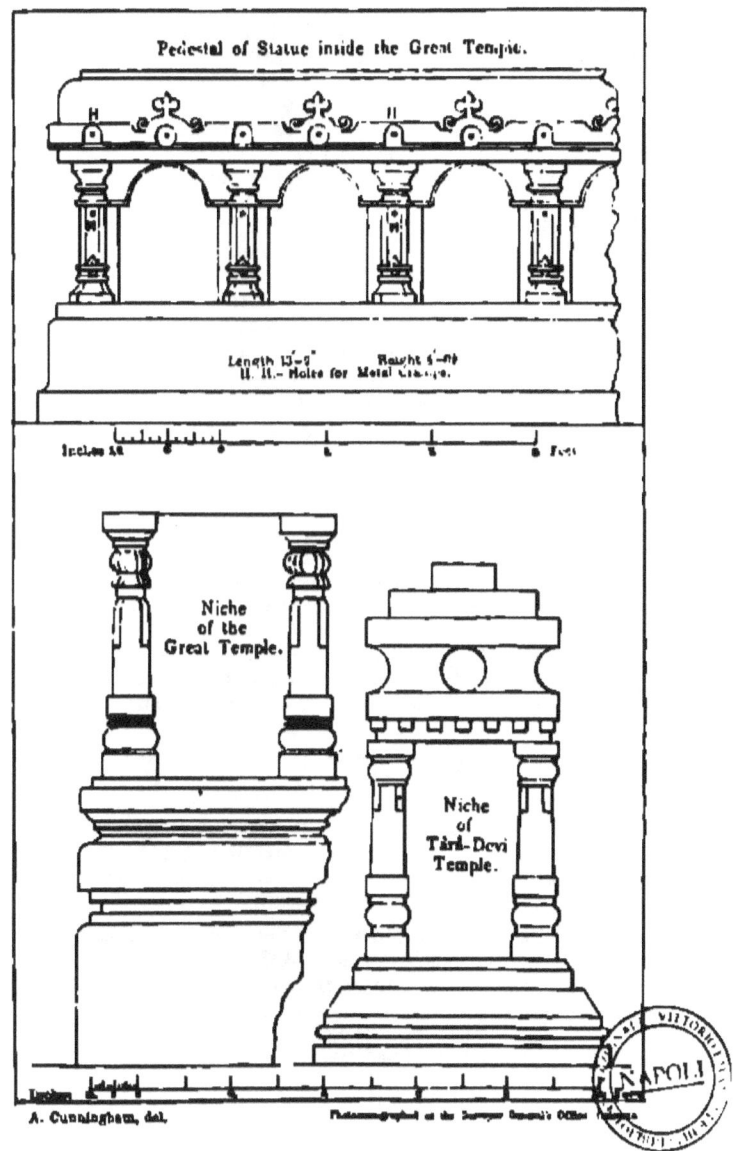

temple, and the erection of an image of Buddha, to the illustrious *Amara Deva*, who is stated to have been one of the nine gems of the court of King Vikramaditya. The last fact serves at once to identify Amara Deva with Amara Sinha, the author of the Amara Kosha, who, as a contemporary of *Vardha Mihira* and *Kálidás*, must have lived in A. D. 500. In this inscription the temple is said to have been erected in compliance with the command of Buddha himself, conveyed to him in a vision. Here then we have the same story that is found in Hwen Thsang. In both statements, a Brahman in a vision receives command from a deity to build a temple with an enshrined figure of a god. The correspondence is complete, excepting only one curious point of difference in the name of the god, whom the Buddhist Hwen Thsang describes as the Brahmanical Mahádeva, but whom the Brahmanist recorder of the inscription calls Buddha himself.

The holy places at Buddha-Gaya were visited between A. D. 399 and 414 by another Chinese pilgrim Fa-Hian, but his account of them is unfortunately very brief. It is, however, sufficient to show that there was no temple in existence at that date. Fa-Hian notes the spot where Buddha, seated on a stone under a great tree, eat some rice presented to him by two maidens. The stone still existed, and is described by him as about 6 feet in length and breadth, and 2 feet in height.* Now, there is a large circular stone, 5 feet 7½ inches in diameter and about 2 feet high, in the small temple of *Vageswari Devi*, which from its dimensions would seem to be the identical stone described by Fa-Hian. It is a blue stone streaked with whitish veins, and the surface is covered with concentric circles of various minute ornaments. The second circle is composed of *Vajras* only. The third is a wavy scroll, filled with figures of men and animals. These circles occupy a breadth of 15 inches, leaving in the centre a plain circle, 3 feet 1¼ inches in diameter, inside which is a square. This simple stone I believe to be the same as that mentioned by Hwen Thsang as a blue stone with remarkable veins.†

From all the facts which I have brought forward, such as the non-existence of any temple in A. D. 400, the recorded erection of a large one by Amara Deva about A. D. 500, and

---

* Beal's Fa-Hian, c. XXXI.
† Julien's Hwen Thsang, II., 471.

the exact agreement in size as well as in material and ornamentation between the existing temple and that described by Hwen Thsang between A. D. 620 and 642, I feel satisfied that the present lofty temple is the identical one that was built by the celebrated Amara Sinha about A. D. 500.

Further information regarding this temple is to be found in the Burmese inscription discovered at Buddha-Gaya by the Burmese Mission in 1833, and translated by Colonel Burney.* Another earlier translation by Ratna Pâla was published by James Prinsep. In this inscription the dates have been read differently by the two translators; Ratna Pâla and James Prinsep reading 667 and 668, while Colonel Burney and his Burmese assistants read 467 and 468. I have carefully copied this inscription, and I am thus enabled to state positively that Colonel Burney was certainly wrong in adopting the earlier date in compliance with the views of the Burmese priests, whose object it was to reconcile the date of the inscription with their own history. James Prinsep remained unconvinced by Colonel Burney's arguments, and appended a note to his translation, in which he states that the first figure of the upper date might be a little doubtful, but that the first six of the lower date seemed to him quite plain, and essentially different from the four which occurs in the second line of the inscription. The two dates of 667 and 668 of the Burmese era, as read by Ratna Pâla, correspond with A. D. 1305 and 1306.

In this Burmese inscription, the erection of the original temple is ascribed to Asoka, as recorded also by Hwen Thsang. Having become ruined, it is said to have been rebuilt by a priest named *Naik Mahanta* according to Ratna Pâla, or by a lord named *Penthagu-gyi* by Colonel Burney. Where the term "priest" is used by Ratna Pâla, Colonel Burney gives "lord," because, as he states, it is not now customary to say *ta-youk* of a priest, although in former times both priests and laymen are said to have been styled *youk*. The Burmese affix *gyi*, which means "great," has apparently been translated into the Indian *Nayak* or Chief; and *Penthagu*, which Colonel Burney regards as a proper name, and which would, therefore, be *Pensagu* in Indian pronunciation, is rendered Mahanta by Ratna Pâla. I cannot

* Bengal Asiatic Researches, XX., 197; and Journal, Bengal Asiatic Society, 1834, p. 214.

BUDDHA—GAYA. Plate VII

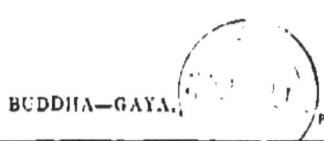

BUDDHA—GAYA.

Plate VI

No. 1 Pavement Slab of Great Temple, S. 1385.

No. 2 Pavement Slab of Great Temple, S. 1238.

A. Cunningham, del.

pretend to reconcile these differences myself; but I submitted a copy of the inscription to Sir Arthur Phayre, whose intimate knowledge, both of the Burmese language and of the Buddhist history, entitles him to give an authoritative opinion on the disputed points of this interesting record. He reads the two dates as 667 and 660, corresponding with A. D. 1305 and 1298.* One thing is quite clear, if these different records are to be reconciled, namely, that *Penthagu-gyi* (or *Naik Muhanta*) should represent the Brahman of Hwen Thsang, and also the celebrated Amara Deva of Wilkin's inscription.

The Burmese inscription goes on to say that the temple, after being again destroyed, was re-built by King *Thado*. Then having once more become ruinous, the "Lord of the White Elephant" and the great "King of Righteousness" deputed *Sri Dharmmapada Rajaguna* to re-build it for a third time. After some delay, the work was begun in A. D. 1305, and the temple was consecrated in the following year 1306.

The granite pavement both inside the temple and in the court-yard outside is covered with rudely carved figures kneeling in adoration after the manner of the Burmese *Shiko*. Two specimens are given in Plate VI. with their accompanying inscriptions. The upper one is dated in Samvat 1365 or A. D. 1328, and the lower one three years later. The inscriptions record the names of the worshippers. On the left of the upper slab the inscription gives the name of a Thákur and of two Thákurins, no doubt his wives, one of whom is called *Jájo*. From the representation of a *stupa* as the object of worship on the right of the upper slab, it would appear that at least one holy *stupa* was still standing at so late a date as A. D. 1328.

In front of the Great Temple there is a small open temple of four pillars covering a large circular stone, with two human feet carved upon it. This temple is now called *Buddha-pad*; but there can be little doubt that it is the same which is mentioned in the Amara Deva's inscription under the name of Vishnu-pad or "Vishnu's feet." Originally the feet may have been those of Buddha, which, on the

---

* In a private letter dated 9th March 1869.

decline of Buddhism, were quietly appropriated to Vishnu by the accommodating Brahmans. There is a short Nâgari inscription on the east side of the stone, giving the date of Sâke 1230, which is equivalent to A. D. 1308.*

There are other points of interest connected with the building of the Great Temple at Buddha-Gaya, such as the date of the Brahmanist King *Sasángka*, who rooted up the Bodhi tree, and placed an image of Mahâdeva in the temple, as well as the date of his contemporary the Buddhist *Purna Varmma*, who renewed the Bodhi tree.

Close to the Great Temple there is a small plain *Samádh*, or cenotaph, over the remains of the earliest Brahmanical *Mahant*. This is of no interest in itself, but the vestibule in front is supported on nine square sand-stone pillars, which have once formed part of a Buddhist railing, similar to those at Sânchi near Bhilsa, and which cannot be of much later date than Asoka. Many similar pillars, but of granite, support the arcades in one of the courts of the Mahant's residence. A few of them bear an inscription in the ancient Pali characters of Asoka's well known records, *Ayáye Kuragiye dánam*, that is, " Gift to the holy Kuragi." There are altogether 33 of these pillars still remaining, of which five or six bear the above inscription. As the pillars are all sculptured, the value of the gift made to the holy *Kuragi* could not have been less than 10,000 Rupees. Some of the sculptured bas-reliefs on these pillars are highly interesting. They show the Buddhistic belief of the donor in the veneration for solid towers and trees ; they show the style of architecture in the representations of temples, houses, gates and city walls ; and the costumes of the people in the dresses of the king, and of other worshippers of each sex.†

Of the 33 ancient pillars above described, there are 10 of sand-stone from some distant quarry, and 23 of granite from the neighbouring hills. They are all of the same dimensions and of the same age ; but as the two sets of

---

* See Plate VII. for a view of this famous stone.

† See Plate VII. for the inscription, and Plates VIII., IX., X. and XI., for the pillars of the Buddhist railing and their sculptured medallions. The excavations which have since been made by Government, on my recommendation, have brought to light a similar series of granite pillars which form an oblong colonnade surrounding the Great Temple, 131 feet from east to west, and 96 feet from north to south. Several of the lower horizontal rails are still attached to the broken pillars.

BUDDHA - GAYA   Plate IX

Buddhist Railing - Middle Pillars
Upper Basreliefs

N° IV.
Granite

N° XIII
Granite

F
Sandstone

N
Granite

A
Sandstone

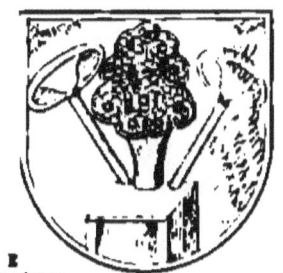

E
Sandstone

A. Cunningham del   Lith Surv Genrl Office Cal June 1871

BUDDHA—GAYA.

Buddhist Railing-Middle Pillars.
Upper Basreliefs.

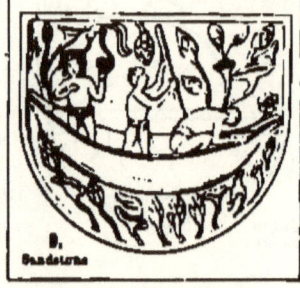
D.
Sandstone.

E.
Sandstone.

L.
Sandstone.

N.
Sandstone.

Granite.

S.
Sandstone.

A. Cunningham, del.

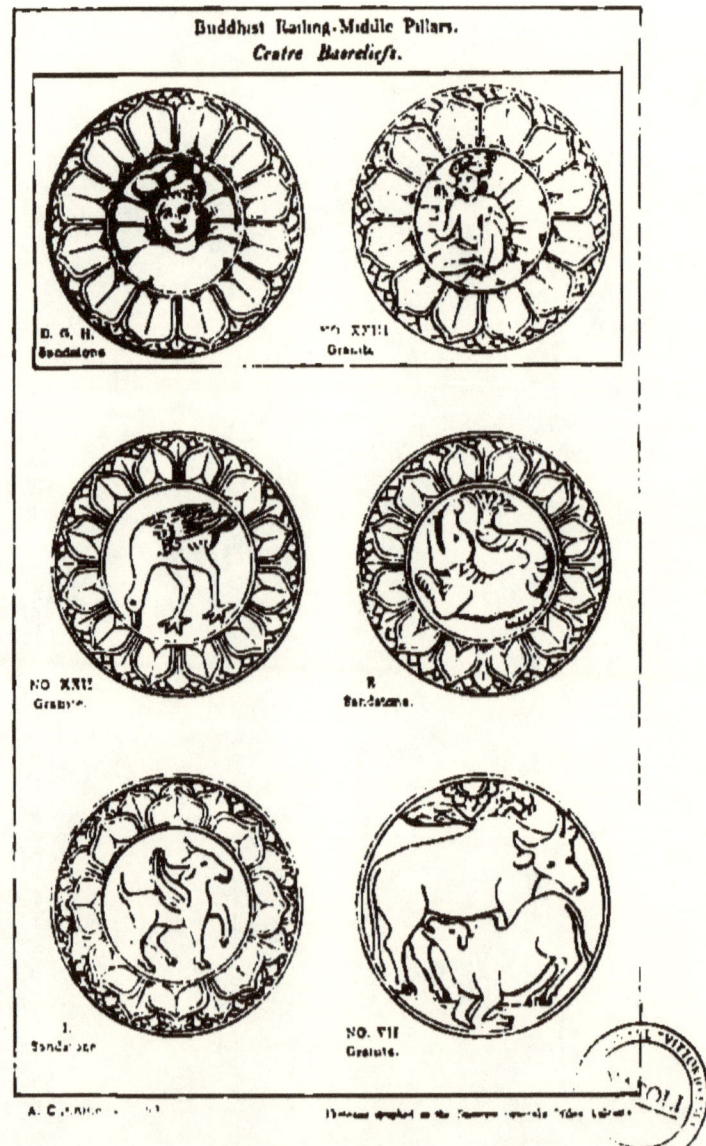

pillars were found in different localities, although not far apart, I believe that they originally formed different enclosures. The sand-stone pillars are said to have been found at the southern side of the Great Temple, and close to the holy Pipal tree. I believe, therefore, that they originally formed an enclosure round the Bodhi tree itself. The granite pillars are said to have been discovered about 50 yards to the east of the Great Temple; and I think it probable that they once formed an enclosure either round the *stupa* which stood on the spot where Buddha received a bowl of rice and milk from two milkmaids. According to Hwen Thsang, this stupa was to the south-west of the Great Temple.*

To the south-east of the Great Temple there is a small tank called *Budhokar Tâl*, which exactly answers the description given by the Chinese pilgrim of the tank of the dragon *Muchalinda.*† This agreement is so striking, that it was seen at once by the members of the Burmese Embassy.

There are two ruined small temples to the east of the Great Temple, the nearer one being called *Tára Devi*, and the further one *Vágesıcari Devi*. But the former temple contains only a standing male figure, with a short inscription over the right shoulder in characters of about A. D. 1000, *Sri Buddha-Dásasya*, "(the gift) of the fortunate slave of Buddha." The goddess Tára belongs to the later days of Buddhism, after the introduction of Tântrika doctrines. The other temple contains a seated male figure, holding a lotus in his left hand, and sword in his uplifted right hand, with a Buddhist tope or solid tower on each side of him.

To the north of the Bodhi tree there is a ruined fortress of earth 1,500 feet long by 1,000 feet broad, attributed to Raja *Amara Sinha Sutira*. This is possibly the same person as the Amara Deva who built the Great Temple, as the arched passage leading to the temple is said to have been built for the convenience of Amara Sinha's Râni when returning from her morning bath in the Nilâjan River to pay her devotions at the shrine. The preservation of the title of Sinha down to the present day would seem to strengthen the supposition of Amara Deva's identity with the author of the Amara Kosha.

---

* I venture to make this guess, as *tûra* or *tûr* is the Sanskrit name for "boiled rice," and *hwen* may, therefore, have been the name of the holy spot where Buddha accepted the offering of the milkmaids. *Hwen* means also a measure of land in Mahratti; the inscription may, therefore, mean simply "Gift to the holy spot of land."

† Julien's Hwen Thsang, II., 478.

The remaining antiquities at Buddha-Gaya consist of numerous Buddhist statues of all sizes, some placed in small temples, and others scattered about the ruins; but the greatest number of them, and by far the finest, are fixed in the walls of the Mahant's residence.

The existing inscriptions at Buddha-Gaya are few in number, and, with one exception, they are of little importance. Two valuable inscriptions, translated by Wilkins and James Prinsep, are no longer to be found; nor does the Mahant know anything about them. This is the more to be regretted, as the former was the record already quoted of Amara Deva, and the other had a doubtful date which might have been re-examined. In searching for these, however, I found a new inscription in the pavement of the gateway of the Mahant's residence. The tenon hinge of the gate works in a socket formed in the very middle of the inscription. There are two socket holes, the second one having belonged to an older gate, or having been cut in the wrong position. This inscription opens with an invocation to Buddha.

III. BAKROR.

To the eastward of Buddha-Gaya, on the opposite bank of the Phalgu or Lilájan River, and immediately to the north of the village of Bakror, there are the ruins of a large brick tope, with a stump of a sand-stone pillar at a short distance to the northward. The ruined mound, which is called Katani, is 150 feet in diameter at base, and 50 feet high. It is built of the usual large bricks, 15¼ × 10¼ × 3¼. Several excavations have been made in it in search of bricks and treasure. About 70 years ago numerous lac seals, impressed with a figure of Buddha, were found in excavating this tope. These are engraved in Moor's Hindu Pantheon, Plate LXX., Figures 6, 7, and 8, where they are said to have been dug up at Buddha-Gaya. My information was, however, derived from the Mahant himself; and as Bakror is only half a mile to the eastward, it would have been more correct to have described the locality as *near*, instead of at, Buddha-Gaya. The stump of the pillar, which is still in situ, is 3 feet 0¼ inch in diameter, and there is another fragment near a well to the north-west that measures 3 feet 0¼ inch in diameter. Both of these pieces belong to the rough bottom portion of the pillar, which must

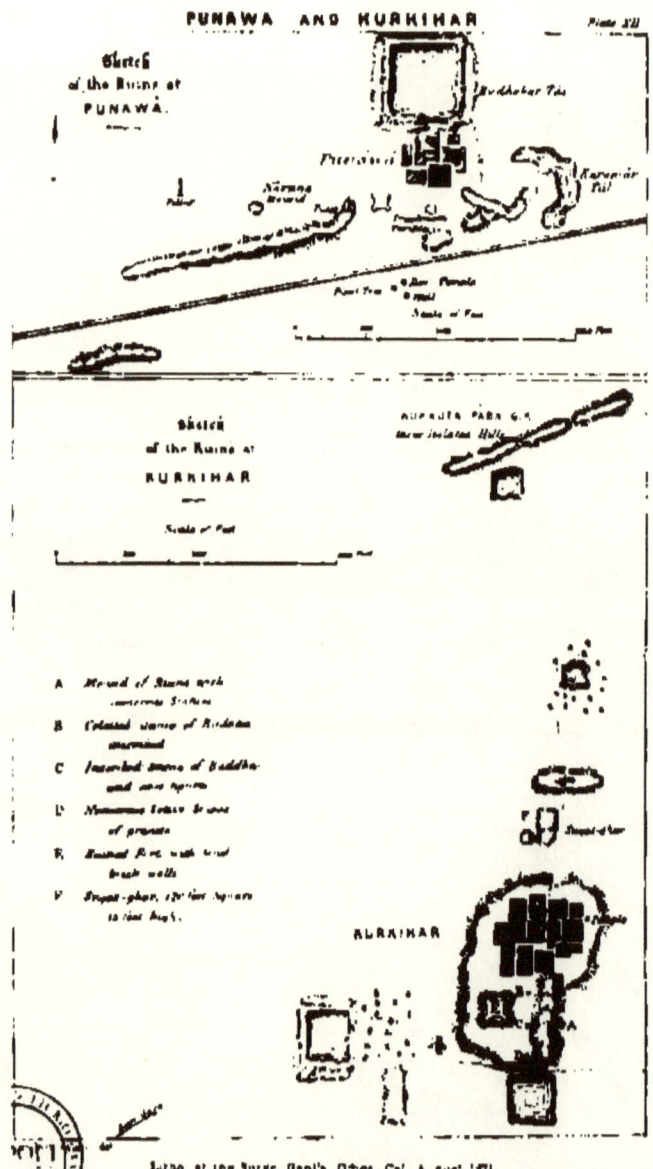

have been imbedded in masonry. The shaft of this pillar is said to have been taken to Gaya by a former Magistrate. Accordingly in Sáhebganj, or the new city of Gaya, there is a sand-stone pillar 2 feet 4¾ inches in diameter, and upwards of 16 feet in height, which was set up as a central point in Sáhebganj, as recorded in a Persian inscription by Charles Búdom Saheb (Boddam) in A. D. 1789.

The tope and pillar of Bakror were visited by Hwen Thsang, who relates a story regarding the capture by a certain king of an "Elephant of Perfume" *(gandha-hasti)*.* In a former existence, as a Bodhisatwa, Buddha was said to have been the son of this Elephant, and a stupa and pillar had accordingly been erected in commemoration of the tradition. There was also a sacred tank, which is, perhaps, represented by a small walled tank generally called *Márttand Pokhar* or *Suraj Kúnd*, that is, the "Tank of the Sun." It is also called *Buddhakúnd;* but this name was applied by some to a large unwalled tank about 800 feet square, immediately to the north of the small tank. An annual fair is held at the Suraj Kúnd, when thousands of pilgrims assemble to bathe in its holy waters. They sit in the water in rows, and repeat, after their attendant Brahmans, the names of all the holy places around Gaya. The ancient name of Bakror is said to have been *Ajayapura*.

IV. PUNAWA.

The village of Punáwá is situated 1·4 miles to the eastward of Gaya, between two hills of grey granite. To the north there is a fine old square tank called *Budhokar Tál*, and to the east another tank called *Karamár Tál*. The principal object is a pillared temple of *Triloknáth*. As it stands at present, this temple is a modern work made up of different sized pillars of various patterns, some with and others without capitals, so as to bring them to the required height. Pilasters have even been made use of as whole pillars, with the old rough engaged backs left exposed. One of the doorways of hard blue stone is richly sculptured. In the centre is a figure of the ascetic Buddha, with a three-pointed crown over his head, and on each side of him nine figures with joined hands

---

* Julien's Hwen Thsang, III., 1.

kneeling towards him. The other doorways are of granite, and, though very plain, are evidently of the same age as the more highly ornamented one.*

Several statues and granite pillars of different sizes are scattered about the foot of the hills. Portions of the usual Buddhist formula, "*Ye Dharmma*," &c., are found upon some of the statues. There are no dates in any of these inscriptions, but the style of their letters fixes their date at about A. D. 1000. To the north-west, on a mound 60 feet square, there are five broken pillars and a broken statue of the three-headed goddess *Vajra-Varáhi*, one of the principal objects of worship amongst the later Buddhists. Two of her heads are human, but the third is that of a hog, and on the pedestal there are seven hogs. The ruined temple on this mound is called *Nárling*.

V. KURKIHAR.

About three miles to the north-east of Punáwá is the large village of Kurkihár. It is not to be found in any of our maps, not even in No. 103 sheet of the Indian Atlas, although it is perhaps the largest place between the cities of Gaya and Bihár. The remains at Kurkihár consist of several ruined mounds, in which numerous statues and small votive topes of dark blue stone have been found. The principal mass of ruin, about 600 feet square, lies immediately to the south of the village.* A second less extensive mound lies to the south-west; and there is a small mound, only 120 feet square, to the north of the village. The last mound is called *Sugatgarh*, or the "house of *Sugata*," one of the well known titles of Buddha. In the principal mass of ruin, the late Major Kittoe dug up a great number of statues and votive topes; and a recent excavation on the west side showed the solid brick-work of a Buddhist stupa. In the north-west corner of this excavation the relic chamber had been reached, and I was privately informed that a small figure and some other remains had been discovered inside. But the head man of the village stoutly denied that anything had been found, and all the villagers *then* denied the discovery also.

---

* See Plate XII.

NĀLANDA

1. Four-armed Female Statue—Kapalera.

2. Bas-relief of Ashta-Sakti.

3. Four-armed Male Figure Trambhak

4. Broken Pedestal

RĀJGIR
5. Son-Bhāndār Cave.

GIRYEK
6. Seated Male Figure.

KURKIHĀR
7. Architrave.

A. Cunningham del.

The principal statue is a squatted figure of the ascetic Buddha under the holy Pipal tree, or *Bodhi-drum*. Overhead there is a representation of the *Nirvána*, or death of Buddha, and on the pedestal there is an inscription in three lines, which is incomplete owing to the loss of a projecting corner of the base. To the right and left there are smaller figures of *Máyá* standing under the Sál tree at the birth of Buddha, and of Buddha himself teaching the law at Banáras after his first attainment of Buddhahood. On the mound to the east there is a standing figure of Buddha, with a small attendant figure holding an umbrella over him. As this attendant has three heads, I believe that it represents the Hindu Triad in the humble position of a servitor of Buddha.

At the north-east corner of the village there is a small rude Hindu temple of brick, in and about which a large number of statues have been collected. The temple is dedicated to Bágheswari Devi (Vyághreswari), but the principal figure inside is a life-size statue of the eight-armed *Durgá* conquering the Maheshásur or Buffalo demon. The figure pointed out to me as that of Bágheswari was a four-armed female seated on a lion with a child in her lap; but I believe that this figure represents either *Indráni* with her son the infant Jayanta, or *Shasti*, the goddess of fecundity, a form of Durgá. The principal figure outside the temple is a life-size statue of *Akshobya*, who is represented squatted under the Bodhi tree, in the same manner as the ascetic Buddha, with the left hand in the lap, and the right hand hanging over the knee. There is a halo round the head inscribed with the usual Buddhist formula, "*Ye Dharmma*," &c.; and near the head there is a short inscription giving the name of the figure "*Tán Akshobya-vajra, hán*."

I procured several short but interesting inscriptions at Kurkihár. The name of *Sákala* is mentioned in several of them, and also *Kerala* in *Dakshinades*.* The age of these inscriptions, judging from the shapes of the letters, must be about A. D. 600 to 1000.

The true name of *Kurkihár* is said to be Kurak-vihár, which I believe to be only a contracted form of *Kúkkutapáda Vihára* or "temple of the cock's foot," which must have been connected with the *Kukkuta-páda-giri* or

---

* See Plate XIII.

Cock's-foot hill, which is described by both Fa-Hian and Hwen Thsang.* The Sanskrit *Kukkuta* is the same word as the Hindi *Kukkar* or *Kurak*, a cock, so that *Kurak-vihár* is clearly the same appellation as *Kukkuta-páda Vihára*. There was a monastery also of the same name, but this was close to *Pátaliputra* or Patna. The *Kukkuta-páda-giri* was a three-peaked hill, which was celebrated as the abode of the great *Kásyapa*, as well as the scene of his death. On this account it was also called *Guru-páda-parvata*, or "Teacher's-foot hill." The situation of *Kurkihár* corresponds exactly with Fa-Hian's account, excepting that there is no three-peaked hill in its neighbourhood. There are, however, three bare and rugged hills which rise boldly out of the plain about half a mile to the north of the village. As these three hills touch one another at their bases, I think that they may fairly be identified with the three-peaked hill of Hwen Thsang.

VI. GIRYEK.

From the neighbourhood of Gaya two parallel ranges of hills stretch towards the north-east for about 36 miles to the bank of the Panchána River, just opposite the village of Giryek. The eastern end of the southern range is much depressed, but the northern range maintains its height, and ends abruptly in two lofty peaks overhanging the Panchána River.† The lower peak on the east is crowned with a solid tower of brick-work, well known as *Jarasandha-ka-baithak*, or "Jarasandha's throne," while the higher peak on the west, to which the name of Giryek peculiarly belongs, bears an oblong terrace covered with the ruins of several buildings. The principal ruin would appear to have been a *vihár*, or temple, on the highest point of the terrace, which was approached by a steep flight of steps leading through pillared rooms.

The two peaks are connected by a steep pavement, which was formerly continued down to the foot of the hill opposite the village of Giryek. At all the commanding points and bends of this road are still to be seen the stone foundations of small brick *stupas* from 5 and 6 feet to upwards of 12 feet in diameter. At the foot of the upper

---

* Beal's Fa-Hian, c. XXIII. ; and Julien's Hwen Thsang, III., 6.
† See Plates III. and XIV. for the position of Giryek.

RAJGIR and GIRYEK

slope, and within 50 feet of Jarasandha's Tower, a tank 100 feet square has been formed, partly by excavation, and partly by building up. There is a second tank, at a short distance to the north, formed by the excavation of the rock for building materials. Both of these tanks are now dry.

The stupa, called *Jarasandha-ka-baithak*, is a solid cylindrical brick tower, 28 feet in diameter, and 21 feet in height, resting on a square basement 14 feet high. The cylinder was once surmounted by a solid dome or hemisphere of brick, of which only 6 feet now remain, and this dome must have been crowned with the usual umbrella rising out of a square base. The total height of the building could not, therefore, have been less than 55 feet or thereabouts. The surface has once been thickly plastered, and the style of ornamentation is similar to that of the Great Temple at Buddha Gaya.[*] I sank a shaft 41 feet in depth from the top of the building right down to the stone foundation; and I continued a gallery, which had been begun many years ago, at the base of the cylinder, until it met the well sunk from above, but nothing whatever was discovered in either of these excavations to show the object of the building.

On the west side of Jarasandha's Tower, and almost touching its basement, I observed a low mound which seemed like the ruin of another stupa. On clearing the top, however, I found a small chamber 5 feet 8 inches square, filled with rubbish. This chamber gradually widened as it was cleared out, until it became 7 feet square. At 6½ feet in depth, the rubbish gave place to brick-work, below which was a stratum of stone, evidently the rough foundation of the building. In the south-west corner of the brick-work, about one foot below the surface, I found 84 seals of lac firmly imbedded in the mud mortar. The seals were all oval, but of different sizes, generally about 3 inches long and 2 inches broad. All, however, bore the same impression of a large stupa with four smaller stupas on each side, the whole surrounded by an inscription in mediæval Nágari characters, *Ye Dharmma hetu prabhava*, &c., being the well known formula of the Buddhist faith. Externally, this building was square with projections in the centre of each face and similar in its ornamentations to the basement of Jarasandha's Tower.

---

[*] See Plate XV. for a sketch of this stupa.

C

On the eastern side of the Panchána River, there is an extensive mound of ruins, being half a mile long from north to south, and 300 yards broad in its widest part. There are the remains of two paved ascents on the river side, and of three more on the opposite side of the mound. In the middle of the mound there is a small mud fort, and at the northern end there are several pieces of sculpture collected together from different places; one of these is inscribed and dated in the year 42 of some unknown era, somewhere about the eleventh century, or perhaps even somewhat later.

At two miles to the south-west of the village of Giryek, and one mile from Jarasandha's Tower, there is a natural cavern in the southern face of the mountain, about 250 feet above the bed of the Bánganga rivulet. This cave, called Gidhadwár, is generally believed to communicate with Jarasandha's Tower; but an examination with torches proved it to be a natural fissure running upwards in the direction of the tower, but only 98 feet in length. The mouth of the cavern, is 10 feet broad and 17 feet high; but its height diminishes rapidly towards the end. The cave is filled with bats, and the air is oppressively warm and disagreeable, which alone is sufficient to prove that there is no exit to the cavern otherwise there would be a draught of air right through it. Vultures swarm about the precipitous cliffs of pale grey horn stone, and I picked up their feathers in the mouth of the cave.

The remains at Giryek, which I have just described, appear to me to correspond exactly with the accounts given by Fa-Hian of the "Hill of the Isolated Rock," where Indra questioned Buddha on 42 points, writing each of them singly with his finger upon a stone, and with that given by Hwen Thsang of the hill of *Indra-sila-guha*, which refers to the same story.* Fa-Hian states that traces of these written questions still existed, and that there was a monastery built upon the spot, but he makes no mention of any stupa. Hwen Thsang states that on the crest of the hill there were marks in two places where the four former Buddhas had sat and walked. On the eastern peak there was a stupa and also a monastery called the "*Hansa Sanghárama*" or "Goose's Monastery," to account for which he relates the

---

* Beal's Fa-Hian, c. 29, and Julien's Hwen Thsang, III., 59.

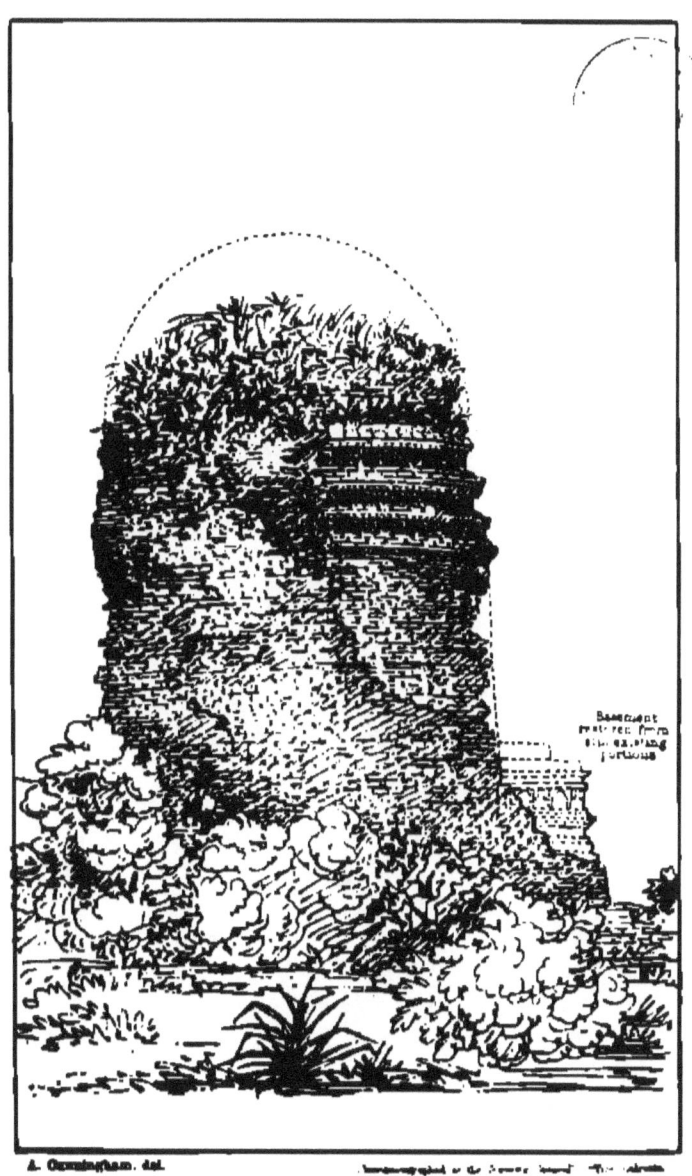

JARASANDHA-KA-BAITHAK

following legend: One day, when taking exercise, a mendicant, who was the steward of the monastery, saw a flock of geese high in the air, and as the monks of his fraternity, although strictly abstemious, had experienced great difficulty in procuring sufficient food, he exclaimed playfully—"To-day the pittance of the monks is insufficient. O noble beings *(Mahásattwas)* you ought to have compassion on our circumstances." No sooner had he spoken these words, than one of the geese fell dead at his feet. The horror-struck mendicant ran to tell the tale to his brethren, who became overwhelmed with grief. "Buddha," said they, "established his law for man's guidance under all circumstances. The *Mahâyâna* (Great Vehicle) is the source of truth, while we have foolishly followed the doctrine of the *Hinâyâna* (Lesser Vehicle). Let us renounce our former opinions. This goose has taught us a salutary lesson, let us do honour to her eminent virtue by transmitting it to the most distant ages." They accordingly built a stupa over the dead goose, which was interred in the base of the monument, and adorned it with an inscription relating the pious devotion of the goose.

If my identification of the Giryek Hill with the *Indrasila-guha* of Hwen Thsang is correct, there can be little doubt that Jarasandha's Tower is the very stupa that was built in honour of the devoted goose. Only this one stupa is mentioned by Hwen Thsang, and Jarasandha's Tower is the only one now existing on the hill. In further corroboration of this identification, I may mention that close by I found a broken figure with a large goose carved on the pedestal; and further, that one of the stupas on the lac seals found on the spot, appears to bear a goose on its summit. As no mention is made of any stupa by Fa-Hian, the erection of this tower most probably took place between his date and that of Hwen Thsang, or about A. D. 500.

The position of Giryek corresponds so exactly both in bearing and distance with that of the hill of *Indra-silaguha*, that I feel quite satisfied of their identity. No etymology has yet been proposed for the name of Giryek; but it seems to me not unlikely that it is nothing more than *Giri-eka*, "one hill," that is, the Hill of the Isolated Rock of Fa-Hian.

Both of the pilgrims mention the cave in the southern face of the mountain, which corresponds exactly with the natural cavern of Gidha Dwár, which I have already described. *Gidha Dwár*, in Sanskrit *Gridhra-dwára*, means the Vulture's pass, or opening. By Hwen Thsang the cave is called *Indra-sila-guha*, or "the cave of Indra's stone," being thus named after the stone on which were delineated the 42 points on which Indra had questioned Buddha. Fa-Hian adds that Indra himself drew the marks upon the stone with his finger.

A second cave is described by Hwen Thsang as the Vulture's Cave in the hill called *Gridhra-kuta-parvata* "or Vulture's Cave hill."[*] This name was derived from the story of Ananda's adventure with the demon Mâra in the shape of a vulture. The demon suddenly stopped before the cave and terrified Ananda, when Buddha passing his hand through the rock laid hold of Ananda's arm, and at once removed his fear. The cleft in the rock said to have been made by Buddha's hand, was seen by Fa-Hian early in the 5th century.[†] Major Kittoe thought that the *Gidha Dwár* Cave was the Vulture's Cave of the Chinese pilgrims, but its distance of 4½ miles from the old capital of *Rájagriha* is too great, as both Fa-Hian and Hwen Thsang place the Vulture's Cave at 15 *li* from old Rájagriha, that is, at only 2½ miles from it. This cave besides answers exactly to that described by Hwen Thsang under the name of *Indra-sila-guha*, and the two caves were certainly distinct. I made every enquiry for another cave, but could only hear of one very close to that of *Gidha Dwár*, which was quite inaccessible. But taking the distance and direction from old Rájagriha, the Vulture's Cave must have been in the lofty precipitous hill now called *Sila-giri*, or the "Rocky Mountain." Gidha Dwár is the name of a narrow pass where the two parallel ranges of hills before described close together within two miles of Giryek, and the Gidha Dwár Cave is immediately above the pass.

VII. RAJGIR.

Whatever doubts may exist regarding the identification of Kurkihár and Giryek, there can fortunately be none

---

[*] Julien's Hwen Thsang, III., 20.
[†] Beal's Fa-Hian, c. 29.

respecting *Rájgir*, as the representative of the ancient *Rájagriha*. The name is still preserved in the modern *Rájgir*, and I found it repeated in numerous inscriptions in the temples on the Baibhár and Vipula Mountains. The old city of Rájagriha is described by Fa-Hian as situated in a valley between five hills, at 4 *li* (or two-thirds of a mile) to the south of the new town of Rájagriha. The same position and about the same distance are given by Hwen Thsang, who likewise mentions the hot springs which exist to this day.*

The old city of Rájagriha is called *Kuságarapura*, or the city of the Kusa grass, by Hwen Thsang, who further describes it as the "town surrounded by mountains." This last is almost a translation of *Giri-vraja*, or the city of "many hills," which is the old name of the capital of Jarasandha, preserved both in the *Rámáyana* and the *Mahábhárata*. Fa-Hian states that the "five hills form a girdle like the walls of a town," which is an exact description of the site of old Rájgir.† A similar description is given by Turnour from the Pali annals of Ceylon, where the five hills are named *Gijjhakuto, Isigili, Webháro, Wepullo*, and *Pandawo*. In the Mahábhárata the five hills are named *Vaihára, Varáha, Vrishabha, Rishigiri*, and *Ghaityaka*; but at present they are called *Baibhár-giri, Vipula-giri, Ratna-giri, Udaya-giri*, and *Sona-giri*.

In the inscriptions of the Jain temples on Mount *Baibhár* the name is sometimes written Baibhára, and sometimes *Vyavahára*. It is beyond all doubt the *Webháro* Mountain of the Pali annals, in which was situated the far-famed *Sattapanni* Cave in front of which was held the first Buddhist Synod in 543 B. C. The Baibhár Hill lies to the west of the hot springs, and the Vipula Hill to the east. In Baibhár there still exists a large cave called *Sou-bhándár*, or the "Treasury of Gold." The situation corresponds exactly with that of the *Pi-po-lo* cave of the two Chinese pilgrims, in which Buddha used to meditate after his noon-day meal.‡ The famous Sattapanni Cave must be looked for in the

---

* Beal's Fa-Hian, c. 28; and Julien's Hwen Thsang, I., 159, III., 22.

† See Plate XIV. for the relative positions of these five hills.

‡ Both M. Julien (in Hwen Thsang, III., 24) and Mr. Beal (in Fa-Hian, c. 30) read *Pi-po-lo* as the *Pippal* tree, but I would suggest that it may be only the Chinese transcript of *Vaibhára*. As, however, the great cave in which the First Synod was held was called the cave of the Nyagrodha tree (Banian, see Adal. Rem. XX., 91), it is very probable that this other cave was called the Pippal tree cave.

northern face of the south-west end of the mountain, at above one mile from the Son-bhândâr Cave.

Mount *Vipula* is clearly identical with the *Wepullo* of the Pali annals, and as its summit is now crowned with the ruins of a lofty *stupa* or *chaitya*, which is noticed by Hwen Thsang, I would identify it with the Chaityaka of the *Mahâ-bhârata*. Regarding the other three mountains, I have nothing at present to offer, but I may mention that they are also crowned with small Jain temples.

The old city between the hills is described by Fa-Hian to be 5 or 6 *li* from east to west, and 7 or 8 *li* from north to south, that is, from 24 to 28 *li* or 4½ miles in circuit. Hwen-Thsang makes it 30 *li* or 5 miles in circuit, with its greatest length from east to west. My survey of the ancient ramparts gives a circuit of 24,500 feet, or 4¾th miles, which is between the two statements of the Chinese pilgrims. The greatest length is from north-west to south-east, so that there is no real discrepancy between the two statements as to the direction of the greatest length of the old city. Each of them must have taken his measurement from the Nekpai embankment on the east (which has been described by Major Kittoe) to some point on the north-west. If taken to the Pânch-Pandu angle of the ramparts, the direction would be W. N. W., and the length upwards of 8,000 feet; but if taken to the temple of Torka Devi, the direction would be N. N. W., and the distance upwards of 9,000 feet.

I have already quoted Fa-Hian's statement that the "five hills form a girdle like the walls of a town." This agrees with Hwen Thsang's description, who says that "high mountains surround it on four sides, and from its *exterior* walls, which have a circuit of 150 *li* or 25 miles. For this number I propose to read 50 *li* or 8½ miles, a correction which is absolutely necessary to make the statement tally with the measurements of my survey. The following are the direct distances between the hills:—

1.	From Baibhâr to Vipula	...	...	...	12,000 feet.
2.	„ Vipula to Batas	...	...	...	4,500 „
3.	„ Ratna to Udaya	...	...	...	8,500 „
4.	„ Udaya to Sona	...	...	...	7,000 „
5.	„ Sona to Baibhâr	...	...	...	9,000 „
			Total	...	41,000 feet.

This is somewhat less than eight miles; but if the ascents and descents are taken into account, the actual length will correspond very closely with the statement of Hwen Thsang when corrected to 50 *li*. The old walls forming this exterior line of rampart are still to be seen in many places. I traced them from Vipula-giri over Ratna-giri to the Nekpai embankment, and thence onwards over Udaya-giri, and across the southern outlet of the valley to Sona-giri. At this outlet, the walls, which are still in good order, are 13 feet thick. To obtain a circuit of 25 miles, as given in Hwen Thsang's text, it would be necessary to carry these ramparts as far as Giryek on the east. As similar ramparts exist on the Giryek Hill, it is perhaps possible that Hwen Thsang intended to include it in the circuit of his outer walls. But this immense circuit would not at all agree with his statement that "high mountains surround the city on four sides," for the distant Hill of Giryek cannot in any way be said to form one of the sides of old Rájagriha.

The new town of Rájagriha is said to have been built by King *Srenika*, otherwise called *Bimbisára*, the father of *Ajátasatru*, the contemporary of Buddha. Its foundation cannot, therefore, be placed later than 500 B. C. according to Buddhist chronology. In Hwen Thsang's time (A. D. 629—642), the outer walls had already become ruinous, but the inner walls were still standing, and occupied a circuit of 20 *li*, or 3⅓ miles. This statement corresponds tolerably well with the measurements of my survey, which make the circuit of the ramparts somewhat less than 3 miles. Buchanan calls new Rájagriha an irregular pentagon of 12,000 yards in diameter. This is clearly a misprint for 1,200 yards, which would give a circuit of 11,303 feet, or 2¼ miles; but this was probably the interior measurement, which, according to my survey, is 13,000 feet. The plan of new Rájagriha I make out to be an irregular pentagon of one long side and four nearly equal sides, the whole circuit being 14,260 feet outside the ditches, or rather less than three miles.*

On the south side towards the hills a portion of the interior, 2,000 feet long and 1,500 feet broad, has been cut off to form a citadel. The stone walls retaining the earthen ramparts of this work are still in good order in many places.

---

* See Plate XIV.

It is possible that this work may be of later date, as suggested by Buchanan, but I am of opinion that it was simply the citadel of the new town, and that its walls have suffered less from the effects of time, owing partly to their having been more carefully and more massively built than the less important ramparts of the town, and partly to their having been occasionally repaired as a military position by the authorities, while the repairs of the town walls were neglected as being either unnecessary or too costly.

The existing remains at Rájagriha are not numerous. The place has been occupied at different times by Musalmáns and Brahmans, by whom the Buddhist stupas and vihárs were pulled down to furnish materials for tombs, masjids, and temples. All the eminences that must once have been crowned by objects of Buddhist worship are now covered with Muhammedan graves; and all the Brahmanical temples about the hot springs have been constructed with the large bricks of Buddhist stupas. One of these last monuments can still be traced outside the south-west corner of the town in a large circular hollow mound, which attracted the notice of both Buchanan and Kittoe. I examined this mound carefully, and I was satisfied that the hollow represented the original site of a stupa from which the bricks had been carried off, while the surrounding circular mound represented the mass of earth and broken brick rubbish left by the workmen. The excavated stupa at Sárnáth, near Banáras, now offers almost exactly the same appearance. According to Hwen Thsang's account, this circular hollow was the site of a stupa 60 feet in height, which was built by Asoka. Beside it there was a stone pillar 50 feet high, on which was inscribed the history of the foundation of the stupa. The pillar was surmounted by an elephant.[*]

On Mount Baibhár there are five modern Jain temples, besides the ruins of an old Saiva temple, of which four granite pillars, 10 feet in height, are still standing, and 50 or 60 smaller pillars are lying confusedly about. At the southern foot of the mountain, the rock has a natural scarp for about 100 yards in length, which, at the western end, has been smoothed to a height of 10 feet, in front of which the rock has been cut away to form a level terrace 90 feet in length by

---

[*] Julien's Hwen Thsang, III., 38.

upwards of 30 feet in breadth. Two caves have been excavated out of the solid rock behind; that to the west, now called the Son Bhándár, or "Treasury of gold," being 34 feet long by 17 feet broad, and that to the east perhaps somewhat less in length, but of the same breadth. This cave has either fallen in naturally through the decay of the rock, or, which is more probable, was blown up by a zemindar in search of treasure, as related by Major Kittoe of the other cave.

The Son Bhándár Cave has one door and one window. Inside there are no traces of seats, or of pedestals of statues, and the walls and roof are quite bare, excepting where a few scarcely legible inscriptions have been cut. There are several short inscriptions on the jambs of the doorway, as well as on the outside. In the principal inscription, which is on two lines outside, the author speaks of this cave as the "auspicious cave," evidently alluding to the fact of its former occupation by Buddha for the purpose of meditating after his noonday meal. This inscription, which is not later than A. D. 200, and is perhaps earlier, records that a certain "Muni, named Vaira Deva, of powerful dignity, was able to obtain emancipation, having shut himself up for spiritual enjoyment in this auspicious cell, a retired abode of Arhantas, fitted for an ascetic for the attainment of liberation." On the east jamb of the door also the same epithet is applied to this cave, as if it was a well known name for it. This cave is excavated in the south face of the hill, where there is a natural scarp for about one hundred yards in length. The face of the cliff at the west end has been smoothed to a height of 19 feet, in front of which the ground has been levelled to form a platform of more than 30 feet. The cave itself is 34 feet long by 17 feet broad and 11½ feet high. To the east there has been a second cave, about 22½ feet long by 17 feet broad; but one half of the roof fell in long ago, and the cave is now filled with masses of rock and earth. The floor of this cave is on a lower level than that of the *Son Bhándár*, but the front is in the same line. Both caves had some building or verandah in front, as there are numerous socket holes cut in the rock above the door for the reception of the ends of beams. The whole length of level clearing in front of the caves is 90 feet.

In the centre of the valley between the five hills, and in the very midst of the old city of Rájagriha, there is a ruined brick mound 19 feet 8 inches in height, which my excavations proved to be an ancient stupa. A diminutive Jain temple, called Maniár Math, stands on the top of the mound. It was built in A. D. 1780. As I expected to find a solid brick building, I sank a shaft outside the Maniár Math with the intention of inclining gradually towards the centre; but I soon found that the core of the mound was a mere mass of rubbish, filling a well 10 feet in diameter. This rubbish was so loose that its removal was dangerous; but by propping up the portion immediately below the little temple, and removing the bricks cautiously, I was enabled to get down to a depth of 21½ feet. At 19 feet I found three small figures. One of them represents Máyá lying on a couch in the lower compartment, and the ascetic Buddha and two attendants above. The second is a naked standing figure, with a seven-headed snake forming a canopy over the head. This is clearly not a Buddhist, but a Jain sculpture. The third is so excessively rude, that it is difficult to identify it. The figure is four-armed, and is seated upon a recumbent animal, which looks more like a bull than anything else. It probably, therefore, represents Mahadeva and his bull Nandi. As all three figures formed only a part of the rubbish, it seems to me certain that the well must once have been empty; and further, that the rubbish was most probably thrown in when the little Jain temple was about to be built.

The natives of the place call this well the Treasury, and they assert that it has never been opened. On my arrival I found a Punjab Sepoy, with a servant, making an excavation on his own account. He had sunk a shaft 3 feet in diameter at 7½ feet from the little temple. The shaft was then 17 feet deep. I examined the bricks which had been taken out, and on finding some with bevelled and rounded edges, and others thickly coated with plaster, I guessed at once that the original structure had been covered with an outer wall, and that the shaft had been sunk just outside the original work. To ascertain whether this conclusion was correct, I laid bare the top of the mound, and soon discovered that the well was surrounded by a wall only 6 feet in thickness. This would give the original stupa a diameter of 22 feet. The Punjab Sepoy continued his shaft down to the stone foundation without finding anything, and then gave up the work.

Having observed that the slope of the mound on the north side was very gentle, I thought it probable that the building must have been approached on this side by a flight of steps. I therefore made an excavation in a line due north from the centre of the mound, and within a couple of hours I found a doorway. Continuing the excavation to the east and west, as well as to the north, I found a small room with brick walls and granite pillars containing two middle-sized sculptured slabs of middle age. Outside the doorway a flight of steps led downwards towards the north; I therefore turned to the south, and continued my excavation until I reached the main building. On examining the wall I found three recesses, the middle one being roofed by overlapping bricks. On clearing out the rubbish, this opening proved to be a carefully built passage only 2 feet 2 inches wide, and 3 feet 4½ inches in height, right through the outer wall of the building. Behind it, but a few inches out of line, there was a similar passage through the original wall, only 2 feet in width. At the end of the passage I found the well filled with the same rubbish as on the south side.

The discovery of this passage shows that the Buddhist Monks had easy access to the interior of the building. I conclude, therefore, that it must originally have contained some relic that was occasionally shown to visitors, and to the public generally, on certain fixed days. I cannot, however, discover in the accounts of Fa-Hian and Hwen Thsang any mention of a stupa inside the walls of old Rájagriha.

The hot springs of Rájagriha are found on both banks of the Sarsuti rivulet; one-half of them at the eastern foot of Mount Baibhâr, and the other half at the western foot of Mount Vipula. The former ar enamed as follows: 1, Gangá-Jumna; 2, Anant Rikhi; 3, Sapt Rikhi; 4, Brahm-kûnd; 5, Kasyapa Rikhi; 6, Biás-kûnd; and 7, Markand-kûnd. The hottest of these are the springs of the Sapt Rikhi. The hot springs of Mount Vipula are named as follows: 1, Sita-kûnd; 2, Suraj-kûnd; 3, Ganes-kûnd; 4, Chandrama kûnd; 5, Rám-kûnd; and 6, Sringgi-Rikhi-kûnd. The last spring has been appropriated by the Musalmáns, by whom it is called Makhdum-kûnd, after a celebrated Saint named Chilla Sháh, whose tomb is close to the spring. It is said that Chilla was originally called Chilwa, and that he was an Ahír. He must, therefore, have been a converted Hindu.

VIII. BARAGAON or NALANDA.

Due north from Rájgír, and seven miles distant, lies the village of Baragaon, which is quite surrounded by ancient tanks and ruined mounds, and which possesses finer and more numerous specimens of sculpture than any other place that I have visited. The ruins at Baragaon are so immense, that Dr. Buchanan was convinced it must have been the usual residence of the King; and he was informed by a Jain priest at Bihár that it was the residence of Raja Srenika and his ancestors. By the Brahmans these ruins are said to be the ruins of *Kunditpur*, a city famed as the birth-place of Rúkmini, one of the wives of Krishna. But as Rúkmini was the daughter of Raja Bhishma, of Vidarbha, or Berár, it seems probable that the Brahmans have mistaken Berár for Bihár, which is only seven miles distant from Baragaon. I therefore doubt the truth of this Brahmanical tradition, more especially as I can show beyond all doubt that the remains at Baragaon are the ruins of Nálanda, the most famous seat of Buddhist learning in all India.

Fa-Hian places the hamlet of Nalo at one *yojan*, or 7 miles from the Hill of the Isolated Rock, that is, from Giryek, and also the same distance from new Rájagriha.[*] This account agrees exactly with the position of Baragaon, with respect to Giryek and Rájgír. In the Pali annals of Ceylon also, Nálanda is stated to be one *yojan* distant from Rájagriha. Again, Hwen Thsang describes Nálanda as being 7 *yojans*, or 49 miles, distant from the holy Pipal tree at Buddha-Gaya, which is correct if measured by the road, the direct distance measured on the map being 40 miles.[†] He also describes it as being about 30 *li*, or 5 miles, to the north of new Rájagriha. This distance and direction also correspond with the position of Baragaon, if the distance be measured from the most northerly point of the old ramparts. Lastly, in two inscriptions, which I discovered on the spot, the place itself is called Nálanda. This evidence seems conclusive; but I may add further that the existing ruins, which I am now about to describe, correspond most minutely with the descriptions of Hwen Thsang.

---

[*] Beal's Fa-Hian, c. XXVIII.
[†] Julien's Hwen Thsang, I, 148.

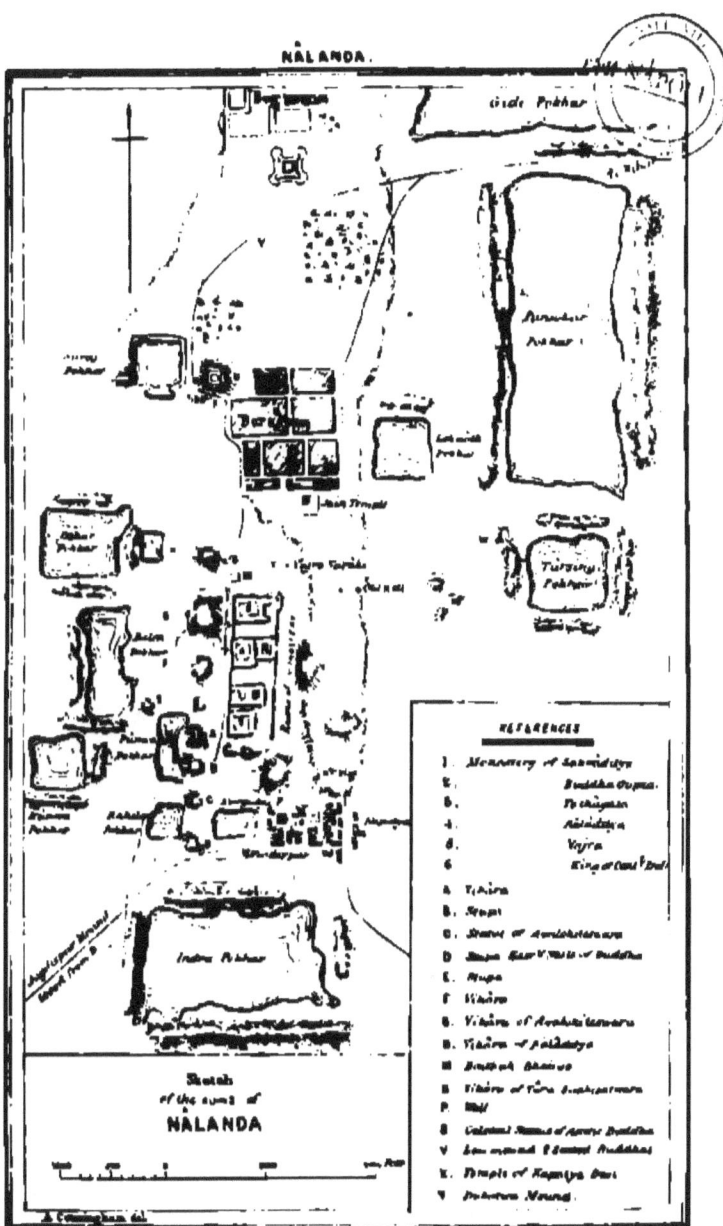

Fa-Hian calls Nâlanda the birth-place of Sâriputra, who was the right hand disciple of Buddha; but this statement is not quite correct, as we learn, from the more detailed account of Hwen Thsang, that Sâriputra was born at *Kalapinâka*, about half-way between *Nâlanda* and *Indra-Sila Guha*, or about 4 miles to the south-east of the former place. Nâlanda has also been called the birth-place of Mahâ Mogalâna, who was the left hand disciple of Buddha; but this is not quite correct, as the great Mogalâna, according to Hwen Thsang, was born at *Kulika*, 8 or 9 *li*, less than 1½ mile, to the south-west of Nâlanda. This place I was able to identify with a ruined mound near Jagdispur, at 1¼ mile to the south-west of the ruins of Baragaon.

The mound of Jagdispur is 200 feet square, and of little height, except in the south-east corner, where there is a considerable eminence, 70 feet square. On the southern edge of this height, there is a magnificent Nim tree, under which several statues have been collected. One of these is the finest and largest piece of sculpture that I have met with. It is a figure of the ascetic Buddha, seated under the Bodhi tree at Buddha-Gaya, and surrounded by horrible demons and alluring females, who are seeking by different means to distract him. On each side other scenes of his life are represented, and over all his *Nirvân*, or death. A large drawing of this elaborate piece of sculpture is given by Buchanan.* The slab is 16 feet high and 9½ feet broad; and, considering the excellence of the sculpture, the multiplicity of the details, and the fine state of preservation, this work is in every way worthy of being preserved by photography. The figure is called Rûkmini by the ignorant villagers, who daily smear its forehead and nose with red lead, and pour milk over the mouth. The offering of milk is considered very efficacious; but the most acceptable offering is a goat; and at the time of my visit, the ground was still wet with the blood of a recently killed goat.

The remains at Baragaon consist of numerous masses of brick ruins, amongst which the most conspicuous is a row of lofty conical mounds running north and south. These high mounds are the remains of gigantic temples attached to the famous monastery of Nâlanda. The great monastery itself can be readily traced by the square patches of cultivation

* Eastern India, I., Plate XIII.

amongst a long mass of brick ruins 1,600 feet by 400 feet. These open spaces show the positions of the court-yards of the six smaller monasteries which are described by Hwen Thsang as being situated within one enclosure forming altogether eight courts. Five of the six monasteries were built by five consecutive princes of the same family, and the sixth by their successor, who is called King of Central India. No dates are given; but from the total silence of Fa-Hian regarding any of the magnificent buildings at Nâlanda, which are so minutely described by Hwen Thsang, I infer that they must have been built after A. D. 410. Fa-Hian simply states that he came to the hamlet of Nalo, "where Sâriputra was born," and this is all that he says of Nâlanda. But surely if the lofty temple of King Bâlâditya, which was 300 feet in height, had then existed, it seems scarcely possible that he should not have noticed it. I would, therefore, assign the probable date of the temples and monasteries of Nâlanda to the two centuries between the visits of Fa-Hian and Hwen Thsang, or from A. D. 425 to 625. This date is further borne out by the fact recorded by Hwen Thsang, that the great temple of Bâlâditya was similar to that near the sacred Pipal tree at Buddha-Gaya. Now, as similarity of style may generally be taken as denoting proximity of date, the erection of Bâlâditya's temple at Nâlanda may, with great probability, be assigned to the same century in which the Buddha-Gaya temple was built. As I have already shown this to be about A. D. 500, the date of the Nâlanda temple will lie between A. D. 450 and 550.

Several inscribed stones lie scattered over the ruins of Bâlâditya's monastery. The letters are only mason's marks, but their forms are those of the 6th and 7th centuries.

To the south of the monastery there was a tank in which the dragon, or Nâga Nâlanda, was said to dwell, and the place was named after him Nâlanda. There is still existing immediately to the south of the ruined monastery a small tank called *Kargidya Pokhar*, which answers exactly to the position of the Nâlanda tank, and is, I have no doubt, the identical pool of the Nâga.

As the people have no particular names for the different masses of ruin, but simply call them collectively "the mounds," I will, for convenience of description, name each of

the principal masses after the ancient tank on its western
side. Other mounds will be described with reference to their
relative positions with respect to the principal ruins. In my
survey of the ruins, I have also attached a letter of the
alphabet to each separate mound.*

Hwen Thsang begins his account with a *cihár*, or
temple, just outside the western wall of the monastery, which
had been erected on a spot where Buddha had dwelt for
three months, explaining the sublime law for the benefit of
the gods. This temple I would identify with the ruined
mound marked A, still 53 feet in height and from 65 to 70
feet in thickness near the top, and which is situated immediately to the westward of the ruined monastery. It stands
to the east of the Pânwa tank, and may, therefore, be called
the Pânwa mound. My excavations, which were carried
down to a depth of 17 feet, exposed the straight walls of a
temple.

To the south, at 100 paces, there was a small stupa,
erected over a spot where a pious mendicant, from a far
country, had performed the *panchánga*, or reverence of the
five members (namely head, hands, and knees) in honour of
Buddha. This stupa is well represented by a small
mound marked B, which is due south of the Pânwa mound.

Still further to the south, there was a statue of Avalokiteswara. As this statue must have had some kind of covering
as a shelter from the weather, I believe that it is represented by another small ruined mound, marked C, immediately to the south of the last.

To the south of the statue there was a stupa, containing
the hair and nails of Buddha. Sick people recovered their
health by making the circuit of this monument. Another
mound, marked D, to the east of the Rabela tank, corresponds with the position of this stupa exactly, as it is due
south of the last mound C. It is still 20 feet high. I made
an excavation in the top, which showed that the mound had
been opened previously, as I found nothing but loose rubbish.
The solid brick-work on all sides, however, satisfied me that
it was the ruin of an ancient stupa.

* See Plate XVI.

Outside the western wall of the monastery, and close to a tank, there was another stupa erected on the spot where Buddha had been questioned by a heretic on the subject of life and death. A small mound, marked E, on the east bank of the *Balen* Tank, corresponds exactly with the position of this stupa.

At a short distance to the east there was a lofty vihár, 200 feet in height, where Buddha had explained the law for four months. In the position here indicated, there stands the highest and largest of all the mounds, marked F. It is still 60 feet in height, with a diameter of 70 feet at 50 feet above the ground, and of 80 feet at 35 feet above the ground. As the outer edges of the walls are much broken, the original size of this massive building at the ground level cannot have been much less than 90 feet square. To ascertain its probable height, we may compare it with the Great Temple at Buddha-Gaya, which has a base of 50 feet square, and a height of 160 feet. But as the copper-gilt *amalaka* fruit which once surmounted it no longer exists, the original height cannot have been less than 170 feet. Now, taking the same proportions for the Nâlanda temple, we may deduce the height by simple rule-of-three, thus as 50 : 170 :: 90 : 300 feet. It is true that Hwen Thsang states the height at only 200 feet, but there is a discrepancy in his statements of the height of another Nâlanda temple, which leads me to propose correcting the height of that now under discussion to 300 feet. In speaking of the Great Temple erected by Bâlâditya, Hwen Thsang in one place makes it 200 feet high, and in another place 300 feet high.[*] In both accounts the enshrined statue is said to be of Buddha himself, as he appeared under the Bodhi tree, and, as the other large temple also contained a statue of Buddha, it seems highly probable that there has been some confusion between the accounts of the two temples.

I am quite satisfied that the lofty mound marked F. is the ruin of a temple, for I discovered three horizontal air holes, each in the form of a cross, at a height of 35 feet above the ground. They measured respectively 6, 8½, and 11¼ feet in length. The last measurement, coupled with the broken state of the brick-work, shows that the walls must have been upwards of 12 feet in thickness. In fact, on the east side,

---

[*] Compare Julien's Hwen Thsang, I. 164, with III, 50.

at 50 feet above the ground, the broken wall is still 15 feet thick. Most probably the walls were not less than 20 feet thick at this height, which would leave an interior chamber 30 feet square. There is now a great hollow in the centre of this mound, which I would recommend to be further excavated down to the ground level, as I think it highly probable that both statues and inscriptions of much interest would be discovered. Perhaps the colossal statue of Buddha, the teacher now standing at the foot of mound II., may have been originally enshrined in this temple.*

In the north-east corner of the square terrace that surrounds this massive ruin, I found the remains of several small stupas, in dark blue stone of various sizes, from 10 to 30 feet in height. The ornamental carvings are still in good order, many of them being very elaborate. Rows after rows of Buddhas of all sizes are the most favourite decoration. The solid hemispherical domes are from 1 foot to 4 feet in diameter. The basement and body of each stupa were built of separate stones, which were numbered for the guidance of the builders, and cramped together with iron to secure greater durability. No amount of time, and not even an earthquake, could have destroyed these small buildings. Their solid walls of iron-bound stones could only have yielded to the destructive fury of malignant Brahmans. I tried to complete a single stupa, but I soon found that several pieces were missing. I believe, however, that a complete one might be obtained by a careful search about the village temples, around the Jain temple, and in the small court-yard opposite Mitrajit's house. If one could be obtained complete, or nearly so, it would form a most striking and ornamental addition to the Calcutta Museum.

---

* This mound was subsequently excavated by order of Government under the superintendence of Captain Marshall. The temple stood on a plinth 12 feet high above the ground level, forming a terrace 15 feet wide all round. The inner room is 30 feet square, with an entrance hall on the east side. The walls, which are of extreme thickness, are built of large bricks laid in mud. There are few remains of plaster, but the lower walls appear to be sound, but externally they are much cracked. The remains of the pedestal occupy nearly the whole west half of the lower room, but there were no traces of any statues. Pieces of broken statues were, however, found in the entrance hall. A portion of the entrance is of more modern date, the same as at Bodh-Gaya. Captain Marshall closes his account of the explorations with the following opinion, which seems to be well founded:— "The general appearance of the building, viz., the false doorway, the abstraction of the idols, and the absence of inside plaster, all give me the notion of the building having been made use of after the glories of the temple had passed away, and then to have fallen to pieces by neglect and consequent decay."

A short distance to the north of the Great Vihár, there was another temple containing a statue of the Bodhisatwa *Avalokiteswara*. This Saint is the same as the *Padma-páni* of the Tibetans, and is always represented with a lotus in his hand. An extensive low mound, marked G., immediately to the north of the great mound, corresponds exactly with the situation of this temple.

To the north of the last temple there was a grand vihár, built by Báládítya, containing a statue of the ascetic Buddha. The height, as I have already noticed, is differently stated by Hwen Thsang at 200 and 300 feet. The lesser height I believe to be the correct one, more especially as Hwen Thsang mentions that in its magnificence, its *size*, and its statue of Buddha, it resembled the Great Temple at Buddha-Gaya. As this last was 170 feet in height, Báládítya's Vihár might very fairly be said to resemble it in *size*, if it was 200 feet high; but if it was 300 feet in height, there could have been no resemblance whatever in the dimensions of a temple that was nearly twice as lofty. A mound, marked II., to the east of the Dchar Tank, corresponds exactly with the situation of this temple. It is still 45 feet in height, with a breadth of 50 feet at top from edge to edge of brick-work. As the facing has disappeared on all sides, the original breadth, at the ground level, could not have been less than 60 feet; and if the relative proportions were the same as those of the Buddha-Gaya Temple, the height of this temple must have been 204 feet, or say, in round numbers, 200 feet, exactly as stated by Hwen Thsang. There is a colossal statue of the ascetic Buddha in a small court-yard called Baithak Bhairav at the foot of this mound, which, in all probability, was the original statue enshrined in Báládítya's Vihár.

Four other buildings and statues, which I have been unable to identify, are next mentioned by Hwen Thsang, who then goes on to describe a brick vihár containing a very lofty copper statue of Tara Bodhisatwa. This was situated at 2 or 3 *li* to the north of the monastery, that is, between one-third and one-half of a mile. Now, at a distance of 2,000 feet to the north of the monastery, and to the east of the Suraj Pokhar, there is a brick ruin of a very large temple, marked N. From its close proximity to the village, this ruin has supplied materials for all the existing houses, and is consequently of much smaller dimensions than those which have been already described. But the removal of the bricks has exposed the actual walls of the temple in several places; and, by making a few excavations, I was able to determine the exact dimensions of the base of this temple. It was 70½ feet by 67 feet, and it stood on a raised terrace 6 feet in height and 125 feet square. If the relative proportion of base to height was the same as that of the Buddha-Gaya Temple, the height of this temple could not have been less than 228 or 240 feet, according to which side of the base is taken for the calculation.

Hwen Thsang also mentions a large well which was just within the gateway on the south side of the surrounding walls of this vihâr. Now, there is a large well, marked P., immediately on the south side of the ruined mound above described, which must be the very one noticed by Hwen Thsang as having owed its origin to Buddha himself.

There are many other objects worthy of notice at Baragaon, which I can only briefly enumerate: 1st, The sculptures collected in the enclosure at Baithak Bhairav, marked M. 2nd, The colossal figure of the ascetic Buddha at S. This statue is remarkable for having the names of the attendant figures inscribed over their heads. Thus we have *Arya Sáriputra* and *Arya Maudgalâyana* inscribed over two flying figures carrying garlands; and *Arya Mitreyanâtha* and *Arya Vasumitra* over two attendant standing figures. An inscription in two lines on the back rail of the seat gives the usual Buddhist formula, and adds that the statue was "the pious gift of *Ganggaká* (a lady who had attained the religious rank of *paramopâsiká*.) This statue is well worthy of being photographed. 3rd, A small temple, marked T., with a figure of the three-headed goddess *Vajra-Varáhi*. The Buddhist formula is inscribed on this figure, which is evidently one of those mistaken by Major Kittoe for Durgâ slaying the buffalo demon Maheshasur. The goddess has one porcine head, and there are seven hogs represented on the pedestal. 4th, A life-size ascetic Buddha in the village of Baragaon, and a number of smaller figures at an adjacent Hindu temple, and also at the house of Mitrajit Zamindar. 5th, Two low mounds to the north of the village marked V., one having a four-armed image of Vishnu on Garud, and the other having two figures of Buddha seated on chairs. The former must clearly have belonged to a Brahmanical temple. 6th, Three statues at W., near the Tár Sing Tank, of which two are females and one a male figure seated with hands on knees. 7th, The small temple in the hamlet of Kapatiya, marked X., where there are several interesting figures collected. Amongst them there is a fine Vajrá Varáhi, and a very good Vágiswari, with an important inscription in two lines, which gives the name of the place Nálanda, and is dated in the year 1 of the reign of the paramount sovereign Sri Gopála Deva.[*] 8th, A large mound at Y., which looked like a ruined stupa. I sank a shaft 20 feet deep in the centre of the mound, and found that it was filled with rubbish. If, therefore, it was a stupa, it had been opened long before; but I am inclined to believe that it was a temple, as a large stone was found in the excavation at a depth of 13 feet. 9th, A Jain temple at Z., which is only remarkable as being of the same style of architecture as the Great Temple at Buddha-Gaya. It is probably of about the same age, or A. D. 500. Its present height is only 36 feet without the pinnacle, which is modern. The whole is white-washed. Inside the temple there are several Jain figures, of which that of *Maháoir* bears the date of Samvat 1504, or A. D. 1447. 10th, On the banks of the Suraj-kúnd many interesting figures are collected. They are chiefly Buddhist, but there are also some figures of Vishnu four-armed, of the Varáha Avatár, of Siva and Párvati, and also of Surya himself.

I cannot close this account of the ancient Nálanda without mentioning the noble tanks which surround the ruins on all sides. To the north-east are the Gidi Pokhar and the Pansokar Pokhar, each nearly a mile in length; while to the south there is the Indra Pokhar, which is nearly half a mile in length. The remaining tanks are much smaller in size, and do not require any special notice.

IX. BIHAR.

The old city of Bihár lies 7 miles to the north-east of Barngaon. In our maps the name is spelt *Behar*, but by the people it is written *Bihár*, which is sufficient to show that it

---

[*] See Plate XIII. for a copy of this inscription.

DHAR.

Plate XVII.

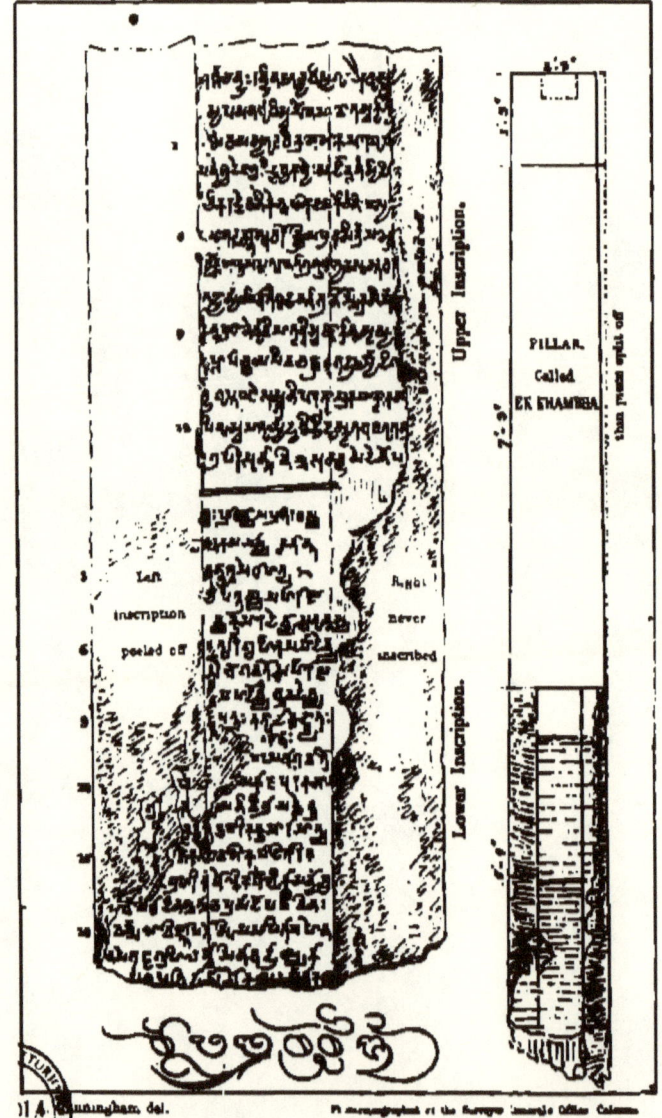

INSCRIPTIONS ON THE DHAR PILLAR.

must once have been the site of some famous Buddhist Vihâr. But the only existing Buddhist remains that I could find were votive stupas and fragments of figures. One of the last was inscribed with characters of about A. D. 000, but the inscription is unfortunately only a fragment.

The city of Bihâr consists principally of one long narrow street, paved with rough stones. There are two bridges with pointed arches over some irrigation canals, the remains of former prosperity; but the whole place is now dirty and decayed. In all directions are seen Musalmân tombs; the smaller ones of brick, the larger ones of squared and carved stones from the usual Muhammadan quarries of ruined Buddhist or Brahmanical buildings. To the north-west of the city there is a long isolated hill, having a precipitously steep cliff on its northern face, and on the southern face an easy slope in successive ledges of rock. The hill is now crowned by some Musalmân buildings, of which the largest is said to be the tomb of Malik Bayâ, but I believe that it is the tomb of one Ibrahim in the reign of Firuz, as I read both of these names in one of the inscriptions. To the north-east of these tombs and distant 1,000 feet, on the highest point of the hill, there is a square platform of brick, which must once have been the basement of a building, perhaps of a stupa, while the more genial site of the Durgâh, where fine trees are now growing, might once have held a Buddhist Vihâr and its attendant monastery.

One mile due east from the Durgâh, and about 100 yards inside the northern gate of the old fort of Bihâr, there lies a sand-stone pillar which bears two separate inscriptions of the Gupta Dynasty. Unfortunately, the surface of the stone has peeled off considerably, so that both of the inscriptions are incomplete. The upper inscription, which is of Kumâra Gupta, has lost both ends of every line, being probably about one-third of the whole. The lower inscription has lost only the left upper corner, and some unknown amount at the bottom, where the pillar is broken off. But as the remaining portion of the *upper* part is letter for letter the same as the opening of the Bhitari pillar inscription, nearly the whole of the missing part of the left *upper* corner can be restored at once.* This record apparently belongs to Skanda Gupta, the son and successor of Kumára Gupta, as the genealogy is continued beyond Kumára in the same words as in the Bhitari inscription.

Outside the northern gate of the old fort, there are some tombs that are said to belong to Christians, as they lie east and west, whilst all Musalmán tombs lie north and south. One of them bears an inscription surmounted by a cross, which proves it to be a Christian tomb. The inscription I believe to be in the Armenian character, but though it does not appear to be old, probably not more than fifty or a hundred years, yet I could not obtain any information regarding the tombs.

The cyclopean walls of the old fort are very curious; but as the fort has been fully described by Buchanan, it is unnecessary for me to do more than make this mention of it.

X. GHOSRAWA.

A Buddhistical inscription from Ghosráwá, a village to the S. S. W. of Bihár, distant 7 miles, was first discovered by Major Kittoe, who published a translation of it made by Dr. Ballantyne. This inscription is a very important one for the illustration of the later history of Buddhism, as it mentions the existence, somewhere about the 8th or 9th century, of several of the most famous places of the Buddhists. For instance, it mentions, 1st, the Kanishka Monastery in the city of Nagarahára, close to Jelalabad in the Kabul Valley; 2nd, the *Vajrásan*, or Diamond throne of Buddha, at Buddha-Gaya; 3rd, the *Indra-Sila* peak, which I have already identified with Giryek; 4th, the Vihár in Nálanda, the city of Yaso Varmma. This part of the translation, however, requires revision, as the name of Nálanda, which occurs twice, has in both instances been rendered as if it was merely a term for some ascetic posture, instead of the proper name of the

---

* See Plate XVII. for the Bihar Pillar inscriptions, and Plate XXVII. for the Bhitari Pillar inscription. Babu Rajendralal Mitra, in the Bengal Asiatic Society's Journal 1864, p. 271, denies the accuracy of my statement. He says "General Cunningham imagines it to be a counterpart of the Bhitari record"—I imagine nothing of the kind. My remarks refer to the upper part of the inscription alone, and this I again assert to be "letter for letter the same as the opening of the Bhitari Pillar inscription." The Babu says that "no specific name is legible." I refer him to his own Nágari transcript of line 4, where he reads *Aricha-putrasya*. This should be *Aneka*, for Ghatot-kacha, the predecessor of Chandra Gupta, whose wife Kumári Devi is mentioned in the next line.

town which contained the most famous monastery in all India. I will submit this inscription for re-translation.

The other remains at Ghosráwá are few and unimportant. There is a mound of brick ruin touching the village, and a small temple on a low mound with some broken figures between Ghosráwá and the small village of Asánagar. The inscription obtained by Major Kittoe is now fixed in the wall of this temple. At the western foot of the Ghosráwá mound there is a four-armed standing male statue of life size, inscribed with the usual formula of the Buddhist faith. In the upper right hand there is a necklace, but the lower hand is open, the upper left hand holds a lotus, and the lower hand a bell. There is a small figure of Buddha in the head dress of the statue, from which I believe that this figure represents Avalokiteswara, as Hwen Thsang describes a similar statue at the Kapotika Sangharáma. The characters of the inscription do not seem to me to be later than A. D. 800.

On the top of the mound I found the lower portion of a female figure, of which the upper part was fixed in the ground near the Asánagar Temple. The statue is two-armed, and holds a lotus in one hand. It probably represents Dharmma. There are two four-armed female attendants, that to the left carrying a human head.

XI. TITARAWA.

At Titaráwa, 2 miles to the north of Ghosráwá, there is a fine large tank 1,200 feet in length, with a considerable mound of brick ruin to the north, and a colossal statue of the ascetic Buddha to the south, which is now called Bhairav. The pedestal is 7 feet broad, and the whole figure is still 9 feet high, although the upper portion is wanting. The usual Buddhist formula is inscribed on the lotus leaves of the pedestal. There are besides several others small and unimportant, one of which bears the Buddhist formula, and another inscription in three lines of small letters. The greater portion of this inscription is injured, but sufficient remains to declare the date of the statue, which I believe to be about A. D. 800; I can read the name of Mahápála at the end of it. On the west side of the statue there is the foundation of a brick stupa, 18 feet in diameter.

The mound of Titarāwn is about 20 feet high, and has a small modern fort on the top, with a round tower at each of the angles. Excavations for bricks are still going on, as at the period of Major Kittoe's visit. I traced the remains of several walls, from which I infer that the mound was the site of a large monastery. There is no mention of this place either in Fa-Hian or Hwen Thsang.

XII. APHSAR.

Five miles to the east of Ghosráwá, and on the eastern bank of the Sakri River, there is a low hill covered with brick ruins, close to a village called Aphsar. The long and important inscription of a second dynasty of Guptas, that was discovered at this place by Major Kittoe, is no longer to be found at Aphsar. The people are unanimous in stating that Major Kittoe removed it to Nowāda for the purpose of copying it; and he himself states that he "brought it away to re-examine it, and to restore it as much as possible before having it fixed in a pedestal near the Varāha" in Aphsar. I enquired for this inscription at Nowāda, at Gaya, and at Banāras, but could not hear any thing of it. The loss of this important inscription is very much to be regretted; but luckily I possess a transcript of it in modern Nagari, which Major Kittoe himself gave me in 1850. This has been submitted to Bábu Rajendralal Mitra for translation.*

XIII. BARABAR.

At 16 miles to the north of Gaya, or 19 miles by the road, there are several groups of granite hills, called *Kawwa-Dol*, *Barábar*, *Nágárjuni*, and *Dharáwat*.† All of these possess some Buddhistic remains, but the most interesting are the caves of *Barábar* and *Nágárjuni*, which were hewn out of the solid rock upwards of two thousand years ago.

Kawwa-Dol is a detached hill nearly one mile to the south-west of the main group of hills, and just six miles

---

* The Bábu's translation will be found in the Bengal Asiatic Society's Journal for 1866, p. 272. The inscription gives the genealogy of nine Gupta Kings. There is apparently nothing to guide us in fixing the date, and, in the absence of the original document, I can only conjecture that these Guptas are of later date than the well-known Gupta dynasty of the Allahabad and Bhitari Pillar inscriptions. I possess gold coins of three later Princes, Vishnu, Kumára, and Jaya, who probably belonged to the family of the Aphsar record.

† See Plate XVIII.

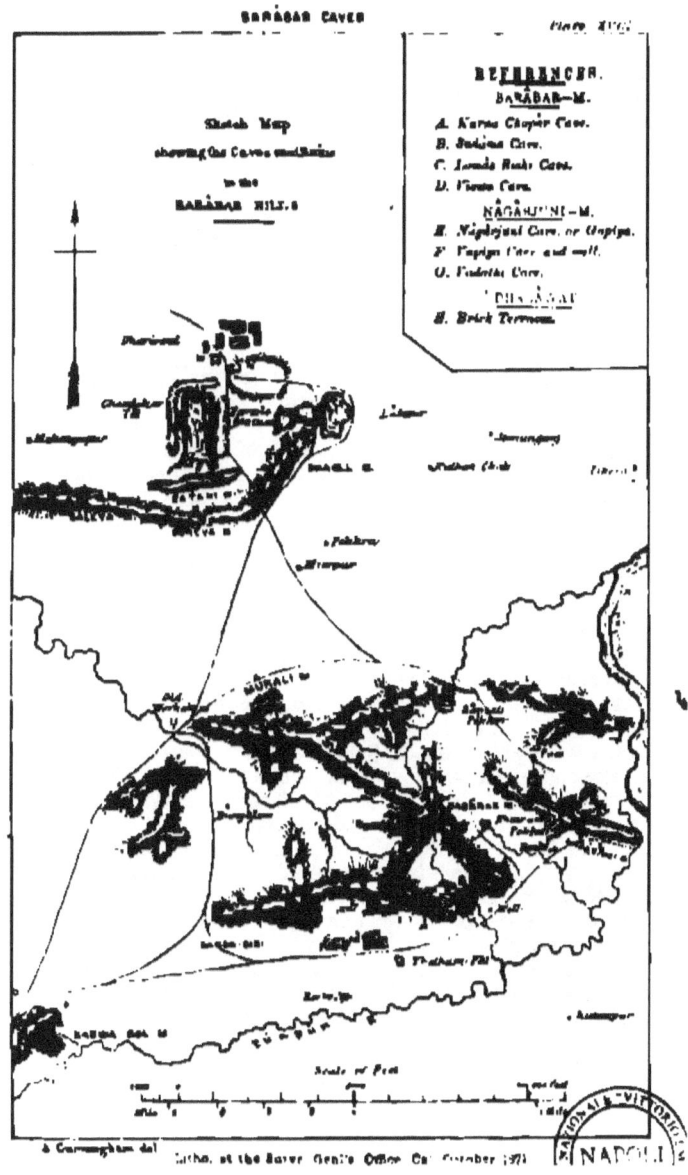

to the east-north-east of the Bela Dāk Bungalow. This hill is quite inaccessible, as it is formed entirely of huge masses of granite piled precipitously above one another, and crowned with a single lofty block that frowns grandly over the plains below. It is said that this pinnacle was formerly topped by another block, which was so nicely balanced that it used to rock even when a crow alighted upon it. From this belief the hill acquired the name of *Kauwa-Dol*, or the "crow's swing," or "rocking-stone."

At the northern foot of the Kauwa-Dol there has formerly been a temple of hewn granite. A large village must also once have existed on the north and east sides of the hill, as the foot of the hill, which is considerably raised above the fields, is strewn with broken bricks, hewn stones, and fragments of pottery. There are several Muhammedan tombs on this mound, built chiefly of pillars and other squared and ornamented stones of some Hindu temple. The name of this old place is said to have been *Samanpur*. Major Kittoe, however, was told that this name applied only to the northern portion of the ruins, the eastern portion being called *Sarain*.

On the rocks of the northern face of the hill, numerous rude figures have been sculptured. One of these is a figure of Ganes, 2½ feet high, beside a lingam. Several of them represent *Gauri Sankar* or *Hara Gauri*; but the most common of these sculptures is the favourite figure of the four-armed Durgā slaying the *Mahesasur*, or Buffalo Demon. In her two right hands she holds a sword and a trident, and in her upper left hand a shield, while her lower left hand grasps the tail of the Buffalo. All of these are Brahmanical figures; but there are also rude figures of Buddha seated, and one female figure which is said to be *Padmavati*, or *Māyā Devi*, but which is most probably only a representation of *Dharmma*. In a recess on the east side of the hill, and amidst the ruins of a large temple, of which several pillars are still standing, there is a colossal figure of Buddha the ascetic, as he appeared when seated in mental abstraction under the Bodhi tree at Buddha-Gaya. A drawing of this figure has been given in Buchanan Hamilton's *Eastern India*.* It is the largest statue that I have seen, the figure

---

* Vol. I., Plate XIV., Fig. 3.

alone being 8 feet high, with a breadth across the shoulders of four feet, and of six feet across the knees. But the great statue in the temple of Buddha-Gaya, which was seen and described by Hwen Thsang, was somewhat more than one-third larger, its dimensions being 11 feet 5 inches in height, 8 feet 6 inches in breadth across the knees, and 6 feet 6 inches across the shoulders.

In the Barábar group of hills there are several distinct peaks, of which the most conspicuous are the *Murali* Peak to the north, and the *Sanda Giri* on the south, both of which join the Barábar or *Siddheswara* Peak on the east. On the summit of the Barábar Peak there is a small Hindu temple dedicated to Mahádeva, which contains a lingam called Siddheswara, and which, from an inscription in one of the caves mentioning this name, we know to be at least as old as the 6th or 7th century. Immediately to the south of the Barábar Peak there lies a small valley, or basin, nearly square in shape, and entirely surrounded by hills, except at two points on the north-east and south-east, where walls have been built to complete the enclosure. Its greatest length, measured diagonally from peak to peak, is just half a mile, but the actual basin is not more than 400 yards in length by 250 yards in breadth.*

Towards the southern corner of the basin, there are two small sheets of clear water, which find an outlet under ground to the south-east and re-appear in the sacred spring called *Pátál Gangá*, where an annual assembly is held in the month of *Bhádrapada* for the purpose of bathing. On this side is the principal entrance to the valley, which lies over large rounded masses of granite, now worn smooth and slippery by the feet of numerous pilgrims. I ascended by this path without any difficulty, after having taken off my shoes, but in descending I found a shorter and quicker way down the mass of loose rough stones at the foot of the enclosure wall on the same side. These stones are the ruins of buildings which once crowned the wall on this side.

Immediately to the south of the water, and in the southern angle of the valley, there is a low ridge of granite rock lying from west to east, about 500 feet long, from 100 to 120

---

* See Plate XVIII.

feet thick, and from 30 to 35 feet in height. The top of the ridge is rounded, and falls rapidly towards the east. It is divided longitudinally by natural cleavage into three separate masses. The block towards the north is much the smallest, being not more than 50 feet long by 27 feet in thickness. Originally it was probably about 80 or 100 feet in length, but its eastern end has been cut away to obtain access to the face of the central mass of rock, in which the *Karna-Chopár* Cave has been excavated. A lingam and two rude Brahminical figures are sculptured on the end of the northern rock. The middle rock is between 200 and 300 feet in length, with a perpendicular face towards the north. The largest mass of rock which faces towards the south is rounded at top, but the lower part has been scarped to form a perpendicular wall for the two large caves now called *Sudáma* and *Lomas Rishi*. A level piece of ground, about 100 feet in width, intervenes between this great rock and the foot of the southern hill. Sheds and temporary buildings are erected on this spot during the annual fair time, when the caves are visited by thousands of pilgrims. The ground is strewn with broken bricks and fragments of pottery, and the rubbish has now accumulated to a height of three feet above the floors of the caves. This will account for the fact of there having been one foot of water in this cave when visited by Buchanan. The water was drained away by Major Kittoe, who dug a trench along the foot of the rock, and brought to light several pieces of stone pillars which probably belonged to some portico or cloister in front of the caves.

The Barábar Basin is naturally a strong defensive position, as it possesses plenty of water, and is only accessible at two points, on the north-east and south-east. Now, both of these points have been closed by walls, and as there are also traces of walls on the surrounding hills, and more particularly on the Siddheswara Hill, it seems certain that the place must once have been used as a stronghold. There is indeed a tradition of some Raja having been besieged in this place, and that he escaped by the narrow passage over the Siddheswara Hill. Its very name of Barábar, that is, *bara* and *awara*, or *Barawara*, the " great enclosure," points to the same conclusion, although this may have been originally applied to the much larger enclosure between the Barábar and Nágárjuni Hills, and the western branch of the Phalgu River, where, according to Buchanan's information, the original Ram Gaya was situated. The numerous heaps of brick and stone that lie scattered over the plain would seem to show that this had once been the site of a large town. The situation is similar to that of old Raja-griha, namely, that of a small valley or basin almost surrounded by hills; but in size it is very much less than the famous *Giriraja*, or hill-encircled city of Jarasandha. This enclosure had the Barábar Hill on the west, the Sangar branch of the Phalgu River on the east, and the two parallel ridges of the Nágárjuni Hills to the north and south. It was upwards of one mile in length, with a mean width of half a mile and a circuit of rather more than three miles. The circuit of the hills surrounding old Raja-griha was about eight miles.

The caves in the Barábar Hills are usually known as the *Sat-ghara*, or "seven houses." Major Kittoe proposed *Sapt-garbha*, or the "seven caves" as the true name; but I think that *Sapta-griha*, or, as it is pronounced in the vernacular of the present day, *Sat-ghara*, is a preferable etymology, as it is the very same name by which this collection of caves is now known.

The Nágárjuni Hills consist of two very narrow ridges of granite running nearly parallel, and about half a mile distant from each other, between the Barábar Peak and the Phalgu River. The northern ridge would appear to be the same as that which Buchanan calls *Murali*,* but my informants applied this name to another peak in the Barábar group. The southern ridge contains the famous old caves, of which the largest one, called the *Gopi* Cave, is on the southern side, with its entrance to the south. The two other caves are situated on the southern face of a small spur, or off-shoot, on the northern side of the hill.

There are, therefore, altogether seven caves in these hills, four of which belong to the *Barábar* or Siddheswara group, and three to the *Nágárjuni* group. I incline, therefore, to believe that the name of *Sat-ghara*, or the "seven houses," belonged originally to the whole of these seven caves, and not

---

* Eastern India, Vol. I, p. 104.

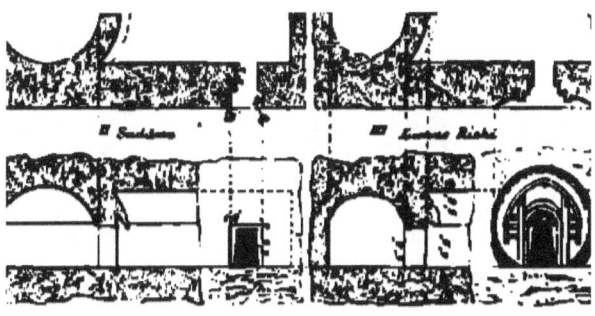

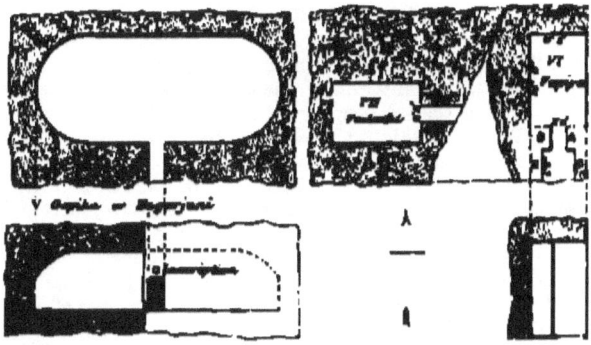

to the four caves with seven chambers in the Barábar group. It is true, indeed, that the Barábar caves are somewhat older than those of Nágárjuni, but the difference of date is very little, being not more than 30 years, as will be shown when I come to speak of the inscriptions.

The *Karna Chopár* Cave, marked A. in the map, is situated in the northern face of the Barábar ridge of granite, which has already been described. The entrance, which is of Egyptian form, faces the north. The cave is 33 feet 6½ inches in length, by 14 feet in width.* The sides of the cave are 6 feet 1½ inch in height, and the vaulted roof has a rise of 4 feet 8 inches, making the total height 10 feet 9 inches. At the western end there is a raised platform 7 feet 6 inches long, 2 feet 6 inches broad, and 1 foot 3 inches high. From its length I infer that this was the pedestal of a statue. The whole of the interior of the cave is polished. On the outside, and at the western corner of the entrance, there is a sunken tablet containing a short inscription of five lines in the ancient character of Asoka's Pillars. It records the excavation of the cave in the 19th year of the reign of Raja *Piyadasi*, that is, of Asoka himself.† This cave, therefore, dates as far back as 245 B. C. The inscription has been so much injured by the weather, that it is very difficult to make out the letters satisfactorily. It also faces the north, so that no advantage can be obtained from the difference of light and shade which is caused by the sun in the hollows of the letters of such inscriptions as face in other directions. There are also several short inscriptions on the jambs of the doorway, such as *Bodhimula* "the root of Intelligence," *Daridra kántára* "the cave of the poor," or "the mendicant's cave," and others the records of mere visitors.

The *Sudáma* Cave, marked B. in the map, is situated in the same granite range, but on the opposite side of it, and with its entrance facing the south. The door-way, which is of Egyptian form, is sunk in a recess 6½ feet square and 2 feet deep. On the eastern wall of this recess or porch, there is an inscription of two lines in the ancient Pali characters of Asoka's Pillars. An attempt has been made to obliterate the greater part of this inscription with a chisel,

---

* See Plate XIX., Fig. 1, for plan and section.
† See Plate XX., No. 1 Inscription.

but owing to the great depth of the letters the work of destruction was not an easy one, and the clearly cut lines of the original letters, with the exception of one, perhaps, at the end, are still distinctly traceable in the midst of the rough holes made by the destroyer's chisel. This inscription records the dedication by Raja *Piyadasi* (that is, Asoka himself), in the 12th year of his reign, of the *Nigoha* cave.* The excavation of this cave, therefore, dates as far back as 252 B. C., the very same year in which many of Asoka's edicts were promulgated, as recorded in his different inscriptions both on pillars and rocks. The cave itself consists of two chambers, of which the inner one is nearly circular with a hemispherical domed roof. This roof, which projects beyond the wall of the circular room into the outer apartment, is considerably under-cut, as if to represent a thatch with its overhanging eaves. The circular room is 19 feet 11 inches in diameter from west to east, and 19 feet from north to south. The outer apartment is 32 feet 9 inches in length, by 19 feet 6 inches in breadth. The walls are 6 feet 9 inches in height to the springing of the vaulted roof, which has a rise of 5 feet 6 inches, making the total height of the chamber 12 feet 3 inches. At the east end of this apartment there is a shallow recess which may have been intended as a niche for a statue, or more probably as an entrance to another projected chamber. But the work was abandoned soon after its commencement, and remains rough and unfinished, while all the rest of the cave, both roof and walls, is highly polished.†

The *Lomas Rishi* Cave, marked C. in the map, is similar to the *Sudama* Cave, both as to the size and arrangement of its two chambers; but the whole of the interior of the circular room has been left rough, and both the floor and the roof of the outer apartment remain unfinished.‡ The straight walls of this apartment are polished, but the outer wall of the circular room is only smoothed and not polished. The chisel marks are yet visible on the floor, while on the roof, which has only been partially hewn, the cuts of the chisels, both broad and narrow, are still sharp and distinct. The excavation of the roof would appear to have been abandoned, owing

---

* See Plate XX., No. 2 Inscription.
† See Plate XIX., Fig. 2.
‡ See Plate XIX., Fig. 6.

PARĀBAR

NĀGĀRJUNI CAVES

IV Gopika, or Nāgārjuni.

V. Vapiyā, or Well Cave.

VI. Vadathi Cave.

VII शावर्ष श्री जहावरू
VIII शावर्षश्रीजहावरू प्रलयसिसि वेद्यर

BARĀBAR CAVES

I. Karna Chopār, at A.

II. Sudāma, at B.

III. Viswamitra, at D.

A. Cunningham, del.

to the work having reached a deep fissure, which forms one of the natural lines of cleavage of the rock. It possesses no inscription.

The door-way of this cave is exactly of the same size and of the same Egyptian form as that of the Sudáma Cave, but the entrance porch has been much enlarged, and has been sculptured to represent what I believe to be the ornamental entrance of a wooden building. A tolerably faithful sketch of this entrance will be found in Buchanan,* but owing to the accumulation of rubbish at the time the sketch was taken, the full height of the work is not shown. The inscriptions also are represented as extending below the top of the doorway on one side, which is not the case, as they are all confined to the semi-circular space above the door. This sketch, however, shows distinctly the ends of the roofing beams and the bambu lattice work of the gable, just such as may still be seen in the wooden buildings of Barmah.

As the inscriptions over the door-way of this cave are all in the same character as those of the later princes of the Gupta dynasty, the date of this sculptured façade may be assigned to the 3rd or 4th century of our era. But as the cave itself corresponds so exactly, both in size and in arrangements, with the Sudáma Cave, I feel satisfied that it must have been excavated at the same time, and that, before the enlargement of the entrance porch, there must have existed an inscription of Asoka, recording the name and purpose of the cave. The present inscriptions are deeply and boldly cut, but the letters are not polished. There are two distinct inscriptions, the upper one, of two lines, being somewhat later in date than the lower one, of four lines, in rather larger letters. Both of these inscriptions have been translated by James Prinsep,† who, owing perhaps to the misplacement of the lines of his *fac-similis*, did not perceive that translations of both had already been published by Wilkins in the second volume of the Asiatic Researches. There is some variation in the two versions of these inscriptions, which will be examined hereafter.

The fourth cave of the Barábar group is that which is called *Viswa Mitra* by Major Kittoe, but which was named

---

* Eastern India, Vol. I., p. 104.
† Bengal Asiatic Society's Journal, 1837, p. 647.

simply *Viswa-jhopri*, or "Viswa's hut," by my informants. This cave, marked D. in the map, is excavated in a large block of granite lying to the eastward of the cave ridge and at a somewhat lower level. It consists of two rooms, an outer apartment or ante-chamber which is polished throughout, and an inner apartment of 11 feet in diameter, which is rough and unfinished. The former is 14 feet long by 8 feet 4 inches broad, and has an inscription on the right hand wall of four lines in the ancient Pali character of Asoka's inscriptions. The last five letters have been purposely mutilated with the chisel, but they are still quite legible.* The inscription, which is otherwise perfect, records the dedication of the cave by Raja *Piyadasi* (that is, Asoka himself,) in the 12th year of his reign, equivalent to 252 B. C. This is the only inscription in this cave which would seem to have escaped the notice of the Brahmanical occupants or visitors of the other caves. On the floor of this outer chamber there are four oblong socket holes, which would appear to have been intended for the reception of timber framing, as suggested by Major Kittoe.

The great cave in the Nágárjuni Hill, marked E. in the map, is excavated in the southern face of the rock, at a height of 50 feet above the country. It is approached by a flight of stone steps, but the entrance is concealed partly by a tree and partly by an *Idgáh* wall, which was built by the last Musalmán occupants. It was inhabited when visited by Major Kittoe in 1847, but was empty when I saw it. This cave is 46 feet 5 inches long and 10 feet 2 inches broad, both ends being semi-circular. The walls are 6 feet 6 inches high, and the vaulted roof has a rise of 4 feet, making a total height of 10 feet 6 inches.† The whole of the interior is polished, but quite plain. There is a low brick platform of modern date at one end, which is said to have been the seat of a Musalmán Saint, who was the disciple and successor of Haji *Hármáyan*. The door-way of the cave is of Egyptian form, being two feet 6 inches wide at top, and 2 feet 11¼ inches at bottom, with a height of 6 feet and half an inch. On the eastern jamb of the door-way there is an inscription in ten lines of the same family and same date as those over the door-way of the Lomas Rishi

---

* See Plate XX., No. 3 Inscription.
† See Plate XIX, Fig. 5.

Cave. This inscription has been translated by Wilkins and by James Prinsep.* On the western jamb of the door there is a short inscription in large letters of the 7th or 8th century. *Achárya Sri Yogananda,* "the teacher Sri Yognananda," whose name will be found repeated in another cave.†

On the outside, immediately over the door-way, there is a small sunken tablet, containing a short inscription of four lines in the ancient Pali characters of Asoka's edicts. This has been translated by James Prinsep.‡ The cave is called *Gopi-ka-kubha,* that is, the "Gopi's or milkmaid's Cave." The inscription records that "The Gopi's Cave, an abode lasting as the Sun and Moon, was caused to be excavated by *Dasaratha,* beloved of the Devas, on his accession to the throne, as a hermitage for the most devoted *Bhadantas* (Buddhist ascetics)."§

The other two caves of the Nágárjuni Group are situated in a low rocky ridge on the northern side of the hill. To the south, and in front of the caves, there are two raised terraces. The lower one to the eastward has a well, 9 feet in diameter and 23 feet deep, immediately in front of the entrance to the eastern cave, which in the inscription is called the "*Vapiya-ka-kubha,*" or "Vapiya Cave," which I believe refers to the well *(vapi)* above described, and which may, therefore, be translated as the "Well Cave." The upper terrace to the westward is 120 feet long from north to south, 60 feet broad from west to east, and 10 feet in height above the plain. The walls are chiefly of brick, but there are several squared stones and granite pillars near the top. These must, I think, have been added afterwards by the Muhammedans when they occupied the caves, for the platform is covered with their small tombs. All around there are heaps of bricks and fragments of carved and squared stones which show that several buildings must once have existed in this place. The upper platform I believe to have been the site of a *vihár* or Buddhist chapel monastery, but there is nothing now remaining to prove any Buddhist occupation, excepting only one fragment of a standing statue.

---

* See Asiatic Researches, I., 282; and Bengal Asiatic Society's Journal, 1837, p. 673.
† See Plate XX., No. 7 Inscription.
‡ Bengal Asiatic Society's Journal, 1837, p. 677.
§ See Plate XX., No. 4 Inscription.

The *Vapiya* Cave, marked F. in the map, has a small porch or ante-chamber, 6 feet long by 5½ feet broad, from which a door-way only 2 feet 10 inches wide leads to the principal room, which is 16 feet 0 inches long and 11 feet 3 inches broad. The roof is vaulted, and 10 feet 6 inches in total height. The whole of the walls are highly polished. On the left hand side of the porch there is an inscription of four lines in the old Pali characters of Asoka's edicts.* In this record the cave is called, as already mentioned, the *Vapiya-ka-kubha*, or "the Well Cave," in evident allusion to the well in front of it. The remainder of the inscription is word for word the same as that of the Gopi's Cave. There are several short inscriptions on the side walls of the porch and on the jambs of the door-way, but they are of little interest, as they merely record the names of visitors. The longest of them reads—

Achârya Sri Yogananda pranamati Siddheswara, "The teacher Sri Yogananda offers adoration to Siddheswara."† In this inscription we find the name of the *lingam* now existing in the temple of the Barâbar Peak, recorded in characters of the 6th or 7th century. James Prinsep refers them to the 6th century. A still older inscription, *Videsa Vasusya Kirttih*, or "the renown of Vasu of Videsa," belongs to the age of the Guptas. According to Buchanan, this cave is called *Mirza Mandai*, or the "Mirza's house."

The third cave of the Nâgârjuni Group, marked G. in the map, is situated immediately to the westward of the last cave, in a gap or natural cleft of the rock, which has probably been enlarged by art. The entrance to the cave lies in this gap facing the east. It is a mere passage, only 2 feet 10 inches in width and 6 feet 1½ inch in height, with a length of 7 feet 2 inches on the northern side, and of 5 feet 9 inches on the southern side. There are socket holes both above and below for the reception of a wooden door. The cave itself is 16 feet 4 inches by 4 feet 3 inches ; but it has been divided into two rooms by a rude brick wall. This must have been the work of some ascetic of former days, as the only opening to the inner room appears to be too small for the passage of any grown-up man, and could only have

---
* See Plate XX., No. 5 Inscription, and Plate XIX., Fig. 6, for plan.
† See Plate XX., No. 6 Inscription.

been used by the occupant for the reception of food. On the right hand jamb of the door-way there is an inscription of four lines in the old Pali characters of Asoka's edicts, in which this cave is called the *Vadathi-kâ-kubha*. The remainder of the record is letter for letter the same as those of the *Gopi* and *Vapiya* Caves. The meaning of the name of *Vadathi* I am not able to explain. The root *vada* means to separate or divide, to surround or encompass, and also to cover. Any one of these meanings might be appropriately applied as descriptive of the peculiar position of this cave, for it is entirely separated from the other cave; it is encompassed by the bluff rocks of the gap in which it is situated, and is so effectually covered or screened from view, that it altogether escaped the notice of Mr. Hathorne when he made copies of the inscriptions in the Gopi and Vapiya caves for James Prinsep. I think, therefore, that the term "secluded" would be descriptive of the position of the cave, and I would suggest that *Vadathika* may probably be a vernacular form of *vada* + *arthika*, the whole meaning simply the cave of the "secluded mendicants." According to Buchanan, this cave is called the abode of Hâji *Harmáyan*.[*]

From the foregoing account of the Barábar caves, it will be seen that the two groups are separated by date as well as by position, the *Satghara* caves having been excavated in the 12th and 19th years of Raja *Piyadisi* (or Asoka) while those of Nâgârjuni were excavated in the first year of *Dasaratha*, the beloved of the Devas. According to the Vishnu Purâna, *Dasaratha* was the grandson of Asoka, and the son of Suyasas; and as the son of *Asoka*, according to the Vayu Purana, reigned only eight years, the accession of Dasaratha must have taken place in 214 B. C. The age of the Nâgârjuni caves is, therefore, 31 years later than that of the Karna-chopâr, and 38 years later than that of the Sudâma and Viswa Caves.

From the various inscriptions we learn that these caves have been successively occupied by Buddhists and by Brahmanists. They were originally excavated for the occupation of Buddhist monks by the Kings Asoka and Dasaratha in the third century before Christ. About the third or fourth century after Christ, the Kings Sârdula Varmma and Ananta Varmma, placed Brahmanical images of *Deva-mátá*, of

---

[*] See Plate XIX., Fig. 7, for plan, and Plate XX., No. 6, for inscription.

Kátyáyani, and of *Mahádeva* and his wife in three of the caves. At a somewhat later date, in the sixth or seventh century, the teacher Yogananda recorded his adoration of the *Siddhesicara lingam*. This occupation by Brahmans in the seventh century may account for the silence of the Chinese pilgrim Hwen Thsang regarding the caves, which, as being in the immediate neighbourhood of Gaya, would otherwise have attracted his attention. At a still later date, somewhere about the twelfth century, the *Jogi-Karnamárga* and the pilgrim *Bhayankara Nátha* visited the caves and inscribed their names.* Still later, the Nâgârjuni caves were occupied by Musalmân Fakîrs. The Idgâh outside the Gopi Cave is said to be only 150 years old, but the numerous graves on the raised terrace in front of the *Vapiya* Cave would seem to denote a much longer occupation of probably not less than 300 or 400 years.

During this successive occupation, the caves would appear to have received new names, as not one of the ancient names recorded in the inscriptions has been preserved. Indeed, the most ancient names would seem to have been lost at a very early date, for the *Gopi* Cave of Dasaratha is designated by Ananta Varmma as "this cavern of the Vindhya mountains," and the *Vadathi* Cave is called simply "this Cave," as if the ancient names had already been forgotten. Similarly, the Lomas Rishi Cave is called *Pravara-giri-guha*, or "the great mountain cave." From these instances, I would infer that the present names of the caves are all of later date than the time of Ananta Varmma in the third or fourth century. That they were also of Brahmanical origin seems to me to be quite certain for the following reasons: *Karna-chopár* I take to be simply *Karna-jhopra*, or " Karna's Hut," so named after *Karna*, King of Angga, the illegitimate son of Pritha, the mother of the Pandus. Similarly, *Lomas Rishi*, who was described to Buchanan as a "very hairy saint," is no doubt the same as *Loma-páda* or "hairy foot," who was also one of the Kings of Angga (or Bhágalpur). But as Lomapáda is only a descriptive appellation of a Prince whose true name was Dasaratha, it would seem as if the name of

---

* See Plate XX., D and B inscriptions from the Vapiya or Well Cave. The other inscriptions given in the same Plate are short desultory records of little importance. No. 16, *daridra-dátára*, "the cave of poverty," and Nos. 18 and 19, *klesa-dátára*, "the cave of affliction," no doubt refer to Buddhism, and show that these caves were inhabited, or at least visited, by Buddhist votaries as late as the third or fourth century A. D.

BARABAR — DHARAWAT. 53

Dasaratha, the founder of the three Nágârjuni Caves, had actually been preserved down to a comparatively late period, and was then ignorantly referred by the Brahmans to the early king of Angga, instead of to the Maurya Prince of Magatha. Regarding the name of *Sudáma* or *Sudháma*, I am unable to offer any conjecture; but *Visvamitra* was one of the most celebrated of the seven Rishis, or great Brahmanical Saints.

The silence of Hwen Thsang regarding the caves has been already noticed; but I have a suspicion that he had heard of the celebrated spring of the *Pátál Gangá* at the foot of the Barábar Hill. According to his account, there was a famous spring of pure water situated at 30 *li* (or 5 miles) to the north of Gaya.* Now, as I could not hear of any spring to the northward of Gaya nearer than Barábar, I would suggest that Hwen Thsang's distance of 30 *li* should be corrected to 130 *li* (or 21¾ miles), which would make his famous spring agree exactly with the position of the *Pátál Ganga*, according to the distance by road, which is 13 miles to the Bela Dák Bungalow + 6 to the Kauwa-Dol Hill + 2 more to the Pátál Gangá. Hwen Thsang adds that "the Indians, following an ancient tradition, called this spring the 'holy water' (l'eau sainte), and that at all times whoever drank of it, or bathed in it, was instantly purified from the stain of his sins." Now the source of the Pátál Gangá is still held in such esteem that, according to Buchanan, from 20,000 to 50,000 people assemble annually in the middle of the month of Bhádrapada to bathe in its waters, and about 500 people bathe daily during the whole of that month.

Should this identification be correct, it would seem to be almost certain that towards the middle of the seventh century of our era, not only were these caves occupied by the Brahmans, but the very memory of their Buddhist origin had either been forgotten or was carefully concealed.

XIV. DHARAWAT.

The *Dhardwat* group of hills lies immediately to the northward of the Barábar hills, about 1¼ mile distant. There are two distinct ridges running from west to east, that to the

* Julien's Hwen Thsang. II., 455.

south being nearly two miles in length with three peaks named *Saleya, Gureya,* and *Dhaoli.** The nearest road from Barâbar to Dharâwat lies through a pass between the Gureya and Dhaoli Hills. The northern ridge consists of a single hill named *Ratani,* which in former days was occupied by some establishment of the Buddhists. On the northern slope of the hill there are two brick terraces which have been built up against the rock. The eastern terrace is 60 feet long by 20 feet broad, and 50 feet above the plain. Near the top the solid brick-work can still be seen for 20 feet in height, below which the brick rubbish reaches to the foot of the hill. The second terrace lies more than 200 feet to the westward of the other; it has a front of 250 feet, but its height is not more than 15 feet above the plain. On this terrace there are two broken Buddhist figures, and beneath it there are four others, of which one bears the usual Buddhist formula of " *Ye Dharmma hetu prabhava,* &c.," in characters of the 9th or 10th century.

To the north of the Ratani Hill there is a large tank called *Chándokhar* Tâl, 2,000 feet in length and 600 feet in width. On the eastern embankment there is a new temple to Mahâdeva, only three years old, and close beside it a very small old temple to Narsingh. Outside this temple there is a very fine life-size statue named Bhairav. The figure stands under a thick stem of lotus which forms an arch overhead, and from which little curling branches strike off on both sides, ending in lotus flowers which support tiny figures of men, women, and animals. The statue has twelve arms, and bears in the head-dress a small figure of Buddha squatted with hands in lap. I recognized it at once as a statue of the famous *Bodhisatwa Avalokiteswara.* Beside the statue, there are several sculptured stones containing rows of Buddhas, and also several fragments of votive stupas, and two slabs with representations of the *Nava-graha,* or "nine planets." There are also numerous fragments of sculpture under a Pipal tree close by, two of which bear inscriptions in characters of the 9th or 10th century.

To the north-east of the Chândokhar Tâl there is an extensive mound of brick ruin, which is probably only the remains of the former town of Dharâwat. In the north-west

* See Plate No. XVIII.

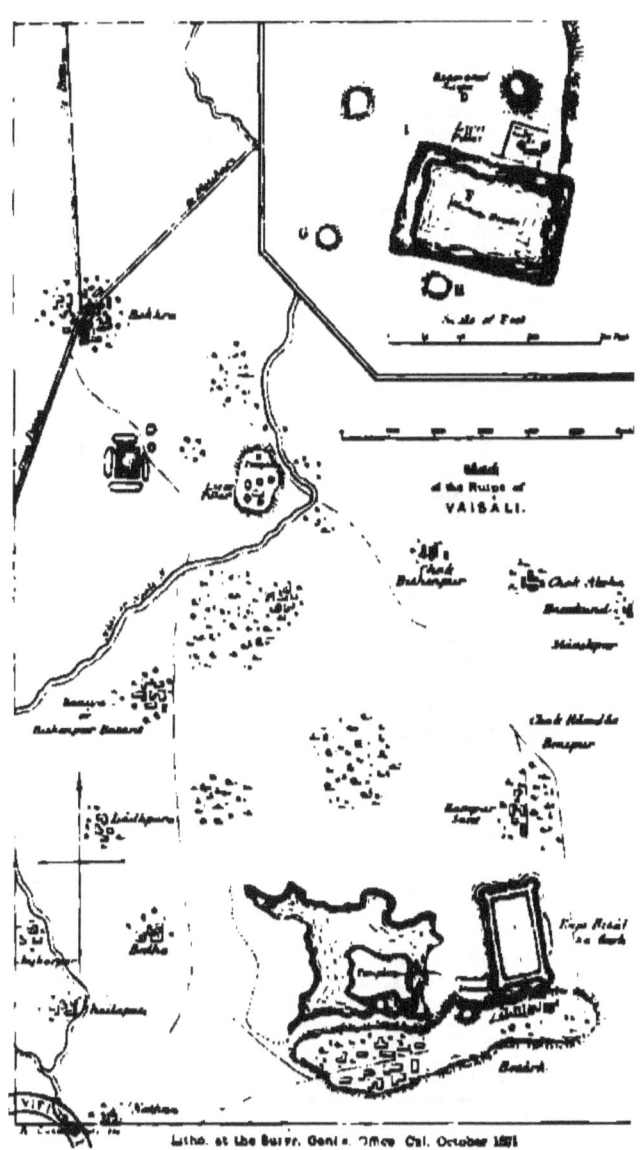

corner of this mound there are two small eminences, which may be the remains of temples, but as the surface of the mound now presents nothing but small fragments of bricks, all the larger bricks having been removed to furnish materials for the present village, it is quite impossible to say what kind of buildings may once have stood upon it. All that can be inferred, I think, from the present remains is, that Dharáwat must at one time, probably about the 8th or 9th century, have been the seat of a considerable Buddhist community. Major Kittoe paid a hurried visit to Dharáwat by moon-light. He notices the twelve-armed figure, which he calls a Buddhist sculpture, as being very remarkable.

XV. BESARH.

The village of *Besárh*, or *Besádh* in Nagari characters, is situated 27 miles, a little to the east of north from Patna, and 20 miles from Hájipur on the left bank of the Ganges. Both the distance and direction from Patna point to this place as the representative of the ancient *Vaisáli*. The name also is the same, as it is written *Besárh* by Abul Fazl in his Ain Akbari.[*] Now, Hwen Thsang places the King's Palace in Vaisáli at 120 *li*, or 20 miles, to the east of north from the northern bank of the Ganges opposite Pátaliputra, that is, from the present Hájipur.[†] He also describes the King's Palace as being from 4 to 5 *li* (from 3,500 to 4,400 feet) in circuit, which agrees with the size of the ruined fort now called *Rája Bisál-ka-garh*, which is 1,580 feet long and 750 feet broad inside, or 4,660 feet in circuit round the crest of the mound. This almost perfect coincidence of name, position, and dimensions, seems quite sufficient to place the identification of Besárh with Vaisáli beyond all reasonable doubt. I will, therefore, now proceed to describe the objects of interest that still remain in Besárh and the neighbouring village of Bakhra, which will afford further proof of the identity of Besárh and Vaisáli.

These ruins were visited by Mr. J. Stephenson in 1834, and described by him in Prinsep's Journal.[‡] They consist of two distinct groups, one at Besárh itself, and the other

---
[*] Gladwin's Translation, II., 188.
[†] Julien's Hwen Thsang, II., 399. To Swetapura 90 *li*, plus 90 *li* to the Ganges. In Vol. I., p. 137, the distance to Swetapura is stated to be 100 *li*.
[‡] Bengal Asiatic Society's Journal, 1835, p. 128.

2 miles to the north-north-west of Besárh, and 1 mile to the south-east of Bakhra. But the whole of these must have belonged to the ancient Vaisáli, as Hwen Thsang describes the old foundations of the city, although even then much ruined, as occupying a circuit of from 60 to 70 li, or from 10 to 12 miles. Now, an oblong square, 3½ miles from north to south, and 2½ miles from west to east, making a circuit of exactly 12 miles, would include both Bakhra and Besárh and all the remains that are at present traceable. This of itself would be sufficient to show that the Bakhra ruins must have formed part of the ancient Vaisáli; but the fact will be placed byond all doubt when I come to describe the ruins themselves, which correspond in the most remarkable manner with the minute details recorded by Hwen Thsang.

The remains at Besárh consist of a large deserted fort, and a ruined brick stupa. The fort is a large brick covered mound of earth, 1,580 feet long from north to south, and 750 feet broad from west to east, measured from edge to edge.* It has round towers at the four corners, and the whole is surrounded by a ditch which was full of water at the time of my visit. The ruined ramparts along the edge, and the four towers at the corners, are somewhat higher than the mass of the mound, which has a general elevation of from 6 to 8 feet above the country. The height of the north-west bastion I found by measurement to be 12 feet above the fields, and 15 feet above the bottom of the ditch, where it was dry. The main entrance was in the middle of the south face, where there still exists a broad embankment across the ditch, as well as a passage through the rampart. In the northern face there was probably only a postern gate, as there is no passage through the rampart, and no trace of any embankment across the ditch, excepting the fact that the only dry part of the ditch is on this face. The only building within the fort is a small brick temple of modern date.

Outside the south-west angle of the fort, and about 1,000 feet distant, there is a ruined mound of solid brick-work, 23 feet 8 inches in height above the fields. The whole of the top has been levelled for the reception of Musalmán tombs, of which the largest, ascribed to Mir Abdál, is said to be 500

---
* See Plate No. XXI.

years old. Mr. Stephenson gives the name of the Saint as Mir Abdullah, and the age of the tomb as 250 years. My informant was the Musalmán whom I found in charge of the tomb. On the south edge of the mound there is a magnificent wide-spreading Banian Tree, supported on numerous trunks, which shades the whole of the tombs. On the same side also a flight of steps leads down to the village of Besárh. This brick mound is the ruin of one of the *stupas*, or solid towers of Vaisáli, of which so many are described by Hwen Thsang. "Both within and without and all round the town of Vaisáli," says he, "the sacred monuments are so many that it would be difficult to enumerate them."* He has, however, described a few of them, which were situated to the south of the town, one of which, I have no doubt, is the solid brick mound that now bears the tomb of the Musalmán Saint, Mir Abdál.

At a short distance to the south of the town, there was a vihâr, and also a stupa in the garden which *Amradárikâ* had presented to Buddha. Beside the garden there was another stupa erected on the spot where Buddha had announced his approaching *Nirvâná* (or death). Beyond this there was a third stupa on the spot where the "thousand sons had recognized their mother." A fourth stupa stood over the spot where Buddha was said to have taken exercise, and a fifth, erected on ancient foundations, commemorated the site on which he had explained certain sacred books. A sixth stupa held the relics of one-half of the body of Ananda, the other half being enshrined at Rája-griha. The bearing of these stupas from the garden of *Amradárikâ* is not stated; but as the mass of the existing brick ruins lies to the westward of the southern entrance of the fort, the whole of these monuments must have been situated in that direction. Of the six stupas described by Hwen Thsang, it is probable that only two were of any size, namely, that erected on the spot where Buddha had announced his approaching *Nirvâná*, and that which contained the relics of the half body of Ananda. It is much to be regretted that the presence of the Musalmán tombs on the top of this ancient stupa effectually precludes any attempt at excavation, otherwise a shaft sunk down through the centre of the mound would probably reveal the purpose for which the monument had been erected. The stupa built by the

* Julien's Hwen Thsang, II., 395.

King of Magadha in Rája-griha, over the other half of the
remains of Ananda, is said by Hwen Thsang to have been a
superb one. An annual fair is held at the Basárh stupa in
the month of *Chaitra*, when many thousands of people assemble at the shrine of Mír Abdál. As the occurrence of
this fair is regulated by the solar reckoning of the Hindus,
and not by the lunar year of the Muhammedans, I conclude
that the festival was established long before the time of the
Musalmán Saint. I would, therefore, as the fair is held
beside the ruined stupa, connect the festival with some
celebration in honour of Buddha, or of one of his disciples.
Two ornamental stone pillars of mediæval date were found a
short time ago in excavating near the foot of the mound.

To the westward of the fort there is a large sheet of
water with an island on the east side, on which is situated a
small temple dedicated to Mahádeva. Inside the temple all
the sculptures found in the ruins of Besárh have been collected. The principal sculpture is a group of Mahádeva
seated on his bull Nandi and caressing Durga, or Gauri, who
is seated on a lion. There is also a standing figure of the
four-armed Vishnu with a radiated halo round his head. In
his hands he holds a club, a ball, a quoit, and a shell. A third
sculpture represents the *Ashta Sakti*, or eight female energies
seated on their respective *vahans* or vehicles. The remaining
sculptures are Buddhistical. One is of Buddha the Ascetic,
two represent the Dhyáni Buddha, Amitábha, while a fourth
is a seated figure of the famous Bodhisatwa Avalokiteswara.

There are several small sheets of water to the north and
north-west of the fort, but when I saw them they were irregular in shape and seemed to me mostly natural hollows filled
with the rain which had recently fallen. The Natives, however, say that formerly there were 52 tanks (*Báwan* Pokhar)
around Besárh, two of which still exist in the neighbourhood
of Bakhra.

The remains at *Bakhra* are all situated on a low mound
just one mile to the south-east of the village, and two miles
to the north north-west of the Fort of Besárh.[*] The greater
portion of this mound is now cultivated, but the whole
surface is covered with small fragments of bricks. The edge
of the mound is best defined on the western side, where it

---
[*] see Plate XXI.

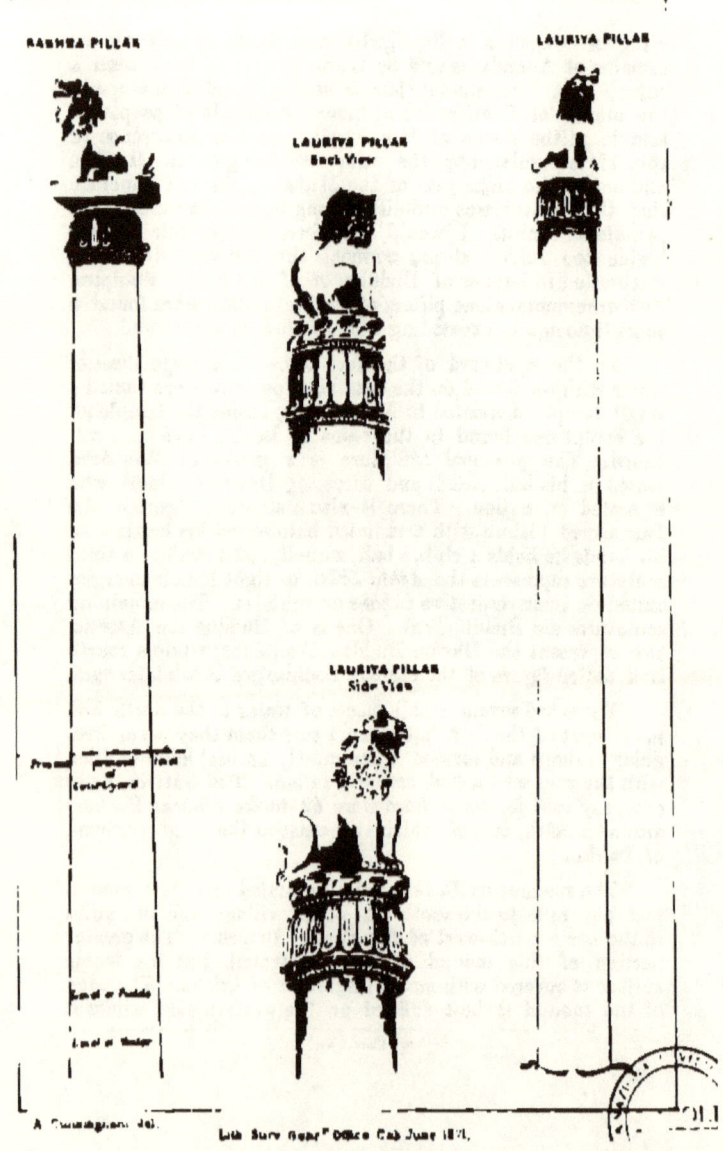

has an elevation of four feet. The remains consist of—1*st*, a stone pillar surmounted by a lion; 2*nd*, a ruined stupa of solid brick; 3*rd*, a tank; 4*th*, four small eminences which mark the sites of ancient buildings; and 5*th*, a very fine life-size statue of Buddha the Ascetic, which was discovered only eight years ago. The pillar and the ruined stupa have already been described by Mr. Stephenson, and the site has already been identified by M. Vivien de St. Martin, as well as by myself, with the Vaisâli of the Buddhists.

The lion pillar of Bakhra is situated in the middle of a small court-yard with small rooms on three sides—the residence of a *Sanyási* who has recently settled at this place. The people call him Baba. He is about 30 years of age, and appeared to me very like a sepoy. He was obliging and communicative, and gave me both assistance and information. If he had been surly and disobliging, he might easily have raised religious scruples, and thus have thwarted me from making an excavation round the pillar, which I was particularly anxious to do, as it was evident to me that the column had sunk considerably into the earth. The man had a few followers, and appeared to be very comfortable. There was plenty of food stored in his house, and a fine old well on the east side of the court-yard.

The shaft of the pillar is a single block of polished sand-stone, 18 feet in height above the present ground level of the court-yard in which it stands, and 27 feet 11 inches above the surrounding fields. The difference between these two measurements, or 9 feet 11 inches, represents the accumulation of rubbish around the pillar above the general level of the country. I made an excavation all round the shaft until I reached water at a depth of 14 feet below the level of the court-yard, and of 4 feet 1 inch below the level of the fields. The water in the old well close by was standing at the same level. As the whole of the shaft exposed by the excavation is polished, it appears to me certain that the pillar must have sunk into the ground at least 4 feet 1 inch in depth, and most probably several feet more, as there was no appearance of any basement at the point reached by my excavation. The whole height of shaft above the water level is 32 feet. I was informed by an old man at Besârh that the Sâheb who excavated the Bakhra stupa left a Bengáli to make an excavation round the pillar, and that just at the water level he found a square pedestal in three steps. Before I began my own excavation, I was told that a previous excavation had been made down to the water level without revealing any inscriptions. I found, however, a few short records in the curious flourished characters, which James Prinsep called "shell-shaped," and which Major Kittoe thought somewhat resembled Chinese. I believe that these characters belong to the 7th or 8th century. But at whatever period these may have been in use, it is certain that at least 4 or 5 feet more of the shaft must then have been exposed to view. The pillar now leans to the westward, and is from 4 to 5 inches out of the perpendicular at the ground level. I attribute the sinking of the pillar partly to the insufficiency of the basement, and partly to the want of stiffness in the sub-soil, which is a loose wet sand. In such a soil the basement should have been well spread out, with its foundation resting on wells, so as to offer an effectual resistance to the thrust of the heavy pillar which, with its capital, must weigh nearly 60 tons. The shaft alone above the water level weighs 37 tons.*

The upper diameter of the pillar is 38·7 inches, and the lower diameter at the water level is 49·8 inches, the mean diameter being 44·2 inches, as the slope of the shaft is quite straight. The pillar is surmounted by a bell-shaped capital, 2 feet 10 inches in height, with an oblong abacus of 12 inches, making the whole height of capital 3 feet 10 inches. This forms the pedestal of a lion statue of life-size. The animal is seated facing the north with his hind legs under him, with his mouth open as if snarling, and his tongue slightly protruded. The attitude is rather stiff, and the fore legs of the animal seem to be both too short and too thick; but the hair of the mane is boldly and cleverly treated, and the general appearance of the statue is certainly striking.

There is no inscription on the pillar to declare the object for which it was erected. It is possible that a short inscription may once have existed, for the surface of the pillar has suffered considerably, and in one part, 2½ feet above the present ground level, the polished surface has peeled off all round. Numerous names of visitors have been cut on the

---

* See Plate XXII. for a view of this pillar.

pillar. Some few are of Musalmáns, several of Hindus, but the most of Christians. The visitors, I was told, wrote their names in charcoal, and a village black-smith afterwards traced them roughly with a chisel The whole surface of the pillar within reach is disfigured with these rude scrawls, of which the neatest and smallest is that of "Reuben Burrow, 1792." Some of the Nágari inscriptions consist of two short lines, but none of them, as far as I could judge, are more than 200 or 300 years old. The pillar is known by the people as *Bhím-Sen-ká-lát* and *Bhím-Sen-ká-danda*.

Immediately to the south of the pillar there is a small tank, 200 feet from east to west, and 150 feet from north to south. It has no name, but is simply called *Kúnd* or *Pokhar*. To the south, at a distance of 35 feet, there is a low mound of broken bricks, which must have been the site of some ancient building. At short distances from the south-west and north-west corners of the tank, there are two similar mounds. The probable identification of the tank and mounds will be noticed hereafter.

Due north from the pillar, and just outside the court-yard, there is a ruined stupa of solid brick surmounted by a fine old Pipal tree. This stupa is 25 feet 10 inches in height above the fields, but only 15 feet 11 inches above the present ground level of the pillar. An excavation has been made right into the centre of the mound from the north-west. The excavation, I was informed by an old man, was superintended by a Bengáli servant of some Sáheb more than 50 years ago, but no discovery was made. This account agrees with that given by Mr. Stephenson, who relates that the excavation was made by a Doctor, resident at Muzafarpur, 30 years ago, that is, previous to 1835, or about A. D. 1805. As the centre of the mass had evidently been reached by the Bengáli, I did not think it necessary to make any further excavation.

To the north-east of the ruined stupa, at a distance of 250 feet, there is a low mound similar to those near the tank, and due north, at a distance of 600 feet, there is a small temple containing a life-size statue of Buddha the Ascetic, which was discovered only eight years ago in digging up some brick walls immediately to the east of the temple. The statue is perfect, not even the nose being broken. There is a small Buddha on each side of the figure, and there are two lions on the pedestal, besides a long inscription, beginning with the usual Buddhist formula. There is no date, but the characters are those of the 8th or 9th century. The spot on which the figure was found was most probably the site of an ancient *vihár* or Buddhist chapel monastery, in which the statue was enshrined. I saw several of the bricks with bevelled edges similar to those that form part of the mouldings of the Great Temple at Buddha Gaya, and of the stupa at Giryek.

The lion pillar and the surrounding remains at Bakhra I would identify with a group of holy buildings described by Hwen Thsang as being situated upwards of one mile to the north-west of the Palace of Vaisáli. The exact distance is not mentioned, but the existing remains correspond so closely with his details regarding the situation and nature of the different objects, that there can be no reasonable doubt as to the identity of the whole group. The first work noticed by Hwen Thsang as being upwards of one mile to the north-west of the Palace of Vaisáli is a stupa that was built by King Asoka, of which the purpose is not stated. Beside the stupa there was a stone column from 50 to 60 feet in height, surmounted by the statue of a lion. To the south of the pillar there was a tank which had been excavated by a flock of monkeys for the use of Buddha. At a short distance to the west of the tank there was a stupa erected on the spot where the monkeys climbed a tree and filled Buddha's begging pot with honey. On the south side of the tank there was another stupa erected on the spot where the monkeys offered the honey to Buddha, and at the north-west angle of the tank there was a statue of a monkey.*

The ruined stupa to the north of the pillar I would identify with Asoka's stupa, and the small tank to the south of the pillar with the celebrated *Markata-hrada* or "Monkeys' Tank," which, as we have already seen, was in the same position with respect to the lion pillar. The two low mounds to the west and south of the tank correspond with the sites of the two stupas built to commemorate the monkey's offering of honey to Buddha; and the low mound to the north-west agrees exactly with the site of the monkey's statue.

---

* Julian's Hwen Thsang, II., pp 386 387.

The correspondence between the several objects so minutely detailed by Hwen Thsang and the existing remains is complete. The only point on which there is any seeming discrepancy is the height of the pillar, which was from 50 feet to 60 feet, while the actual pillar may, perhaps, be less. The height of the lion statue is 4 feet 6 inches, that of the capital is 3 feet 10 inches, and that of the polished shaft down to the water level is 35 feet 10 inches, making altogether a height of only 44 feet 2 inches; but as neither the basement of the pillar nor the end of the polished portion of the shaft have been reached, it is quite certain that the pillar must have been higher than this measurement. I would, therefore, fix its probable original height at about 50 feet, which would then agree with the measurement of Hwen Thsang.

Vaisáli, the Capital of the *Lichchhavi* family, was especially famous as the scene of the second Buddhist Synod in 443 B. C. The assembly was held, according to Hwen Thsang, at a spot 2½ miles to the south-east of the city, but I could find no remains in that direction. Vaisáli was also celebrated as the place where Buddha had announced his approaching *Nirvána*. The actual spot was to the westward of the town, but after the announcement, Buddha, with his cousin disciple Ananda, repaired to the *Kutágára* hall, where he addressed his followers for the last time. Kutágára, which means the " upper-storied hall," was a famous edifice situated in the *Mahávano Viháro*, in which Buddha had dwelt during the 5th year of his teaching.* *Mahávano Viháro* means " the Chapel Monastery of the Great Forest." Fa-Hian speaks of " a great forest and a chapel of two stories;" but Hwen Thsang makes no allusion to the upper-storied hall, although, as we know from the *Mándhátri Sutra* of the *Divya Avadána*, translated by Burnouf, the *Kutágára* Hall was situated on the bank of the *Markata-hrada*, or " Monkey Tank."† From Hwen Thsang's silence I infer that this once famous hall, which Fa-Hian had seen about A. D. 410, must have become ruined before A. D. 640. Altogether, the agreement of these details is so very close that I think there can be little, if any, doubt that the Bakhra ruins represent the site of the group of sacred objects described by Hwen Thsang. Even the great forest can still be traced in the numerous fine

* Turnour in Bengal Asiatic Society's Journal, 1834, pp. 791 and 1890.
† Introduction à l'Histoire du Buddhisme Indien, p. 74.

groves of trees which surround the ruins on all sides. The name of Bakhra may possibly have been derived from *Vak* (S. Vach) "to speak," from the fact that in the *Kutágára* Hall Buddha had addressed his disciples for the last time.

XVI. KESARIYA.

To the north-north-west, distant 30 miles from Besárh, and somewhat less than two miles to the south of the large village of Kesariya, stands a lofty brick mound capped by a solid brick tower of considerable size. This ruin has already been brought to notice by Mr. B. H. Hodgson, but no description has been published, and in the sketch taken by his Native artist, the mound appears much too high for its breadth, while the stupa (or dahgopa) on the top is made much too small.*

The mound of Kesariya is a ruined mass of solid brick-work, 62 feet in height, and 1,400 feet in circumference at the base of the ruins. On the top of this there is a solid brick stupa, the whole surface of which is ruined, excepting at the base, which is still perfect in several places. In the most perfect part there are 15 courses of surface brick-work still in good order, and in two other places there are 10 and 11 courses perfect. From these three points I made out the base of the stupa to be 68 feet 5 inches in diameter. My measurement of the height was necessarily rough, as there was no defined edge at the top, the whole being thickly covered with long grass. After much trouble I made out a height of 38 feet 7¼ inches for the cylindrical portion, and of 12 feet 10¼ inches for the dome, or altogether of 51 feet 6 inches. But as the height of the dome cannot have been less than the half diameter of the building, or 34 feet 2½ inches, the original height of the solid brick-work of this stupa must have been 72 feet 10 inches, and the whole height of the stupa with its pinnacle not less than from 80 to 90 feet, or including the ruined basement on which it stands, not less than 150 feet above the ground. †

From the ruined state of the lower mound, compared with the perfect state of the base of the upper stupa, I am

---
* Bengal Asiatic Society's Journal, 1835, Plate VII.
† See Plate XXIII. for a plan of the ruins of Kesariya; and Plate XXIV. for a view of the stupa.

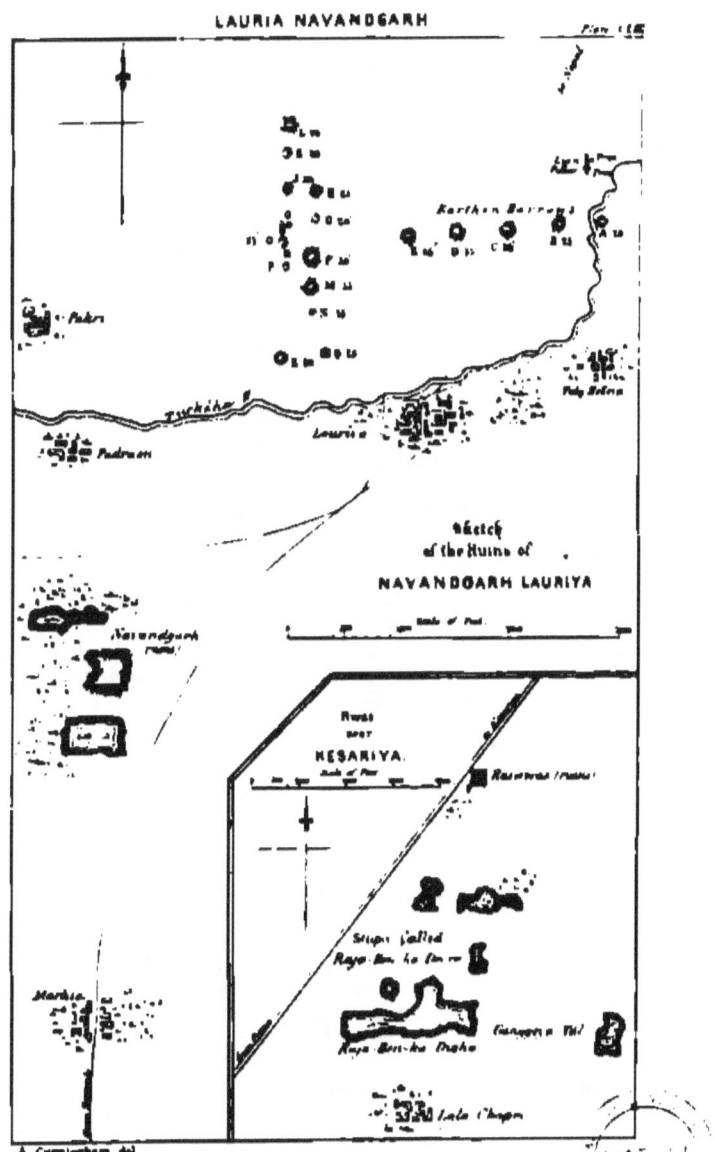

of opinion that the present stupa is of middle age, say from A. D. 200 to 700, and that it was built upon the ruined mass of a much older and much larger stupa. That such a practice was not uncommon, we learn from Hwen Thsang, who describes two stupas at Vaisáli as having been erected on ancient foundations. I feel quite satisfied that such has been the case with the Kesariya Monument, and as all the early stupas are found to be hemispherical, I infer that the lower and earlier stupa must have been of that form. Its great size may be deduced from the breadth of the base of the upper stupa, namely, 68 feet 5 inches, at a height of 62 feet above the ground; and as there must have been a clear terrace all round this stupa, for the perambulation of pilgrims, the actual thickness of the early stupa at this height cannot have been much less than 100 feet, which would give a diameter at base of 160 feet. The height of the hemisphere would, of course, have been 80 feet, but with the usual square Buddhist capital surrounded by an umbrella, or other pinnacle, the stupa could not have been less than 100 feet.

This ancient monument is known to the people as *Rája Ben ka Deöra*. The similar but smaller stupa at Kasiya is also called a *Deöra*, or, as it is written by Buchanan, *Dewkara*. In both cases the name belongs to the upper stupa, and not to the whole mass, as all mounds, whether of earth or brick, in this part of the country, are named *Bhisa*. Doöriya, which is a very common village name in the districts of Tirhut, Champáran, and Gorakhpur, is applied, I believe, only to such places as possess either a temple or some other holy buildings. Of *Raja* Ben the people have no tradition, except that he was one of the five Supreme Emperors of India, and he is, therefore, called *Raja Ben Chakravartti*. The piece of water immediately to the south of the stupa is also named after him, *Rája Ben ka Digha*, or Raja Ben's Tank. I know only of one Raja *Vena*, whom the Rishis are said to have inaugurated as "Monarch of the Earth," but whom they afterwards slew, because he would not allow them to worship Vishnu—"Who," exclaimed he, "is this Hari whom you style the lord of sacrifice?" From Vena's right arm, when rubbed by Brahmans, was produced a son named Prithu, who, according to the Vishnu Purána, also become a *Chakravartti Raja*. This Vena Chakravartti is most probably the great Raja Ben to whom the tradition refers.

Now it is remarkable that, according to the account of Hwen Thsang, this stupa was also referred to a Chakravartti Raja by the Buddhists of the 7th century. He states that at somewhat less than 200 *li* (that is, less than 33 miles, or say about 30 miles) to the north-west of Vaisáli, which is the exact position of the Kesariya stupa, there was an ancient town which had been deserted for many ages. It possessed a stupa built over the spot where Buddha had announced that in one of his former existences he had been a Bodhisatwa, and had reigned over that town as a *Chakravartti Raja*, named *Mahadeva*.* It can hardly, I think, be doubted that the tradition of Raja Ben preserves the very same story which is recorded by Hwen Thsang. That the stupa was intended to commemorate a Chakravartti Raja might also have been inferred from its position at the meeting of four principal roads. "For a Chakravartti Raja," said Buddha addressing Ananda, "they build the *thupo* at a spot where four principal roads meet." Now to the south of Kesariya, within one-quarter of a mile of the stupa, the two great thoroughfares of the district cross each other, namely, that from Patna northward to Bettiah, and that from Chapra across the Gandak, north-eastwards to Nepál.

On the east side of the Kesariya stupa a gallery has been excavated right to the centre of the building. This is said to have been done upwards of 40 years ago by one Kási Náth Babu, the servant of a Colonel Sáheb. As the name of "Lieutenant-Colonel Mackenzie, Madras Engineers, 1814," is inscribed on the Bakhra Pillar, I think it probable that the excavation was made by his orders. No discovery was made, and, if I am right in my identification of this stupa with that which was erected on the spot where Buddha announced his previous existence as a Chakravartti Raja, it is almost certain that it would not have been the depository of relics or of other objects. The monument was, in fact, only a memorial stupa, erected to perpetuate the fame of one of Buddha's acts, and not a sepulchral stupa for the reception of relics.

To the north north-east of the stupa, and rather less than half a mile distant, there is a small mound which has been partially excavated to furnish materials for the bridges on the high road, which, within the last few years, have been

* Julien's Hwen Thsang, II., 384.

made from Bakhra to Motihari *viâ* Kesariya. The excavations have disclosed the walls of a small temple, 10 feet square inside, and the head and shoulders of colossal figure of Buddha, with the usual crisp curly hair. The mound, which is about 200 feet square, is called *Ranivâs*, and also Gorai, and the buildings are attributed to some ancient Râni. It appears to me to have been the site of a Vihâra or Temple Monastery, as portions of cells are still traceable on the eastern side. At the south-west angle there is another smaller mound of brick ruin, 120 feet from north to south and 60 feet from west to east. It is probably the ruin of a temple.

XVII. LAURIYA ARA-RAJ.

Between Kesariya and Bettiah, at a distance of 20 miles to the north-west of the Kesariya stupa, and one mile to the south-west of the Hindu temple of Ara-Râj Mahâdeo, there stands a lofty stone column which bears in well-preserved and well-cut letters several of the edicts of King Asoka. The pillar itself is simply called *Laur*, that is, "the *phallus*," and the neighbouring village, which lies not more than 100 yards to the westward, is called *Lauriya*. This is the pillar which, on the authority of Mr. Hodgson, has been called the Radhia Pillar. Now, as the other pillar to the north of Bettiah is also called *Laur*, and the large village close to it *Lauriya*, while Mr. Hodgson has named it *Mathiah*, I presume that his Munshi intentionally suppressed the phallic name of *Lauriya*, and named the two pillars at random after some of the neighbouring villages. Thus Rahariya (Rurheea of Indian Atlas Sheet No. 102), which is Mr. Hodgson's Radhia, lies 2½ miles to the west north-west of the southern pillar, while Mathiah lies 3 miles due south from the northern pillar. In describing these pillars I will preserve the characteristic name of *Lauriya*, and for the sake of distinguishing the one from the other, I will add to each the name of the nearest village, thus the village near the southern pillar I shall call *Lauriya Ara-Raj*, and that near the northern pillar *Lauriya Navandgarh*.

The Ara-Raj Pillar is a single block of polished sandstone, 36½ feet in height above the ground, with a base diameter of 41·8 inches, and a top diameter of 37·0 inches. The weight of this portion only is very nearly 34 tons, but as there must be several feet of rough shaft sunk in the earth, the actual weight of the single block must be about 40 tons. This pillar has no capital, although there can be little, if any, doubt that it must once have been crowned with a statue of some animal. The people, however, know nothing of it, and not a fragment of any kind now exists to suggest what it may have been. The site of the village is a very secluded one, and there are no ruins or other remains to attract attention. It has accordingly escaped the notice of travellers, and the disfigurement of their names—the only record being that of "Reuben Burrow, 1792," besides a few flourished letters, or marks, of the kind which James Prinsep called shell-shaped characters.

The edicts of Asoka are most clearly and neatly engraved, and are divided into two distinct portions,—that to the north containing 18 lines, and that to the south 23 lines. I made a copy of the inscription by the eye, which I then compared with James Prinsep's text, and afterwards I re-examined every letter in which our copies differed. I also made an inked impression of the whole inscription on paper. But, though the variations from Prinsep's text are not many, yet, as no facsimile has yet been made public, it is important, for the sake of comparison, to afford access to one which has been carefully copied in every letter.

XVIII. LAURIYA NAVANDGARH.

The lion pillar of Lauriya Navandgarh, which after Mr. Hodgson has hitherto been called the Mathiah Pillar, is situated at rather less than half a mile to the north-east of the large village of Lauriya, at 15 miles to the north north-west of Bettiah, and at 10 miles from the nearest point of the Gandak River. As Mr. Hodgson's name of Mathiah serves only to mislead, I propose to call the site of this pillar Lauriya Navandgarh, by adding the name of a very remarkable deserted fort which stands just half a mile to the south-west of Lauriya. The village of Mathiah lies no less than 3 miles to the south of the pillar, and is besides both smaller and of less consequence than Lauriya. The name of this Lauriya is printed in Roman letters in the Indian Atlas Sheet No. 102, and even the "stone pillar" itself is inserted in its proper place to the north-east of the village. The deserted

Barrow D Barrow R Barrow P Barrow G Barrow H Pipal Tree

fort of Navandgarh is omitted, but it will be found in the Calcutta Map, on the 8-mile scale, as Naonad-garh. The mound is from 250 to 300 feet square at top, and 80 feet in height. On account of its height it was chosen as one of the stations of the Trigonometrical Survey, and for the same reason it commands a most extensive and beautiful view of the well-wooded country around it.*

The remains at Lauriya Navandgarh are particularly interesting, as they are very extensive, and at the same time quite different in character from any others that I have examined. These remains consist of three rows of earthern barrows or huge conical mounds of earth, of which two of the rows lie from north to south, and the third from west to east. The stupas hitherto met with have been made either of stone or of brick; but the earliest stupas were mere mounds of earth, of which these are the only specimens that I have seen. I believe that they are the sepulchral mounds of the early kings of the country, prior to the rise and spread of Buddhism, and that their date may, therefore, be assumed as ranging from about 000 to 1500 B. C. The word stupa meant originally only "a mound of earth," and this is the rendering given to the word by Colebrooke in his translation of the Amarakosha. In the time of Asoka all the stupas were certainly built either of stone or brick, as recorded by Hwen Thsang; and, although he is silent regarding the material of the earlier stupas of Ajâtasatru and other contemporaries of Buddha, yet, as he makes no mention anywhere of earthen stupas, I presume that all the Buddhist monuments were either of brick or stone. The earthen barrows I would, therefore, refer to an earlier period, as the stupas or sepulchral mounds raised over the ashes of the rulers of the country, the larger mounds belonging, perhaps, to the greater or more famous monarchs who had assumed the title of *Chakravartti* Râjas. Every mound is called simply *Bhisa*, and the whole are said to have been the fortified residences of the ministers and nobles of Raja *Uttânpat*, while the Fort of Navandgarh was the Raja's own residence. *Uttânapâda*, King of Brahmavarta or Bharatkhand, that is, of the Gangetic Doab, was the son of the Manu *Swayambhuva*, the first-created of Brahma, and the progenitor of

---

* See Plate XXIII. for a plan of these ruins, and Plate XXV. for a view.

mankind. Raja Vena, to whom the Kesariya Monument is assigned, was the seventh in descent from Uttánapáda. Another decisive evidence in favour of the great antiquity of these barrows is the fact that Major Pearse, of the Madras Artillery, found one of the small punch-marked silver coins in his excavations amongst them These coins are certainly anterior to the time of Alexander the Great, and I believe that many of them are as old as 1000 B. C., and, perhaps, even older.

There are three rows of these earthen mounds, of which one line runs from east to west, and the other two lines from north to south. There are five barrows in the east and west row and six barrows in the inner north and south row, while the outer north and south row has four large and at least seven small barrows.* There are probably several more small mounds which escaped my observation in the jungle surrounding some of the larger mounds, but I do not believe that any barrow of greater height than 5 or 6 feet remains unnoticed. In my survey of these remains I have attached a separate letter of the alphabet to each mound for the sake of greater clearness of description.

In the east and west line there are five mounds marked A. to E. Four of these mounds, A., C., D., and E., are covered with fragments of brick, and there are also traces of the walls of small brick buildings on their summits. Mound A. is 20 feet in height. Within 5 feet of its top, I excavated a portion of a circular foundation wall, 10 inches thick, formed of single bricks 20½ inches long and 4 inches thick. There were only four courses of bricks resting on the earth of the mound. This work may either have been the retaining wall of a circular terrace which once crowned the top of the mound, or it may have been the foundation of a tower; but

---

* See Plate XXIV. for a view of these earthen mounds and of the Lion pillar. The following extracts from the Bengal Administration Report for 1868-69 show the nature of the discoveries to be expected in these mounds. The excavations were made on my recommendation:

"*Para.* 273.—" At Lowrya, 15 miles north-west of Bettiah, there is one of Asoka's edict or boundary pillars. It is of granite, 40 feet high and 9 feet in circumference at base. It has an entablature at top surmounted by a lion couchant. A short time ago, close by it, were found some leaden coffins containing unusually long human skeletons."

A second paragraph, perhaps, refers to a different discovery, but I suspect it must be the same described by a different person.

* Some tumuli have been discovered in the Bettiah sub-division, from one of which two iron coins were obtained, and from another an iron coffin 9 feet or so in length; in this were human bones. The coffin was greatly corroded, and fell to pieces."

as the wall was only 10 inches thick, the former would seem to be the more probable supposition. Mound B. is a simple earthen barrow, 25 feet in height. Mound C., which is 30 feet in height, is thickly covered with broken brick. There are traces of foundation walls on the top, but a former excavation shows that the whole mass is plain earth. There are traces also of walls on the slopes of the mound; and in an excavation amongst these superficial brick ruins made by Mr. Lynch, Deputy Magistrate of Motihári, there was found a seal of black earthen-ware, bearing a short inscription in characters of the Gupta period, that is, of the 2nd and 3rd century after Christ. The inscription, which consists of four letters, reads *Atavijá*. This is most probably only a name which may mean either *Atavi + ja*, "the forest born," or less probably *Ata + rija*, "the cause of motion." At the end of the name there is the *Swástika*, or mystic cross, and over the name in the middle there is the symbol of *Dharmma*, and to the left, in a slanting direction, a trident, or *trisúl*. The discovery of this seal shows that Navandgarh Lauriya was certainly occupied by the Buddhists as late as the 2nd or 3rd century A. D. Doubtless their occupation continued to a later period; for, although both Fa-Hian and Hwen Thsang make no allusion to it, their silence is easily accounted for by the fact that the course of their travels did not take either of them into the Bettiah District. The two remaining barrows of this row are somewhat higher, mound D. being 35 feet, and E. 45 feet. Both of them are covered with broken brick. The top of D. had already been opened, and I myself made an excavation on the top of mound E. Both had flat tops, as if terraces had once existed on their summits, and with this impression I began my excavation. At the depth of 4 feet all trace of brick disappeared, the mass of the mound being plain earth. The bricks were large, 15" × 9" × 2½."

None of the barrows of the middle line have any traces of brick upon them, but seem to be made of plain earth. They are all covered with low thorny jungle. The most northerly mound of this line, marked H., is 25 feet in height; the next mound, marked G., is 20 feet; the next F. is 50 feet; and the next M. is 55 feet. The last two are the highest of all the barrows at Navandgarh Lauriya. The next mound N. is only 15 feet high, and the next southerly mound, marked Q., is 25 feet in height. About one-half of the mass of the last mound has been excavated and carried away to Bettiah on bullocks and donkeys. The whole heart of the mound is formed of an extremely hard whitish clay, which is used by the people as a light coloured clay-wash for the walls of their houses. This clay is, indeed, so hard that it turns the edges of common digging tools. When freshly cut, it glistens, and has a bluish tint. From whence was this clay obtained? There is none now anywhere near the place, the soil being generally light and sandy. Can it have been found here formerly, or was it brought from a distance?

In the outer line there are only four large barrows, the most northerly, marked L., being 20 feet in height, and the other three, marked K., J., and R., being each 30 feet. The last mound R., which is the most southerly of this line, has also been excavated for the sake of its still white clay, which is similar to that of mound Q. of the middle line. Between J. and R. I traced seven small mounds, of which the largest, marked O., is only 8½ feet in height. I made an opening in this mound down to the ground level, but without any result, except that it proved the mound to be formed of common hard earth, and not of the indurated glistening white clay, which forms the masses of the two barrows Q. and R.

There is another question regarding these barrows which is, perhaps, quite as puzzling as that of their origin, namely, from whence was the earth for so many large mounds procured, for there is not a single hollow or excavation of any kind in their neighbourhood? On three sides of the huge mound of Navandgarh the tanks still exist to show from whence its material was obtained, but with respect to the material for the tumuli we are left entirely to conjecture. Between the mounds and the village of Lauriya there is the dry bed of an annual flood stream called the *Tarkáha Nála*, but its soil is light and sandy, excepting only in the deeper pools, where the water lies for several months. It seems scarcely possible that the earth could have been taken from this sandy channel, and yet it is equally impossible to say from what other place it could have been obtained.

The lion pillar of Lauriya Navandgarh stands to the north of the mounds A. and B., at a distance of less than 500 feet from each. Its shaft is formed of a single block of polished sand-stone, 32 feet 9½ inches in height, with a diameter at base of 35·5 inches and of 20·2 inches at top. The capital, which is 6 feet 10 inches in height, is bell-shaped, with a circular abacus supporting the statue of a lion facing the north.* The abacus is ornamented with a row of Brahmani geese pecking their food. The column has a light and elegant appearance, and is altogether a much more pleasing monument than the stouter and shorter pillar of Bakhra. The lion has been injured in the mouth, and the column itself bears the round mark of a cannon shot just below the capital, which has itself been slightly dislodged by the shock. One has not far to seek for the name of the probable author of this mischief. By the people the outrage is ascribed to the Musalmáns, and on the pillar itself, in beautifully cut Persian characters, is inscribed the name of *Mahi-ud-din Muhammad Aurangzib Pádsháh Alamgir Gházi, Sanh*, 1071. This date corresponds with A. D. 1660-61, which was the fourth year of the reign of the bigotted Aurangzib, and the record may probably have been inscribed by some zealous follower in Mir Jumla's Army, which was then on its return from Bengal, after the death of the Emperor's brother Shuja. The Navandgarh Pillar is much thinner and much lighter than those of Ara-Ráj and Bakhra. The weight of the polished portion of its shaft is only 18 tons, or rather less than half that of the Bakhra Pillar, and somewhat more than half that of the Ara-Ráj Pillar.

The pillar is inscribed with the edicts of Asoka in the same clear and beautifully cut characters as those of the Ara-Ráj Pillar. The two inscriptions, with only a few trifling variations, correspond letter for letter. I made a careful copy of the whole for comparison with the text made public by James Prinsep. I made also a facsimile impression in ink.

The Navandgarh Pillar has been visited by numerous travellers, as it stands in the direct route from Bettiah to Nepal. There are a few unimportant inscriptions in modern Nágari, the oldest being dated in *Samvat* 1566, *chait badi* 10, equivalent to A. D. 1509. One of them, without date, refers to some petty Royal Family, *Nripa Narayana Suta*, *Nripa Amara Singha*, that is, "King Amara Singha, the son of King Narayana." The only English inscription is the name of *Rn. Burrow*, 1792.

---

* See Plate XLII. for a view of this pillar.

K

The pillar itself has now become an object of worship as a phallus or lingam. Whilst I was copying the inscription, a man with two women and a child set up a small flag before the pillar, and placed offerings of sweetmeats around it. They then all knelt before it, bowing down their heads to the ground with their hands behind their backs, and repeating some prayer. The erection of the pillar is ascribed to Raja *Bhim Mári*, one of the five Pandava brothers to whom most of the pillars in India are now ascribed. I could not learn anything regarding the title of *Mári*. There are two fine Banian trees close to the pillar,—one to the north, and the other to the south;—but there are no traces of buildings of any kind near it.

XIX. PADARAONA.

The large village of *Padaraona*, or *Padaravana*, is situated 12 miles to the west of the River Gandak, 27 miles in a direct line to the north north-west of Navandgarh Lauriya, and 40 miles to the north north-east of Gorakhpur. I believe that it is the ancient *Páwá*, as it is situated just 12 miles from Kasia, which agrees with the position assigned to *Páwá* in the Pali Annals with respect to Kusinagara. The very name of *Páwá* also seems to be only a corruption of *Padura-vana*, or *Padar-ban*, which might easily be shortened to *Parban*, *Páwan*, and *Páwá*.

The remains at Padaraona consist of a large mound covered with broken brick and a few statues. The mound is 220 feet in length from west to east, 120 feet in breadth from north to south, and 14 feet in height at the western end above the fields. The long trench mentioned by Buchanan still exists on the west side, and looks as if a wall had been dug out for the sake of the bricks. About eight years ago a large hole was excavated to the east of the trench by a zemindar for the sake of bricks. Two houses were built of the materials then obtained, but sufficient trace of the walls still remains to show that they were in straight lines, one of them being paralled to Buchanan's trench. From this I infer that there was a court-yard about 100 feet square, with cells on each side for the accommodation of monks. In the centre there was probably either a stupa or a temple. But if I am right in my identification of Padaraona with *Páwá*, the building would almost certainly have been a stupa; for we know that the people of Páwá, after the cremation of Buddha's body, obtained one-eighth of the relics, over which they erected a stupa. The entrance to the court-yard would appear to have been on the east side, where the mound is now low and thickly covered with bricks.

In a small roofless brick building at a short distance to the northward, there are a few old figures. This temple is dedicated to Háthi Bhawâni, or the Elephant Goddess, who is accordingly propitiated with rude votive figures of elephants in baked clay, of which numbers lie scattered about the temple, both inside and outside. The statue called Háthi Bhawâni represents a squatted male figure with a triple umbrella over his head. The figure appears to be naked, and if so, it must belong to the Jains, and not to the Buddhists. A drawing of it is given by Buchanan.* There are also two fragments with seated Buddhas, and a third with the upper half of a female figure. On referring to Buchanan I recognized all three fragments as having belonged to the statue sketched as fig. 2 in his plate. The principal figure is now gone, but there are a few unimportant fragments not noticed by Buchanan, and in the village there is the pedestal of a statue.

I made an excavation on the highest part of the mound on the west side, and to the northward of the zemindar's excavation. In this I found bricks with rounded edges such as I had noticed in the mouldings of the Great Temple at Buddha-Gya, and of the stupa at Giryak. I found also wedge-shaped bricks of two sizes. The largest ones being only fragments, I was unable to ascertain their length, but their breadth was 20¾ at the end, and 19¼ inches at 6 inches distance. As the larger end was rounded, these bricks must have formed part of some circular building and most probably of a solid stupa, which would have been just 30 feet in diameter. The smaller bricks were 8¼ inches long 5¾ inches broad at the widest end, and 5 inches at the narrow end, with a thickness of 2¼ inches. These may have belonged to a small stupa about 9 feet in diameter. In my excavation I found also the base of a pillar of coarse grey sandstone. It was 15 inches square and 6¼ inches high, with a few plain

---

* Eastern India, II., Plate L, Fig. 2.

mouldings at the upper edge. The complete excavation of this mound would not be difficult, and the work might be superintended by the civil authorities of the place, who live close by.

XX. KASIA.

The village of *Kasia* is situated at the crossing of two great thoroughfares, at a distance of 35 miles due east from Gorakhpur. The name is written *Kasia*, with the short *a* in the first syllable; but I have little doubt that it should be written *Kusia* with the short *u*, for the place corresponds, both in position and in name, with the celebrated *Kusinagara* or "Town of the Kusa-grass," which, as the scene of Buddha's death, was famous throughout India. This sacred spot was visited both by Fa-Hian and by Hwen Thsang; and the latter has left a detailed account of the various *stupas* which still existed in his time. Most of these have now disappeared, owing partly to the removal of bricks by the people, but chiefly, I believe, to the inundations of the Little Gandak River, which at some former period must have flowed close by the sacred buildings of *Kusinagara*, as there are several old channels between the two principal masses of ruins, which are still occasionally filled during the rainy season.

The existing remains have already been described by Buchanan[*] and by Mr. Liston;[†] but their accounts are very brief, and offer no attempt to identify the ruins with any of the ancient cities which are known to have existed in this part of the country. The remains consist of—1*st*, a lofty mound of solid brick-work called *Devisthán* and *Rámábhár Bhawáni*; 2*nd*, an oblong mound called the Fort of *Mithá Kuár*, which is covered with broken brick and jungle, and on which stands a brick stupa much ruined; 3*rd*, a large statue of Buddha the Ascetic; 4*th*, a low square mound covered with broken brick near the village of *Anrudhica*; and 5*th*, a number of low earthern mounds, like barrows, which are scattered over the plain to the north and east of the great mound.[‡]

---

[*] Eastern India, II., p. 357.
[†] Bengal Asiatic Society's Journal, 1837, p. 477.
[‡] See Plate XXVI. for a Map of Kasia. I opened several of these barrows, but without any result. I believe now that I did not dig deep enough. That they are tombs I feel quite certain, as Megasthenes describes the Indian "sepulchres as plain, and the tumuli of earth low." Strabo, XV., L. 54.

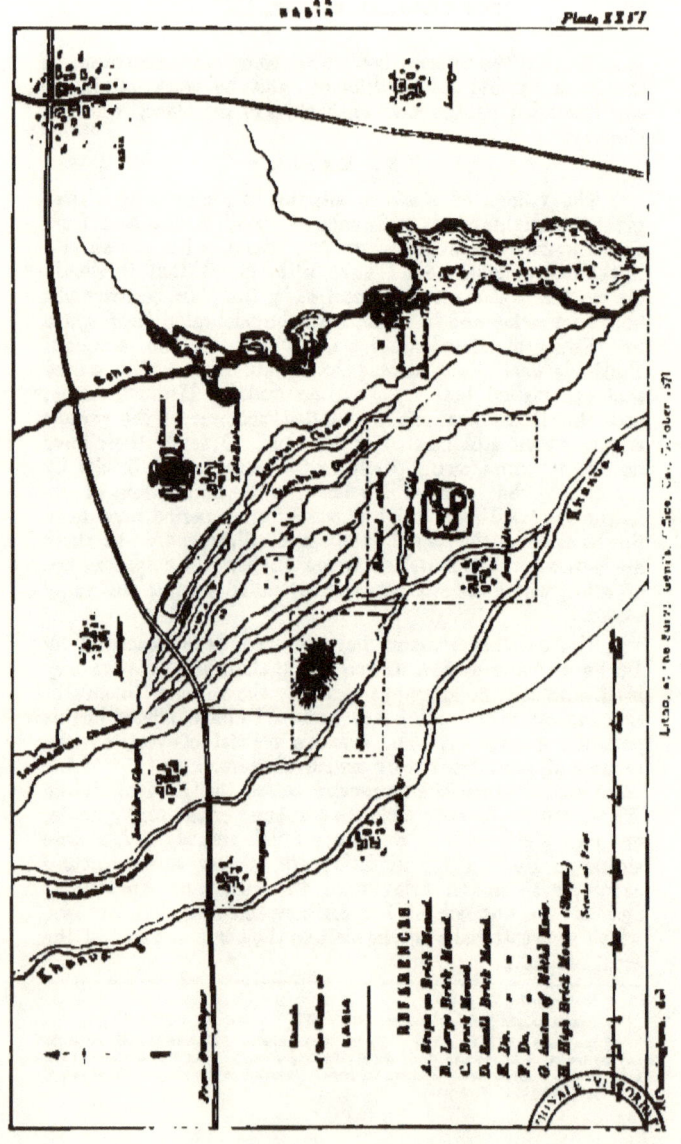

The mound called *Devisthán* and *Rámábhár Tíla* is the ruin of a large ancient stupa of solid brick-work, which is still 40 feet in height above the fields. It is situated somewhat less than one mile to the south-west of Kasia. On the top, under a fine old Banian Tree, is the shrine of the goddess Devi. There is neither statue nor building, but only some votive figures in baked clay, the offerings of the poor people to their favourite Devi. The goddess is also called *Rámábhár Bhawáni*, because the mound is situated on the western bank of the *Rámábhár Jhíl*, a large natural sheet of water, which forms part of the bed of the *Roha Nála*, one of the old channels of the Little Gandak. As the mound is also called Rámábhár Tíla, it is possible that this name may have originally belonged to the stupa. I attempted to make an excavation at the top of the mound, but the large interlaced roots of the Banian Tree soon forced me to give up the work. At the south-eastern foot of the mound I discovered a portion of a small stupa formed of very large bricks, averaging 5 inches in thickness. These bricks were 17½ inches in length and wedge-shaped, being 8½ inches broad at one end, and only 7 inches at the other end. These dimensions would give a diameter of only 16½ feet to the stupa.

The large mound called *Máthá-Kuar-ka-kot*, or the "Fort of Máthá-Kuár," is 600 feet in length from north-west to south-east, and from 200 to 300 feet in breadth. At its highest point, which is 30 feet 3 inches in height above the plain, the mound is formed entirely of solid brick-work, which I believe to be the remains of a very ancient stupa. On this point stands a solid tower of brick-work with sides much ruined, and its top covered with long grass. This is undoubtedly a stupa, and from its position it must be of much later date than the ancient mass of brick-work on which it stands. I conclude that it is a work of middle age, or between A. D. 200 and 600. At present the mass of the tower is only 2½ feet thick, but by clearing away the rubbish, I measured a circumference of 86 feet, which gives a diameter of nearly 27¼ feet. The present height of the lower portion is only 15 feet, and that of the grass-covered top, 12 feet 9 inches, the whole being 27 feet 9 inches above the ancient foundation, and 58 feet above the plain. But as the original height of this later work was most probably equal to two diameters, or 55 feet, the whole height of the stupa above the plain would have been 85 feet. I drove a horizontal gallery into the centre of the building at its base without making any discovery. I confess that I did not expect to find anything, as, I believe, that whatever relics may have been deposited on this spot, they would have been placed in the more ancient stupa below, which forms the foundation of the present monument. There is a fine Pipal Tree close to this stupa.*

The mound called the Fort of Máthá Kuár is situated nearly 1,600 yards to the north north-west of the ruined stupa called Rámábhár. Buchanan gives the distance as 400 yards, which is most probably a misprint for 1,400 yards. My distance was measured from centre to centre; if taken from foot to foot, the distance would be a little over 1,400 yards. This mound would seem to have been formed of the ruin of two large buildings and of several small ones. The site of one of the larger ones has just been described; that of the other is to the north-westward, the summit of the mound at this point, which is crowned by a large Pipal Tree, being 20 feet in height above the plain. To the east of the stupa there is also a small detached mound, 16 feet 3 inches in height. I made an excavation in the top of this mound, which I abandoned after reaching a depth of 4 feet 3 inches, as I found only broken bricks mixed with earth. Both to the north and south of the stupa there are low mounds, which are probably the remains of small detached towers or other buildings. The top of the large mound is in most parts thickly covered with bricks, but towards the north-west end, where the elevation is low, there are some rather large spaces quite clear of bricks, which may be supposed to represent the court-yards, or vacant spots between the buildings. I noticed many wedge-shaped bricks, which must have belonged to stupas of small size, besides several bricks with one-half face bevelled like those in the mouldings of the Great Temple at Buddha-Gaya and of Jarasandha's Tower at Giryek. I was unable to trace any straight lines of surrounding walls, and, from the irregular outline of the mound, I incline to believe that it has been formed by the ruin of a considerable number of independent buildings, such as a cluster of stupas of all sizes. From the total absence of statues, I infer that there were probably but few temples on this site.

The large statue known as that of *Máthá Kuár*, or the "Dead Prince," is now lying on the ground at a distance of

---
* See Plate XXVII. for a view of these ruins.

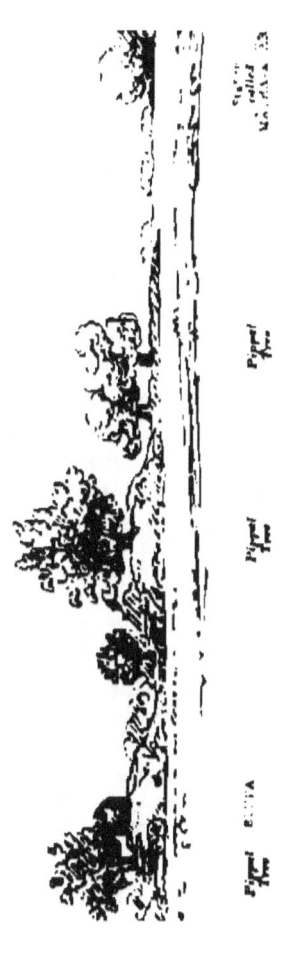

1,100 feet from the brick stupa above described. Quite close beside it, to the eastward, there is a low square mound which I believe to be the remains of a temple in which the image was formerly enshrined. The statue which is made of the dark blue stone of Gaya, is split into two pieces from top to bottom, and is otherwise much injured. The short inscription on its pedestal has been almost worn out by the villagers in sharpening their tools, but the few letters which remain are sufficient to show that the statue is not of older date than the 11th or 12th century. The figure itself is colossal, and represents Buddha the Ascetic seated under the Bodhi Tree at Budha-Gaya. The whole sculpture is 10¼ feet in height by 4¾ feet in breadth. The height of the figure alone is 5 feet 4½ inches, the breadth across the shoulders being 3 feet 8½ inches, and across the knees 4 feet 5 inches. A sketch of this sculpture is given by Buchanan.*

Between the Fort of *Máthá Kuár* and the great stupa on the *Rámábhár Jhíl*, there is a low mound of brick ruins about 500 feet square, which is said to have been a *kot* or fort, and to which no name is given; but as it lies close to the village of Anrudhwá on the north-west, it may be called the Anrudhwá mound. There is nothing now left to show the nature of the buildings which once stood on this site; but from the square shape of the ruins, it may be conjectured with some probability that they must be the remains of a monastery. There are three fine Pipal Trees now standing on the mound.

To the north and east of the mound of Máthá Kuár the plain is covered with a number of low grassy mounds from 3 to 6 feet in height, and from 12 to 25 feet in diameter. Regarding these barrows the people have a tradition that gypsys were formerly very numerous about Kasia, and that these mounds are the tumuli of their dead. I opened three of them, but without making any discovery. They were all formed of plain earth, without any trace of bones, or ashes, or broken bricks. The people call them simply mounds, but I was informed by an old man that he had heard them styled *Bhímáwát*, and that ghosts were sometimes seen flitting about them. If the name of *Bhímáwát* has any reference to these ghosts, it might, perhaps, be translated as the "fear-

---

* Eastern India, II., Plate LI.

some place;" but I cannot bo certain of the spelling, and it is also possible that the old man may not have remembered the name correctly. I counted 21 of these mounds, but as they are generally not more than 3 or 4 feet in height, it is probable that their actual number is much greater.*

I have already stated that the site of Kasia corresponds both in position and in name with the ancient city of *Kusinagara*, which was famous throughout India as the scene of Buddha's death. According to Hwen Thsang, Kusinagara was situated at 700 *li*, or 110 miles to the north-east of Benares. Now *Kasia* is 112 miles to the north north-east of Benares in direct line. Fa-Hian also places Kusinagara at a distance of 23 *yojans* to the north-west of a place which was situated only 8 or 10 miles to the north of Vaisáli, where the *Lichchhavi* Nobles had taken a last farewell of Buddha. At 7 miles to the *yojan* Fa-Hain's measurement would place Kusinagara at 148 or 150 miles to the north-west of Vaisáli. Now the distance by the route which I marched is exactly 140 miles in a north-west direction, but as this measurement was taken along the straight lines of road which have been laid out by the British authorities, the actual distance by the old winding Native roads must certainly have been somewhat greater, or as nearly possible 150 miles.

The only name now associated with the ruins near Kasia is that of *Matha Kuár*, or the "*Dead Prince.*" Mr. Liston gives the name as *Mata*, but a Brahman of the neighbouring village of Bishanpur, who wrote the name for me, spelt it as I have given it, *Máthá*. As this spelling points to the derivation of the word from *Máthá*, or *Máthá*, "to kill," I have translated *Máthá Kuár* as the "Dead Prince," which I refer to Buddha himself after his death, or, in the language of the Buddhists, after his obtainment of *Nirvana*. Hwen Thsang, when speaking of *Sakya's* assumption of the mendicant's dress, calls him *Kumára Rajá*, or the "Royal Prince;" but, although this title was never, I believe, applied to him by the learned after his assumption of Buddhahood, it does not seem at all improbable that it may have remained in common use amongst the people. We

---

* See a previous note at p. 78, quoting the description of Megasthenes, that the Indian tumuli were "low mounds of earth."

know from Hwen Thsang that on the spot where Buddha died there was a brick *vihár* or.temple monastery in which was enshrined a recumbent statue of Buddha on his death-bed, with his head turned to the north. Now this statue would naturally have been the principal object of veneration at Kusinagara; and, although amongst the learned it might have been called the "statue of the *Nirvána*," yet I can readily believe that its more popular name amongst all classes would have been the "statue of the Dead Prince." I am, therefore, of opinion that the name of *Máthá Kúar*, which still clings to the ruins of Kasia, has a direct reference to the death of Buddha, which, according to his followers, took place at Kusinagara on the full moon of Vaisákh, 543 B. C.

Owing to the wanderings of the Little Gandak River, it is somewhat difficult to follow Hwen Thsang's account of the sacred edifices at Kusinagara. The whole of the existing remains are situated to the eastward of the *Khanúa Nála*, which is only a branch or inundation channel of the Little Gandak River. All the old channels are called *Chawar*; the *Lombuha Chawar*, running between the two ancient stupas, and the *Roha Chawar*, or Roha Nála, to the east of the Rámábhár Tila. An intelligent man, whom I met at Padraona, called the stream to the westward of *Kasia* the *Hirana*, but the people in the villages about the ruin knew only the *Khanúa Nála*, and had never heard of the *Hirana*. Buchanan, however, calls the *Hirana* a considerable rivulet which has a course of about 15 miles, and makes it a feeder of the Little Gandak;* but there is some confusion in his description of this river. The changes of name would, however, appear to have been as numerous as the changes of channel; for, in the time of Hwen Thsang, this stream was called the *Ajitavati*, its more ancient name having been *Hiranyavati*, while the present name is Chota Gandak, and the eastern inundation branch is called *Khanúa*. There is now no trace of Hwen Thsang's *Ajitavati*, but the name of *Hiranyavati* is still preserved in the *Hirana* of my Padraona informant.

At the time of Hwen Thsang's visit, the walls of Kusinagara were in ruins, and the place was almost deserted; but the brick foundations of the old Capital occupied a

---

* Eastern India, II., p. 316.

circuit of about 12 *li*, that is, of about two miles. After a long and attentive comparison of all our available information, I have come to the conclusion that the famous city of Kusinagara must have occupied the site of the mound and village of Anrudhwá. The ruined mound, which is about 500 feet square, I would identify as the site of the Palace of the Mallian Kings, which was in the midst of the city, and to the city itself I would assign an extent of about 1,000 feet on all sides of the palace. This would give a square area of 2,500 feet, or nearly half a mile on each side, with a circuit of 10,000 feet, or nearly 2 miles, as recorded by Hwen Thsang. I will now compare the existing remains with the account of the Chinese pilgrim, and with the details given in the Páli Annals of Ceylon, as translated by Turnour.

The spot where Buddha died is fixed by Hwen Thsang at 3 or 4 *li*, or rather more than half a mile, to the north-west of the city, in a forest of *sál* trees, at a short distance from the western bank of the *Ajitavati* River. The distance and direction correspond exactly with the site of the great mound now called the Fort of *Máthá Kuár*. On this spot was erected a great brick *vihár* or temple monastery, in which was enshrined a statue of Buddha in a recumbent posture as he appeared when about to enter *Nirvána*. This *vihár* I would identify with the extensive mass of ruin marked K. in my survey of the site at the western end of the mound. Beside the vihár there was a stupa, 200 feet in height, built by Asoka, and a stone pillar, on which was recorded the history of the *Nirvána*, or death of Buddha. This stupa I would identify with the foundation or lower part of the brick tower marked A., now standing on the mound, and of which an account has already been given. Hwen Thsang describes two smaller stupas, and then a third grand stupa which stood on the spot where Brahman Subhadra had entered into *Nirvána*.* As the whole of the buildings above described as well as three small stupas were clustered together around the spot where Buddha was said to have died, their ruins, in the lapse of ages, would naturally have formed a single large mound of irregular outline, in all respects similar to the mass of ruins now called *Máthá-Kuár-ka-kot*. I think, therefore, that no reasonable doubt can now remain against the identification of Kasia with the ancient Kusinagara. With

---

* This last I would identify with the high point in the centre of the mound marked B.

regard to the slight difference of name, I have already stated my belief that the name of the present village should in all probability be written *Kusia* instead of *Kasia*, and in favour of this spelling I may add that the name is variously spelt in the Buddhist Books as *Kusigrámaka*, *Kusinára*, *Kusinágara*, and *Kusinagari*.

After the death of Buddha, the assembled Bhikshus (or mendicants) were consoled by the Venerable Aniruddha, who assured them that he saw the Devatas looking down from the skies upon earth, and weeping and bewailing with dishevelled hair and up-lifted arms.* Aniruddha was the first cousin of Buddha, being the second son of Amitodana, one of the brothers of Suddhodana, the father of Sákya Sinha. He was one of the ten great disciples of his cousin, and was renowned for his penetrating sight. Accordingly, on the death of Buddha, he took the lead of all the disciples present, and conducted their proceedings. By his directions Ananda made known the death of Buddha to the Mallian Nobles, who at once proceeded to the spot with garlands of flowers, and numerous cloths and music. For six days the body lay in state, attended by the people of Kusinâra. On the seventh day, when eight of the Mallian Nobles, who had been selected to carry the corpse to the place of cremation, attempted to lift it, they found themselves unable to move it. The amazed Nobles, on enquiring of the Venerable Aniruddha the cause of this prodigy, were informed that their intention of carrying the corpse through the southern gate to the south of the city was contrary to the intention of the Devatas. "Lord," said the Mallian Nobles, "whatever be the intention of the Devatas, be it acceded to." Accordingly, the corpse was borne by the eight Mallian Chieftains, on a bier formed of their lances, through the northern gate to the centre of the town, and then through the eastern gate to the coronation hall of the Mallians, where the funeral pile had been prepared. Four Noble Mallians then advanced and applied their torches to the funeral pile, but they were unable to ignite it. Again the baffled Nobles inquired of Aniruddha the cause of this second prodigy, who informed them that it was the intention of the Devatas that the corpse should not be burnt until the arrival of Mahá Kásyapa, the chief disciple of Buddha. At that

---

* Turnour in Bengal Asiatic Society's Journal, 1838, p. 1009.

moment Kasyapa was on his way from *Páwá* to *Kusinára*. On his arrival he perambulated the pile three times, and then opening it at the end, he reverentially bowed down his head at the feet of Buddha. As he rose, the pile spontaneously ignited, and the corpse of the great teacher was consumed.

I have given this long account of the obsequies of Buddha for the express purpose of showing the very prominent part that was taken by Aniruddha in all the proceedings. He first consoled the disciples on the death of Buddha; he then explained the causes of the miracles why the Mallian Nobles were unable at first to lift the corpse of Buddha, and afterwards to ignite the funeral pile; and lastly, according to Hwen Thsang, he ascended to the heavens to inform Máyá Devi, the mother of Buddha, of her son's death. As the whole of these acts were performed at Kusinára, we might not unreasonably suppose that some memorial monument of Aniruddha would have been erected there. There is, however, no record of such a monument in Hwen Thsang's account of the sacred edifices at Kusinagara; but I think it more than probable that the village of Anrudhwá must have received its name from some former memorial of the farsighted Aniruddha, the cousin of Buddha. In Sheet 102 of the Indian Atlas the name of this village is spelt Aniroodwa, which is more correct than the name written down for me by a Brahman of the place. The existence of this name in the immediate vicinity of the ancient monuments of *Kusía* must, I think, add considerable weight to all the other evidence in favour of the identification of *Kusía* with the ancient *Kusinagara*.

There is a discrepancy between the Ceylonese annals and the accounts of the Chinese pilgrim regarding the site of Buddha's cremation. According to the Pali annals above quoted, the corpse must have been burnt somewhere to the eastward of the city, and with this account Fa-Hian would seem to agree, for he places the scene of Buddha's death to the northward of the town. Hwen Thsang, however, places the site of the cremation to the northward of the city, across the River Hiranyavati. I think that these different accounts may, perhaps, be reconciled by identifying the stupa of the cremation with the large brick mound called the *Rámábhár Tila*, which being situated opposite to the north-east corner of the Anrudhwa mound (or ancient city as I suppose), might

BHUIKHUNDU and KANADI   Plate XXVIII

have been loosely described by one party as lying to the *north*, and by the other as lying to the *east*.

But the Rámábhár Tila, perhaps, corresponds more exactly with the site of another stupa, which is described by Hwen Thsang as having been built by Asoka near the ancient dwelling of Chanda, to the north-east of the city gates. This account, however, is somewhat vague, as no particular gate is specified. The existence also of a second stupa at the south-east foot of the *Rámábhár Tila* is against this identification, as only one stupa is mentioned on this site by Hwen Thsang. I am, therefore, strongly inclined to identify the *Rámábhár Tila* with the famous cremation stupa ; but if this position should be considered too far to the eastward to agree with Hwen Thsang's description, then the cremation tower must have occupied some position to the north of the Anrudhwá mound in the very midst of the ancient channel of the little Gandak River. I confess, however, that my own opinion is against this conclusion, and in favor of the identification of the Rámábhár Tila with the cremation stupa.

XXI. KHUKHUNDO.

On leaving Kusinagara Hwen Thsang directed his steps towards Banáras, and, after having travelled about 200 *li*, or upwards of 30 miles, to the south-west, he reached a large town, in which dwelt a very rich Brahman devoted to Buddhism.[*] If we adhere closely to the south-west bearing, we must identify this large town with Rudrapur, an ancient place 30 miles to the south-east of Gorakhpur, and 28 miles in a direct line from *Kasía*. But as Hwen Thsang speaks of the Brahman's hospitality to travellers going and coming, it would appear certain that the town must have been on the high road leading from Kasia to Banáras. Now the high road can never have passed through Rudrapur, as it would have entailed the passage of the *Rapti* in addition to that of the *Ghágra* River. I have had some experience in the laying out of roads, and I feel quite satisfied that the old high road must have crossed the Ghágra somewhere below its junction with the Rapti. According to the people, the old passage of the Ghágra was at *Maili*, four miles to the south of Kahnon, and three miles to the north of Bhágalpur. From

---

[*] Julien's Hwen Thsang, II., p. 349.

Kasia to this ghât on the Ghágra, the road would have passed through the ancient town of *Khukhundo*, and the large villages of *Kahaon* and *Bhigalpur*. Of these three, Khukhundo corresponds best with the description of a large town; and as it is 27 miles from Kasia by the present straight road, it must have been about 30 miles by the winding Native tracks. I believe, therefore, that it is the large town described by Hwen Thsang in which a rich Brahman had spent his wealth in the magnificent decoration of a Buddhist monastery. Khukhundo is not now a place of any note amongst the Brahmans, but it is often visited by Agarwâl Sráwaks from Gorakhpur and Patna, who have built a small Jain temple amongst the ruins. By them its proper name is said to be *Kishkindapura*, so called from *Kishkinda*, a mountain in the south of India, famous in the history of Rama. Khukhundo must, therefore, have been a Brahmanical town.

The remains at Khukhundo consist of a few large tanks, and a number of low mounds covered with broken brick and thick jungle. The ruins which lie scattered about over the plain, and amongst the fields to the south of Khukhundo, cover nearly one square mile of ground. All the larger mounds are square in form, and are beyond all doubt the ruins of temples. There are a few low oblong heaps which may possibly be the ruins of long ranges of inferior buildings, but I think it more probable that they are only the collections of brick from the fields. Every large mound has at least one fine lofty tree growing on its summit, and to the destructive power of the roots of these trees I would attribute the overthrow of the Khukhundo temples. I verified this opinion in one instance, that of mound K., by an excavation which showed the floor of a temple completely broken up by the wide-spreading roots of a fine Tamarind tree. Another notable instance is that of a temple at Kahaon, which was standing at the time of Buchanan's visit, but which is now only a low mound of brick ruin. Its overthrow is attributed by all the villagers to a Pipal tree, which stands close by the ruin.

The mounds of Khukhundo are about 30 in number, but not more than three of them have any names, the rest being called simply *Deóra*, or "mounds." In my survey of the ruins I have distinguished them by different letters of the alphabet, and under these letters I will now describe them.*

Mound A. is 100 feet square at base and 6 feet in height. There is a *Bel* tree (Egle Marmelos) on the top, and a *Pákar* (Ficus Venosa) on the west side. Under the Bel tree there is a good figure of the four-armed Vishnu in sandstone, with a peculiar rayed halo, which is boldly pierced through the slab.

Mound B., which is 50 feet square at base and 10 feet high, is called *Siva-ka-Tila* or Siva's mound, because there are the foundations of a *lingam* temple on its summit; the temple was only 8 feet square, but the *lingam* in blue stone is still perfect. There is one good piece of sculpture representing two seated figures, male and female, the latter with a child in her arms. A tree rises behind them, and with its branches forms a canopy over their heads. The figures, which appear to be entirely naked with the exception of some ornaments, are, I believe, Mahadeva and his wife Devi, or Bhawáni, represented as the goddess of fecundity, with a child in her arms. Another sculpture represents a four-armed female standing in what appears to be the prow of a boat. The subordinate figure of Ganesa, on the upper right hand, shows that the principal figure must be Párvati, the wife of Siva.

Mound C. is 120 feet in length, by 110 feet in breadth, and 15 feet in height. On the top there are the ruined walls of a brick temple, from 4 to 5 feet in height, forming a room of 9 feet square, with a *lingam* in the centre. To the south-west there is a walled entrance built of bricks of different sizes, and containing one piece of moulded bricks with a flower ornament. The small size of the room, the mixture of large and small bricks in the walls, and the unusual direction of the entrance, all lead me to conclude that this is an insignificant modern structure, built of bricks of all kinds found on the surface of the mound.

On both sides of the entrance there are several sculptures in sandstone, of which the principal is a statue of Ganesa. The other sculptures are a broken statue of Ganesa with his rat; the pedestal of a statue with a foot resting on a bull;

---

* See Plate XXVIII. for a plan of these ruins.

a four-armed female, most probably Párvati, attended by two heavenly musicians; and a slab containing personifications of the *Navagraha*, or "Nine Planets."

Mound D., which is 100 feet square at base and 15 feet in height, is crowned with a fine Banian tree. Beneath the tree are collected several pieces and fragments of sculpture, which are partly Brahmanical and partly Jain. The principal sculpture represents a four-armed seated male figure, with beard and moustaches, his right foot resting on a bull. In his four hands he holds a two-pronged sceptre, a necklace, a ball, and square pole. This is probably a figure of Siva. A second statue represents the four-armed Vishnu standing, and holding in three hands a club, a quoit, and a shell, the fourth hand being open with a lotus flower marked on the palm. A third sculpture is the pedestal of a statue with some naked figures on the face of it, and an antelope in the middle. The antelope is the cognizance of Santanath, the 16th Jain hierarch. A fourth stone is simply the pedestal of a lingam. The remaining sculptures are two pairs of apparently naked figures, male and female, seated—the latter with a child in her arms. These two sculptures are similar to one in the *Siva* Temple on mound B., which I have supposed to represent Mâhadeva and his wife Bhawâni as the goddess of fecundity. But in these two sculptures the god has a small naked figure of Buddha fixed in the front of his head-dress, from which I infer that these figures probably belong to the Jain religion, while that on mound B. certainly belongs to the Brahmanical *Shashti*, the goddess of fecundity.

Mound E. is about 75 feet square and 15 or 16 feet in height. It is now quite bare, the whole surface having been recently excavated for bricks. Any figures that may have been discovered were probably removed to Mound D., which would account for the mixture of Saiva and Vishnava sculptures now lying on its summit.

Mound F. is 150 feet in length, by 120 feet in breadth, and 18 feet in height. On the south slope of the mound there is a fine statue of the four-armed Vishnu in blue stone from the quarries near Gaya.

G. and H. are small low mounds from which bricks have been recently excavated. They are probably the remains of inferior temples.

Mound J., which is 75 feet square at base, and 15 feet in height, has also been recently excavated. I was able to trace the straight walls of a temple, and in the excavated holes I found large thick pieces of plaster, which had once covered the walls. There are no sculptures now lying about this mound, but immediately to the south of it, and outside a small modern Jain temple, there is a very fine standing figure of the four-armed Vishnu in blue stone. The head and arms are gone, but the rest of the sculpture is in good order. On the left side there are the Fish, the Tortoise, and the Boar *Avatárs*; and on the right the Buddha and the *Kalki Avatárs*. The five missing incarnations must have been lost with the head of the figure. This fine statue was probably enshrined in a temple now represented by mound J.

The Jain temple is a small square flat-roofed brick building of recent date. There are no Jains now living at Khukhundo, but the temple is visited by the Baniyas and Bankers of Gorakhpur and Patna. Inside the temple there is a large naked figure in blue stone, sitting squatted with his hands in his lap. Overhead there is a triple umbrella, and above that a *Dundubhi* Musician flying with his drum. On the pedestal there is a bull with a lion on each side. Now the bull is the cognizance of Adi Buddha, the first of the 24 Jain Pontiffs. The people are, therefore, mistaken in calling the figure a statue of *Párswanáth*, whose well known symbol is a snake. Outside the temple, however, there is another naked Jain statue which has two snakes twisted around its pedestal, and is, therefore, most probably a figure of *Párswanáth*. It is possible that this may have been the original figure enshrined in the temple. Another sculpture, in coarse sand-stone, represents the same naked couple, male and female, whom I have before described. A tree rises behind them, and with its boughs forms a canopy over their heads. Over all there is a small squatted figure like a Buddha, but naked. The male figure in this sculpture has a lotus in his right hand.

Mound K., which is crowned with a fine Tamarind tree, is the largest mass of ruin at Khukhundo. It is 120 feet square at base and 10 feet in height. At 10 feet above the ground level I made an excavation at a point on the western edge, where I observed something like a piece of terraced flooring. My excavation uncovered a portion of terraced

M

floor 9 feet square, but completely broken up by the wide-spreading roots of the Tamarind Tree, which have pierced the mound in all directions. I found several ornamental bricks with boldly cut-flowers and leaves 1½ inch in depth. Two of these bricks, with opposite curves forming an ogee, had evidently belonged to a cornice. The outer faces of all the bricks are ground smooth, and all the edges are so sharp and clean that the joints between the courses of bricks must have been very fine indeed. As I saw no fragments of figures about this mound, I think it is very probable that the statue belonging to it may be one of those now standing outside the Jain temple.

Mound N. is low and clear of jungle, having been excavated for bricks within the last few years. It is 45 feet square at base, but only 8 feet high. From its being both low and clear I thought it favourable for excavation. I dug a circular hole of about 8 feet diameter in the top of the mound, and near the middle, at a depth of only 1 foot I came upon a stone *Yoni*, or receptacle for a *lingam*, fixed in its original position, with the spout end turned towards the north. Further excavation showed that the floor had been broken up, but the marks of the original floor level were quite distinct on the centre stone. As there were no traces of any figures, I gave up the excavation, which had already been sufficient to determine that the mound N. is the ruin of a *linga* temple, dedicated to the god Mahádeva.

Mound S. is 100 feet in length, by 60 feet in breadth, and 12 feet in height towards its western end. The top is crowned with two fine *Siris* Trees, under which there is a life-size standing figure in sand-stone. The nose and forehead have been lost by a split of the stone, which must have been as old as the figure itself, for there are two holes in the split face which still retain bits of the metal clamps that were used in repairing the statue. The figure has apparently had four arms, and is called *Jug-bhíra*, or *Jug-víra*, " the Champion of the Age," a title which might be applied appropriately to *Víra*, or Mahávíra, the last of the 24th Jain hierarchs and the pontiff of the present age.

Mound Z. is a long low mass of ruin to the south-west of Khukhundo, half hidden amidst bambus. I found a recent excavation at the western end of the mound, from which the bricks could not have been removed above a few days, as the sides of the excavated hole still preserved the shape of the walls exactly. In form the building was an octagon of 14 feet across, with projections on the four sides facing the cardinal points. On the north-east side a portion of solid brick-work still remained, but not of sufficient thickness to show whether the building had been solid or hollow. As far as my experience goes, the only buildings of this shape are Buddhist *stupas*, as at *Dhamnár* and *Kholsi* in Malwa, or *Baragaon* (or *Nálanda*) in Bihár, and throughout Pegu and Burmah. In all instances the four projecting sides form niches for statues of the previous Buddhas. In the gigantic *Shwe-Dagon* stupa at Rangoon, these niches are expanded into distinct temples enshrining colossal figures. I incline, therefore, to conclude that the building recently excavated in mound Z. was a Buddhist stupa. But if Brahmanical temples of this form have ever been built, I should certainly prefer to consider mound Z. as the ruin of another orthodox temple, and to add one more to the long list of Brahmanical remains at Khukhundo.

With the exception of *Baragaon* (the ancient *Nálanda*), I have seen no place where the ruins offer such a promise of valuable discovery as at Khukhundo. The mounds are all low, and as they appear to be the ruins of temples, the work of excavation would be comparatively easy. I think that it would be sufficient to remove the top of each mound down to the level of the floor of the building, clearing away the rubbish entirely, but leaving the walls standing to show the plan of the building. Amongst the rubbish we might expect to find both statues and inscriptions, and perhaps other objects, all of which would help to throw light on the rise and progress of modern Brahmanism, more particularly during the long period of its struggles with expiring Buddhism.[*]

XXII. KAHAON.

The village of Kahaon is situated eight miles to the south of Khukhundo, and 46 miles to the south-east of Gorakhpur in a direct line. To the north of the village there is a stone pillar, and also some other remains, which have been

---

[*] As far as I am aware nothing has yet been done towards the excavation of these mounds.

described by Dr. Buchanan* and by Mr. Liston.† Dr. Buchanan calls the village *Kangho*, but the name is written *Kahaon*, or *Kahāwan*, by the people of the place, and I can only surmise that Buchanan's *Kangho* may have been originally written *Kanghon*, and that the final nasal has been omitted by mistake, either in copying or in printing. In the inscription on the pillar the village would seem to be called *Kakubharali*; and from some compound of *Kakubha*, such as *Kakubhawan*, the name of *Kahdwan* would be naturally derived.

The remains at *Kahaon* consist of an inscribed stone pillar, an old well, two ruined temples, and several tanks. The whole of these, together with the village itself, are situated on a low but extensive mound of brick ruin. Although the mound is of rather irregular outline on the east side, it may be best described as a square of nearly 500 yards.‡ The village occupies the south-western quarter of the square, and contains some fine old wells built of very large bricks, which are a sure sign of antiquity. The tanks, which would seem to have been connected with the old buildings, are all called *gar*, the meaning of which I was unable to ascertain, but which, as applied to water, must certainly be derived from the Sanskrit *gri*, to wet. These tanks are, 1st, the *Purena-gar*, a dirty pond immediately to the north of the village; 2nd, the *Karhahi-gar*, a small deep pond at the north-west angle of the ruins; 3rd, the *Jhakrahi-gar*, another small pond at the north-east angle, which is also called *Sophā-gar*; and 4th, a large sheet of water to the east of the village called *Askāmini*, or *Akāskdmini-gar*. This is the tank which Buchanan calls *Karhahi*, a misprint probably for *Kāmini*. From the size and appearance of the *Askāmini* Tank, I conclude that from it must have been excavated all the bricks and earth for the construction of the temples and village of Kahaon.

The Kahaon Pillar is a single block of coarse grey sandstone, 24 feet 3 inches in height from the ground to the metal spike on the top. The existence of this spike shows that the pillar has once been crowned by a pinnacle of some kind, perhaps by a statue of a lion, or of some other animal

---

* Eastern India, II., p. 366.
† Bengal Asiatic Society's Journal, 1838, p. 33.
‡ See Plate XXVIII.

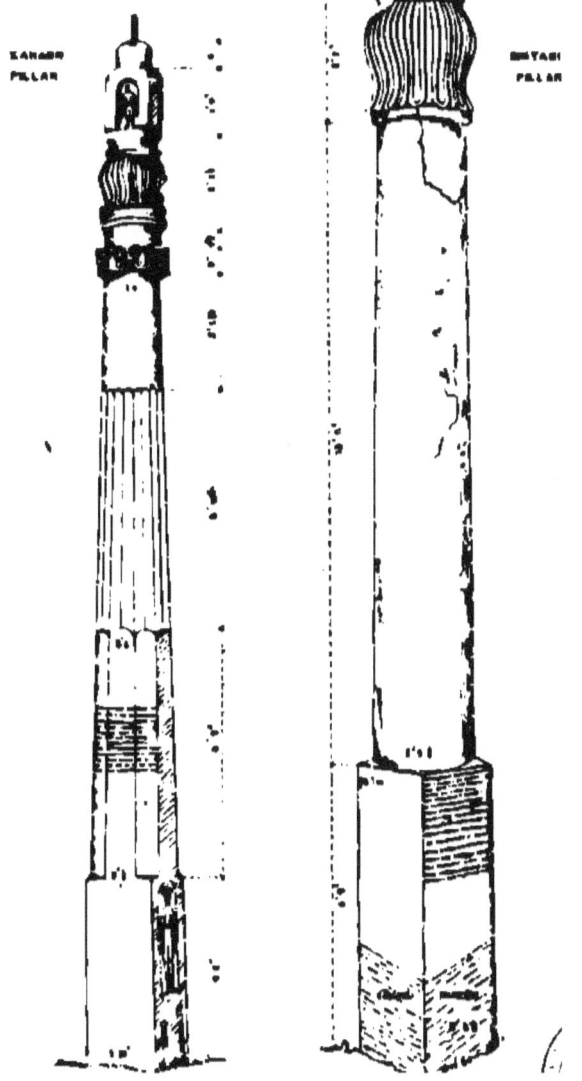

rampant; but whatever the pinnacle may have been, its height could not have exceeded 2½ or 3 feet. The total height of the column, therefore, must have been about 27 feet. The lower part of the shaft, to a height of 4½ feet, is a square of 1 foot 10 inches; above this, for a height of 0 feet 3 inches, it is octagonal; then sixteen-sided for a height of 5 feet 10½ inches; and then circular for a height of 2 feet 1½ inch. Above this, for a height of 9 inches, the pillar becomes square with a side of 18 inches, and then circular again for a height of 4½ inches, making the total height of the shaft 19 feet 10½ inches. The height of the capital, in its present incomplete state, is 4 feet 4½ inches. The lower portion, which is 2½ feet high, is bell-shaped, with circular bands of moulding both above and below. The bell itself is reeded, after the fashion of the Asoka pillars. Above this the capital is square, with a small niche on each side holding a naked standing figure. The square top slopes backward on all sides, and is surmounted by a low circular band, in which is fixed the metal spike already described.[*]

On the western face of the square base there is a niche holding a naked standing figure, with very long arms reaching to his knees. Behind, there is a large snake folded in horizontal coils, one above the other, and with its seven heads forming a canopy over the idol. Two small figures, male and female, are kneeling at the feet, and looking up to the idol with offerings in their hands.

On the three northern faces of the octagonal portion of the pillar, there is an inscription of 12 lines in the Gupta characters of the Allahabad Pillar.[†] There is a good copy of this inscription in Buchanan,[‡] and another and better copy in Prinsep's Journal.[§] In the translation given by James Prinsep, the date was read as being 133 years after the decease of *Skanda Gupta*, instead of in the year 133, after the death of Skanda. The true number of the year is 141, as pointed out by Professor FitzEdward Hall, but the epoch or era in which the years are reckoned is doubtful. Professor Hall, on the authority of *Bápu Deva Sástri*, the

---

[*] See Plate XXIX.
[†] See Plate XXX.
[‡] Eastern India, II., Plate V.
[§] Bengal Asiatic Society's Journal, 1838, Plate I.

learned Astronomer of the Banáras College prefers the era of *Vikramáditya*, but I am inclined to adopt that of *Sake*; and this era, I believe, is also preferred by Mr. Thomas. The difference between the two is 135 years. If dated in the Vikrama era, the pillar must have been erected in 141—57 = 84 A. D.; but if dated in the Sake era, the period of its erection will be 141 + 78 = 219 A. D. The latter date, I think, accords best with the now generally admitted epoch of the overthrow of the Gupta Dynasty in A. D. 319.

The purport of the inscription, as translated by Prinsep, is simply to record the dedication of five images of Indra by one *Madra*, who calls himself " the constant and friendly patron of *Brahmans, Gurus*, and *Yatis*," or Brahmans, religious teachers, and sages," or Ascetics who have subdued their passions. In the present day the term *Yati* is, I believe, applied only to a Jain Priest; and, although at first the mention of Brahmans would seem to preclude any reference to the Jain religion, yet the *Yatis* themselves are usually, if not always, Brahmans, and the naked figures with crisp curled hair, on the base and capital of the pillar, must belong either to the Jains, or to the latter *Tántrika* Buddhists. I found a similar naked standing figure, canopied by a seven-headed snake, inside the great mound of old Rájagriha.

Both of the temples described by Buchanan[*] are now in ruins; and as they are not mentioned by Mr. Liston in 1837, they must have fallen before his visit. Buchanan describes them as pyramidal in form, with two apartments, one over the other, as in the great temple at Buddha-Gaya. Inside he found only two fragments of images, of which one showed the feet of a standing figure with a female votary seated at one side. I made an excavation in the northern ruin, and found that the temple had consisted of a room 9 feet square with walls only 1 foot 9 inches in thickness. The building, therefore, was only 12 feet 6 inches square on the outside. In the slight sketch of this temple given by Buchanan, no dimensions are noted, but the height of the building is twice and a half its width, or about 30 feet, according to the measurement obtained by my excavation. On the ruin of the southern temple, I found a naked standing figure of life-size, similar to that on the base of the pillar.

---

[*] Eastern India, II., p. 367.

Inscription on the Bhitari Pillar.

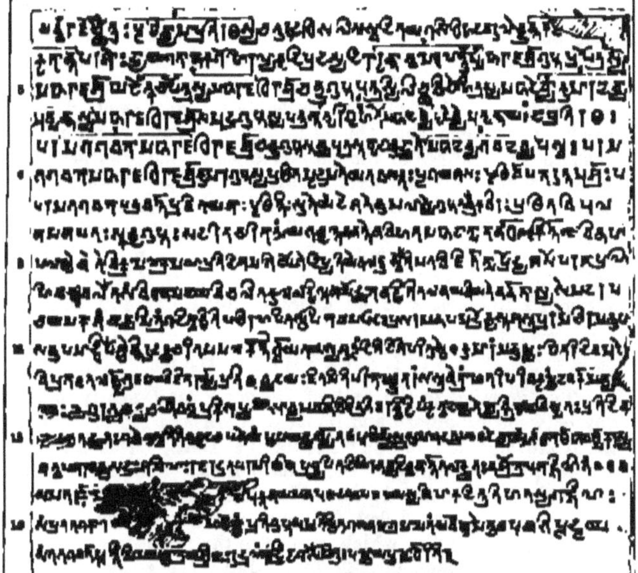

N. B. The thin lines with No. over them denote the corresponding lines of the lower inscription on the Bihar Pillar.

Inscription on the Kahaon Pillar.

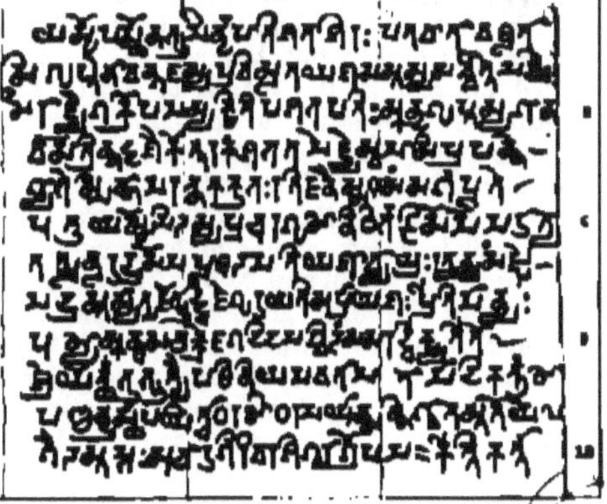

Bhitari Seals.

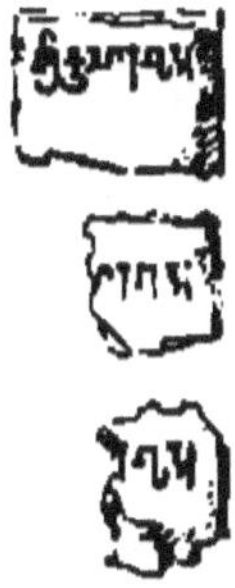

A. Cunningham, del.

Photozincographed at the Surveyor General's Office, Calcutta.

BHITARI AND KAHAON PILLARS.

Immediately to the north of the pillar, and on the highest point of the mound, there are traces of the brick walls of some buildings; and to the south-east, there is an old well which has been lately filled up. Buchanan describes the pillar as having originally "stood in a small quadrangular area, surrounded by a brick wall, and probably by some small chambers." I presume that the pillar must have been placed opposite the entrance of the temple, in which the *Panchendra* or five images of Indra were enshrined. It is probable that there were several temples and other buildings crowded around the pillar, otherwise it will be difficult to account for the great size of the mound, which, though not more than 6 feet in height above the fields, extends from west to east upwards of 1,200 feet, with an average breadth of 400 feet.

XXIII. HATHIYA-DAH.

Twelve miles to the east of Deogong, and nearly midway between Azimgarh and Banâras, there is an old dry tank, called *Hathiya-dah*, or the "Elephant's Tank," with an inscribed pillar standing in the middle of it. The pillar itself is called *Hathiya-dah-ka-lât*. The name is derived from a large stone elephant, 5 feet 6 inches in length, and 4 feet 10 inches in height, which stands to the north-west of the pillar, at a distance of 138 feet. Both the pillar and the elephant are formed of a coarse grey sand-stone, and they have accordingly suffered from exposure to the weather, and are now much worn. The shaft of the pillar is a single block, 12 feet 9 inches in height and 1 foot 5¼ inches in diameter, both at base and top. Originally it must have been several feet higher, but the bed of the tank has gradually silted up, and in the month of March bore a fine crop of wheat. The capital is a flat circular slab, slightly rounded on the upper edge, and quite plain. In fact, the pillar is a mere cylindrical block intended apparently for the sole purpose of exhibiting the inscription. To the west of the pillar there is a low mound of brick ruins, 170 feet in length from north to south, and 25 feet broad. It is called *Siwarika-Tila*, or "Siwaris' Mound;" but the people have no tradition about it, and do not know what is the meaning of the names. Most probably it has some reference to a temple of Siva, which may have stood there in former days. The villages nearest to the pillar are *Singhpura* to the north,

Nowa Rasíya to the east, *Pakari* to the south-east, *Debhao* to the south-west.

The pillar is said by the people to have been set up by Raja Gajpat Singh in Samvat 207, or A. D. 150; but both name and date are wrong. *Gajapati*, or "Lord of Elephants," is only one of the titles of the king in whose reign the pillar was erected, and the date is Samvat 1207, or A. D. 1150. This inscription occupies 10 lines, but as the letters are large and coarsely cut, it is not a long one. It records the excavation of the tank by several *Thákurs*, of whom the chief is "*Bellan Thákur*, the Treasurer (Bhándagárika) of *Gosalla Devi*, the Queen *(Mahárájí)* of Raja Govinda Chandra Deva, the Lord of Horses, Lord of Elephants, and Lord of Men, on Thursday, the 5th of the waning moon of *Ashárh*, in Samvat 1207." The record is not of much value, but it is of later date, by 25 years, than any inscription hitherto found of the Ráhtor Prince Govinda Chandra Deva of Kanoj.

XXIV. BHITARI.

The large village of Bhitari is situated on the left bank of the *Gángi Nadi* nearly midway between Banáras and Gházipur, and five miles to the north north-east of *Saidpur*. The Gángi River, which surrounds the village on three sides, is crossed by an old stone bridge of early Muhammedan style. The oldest bridge consisted of only two small arches, to which two others have since been added at different times. Bhitari has once been a town of some consequence, and it is still a considerable village, with a great number of brick-houses. Both in speaking and in writing, its name is usually coupled with that of another place in its vicinity as *Saidpur Bhitari*. It is thus designated in the Ain Akbari, but the name has been strangely misread by Gladwin as *Syedpoor Nemedy*,[*] a mistake that must be due to the faulty nature of the Persian character in which his original was written, as its alphabet is utterly unsuited for the correct record of proper names.

The remains at Bhitari consist of several ruined brick mounds, an inscribed stone pillar, and a few pieces of sculp-

---

[*] English Translation, II., p. 82.

ture. Some of the mounds appear to be mere heaps of broken stone and brick—the gatherings from the fields after each season's ploughing. The larger mounds, which run parallel to each other from the bridge towards the village, seem to me to be only the ruins of houses that once formed the two sides of a street. The remaining mounds, which are of square form and isolated, are at present covered with Musalmán tombs; but I have little doubt that all of them were originally either temples or other Hindu buildings. That one of these mounds belonged originally to the Hindus, we have an undoubted proof in the existence of the inscribed stone pillar, which stands partially buried in the rubbish of its eastern slope, and in the discovery at the foot of the pillar of an old brick inscribed with the name of *Sri Kumára Gupta.* The early occupation of the place by the Hindus is further proved by the discovery of several Hindu statues and *lingams* in the rubbish about the mounds, and by the finding of numerous bricks inscribed with *Kumára Gupta's* name in the fields.* I obtained further proof of the same by the purchase on the spot of three Indo-Sassanian coins of base silver, which probably date from the 8th or 9th century, and of one small round copper coin with an elephant on the obverse, and a peculiar symbol, supposed to be a *Chaitya,* on the reverse, which cannot, in my opinion, be of later date than the invasion of Alexander the Great.

The Bhitari Pillar is a single block of reddish sand-stone, apparently from one of the Chunar quarries. The shaft of the pillar is circular, with a diameter of 2 feet 4½ inches, and a height of 15 feet 5 inches.† The base is square, but its height is rather uncertain. The upper portion, on which the inscription is cut, has been smoothed, but the lower portion, as far as my excavation went, still bears the marks of the chisel, although not very deep. My excavation was carried down to the level of the adjoining fields, a depth of 6 feet 9 inches below the top of the base, without finding any trace of a pedestal; and as it is most probable that the inscription was placed on a level with the eye, I would fix the height of the original base at about 6 feet, thus giving it an elevation of only 9 inches above the level of the country.

---

* See Plate XXX, for sketches of these bricks.
† See Plate XXIX, for a view of this pillar.

The capital is 3 feet 2 inches in height, bell-shaped, and reeded like the capitals of the Asoka Pillars. A large portion of the capital is broken off on the western side, thus exposing a deep narrow socket, which could only have held a metal spike. The upper portion of the shaft also is split to a depth of about 2 feet. The people say that the pillar was struck by lightning many years ago. It certainly was in the same state when I first saw it in January 1836, and I know of only one reason to make me doubt the accuracy of the people's statements, namely, that both the iron pillar at Delhi, and the stone pillar at *Nacandgarh Lauriya*, have been wantonly injured by cannon shot. If the capital of the Bhitari Pillar had been surmounted by a statue of any kind, as it most probably was when the Muhammadans first settled there, I think that the breaking of the capital may be attributed to their destructive bigotry with quite as much probability as to lightning. I found a portion of the broken capital in my excavation at the foot of the pillar.

The inscription, which is cut on the eastern side of the base, consists of 19 lines of well shaped characters of the early Gupta period. Unfortunately, this face is much weather-worn, and the stone has also peeled off in several places, so that the inscription is now in even a worse condition than when I first saw it in January 1836. The copy which I then made by eye I compared letter by letter with the original inscription on the spot, and, although I found several errors in different parts of the inscription, yet the only serious one is an omission of five letters in the 15th line. I made also an impression of the inscription over which I pencilled all the letters as they appeared to the eye. This is, indeed, the only successful method of copying a weather-worn inscription; for the edges of the letters being very much rounded, an impression gives only a number of confused and shapeless spots, although many of the letters being deeply cut are distinctly legible, and may easily be copied by the eye. The value of an impression thus pencilled over is very great, as it ensures accuracy in the number of letters, and thus most effectually prevents all errors, both of insertion and omission. The copy which I have thus made is, I believe, as perfect as it is possible to obtain now, considering the weather-worn state of the letters.*

---

* See Plate XXX. for a copy of this inscription.

From the copy which I prepared in January 1836, a translation was made by Dr. Mill, which was published in Prinsep's Journal for January 1837. My re-examination of the inscription has corrected some of Dr. Mill's proposed readings, while it has confirmed many of them, a few being still doubtful owing to the abraded state of the letters. As translated by Dr. Mill, the inscription refers chiefly to the reign of *Skanda Gupta*, closing with his death, and the accession of his infant son. The object of the inscription was to record the erection of a sacred image, the name of which Dr. Mill was unable to read, but which may possibly be recovered when my new copy is re-translated by some competent scholar. In my remarks on the lower inscription on the Bihár Pillar, I have already noticed that all the remaining part of the *upper* portion of it, which contains the genealogy, is letter for letter identical with the first part of Bhitari record, and I repeat the notice here for the purpose of adding that, by a comparison of the two inscriptions, every letter of the upper part of both, or about one-third of the whole, may be restored without chance of error.*

The sculptures now to be seen at Bhitari are very few, but they are sufficient to show the former existence of several large stone temples. In the village there is a colossal figure of *Ganesa*, and a broken bas-relief of the *Navagraha*, or "Nine Planets." The colossal statue must almost certainly have been the principal figure enshrined in a temple dedicated to *Ganesa*. There is also a large slab with a half-size two-armed female figure, attended by another female figure holding an umbrella over her, both in very high relief. The figures in this sculpture are in the same style and in the same attitudes as those of the similar group of the Rája and his umbrella attendant on the gold coins of the Gupta Princes. This sculpture, I believe, represents a queen on her way to worship at the temple. The group is a favorite one with Hindu artists, and, as far as my observation goes, it is never used singly, but always in pairs—one on each side of the door-way of a temple. The age of this sculpture I am inclined to fix as early as the time of the Gupta Kings, partly on account of the similarity of style to that of their gold coins, partly also because the pillar belongs to one of

---

* The two inscriptions may now be compared in Plates XVII. and XXX.—&c my previous remark in note in page 58.

that family, but chiefly because the bricks found in various parts of the ruins are stamped with the name of *Sri Kumára Gupta*.

If I am right in attributing the sculptures to the time of the Gupta Dynasty, or from A. D. 100 to 300, then the Bhitari ruins will be amongst the oldest Brahmanical remains now known to us. For this reason alone I would strongly advocate the excavation of all the isolated mounds, and more particularly of the pillar mound, in which we might expect to find not only all the fragments of the original capital, but also many sculptures and other objects belonging to the temple in front of which the pillar was erected. I have already stated that the bridge over the Gângi River is built entirely of stones taken from the ancient buildings of Bhitari. Many of these stones are squared, and ornamented with flowers and various mouldings, and on one of them I observed the syllable *si*. This is a mere mason's mark, but as the shape of the letter is the same as that of the Gupta alphabet, the discovery of this single character tends strongly to confirm the accuracy of the date which I have already assigned to the Bhitari ruins on other grounds. As Bhitari is in the *Jághir* of the enlightened Rája Deo Náráyan Singh, every facility for excavation would, of course, be obtained on application to him.

At my recommendation the Government afterwards authorized a small sum for excavations, and, at my request, my friend Mr. C. Horne, of the Civil Service, then Judge of Banáras, kindly undertook to superintend the work. His report, which follows, gives a tolerably full and interesting account of this ancient place:

"Bhitari is a small bazaar and village situated on the Gângi Nadi, about 4½ miles north-east by north of Syedpur, on the high road from Banáras to Ghâzipur. It is called Syedpur Bhitari, and Rája Deo Narain Singh derives his title from it. On approaching from the south-west by a good fair weather road, it presents the appearance of a very large ruined earthen fort. In general form it is nearly a rectangle,* and the only deviation from that form is caused by an eminence or spur running from the south-west corner, and which has evidently been always crowned by some

---

* East face 540 yard., South 525 yards, West 605 yards, North 700 yards.

imposing edifice. The nature of the ground has been skilfully brought to bear; and it would seem that the west face was merely scarped towards the river, having been originally very high (perhaps thirty feet), whilst to the east a large space has been lowered a few feet to provide earth to raise an embankment, in digging through which no traces of masonry can be found. On the south face the line is by no means straight, the nature of the ground having been followed, and the high bank of a tank already formed having been merely added to the north face is more regular.

"Each of these sides had large mounds, upon which were either temples or forts. There is one of these at each corner, and one-half way on each side, whilst the spur before alluded to, which forms the south-west corner, has certainly been long ago crowned with a large Buddhist temple, now re-placed with a shabby Idgah. Within this enclosure were evidently many large buildings, and their former presence is attested by the *kheras* or mounds of broken brick and earth scattered in every direction. At present there is a small winding bazar of insignificant shops, all, however, built of old bricks. There is also a large suburb, if it may be so termed, of ruinous brick houses with but few inhabitants. The surrounding mounds and embankments are dotted over with Muhammadan tombs, mostly of very recent erection, and many of which are built with the large nearly-square Buddhist bricks.

"But to proceed to the object of this notice, *viz.*, the Buddhist remains at Bhitari—1*st*, there is a large monolith standing, as nearly as possible, in the centre of the place. This is 28½ feet in height, and stands upon a rough stone 7 or 8 feet below the present level of the soil. For the first 10 feet 2 inches it is square, and stands, as nearly as possible, facing the cardinal points. At the top of the square part is an inscription which is stated by General Cunningham to contain a record of Skanda Gupta; this faces east. The upper part, including the capital which takes up about three feet, is circular, and where it joins the square part is 2 feet 3 inches in diameter, and apparently of even thickness in its whole length. The capital is handsomely fluted, and has a slice broken off it. There is also a flaw near the top in the pillar itself, which is one solid piece of sand-stone, resembling that found at Chunar, being of the hard kind.

"The monolith is out of the perpendicular, and this deviation, as well as the cracked capital, is said to have been occasioned by lightning long ago.

"I laid bare the east face of the foundation as the column slopes to the north, and found that the base was displaced three inches off the foundation-stone on the south side, and that there were two iron wedges driven under it, and that at some remote period stone-work of a massive character had been placed around to prevent further declension. I then cleared the mound away which abutted on the column, hoping to find some traces of foundations at least of the building to which the monolith might have formed an adjunct. This mound, from 12 to 16 feet in height, and extended some distance, and, as far as I could ascertain by cutting a trench and levelling, consists entirely of broken bricks and earth.

"I will now refer to the old Buddhist temple, which must formerly have stood on the high spur to the south-west. Owing to the presence of the Idgah, the number of tombs, and my limited time, I made no excavations on this spot; but I was easily enabled to trace the various parts of the temple scattered over the place and performing various functions. Firstly, there were the pillars of the shrine, with their carved suns, and grotesque faces with foliage flowing from their mouths and eyes, and the constantly recurring flat vase, all used by the Muhammadans in their mosque. Then there were the plainer columns of the cloister, square below, and octagonal above. These latter I found rounded off and set up as Muhammadan head-stones to graves, the light being burnt on the top of them! Until I discovered two of these *in situ*, or at the graves, the Musalmans assured me they were Hindu conversions of the Buddhist pillars into emblems employed in the worship of Mahádeo. Secondly, there were the stone beams used also in the mosque, both as beams, and as uprights at the wells and in houses. And, lastly, there were the roofing stones used as pavement and for putting over graves.

"In compliance with the extract of General Cunningham's report, several cross cuttings were made: The one through the surrounding mounds to see what kind of wall had been erected, if any,—the result of this has been before alluded to; Another cutting was made through an isolated mound of some 9 feet in height, the result of which merely proved it to have an ancient dust heap; A third, through a very high and likely mound resulted in nothing but earth and broken bricks; Another has since been made, but the results were the same as in the other cases. The reason for this is very plain: Each of these mounds represents an ancient edifice not, perhaps, of the time of the Buddhists (for the bricks do not bear that character), but the constant excavation of foundations for the past 200 years for the purpose of building has produced the results above alluded to. Each party has taken the bricks he needed and filled in again the rubbish.

"Just below the Idgah and exterior to the work is an old Muhammadan bridge across the Gángí Nadi, which might be repaired with advantage. This has been entirely constructed with the cut-stones taken from the Buddhist structure above. The date of its erection may have been from 200 to 250 years, since or subsequent to the erection of that of Jonpur, which it resembles in many points. The carved work is built inwards.

"There are around Bhitari, at some little distance, say a quarter or half a mile, a number of detached mounds evidently of Buddhist origin, and apparently of artificial construction. These might repay excavation.

"In conclusion, I would beg to suggest with all deference, and without access to books, my knowledge must be limited that Bhitari was of old a strongly fortified earthen camp, in which there was at least one large Buddhist temple and several edifices in connection with the same; but nothing short of a lengthened residence on the spot, together with careful exploration, can ever accurately determine the nature of the latter. It is difficult to account for the base of the monolith being so far below the present level of the soil with which it does not appear to me ever to have been even."

XXV. BANARAS, SARNATH.

Banáras is celebrated amongst the Buddhists as the scene where their great teacher first expounded his doctrine, or, as they metaphorically express it, where he first began to "turn the wheel of the law." This is one of the four great events in the life of Buddha, and accordingly it forms one of the most common subjects of Buddhist sculpture. In the great Buddhist establishment near Banáras, which is described by Hwen Thsang the principal statue enshrined in a temple 200 feet in height, was a copper figure of Buddha represented in the act of "turning the wheel of the law." I found numerous statues of Buddha in the same attitude during my explorations about Sárnáth in 1835-36, and Major Kittoe discovered several more in 1851-52. I found also many others figures, but those of Buddha, the "Teacher," were the most numerous. The inscribed pedestal found by Dewán *Jagat Singh* in 1704, also belonged to a statue of Buddha, the Teacher. Similarly at Buddha-Gaya, where Sákya Sinha sat for six years meditating under the Bodhi Tree, the favourite statue is that of Buddha the Ascetic.

The city of Banáras is situated on the left bank of the Ganges, between the *Barná Nadi* on the north-east, and the *Asi Nála* on the south-west. The *Barná*, or *Varaná*, is a considerable rivulet, which rises to the north of Allahabad, and has a course of about 100 miles. The *Asi* is a mere brook of no length, and, owing to its insignificant size, it does not appear in any of our most detailed maps. It is not entered in the Indian Atlas Sheet No. 88, which is on the scale of four miles to the inch, nor even in the larger lithographed map of the District of Banáras on the double scale of two miles to the inch. This omission has led the learned French Academician M. Vivien de Saint Martin to doubt the existence of the *Asi* as a tributary of the Ganges, and he conjectures that it may be only a branch of the *Barna*, and that the joint stream called the *Varanasi* may have communicated its name to the city. The *Asi Nala*, however, will be found, as I have described it, in James Prinsep's map of of the city of Banáras, published by Hullmandel, as well as in the small map which I have prepared to illustrate this account.[*] The position of the *Asi* is also accurately described by H. H. Wilson in his Sanskrit Dictionary, under the word *Varanasi*. I may add that the road from the city to *Ramnagar* crosses the *Asi* only a short distance from its confluence with the river. The points of junction of both streams with the Ganges are considered particularly holy,

---

[*] See Plate XXXI.—The Asi is mentioned by Abul Fazl in Ait Ain Akbari, II., p. 28; and by Bishop Heber, I., 357, and more particularly in p. 399, where he speaks of "the small river."

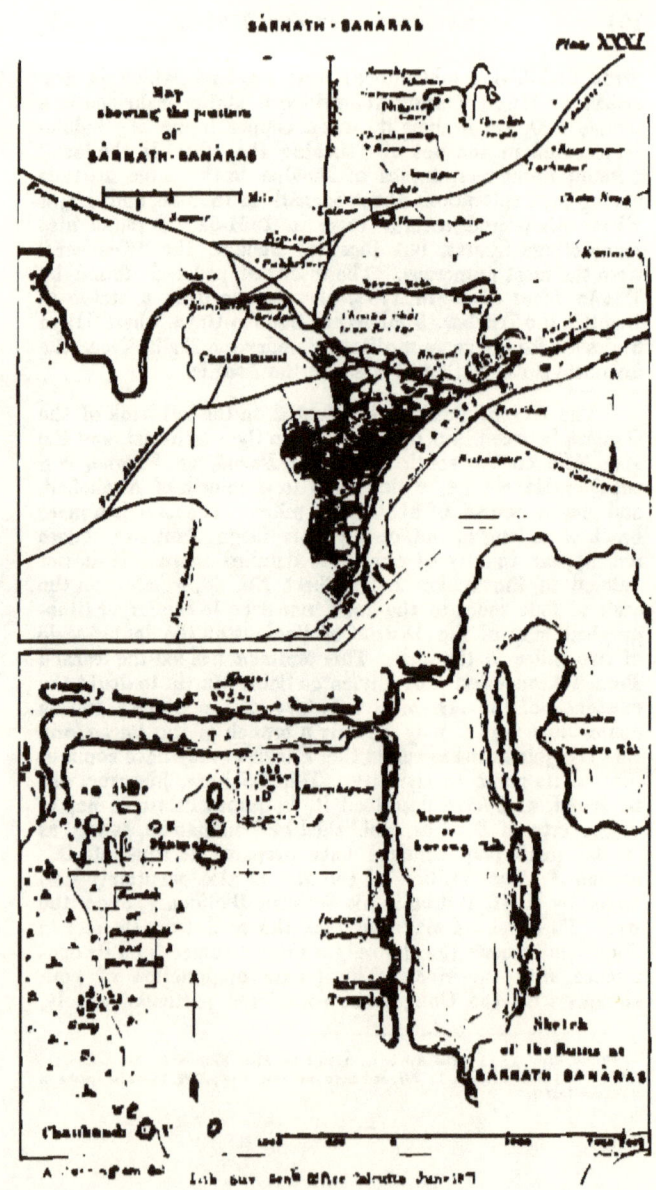

and accordingly temples have been erected both at *Barna Sangam* below the city, and at *Asi Sangam* above the city. From the joint names of these two streams, which bound the city to the north and south, the Brahmans derive *Varanasi* or *Vâranasi*, which is said to be the Sanskrit form of the name of Banâras. But the more usual derivation amongst the common people is from Râja *Banâr*, who is said to have re-built the city about 800 years ago.

The Buddhist remains of Banâras are situated nearly due north, and about 3½ miles distant from the outskirts of the city, at a place popularly known by the name of *Sârnâth*. This name, which is usually applied to the great Buddhist tower, or stupa, belongs properly to a small Brahmanical temple on the western bank of the lake, while the great tower itself is called *Dhamek*. An annual fair is held close to the temple of Sârnâth, and there is an indigo factory only 200 yards to the north of it. The name of Sârnâth was, accordingly, well known both to the Natives and to the English, and when the neighbouring ruins first attracted attention, they were always referred to by that name. The earliest mention of them is by Jonathan Duncan in 1794, in his account of the discovery of two Urns by Babu Jagat Singh "in the vicinity of a temple called Sârnâth."[*] It is possible that Duncan here refers to the Brahmanical "temple;" but in the subsequent notices by Wilford and James Prinsep, both of whom had resided for many years at Banâras, the name of Sârnâth is always applied to the great tower. The same name is given to the tower in an engraving which was published in 1834 in Captain Elliot's Views in India.

Sârnâth means supply the "best Lord," which title is here applied to the god Mahâdeva, whose symbol, the *lingam*, is enshrined in the small temple on the bank of the lake. I believe, however, that the name is only an abbreviation of *Sâranggânâtha*, or the "Lord of Deer," which would also be an appropriate epithet for Mahâdeva, who is frequently represented as holding a deer in his left hand. As the lake in front of the temple is still occasionally called "*Sârang Tâl*," my conjecture that the true name was *Sarangga Nath* seems a very probably one; but I would refer the epithet to Buddha himself, who in a former existence was fabled to have roamed

---

[*] Asiatic Researches, V., p. 131.

the woods in this very spot as the king of a herd of deer. But this spot was specially esteemed by the Buddhists on account of a curious story which is given at some length by Hwen Thsang, and which, as illustrative of the Buddhist tenderness for life, I will now relate.*—" The Rája of Banáras, who was fond of sport, had slaughtered so many deer that the king of the deer remonstrated with him, and offered to furnish him with one deer daily throughout the year, if he would give up slaughtering them for sport. The Rája consented. After some time, when it came to the turn of a hind, big with young, to be presented to the Rája, she objected that, although it might be her turn to die, yet the turn of her little one could not yet have arrived. The king of the deer (that is, Buddha) was struck with compassion, and offered himself to the Rája in place of the hind." On hearing the story the Rája exclaimed—" I am but a deer in the form of a man, but you are a man in the form of a deer." He at once gave up his claim to the daily gift, and made over the park for the perpetual use of the deer, on which account it was called the ' Deer Park' *(Mrigadáva)*. It is curious to learn that a *ramna*, or antelope preserve still exists in the neighbourhood of *Sárnáth*.

The principal remains at Sárnáth are the following:

1st.—The great stone tower call *Dhamek*; *2nd*, the remains of a large brick tower opened by Jagat Sing; *3rd*, the traces of buildings excavated by myself in 1835-36; *4th*, the remains of buildings excavated by Major Kittoe in 1851-52; and *5th*, a high mound of solid brick-work crowned with an octagonal brick tower, called *Chaukandi*, and situated at rather less than half a mile from the great tower of Dhamek. With the simple exception of *Chaukandi*, the whole of these remains are situated on an extensive mound of brick and stone ruins about half a mile long, and nearly a quarter of a mile broad. On the north and east there are three large sheets of water which communicate with one another. To the east lies the *Narokar* or *Sárang Tál*, which is 3,000 feet long and 1,000 feet broad. On the north-east this communicates with the *Chandokar* or *Chandra Tál*, which is of about the same size, but of less regular shape. On the north lies

---

* Julien's Hwen Thsang, II., p. 361.

the *Naya Tal*, or "New Tank," which is upwards of half a mile in length, but little more than 300 feet in width.*

At the north-eastern end of the mass of ruin is situated the village of *Bardhi*, which, as I infer from the spelling, must have been named after *Vajra Vardhi*, a goddess of the later Buddhists. To the west, beyond the bend of the Naya Tál, lies *Guronpur*, or the "Village of Teachers," which in its day was probably inhabited by Buddhist *Gurus*. The *Mrigadáva*, or "Deer Park," is represented by a fine wood, which still covers an area of about half a mile, and extends from the great tower of *Dhamek* on the north to the *Chaukandi* mound on the south. To the south-west of the great tower the Jains have erected a modern temple of *Párswanáth*. The temple is white-washed and surrounded by a wall enclosing an area 167 feet square. Since I first surveyed these ruins in 1835, a second or outer enclosure has been added on the east side, the walls of which run right up to the great tower and cause much inconvenience to visitors, by obstructing their free passage round the building.

The most remarkable of the Sárnáth Monuments is the great tower called *Dhamek*. Mr. Fergusson† has stated that "this building was opened by Major Cunningham, *under Mr. Prinsep's auspices ;*" but this statement is incorrect, as the operations were begun by myself before any communication was made to James Prinsep, and were afterwards continued entirely under my own guidance. The cost of opening the tower was shared between James Prinsep, Captain Thoresby, Major Grant, and myself, but the work had been commenced "under my own auspices," and was not suggested to me by James Prinsep. The excavation was begun in December 1834, and closed in January 1836, at a cost of Rupees 517-3-10. But, before detailing these operations, I will describe the tower itself.

The Buddhist *stupa* called *Dhamek* is a solid round tower, 93 feet in diameter at base and 110 feet in height above the surrounding ruins, but 128 feet above the general level of the country. The foundation or basement, which is made of very large bricks, has a depth of 28 feet below the level of the ruins, but is sunk only 10 feet below the surface of the

---

* See Plate XXXI.
† Handbook of Architecture, I., p. 15.

country. The lower part of the tower, to a height of 43 feet, is built entirely of stone from one of the Chunar quarries, and with the exception of the upper five courses, the whole of this part of the building is a solid mass of stone, and each stone, even in the very heart of the mass, is secured to its neighbours by iron cramps. The upper part of the tower is built entirely of large bricks, but as the outer facing has long ago disappeared, there is nothing now left to show whether it was formerly cased with stone, or only plastered over, and coloured to imitate the stone-work of the lower portion. I infer, however, that it was plastered, because the existing stone-work terminates with the same course all round the building, a length of 292 feet. Had the upper part been cased with stone, it is scarcely possible that the whole should have disappeared so completely that not even a single block out of so many thousands should now remain in its original position. In one part I observed some projecting bricks which appeared very like the remains of a moulding at the base of the dome. On the top I found a small brick cap, 8 feet in diameter and only 4 feet high. From its size I infer that this was the ruin of the base of a small pinnacle, about 10 feet square, which most probably once supported a stone umbrella. I infer this because the figures of Buddha the Teacher are usually represented as seated under an umbrella.

The lower part of the monument has eight projecting faces, each 21 feet 6 inches in width, with intervals of 15 feet between them. In each of the faces, at a height of 24 feet above the ground, there is a semi-circular headed niche, 6½ feet in width, and the same in height. In each of the niches there is a pedestal, 1 foot in height, and slightly hollowed on the top to receive the base of a statue; but the statues themselves have long ago disappeared, and I did not find even the fragment of one in my excavation at the base of the monument. There can be little doubt, however, that all the eight statues represented Buddha the Teacher, in the usual form, with his hands raised before his breast, and the thumb and fore-finger of the right hand placed on the little finger of the left hand for the purpose of enforcing his argument. Judging by the dimensions of the niches, the statues must have been of life-size.*

---

* I would suggest that one of the many sitting statues of Buddha the Teacher, which have since been discovered, and are now deposited at the Banaras College, should be placed in one of these niches.

From the level of the base of the niches the eight projecting faces lessen in width to five feet at the top; but the diminution is not uniform, as it begins gradually at first, and increases as it approaches the top. The outline of the slope may have been possibly intended for a curve, but it looks much more like three sides of a large polygon. Around the niches seven of the faces are more or less richly decorated with a profusion of flowing foliage. The carving on some of the faces has been completed, but on others it is little more than half finished, while the south face is altogether plain. On the unfinished faces portions of the unexecuted ornamentation may be seen traced in outline by the chisel, which proves that in ancient times the Hindus followed the same practice as at present, of adding the carving after the wall was built.

On the western face the same ornamentation of flowing foliage is continued below the niche, and in the midst of it there is a small plain tablet, which can only have been intended for a very short inscription, such, perhaps, as the name of the building. A triple band of ornament, nearly 9 feet in depth below the niches, encircles all the rest of the building, both faces and recesses. The middle band, which is the broadest, is formed entirely of various geometrical figures, the main lines being deeply cut, and the intervening spaces being filled with various ornaments. On some of the faces where the spaces between the deeply cut lines of the ruling figures are left plain, I infer that the work is unfinished. The upper band of ornamentation, which is the narrowest, is generally a scroll of the lotus plant with leaves and buds only, while the lower band, which is also a lotus scroll, contains the full blown flowers as well as the buds. The lotus flower is represented full to the front on all the sides except the south south-west, where it is shown in a side view with the *Chakwa* or Brahmani Goose seated upon it. This, indeed, is the only side on which any animal representations are given, which is the more remarkable, as it is one of the recesses and not one of the projecting faces. In the middle of the ornament there is a human figure seated on a lotus flower and holding two branches of the lotus in his hands. On each side of him there are three lotus flowers, of which the four nearer ones support pairs of Brahmani Geese, while the two farther ones carry only single birds. Over the nearest pair of geese, on the right hand of the figure, there is a frog. The attitudes of the birds are all good, and even that of the human figure is easy, although formal. The lotus scroll with its flowing lines of graceful stalk, mingled with tender buds and full blown flowers, and delicate leaves, is very rich and very beautiful. Below the ornamental borders there are three plain projecting bands.

I employed two expert masons for twelve months in making full-size drawings of the whole of these bands of ornament. Two plates of the east south-east and south south-west sides were afterwards engraved in Calcutta under my own guidance, for publication by James Prinsep in the Asiatic Researches; but his lamented illness put a sudden stop to the work, as his successor, Mr. Curnin, would not allow the mint engraver to continue it.

Near the top of the north-west face there are four projecting stones placed like steps, that is, they are not immediately over each other, and above them there is a fifth stone which is pierced with a round hole for the reception of a post, or more probably of a flag-staff. The lowest of these stones can only be reached by a ladder, but ladders must have been always available, if, as I suppose, it was customary on stated occasions to fix flags and steamers on various parts of the building, in the same manner as is now done in the Buddhist countries of Burmah and Ladák.

With the single exception of the Táj Mahal at Agra, there is, perhaps, no Indian building that has been so often described as the great Buddhist tower near Sárnáth. But strange to say, its dimensions have always been very much under-stated, although the circumference might have been very closely ascertained with the greatest ease in a few minutes, by measuring, either with a walking stick or with the fore-arm, the breadth of one projecting face and of one recess, which together form one-eighth of the whole. H. H. Wilson, quoting Wilford, states that "Sárnáth is about 50 feet high, and may be as many paces in circumference." Miss Emma Roberts states that it is "about 150 feet in circumference," and "above 100 feet in height." Mr. Fergusson calls it between 50 and 60 feet in diameter, and 110 feet in height. This last statement of the height is correct, having been taken from a note of mine, which was published by Mr. Thomas in the Bengal Asiatic Society's Journal. This height was carefully measured by myself with an iron chain in January 1835, by means of the scaffolding which I had put up for the purpose of opening the tower. By a previous measurement with a theodolite I had found the height to be 109 feet 10 inches. The breadth of one projecting face and of one recess is 36 feet 6 inches, which multiplied by 8 gives 292 feet as the circumference, and a trifle less than 93 feet as the diameter, or nearly double the thickness stated by any one of the authorities just quoted.

On the 18th January 1835 my scaffolding was completed, and I stood on the top of the great tower. On cutting the long grass I found two iron spikes, each 8 inches long, and shaped like the head of a lance. On the following day I removed the ruined brick pinnacle and began sinking a shaft or well, about 5 feet in diameter. At 3 feet from the top I found a rough stone, 24 inches x 15 inches x 7 inches, and on the 25th January, at a depth of 10½ feet, I found an inscribed slab 28¾ inches long, 13 inches broad, and 4¾ inches thick, which is now in the Museum of the Bengal Asiatic Society. The inscription consists of the usual Buddhist formula or profession of faith beginning with the words "*Ye Dharmma hetu prabhavá, &c.*," of which translations have been given by Mill, Hodgson, Wilson, and Burnouf. The following is Hodgson's translation, which has received the approval of Burnouf: "Of all things proceeding from cause, their causes hath the *Tathágata* (Buddha) explained. The Great Sramana (Buddha) hath likewise explained the causes of the cessation of existence." The letters of this inscription, which are all beautifully cut, appear to me to be of somewhat earlier date than the Tibetan alphabet, which is known to have been obtained from India in the middle of the 7th century. I would, therefore, assign the inscription, and consequently the completion of the monument, to the 6th century.[*]

On the 22nd January I began to excavate a horizontal gallery on the level of the top of the stone-work, and on the 14th of February, at a distance of 44 feet, the gallery joined the shaft, which had been sunk from above. As I now found that the upper course of stone was only a facing, I sank the

[*] See Bengal Asiatic Society's Journal, 1835, p. 133, for different translations, and Plate IX. for a copy of the inscription. The original stone is now in the Museum of the Asiatic Society in Calcutta.

gallery itself down to the level of the stone-work, and continued it right through to the opposite site. I thus discovered that the mass of the inner stone-work was only 33 feet in height, while the outer stone-work was 43 feet. In the middle, however, there was a pillar of stone-work, rising 6 feet higher than the inner mass. This was, perhaps, used as a point from which to describe the circle with accuracy. Small galleries were also made to reach the tops of the east and west faces, but nothing was discovered by these works.

The labor of sinking the shaft through the solid stone-work was very great, as the stones which were large (from 2 to 3 feet in length, 18 inches broad, and 12 inches thick) were all secured to each other by iron cramps. Each stone had usually eight cramps, four above, and as many below, all of which had to be cut out before it could be moved. I therefore sent to Chunar for regular quarrymen to quarry out the stones, and the work occupied them for several months. At length, at a depth of 110 feet from the top of the monument, the stone gave place to brick-work, made of very large bricks. Through this the shaft was continued for a further depth of 28 feet, when I reached the plain soil beneath the foundation. Lastly, a gallery was run right through the brick-work of the foundation, immediately below the stone-work, but without yielding any result.

Thus ended my opening of the great tower after 14 months' labour, and at a cost of more than Rs. 500. When I began the work I was not aware that many of the most hallowed of the Buddhist Monuments were only memorial *stupas*, raised over spots rendered famous by various acts of Buddha, such as we know from Hwen Thsang's account was the great tower near Banáras, which was erected by Asoka near the spot where Buddha had begun to " turn the wheel of the law," that is, to preach his new doctrine. The " tower of the Deer Park near Banáras" is likewise enumerated by another Chinese author as one of the " eight divine towers" erected on sites where Buddha had accomplished "many important acts of his terrestrial career," the particular act which he had accomplished at Banáras being his preaching. This tower was seen by Fa-Hian in the beginning of the 5th century, who notices that Buddha, when he began to "turn the wheel of the law," sat down looking towards the west. Now, on the western face of the great tower there is a small plain tablet, which, as I have said before, could only have been intended for some very short inscription, such as the name either of the tower itself, or of the event which it was intended to commemorate. But, whatever it may have been intended for, its position was no doubt significant, and, as at Buddha Gaya, where Sâkya had been seated facing the east, his statue was placed in the same position, so at Banâras, where, when he began to preach he had been seated facing the west, his statue must have been placed in the same direction. I conclude that the western face of the monument erected to commemorate that event would have been the principal side, and that any inscription would certainly have been placed on that side.

It now only remains to notice the name by which this great tower is known amongst the people of the neighbouring villages. This name is *Dhamek*, of which no one knows the meaning. It is evidently some compound of *Dharmma*, and, bearing in mind that on this spot Buddha first began to "turn the wheel of the law," I would suggest that *Dhamek* is only an abbreviation of the Sanskrit *Dharmmopadesaka* or "Preacher of *Dharmma*," which is, indeed, the common term now in use to designate any religious teacher. The term is also used in the simpler form of *Dharmma desaka*, which, in familiar conversation, would naturally be shortened to *Dhamadek* and *Dhamek*. The special fitness of this name for the great tower in the Deer Park at Banâras is so obvious and striking, that I think it needless to offer any further remarks on the subject.

At a distance of 520 feet to the westward of *Dhamek*, there is a large circular hole, upwards of 50 feet in diameter, surrounded by a very thick brick wall. This is the ruin of the large brick *stupa* which was excavated by Bábû Jagat Singh, the Dewân of Râja Chait Singh, of Banâras, for the purpose of obtaining bricks for the erection of Jagatganj. In January 1794 his workmen found, at a depth of 27 feet, two vessels of stone and marble, one inside the other. The inner vessel, according to Jonathan Duncan's account,[*] contained a few human bones, some decayed pearls, gold leaves, and other jewels of no value. In the "same place" underground, and on the "same occasion," with the discovery of the urns, there was found a statue of Buddha, bearing an

---

[*] Asiatic Researches, V., p. 131.

inscription dated in *Samvat* 1083, or A. D. 1026. An imperfect translation of this inscription was given by Wilford, accompanied by some remarks, in which he applies the statements of the record to the great tower of Dhamek, instead of to the building in which it was actually discovered.*

At my suggestion Major Kittoe made a search for this statue amongst the plundered stones of Jagatganj, where it was found broken and mutilated. The inscription, however, was still legible, and the remains of the figure are sufficient to show that the statue was a representation of Buddha the Preacher, and not of Buddha the Ascetic. Major Kittoe sent me a transcript of the inscription in modern Nágari, which I strongly suspect to have been *Brahmanized* by his BanArus Pandits. In its modern Nágari form, as translated for me, it records that "*Mahi Pála*, Rája of *Gauda*, having worshipped the lotus-like foot of Sri *Dhámurási* ("heap of light" ? Buddha) grown in the lake of Váránasi, and having for its moss the hair of prosperous kings, caused to be erected in Kási hundreds of *Isána* and *Chitraghanta*. Sri *Sthira Pala* and his younger brother, Sri *Vasanta Pala*, having restored religion, raised this tower with an inner chamber and eight large niches.†" Wilford read *Bhupálu* instead of Isána, but I am unable to offer any conjecture as to the true reading, as I know not where the original is now deposited. Major Kittoe's facsimile of the inscription is, perhaps, amongst those deposited by him in the Asiatic Society's Museum.

My reasons for fixing on the large round hole, 520 feet to the west of the great tower, as the site of the stupa excavated by Jagat Singh, are the following: In 1835, when I was engaged in opening the great tower itself, I made repeated enquiries regarding the scenes of Jagat Singh's discovery. Every one had heard of the finding of a stone box which contained bones, and jewels, and gold, but every one professed ignorance of the locality. At length, an old man named *Sangkar*, an inhabitant of the neighbouring village of Singhpur, came forward and informed me that, when he

---

* Asiatic Researches, IX, 204.

† *Isána* means "light, splendour," and was probably the technical name of a "lamp-pillar" for illumination. *Chitraghanta* means a variegated or "ornamented bell." I would, therefore, translate the two words as "lamp-pillars and ornamental bells." *Gauda* is the name of the country to the north of the Ghághra River. *Gauda* was also the name of the old capital of Bengal.

was a boy, he had been employed in the excavations made by Jagat Singh, and that he knew all about the discovery of the jewels, &c. According to his account the discovery consisted of two boxes, the outer one being a large round box of common stone, and the inner one a cylindrical box of green marble about 15 inches in height and 5 or 6 inches in diameter. The contents of the inner box were 40 to 46 pearls, 1 ½ rubies, 8 silver and 9 gold earrings *(karn phul)*, and three pieces of human arm bone. The marble box was taken to the Bará Sáhib (Jonathan Duncan), but the stone box was left undisturbed in its original position. As the last statement evidently afforded a ready means of testing the man's veracity, I enquired if he could point out the spot where the box was left. To this question he replied without any hesitation in the affirmative, and I at once engaged him to dig up the box. We proceeded together to the site of the present circular hole, which was then a low uneven mound in the centre of a hollow, and, after marking out a small space about 4 feet in diameter, he began to work. Before sunset he had reached the stone box at a depth of 12 feet, and at less than 2 feet from the middle of the well which he had sunk. The box was a large circular block of common Chunar sand-stone, pierced with a rough cylindrical chamber in the centre, and covered with a flat slab as a lid. I presented this box, along with about 60 statues, to the Bengal Asiatic Society, and it is now in their Museum, where I lately recognized it. In their catalogue, however, it is described as "042B, a Sarcophagus found in the tope of *Manikyala* (!); Donor, Lieutenant A. Cunningham."

The discovery of the stone box was the most complete and convincing proof that I could wish for of the man's veracity, and I at once felt satisfied that the relics and the inscribed figure of Buddha found by Jagat Singh's workmen had been discovered on this spot, and consequently that they could not possibly have any connexion with the great tower of *Dhamek*. My next object was to ascertain the nature of the building in which the box was deposited. As I had found the box standing on solid brick-work, I began to clear away the rubbish, expecting to find a square chamber similar to those which had been discoverd in the topes of Afghanistan. My excavations, however, very soon showed that, if any chamber had once existed, it must have been demolished by

Jagnt Singh's workmen. Sangkar then described that the box was found in a small square hole or chamber only just large enough to hold it. I cleared out the whole of the rubbish until I reached the thick circular wall which still exists. I then found that the relic box had been deposited inside a solid brick hemispherical *stupa*, 40 feet in diameter at the level of the deposit, and that this had been covered by a casing wall of brick, 10½ feet in thickness; the total diameter at this level was, therefore, 82 feet. The solid brick-work of the interior had only been partially excavated by Jagnt Singh's workmen, nearly one-half of the mass, to a height of 6 feet above the stone box, being then untouched. I made some excavations round the outer wall to ascertain its thickness, but I left the brick-work undisturbed.

About 18 years afterwards, the excavation of this stupa was continued by Major Kittoo and Mr. Thomas until the whole of the inner mass had been removed, and the foundation of the outer casing exposed. The inner diameter is given by Mr. Thomas as 40 feet 6 inches, the slight excess over my measurement being due to the thickness of a base moulding of the original stupa. I have again carefully examined the remains of this monument, and I am quite satisfied that in its original state it was an ancient hemispherical stupa, 40 feet in diameter at base, and about 35 or 40 feet in height, including the usual pinnacle. Afterwards, when, as I suppose, the upper portion had become ruinous, it was repaired by the addition of a casing wall 10½ feet in thickness. The diameter of the renewed edifice thus became 82 feet, while the height, inclusive of a pinnacle, could not have been less than 50 feet.

On a review of all the facts connected with this ruin, I incline to the opinion that the inner hemisphere was an ancient relic *stupa*, and that this having become ruinous, it was repaired, and an outer casing added by the brothers *Sthira Pála* and *Vasanta Pála* in A. D. 1026. In the *Mahāwanso* we find the record of similar additions having been made to some of the *stupas* in Ceylon, and I know from personal inspection that many of the great *Dhagopas* of Burmah have been increased in size by subsequent additions.

Due south from the great tower of Dhamek, and at a distance of 2,500 feet, there is a lofty ruined mound of solid

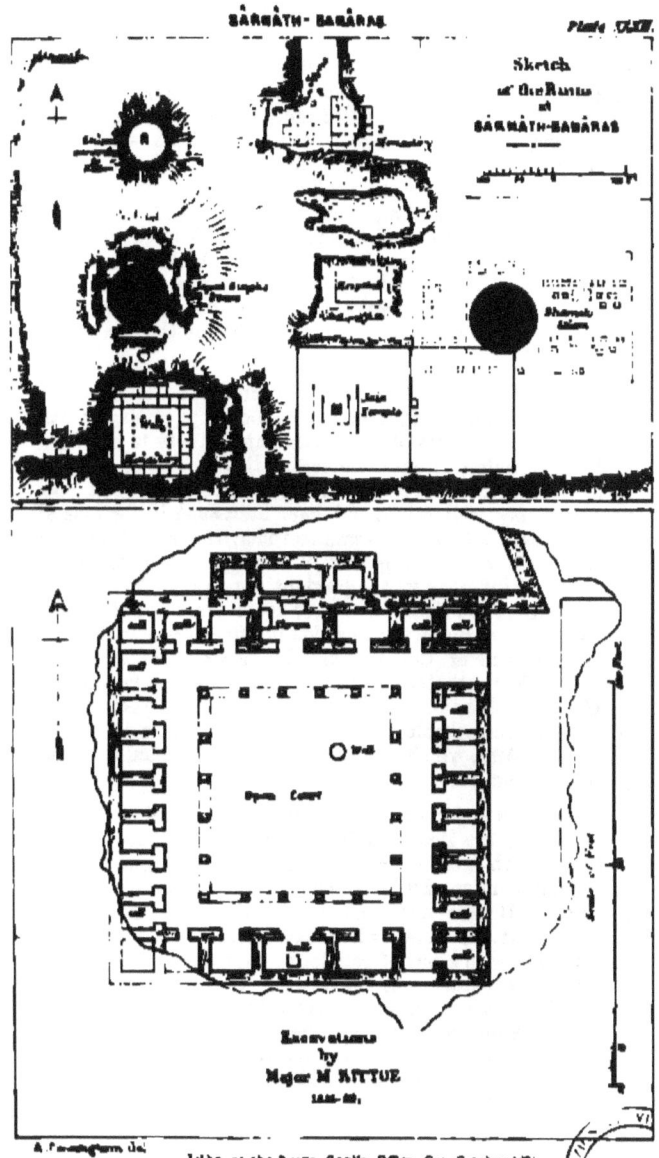

brickwork, surmounted by an octagonal building. When I first lived at Banáras, this mound was always known by the name of *Chaukandi*, of which no one knew the meaning. But during my late visit I found that the old name was nearly forgotten, having been superseded by *Luri-ka-kodan* or "Luri's leap." *Luri* was an *Ahir*, who jumped from the top of the octagonal building some years ago, and was killed. The mound itself is 74 feet in height to the floor of the octagonal building which rises 23 feet 8 inches higher, making a total height of 97 feet and 8 inches. An inscription over one of the door-ways of the building records that it was built in the reign of *Humáyun*, as a memorial of the emperor's ascent of the mound.

In 1835 I opened this mound by sinking a well from the floor of the building right down to the plain earth beneath the foundation. I also drove a horizontal gallery to meet the well about half way up the ascent. But as neither of these excavations resulted in any discovery, I then thought it possible that my well might not have been sunk in the axis of the building. I therefore began to widen the well from the point of junction of the gallery until it was nearly 20 feet in diameter. This work was stopped at a depth of 27 feet by my departure from Banáras. I have again examined this ruin, and I am now quite satisfied that my first well was sunk in the very centre of the mound. The absence of any relic chamber shows that this was not a relic tower, a conclusion which is fully borne out by Hwen Thsang's description of one of the most remarkable of the sacred edifices near the Deer Park at Banáras, which, I believe, may be identified with the *Chaukandi* mound.

At 2 or 3 *li* (or rather less than half a mile) to the south-west of the Deer Park Monastery, Hwen Thsang places a *stupa* which was no less than 300 feet in height.* This lofty monument sparkled with the rarest and most precious materials. It was not ornamented with rows of niches, neither had it the usual bell-shaped cupola, but its summit was crowned with a sort of religious vase, turned upside down, on the top of which was an arrow. This is the whole of Hwen Thsang's account of this remarkable building, which, although too meagre to gratify curiosity, is still sufficient for

---

* Julien's Hwen Thsang, II., p. 363.

the purpose of identification. In position it agrees almost exactly with that of the great brick mound of *Chaukandi*, which I have just described. The distance of this last from the ruined mound on which the village of Barábipur stands, and which I have already identified with the position of the Deer Park Monastery, is just half a mile, but the direction is south south-west instead of south-west. With regard to size, it is difficult to say what may have been the height of the *Chaukandi* edifice. My excavations have proved that the centre of the present mound is all solid brick-work; but the subsequent explorations of Major Kittoe have brought to light three immense straight walls about mid-way up the eastern side, and two more on the western side, which have all the appearance of gigantic buttresses. Now, as these walls could not possibly have been required for the stability of the great solid mass below, it seems not unreasonable to conclude that they must in some way have been connected with the support of the upper portion of the building, which no longer exists. Hwen Thsang's account is somewhat vague, but I believe his intention was to describe a dome or cupola narrowed at the base, like the neck of a religious vase reversed. He distinctly states that it was not a bell-shaped cupola, that is, the dome did not spread outwards in the form familiar to us in the great *Dhagopas* of Rangoon and Pegu. An excellent illustration of the reversed vase form may be seen in a rock-cut temple at Ajanta, given by Fergusson.*

I will conclude this notice of the remains at Sárnáth Danáms with a short account of the excavations which have been made at different times during the last seventy years in the vicinity of the great tower of Dhamek.

The earliest excavations of which we possess any record were those made by Bábá Jagat Singh in 1793-94, for the purpose of obtaining materials, both stones and bricks, for the erection of a market-place, in the city, which was named after himself, *Jagatganj*. I have already noticed his discovery, in January 1794, of the two stone boxes containing a few bones, with some decayed pearls and slips of gold. A brief account of this discovery was published by Jonathan

---

* Hand-book of Architecture, I, p. 20.

Duncan,* and a more detailed notice by Wilford in a later volume of the same work. I can add little to their accounts, except that the original green stone vase, which Jonathan Duncan presented to the Asiatic Society in 1794, had disappeared before 1834, when I wrote to James Prinsep about it. I may mention also, on the authority of the work-people, that the dilapidated state of the lower part of the Dhamek Tower is due entirely to the meanness of Jagat Singh, who, to save a few rupees in the purchase of new stones, deliberately destroyed the beautiful facing of this ancient tower. As each stone was slowly detached from the monument by cutting out all the iron cramps by which it was secured to its neighbours, the actual saving to the Bábú could have been but little; but the defacement to the tower was very great, and, as the stones were removed at once, the damage done to the tower is quite irreparable.

Jagat Singh's discovery would appear to have stimulated the curiosity of the British officers, for Miss Emma Roberts, writing in 1834, relates that "some 40 or 50 years ago" (that is, about 1794) " the ruins near Sárnáth attracted the attention of several scientific gentlemen, and they commenced an active research by digging in many places around. Their labours were rewarded by the discovery of several excavations filled with an immense number of flat tiles, having representations of Buddha modelled upon them in wax. It is said that there were actually cart loads of these images found in the excavations before mentioned. Many were deposited in the Museums and collections of private individuals; but whether they were ever made the subject of a descriptive account seems doubtful, there being at least no public document of the kind."† I can add nothing to Miss Roberts' account, as all my enquiries have failed to discover any of the wax seals of Buddha above mentioned. I may note, however, that in the temples of Ladák I have seen small chambers quite full of similar little figures of deceased Lámas. In Burmah also I have seen small figures of Buddha in burnt clay accumulated in heaps equal to cart loads, both in the caves and in the temples. The figured seals discovered near Sárnáth would appear to have been of a similar kind to those which I extracted from the ruined building close to

---

* Asiatic Researches, V., p. 131.   † Views in India, &c., II., p. 8.

Jarasandha's Tower at Giryek, and also to those which I have described as having been found in the ruins at Bakror, opposite to Buddha Gaya.

The next excavations, as far as I am aware, were those undertaken by myself in 1835-36. These excavations, as well as the drawings of the elaborate ornament of the great tower, were made entirely at my own expense, the cost during 18 months having been Rs. 1,200. I made several desultory excavations wherever I saw traces of walls, but they all proved to belong to temporary habitations of a late period. At last, after a heavy fall of rain, I observed a piece of terraced floor which I ordered to be cleared for the purpose of pitching my tent upon it. After a few hours' labour, however, the flooring terminated on what appeared to be the edge of a small tank, which was only 19 feet 9 inches square. Continuing the work, I found the bases of pillars in pairs surrounding the square. Amongst the rubbish inside the square, I found an elaborately sculptured bas-relief, in grey standstone, representing the *Nirvāna* of Buddha. The stone had been broken into four pieces, of which one was missing, but the remaining three pieces are now in the Calcutta Museum. This sculpture, I consider, particularly interesting, as the subject is treated in a novel and striking manner. In the ordinary representations of the death-bed scene, the spectators are confined to a few attendants, who hold umbrellas over the body or reverentially touch the feet. But in the present sculpture, besides the usual attendants, there are the *Navagraha* or "Nine Planets" in one line, and in a lower line, the *Ashta Sakte* or "eight female energies," a series of goddesses apparently belonging to one of the later forms of Buddhism. This sculpture is well worthy of being photographed.

Further excavation showed that the small pillared tank, or court-yard, was the centre of a large building, 68 feet square, of which the outer walls were 4½ feet thick. My exploration was not completed to the eastward, as the walls of the building in that direction had been entirely removed by some previous excavation, with the exception of detached portions of the foundation, sufficient to show that it corresponded exactly with the western half of the building. The central square was apparently surrounded by an open verandah, which gave access to ranges of five small rooms or cells

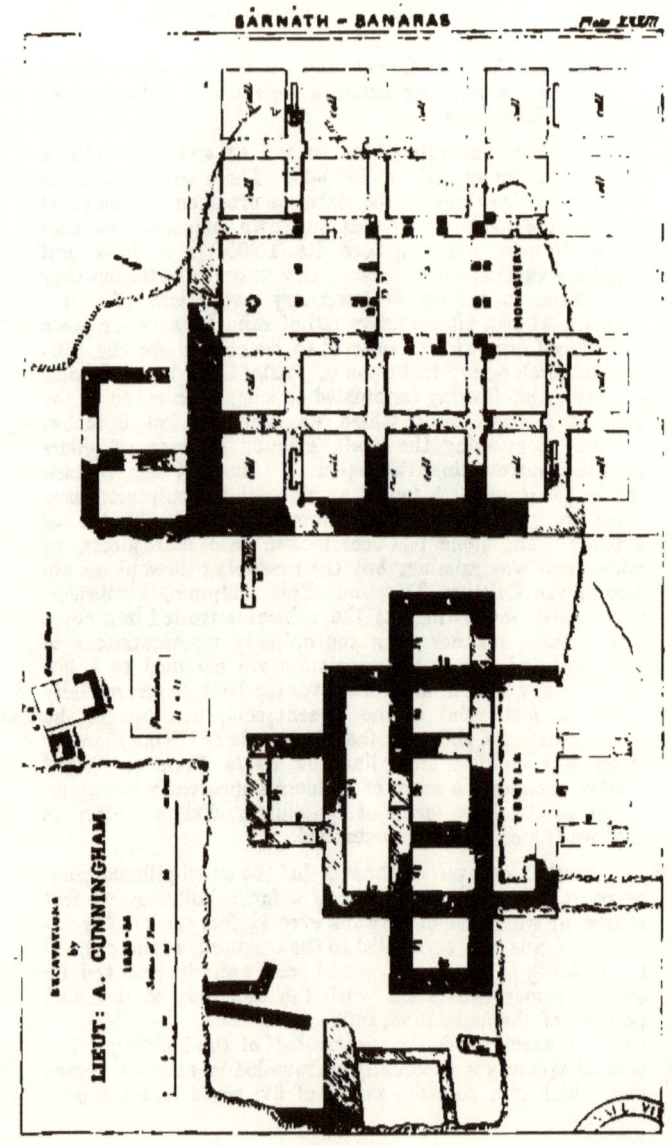

each of the four sides of the building. In all the cells I
found pieces of charred wood, with nails still sticking in
some of them, and in the middle cell on the western side I
found a small store of unhusked rice only partially burnt.
In a few places I found what appeared to be pieces of terraced roofing, and in one place a large heap of charcoal. On
the south side the central room was lost by previous excavation, but on the north side I found a room entirely open
towards the verandah, as if it was a hall, or place of general
meeting for the resident monks. Inside this room there was
the base or pedestal of what I believe to have been a small
votive *stupa*, the top of which probably reached to the roof
and took the place of a pillar. A small drain led underground from the north-west corner of the central square to
the outside of the building on the north, for the purpose, as
I conclude, of carrying off the rain-water.*

The building which I have just described would appear
to have been a *Vihára*, of "Chapel Monastery," that is, a
monastery with a chapel or temple forming an integral part
of the building. From the thickness of the outer wall I
infer that this edifice was not less than three or four stories
in height, and that it may have accommodated about 60
monks. The entrance was probably on the south side, and I
think that there must have been a statue of Buddha in the
northern verandah. The bas-relief which I found in the
central square almost certainly formed one of the middle
architraves of the court.

Continuing my excavations in the high ground to the
westward, I came upon the remains of a building of a totally
different description. The walls of this edifice were 3 feet
thick throughout, and I found the plaster still adhering to
the inner walls of what I will call the verandahs, with
borders of painted flowers, quite fresh and vivid. The mass
of the building consisted of a square of 34 feet, with a small
porch on each of the four side. The building was divided
into three parts from west to east, and the central part was
again sub-divided into three small rooms. I think it probable that these three rooms were the shrines of the Buddhist
Triad *Dharmma*, *Buddha*, and *Sangha*, and that the walls of

---

* See Plate XXXII. for the plans of three buildings. The position is marked by
the letter P. in the sketch of the ruins in Plate XXXI.

the two long rooms or verandahs to the north and south were covered with statues and bas-reliefs. The entrance verandah of one of the vihár caves at *Kánhari*, in Salsette, is adorned in a similar manner; and even in the present day the inner walls of the temples, both in Ladák and in Barmah, are covered with figures of Buddha. This also, as we know from Hwen Thsang's account, was the style of the walls of the great vihár in the Deer Park at this very place, and a similar style of ornamentation prevailed both at Buddha Gaya and at Nálanda. Outside the walls also I found a great number, about 50 or 60, of large deeply carved stones, which had once formed part of a magnificent frieze, with a bold projecting cornice. The face of the frieze was ornamented with small figures of Buddha seated at intervals in peculiar shaped niches, which I have traced from the rock hewn caves of Dhamnár, in Malwa, to the picturesque but fantastic *Kyoungs* of Burmah. A few of these stones may now be seen in the grounds of the Sanskrit College at Banáras. As I found no traces of burnt wood, I am inclined to believe that the roof of the building was pyramidal, and that the general appearance of the edifice must have been strikingly similar to that of the great temple of Brambanan, depicted in the 2nd Volume of Raffles' Java.

Whilst engaged in excavating the walls of this temple, I was informed by *Sangkar*, Rájbhar of Singpur, the same man who had pointed out to me the position of the relic box in Jagat Singh's *stupa*, that, whilst he was engaged in digging materials for Jagatganj, the workmen had come upon a very large number of statues, all collected together in a small building. The walls were pulled down and the bricks were carried away, but the statues were left untouched in their original position. I at once commenced an excavation on the spot pointed out by Sangkar, which was only a few feet to the north of the temple just described. At a depth of 2 feet below the surface, I found about 60 statues and bas-reliefs in an upright position, all packed closely together within a small space of less than 10 feet square. The walls of the building in which they had been thus deposited had been removed as stated by Sangkar, but the remains of the foundation showed a small place of only 11 feet square outside. I made a selection of the more perfect figures which, together with the bas-reliefs, I presented to the Asiatic

SÁRNÁTH-BANÁRAS.

Society. A sketch of the principal bas-relief, which represents the four great events in the career of Sákya Muni, has been published by M. Foucaux.* A second bas-relief represents the same four scenes, but on a smaller scale. A third bas-relief, which gives only three scenes, omitting the *Nirvána*, has a short inscription below in two lines, which records the sculpture to have been the gift of Hari Gupta. The characters of this inscription, which are of the later Gupta type, shows that this piece of sculpture is certainly as old as the 3rd or 4th century. A fourth bas-relief gives five scenes, the additional scene being the conception of Máyá Devi on the appearance of the *Chhadanta* Elephant. Some of the seated figures were in excellent preservation, and more particularly one of Buddha the Teacher, which was in perfect condition, and coloured of a warm red hue. The remaining statues, upwards of 40 in number, together with most of the other carved stones which I had collected, and which I left lying on the ground, were afterwards carted away by the late Mr. Davidson and thrown into the Barna River under the bridge to check the cutting away of the bed between the arches.

As the room in which I found all these sculptures was only a small detached building, and as it was quite close to the large temple which I have just described, I conclude that the whole of the sculptures must have belonged to the temple, and that they were secreted in the place where I discovered them, during a time of persecution, when the monks were obliged to abandon their monasteries and take refuge in Nepál. This conclusion is partly borne out by the fact that I found no statues within the walls of the temple itself.

To the north of the temple, at a distance of 26 feet, my excavations uncovered a large single block of stone, 6 feet in length, by 3 feet in height, and the same in thickness. The stone had been carefully squared, and was hollowed out underneath, forming a small chamber, 4 feet in length, by 2 feet in breadth, and the same in height.† This large stone has also disappeared, which is the more to be regretted, as I think it highly probable that it was the celebrated stone,

---

* Translation of the Tibetan History of Buddha, Plate I.
† See sketch of the ruins in Plate XXXII, letter Q. This stone has now disappeared.

described by Hwen Thsang, on which Buddha had spread out his *kasháya* to dry after washing it in the neighbouring tank. Certain marks on the stone appeared to the Buddhists to represent the thread lines of the web of Buddha's cloth "as distinctly as if they had been chiselled." Devout Buddhists offered their homage before the stone daily; but whenever heretics, or wicked man, crowded round the stone in a contemptuous manner, then the dragon *(Nága)* of the neighbouring tank let loose upon them a storm of wind and rain.*

My excavations at Sárnáth were brought to a close suddenly by my removal to Calcutta. Luckily I had prepared plans of the buildings while the exhumation was going on, for nothing whatever now remains of all my excavations, every stone and every brick having been removed long ago.

The last excavations at Sárnáth were made at the expense of Government under the personal superintendence of Major Kittoe. On his departure for England in January 1853, in ill health, he carried away all his measurements and memoranda for the purpose of compiling an account of his discoveries for publication. His continued ill health and early death effectually prevented fulfilment of this intention, and no one, as far as I can learn, knows what has become of his papers. His drawings, which were numerous and valuable, were sent to the India House Museum by Mr. Thomason. One of them has since been published in 1855 by Mr. Fergusson, and another in 1850 by Mrs. Spiers.† Major Kittoe's inscriptions were entrusted to the charge of the Asiatic Society in Calcutta, evidently in deposit for the sake of safety, as he hoped to return again to India, and to prepare them for publication with his own hand.

My account of Major Kittoe's discoveries must necessarily be brief, as the only information which I possess is contained in a long letter from himself, dated 10th May 1852, and in Mr. Thomas' "Note on the excavations at Sárnáth."‡ In writing to Major Kittoe previously, I had mentioned the

---

* Julien's Hwen Thsang, II., 360.

† See "Handbook of Architecture," Vol. I., p. 7, and "Life in Ancient India," p. 267. I have since seen these drawings in the Library at the India Office. They number about 150, but their value is much impaired by the general want of names and descriptive titles.

‡ Bengal Asiatic Society's Journal, 1854, p. 469.

three stupas which I had myself opened, and which I have already described. In reply he wrote—" How do you make out *three* towers at Sárnáth ? I make out *four*, to say nothing of innumerable smaller affairs down to the size of a walnut, which I have laid bare." Attached to this he gave a rough sketch of the ground, showing the position of the fourth tower to be immediately to the north of Jagat Singh's stupa, where I have accordingly inserted it, on his authority, in my survey of the ruins. Further on he writes—" I have laid bare *chaityas* upon *chaityas*, four and five deep, built one over the other." In another place he describes the oblong courtyard which was excavated by himself at a distance of 125 feet to the westward of the great tower, as a "large quadrangle, or *hospital*, for I have found pestles and mortars (*sills* or flat stones for mashing), *loongas*, &c., &c." This is the quadrangle marked Z. in my plan of the ruins. It is 60 feet long from west to east, and 42 feet broad, and is surrounded by a low wall 3 feet thick and 1½ foot high above the level of the terraced floor, parts of which still remain. Fixed in this wall are the stumps of twelve stone pillars, which are split in all directions as if destroyed by fire. I agree with Major Kittoe in thinking that this quadrangle is probably the ruin of a hospital.

In reply to a question about stone umbrellas, Major Kittoe wrote to me as follows: "I have got hold of two, one in fragments (*burnt*), of say 6 feet diameter, mushroom-shaped, and another, *also burnt*, but not broken, elegantly carved in scroll on the inside, but nearly defaced by the action of saltpetre."

Of the great tower itself, Major Kittoe's opinion was, that " the arrangement was precisely the same as at Rangoon, rows and rows of small temples, umbrellas, pillars, &c., around the great tope. They all run north and south, and east and west, large and small." To this account he added a small rough sketch showing the arrangement of the smaller stupas about the great tower. This sketch I have inserted in my survey in dotted lines.* Judging from the arrangement of the subsidiary buildings about the great stupas of Burmah and Ladák, with which I am personally acquainted, I have every

---
* See sketch of the ruins in Plate XXXII.

reason to accept Major Kittoe's sketch as a correct outline of what he had himself ascertained by excavation; but as the sketch is not drawn to scale, the relative sizes and distances may not, perhaps, be quite accurate.

Of his other discoveries he wrote as follows : " I have got fine specimens of carved bricks and two heads of Buddha, made of pounded brick and road-earth coated with fine shell lime, in beautiful preservation. I have a fine head of a female in white marble (partly calcined), and a portion of the arm. It has been a nearly life-size figure of *Pàrvati*."

It will have been observed that every excavation made near Sárnáth has revealed traces of fire. I myself found charred timber and half burnt grain. The same things were also found by Major Kittoe, besides the evident traces of fire on the stone pillars, umbrellas, and statues. So vividly was the impression of a great final catastrophe by fire fixed in Major Kittoe's mind, by the discoveries made during his excavations that he thus summed up his conclusions to me in a few words : " *all has been sacked and burnt*, priests, temples, idols, all together. In some places, bones, iron, timber, idols, &c., are all fused into huge heaps; *and this has happened more than once*." Major Kittoe repeated this opinion in almost the same words when I saw him at Gwalior in September 1852. I will recur to this subject again before I conclude my account of the discoveries at Sárnáth.

On Major Kittoe's departure from Banáras, the excavations were continued at first under Mr. E. Thomas, and afterwards under Professor FitzEdward Hall. To the former gentleman we are indebted for a general account of the state of the excavations at the time of his assuming charge, and more especially for a very clear and interesting description of the ancient monastery which was then being exhumed, and of the various articles which were discovered within its precincts. This work was subsequently completed by Mr. Hall, and I have made a plan of the building as it now appears.* Mr. Thomas calls it an "old Buddhist monastery," and with this identification I fully agree. According to Hwen Thsang, there were no less than 30 monasteries about the Deer Park at Banáras, which together contained 3,000 monks, or an average of 100 monks each. Now the building under review

---

* See Plate XXXII., excavations by Major Kittoe, which were afterwards completed by Mr. Thomas and Dr. Hall.

contains no less than 28 separate apartments, and if one of these be set aside as a shrine for a statue of Buddha, and a second as a hall for teaching, there will remain 26 cells for the accommodation of monks. Again, judging from the thickness of the walls, I am of opinion that the building could not have been less than 3 or 4 storeys in height. Assuming the latter to have been the actual height, the building would have contained 104 cells, and, therefore, may possibly have been one of the 30 monasteries noted by Hwen Thsang.

The ground plan of the monastery shews a central court 50 feet square, surrounded by pillars which must have supported an open verandah or cloister in front of the four ranges of cells. In the north-east corner of the court-yard there is an old well, 4 feet 10 inches in diameter, and 37 feet deep. As this well is placed on one side, I infer that the middle of the court was occupied by a *stupa* or a statue, or more probably, perhaps, by a holy tree, as I could not find any traces of the foundation of a building. On the outside, the building is 107 feet square. In the centre room on the north side, which is 18 feet in length, there are two large stones placed against the walls as if intended for the reception of statues. This also was Mr. Thomas' opinion. This room, I believe, to have been the shrine of the monastery. In the centre room on the south side there is a "square, elaborately corniced block," which Mr. Thomas believed to have been the throne for a seated figure of Buddha. I incline, however, to the opinion that this was the seat of the teacher for the daily reading and expounding of the Buddhist Scriptures. The cells on each side of these two central rooms are somewhat larger than those on the eastern and western sides of the court, and were, therefore, probably assigned to the senior monks. The common cells are 8½ feet by 6 feet, and each has a separate door.

The ground plan of this monastery is similar to that of the large caves at Bágh and Ajanta, sketches of which have been given by Mr. Fergusson.* The plan is in fact almost identical with that of the Bágh Cave, the only difference being the want of cells in the cave monastery on the side

---

* Handbook of Architecture, I., pp. 33, 34.

opposite to the sanctuary, which was necessarily left open for the sake of affording light to the interior. The great cave at Junir is also similar in plan, but it is apparently of older date, as it wants the sanctuary opposite the entrance.

The destruction of this large monastery would appear to have been both sudden and unexpected, for Mr. Thomas records that Major Kittoe found "the remains of ready-made wheaten cakes in a small recess in the chamber towards the north-east angle of the square." Mr. Thomas himself also found portions of wheat and other grain spread out in one of the cells. These discoveries would seem to show that the conflagration had been so sudden and rapid as to force the monks to abandon their very food. Such also is Mr. Thomas' opinion, conveyed in the following vivid description: "The chambers on the eastern side of the square were "found filled with a strange medley of uncooked food, hastily "abandoned on their floors,—pottery of every-day life, nodes "of brass produced apparently by the melting down of the "cooking vessels in common use. Above these again were "the remnants of the charred timbers of the roof, with iron "nails still remaining in them, above which again appeared "broken bricks mixed with earth and rubbish to the height "of the extant walls, some 6 feet from the original flooring. "Every item here bore evidence of a complete conflagration, "and so intense seems to have been the heat that, in "portions of the wall still standing, the clay which formed "the substitute for lime in binding the brick-work is baked "to a similar consistency with the bricks themselves. In "short, all existing indications lead to a necessary inference "that the destruction of the building, by whomsoever caused, "was effected by fire applied by the hand of an exterminating "adversary, rather than by any ordinary accidental con-"flagration."*

This opinon was expressed by Mr. Thomas in 1854, before the whole of the monastery had been exhumed. A later account has since been published by Dr. Butter in 1856, who stated his opinion that "the burnt grain and masses of half fused iron discovered by Mr. Hall corroborate the

---

* Bengal Asiatic Society's Journal, 1854, p. 472.

conclusions drawn by previous explorers, that the monastery had been destroyed by fire."*

During my stay at Banáras, I examined the collection of articles found by Professor Hall in the various excavations which he conducted at Sárnáth, and which are now deposited in the Museum of the College. The only article requiring special notice is No. 18, an impression in burnt clay, of a seal 1½ inch in diameter with two lines of Sanskrit, surmounted by a lozenge-shaped device, with two recumbent deer as supporters. The device of the two deer is significant, as it no doubt shows that the seal must have belonged to some person or establishment attached to the monastery of the Deer Park. The end of the upper line and the whole of the lower line of the inscription are too much injured to be made out satisfactorily. The inscription begins with the word *Sri Saddharmma*, "the auspicious true *Dharmma*," and the letters at the end of the first line look very like *Rakshita* the "Preserver." This would be a man's name *Sri Saddharmma Rakshita*, "the Cherisher of the true Dharmma," a title not uncommon amongst the Buddhists. Of the lower line I am unable to suggest any probable rendering.

In the absence of any general plan of the ruins, showing the extent of the explorations carried on by Major Kittoe and his successors, I do not think it would be advisable to undertake any further excavations at Sárnáth, Banáras; I have already suggested that the ground immediately around the great tower should be levelled for the purpose of affording easy access to visitors.† In carrying out this operation, every fragment of sculpture should be carefully preserved, as I think it very probable that some portions of the statues, which once adorned the eight niches of the great tower, may be discovered in the masses of rubbish now lying in heaps at its foot. It might, perhaps, be worth while to make a few tentative excavations in the mass of ruins to the north and north-west of the great tower, by digging long narrow trenches from west to east, and from north to south. Should these trenches uncover the remains of any large buildings,

---

* Bengal Asiatic Society's Journal, 1856, p. 396.
† This clearance of the ruins around the great stupa has since been made by Mr. Horne, to a breadth of 25 feet.

the work might then be continued. But should nothing promising be discovered, I would recommend the immediate stoppage of the work.

Since this report was written, the Reverend Mr. Sherring has published a very full and interesting account of Banáras, in which a whole chapter is dedicated to the Buddhist ruins at Sárnáth.* In Appendix B, he has also given a translation of Hwen Thsang's description of the holy places at Banáras, which is a most valuable addition, as M. Julien's French translation is not easily procurable.

---

* See Chapter XVIII., p. 233 of "The Sacred City of the Hindus," an account of Banáras in ancient and modern times,—by the Reverend M. A. Sherring, with an introduction by Fitz Edward Hall, Esq.

Report of Operations of the Archæological Surveyor to the Government of India during season 1862-63.

NOTE.

In A. D. 634, when the Chinese pilgrim Hwen Thsang crossed the Satlaj from the westward, the first place that he visited was Po-li-ye-to-lo, or *Pariyatra*, which has been identified by M. St. Martin with *Vairát*, to the northward of Jaypur. This place I have not yet visited, as my explorations during the cold season of 1862-63 were confined to Delhi, Mathura, and Khálsi, on the line of the Jumna and to the ancient cities lying north of that river in the Gangetic Doab, Oudh, and Rohilkhand. In these provinces, I have followed Hwen Thsang's route from *Mathura* to *Srávasti;* and, with his aid, I have been successful in discovering the once famous cities of *Ahi-chhatra, Kosámbi, Sháchi,* and *Srávasti*. The sites of other celebrated places have likewise been determined with almost equal certainty, as *Srughna, Madipur, Govisana, Pilosana, Kusapura,* and *Dhopápapura*. I begin the account of my explorations at Delhi, which is the only place of note not visited by the Chinese pilgrim, whose route I take up at Mathura, and follow throughout Rohilkhand, the Doab, and Oudh. The places visited during this tour are accordingly described in the following order:

  I. Delhi.
  II. Mathura.
  III. Khálsi.
  IV. Madáwar, or *Madipur.*
  V. Káshipur, or *Govisana.*
  VI. Rámnagar, or *Ahi-chhatra.*
  VII. Soron, or *Sukrakshetra.*
  VIII. Atranjikhera, or *Pilosana.*
  IX. Sankisa, or *Sangkasya.*
  X. Kanoj, or *Kanyakubja.*
  XI. Kákupur, or *Ayuto.*
  XII. Daundiakhera, or *Hayamukha.*
  XIII. Allahabad, or *Prayága.*

XIV. Kosam, or *Kosámbi*.
XV. Sultánpur, or *Kusapura*.
XVI. *Dhopápapura*.
XVII. Ajudhya, or *Sákcta*.
XVIII. Hátila, or *Asokpur*.
XIX. Sahet-Mahet, or *Srávasti*.
XX. Tanda.
XXI. Nimsar.
XXII. Bári-khar.
XXIII. Dewal.
XXIV. Parasún Kot.
XXV. Bilai-khera.
XXVI. Kúbar.

I. DELHI.

The remains of Delhi are graphically described by Bishop Heber* as "a very awful scene of desolation, ruins after "ruins, tombs after tombs, fragments of brick-work, free- "stone, granite, and marble, scattered everywhere over a soil "naturally rocky and barren, without cultivation, except in "one or two small spots, and without a single tree." This waste of ruins extends from the south end of the present city of Shahjahánábád to the deserted forts of Rai Pithora and Tughlakabad, a distance of 10 miles. The breadth at the northern end, opposite Firuz Shah's Kotila, is about 3 miles, and at the southern end, from the Kutb Minar to Tughlakabad, it is rather more than 6 miles; the whole area covered with ruins being not less than 45 square miles. It is most probable, however, that not more than a third of this extent was ever occupied at any one period, as the present ruins are the remains of seven cities, which were built at different times by seven of the old Kings of Delhi.†

Other forts are recorded to have been built by the Emperors Balban, Kai-Kubád, and Mubárak; but there are no remains of them now existing, and the very sites of them are doubtful. It seems even probable that there were no remains of these three cities so far back as A. D. 1611, in the reign of Jahángir, when the English merchant, William Finch, travelling from Agra to Delhi, entered the Mogul

* Journal II., page 280.
† See Plate No. XXXV, for a map of the ruins at Delhi.

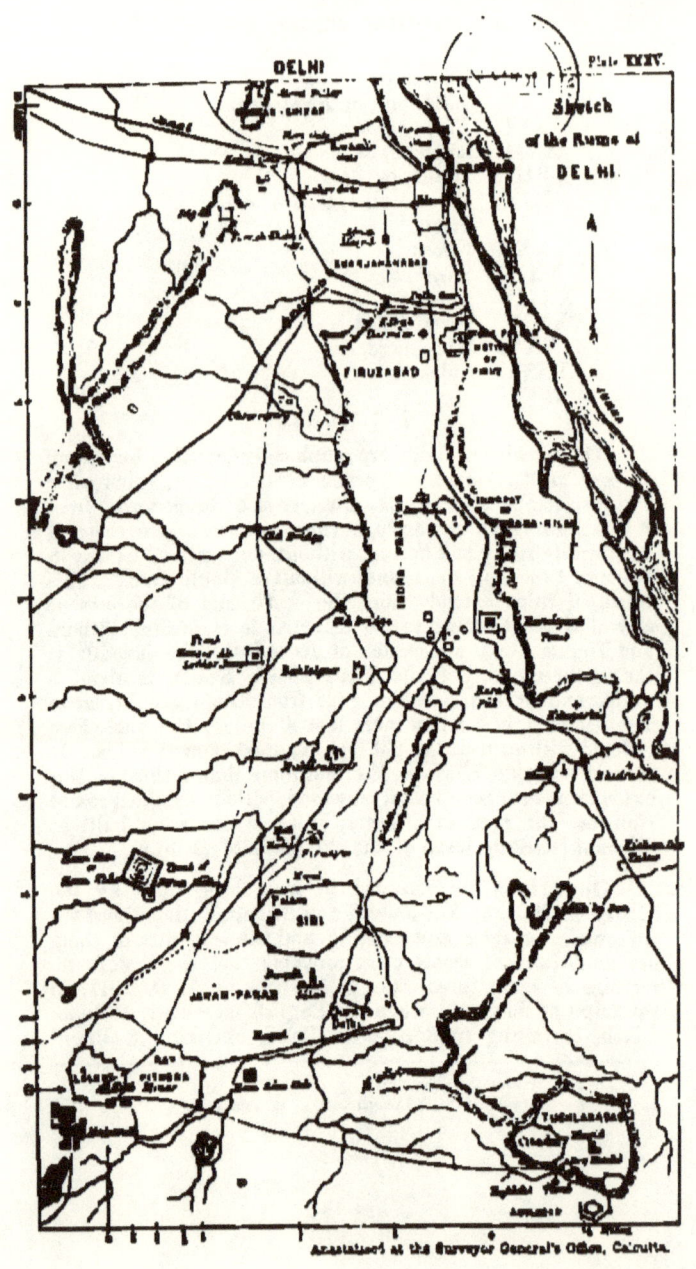

Capital from the south, for he states that on his *left* hand he saw the ruins of "*old Delhi, called the 7 castles and 52 gates,*" a name by which these ruins are still known in the present day. With regard to the work of the Emperor *Ghiás-uddin-Balban*, who reigned from A. D. 1266 to 1288, I think that too great importance has been attached to its name of *Kila* or fort. The Kila *Marzghan*, which Syad Ahmed places at *Ghiáspur*, near the tomb of *Nizám-uddin Aulia*, was built as an asylum, *marja*, or place of refuge for debtors. Now, this asylum for debtors was still existing in A. D. 1335 to 1340, when Ibn Batuta was one of the Magistrates of Delhi. He describes it as the *Dár-ul-aman*, or "House of Safety," and states that he visited the tomb of Balban, which was inside this *house*. From this, as well as from its name of *Dár-ul-aman*, I infer that the building was a walled enclosure of moderate size, perhaps not much larger than that which now surrounds the tomb of Tughlak Shah. This inference is rendered almost certain by Ibn Batuta's description of Delhi,* which, he says, "now consists of *four* cities, which becoming contiguous, have formed *one*." Now three of the four cities here alluded to are certainly those of *Rai Pithora*, *Jahán-panáh*, and *Siri* (of which the continuous walls can be easily traced even at the present day), and the fourth city must have been Tughlakabad. No particular date can be assigned to Jahán-panáh which was an open suburb until the time of Muhammad Tughlak, who first enclosed it with walls; but as Ibn Batuta was one of the Magistrates of Delhi under this Emperor, it is certain that Jahán-panáh must have been one of the four cities described by him. I feel quite satisfied, therefore, that the *Kila-Marzghan*, called also *Dár-ul-aman*, or "House of Refuge," was not a fortress, or large fortified city, but only a small walled enclosure surrounding his own tomb, and forming, at the same time, a place sufficiently large as an asylum for debtors and criminals.

The city of Kai-Kubád, called *Kilu-gharí*, was certainly situated on the bank of the Jumna,† where the name is still

---

* Travels, translated by Dr. Lee, p. 111.
† Gladwin's Ain Akbari, II., p. 86; and Brigg's Ferishta, I., p. 274.

found attached to a small village on the south-east of Humáyun's tomb. The new city of Mubárak, named Mubárakábád, was also situated on the bank of the Jumna.*

The "seven forts" of old Delhi, of which remains still exist, are, according to my view, the following:

1. —*Lálkot*, built by Anang Pál about A. D. 1052.
2. —*Kila Rai Pithora*, built by Rai Pithora about A. D. 1180.
3. —*Siri*, or *Kila-Alai*, built by Ala-uddin in A. D. 1304.
4. —*Tughlakabad*, built by Tughlak Shah in A. D. 1321.
5. —*Citadel* of Tughlakabad, ditto ditto.
6. —*Adilabad*, built by Muhammad Tughlak about A. D. 1325.
7. —*Jahán-Panáh*, enclosed by ditto.

In this list there is no mention of *Indraprastha*, because this celebrated capital of the Pándus is always described as being situated on the bank of the Jumna, which would have been on the right hand of the English traveller, and because the present fort of Indrapat, no doubt, represents some portion of the actual site, as well as the name of the famous city of Yudhishthira. *Indraprastha* and *Delhi* were, therefore, two different cities, situated about 5 miles apart,—the former on the bank of the Jumna above Humáyun's tomb, and the latter on a rocky hill to the south-west, surrounding the well known Iron Pillar. At the time of the Muhammadan conquest, the Hindu city of *Dilli* was confined to the two forts of *Lálkot* and Rai Pithora; but after Firuz Shah had moved the seat of Government to Firuzabad on the very site of the ancient *Indraprastha*, the name of *Dilli* was some times applied to the whole of the old city, including the Musalmán fort of *Siri* and the fortified suburbs of *Jahánpanáh*. Sharf-uddin, the historian of Timur, restricts the name of old Delhi to the two Hindu forts, and describes the cities of *Siri* and *Jahán-panáh* separately. Ferishta also does the same in his account of the latter kings of the Tughlak dynasty. But after Humáyun had re-built *Indrapat*,

---

* Brigg's Ferishta I. p. 5 829; see also the contemporary statement of the author of the Tárikh-i-Mubárak Sháhí, quoted by Mr. Thomas—"Chronicles of the Pathán Kings, p. 332, note.

under the name of *Din-panáh*, and after Shir Shah had founded his fort of *Kila-Shir-Shah* on the site of Firuzabad and Indraprastha, the common people began to use the names of old Delhi and new Delhi—the former being confined to the cluster of cities about the Hindu *Dilli*, while the latter was applied to those situated on the Jumna, on the site of the ancient Indraprastha.

Indraprastha or *Indrapat*.—At the time of the *Mahábhárata*, or "Great War" between the Pándus and Kurus, this was one of the well known five *pats* or *prasthas* which were demanded from Duryodhan by Yudhisthira as the price of peace. These five *pats* which still exist, were *Pánipat Sonpat, Indrpat, Tilpat*, and *Bághpat*, of which all but the last were situated on the right or western bank of the Jumna. The term *prastha*, according to H. H. Wilson, means anything "spread out or extended," and is commonly applied to any level piece of ground, including also tableland on the top of a hill. But its more literal and restricted meaning would appear to be that particular extent of land which would require a *prastha* of seed, that is, 48 double handfulls, or about 48 imperial pints, or two-thirds of a bushel. This was, no doubt, its original meaning, but in the lapse of time it must gradually have acquired the meaning, which it still has, of any good sized piece of open plain. *Indraprastha* would, therefore, mean the plain of Indra, which was, I presume, the name of the person who first settled there. Popular tradition assigns the five *pats* to the five Pándu brothers.

The date of the occupation of Indraprastha as a capital by Judhisthira, may, as I believe, be attributed, with some confidence, to the latter half of the 15th century before Christ. The grounds on which I base this belief are as follows: 1st, that certain positions of the planets, as recorded in the *Mahábhárata*, are shown by Bentley to have taken place in 1824-25 B. C., who adds that "there is no other year, either before that period or since, in which they were so situated;" 2nd, in the Vishnu Purána it is stated that at the birth of *Púrikshita*, the son of *Arjuna Pándava*, the seven Rishis were in *Maghá*, and that when they are in *Purva Ashárha* Nanda will begin to reign. Now, as the seven Rishis, or stars of the Great Bear, are supposed to pass from one lunar asterism to another in 100 years, the interval between Párikshita and Nanda will be 1,000 years. But in the Bhágavata Puráṇa this interval is said to be 1,015 years, which added to 100 years, the duration of the reigns of the nine Nandas, will place the birth of Párikshita 1,115 years before the accession of Chandra Gupta in 315 B. C., that is, in 1430 B. C. By this account the birth of *Párikshita*, the son of *Arjuna*, took place just six years before the Great War in B. C. 1424. These dates, which are derived from two independent sources, mutually support each other, and therefore seem to me to be more worthy of credit than any other Hindu dates of so remote a period.

Indraprastha, the city of Yudhisthira, was built along the bank of the River Jumna between the Kotila of Firuz Shah and the tomb of Humáyun. At that time the river flowed upwards of one mile to the westward of its present course, and the old bed is still easily traceable from Firuz Shah's Kotila, past Indrpat and Humáyun's tomb to *Ailu Ghari*. The last place was on the immediate bank of the river, so late as the reign of Kaikubád in A. D. 1290, as his assassins are reported to have thrown his body out of the palace window into the Jumna. The name of Indraprastha is still preserved in that of Indrpat, a small fort, which is also known by the name of *Puráṇa Kila* or the "old fort." This place was repaired by the Emperor Humáyun, who changed its name to *Din-pánah*; but none, save educated Musalmáns ever make use of this name, as the common people invariably call it either Indrpat or Puráṇa Kila. In its present form, this place is altogether a Muhammadan structure; and I do not believe that there now exists even a single carved stone of the original city of Yudhisthira. The only spot that has any claim to have belonged to the ancient city is a place of pilgrimage on the Jumna called *Nigambod Ghát*, which is immediately outside the northern wall of the city of *Shahjuhánábád*. This ghát is celebrated as the place where Yudhisthira, after his performance of the *Aswamedha*, or "horse sacrifice," celebrated the *Hom*. A fair is held at Nigambod whenever the new moon falls on a Monday. It is said to be held in honor of the River Jumna.

According to the Bhágavata Puráṇa, Yudhisthira was the first King of Indraprastha, and the throne was occupied by the descendants of his brother Arjuna for 30 generations down to Kshemaka. This last prince was deposed, according to all the copies of the Rajávali, by his Minister Visarwa, of whose family 14 persons are said to have held the throne for 500 years. They were succeeded by a dynasty of 15 *Gautamas*, or *Gotama-vansas*, who were followed by a family of nine *Mayuras*. *Raja-pála*, the last of the Mayuras, is stated to have been attacked and killed by the Raja of Kumaon, named *Sakáditya*, or "Lord of the Sakas." But this was only the title, and not the name, of the conqueror; for Vikramáditya is said to have obtained his title of *Sakári* by defeating him.

At this point of the traditional histories, the name of Dilli makes its first appearance;* but nothing is recorded regarding the change of name, and we are left to conjecture whether the city of *Dilli* had already been founded, or whether this name has been used instead of that of Indraprastha through simple inadvertence. According to one tradition, which is but little known, the city of Dilli was founded by Raja *Dilipa*, who was the ancestor in the fifth generation of the five Pandu brothers. But this story may be dismissed at once as an ignorant invention, as Dilli is universally acknowledged to be of much later date than Indraprastha, the city of Yudhisthira himself.

According to a popular and well known tradition, *Dilli* or *Dhili*, was built by Raja *Dilu*, or *Dhilu*, whose date is quite uncertain. This tradition was adopted by Ferishta, who adds that Raja *Dilu*, after a reign of either 4 or 40 years, was attacked and killed by Raja *Phur*, or Porus, of Kumaon, who was the antagonist of Alexander the Great. If this statement could be depended upon, it might perhaps be entitled to some consideration, as giving the probable period of the foundation of Dilli. But unfortunately Ferishta's ancient chronology is a mere jumble of errors; thus, for instance, Phur's nephew, *Juna*, who should have been a contemporary of Seleukos Nikator, is said to be a contemporary of Ardashir Babekan, the founder of the Sassanian dynasty in A. D. 226. But Ardashir himself is afterwards made a contemporary of Vikramáditya of Ujain in 57 B. C. The most probable explanation of these different dates would seem

---

* In Chand's Prithi-Raj-Raisa, the name is invariably written *Dilli*, with the first vowel short, and the other long. In one place I have found the city called *Dillipur*, which might as probably be derived from *Dillip* as from *Dilu*.

to be some confusion regarding the name of Ardashir, and
perhaps the safest plan will be to accept the author's last
statement, that Raja *Dilu* was a contemporary of Vikramáditya.

Now the story of *Dilu*, and of his defeat by Phur, Raja
of Kumaon, is exactly the same as that of *Raja Pál*,
King of Dilli, and of his defeat by *Sukwanti* (or *Sukdat*
or *Sukáditya*), Raja of Kumaon, as related in several
different copies of the Rajávali. As in all of these the invader is said to have been defeated and slain by *Vikramáditya Sakári*, the date of this event must be assigned either
to 57 B. C. or to A. D. 79. The latter date is the true one,
according to Abu Rihán; and as Sakáditya is said to have
reigned 14 years in Dilli, his conquest must have taken place
in A. D. 65. I confess, however, that I have but little faith
in the dates of any Hindu traditionary stories, unless they
can be supported by other testimony. That the city of Dilli
was founded by a Raja of similar name, is probable enough,
for it is the common custom of India, even at the present
day, to name places after their founders. But there is unfortunately so much uncertainty about the dates in all the
stories connected with the foundation of Dilli, that it is
difficult to form any satisfactory conclusion as to the
truth.

According to Kharg Rai, the Gwalior Bhát, who wrote
in the reign of Shahjahán, the last Pándu Prince, named
Niláyhpati, was King of Dilli when 3000 years of the Káliyuga had expired, that is, in 101 B. C. In that year he was
attacked by a Raghuvansi Raja, named *Sankhdhwaj*, with
whom he fought 17 battles, but was eventually defeated and
killed after a reign of 44 years, which brings us to 57 B. C.
Sankhdhwaj himself is said to have been defeated and killed by
the famous Vikramáditya of Ujain, who thus became King
of Dilli *(Dilli-pat-kaháyo)*. His descendants are recorded
to have reigned in Ujain for 792 years, during the whole of
which time Dilli was deserted *(ujarh rahi)*. At the end of
these 792 years, or in $792 - 56\frac{3}{4} = 735\frac{1}{4}$ years complete, or
A. D. 736, Dilli was re-peopled by *Bilan De Tomar*, whose
descendants occupied the throne until displaced by the Chohans under *Bisal De*, who is no doubt the *Visala Deva* of the
two inscriptions on Firuz Shah's Pillar.

In this account of Kharg Rai, I recognize another version of the former story of the Raja of Dilli being overcome by the King of the Sakas, who was himself afterwards defeated by Vikramáditya. The name of *Sankhdhwaj* would appear to be only a misreading either of *Sakwant*, or of Sakdat or Sakáditya; but *Niláyh-pati* is quite unlike Raja Pál, although it might be a mistake for Tilak pati, and would thus, perhaps, have some connection with the name of Raja Dílu.

I think also that I can recognize another version of the same legend in the story of *Rásal*, King of Hind, and his sons Rawál and Barkamárys, as preserved in the Mojmal-ut-tawárikh of Rashiduddin.* In this version King Rásal, whom I would conjecturally identify with Raja Pál of the Rajávali, is driven from his throne by a rebel, who is afterwards conquered by *Barkamárys*, a name in which, though slightly altered, I still recognize the famous *Bikramádit* or Vikramáditya.

The overthrow of the Sakas is universally attributed to the Vikramáditya who assumed the title of *Sakári*, and established the era which still bears his name, beginning in 57 B. C. But if the prince who founded this era was a contemporary of Pravarasena, Raja of Kashmir, and of the poet Kálidása, as well as of the Astronomer Varáha Mihira, as there seems good reason to believe, it is quite certain that he cannot be dated earlier than the beginning of the sixth century of the Christian era. This conclusion is supported by the strong testimony of Abu Rihán, who states that the great victory over the Sakas was gained at a place called *Koror*, between Multan and Loni, by a prince named Vikramáditya, just 135 years after the prince of the same name who founded the Vikrama Samvat. As the date of this event corresponds exactly with the initial point of the *Saka*-era which was established by *Sálivahána*, it results that the Vikramáditya of Abu Rihán is identical with the Sáliváhana of the popular Indian traditions. This conclusion is further strengthened by the fact that in Colonel James Abbott's list of the Rajas of Syálkot, a reign of 90 years is assigned to Sálivahána, which is exactly the same as is

---

* Reinaud, "Fragments Arabes," &c., p. 17.

allotted to Vikramáditya, the conqueror of the Sakas, in all the seven copies of the Rajávali that I have seen. On these grounds, I venture, with some confidence, to fix the date of the defeat of the Saka conqueror of Dilli in A. D. 78, which is the initial point of the Sake-era of Sáliváhana.

Accepting this date as tolerably well established for an event in ancient Indian history, the foundation of *Dilli* must be placed at some earlier period, and perhaps the date of 57 B. C., or contemporary with Vikramáditya, as recorded by Ferishta, may not be far from the truth. Regarding the widely spread tradition that Dilli was deserted for 792 years, from the conquest of Vikramáditya to the time of the first Tomara Raja Anang Pál, I think that it may be fully explained by supposing that during that period Dilli was not the residence of the King. It is almost certain that it was not the capital of the powerful family of the Guptas, who most probably reigned from A. D. 78 to 319 ; and it is quite certain that it was not the capital of the great King Harsha Vardhdhana and his immediate predecessors, whose metropolis was Kanoj during the latter half of the sixth, and the first half of the seventh century. That Dilli was most probably occupied during this period, we may infer from the erection of the Iron Pillar by Raja *Dháva*, the date of which is assigned to the third or fourth century by James Prinsep.[*] Mr. Thomas "considers that Prinsep has assigned too high an antiquity to the style of writing employed on this monument;" but on this point I venture to differ, as I find, after a careful examination of the inscription, that the whole of the letters are the same as those of the records of the Gupta dynasty, whose downfall is assigned to A. D. 319 by Abu Rihán. I think it probable that Raja Dháva may have been one of the princes who assisted in the overthrow of the once powerful Guptas, and I would, therefore, fix on A. D. 319 as an easily remembered and useful approximation to his true date.

A still earlier mention of Dilli may possibly be found in Ptolemy's *Daidala*, which is placed close to *Indabara* (perhaps Indrpat,) and midway between *Modura* or Mathura, and *Batan Kaisara*, or Sthâneswara. For the last name I propose to read *Satanaisara* as its position between Mathura and

---

[*] Bengal Asiatic Society's Journal, 1838, p. 629.

DELHI.   111

Zulindrine or the *Jálandhar* Doab renders it almost certain that it must be Sthâneswara or Thânesar. The close proximity of *Daidala* to *Indabara*, joined to the curious resemblance of their names to Dilli and Indrpat, seems to me to offer very fair grounds for assuming their probable identity with these two famous Indian cities.

The ancient city of Dilli may, with tolerable certainty, be considered to have occupied almost the same site as the fort of Rai Pithora, as it is to be presumed that the Iron Pillar must have been erected in some conspicuous position, either within the old city, or close to it. With the solitary exception of the Iron Pillar, I am not aware that there are any existing remains that can be assigned with certainty to the old Hindu city of Dilli. A single pillar, amongst the many hundreds that now form the colonnades of the Kutb Minar, may perhaps belong to the old city, as it bears a figure either of Buddha the Ascetic seated in contemplation, or of one of the Jain hierarchs. No doubt some, and perhaps even many, of the pillars of these colonnades may have belonged to temples of the old Hindu city; but after a minute examination on three successive days, of the sculptures on the pillars, and of all the letters and mason's marks on the pillars and walls, I came to the unwilling conclusion that (with the two exceptions just noted) there is nothing now existing that is older than the tenth or eleventh century.

According to the tradition which is universally accepted by all Hindus, the city of Dilli was re-built by Anang Pâl, the first King of the Tomar dynasty. The manuscript of Kharg Rai, which I obtained at Gwalior, names him *Bilan De*, and a second manuscript, received from Bikaner, calls him *Bilan Deo* or *Anang Pâl*; but Abul Fazl, Colonel Tod, and Syad Ahmad call him simply Anang Pâl; and he is so named in two inscriptions which are found on the Iron Pillar. The date of Anang Pâl, the founder of the Tomar dynasty, is variously given by the different authorities; but even the most discrepant of these dates, when carefully examined, will be found to agree within a few years of the others. The different dates given are as follows:

1st.—*The Gwalior manuscript of Kharg Rai.*—This date has already been referred to. Kharg Rai states that Dilli was deserted for 792 years after

Vikramâditya, when it was re-founded by Bilan De Tomar. This gives the year A. D. 736 as before noted. Colonel Tod refers to the same tradition when he states that Delhi lay waste for eight centuries.* But I am satisfied that he had the well known number of 792 recorded in his notes, for, in the very same page in which he makes the above statement, he gives the date of the re-building of Dilli by Anang Pâl as *Samvat* 848, which, by using his erroneous difference of 56 years, instead of 57, is equivalent to A. D. 792. But in another part of his work, Colonel Tod states that he possessed the original Hindu manuscript which Abul Fazl had used, and that the date of the re-building of Dilli by Anang Pâl was *Samvat* 829 instead of S. 429. I strongly suspect that Colonel Tod has made a mistake in this last statement, for I found, on examining the bard *Mûk-ji's* manuscript, then in the possession of his sons, that S. 821 is the date assigned to the *overthrow* of the Tomaras, and not to their *rise*. From these different statements I feel assured that he must have found the number 792 recorded in his notes without any explanation, and that he erroneously adopted it as the date of the re-founding of Dilli.

2nd.—In the Ain Akbari of Abul Fazl, the date of Anang Pâl is placed in *Samvat* 420, and the end of the Tomar dynasty in S. 848;† thus limiting the rule of the *Tomaras* to 419 years, while his detailed account of the lengths of reigns amounts to 437 years. The former period has been adopted by Syad Ahmad, as I think, judiciously, because of the increased chances of error in the detail of twenty reigns. On the *Iron Pillar* this date is given as S. 419, and the fall of the dynasty is assigned to S. 648,

---

* Rajasthan, I., p. 87.
† Gladwin's Translation, I., pp. 96 and 97.

which is most probably an error of the engraver for S. 846. The difference between these dates is 427 years.

3rd.—In two manuscripts from Kumaon and Garhwâl, the date of the first Tomara Raja is given as 13th Bhâdon S. 846, which is equivalent to A. D. 789.* But as both of these manuscripts omit the first three names, which are found in all the other manuscripts, I conclude that the date therein given is that of the fourth prince of the other lists. Deducting, therefore, from the above date the sum of the three omitted reigns, which amount to 58 years, we obtain A. D. 731 as another period for the re-building of Dilli by Anang Pâl.

It will be observed that the three manuscripts from Gwalior, Kumaon, and Garhwâl, place the date of the refounding of Dilli in the eighth century A. D., whereas Abul Fazl and the inscription on the Iron Pillar refer this event to the fourth century A. D.; and so also does the author of the *Araish-i-Mahfil*, who gives S. 440. Now, although Abul Fazl specially notes that his date of 420 is of the era of Vikramâditya, yet he is most undoubtedly wrong, as I will now show from other statements of his own. According to this account, the Tomar dynasty, which lasted 419 years, was succeeded by the Chohan dynasty, which ruled for 83 years, and was then overcome by Sultan *Muâz-uddin Sâme*. The period of this event is stated to be A. H. 588, or A. D. 1192. Now, deducting 419 + 83, or 502 years, from A. D. 1192, we obtain A. D. 690 as the true date of Anang Pâl according to Abul Fazl's own figures, instead of S. 420—57, or A. D. 372, as stated in his text. But as the rule of the Chohans is limited to 41½ years in my two manuscripts from Kumaon and Garhwâl, and to 40 years in my Gwalior manuscript, I think that the authority of these three records may be taken as at least of equal weight with that of the Ain Akbari. The true periods of the two dynasties will, therefore, be 419 + 41 = 460 years, which deducted from A. D. 1191, the corrected date of Muâz-uddin's conquest, will

---

* A third MS. from Kadârnâth agrees generally with the two previously obtained from Dhiantal and Srinagar.

give A. D. 731 for Anang Pál's re-building of Dilli, which is within five years of the traditional date of A. D. 736, already noticed.

The only explanation which I can propose of the great discrepancy between the true date and that which is stated in the Ain Akbari is, that Abul Fazl simply mistook the era in which he found the date recorded. Now, if we suppose that the era of his dates was that of *Balabhi*, which began A. D. 319, we shall have S. 429 + 318 = 747 A. D. as the corrected date for the re-building of Dilli by Anang Pál according to Abul Fazl. But by using the date of S. 419, which is recorded on the Iron Pillar, we shall obtain A. D. 737, which is within one year of the date already fixed by the traditional story of Dilli having lain waste for 792 years, and which agrees also with the date derived from the lengths of reigns by working backwards from A. D. 1193, the period of Muñz-uddin's conquest. I therefore look upon the date of A. D. 736 for the re-building of Dilli under Anang Pál as being established on grounds that are more than usually firm for early Indian History. The famous poet Mir Khusru, of Delhi, who wrote both before and after A. D. 1300, gives an amusing anecdote of Anang Pál, "a great Rai, who lived five or six hundred years ago." "At the entrance of his palace he had placed two lions, sculptured in stone. He fixed a bell by the side of the two lions, in order that those who sought justice might strike it, upon which the Rai would order them to be summoned, would listen to their complaints, and render justice. One day a crow came and sat on the bell, and struck it, when the Rai asked who the complainant was. It is a fact, not unknown, that bold crows will pick meat from between the teeth of lions. As stone lions cannot hunt for their prey, where could the crow obtain its usual sustenance? As the Rai was satisfied that the crow justly complained of hunger, having come to sit by his stone lions, he gave orders that some goats and sheep should be killed, on which the crow might feed himself for some days."*

---

* Sir H. M. Elliot's Muhammadan Historians of India, edited by Dowson, III., 565. From this story we learn that so early as A. D. 1300 Anang Pál was believed to have reigned in Delhi between 700 and 800 A. D., which agrees exactly with the statements of the chroniclers.

Accepting this date of A. D. 736, we have to account for the period of 702 years during which Dilli is said to have lain waste, when it is almost certain that the city must have been occupied at the time when Raja *Dháva* erected the Iron Pillar. Perhaps the simplest explanation is that which I have already given, *viz.*, that during this period Dilli was not the metropolis of the Kings of Upper India. The silence of the Chinese pilgrims Fa Hian and Hwen Thsang regarding Dilli may, perhaps, be considered as a strong proof of the smallness of the city from A. D. 400 to 640. Fa Hian, however, does not mention any place between Taxila and Mathura, and Hwen Thsang could only have passed through Dilli once, *viz.*, when he returned from Mathura to Thanesar. It is even possible that he may have travelled by Mirat, which then possessed one of Asoka's Pillars, for, if Dilli was not a famous place amongst the Buddhists, as I believe it was not, it is improbable that he would have visited it.

Dilli must, however, have been the Capital of Anang Pál, and most probably also of several of his successors; but I have a strong suspicion that the later Rajas of the Tomar dynasty resided at Kanoj. M. Reinaud remarks that Otbi, the historian of Mahmud, makes no mention of the city of Dilli, and that only a single allusion to it is made by Abu Rihán in his *Kánun-al-masudi*. It is, indeed, a fact worthy of special notice that Dilli is not once mentioned in Abu Rihán's geographical chapter, which gives the routes between all the principal places in Northern India. He notices Thanesar, and Mathura, and Kanoj, but Dilli is never mentioned, an omission which could hardly have happened had Dilli been the capital of the famous Tomar Rajas at that time. I conclude, therefore, that Dilli was not their residence in the beginning of the eleventh century, and I think that I can show with much probability that Kanoj was the metropolis of the Tomar Rajas for several generations prior to the invasion of Mahmud of Ghazni.

In A. H. 303, or A. D. 915, India was visited by the well known Geographer Masudi, who records that "the King of Kanoj, who is one of the Kings of es-Sind, is *Budak*; this is a title general to all Kings of el-Kanoj."* The name

---
* Sir H. M. Elliot—Historians of India, I., 57.

which in the above extract is read as *Budah* by Sir Henry
Elliot is said by Gildemeister,* to be written *Bocarah* in the
original, for which he proposes to read *Porarah*, for the well
known *Paurara*. From the King of Oudh's Dictionary two
different spellings are quoted, as *Porán*, and *Forán;* while
in Ferishta the name is either *Korrah*, as written by Dow,
or *Kuwar*, as written by Briggs. In Abulfeda the name is
Nodah. Now, as the name, of which so many readings have
just been given, was that of the King's family or tribe, I
believe that we may almost certainly adopt *Torarah*
as the true reading according to one spelling, and *Torah*,
according to the other. In the Sanskrit inscriptions of the
Gwalior dynasty of this name, the word is invariably spelt
Tomara. Kharg Rai writes *Toár*, which is much the same
as Colonel Tod's *Tuār*, and the *Tucár*, of the Kumaon and
Garhwál manuscripts. Lastly, in Gladwin's Ain Akbari
I find *Tenore* and *Toonoor*, for which I presume that the
original has simply, *Tunwar*. From a comparison of all
these various readings, I conclude that the family name of the
Raja of Kanoj in A. D. 915, when Masudi visited India,
and again in A. D. 1017 and 1021, when Mahmud of
Ghazni invaded India, was in all probability *Tocar* or *Tomar*.
In favour of this conclusion there is the further testimony
of Masudi that in A. D. 915 the four great Kings of India
known to the Musalmáns were, 1st, the *Balhará*, who lived
in *Mánkír;* 2nd, the King of *Kanoj;* 3rd, the King of
Kashmir; and 4th, the King of *Sind*. As no King of Dilli
is mentioned, it seems not unreasonable to infer that at that
time, in A. D. 915, the powerful *Tomars* most probably held
their Court at Kanoj.

If I am correct in the above identification, then the
name of the King at the time of Mahmud's invasion should
correspond with that of the *Tomar* Raja, who, according to
the genealogical lists, was reigning at that particular period.
According to *Otbi*† the name of this Raja of Kanoj
was *Raj Pál*, or *Rájaipál*, which I take to be equivalent
to Raja *Jaypál*. Now the 14th prince in Abul Fazl's list‡

---

* Scriptorum Arab de rebus Indicis, p. 160.
† Bernard Fragments, Arabes, p. 263.
‡ Ain Akbari, II—94.

is *Jaypál*, whose death, according to the lengths of reigns given in the Ain Akbari, occurred 287 years and 6 months after the re-building of Dilli by Anang Pál. Adding this number to A. D. 736½, we obtain the year 1023¾ as that of the death of Jaypál. By comparing the lists of Abul Fazl and Syad Ahmad with those of my Gwalior, Kumaon, and Garhwál manuscripts, and taking the lengths of reigns according to the majority of these five authorities, the period elapsed from the accession of Anang Pál to the death of Jaypál, amounts to 285 years and 6 months. Adding this number to A. D. 736½, we get 1021½ as the date of Jaypál's death, which is, I believe, within a few months of the true date. According to Ferishta,[*] Mahmud first heard of the alliance of the Hindu princes against his tributary the King of Kanoj, some time in the Hijra year 412, which began on 17th April 1021. As several other events are previously recorded, and as Mahmud is said to have marched to his aid at once, I conclude that he may have left Ghazni about *October* 1021, and as Kanoj is three months' march distant from Ghazni,[†] he must have reached that city in January 1022. On his arrival, Mahmud found that the King of Kanoj had already been attacked and killed. The death of Jaypál must, therefore, have occurred about December 1021, which agrees almost exactly with the date of his death, which I have already deduced from the genealogical lists. Precisely the same date also is obtained by working backwards by lengths of reigns from the date of Munzuddin's conquest of Dilli in A. D. 1101.

Since this account was written, the 2nd volume of Professor Dowson's edition of Sir H. M. Elliot's Muhammadan Historians of India has appeared, which contains;[‡] a translation of the *Mirát-i-Asrár*, being a fabulous relation of the acts of Sálár Sáhu and his son Sálár Masáud. The latter is said to have captured Dehli, and to have killed the King named Mahipál. But as Masáud was born in A. D. 1014, and was 18 years of age when he reached Oudh, after passing Delhi and Kanoj, the capture of Delhi cannot have taken place earlier than A. D. 1030, when he was 17 years of age.

---

[*] Briggs, 1—63.
[†] Briggs's Ferishta, 1.—57.
[‡] Appendix, pp. 513—519.

But as the King of Kanoj is called Jaypál, whom we know to have been killed in A. D. 1021, I have no faith in the truth of the narrative, which was compiled by a credulous author in the reign of Jahángir. There are two Mahipáls in the lists, one of whom formed the lake and gave his name to the village of Mahipálpur, but neither of their dates fits with that of Sálár Masáud. The silence of the contemporary historian Otbi regarding Delhi, and its immunity from attack during the long reign of Mahmud, when the neighbouring cities of Thánesar, Mirat, Mathura, and Kanoj, were all captured, seem to me quite incredible on any other supposition than that which I have endeavoured to prove, namely, that Delhi was then a comparatively unimportant town, without any means of defence, as Lálkot had not then been built, and without the wealth of a capital, to attract the cupidity of an invader. The occurrence of the two names of Jaypál and Kuwar Pál in the list of Tomar Princes of Delhi *at the very time* that the same names are given by the Muhammadan historians as those of two Kings of Kanoj, seems to me to admit of only one explanation—that they were identical.

The following lists of the Tomar dynasty of Dilli contain all the information which, up to this time, I have been able to collect. The list of Abul Fazl is given in the Ain Akbari; and Syad Ahmad's list is printed in his *Asár-us-Sunáddid*. The Bikaner manuscript, which I obtained in 1840, agrees exactly in the order of the names, and very closely also in the spelling of them, with those of the printed lists just noticed; but it unfortunately wants the lengths of reigns. The Gwalior manuscript, which I procured in 1849, agrees very closely with the others as to the lengths of reigns, but it differs slightly in the order of the names. As this list is appended to Kharg Rai's History of Gwalior, which was composed in the reign of Shahjahan, it is valuable as an independent authority. The Kumaon and Garhwál manuscripts, which were obtained in 1859 and 1862, respectively, are imperfect in the same places, which shows that they must have been derived from a common source.[*] They are valuable, however, for their agreement in omitting the last king of the other lists, named *Prithei Rai* or *Prithivi Pála* who

---

[*] A third MS. since obtained from Kotkattah, agrees very closely with these MSS. from Bhim Tál and Srinagar. A list published by Mangal Sen, in his History of Bulandshahr, agrees with that of Syad Ahmad, except in No. 6, which he gives as Bhim Raj.

DELHI.

would appear to be the same as the Chohán Prithivi Raja, commonly called Rai Pithora. In proof of this, I may adduce the fact that the promised number of *nineteen Tomara Rajas* is complete without this name.

THE TOMARA, OR TOAR, DYNASTY OF DILLI.

	Abul Fazl, Syed Ahmad, Bhaner MS.	Gwalior MSS.	Husnaco, Garhwal MSS.	Reigns. Y. M. D.	Accession. A. D.
1	Ananga Pála	Bilan De	(caret)	46 0 0	736 5 0
2	Vasu Deva	(caret)	(caret)	19 1 14	734 5 0
3	Gangya	Gangyeva	(caret)	21 8 25	778 6 19
4	Prithivi Malla*	Prathama	Mahi P.	19 6 29	794 8 26
5	Jaya Deva	Saha Deva	Jadu P.	20 7 25	814 9 5
6	Nira, or Ihra P.	Indrajita	Kal P.	24 1 0	836 10 3
7	Udiral, or Aderah	Nara P.	Jaya Deva P.	36 7 21	840 8 19
8	Vijaya, or Vacha	Indrajita	Chamra P.	17 1 15	875 10 25
9	Bhisha, or Amit	Vacha Raja	Bhisam P.	23 5 26	897 1 0
10	Riksha P.	Vira P.	Suhla P.	17 6 4	910 6 23
11	Sukh, or Nek P.	Gopala	Teja P.	20 4 6	948 10 17
12	Gopala	Tilhan De	Mahi P.	18 9 15	981 6 1
13	Sallakshana P...	Suvari	Suran	15 10 10	979 6 15
14	Jaya P.	Gan P.	Jaik P.	16 4 3	1005 4 25
15	Kamwyl P.	Kumára P.	(caret)	29 9 15	1071 8 29
16	Ananda, or Anek	Ananda P.	Anek P.	29 6 15	1051 6 17
17	Vijaya Pala, or Pal	Teja P.	Teja P.	24 1 6	1081 1 5
18	Mahaimal, Mahi P.	Mahi P.	Jpán P.	25 3 23	1105 2 11
19	Akr Pál, Akhmal	Mahomed P.	Ana P.	23 7 15	1130 5 6
				Capture of Dilli	2151 7 29
20	Prithivi Rája	Prithivi P.	(caret)	23 7 10	

* Or Pála.

In the above list I have adopted as a starting point the exact amount of 702 years complete from the time of Vikramaditya; or 792 — 56¾ = 735¼ years complete, or April A. D. 736. But it is obvious that the period elapsed is more likely to have been 702 years and some months over than the exact number of 702 years. For instance, 702¼ years would place the death of Jaya Pála in A. D. 1021-11-20, that is, on the 29th December A. D. 1021; but as the exact date of this event is not recorded by the Muhammadan Historians, I have thought it best to adhere to the date obtained from the complete period of 792 years.

I will now consider the claim which I have put forward on the part of the *Tomara* dynasty as Rajas of Kanoj. We know that, after the conquest of Kanoj by Mahmud early in A. D. 1022, the reigning family changed its residence to *Bári*, which was three days' journey distant, on the east side of the Ganges. Mirkhond states that it was situated at the confluence of three rivers, namely, the *Saro*, the *Kábín*, and the *Rakab*.* According to Rashiduddin, the three rivers are the *Rahet*, the *Gomati*, and the *Sarju*.† The second of these rivers is undoubtedly the *Gumti*, which in Sanskrit is the *Gomati*. The first is either the *Behta*, or else the *Bahria*, which joins the Behta, and the third is the *Sarain*, a good sized stream which passes by Sitapur. Both the Behta and Sarain join the Gumti near *Bári*, which still exists as a good sized village. As Abu Rihán, who records this change of capital, was actually resident in India at the time when it took place, and as his work was written in A. D. 1031, we have the most complete authentication of Mirkhond's date of this event. I presume that the change was made on account of the exposed situation of Kanoj, which had so lately been twice captured, first, in A. D. 1017 by Mahmud, and again in A. D. 1021 by the Raja of *Kalanjar* and his allies. I conclude, therefore, *Kuuwar Pál*, or *Kumára Pál*, who was the successor of Jaypál, reigned at *Bári* from A. D. 1021 to 1051.

About this very time also, as we learn from several inscriptions, the kingdom of Kanoj was conquered by *Chandra Deva*, the founder of the Rahtor dynasty of Kanoj. We possess no inscriptions of Chandra Deva himself, but there is one of his son, Madana Pála, which is dated in S. 1154 or A. D. 1007; and two of his grandson, Govinda Chandra, dated in S. 1177 and S. 1210 or A. D. 1120 and 1162. We know also from other inscriptions that Govinda's grandson ascended the throne between A. D. 1172 and 1177, or say in A. D. 1175. With these dates before us, we may safely fix Govinda's accession in A. D. 1110 or 1115, and

---

* Reinaud, " Fragments Arabes," &c., —See pp. 99—100, note.
† Sir H. M. Elliot's Muhammadan Historians of India, p. 32.

that of his grandfather, Chandra Deva, the founder of the dynasty, in A. D. 1050. Now this is the very date, as we learn from other sources, at which Anang Pál II., the successor of Kumára Pála, established himself at Dilli, and built the fort of *Lálkot.* On the Iron pillar there is a short inscription in three lines, which appears to be a contemporary record of Anang Pál himself, as the characters are similar to those of the mason's marks on the pillars of the colonnade of the Great Mosque, but are quite different from those of the two modern Nágari inscriptions, which are close beside it. The following are the words of this short record: "*Samvat Dihali* 1109 *Ang Pál bahi,*" which may be translated thus—"In *Samvat* 1109, or A. D. 1052, *Ang* (or *Anang*) *Pál* peopled *Dilli.*" This statement is borne out by the testimony of the Kumaon and Gárhwal manuscripts, in which, opposite the name of Anek Pál, I find recorded that in *Samvat* 1117, or A. D. 1060, on the 10th of *Márgasiras Sudi* "he built the Fort of Dilli and called it *"Lálkot" (Dilli ka kot karáya, Lálkot kaháya").* This name was still in use during the reign of the first Musalmán King, Kutbuddin Aibeg, as I find in the manuscripts of *Mák-ji,* the bard of the *Khichi* Chohans, that Kutbuddin, soon after his accession, issued seven orders to the Hindu Chiefs, of which the fifth is "*Lálkot tai nugáro bájto a,*" or "kettle-drums are not to be beaten in Lálkot." This is a rule which is still observed, as none but the royal drums are beaten where the sovereign is present. Kutbuddin must, therefore, have taken up his residence in Lálkot, or the fortified city of Anang Pál.*

Now this date, recorded on the Iron Pillar, agrees so exactly with the period of the Rahtor conquest of Kanoj, that I think we may infer, with considerable probability, that the re-building of Dilli by Anang Pál was owing to the loss of the territory of Kanoj along with its new Capital of Bári in Oudh.† The accession of Anang Pál II., according

---

* This is confirmed by the Muhammadan Historians, who state that the first two Kings, Kutb-ud-din Aibeg and Shamsuddin Altamsh resided in the Fort of Rai Pithura. See Ain Akbari by Gladwin, II., p. 56.

† The loss of power by the Tomar Princes of Delhi at this very time would seem to be confirmed by the asserted supremacy of Chandra Deva, the Rathor Raja of Kanoj, who is called the "protector of the sacred places at Kási, Kusika, Northern Kosala, and Indrasthána," of which the last is only another name for Indraprastha, or Delhi.—See Dr. Hall's translation of Madana Pála's Inscription in the Bengal Asiatic Society's Journal, 1858, p. 234.

to the genealogical lists, took place in A. D. 1051, and in 1052 we find a record of him on the Iron Pillar at Dilli. If, then, we suppose that he commenced re-building at once, there is every probability in favour of the accuracy of the statement that he finished the *Lálkot*, or "Red Fort," of Dilli in A. D. 1060. If the site of the Red Fort may be fixed by the position of the *Anang Tál*, as well as by that of the Iron Pillar which records the work, then the grand old fort which now surrounds the Kutb Minar is in all probability the very Lálkot that was built by Anang Pál. But there are also three other points in favour of this identification, *viz.*, 1st, that all the 27 temples destroyed by the Musalmáns would appear to have stood inside the walls of Lálkot; 2nd, that one of these 27 temples was almost certainly built in the reign of Anang Pál; and 3rd, that the Fort of Rai Pithora is only an extension of the older fort, which now surrounds the Kutb Minar. For these reasons I believe that this massive old fort, which is still in very good order in many places, is the identical Lálkot of Anang Pál. The circuit of its walls, according to my survey, is 2¼ miles.

To this Anang Pál I attribute the construction of a very deep tank situated one-quarter of a mile to the north-west of the Kutb Minar, and which is still called Anang Tál. This tank is 160 feet long from north to south, and 152 feet broad from east to west, with a depth of 40 feet. It is now quite dry, but Syad Ahmad quotes a statement that, in the time of Sultán Ala-uddin Khilji (A. D. 1296—1316), the water used for the mortar of the great unfinished Minar was brought from this tank. I refer also to this Anang Pál the founding of a village in the Balamgarh District, which is still called *Anekpur*. According to Syad Ahmad, the popular date of this work is S. 733, or A. D. 676; and he attributes it to Anang Pál 1st, the founder of the dynasty. But I think it more probable that the date refers to the Balabhi era of A. D. 319, which will place the building of the village in 733 + 318 = A. D. 1051, in which year Anang Pál 2nd, the true founder of Dilli, succeeded to the throne. Another work of the same time is the *Suraj Kund*, a fine deep tank near Anekpur, the building of which is attributed to Suraj Pál, one of Anang Pál's sons, in S. 743, which, referred to the Balabhi era, is equivalent to A. D. 1061, a date which

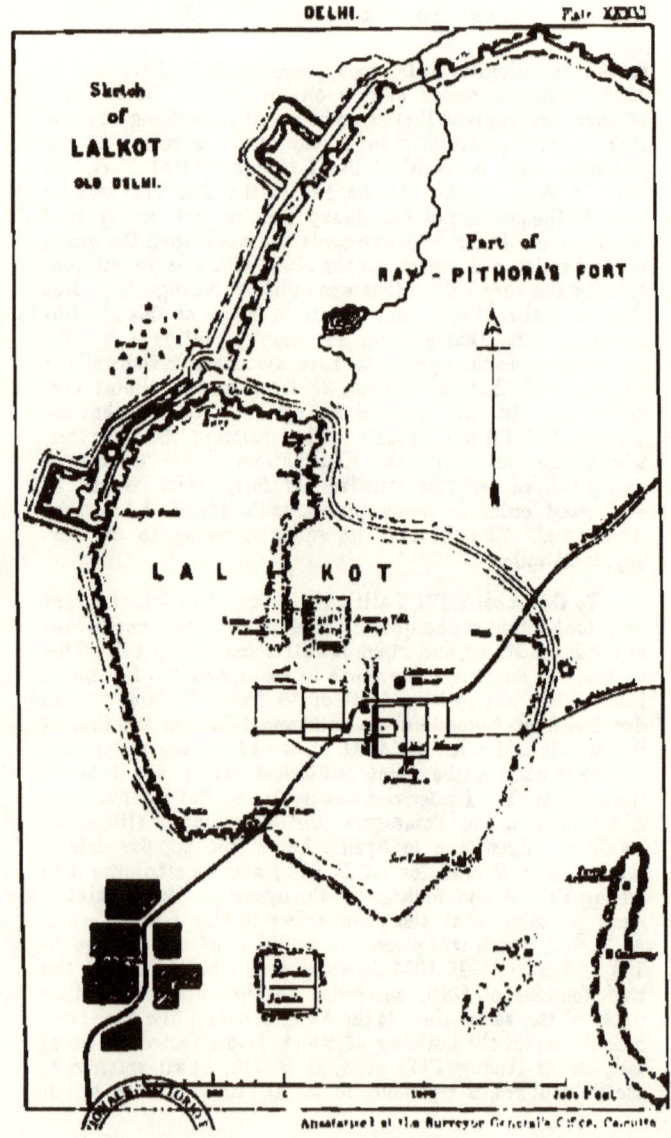

corresponds most exactly with those which we have already obtained.

To Anang Pál I attribute also the erection of at least one of the 27 temples which once stood around the Iron Pillar. Many of the pillars and beams of this temple have been made use of by the Musulmáns in the construction of the south-east corner of the colonnade of the Great Mosque. Most of them are inscribed with mason's marks, as will be noticed at length when I come to speak of the ruins in detail; and one of them bears the date of 1124, which, referred to the era of Vikramáditya, is equivalent to A. D. 1067, in the very middle of the reign of Anang Pál II.

According to the traditions of the people, which I managed to pick up, the following were some of the numerous sons of Anang Pál:

1st.—*Tej Pál*, or *Tejran*, who founded *Tejára*, between Gurgaon and Alwar. In the Bikaner MS. this prince is called Vijaya Sál, or Pál.

2nd.—*Indra Raj*, who founded *Indragarh*.

3rd.—*Rang Raj*, who founded two places named *Tárágarh*, of which one is said to be near Ajmer.

4th.—*Achal Raj*, who founded *Acheca*, or *Achner*, between Bharatpur and Agra.

5th.—*Draupada*, who is said to have lived at Asi, or Hansi.

6th.—*Sian Pál*, who founded *Sirsa* and *Siswal*, said to be same as *Sirsi Patan*.

If these traditions are of any value, they will enable us to judge of the extent of Anang Pál's dominions by the names of the places which were founded or held by his sons. According to this test his dominions extended from Hánsi on the north to Agra on the south, and on the western side they reached nearly as far as Alwar and Ajmer. To the eastward they were most probably bounded by the Ganges, beyond which the whole country was then held by the Katehria Rajputs. I see nothing improbable in these traditions of the *Tomar* possessions, and I am, therefore, willing to accept them as valuable additions to our present scanty knowledge of Hindu history.

v

There are traditions of a similar kind regarding the sons of another Tomar Raja, called *Karna Pál :* but his name is not to be found in any of the lists. As, however, one of his sons was called *Bach Deo*, a name which is given in three of the lists as *Vachu Raja*, in a fourth list as *Vijaya Raja*, and in two others as *Bibasa Pála*, I think that we have some grounds for identifying *Karna Pál* with the father of *Vacha Deva* of the lists, more especially as the lists differ so much amongst themselves regarding the name of the father who is called both Nar Pál and Har Pál, either of which may be derived from Karn. He is variously called *Adereh, Udi-Ray, Indrajit,* and *Chanra* Pál, of which the first three names are evidently only various readings of one original name. The sons of Karna Pál, according to the popular tradition, were the following:

1st.—*Bach Deo*, who founded *Baghor*, near Narnol, and *Buchera* or *Baghera* near Thoda Ajmer.

2nd.—*Nág Deo*, who founded *Nágor* and *Nóyda* near Ajmer.

3rd.—*Krishn Ray*, who founded *Kishengarh*, 10 miles to north north-east of Alwar, and *Khds Ganj* between Soron and Etah.

4th.—*Nihál Ray*, who founded *Náráyanpur*, 10 miles to west of Alwar.

5th.—*Somasi*, who founded *Ajabgarh*, between Alwar and Jaypur.

6th.—*Har Pál*, who founded *Harsora*, 16 miles to north north-west of Alwar, and *Harsoli*, 23 miles to north of Alwar.

To this list I may add *Bahádurgarh*, 7 miles to north-east of Alwar, which is said to have been founded by *Karna Pál* himself.

The only other work of the Tomaras which has come to my knowledge is the village of *Mahipálpur*, situated two miles to the east north-east of the Kutb Minar, with its great embanked lake, three-quarters of a mile long and one-quarter broad. Mahi Pál, the grand-father of Jay Pál, is the 12th in the list, and reigned from A. D. 061 to 079.* The embankment was the work of Firuz Tughlak.† A second Mahi Pál reigned from A. D. 1103 to 1130.

If these traditions are true, the dominion of the Tomaras must at one time have extended to the westward as far as Sirsa and Nâgor. To the south-west there is the district of *Toârvati*, or *Tomaravati*, between Alwar and Shekhâvati; and to the south-east there is the district of *Toârghár*, or *Tomarghár*, between Dholpur and Gwalior, both of which still preserve the name of this once powerful clan. The Tomara dynasty of Gwalior, which held that strong fort for nearly a century and a half, traced its descent from Anang Pál of Dilli, and the present Chief of Toârvati, as well as the Tomar Zemindars of Toârghár, still proudly lay claim to the same origin.

Anang Pál II. was succeeded by three other Rajas of the Tomar family, of whom the last was a prince of the same name, Anang Pál III. During the reign of this last King, Dilli was captured by the Chohâns under *Visala Deva*, but the date of this event has not yet been satisfactorily ascertained. According to Abul Fazl it occurred in S. 849, which, referred to the Balabhi era, gives A. D. 1166; but as the date of *Visala's* inscription on Firuz Shah's Pillar is S. 1220 of *Vikrama*, or A. D. 1163, it is certain that the capture of Dilli must have preceded the conqueror's advance to the foot of the hills near Khizrabad, where this pillar was then standing. This position at the foot of the Himâlaya Mountains is specially referred to in the record where Visala speaks of having made tributary all the regions between Himâvat and Vindhya.‡ *Màlk-ji*, the bard of the Khichi Chohâns, gives the date as S. 821, which, compared with Abul Fazl's date, is probably too early. The author of the *Araish-i-mahfil* says that it was rather more than 1200 *Samvat*, that is, somewhat later than A. D. 1143.

* The Hindu pillars of white marble and red sandstone which are found in the gateway and colonnade of Sultan Ghári's tomb, were most probably the spoils of a temple to Siva, built by Mahi Pal on the bank of the Mahipalpur Lake, which is only half a mile distant from the tomb. I found a marble argha, or yoni receptacle of the fingers of Mahâdeva in the pavement of the colonnade of the tomb between two marble pillars.

† Journal of Archæological Society of Delhi; September 1850, p. 92.

‡ The actual "Capture of Delhi" by the Chohâns is mentioned in Tod's Bijoli Inscription dated in S. 1226, or A. D. 1169,—"Rajasthan," II., p. 743. It must, therefore, have occurred some time earlier.

The Kumaon and Garhwâl manuscripts place it in S. 1191, or A. D. 1134; but as they also place the final conquest of the Muhammadans in S. 1231, or A. D. 1174, or just 17 years too early, it seems probable that the capture of *Dilli* by the Chohâns may also be ante-dated by about the same number of years. Admitting this view as probably correct, the capture of Dilli by the Chohâns will be referred to A. D. 1151. Lastly, by the list which I have already given of the Tomar dynasty, the close of Anang Pâl's reign is placed in the latter half of A. D. 1151, or early in 1152, by accepting the longer reign of 21 years 9 months and 16 days, which is found in the Gwalior manuscript.*

By a comparison of all these dates with the period assigned to the Chohân dynasty, it seems most probable that the true date of the capture of *Dilli* by the Chohâns must have been about A. D. 1151. The period assigned to the Chohâns varies from 40½ years to 41¾. By deducting the former number from A. D. 1191, the date of Muâzuddin Sâm's conquest, we obtain A. D. 1154 as the probable period of the capture of Dilli by Visala Deva, when, according to the Kumaon and Garhwâl manuscripts, *Chaucân takht baitha, Dilli Râj kiya,*—"the Chohân sat on the throne and established his kingdom in Dilli." But although Visala thus became the actual lord of Dilli, it is almost certain that Anang Pâl was left in possession of his ancient kingdom as a tributary of the Chohân, while Someswara, the son of Visala, received Anang Pâl's daughter in marriage. The issue of this union, the famous *Prithvi Raj,* or *Rai Pithora,* became the adopted son of the Tomar King, and was formally acknowledged as heir to the throne of Dilli. According to the *Prithvi-Rai-Charitra,* this adoption took place in A. D. 1169, at which date Prithvi Râj must have been about 16 years of age.† Now, as the bard Chand records that the adoption took place during the life-time of Anang Pâl, this last of the Tomar Kings was still reigning in A. D. 1169. We may, therefore, safely fix the close of his reign, and of the Tomar dynasty, to the close of the same year, or the

---

* This leaves 40 years for the reign of the Chohân dynasty in Dehli, which agrees with the period assigned to this race in the details of the Gwalior, Kumaon, and Garhwâl MSS.

† See Wilford in Asiatic Researches, IX., p. 175, quoting the *Prithvi-Rai-Charitra,* says 1173; but as Wilford used the wrong equation for the Vikramaditya era, the true date must be A. D. 1169.

beginning of 1170. This will give a reign of 22 years to Prithvi Raja, which is the very term assigned to him in all the manuscripts, at the end of the Tomar dynasty. It will also add about 18 years to the length of Anang Pál's reign, during which time I suppose him to have been tributary to Visala Deva.

The subject of the Chohán dynasty has been so much confused by the conflicting accounts given by Colonel Tod,[*] that I have found it impossible to make any satisfactory arrangement, either of the names of the Princes, or of the lengths of their reigns. So far as our information goes, the only Chohán Princes of Ajmer, who were at the same time actual Kings of Dilli, were Visala Deva and Prithvi Raja. During the latter half of Anang Pál's reign, I consider him to have been only the titular King of Dilli, and tributary to the paramount sovereign of Ajmer. On his death in A. D. 1170, the throne of Dilli would of course have fallen to Prithvi Raja by his adoption as the successor of the Tomar Prince. On Visala's death, which could not have occurred earlier than A. D. 1163, I infer that Someswara succeeded to the throne of Ajmer. When he was killed in battle seven years afterwards, or in A. D. 1170, the throne of Ajmer would have fallen to Prithvi Raja. But in the genealogical lists between Someswara and his son Prithvi Raja we find the names of *Châhara Deva* and *Nâga Deva* (or *Jaga Deva*), and I can only account for their insertion by supposing that they were the tributary Rajas of Dilli under Prithvi Raja as lord paramount. This seems highly probable if we may place any dependence on the latter part of Colonel Tod's genealogical list of the Chohâns, in which *Châhara Deva* is made the younger brother of Prithvi Raja. That *Châhara*, or *Châhada Deva*, was a person of some consequence, we know from his coins, which are less uncommon than those of Prithvi Raja himself. Perhaps *Nâga Deva* may have been another brother or a near relative.[†]

Colonel Tod gives the substance of an inscription discovered at Bijoli, which is dated in S. 1226, or A. D. 1169,

---

[*] Compare Tod's Rajasthan, II., 451, with II., 763, and Royal Asiatic Society's Transactions, I., p. 145.

[†] In a fine MS. of Chand's Prithi Râj Raisa in my possession I find Prithvi Raja recorded as the son of Someswara, and the grandson of Visala Deva, and the 7th in descent from Vira-Visala. This clears up most of our difficulties, as we now have a Visala Deva contemporary with the record of the Delhi Pillar, a name which is wanting in all the other lists.

during the life-time of Someswara.* In this inscription it is stated that Someswara was originally called Prithvi Raja, but "having obtained the regal dignity through Someswara, he was thence called Someswar." Now, if the date of this inscription has been rightly read, it seems most probable that the Hansi inscription, which mentions a Prithvi Raja in S. 1224, or A. D. 1167, or just two years earlier, must refer to the father, who afterwards obtained the name of Someswara, and not to the son, who is popularly known as *Rai Pithora*.† This assignment of the Hansi inscription to the father is rendered certain by another fact recorded in it, which has escaped the notice of Colebrooke, Fell, and Tod, namely, that *Kirana*, or *Kilhana* of the *Guhila* or Grahilot race, was the maternal uncle of Prithvi Raja. Now, if there is one point undisputed in the history of Rai Pithora, it is that his mother was the daughter of the Tomar Raja Anang Pâl. I conclude, therefore, that the Prithvi Raja, whose mother was a Grahilot, must have been Someswara, whose original name, before his accession to the throne, was also Prithvi Raja.

With the above explanations, I now give all the lists of the Chohán dynasty which I have been able to collect, excepting those of *Tod* and *Mûk-ji*, the Khichi bard, which disagree with the others in so many names that they would be of no use for comparison:

THE CHOHAN DYNASTY OF DILLI.

Abul Fazl, Syad Ahmed.	Gwalior, Kamaon, Garhwal MS.	Length of Reign.	Prithi-Raj Rasa MS.	Inscriptions.
		Y. M. D.		
Bil Deo ...	Visala Deva ...	6 1 4	Visala Deva ...	Visala Deva, S. 1220 or A. D. 1163.
Amara Ganga ...	Gangeya, or Amara Deva ...	5 2 3		
Kehar Pâl ...	Pahadi, or Pada Deva ...	8 1 5		
Samer ...	Samas, or Saveras	7 4 2	Someswara ...	Someswara, S. A. D. 1224=1167. 1220=1163.
Jahir ...	Vehan De, or Bala Deva ...	4 6 1		
Nâg Deo ...	Jag Deo, or Jagarmangur ...	3 1 5		
Pithora, or Prithvi Raja ...	Prithvi Raja ...	0 1 1	Prithvi Raja.	
		40 2 21		

* Rajasthan, II., 713.
† See Captain Fell in Asiatic Researches, XV., 443; and Tod in Royal Asiatic Society's Transactions, I., 154 and 261.

DELHI. 159

On comparing these lists, I think that *Bil Deo* of Abul Fazl may be identified with *Visala Deva* of the inscription on Firuz Shah's Pillar, and that *Sumer* or *Samas* are only corruptions of Someswara. The other names require no remarks.

The reign of Prithvi Raj has been rendered memorable by three events which form separate parts of the rather voluminous work of the bard *Chand*, named *Prithvi Ráj-Rása*. The work is divided into several *Khands*, or books, which are generally known by the names of the subjects of which they treat; thus, the *Kanoj Khand* gives the story of the forcible abduction of the not unwilling daughter of Jaya Chandra, the Rahtor Raja of Kanoj; while the *Mahoba Khand* relates the various fortunes of the successful war with *Parmálik* or *Paramárdi Deva*, the Chandel Raja of Mahoba, and the last books are devoted to the great struggle between the Hindus and Musulmáns, which ended in the final overthrow of Prithvi Ráj, and the establishment of Kutb-ud-din Aibeg on the throne of Dilli as a dependant of the paramount Sovereign Muaz-ud-din Ghori.

The date of the abduction of the Kanoj Princess may be assigned with great probability to the year A. D. 1175, as we know from inscriptions that *Vijaya Chandra*, the father of *Jaya Chandra*, was still living in 1172, and that Jaya Chandra had succeeded to the throne *before* 1177. This event cannot, therefore, be placed earlier than 1175; and as Prince *Rainsi*, the issue of this union, was able to bear arms in the last fatal battle with the Musulmáns in 1193, in which he was killed, it is not possible to place the date of the abduction *later* than 1175.

The date of the great war with the Chandel Prince of Mahoba is given in the *Mahoba Khand* of Chand's poem as Samvat 1241, or A. D. 1184. My copy of this portion of the poem was obtained in Mahoba itself, and I have every reason to believe in the correctness of the year named, as it is borne out by two existing inscriptions of *Paramárddi Deva*, the Chandel Raja, which are dated, respectively, in Samvat 1224 or A. D. 1167, and S. 1241 or A. D. 1184. The date of the final conquest of Dilli by the Musulmáns is variously given by the different authorities. Thus Ibn Batuta has A. H. 584, or A. D. 1188; Abul Fazl has A. H. 588, or A. D. 1192; and Ferishta has A. H. 589, while Syad Ahmad has adopted A. H. 587, founded on his reading of the written date on the Eastern Gateway of the Kutb Masjid. He reads the unit of this date as *Saba*, or 7, whereas I make it *tisa*, or 9. The difference arises from the various reading of two easily mistakeable words *sabá* and *tisá*. My attention was particularly drawn to this date by Mr. Thomas's note on Syad Ahmad's date, which, as he says, "anticipates the epoch ordinarily assigned to the Muhammadan conquest of India by two years." I examined this portion of the inscription minutely with a telescope, and I found two dots or points, which are omitted in Syad Ahmad's lithographed copy of the inscription, quite distinct, *one over the other*, between the words *Sauk* and *wa*, and immediately over the unit of the date, which is placed below those words. If these dots belong to the unit of the date, we must accept the reading of *tisa* and adopt 589 A. H. or A. D. 1193 for the capture of Delhi.*

The only work which is attributed to Prithvi Raja is the extensive fort to the north and east of Anang Pál's Lálkot, which is still called *Kilah Rai Pithora*, or "Pithora's Fort." From the north-west angle of Lálkot the lines of Rai Pithora's walls can still be distinctly traced, running towards the north for about half a mile. From this point they turn to the south of east for one and a half miles, then to the south for one mile, and lastly, to the west and north-west for three-quarters of a mile, where they join the south-west angle of Lálkot, which being situated on higher ground forms a lofty citadel that completely commands the Fort of Rai Pathora. The entire circuit of the walls of the two forts is 4 miles and 3 furlongs, or rather more than half the size of the modern city of Shahjahánábád.†

Up to this point I have endeavoured to trace the outline of the history of Hindu *Dilli*, partly from existing monuments, partly from inscriptions, and partly from other records,

---

* This important date had so attracted the attention of Mr. Thomas, that he erected a scaffolding for the purpose of more carefully studying the original, and he has since had the doubtful passage examined by a most competent authority. As both agree that the true reading is *saba* and not *tisa*, I adopt the reading of A. H. 587, or A. D. as the true date of the first capture of Delhi by the Muhammadans. See Mr. Thomas's Chronicles of the Pathan Kings of Delhi, p. 23, note, for full notice of this date, which he supports by the authority of Hasan Nizámí and Minhájus-Siráj.

† See Plates XXV. and XXXVI. for the relative positions and plans of *Lálkot* and Rai Pithora's Fort.

both printed and manuscript. The history of Muhammadan *Dihli*, or *Delhi*, according to our corrupt spelling, will be found in ample detail in Ferishta and other Moslem authors. I will now, therefore, confine my remarks to a description of the many noble remains of by-gone days, which, either by their grand size, their solid strength, or their majestic beauty, still proudly testify that this vast waste of ruins was once Imperial Delhi, the Capital of all India.

HINDU REMAINS.

The most ancient monuments of Delhi are the two Stone Pillars bearing the edicts of Asoka, both of which were brought to the Capital by Firuz Shah Tughlak, about A. H. 757, or A. D. 1350. The account of the removal of these pillars from their original sites is given in detail by *Shams-i-Siráj*, who was most likely an eye-witness of the re-erection in Firuzábád, as he records that he was 12 years of age at the time when they were set up.[*] This circumstantial account of a contemporary writer at once disposes of Colonel Tod's story[†] that Firuz Shah's Pillar was originally standing "at *Nigambod*, a place of pilgrimage on the Jumna, a few miles below Delhi, whence it must have been removed to its present singular position." *Nigambod* still exists as a place of pilgrimage, being a *ghát* immediately outside the northern wall of the city of Shahjahánábád. It is, therefore, *above* the city of Delhi, instead of being a few miles *below* it, as described by Colonel Tod.

Firuz Shah's Pillar, according to Shams-i-Siráj, was brought from a place which is variously called *Topur, Topera, Toparsuk, Tohera, Tawera,* and *Nahera.*[‡] The place is described as being "on the bank of the Jumna, in the district of Salora, not far from Khizrabad, which is at the foot of the mountains, 90 koss from Delhi." The distance from Delhi and the position at the foot of the mountains point out the present Khizrabad on the Jumna, just below the spot where the river issues from the lower range of Hills, as the place indicated by Shams-i-Siráj. *Salora* is, perhaps, Sidhora, a

---

[*] Journal of Archæological Society of Delhi, I., 74.
[†] Rajasthan, II., 458.
[‡] Journal of the Archæological Society of Delhi, I., pp. 29 and 75. See also Sir H. M. Elliot's Muhammadan Historians, by Dowson, III., p. 350, where the name of the village is given as *Tobra*.

large place only a few miles to the west of Khizrabad. From the village where it originally stood, the pillar was conveyed by land on a truck to Khizrabad, from whence it was floated down the Jumna to Firuzabad, or new Delhi. From the above description of the original site of this pillar, I conclude that the village from whence it was brought was, perhaps, the present *Paota*, on the western bank of the Jumna, and 12 miles in a direct line to the north-east of Khizrabad. Now, in this immediate neighbourhood on the western bank of the Jumna, and at a distance of 66 miles from Thanesar, Hwen Thsang places the ancient Capital of *Srughna*, which was even then (A. D. 630—640) in ruins, although the foundations were still solid. The Chinese pilgrim describes *Srughna* as possessing a large *Vihár*, and a grand stupa of Asoka's time containing relics of Buddha, besides many other stupas of *Sáriputra Maudgalyayana*, and other holy Buddhists. The village of *Topar*, which was the original site of Firuz Shah's Pillar, was certainly within the limits of the ancient kingdom of Srughna, and I think it probable that in the work *Suk*, which is appended to one of the various readings of the name of the village of *Topar*, we still have a fair approximation to *Sughan*, the popular form of the Sanskrit *Srughna*.

When the pillar was removed from its original site, a large square stone was found beneath it, which was also transported to Delhi.* This stone was again placed beneath the pillar in its new situation on the top of the three-storied building called Firuz Shah's Kotila, where it may now be seen, as a gallery has been pierced through the solid masonry immediately beneath the base of the pillar. According to Shams-i-Siráj, the whole length of the shaft was 32 *gaz*, of which 8 gaz were sunk in the building. As the pillar at present stands, I found the total height to be 42 feet 7 inches, of which the sunken portion is only 4 feet 1 inch. But the lower portion of the exposed shaft to a height of 5 feet is still rough, and I have little doubt, therefore, that the whole of the rough portion, 9 feet in length, must have been sunk in the ground on its original site. But according to Shams-i-Siráj, even more than this, or one-fourth of its whole length, that is, 10 feet 8 inches, was sunk in the masonry of Firuz

---

* A similar large square stone was found under the Pahládpur Pillar, when it was removed to the grounds of Queen's College at Banáras.

Shah's Kotila. This I believe was actually the case, for on the west side of the column there still remain *in situ* the stumps of two short octagonal granite pillars that would appear to have formed part of a cloister or open gallery around a fourth story, which cannot have been less than 6½ or 7 feet in height. I conclude, therefore, that the statement of Shams-i-Siráj is quite correct.

When the pillar was at last fixed, the "top was ornamented with black and white stone-work surmounted by a *gilt* pinnacle, from which no doubt it received its name of *Minár Zarin*, or 'Golden Pillar.' This gilt pinnacle was still in its place in A. D. 1611, when William Finch entered Delhi, as he describes the Stone Pillar of *Bimsa*, which, after passing through *three* several stories, rising 24 feet above them all, having on the top *a globe surmounted by a crescent*." The 24 feet of this account are probably the same as the 24 *gaz* of the other, the *gaz* being only a fraction less than 16 inches.

The great inscription of Asoka, which is engraved on this pillar, attracted the notice and stimulated the curiosity of Firuz Shah, who assembled a number of learned Brahmans to decypher it, but without success. "Some, however, interpreted the writing to signify that no one would ever succeed in removing the pillar from the spot on which it originally stood, until a King should be born, by name Firuz Shah." This sort of unblushing mendacity is still but too common in India. Almost everywhere I have found Brahmans ready to tell me the subject of long inscriptions, of which they could not possibly read a single letter. Equally untrue, although not so shameless, are the accounts of this inscription given by Tom Coryat. In a letter to L. Whittaker,* he says—" I have been in a city of this country called Delee, where Alexander the Great joined battle with Porus, King of India, and defeated him, and where, in memory of his victory, he caused to be erected a brazen pillar, which remains there to this day." The same story, with additions, was repeated to the unsuspecting Chaplain Edward Terry,† who says—" I was told by Tom Coryat (who took special note of this place) that he, being in the city of Delee, observed a very great

---

* Kerr's Voyages and Travels, IX., 423.
† Journal, p. 82.

pillar of marble, with a *Greek* inscription upon it, which time hath almost quite worn out, erected (as he supposed) there and then by Great Alexander to preserve the memory of that famous victory." This erroneous opinion of Coryat was adopted by most of the early English travellers, as noticed by Purchas,* who states that these inscriptions are in *Greek* and *Hebrew*, and that some affirm the pillar was erected by Alexander the Great. Coryat's mistake about the Greek most probably arose from an actual inspection of the inscription, in which he would naturally have recognized the Old Páli *th, chh, t, k, g, r, b, j,* and *e,* as Greek letters. The similarity struck James Prinsep also. A noteable exception to the other English travellers is William Finch, who simply states that " it has inscriptions."

The mistakes that have been made about this column are, however, not confined to its inscriptions, as we have seen above, were Coryat calls it a "*brazen* pillar." Strange to say a similar mistake has been made by the generally accurate Bishop Heber, who calls it " a high black pillar of *cast-metal;*" and, again, in describing the iron pillar, he calls it a metal pillar like that in Firuz Shah's Castle.† Again Colonel Tod has identified this pillar with the Nigambod column alluded to by the bard Chand " as telling the fame of the Chohán." It is quite possible that some other pillar may once have stood at Nigambod; but as the golden column of Firuz really does "tell the fame of the Chohán," and as its inscriptions were recorded only thirty years prior to Chand's death, it seems most probable that his allusion must be to this particular pillar. The name of Nigambod may, perhaps, be a corruption of the real name of the place where the column then stood, or an ignorant interpolation in the text of a date later than Firuz Shah.

The "Golden Pillar" is a single shaft of pale pinkish sand-stone, 42 feet 7 inches in length, of which the upper portion, 35 feet in length, has received a very high polish, while the remainder is left quite rough. Its upper diameter is 25·3 inches, and its lower diameter 38·8 inches, the diminution being ·39 inch per foot. Its weight is rather more than 27 tons. In its dimensions it is more like the Allahabad

---

* Kerr, VIII, 293, note 6.
† Journal, II., pp. 291—307.

pillar than any other, but it tapers much more rapidly towards the top, and is, therefore, less graceful in its outline.

There are two principal inscriptions on Firuz Shah's pillar, besides several minor records of pilgrims and travellers from the first centuries of the Christian era down to the present time. The oldest inscriptions for which the pillar was originally erected comprise the well known edicts of Asoka, which were promulgated in the middle of the third century B. C. in the ancient *Páli*, or spoken language of the day. The alphabetical characters, which are of the oldest form that has yet been found in India, are most clearly and beautifully cut, and there are only a few letters of the whole record lost by the peeling off of the surface of the stone. The inscription ends with a short sentence, in which King Asoka directs the setting up these monoliths in different parts of India as follows:[*] "Let this religious edict be engraved on stone pillars *(sila thambha)* and stone tablets *(sila phalaka)* that it may endure for ever." In this amended passage we have a distinct allusion to the rock inscriptions, as well as to the pillar inscriptions. As this is the longest and most important of all the pillar inscriptions of Asoka, I made a careful impression of the whole for comparison with James Prinsep's published text. The record consists of four distinct inscriptions on the four sides of the column facing the cardinal points, and of one long inscription immediately below, which goes completely round the pillar. I may mention that the word *Ajakándni*, at the end of the 7th line south face, was not omitted "accidentally," as James Prinsep supposed, by the original engraver, but has been lost by the peeling away of the stone for about 4 inches. The vowel *i* attached to the final letter is still quite distinct. The penultimate word on the eastern face is not *agnim*, as doubtfully read by Prinsep, but *abhyum*, and, as he rightly conjectured, it is the same word that begins the 19th line. The last word in the 11th line, which puzzled Prinsep, is not *atikata*, but *atikantam*, the same as occurs near the beginning of the 15th line. The few corrections which I have noticed here show the accuracy of Burnouf's opinion, that a new collation of

---

[*] See James Prinsep in Bengal Asiatic Society's Journal, 1837, p. 602. He reads *siladhalakini*, instead of *phalakini*, which is quite distinct on the pillar.

the pillar inscriptions would be of the greatest value. I am happy to say that I have now made new copies of the inscriptions on the pillars at *Delhi*, *Ararâj*, and *Navandgarh*, for collation by competent scholars.

The last 10 lines of the eastern face, as well as the whole of the continuous inscription round the shaft, are peculiar to the Delhi pillar. There is a marked difference also in the appearance of this part of the inscription. The characters are all thinner and less boldly cut; the vowel marks are generally sloping instead of being horizontal or perpendicular, and the letters *j*, *t*, *s* and *h* are differently formed from those of the preceding part of the inscription. These new forms are exactly the same as those of the rock inscription near Khâlsi, on the Jumna, which is only a few miles above *Paota*, the probable site from whence the pillar was brought by Firuz Shah.

The second inscription is that which records the victories of the Chohân Prince Visala Deva, whose power extended "from Himâdri to Vindhya." This record of the fame of the Chohân consists of two separate portions, the shorter one being placed immediately above Asoka's edicts, and the longer one immediately below them. But as both are dated in the same year, *viz.*, S. 1220, or A. D. 1163, and refer to the same Prince, they may be considered as forming only one inscription. The upper portion, which is placed very high, is engraved in much larger characters than the lower one. A translation of this inscription was published by Colebrooke, and his rendering of the text has been verified by H. H. Wilson from a copy made by Mr. Thomas.[*] The reading of Sri *Sallakshana* proposed by Mr. Thomas is undoubtedly correct, instead of *Sri Mad Lakshana*, as formerly read. I would suggest also that the rendering of *Châhumâna tilaka*, as "most eminent of the tribe which sprang from the arms" (of Brahma), seems to me much less forcible than the simple translation of "Chief of the *Châhumânu*" or Chohân tribe. I believe also that there is an error in referring the orgin of the Chohâns to Brahma, as *Mûk-ji*, the Bard of the Khichi Chohâns, distinctly derives them from the *Anal kund*, or fount of fire on Mount Abu, an origin which

---

[*] Colebrooke in Asiatic Researches, III, 130; and Thomas's Prinsep's Essays, I, 325.

corresponds with that assigned to them by Colonel Tod. It is *Cháluk Rao*, the founder of the *Chálukya*, or *Soláukhi* tribe, that is fabled to have sprung from Brahma.

The minor inscriptions on Firuz Shah's Pillar are of little interest or importance. They are, however, of different ages, and the more ancient records must have been inscribed while the pillar yet stood on its original site, under the hills to the north of *Khizrabad*. One of the oldest is the name of *Sri Bhadra Mitra*, or *Subhadramitra*, in characters of the Gupta era. This is written in very small letters, as are also two others of the same age. In larger letters of a somewhat later date, there are several short inscriptions, of which the most legible is *Surya Vishnu Subarnakakana*. A second begins with *Hara Singha Subarnakakana*, the remainder being illegible, with exception of the word *Kumára*. A third reads *Charma Subana*, the second letter being somewhat doubtful. This record is extended in another place to *Charma Srbanakshdra*. Of a much later date is the name of the *Saiva* mendicant *Siddh Bhayaukarnáth Jogi*, followed by a *trisul*. The name of this wandering mendicant is also recorded in the very same characters, but simply as "*Bhayankar Náth*," in one of the *Barábar* caves in Bihár.* On the northern face there are two still later inscriptions in modern Nágari, both of which bear the same date of Wednesday, 13th, waning moon of *Chaitra*, in *Samvat* 1581, or A. D. 1524. The longer inscription contains the name of *Suritan Ibráhim*, or Sultan Ibrahim Lodi, who reigned from A. D. 1517 to 1525.

The second of Asoka's Delhi Pillars is now lying in five pieces near Hindu Rao's house on the top of the hill to the north-west of Shahjahánábád. The whole length of these pieces was 32¾ feet, but the upper end of the middle piece, which was inscribed with Asoka's edicts, was sawn off some years ago, and sent to Calcutta, where it may now be seen in the Asiatic Society's Museum.† The portion of the shaft that was below the inscription still measures 18 feet, and that which was above it, 12 feet. As the end of the shaft is still rough, it seems probable that the polished portion could not

---

* See p. 22, and Plate XX.

† This has now been returned to Delhi, and the pillar has been restored; but I think that it ought rather to have been set up at Mirat, from whence it was originally brought by Firuz Shah.

have been more than 32 feet in height, which is somewhat less than that of the other known pillars of Asoka. Indeed, this pillar is described by Shams-i-Siráj as being smaller than the other, a description which can apply only to its height, as its diameter is somewhat greater. From its broken state it is not easy to obtain correct measurements of its thickness. At the point where the inscribed piece was sawn off, the diameter is 33·44 inches; and my measurements make the upper diameter $20\frac{1}{4}$ inches, and lower diameter of the smoothed portion 35·82 inches. The rough thick end is about 38 inches in diameter. These measurements make the diminution of the pillar just one-fifth of an inch per foot.

According to Shams-i-Siráj this column was brought from Mirat by Firuz Shah, and erected near its present position in the *Kushak Shikar*, or "hunting palace." The position of the palace has already been determined by the researches of Messrs. Cope and Lewis;* but the following statements of William Finch will place this identification of site beyond all dispute. In A. D. 1611 he describes the city (that is, of Shir Shah) as being 2 koss, or $2\frac{1}{2}$ miles, in length from gate to gate, and about 2 koss from thence he places "the ruins of a hunting seat or *mole* (*Mahal*) built by *Sultan Bemsa*, a great Indian Sovereign."† This description agrees exactly with the position of the broken pillar, which is about $2\frac{3}{4}$ miles to the north-west of the *Lál Darwáza*, or north gate of the old city of Shir Shah, which is itself about $2\frac{1}{4}$ miles distant from the south gate, to the westward of *Dinpandh*, or *Purana Killah*.

According to the popular belief, this pillar was thrown down by an accidental explosion of a powder magazine in the time of Farokhsir, who reigned from A. D. 1713 to 1719. This tradition is rendered almost certain by the statements of Padre Tieffenthaler, who resided in India between A. D. 1743 and 1786. He saw the pillar lying just as it is now in five pieces; but he was informed that it was standing erect not long before, and that it was thrown down by an explosion of gunpowder.

---

* Journal of Archæological Society of Delhi.
† Kerr's Voyages and Travels, VIII., 292.

The inscriptions on this pillar are very imperfect, owing to the mutilated and worn surface of the stone. Such portions as remain have been carefully examined by James Prinsep, who found them to be "so precisely the duplicates" of the other inscription that he did not think "it worth while to make them the subject of a separate note."* The remaining portions, which correspond with parts of the inscriptions on the north, south, and west faces of the other pillar, have been lithographed by Prinsep in Plate XLII., Vol. VI. of his Journal.

The *Iron Pillar* of Delhi, which is the next work in point of antiquity, is one of the most curious monuments in India. Many large works in metal were no doubt made in ancient times, such, for instance, as the celebrated Colussus of Rhodes, and the gigantic statues of the Buddhists, which are described by Hwen Thsang. But all of these were of brass or copper, all of them were hollow, and they were all built up of pieces rivetted together, whereas the Delhi Pillar is a solid shaft of wrought iron upwards of 16 inches in diameter, and upwards of 40 feet in length. It is true that there are flaws in many parts, which shew that the welding is imperfect; but when we consider the extreme difficulty of manufacturing a pillar of such vast dimensions, our wonder will not be diminished by knowing that the welding of the bar is defective. The total height of the pillar above ground is 22 feet, but the smooth shaft is only 15 feet, the capital being 3½ feet, and the rough part of the shaft below also 3½ feet. But its depth under ground is asserted to be considerably greater than its height above ground, as a recent excavation is said to have been carried down to 26 feet without reaching the foundation on which the pillar rests.† The whole length of the Iron Pillar is, therefore, upwards of 48 feet, but how much more is not known, although it must be considerable, as the pillar is said not to have been loosened by the excavation. I think, therefore, it is highly probable that the whole length is not less than 60 feet. The lower diameter of the shaft is 16·4 inches, and the upper diameter is 12·05 inches, the diminution being ·29 of an inch per foot. The pillar contains about 80 cubic feet of metal, and weighs upwards of 17 tons.

---

* Journal of Asiatic Society, Bengal, VI., 704.

† Mr. Cooper told me 26 feet, but the man in charge assured me that the actual depth reached was 35 feet.

When I wrote this report in 1863 I described the pillar as formed of "mixed metal." This I did on the authority of the late Mr. Fred. Cooper, Deputy Commissioner of Delhi. He was then preparing a hand-book for Delhi, in which I find the pillar is thus described—"The celebrated *Loha-ka-lát* or iron pillar, which is, however, a misnomer, for it is a compound metal resembling bronze." On thinking over this question some months afterwards it struck me that a *bronze* pillar would never have escaped the rapacity of the Muhammadan conquerors. I, therefore, obtained a small bit from the rough lower part of the pillar, which I submitted to Dr. Murray Thomson for analysis, who informed me that the metal was "pure malleable iron of 7·66 specific gravity." I have since referred to various books to see what account was given of this pillar by different tourists; and I find that the opinion that the pillar was made of mixed metal or bronze has certainly prevailed since the beginning of the century.* But it is most probably of even older date, as the notorious Tom Coryat speaks of the *brazen* pillar which he had seen at "Delee." There can be little doubt that this was also the Native belief in former times, as it certainly is at present; for I presume that the early English residents at Delhi adopted what they were told by the people without either question or examination, although the one continued to call it the *Lohi-ki-lát*, and the other the "Iron Pillar." The belief, perhaps, arose from the curious yellow appearance of the upper part of the shaft, which I myself observed, and which induced me to accept Mr. Cooper's statement.

The Iron Pillar records its own history in a deeply cut Sanskrit inscription of six lines on its western face. The inscription has been translated by James Prinsep, who remarks that "the pillar is called the arm of fame" (*Kirtti bhuja*) "of Raja Dhára, and the letters cut upon it are called the typical cuts inflicted on his enemies by his sword, writing his immortal fame."† It is stated that he subdued a people

---

* In 1816 the pillar was seen by a lady, "Tour in the Upper Provinces by A. D.," p. 165, who describes it as "the wonderful brazen pillar." Bishop Heber, "Travels, II., 291, 317," calls it a "metal pillar" or a "black pillar of cast metal." In 1834 Miss Emma Roberts, "Views in India, I., 40," speaks of it as "a pillar of mixed metal;" and in 1844 Colonel Sleeman, "Rambles, II., 256," writes that the small pillar is of bronze, or a metal which resembles bronze, and is softer than brass.

† Bengal Asiatic Society's Journal, VII., p. 630.

on the *Sindhu*, named *Tahlikas*, and "obtained with his own arm an undivided sovereignty on the earth for a long period." The above is the whole of the meagre information that can be gathered from this inscription, save the bare fact that the Raja was a worshipper of Vishnu. The date of the inscription is referred by James Prinsep to the third or fourth century after Christ; but Mr. Thomas considers that this is "too high an antiquity for the style of writing employed on the monument." I agree, however, with Prinsep, as the characters appear to me to be exactly the same as those of the Gupta inscriptions. I have already suggested the year A. D. 319, which is the initial point of the Balabhi or Gupta era, as an approximate date, as I think it not improbable that the Raja may have assisted in the downfall of the powerful Gupta dynasty. I read his name preferably as *Bháva*, the letter *bh* having got closed by the accidental slip of the punching chisel. The letter is different from every other *dh* in the inscription.

According to universal tradition, the Iron Pillar was erected by *Bilan Deo*, or Anang Pál, the founder of the Tomara dynasty, who was assured by a learned Brahman that, as the foot of the pillar had been driven so deep into the ground that it rested on the head of *Vasuki*, King of the Serpents, who supports the earth; it was now immoveable, and that dominion would remain in his family as long as the pillar stood. But the Raja, doubting the truth of the Brahman's statement, ordered the pillar to be dug up, when the foot of it was found wet with the blood of the serpent king, whose head it had pierced. Regretting his unbelief, the Iron Pillar was again raised; but, owing to the king's former incredulity, every plan now failed in fixing it firmly, and, in spite of all his efforts, it still remained loose (*dhíla*) in the ground, and this is said to have been the origin of the name of the ancient city of *Dhili*.

This tradition has been variously reported by different authorities, but the main points are the same in all. Colonel Tod states that the Iron Pillar is said to be resting on the head of the *Sahes Nág*, who is the same as *Vasuki*, the Serpent King. A lady traveller, who visited Delhi between 1804 and 1814, heard the tradition in a somewhat different way.* A Brahman told the king that if he could place the seat of his government on the head of the snake that supports the world,

---

* "Tour in the Upper Provinces," by A. D., p. 166.

his kingdom would last for ever. The Iron Pillar was accordingly driven into the ground on its present site, under the superintendence of the Brahman, who announced that the lucky spot had been found. On hearing this, a courtier, jealous of the Brahman's influence, declared that the pillar was not placed over the serpent's head, but that he could point out the true place, which he had seen in a dream. The pillar was accordingly taken up by the Raja's order, and, agreeably to the Brahman's prediction, the foot of it was found wet with the blood of the serpent's head. This tradition is also imperfectly related in Purchas's Pilgrims, on the authority of English travellers who visited India during the reigns of Jahángir and Shahjahan. Purchas states that the *Rase* (Raja) who founded Delhi, "by advice of his magicians, tried the ground by driving an iron stake, which came up bloody, having wounded a snake. This the *Ponde* (Pándo or Pandit), or magician, said was a fortunate sign."* In all these different versions of the erection of the Iron Pillar, the main points of the story are the same, and the popular belief in this tradition is confirmed by the well known verse—

"*Kílli to dhílli bhai,*
"*Tomar bhoya mat kin.*"
"The pillar has become loose,
"The Tomar's wish will not be fulfilled."†

This tradition is related in a more poetical form by Kharg Rai, who wrote in the reign of Shahjahan. According to him, the Tomar Prince was provided by the sage *Vyás* with a golden nail, or spike, 25 fingers in length, which he was told to drive into the ground. At a lucky moment, on the 13th day of the waning moon of *Vaisákh*, in the *Samvat* year 702, or A. D. 736, when the moon was in the mansion of *Abhijit*, the spike was driven into the ground by the Raja. Then said Vyás to the King—

"*Tum se ráj kadi jaëga nahi,*
"*Yih khunti Vasug ki máthe gadhi hai.*"
"Ne'er will thy kingdom be bespod,
"The spike hath pierced Vasuki's head."

---

* Kerr's Voyages and Travels, VIII, 592, note.
† My assistant, Mr. J. D. Beglar, has pointed out to me that *towar* is a common construction for *tumhára*, "your." I believe, therefore, that a pun is intended, and that the second line may be translated—"Your wish will not be fulfilled."

Vyâs had no sooner departed, than the incredulous Raja boldly declared his disbelief in the sage's announcement, when immediately

"*Bilan De khunti ukhârh dekhi,*
"*Tab lohu ac chuchâti nikali.*"
" He saw the spike thrown on the ground,
" Blood-dropping from the serpent's wound."

The sage was recalled by the horrified king, who was directed to drive the stake into the ground a second time. Again he struck, but the spike penetrated only nineteen fingers, and remained *loose* in the ground. Once more then the sage addressed the Raja prophetically,—" Like the spike *(killi)* which you have driven, your dynasty will be unstable *(dilli)*, and after ' nineteen' generations it will be supplanted by the Chobáns, and they by the Turkâns." Dilan De then became King of *Dilli*, and with his descendants held the throne for nineteen generations, according to the number of fingers' lengths which the spike had been driven into the ground.

What was the origin of this tradition, and at what time it first obtained currency, may never, perhaps, be known; but I think we are justified in hazarding a guess that the long reign of the Tomar dynasty must first have led to an opinion of its durability which would then have been naturally compared with the evident stability with which the Iron Pillar was fixed in the ground. We have an exactly parallel case in the well known saying about Rome and the Coliseum—" *Quamdiú stabit Colysens, stabit et Roma quando cadit Colysens cadit Roma,*" which the verse of Byron has rendered famous.—

" While stands the Coliseum, Rome shall stand,
" When falls the Coliseum, Rome shall fall."

This, indeed, is the oldest form of the Indian tradition that I have been able to trace. When the Muhammadan conqueror first took possession of Delhi, he was informed that the inscription on the Iron Pillar declared that the Hindu rule would last as long as the pillar remained standing; on hearing which, to show his contempt of the prophecy, the proud victor allowed the pillar to stand. This same story must have been told to Bishop Hober, but he has jumbled it up with his account of Firuz Shah's Pillar.* That the story which he heard must have belonged to the Iron Pillar is rendered certain by his referring it to the period of "the conquest of the country by the Musulmáns." About the same time also a similar story was heard by Major Archer,† who records that, "as long as the pillar stood, so long would Hindustan flourish." At a later date, a similar story was repeated to Mrs. Colin Mackenzie,‡ who says that the Iron Pillar bears a Sanskrit inscription, "the purport of which is that, as long as this pillar stands, the *Ráj* or kingdom has not finally departed from the Hindus." Lastly, Syad Ahmad relates that the pillar was driven into the head of *Vasuki*, King of the Snakes, to make his empire lasting.

If I am right in ascribing the origin of this tradition to a late period in the history of the Tomars, when the long duration of their rule had induced people to compare its stability with that of the Iron Pillar, I think that the saying may be referred with considerable probability to the prosperous reign of Anang Pál II., whose name is inscribed on the shaft with the date of *Samvat* 1109 or A. D. 1052.

The account given above was written in 1863, shortly after which I found the original version of the story in the 3rd book of my copy of Chand's Prithi Ráj Ráisa, which is appropriately named *Killí-dhilli-kathá*, or "story of the Loose Pillar." Chand, however, refers the event to the time of the last Anang Pál, who wished to ascertain the fortunate hour for holding a great festival in honour of the birth of his grandson, Prithi Ráj. He enquired from Vyás, a Jagjoti Brahman, who after a short consideration replied—"Now is the lucky time, your dynasty will become immoveable, and its root will strike into the head of Seshnág.§ But the Raja was incredulous, when Vyás taking an iron spike drove it down 60 fingers deep until it reached the serpent's head,¶ and drawing it out he showed it to the Raja covered with blood. Then addressing Anang Pál, he said—"Your kingdom like the spike has become unstable."

---

* Journal II., 291.
† Tour in Upper India, I., 121.
‡ 2nd edition, p. 47
§ Seshnág or Vásuki is the King of the Serpents, on whose thousand heads the earth itself is said to be supported.
¶ *Sattiun angula lohah killiya, Sahas Seshkh sir milliya.*

Thus saith the Seer Vyás,
Things that must come to pass:
Now the *Tomars*, next *Chohâns*,
And shortly after the *Turkâns*.*

The Raja in a rage expelled Vyás, who retired to Ajmer, where he was hospitably received by the Chohâns on account of his prophecy in favour of their race.

The remaining inscriptions on the Iron Pillar are numerous but unimportant. There are two records of the Chohân Raja *Chatra Sinha*, both dated in *Samvat* 1883, or A. D. 1826. They state that the Raja was descended from *Prithivi Raja* in 20 generations, which is quite possible, although the period allowed for each generation is under 23 years. The date of Prithivi Raja is given as *Samvat* 1851, or A. D. 1094, which is just 99 years too early, an amount of error which agrees with the false dates which have been inserted in the text of the *Prithi Ráj Rása* of the Bard *Chand*. There is also another modern Nagari inscription of six lines, dated in *Samvat* 1707, or A. D. 1710, of the Bundela Rajas of *Chúnderi*. Below this there are two Persian inscriptions, dated in A. H. 1060 and 1061, or A. D. 1651-52, which merely record the names of visitors.

The only other remains of Hindu Delhi are the numerous pillars which form the colonnades of the Court of the Great Masjid close to the Kutb Minar. The Arabic inscription over the eastern entrance of this Court-yard states that the materials were obtained from the demolition of 27 idolatrous temples, each of which had cost the sum of 20 *lakhs* of *Diliâls*. I agree with Mr. Thomas† that the *Diliâl* must have corresponded with the original billon currency of Prithivi Raja. Now the value of the Diliâl was as nearly as possible the same as that of the *Jital* or *Chital* of Ala-uddin Khilji, 50 of which, as we learn from Ferishta,‡ were equal to one Rupee. The cost of each of these temples would not, therefore, have been more than Rs. 40,000, and that of the whole number, only Rs. 10,80,000, or £108,000. The cost of these temples seems excessive when expressed in such

---

* *Káhe Vyás Jogjati ogamu ágamu á-jánao,
Tomar, tai Chuhuwân hoi, puni puni Turkánao.*

† Prinsep's Essays, I., 325.

‡ Briggs, I., 360.

small money as *Diliāls*, each coin being worth only a little more than a half-penny; but the sum is moderate enough when it is named in rupees.

Mr. Fergusson* has expressed an opinion that "it is not "easy to determine whether the pillars now stand as ori- "ginally arranged by the Hindus, or whether they have been "taken down and re-arranged by the conquerors." In this instance he thinks it "most probable that the former was "the case, and that they were open colonnades surrounding "the palace of Prithivi Raja;" but he presently adds that, "if this is so, it is the only instance known of Hindu pillars "being left undisturbed." When Mr. Fergusson formed this opinion, he was not aware of the fact recorded over the eastern gateway by the Musulmán conqueror, that the Great Masjid had been built of the materials of no less than *twenty-seven Hindu temples*. He knew only the common tradition that on this site once stood the palace and temple attributed to Prithivi Raja. On this account he may have supposed that most of these pillars must have belonged to those buildings, and, therefore, that some of them might *possibly* still be in their original positions. But evidently he had strong doubts on the subject; for he repeats his opinion that, "if the pillars at Kutb are *in situ*, it is the only instance "known of such being the case." In February 1853 I examined very minutely the pillared cloisters of the Great Mosque, and I then came to the conclusion, as recorded in my note-book at the time, that "the square about the Iron "Pillar is all made up; the outer-walls are not Hindu; the "pillars are all made up of pieces of various kinds; the "shaft of one kind being placed above that of another for "the purpose of obtaining height. The general effect is good; "but a closer inspection reveals the incongruities of pillars, "half plain and half decorated, and of others that are thicker "above than below." Just ten years later, in January 1863, with Mr. Fergusson's book in my hand I re-examined the whole of these pillars with exactly the same result. Every single pillar is made up of *two* separate Hindu shafts, placed one above the other; and as those shafts are of many various sizes, the required height is obtained by the insertion of other pieces between the shorter shafts.† In one instance

---

* Hand-book of Architecture, 1418.

† I have a suspicion that some of the pillars in the Masjid itself may be in their original positions. They are single pillars of a large temple. I will examine them minutely during the ensuing cold season, 1871-72.

in the north cloister there is a pillar made up of no less than three shafts of exactly the same pattern, piled one over the other. This may be seen in Beato's photograph of this cloister (see the 4th pillar on the left hand). The general effect of these large rows of made-up columns is certainly rich and pleasing; but this effect is due to the kindly hand of time, which has almost entirely removed the coating of plaster with which the whole of these beautifully sculptured pillars were once barbarously covered by the idol-hating Musalmáns.

The same doubling up of the old Hindu pillars has been followed in the cloisters of the outer court of the Kutb Mínar, the shaft of one plain pillar being placed over another to obtain height. A similar re-arrangement may be observed in the Court of the Júmai or Dína Masjid of Kanoj, commonly called *Sita-ka-Rasúi*, or "Sita's kitchen."

The number of decorated pillars now remaining in the court-yard of the Great Mosque around the Iron Pillar is, as nearly as I could reckon them, 340; but as the cloisters are incomplete, the original number must have been much greater. My reckoning makes them 450. In the interior of the Great Mosque itself there are 35 pillars now remaining, of a much larger size and of a somewhat different style of decoration. When the Mosque was complete there must have been not less than 70 of these pillars. Of the plainer pillars in the court-yard of the Kutb Mínar I counted 370, but the total number required to complete the cloisters would be about 1,200.

I have given these figures in detail for the purpose of corroborating the statement of the Musalmán conqueror, with regard to the number of temples that were standing in Dilli at the close of the Hindu power. The usual number of columns in a Hindu temple is from 20 to 30, although a few of the larger temples may have from 50 to 60. But these are exceptional cases, and they are more than balanced by the greater number of smaller temples, which have not more than 12 or 16 pillars. The great temple of *Vishnupad* at Gaya has 50 pillars, and Mr. Fergusson mentions that a temple of 56 pillars was the most extended arrangement that he had met with under a single dome.[*] The magnificent

---

[*] Illustrations of Indian Architecture, folio ed., p. 18.

temple at *Chandrávati*, near *Jhálra Pátan*, and the pillared temple of *Ganthai*, at *Kajráho*, have only 28 columns each. The *Baroli* temple has 24 columns, the great temple at *Bindrában* has only 16, and the *Chaori*, in the *Mokandra Pass*, has not more than 12. But there are many temples that have even fewer pillars than these; as, for instance, that of *Mála Devi*, in Gwalior, which has only 6 pillars, and that of *Chatur Bhuja*, also in Gwalior, which has not more than 4 pillars. Taking these temples as fair specimens of many various styles and ages, the average number of pillars in a Hindu fane is between 24 and 25, or, if the extremes be omitted, the average number is 21. Accepting these numbers as a fair guide, we may set down the 76 pillars of the Great Masjid as the spoils of at least 2, but more probably of 3 temples, each equal in size to the magnificent fane at Chandrávati. Similarly the 453 pillars of the court of the Masjid will represent the spoils of not less than from 18 to 22 temples, of 20 and 25 columns each. These numbers added together give a total of from 20 to 25 temples, which agrees so nearly with the number recorded in the Muhammadan inscription, as to leave no doubt whatever of the truth of the conqueror's boast that the Masjid was built of the spoils of 27 temples.

A curious confirmation of the average size of those temples has been afforded by a discovery which I first made in 1853, and which I completed during the present year 1863. In the south-east corner of the cloisters of the Great Mosque, the pillars, with bases and capitals complete, are nearly all of one style and size, and quite different from the other columns. Now, the bases, shafts, and capitals of these pillars are *numbered*, the highest number discovered being 19. I found 15 numbered shafts, of which No. 13 is in the north cloister, far away from its fellows. I found also 13 numbered bases, and 7 numbered capitals; but only in one instance, that of No. 10, do the numbers of base, shaft, and capital, as they now stand, agree. Here, then, we have a direct and convincing proof that these particular pillars have all been re-arranged. The total number of shafts discovered was only 15, but they were all numbered. Of the bases I discovered 19, of which 4 were square, and 15 had the angles recessed like all the shafts. Of the capitals, all of one uniform pattern, I found 20, of which one was inscribed with the No. 19. From all these

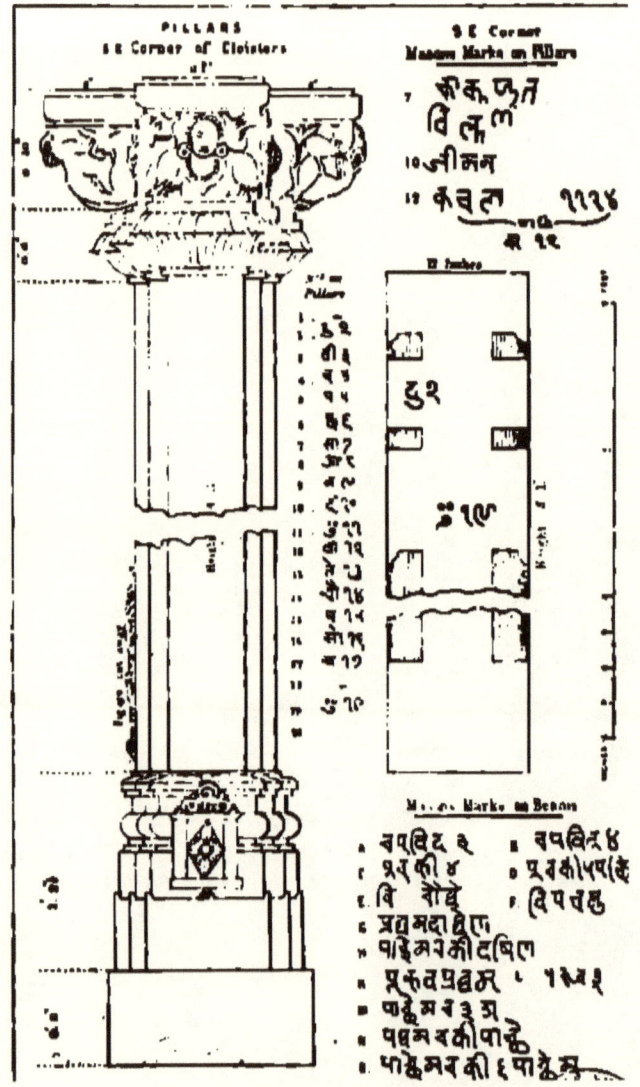

facts I conclude, with a probability amounting almost to certainty, that the temple from which these pillars were obtained consisted of 20 columns only. On No. 12 shaft there is the word *Kachal* in Nagari letters on one face, with the date of 1124 on another face, which, referred to the Vikramáditya *Samvat*, is equivalent to A. D. 1067, at which time Anang Pál II., the founder of Lalkot, was reigning in Dilli.

But the mason's marks on the stones of this temple were not confined to the pillars, as I discovered them on no less than 13 different portions of its entablature. These marks are more than usually detailed; but, unfortunately, in spite of their length and apparent clearness, I am still unable to make them out completely.[*]

The marks are the following:

A.—*Chapa Vida* 3	Upper *Vida* (?) No. 3
B.—*Chapa Vida* 4	Ditto (?) No. 4
C.—*Páchuki* 4	Rear (?) No. 4
D.—*Pachuki* 5 pachhim	Rear (?) No. 5 west.
E.—*Ti Chaothe*	*Vida* (?) fourth.
F.—*Ti panchama*	*Vida* (?) fifth.
G.—*Prathama Dáchen*	First Architrave.
H.—*Pachchhim Raki Dáchen* ...	West side Architrave.
K.—*Purab Prathama*	East first.
L.—*Purab* 3	East No. 3.
M.—*Pachchhim Ra* 3 *A-*(ge ?) ...	West side No. 3., front?
N.—*Pachchhim Raki pachchhe* ...	West side back.
O.—*Pachchhim Raki* 6 *pachchhe* ...	West side No. 6, back.

There is a peculiarity about the numbers of the pillars which is worthy of note. Each cypher is preceded by the initial letter of the word for that number. Thus, 3 is preceded by *ti* for *tin*, 10 by *da* for *das*, and 16 by *so* for *solah*. The same style of marking would appear to have been used for a second temple, as I found a pillar of another pattern with the number *da* 2, and a pilaster of the same kind with

---

[*] See Plate XXXVII. for copies of these mason's marks, and a drawing of one of the pillars. During a visit of a few hours in the present year, 1874, I found two numbered pillars of a different kind, with the Nos. 2 and 19, showing that a second temple, destroyed by the Muhammadans, must have been supported on not less than 20 pillars. I found also a mason's record of five lines on a third variety of pillar, but the letters are faint and difficult to read. I can make out a notice of 7+6+5+8, or 26 pillars altogether, of which I discovered 5 in the cloisters.

§ 19.* Sixteen bases of the first pillar have recessed angles, and four are plain squares. In this case the temple would have had 4 pillars (probably an outer row) of one pattern, and 16 of another kind, but all of the same height.

The dimensions of these inscribed pillars are as follows:

		Ft. In.	Ft. In.
Capital	Upper member, with brackets...	0 10	
	Lower ditto ...	0 6	
			1 4
Shaft	... ...	...	4 11¼
Base	Upper portion, ornamented ...	1 2½	
	Lower ditto plain ...	0 9	
			1 11¼
	Total height ...		8 3

The only other Hindu remains are the two forts of *Lálkot* and *Rai Pithora*, which together formed the old Dilli of the Musalmáns, after the building of a new fort of *Siri* by Ala-ud-din Khilji. Of these two, the older fort of *Lálkot* has hitherto remained unknown, being always described by Musalmáns as a part of the fort of Rai Pithora. It is called *Siri* by Lieutenant Burgess, who made a survey of the ruins of Dilli in 1849-50, and the same name is given to it by Messrs. Cope and Lewis in their interesting account of Firuzabad, published in the Journal of the Archæological Society of Delhi for 1850. The reasons which induce me to identify this fort with the *Lálkot* of Anang Pál have already been given when speaking of the re-founding of *Dilli*, and the reasons which compel me to reject its identification with *Siri* will be detailed when I come to speak of that place.

The Fort of *Lálkot*, which was built by Anang Pál in A. D. 1060, is of an irregular rounded oblong form, 2¼ miles in circumference. Its walls are as lofty and as massive as those of *Tughlakábád*, although the blocks of stone are not

---

* These two pillars are 4 feet 10½ inches high, and 11¾ inches square. I found 13 pillars of almost the same pattern, but of somewhat larger dimensions, being 5 feet 3½ inches high, and 13½ inches square. The commonest pillar is of a similar pattern, but with the addition of human figures on the lower faces of the shaft, and a deep recessed ornament at the top of the shaft. Of this kind I counted 76 pillars during my last visit in the present year 1871.

so colossal. By different measurements I found the ramparts to be from 28 to 30 feet in thickness, of which the parapet is just one-half. The same thickness of parapet is also derived from the measurement given by Ibn Batuta in A. D. 1340, who says that the walls were *eleven* cubits thick. Accepting this measure as the same that was in use in Firuz Shah's time, namely, of 16 inches, as derived from the length of Firuz Shah's pillar, the thickness of the walls of old Dilli was 14⅔ feet. These massive ramparts have a general height of 60 feet above the bottom of the ditch, which still exists in very fair order all round the fort, except on the south side, where there is a deep and extensive hollow that was most probably once filled with water. About one-half of the main walls are still standing as firm and as solid as when they were first built. At all the salient points there are large bastions from 60 to 100 feet in diameter. Two of the largest of these, which are on the north side, are called the *Fateh Búrj* and the *Sohan Búrj*. The long lines of wall between these bastions are broken by numbers of smaller towers well splayed out at the base, and 45 feet in diameter at top, with curtains of 60 feet between them. Along the base of these towers, which are still 30 feet in height, there is an outer line of wall forming a *raoni* or faussebraie, which is also 30 feet in height. The parapet of this wall has entirely disappeared, and the wall itself is so much broken, as to afford an easy descent into the ditch in many places. The upper portion of the counterscarp walls has all nearly fallen down, excepting on the north-west side, where there is a double line of works strengthened by detached bastions.

The positions of three of the gateways in the west half of the fort are easily recognized, but the walls of the eastern half are so much broken that it is now only possible to guess at the probable position of one other gate. The north gate is judiciously placed in the re-entering angle close to the Fateh Búrj, where it still forms a deep gap in the lofty mass of rampart, by which the cowherds enter with their cattle. The west gate is the only one of which any portion of the walls now remains. It is said to have been called the *Ranjit* gate. This gate-way was 17 feet wide, and there is still standing on the left hand side a large upright stone, with a grove for guiding the ascent and descent of a portcullis. This stone is 7 feet in height above the rubbish, but it is probably not less than 12 or 15 feet. It is 2 feet 1 inch broad and 1 foot 3 inches thick. The approach to this gate is guarded by no less than three small out-works. The south gate is in the southmost angle near Adham Khan's tomb. It is now a mere gap in the mass of rampart. On the south-east side there must, I think, have been a gate near Sir Thomas Metcalfe's house, leading towards Tughlakabad and Mathura.*

Syad Ahmad states, on the authority of Zia Barni, that the west gate of Rai Pithora's Fort was called the *Ghazni* Gate after the Musalmán conquest, because the *Ghazni* troops had gained the fortress by that entrance. I feel satisfied that this must be the *Ranjit* Gate of Lálkot for the following reasons :

1st.—The Musalmáns never make any mention of Lálkot, but always include it as a part of Rai Pithora's Fort.

2nd.—The possession of the larger and weaker fortress of Rai Pithora could not be called the conquest of Delhi, while the stronger citadel of Lálkot still held out.

3rd.—The evident care with which the approach to the *Ranjit* Gate has been strengthened by a double line of works, and by three separate out-works immediately in front of the gateway itself, shows that this must have been considered as the weakest point of the fortress, and therefore that it was the most likely to have been attacked. For this reason I conclude that the *Ranjit* gate was the one by which the Musalmáns entered Lálkot, the citadel of Dilli, and that, having proved its weakness by their own success, they at once proceeded to strengthen the works at this point for their own security. A case exactly similar occurred less than forty years afterwards, when the Emperor Altamsh, having gained an entrance into the fortress of Gwalior by the deep ravine on the west side called *Urwáhi*, immediately closed it by a massive wall, to prevent his enemies from taking advantage of the same weak point. I believe that the western

---

* See Plate No. XXXVI. for an enlarged plan of Lálkot, showing the positions of the different gates. It seems probable that the western half of Lálkot was once cut off from the eastern half, as there are traces of walls and ramparts running from the Buban Bar) on the north direct south towards Adham Khan's tomb. I traced these walls as far as the ruined building to the west of Anang Pál's tomb. The western portion would have been the citadel of Lálkot under Anang Pál, before the accession of Rai Pithora. My Assistant, Mr. J. D. Beglar, has discovered a gateway in the southern half of this wall, between Adham Khan's Tomb and the Jug Maya temple.

gate was called the Ghazni Gate for the simple reason only that Ghazni lies to the west of Delhi.

The Fort of Rai Pithora, which surrounds the citadel of Lâlkot on three sides, would appear to have been built to protect the Hindu city of *Dilli* from the attacks of the Musalmâns. As early as A. D. 1100, the descendants of Mahmud, retiring from Ghazni before the rising power of the Saljukis, had fixed their new capital at Lahor, although Ghazni still belonged to their kingdom, and was occasionally the seat of Government. But a new and more formidable enemy soon appeared, when the celebrated Muâz-uddin Sâm, commonly called Muhammad Ghori, after capturing the cities of Multan and Parshâwar, appeared before Lahor in A. D. 1180, and put an end to the Ghaznavide dynasty by the capture of their capital in A. D. 1186. The danger was now imminent, and only a few years later we find the Ghori King in full march on Ajmer. But the Raja of Dilli was well prepared for this invasion, and, with the aid of his allies, he defeated the Musalmâns with great slaughter at *Tilaori*, midway between Karnâl and Thanesar. As the first appearance of the formidable Ghoris before Lahor corresponds so nearly with the accession of Prithivi Raja, I think it very probable that the fortification of the city of Dilli was forced upon the Raja by a well-grounded apprehension that Dilli itself might soon be attacked; and so it happened, for within two years after the battle of *Tilaori* the Raja was a prisoner, and Dilli was in the possession of the Musalmâns.

The circuit of Rai Pithorn's Fort is 4 miles and 3 furlongs, or just three times as much as that of *Lâlkot*. But the defences of the city are in every way inferior to those of the citadel. The walls are only half the height, and the towers are placed at much longer intervals. The wall of the city is carried from the north bastion of Lâlkot, called *Fateh Bûrj*, to the north-east for three-quarters of a mile, where it turns to the south-east for 1½ mile to the *Damdama Bârj*. From this bastion the direction of the wall for about one mile is south-west, and then north-west for a short distance to the south end of the hill on which Azim Khan's tomb is situated. Beyond this point the wall can be traced for some distance to the north along the ridge which was most probably connected with the south-east corner of Lâlkot, somewhere in the neighbourhood of Sir T. Metcalfe's house.

The Fort of Rai Pithora or Delhi Proper is said to have had nine gates besides the Ghazni Gate,* most of which can still be traced. Three are on the west side, of which two belong to the citadel of Lalkot, and the third has a small outwork. There were five on the north side, towards Jahanpanah, and one on the east side, towards Tughlakabad, which must have been the Badaon Gate, that is so often mentioned in early Muhammadan history. There must also have been one gate on the south side, which would have been close to Sir T. Metcalfe's house. Such was the Hindu City of Dilli when it was captured by the Musalmáns in January 1191. The circuit of its walls was nearly 4½ miles, and it covered a space of ground equal to one-half of the modern Shahjahánábád, the Capital of the Mogul Sovereigns of India. It possessed 27 Hindu temples, of which several hundreds of richly carved pillars still remain to attest both the taste and the wealth of the last Hindu Rulers of Dilli.

MUHAMMADAN REMAINS.

The first Musalmán Sovereigns of Delhi are said to have remained content with the fortress of Rai Pithora, although it seems highly probable that they must have added to the defences of the west gate, by which they had entered Lálkot, the citadel of the Hindu Kings. But though the first Musalmán Kings did not build huge forts or extensive cities to perpetuate their names, yet in the Great Mosque and magnificent column of Kutb-uddin Aibeg, as well as in the richly carved tomb of Altamsh, they have left behind them a few noble works, which are in every way more worthy of our admiration.

The Great Mosque of Kutb-uddin was called the *Jáma Masjid*, according to the inscription over the inner archway of the east entrance. But it is now more commonly known as the *Masjid-i-Kutb-ul Islám*, or the "Mosque of the Pole Star of Islamism," a name which appears to preserve that of its founder. It seems probable, however, that the Kutb Mosque, as well as the *Minár*, may have been named after the contemporary Saint *Kutb-uddin Ushi*, whose tomb is close by. Syad Ahmad adds that the Mosque was also called

---

* Malfuzát-i Timúri, or Autobiography of Timur, in Dowson's edition of Sir H. M. Elliot's History—III, 448.—So also Shamshuddin in the Zafar Náma, in Dowson's Elliot, III., 501.

the Adina Masjid. This Great Mosque, which even in ruin is one of the most magnificent works in the world, was seen by Ibn Batuta* about 150 years after its erection, when he describes it as having no equal, either for beauty or extent. In the time of Timur, the people of old Delhi prepared to defend the Great Mosque, but they were all, according to the Muhammadan Historian Sharaf-uddin, despatched by the sword "to the deepest hell." The Mosque is not mentioned by Baber, although he notices the Minar and the tomb of Khwaja Kutb-uddin, which he perambulated.† It is not mentioned either by Abul Fazl; but no inference can be drawn from his silence, as he does not even allude to the Kutb Minâr. The Minar itself was repaired during the reign of Sikandar Lodi; but we hear nothing of the Great Mosque, from which, perhaps, it may be inferred either that it was still in good order, or that it was too much ruined to be easily repaired. I conclude that the latter was the case, as it seems probable that the permanent removal of the court from Delhi to Firûzabad must have led to the gradual abandonment of the old city. We have a parallel case in the removal of the Hindu court from Kanoj to the Bâri in the time of Mahmud of Ghazni. This removal took place in A. D. 1022 and in A. D. 1031, or within ten years, Abu Rihan records that Kanoj having been deserted by its ruler, "fell to ruin."

The Great Mosque of Kutb-uddin was begun immediately after the capture of Delhi in A. H. 587, or A. D. 1191, as recorded by the King himself in the long inscription over the inner archway of the east entrance. This is the reading of the date given by Syad Ahmad, and Mr. Thomas has shown good grounds for its being the true date. My own reading was 589, taking *tisa* or nine, where Syad Ahmad reads *saba* or seven, but the two words are so much alike that they may be read differently by different people. Mr. Thomas has pointed out that Ibn Batuta read the unit as *arba* or four. In this inscription, as well as in the shorter one over the outer archway of the same gate, Kutb-uddin refrains from calling himself by the title of Sultân, which he bestows on his Suzerain Muñz-uddin in the inscription over the north

---

* Travels, p. 111.
† Memoirs, p. 308.

gateway. This last inscription is dated in A. H. 592. And here I have to notice the omission of two points in the Syad's copy of the second number of the date. In my copy, which was taken in 1839, I find the word *tisnīn*, or "ninety," quite complete. This inscription records that the foundation of the Masjid was laid in the reign of the Sultan *Muā:-uddin Muhammad, bin Sâm* (in the time of the Khalif) *Nasīr*, Chief of the Faithful. The date of A. H. 592, or A. D. 1196, must, therefore, I think, be referred to the completion of the building. It is true that five years may seem but a short time for the erection of this large mosque, yet, when we remember that the whole of the stones were obtained ready squared from the Hindu temples on the spot, our wonder will cease, and any doubts that might have arisen in our minds will be dissipated at once.

The *Jāma Masjid* is not so large as many buildings of the same kind that have been raised in later years, such as the great Mosques of Jonpur and others; but it is still unrivalled for its grand line of gigantic arches, and for the graceful beauty of the flowered tracery which covers its walls. The front of the Masjid is a wall 6 feet thick, pierced by a line of five noble arches. The centre arch is 22 feet wide and nearly 53 feet in height, and the side arches are 10 feet wide and 24 feet high. Through these gigantic arches the first Musalmāns of Delhi entered a magnificent room, 135 feet long and 31 feet broad, the roof of which was supported on five rows of the tallest and finest of the Hindu pillars. The Mosque is approached through a cloistered court, 145 feet in length from east to west, and 96 feet in width. In the midst of the west half of this court, stands the celebrated Iron Pillar, surrounded by cloisters formed of several rows of Hindu columns of infinite variety of design, and of most delicate execution. There are three entrances to the court of the Masjid, each 10 feet in width, of which the eastern entrance was the principal one. The southern entrance has disappeared long ago, but the other two are still in good order, with their interesting inscriptions in large Arabic letters.

I have already noticed that the whole of the beautiful Hindu pillars in these cloisters were originally covered with plaster by the idol-hating Musalmāns as the readiest way of removing the infidel images from the view of true believers. A distinct proof of this may be seen on two stones in the north

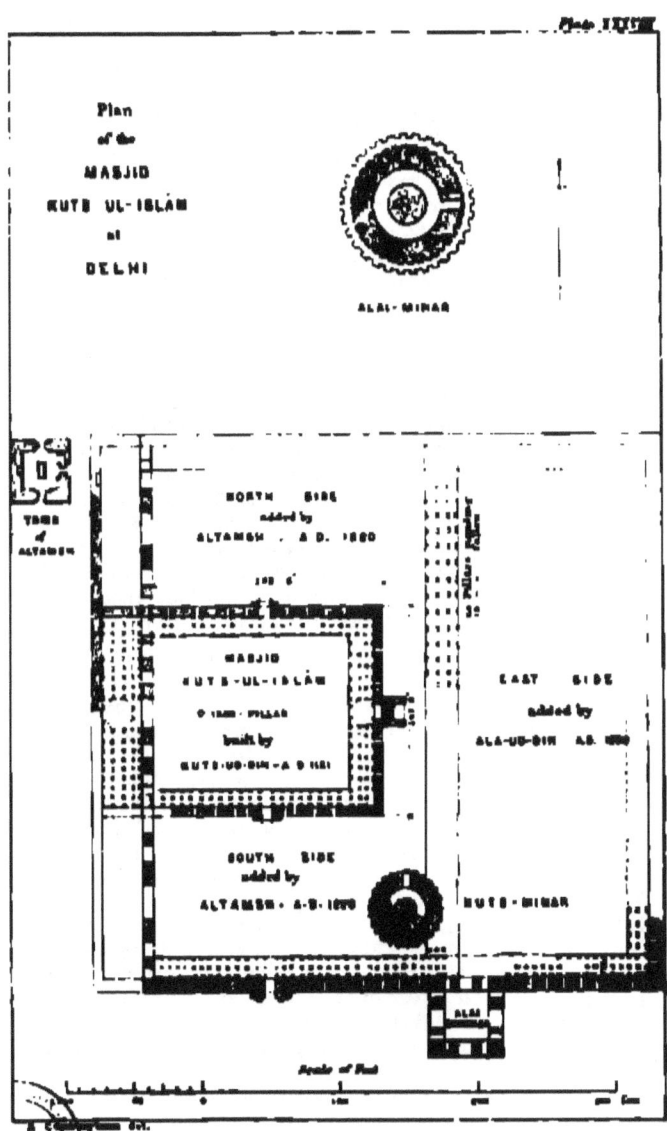

side of the court, one fixed in the inner wall in the north-east angle just above the pillars, and the other in the outer wall between the north gate and the north-east corner. The inner sculpture represents several well known Hindu gods,—1st, *Vishnu*, lying on a couch with a lotus rising from his navel, and covered by a canopy, with two attendants, one standing at his head and one sitting at his feet; 2nd, a seated figure not recognized; 3rd, *Indra*, on his elephant; 4th, *Brahma*, with three *heads* seated on his goose; 5th, *Siva*, with his trident seated on his bull *Nandi;* 6th, a figure with lotus seated on some animal not recognized. The outer sculpture is of a different description. The scene shows two rooms with a half-opened door between them. In each room there is a female lying on a couch with a child by her side, a canopy over her head, and an attendant at her feet. In the left-hand room two females are seen carrying children towards the door, and in the right-hand room two others are doing the same. The whole four of these females appear to be hastening towards the principal figure in the right-hand room. I am unable to offer any explanation of this very curious scene,* but as it is very unlikely that these figures would have been exposed to the sight of the early Musalmans, I conclude that these stones must also have been carefully plastered over.

During the reign of Altamsh, the son-in-law of Kutbuddin, the Great Mosque was much enlarged by the addition of two wings to the north and south, and by the erection of a new cloistered court on the north, east, and south sides, so as to include the Kutb Minar in the south-east corner of the enclosure. The fronts of the two wing buildings are pierced by three arches each, the middle arches being 2½ feet span, and the side arches 13 feet. The walls are of the same thickness, and their ornamental scrolls are of the same delicate and elaborate tracery as those of the original Mosque.* The whole front of the Jáma Masjid, with its new additions, is 381 feet in length, which is also the length of its cloistered court, the breadth being 220 feet. The wall on the south side of the court, as well as the south end of the east wall, are fortunately in good preservation, and, as about three-fourths of the columns are still standing, we are able to measure the size of the enclosure with precision, and to reckon the number

---

* See plate No. XXXVII. for a plan of the original Masjid and its additions.

of columns with tolerable certainty. The number of columns in the new cloisters must have been as nearly as possible 300, and as each of them consists of two Hindu shafts, the whole number of Hindu pillars thus brought into use could not have been less than 600. By my measurements the new court is 302 feet long and 220 feet broad, inside the the walls, of which the west wall, which is the front of the Masjid, is only 8 feet thick, the other walls being 11 feet thick. In the south-east corner of this great quadrangle stands the majestic column called *Kutb Minar*, within 11 feet of the line of cloister pillars on the south, and extending into the middle of the cloister on the east side.

At a later date the court of the Great Mosque was still further enlarged by Alauddin Khilji, by the addition of a large cloistered enclosure on the east side, equal in size to more than one-half of the court of Altamsh. This work is described by the contemporary poet Amir Khusru,[*] who says that the "Sultan determined upon adding to and completing the Masjid-i-Jámi of Shams-uddin by building beyond the three old gates and courts a fourth with lofty pillars, and upon the surface of the stones he engraved verses of the Kurán in such a manner as could not be done even on wax; ascending so high that you would think the Kurán was going to heaven, and again descending in another line so low that you would think it was coming down from heaven. * * * He also repaired the old Masjids, of which the walls were broken or inclining, or of which the roof and domes had fallen." I have given this important passage at some length, as its purport does not seem to be quite clear. Mr. Thomas understands it to affirm that the long line of noble arches of the great Masjid itself were built by Alauddin,[†] and certainly the description of the engraved lines of the Kurán *ascending and descending* is more applicable to these arches than to any other portion of the Great Kutb buildings. I think, however, that Amir Khusru must refer to the engraved lines of *Tughra* on the *Alai Darwáza*, which *ascend and descend* in the same way as those on the great arches of the Mosque. It may be argued that the inscriptions may have been added by Alauddin to the arches built by his predecessors Aibeg and Altamsh.

---

[*] Sir H. M. Elliot's Muhammadan Historians, by Dowson, III., 63.
[†] Chronicles of the Pathan Kings of Delhi, p. 156.

I confess, however, that my own opinion is strongly in favour of the contemporaneous engraving of the inscriptions, and of the erection of the long line of noble arches by the earlier Kings Aibeg and Altamsh. I rest my opinion not only on the positive statement of Hasan Nizámi, a contemporary of Aibeg, who records that Kutb-uddin " built the Jámi Masjid at Delhi," and covered it with " inscriptions in *Tughra* containing the divine commands,"* but also on the shape and construction of the arches, and the form of the letters, both of which correspond with those of the Altamsh Masjid at Ajmer, while they differ entirely from those of the Alai Darwáza and Khizri Masjid of the time of Alauddin. I note first that the four remaining arches of Kutb-uddin's Mosque are ogee in shape like those of the Great Mosque at Ajmer, and quite different from the pointed and horse-shoe arches of Alauddin. I note next that the upright letters of the Kutb Masjid are very nearly of uniform thickness, thus agreeing with those of the dated inscriptions on the gateways, while those of Alauddin's time are invariably much broader at top than at bottom. Lastly, I note that the undulated flower stem, which forms the ornament of the main line of inscription on the central arch of the Mosque, is exactly the same as that of the inscription on the north gate which is dated in A. H. 594.†

During the present century, much speculation has been wasted as to the origin of the Kutb Minar, whether it is a purely Muhammadan building, or a Hindu building altered and completed by the conquerors. The latter is undoubtedly the common belief of the people, who say that the pillar was built by Rai Pithora for the purpose of giving his daughter a view of the River Jumna. Some people even say that the intention was to obtain a view of the Ganges, and that the Kutb Minar having failed to secure this a second pillar of double the size was commenced, but the work was interrupted by the conquest of the Musalmáns. The first part of this tradition was warmly adopted by Sir T. Metcalfe, and it has since found a strong advocate in Syad Ahmad, whose remarks are quoted with approval by Mr. Cooper in his recent hand-book for

---

* Sir H. M. Elliot's Historians, by Dowson, II., p. 222.
† Compare this desert inscription No. 7, plate XIII. of the Asár us Sanadíd, with any large photograph of the Kutb arches.

Delhi. Syad Ahmad, however, refers only tho basement storey to Rai Pithora; but this admission involves the whole design of the column, which preserves the same marked character throughout all the different storeys. The Hindu theory has found a stout opponent in Colonel Sleeman, who argues that the great slope of the building "is the peculiar characteristic of all architecture of the Pathans," and that the arches of the Great Mosque close by it "all correspond in design, proportion, and execution to the tower."*

Mr. Cooper † recapitulates Syad Ahmad's arguments, and finally states as his opinion that it "remains an open question whether this magnificent pillar was commenced by the Hindus or Muhammadans." I must confess, however, that I am myself quite satisfied that the building is entirely a Muhammadan one, both as to origin and to design; although, no doubt, many, perhaps all, of the beautiful details of the richly decorated balconies may be Hindu. To me these decorations seem to be purely Hindu, and just such as may be seen in the honey-comb enrichments of the domes of most of the old Hindu temples. The arguments brought forward in support of the Hindu origin of the column are the following:

1st.—"That there is only *one Minar*, which is contrary to the practice of the Muhammadans, who always give two Minars to their Masjids." I allow that this has been the practice of the Muhammadans for the last three hundred years at least, and I will even admit that the little corner turrets or pinnacles of the *Kála*, or *Kalán*, *Masjid* of Firuz Shah, may be looked upon as Minars. This would extend the period of the use of two Minars to the middle of the 14th century; but it must be remembered that these little turrets of Firuz Shah's Masjid are not what the Musalmans call *Mízinahs*, or lofty towers, from the top of which the Muazzin calls the faithful to prayer. But the Kutb Minar is a *Mizinah;* and that it was the practice of the early Muhammadans to build a single tower, we have the most distinct and satisfactory proofs in the two Minars of Ghazni, which could not have belonged to one Masjid, as they are half a mile apart, and of different sizes. These Minars were

---
* Rambles of an Indian Official, II., 251.
† Hand-book for Delhi, p. 73.

built by Mahmud in the early part of the 11th century, or about 180 years prior to the erection of the Kutb Minar. Another equally decisive proof of this practice is the solitary Minar at Koel, which was built in A. H. 652, or A. D. 1254, by *Kullugh Khan*, during the reign of Násir-uddin Mahmud, the youngest son of Altamsh, in whose time the Kutb Minar itself was completed. These still existing Minars of Ghazni and Koel show that it was the practice of the early Muhammadans to have only one Minar even down to so late a date as the middle of the 13th century.

2nd.—It is objected that the slope of the Kutb Minar is much greater than that of any other known Minars. This objection has already been satisfactorily answered by Colonel Sleeman, who says truely that "the slope is the peculiar characteristic of the architecture of the Pathans."

3rd.—Syad Ahmad argues that, if the Minar had been intended as a *Mázinah* to the Great Mosque, it would have been erected at one end of it, instead of being at some distance from it. In reply to this objection I can point again to the Koel Minar, which occupies exactly the same detached position with regard to the Jáma Masjid of Koel as the Kutb Minar does with respect to the Great Mosque of Delhi. Both of them are placed outside the south-east corner of their respective Masjids. This coincidence of position seems to me sufficient to settle the question in favor of the Kutb Minar having been intended as a Mázinah of the Great Mosque.

4th.—Syad Ahmad further argues "that the entrance door faces the north, as the Hindus always have it," whereas the Muhammadans invariably place it to the eastward, as may be seen in the unfinished "Minar of Alauddin to the north of the Kutb Minar." Once more I appeal to the Koel Minar, which, be it remembered, was erected by the son of the Emperor who completed the building of the Kutb Minar, and which may, therefore, be looked upon as an almost contemporary work. In the Koel Minar the entrance door is to the north, exactly as in the Kutb Minar. In both instances, I believe that it was so placed chiefly for the convenience of the Muazzin when going to call the faithful to prayer. It think, also, that Syad Ahmad has overlooked the fact that the Minars of modern days are "engaged" towers, that is, they form the ends of the front wall of the Mosque, and, as the back wall of every Mosque is to the westward, the entrances to the "engaged" Minars must necessarily be to the eastward. But the case is entirely different with a solitary disengaged Minar, of which the entrance would naturally be on the side *nearest* to its Masjid. But waiving this part of the discussion, I return to the fact that the entrance of the Kool Minar is to the northward, exactly the same as in the Kutb Minar, and that the entrances to the two great tombs of *Bahawal Hak,* and *Rukn-uddin* in Multan are not to the eastward but to the southward, as are also those of the Táj Mahal, and of most other modern tombs. The only exception that I know is the tomb of Altamsh, of which the entrance is to the eastward. The argument of Syad Ahmad includes also the position of the entrance doors of Hindu buildings, which, as he says, are always placed to the northward. But this is an undoubted mistake, as a very great majority of Hindu temples have their entrances to the eastward. On referring to my Note books, I find that, out of 50 temples, of which I have a record, no less than 38 have their entrances to the east, 10 to the west, and only 2 to the north, both of which last are in the Fort of Gwalior.

4th.—Syad Ahmad further objects that "it is customary for the Hindus to commence such buildings without any platform (or plinth), whereas the Muhammadans always erect their buildings upon a raised terrace or platform, as may be seen in the unfinished Minar of Alauddin Khilji." In this statement about the Hindu buildings, Syad Ahmad is again mistaken, as it is most undoubtedly the usual custom of the Hindus to raise their temples on plinths. I can point to the gigantic Buddhist temple at Buddha Gaya as springing from a plinth nearly 20 feet in height. The two largest temples in the Fort of Gwalior, one Brahmanical and the other Jain, are both raised on plinths, so also are the elaborately sculptured temples of Kajráha, and so are most of the temples in in Kashmir. Lastly, the Great Pillar at Chitor has a plinth not less than 8 or 10 feet in height, as may be seen in Forgusson's and Tod's Drawings, and which Tod[*] describes as "an ample terrace 42 feet square." The smaller pillar at Chitor must also have a good plinth, as Fergusson describes the entrance as at some height above the base. That the

---

[*] Rajasthan, II., 761.

Muhammadans in India also erect their buildings on plinths or raised terraces, I readily admit; for, on the same principle that a Cuckoo may be said to build a nest, the Musalmáns usually placed their buildings on the sites of Hindu temples which they had previously destroyed. The Mosques at Mathura, Kanoj, and Jonpur, are signal examples of this practice. The raised terrace is, therefore, only an accidental adjunct of the Muhammadan building, whereas it is a fundamental part of the Hindu structure. But the early Musalmáns did *not* place their buildings on raised terraces or platforms, as may be seen by a reference to the Drawings of Mosques in Syria and Persia, which are given in Fergusson's Hand-book.* The Ghaznivides also, who were the more immediate predecessors of the Indian Musalmáns, built their Minars at Ghazni without plinths. The contemporary tomb of Altamsh is likewise without a plinth. From all these facts I infer that the early Musalmán structures in India were usually built without plinths, and therefore that the Kutb Minar is undoubtedly a Muhammadan building.

5*th*.—The last argument brought forward by Syad Ahmad is, that bells, which are used in Hindu worship, are found sculptured on the lower part of the basement storey of the Kutb Minar. It is true that bells are used in the daily worship of the Hindus, and also that they are a common ornament of Hindu columns, as may be seen on most of the pillars in the cloisters of the Great Mosque. But bells are no more idolatrous than flowers, which are used in such profusion in the daily service of the Hindu temples. The fact is that, where Muhammadan mosques have been built of the materials stolen from Hindu temples, such portions of architectural ornament as were free from figures either of men or of animals, were invariably made use of by the conquerors. For this reason most of the ornamentation of the early Musalmán buildings is purely Hindu. For instance, in the Jáma Masjid of Kanoj, which is built entirely of Hindu materials, the whole of the concentric circles of overlapping stones in the central dome, with only one exception, still preserve the original Hindu ornament unaltered. The exception is the lowest circle, which is completely covered with Arabic inscriptions. One of the Hindu circles is made up solely of the *Swastika* or mystic cross of the early Indians. This symbol is essentially an idolatrous one, although it is

---

* Vol. I, p. 115.

most probable that the Musalmáns were not aware of its significance. But if the ornamental bells of the Kutb Minar are to be taken as a proof of its Hindu origin, even so must the ornamental *Swastikas* of the Kanoj Masjid be accepted as evidence to the same effect. It is admitted that this Masjid is built up entirely of Hindu materials, but these have been skilfully re-arranged by the Moslem Architect to suit the requirements of a mosque, so that the design of the building is strictly Muhammadan, while its ornamentation is purely Hindu. I may add that one of the western pillars that supports the central dome of this mosque *is made up of two old shafts*, both of which are decorated with the Hindu bell and suspending chain.

The strong evidence which I have brought forward in reply to the arguments of Syad Ahmad and others, appears to me to be quite conclusive as to the origin of the Kutb Minar, which is essentially a Muhammadan building. But the strongest evidence in favor of this conclusion is the fact that the Musalmáns of Ghazni had already built two separate Minars of *similar design* with angular flutes, whereas the only Hindu pillar of an early date, namely, the smaller column at Chitor, is altogether dissimilar, both in plan and in detail. The entrance to this Hindu tower is at some height above the ground, while that of the Kutb Minar is absolutely on the ground level. The summit of the Hindu tower is crowned by an open pillared temple of almost the same width as the base of the building, whereas the cupola of the Kutb Minar is little more than one-sixth of the diameter of its base. But this small cupola of less than 9 feet in diameter was peculiarly adapted for one special purpose connected with the performance of the Muhammadan religion. From this narrow point the Muazzin could summon the faithful to prayer from all sides by simply turning round and repeating the *Izán*, and on all sides he would be visible to the people. The small size of the cupola, which crowns the Kutb Minar, is a characteristic peculiar to Muhammadan towers for the special reason which I have just mentioned. On this account, therefore, I conclude that the Kutb Minar is a *Mázinah* or Muazzin's tower.

That the Kutb Minar was actually used as a *Mázinah*, we may infer from the records of Shamsi Siráj, who about A. D. 1380, records that the magnificent Minár in the Jáma Masjid of old Delhi was built by Sultan Shams-uddin

Altamsh. But the fact is placed beyond all doubt by Abulfeda, who wrote about A. D. 1300. He describes the *Mazinah* of the Jâma Masjid at Delhi as made of red stone and very lofty, with many sides and 360 steps. Now this description can be applied only to the Kutb Minar, which, as it at present stands, has actually 379 steps; but we know that the Minar was struck by lightning in the reign of Firuz Shah, by whose orders it was repaired in A. D. 1368. There is, therefore, nothing improbable in the account of Abulfeda that the Minar in his time had only 360 steps. On the contrary I accept the statement as a valuable hint towards ascertaining the height of the original Minar as completed by the Emperor Altamsh.*

The object of building this lofty column seems to me to be clear enough. The first Musalmán conquerors were an energetic race, whose conceptions were as bold and daring as their actions. When the zealous Muhammadan looked on the great city of Delhi, the metropolis of the princely Tomars and the haughty Chohans, his first wish would have been to humble the pride of the infidel; his second, to exalt the religion of his prophet Muhammad. To attain both of these objects, he built a lofty column, from whose summit the *Muazzin's* call to morning and evening prayer could be heard on all sides by Hindus as well as by Musalmáns. The conqueror's pride was soothed by the daily insult and indignity thus offered to the infidel, while his religious feelings were gratified by the erection of a noble monument which towered majestically over the loftiest houses in the city.

The Kutb Minar, as it stands now, is 238 feet and 1 inch in height, with a base diameter of 47 feet 3 inches, and an upper diameter of nearly 9 feet. The base or plinth of the pillar is 2 feet in height, the shaft is 234 feet and 1 inch, and the base or stump of the old cupola is 2 feet more; thus making the whole height 238 feet 1 inch. The shaft is divided into five storeys, of which the lower storey is 94 feet 11 inches in height, and the upper storey is 23 feet 4 inches, the two

---

* See Gildemeister Scriptorum Arabum de rebus Indicis. He describes it as built of red stone.

Of the 379 steps 3 belong to Major Smith's cupola, and 37 to the upper storey of 22 feet 4 inches, which leave 339 steps to the four lower storeys. In the time of Abulfeda, there must consequently have been 21 steps above the fourth storey to make up his total of 360 steps. These would be equal to 13 feet in height, making the total height in his time 228 feet 9 inches, or 9 feet 4 inches less than at present. This agrees with the statement of Firuz Shah, who says—"The *Minâra* of Sultan Muir-uddin Aim had been struck by lightning. I repaired it, and raised it *higher than it was before*.—See Dowson's edition of Sir H. M. Elliot's Historians, III, 353. Futuhát i Firuz Shahi.

measurements together being just equal to one-half of the height of the column. The height of the second storey is 50 feet 8½ inches, that of the third storey is 40 feet 9½ inches, and that of the fourth storey is 25 feet 4 inches, or just one-half of the height of the second storey. There are two other proportions which may be noticed, as they most probably entered into the original design of the building. The column, as it stands now, omitting only the stump of the old cupola, is just five diameters in height; thus, 47 feet 3 inches, multiplied by 5, gives 236 feet 3 inches as the height of the column, which is only 2 inches in excess of the mean measurement. Again, the lower storey is just two diameters in height. Both of these proportions were, I presume, intentional. But there is another coincidence of measurements, which is, I think, too curious to have been intentional, namely, that the circumference of the base is equal to the sum of the diameters of the six storeys of the building, the old cupola being considered as a sixth storey.*

As some of the dimensions here given differ from those recorded by Ensign Blunt in the Asiatic Researches, it is necessary that I should state that they are the mean results of two sets of measurements, the first taken by myself in 1839, and the other by Sir Frederick Abbott in 1846. I now give these measurements in detail for comparison:

		A. D. 1839.		A. D. 1846.		Mean.		Blunt.	
		Ft.	In.	Ft.	In.	Ft.	In.	Ft.	In.
Upper storey	...	21	10	22	10	22	4	02	6
4th "	...	25	4	25	4	25	4	23	0
3rd "	...	40	9	40	10	40	9½	40	0
2nd "	...	50	10	50	7	50	8½	50	0
Basement "	...	95	3	94	7	94	11	90	0
		234	0	234	2	234	1		
Plinth	...	2	0	2	0	2	0		
		236	0	236	2	236	1		
Stump of old cupola	...	2	0	2	0	2	0		
Total present height	...	238	0	238	2	238	1	242	0

* If the fifth storey of the original pillar bore the same proportion to the third storey of eighteen-nineteenths which the latter bears to the first storey, then its height would have been nearly 17 feet, instead of 13 feet, as mentioned in the previous note. But as the height of the steps in each of the four lower storeys averages from 7½ to 7¼ inches, it is most probable that they were of the same dimensions in the fifth storey as they are now, or somewhat over 7 inches.

The only way in which I can account for the great difference of 5 feet in the height of the lower storey between Blunt's measurements taken in 1794 and the actual height as it now stands, is by supposing that there must have been an accumulation of rubbish at the foot of the tower which would have diminished the actual height of the basement storey. His heights of the second and third storeys agree very closely with my measurements, but that of the fourth storey is more than 2 feet short of the true height. The height of the fifth storey is not given.

In recording Blunt's measurements Mr. Fergusson has, I think, made a mistake in excluding the cupola from the ascertained height of 242 feet 6 inches. Blunt distinctly states that the height of the third storey was 180 feet, which, deducted from 242½, will give no less than 62½ feet for the height of the two upper storeys. But this height, as we know from present measurements, is only 25 feet 4 inches, plus 22 feet 4 inches, or altogether 47 feet 8 inches, which, deducted from 62½ feet, leaves 14 feet 10 inches unaccounted for. I conclude, therefore, that this must have been the height of the cupola as it stood in A. D. 1794. Accepting this view as correct, the true height of the Kutb Minar in 1794 must have been 236 feet 1 inch, plus 14 feet 10 inches, or 250 feet 11 inches.

The base or plinth of the Kutb Minar is a polygon of 24 sides, each side measuring 6 feet 1¼ inches, or altogether 147 feet. The basement storey has the same number of faces formed into convex flutes, which are alternately angular and semi-circular. This last fact alone is sufficient to show the inaccuracy of Blunt's description of the plan as a polygon of 27 sides,[*] as any uneven number of faces would have brought two flutes of the same kind together. In the second storey the flutes are all semi-circular, and in the third storey they are all angular. The fourth storey is circular and plain, and the fifth storey is partially fluted with convex semi-circular flutes. Round the top of each storey runs a bold projecting balcony, which is richly and elaborately decorated. The three lower storeys are also ornamented with belts of Arabic writing, bordered with richly decorated bands. These three storeys are built entirely of red sand-stone, but there is a

---

[*] Asiatic Researches of Bengal, IV., 321.

difference in the colours of the stone, that of the second storey being generally a pale pinkish buff, while that of the third storey is a dark red. The whole of the upper part of the fourth storey is built of white marble, and there are also two ornamental bands of white marble in the fifth storey. According to Ibn Batuta,* the pillar was said to have been built "of stones from *seven* different quarries;" but I could not trace more than *three* different kinds of stone, *viz.*, the grey quartzose rock of Delhi, the white marble of Jaypur, and the red sand-stone of the hills to the south of Delhi. If, however, the different colours of the sand-stone be taken into account, there are certainly three distinct colours, or buff, pink, and red, which may be considered as forming three distinct varieties of sand-stone. The grey quartzose stone is used only in the interior of the building, and the white marble is confined to the two upper storeys. Inside the pillar there is a spiral staircase of 376 steps from the ground level to the balcony of the fifth storey. Above this, there are three steps more to the present top of the stone-work, which once formed the floor of the paltry pavilion which Major Robert Smith was allowed to stick on the top of this noble column.

In 1794, when Ensign Blunt sketched the Kutb Minar, the old cupola of Firuz Shah was still standing, although much ruined. Blunt's rude sketch, as given in the Asiatic Researches, conveys no intelligible idea of the old cupola, and is sarcastically compared by Robert Smith to "a large stone harp." A better idea of the old cupola will be formed from an aqua-tint view of the pillar given in Blagdon's "Brief History of India," which was published about 1805.† By comparing this view with the statement of the Natives that the old cupola was a "plain square top on four stone pillars,"‡ I think that it would be quite possible to restore the upper part of the pillar in a style that would harmonize with the rest of the building. It is difficult, indeed, to conceive anything more incongruous than the flimsy Mogul pavilion, which Robert Smith fixed on the "top of this grand and massive specimen of Pathán architecture." In my Note-book of 1839, I find a remark that "the balustrades of the

---

* Travels by Dr. Lee, p. 111.

† Most of the views of this book are by Daniell. The value of the latter press may be judged by the name given to the pillar, "Kuttull Minor of Delhi."

‡ Robert Smith's Report in Journal, Archæological Society of Delhi.

balconies and the plain slight building on the top of the pillar do not harmonize with the massive and richly ornamented Pathán architecture.". Major Smith's pavilion was taken down in 1847 or 1848 by order of Lord Hardinge. I presume that this was done at the suggestion of his eldest son, the present Lord Hardinge, whose known artistic taste and skill would at once have detected the architectural unfitness of such a flimsy pavilion for the summit of this noble column.

On the 1st of August 1803, the old cupola of the Kutb Minar was thrown down, and the whole pillar seriously injured by an earthquake. A drawing of the pillar, while it was in this state, was made by Captain Elliot upwards of two years after the earthquake, but the engraving of this drawing is too small to show the nature of the balustrades of the balconies. About this time the dangerous state of the pillar was brought to the notice of the Governor General, who authorized the necessary repairs to be begun at once. This difficult work was entrusted to Major Robert Smith, of the Engineers, and was completed by the beginning of the year 1828, at a cost of Rs. 17,000, with a further charge of more than Rs. 5,000 for clearing the ruins around the pillar. The intricate nature of some of these repairs can be best seen and understood by an examination of Mallitte's large photograph of the lower balcony. All the forms of the mouldings have been carefully preserved, but the rich ornamentation has been omitted as too costly, and the new stonework is, therefore, quite plain throughout. This part of the work appears to have been done with much patience and skill, and Major Smith deserves credit for the conscientious care which he bestowed upon it. But this commendation must be confined to the *repairs*, for the *restorations* of the entrance door-way, of the balustrades, and of the cupola, are altogether out of keeping with the rest of the pillar.

It appears from Major Smith's report that the old entrance doorway was still in existence at that time, although much broken. This being the case, he should have adhered strictly to the original design, instead of which, to use his own words, " the former rude and fractured entrance door of the base of the column (was) repaired, and *improved with new mouldings, frieze,* and repair of the inscription tablet." From this statement I infer that the whole of the entrance doorway is Smith's own design, a conclusion which has already been drawn by Mr. Fergusson, who denounces this work as being "in the true style of Strawberry Hill Gothic." Perhaps it may not now be possible to recover the original design, but its main features may be ascertained from the other three existing doorways. All of these are plain, and it is evident from Major Smith's account that the lower doorway was also plain, or, as he calls it, "rude," and without frieze or mouldings, which were added by himself. I confess, therefore, that I should like to see Smith's doorway altogether removed, and the old entrance restored in the simple but massive style of the other doorways. The entrance of the Koël Minar, which is still in existence, is also plain, and might be studied with advantage.

The flimsy balustrades are even a greater eye-sore than the modern entrance, as they form a prominent part in every view of the building. But although not ornamental, they are useful, and might on that account alone be tolerated. It would not, however, be either difficult or expensive to remove them, and to furnish new balustrades more in harmony with the rich style of the balconies. Ensign Blunt describes the old balustrades as "small battlements;" and such, I believe, must have been the nature of the original balustrades, at once rich and massive, like the battlements of the older tombs. The present balustrades might be sold with advantage in Delhi, as they belong to the flimsy style of garden-house architecture of the present day.

The history of the Kutb Minar is written in its inscriptions. In the basement storey there are six bands or belts of inscriptions encircling the tower. The uppermost band contains only some verses from the Koran, and the next below it gives the well known ninety-nine Arabic names of the Almighty. The third belt contains the name and praises of *Muáz-uddin, Abul Muzafar, Muhammad Bin Sám.* The fourth belt contains only a verse from the Koran, and the fifth belt repeats the name and praises of the Sultan Muhammad Bin Sám. The lowermost belt has been too much injured, both by time and by ignorant restorations, to admit of being read, but Syad Ahmad has traced the words "*Amir-ul-Umra,* or Chief of the "nobles." The inscription over the entrance doorway records that "this Minar of Sultan Shams-uddin Altamsh having been injured, was repaired during the reign of Sikander Shah, son of Bahlol, by Fateh Khan, the son of Khawas Khan, in A. H. 909 or A. D. 1503.

In the second storey the inscription over the doorway records that the Emperor Altamsh ordered the completion of the Minar. The lowermost belt contains the verses of the Koran respecting the summons to prayers on Friday, and the upper line contains the praises of the Emperor Altamsh. Over the door of the third storey the praises of Altamsh are repeated, and again in the belt of inscription round the column. In the fourth storey the door inscription records that the Minar was ordered to be erected during the reign of Altamsh. The inscription over the door of the fifth storey states that the Minar having been injured by lightning, was repaired by the Emperor Firuz Shah in A. H. 770 or A. D. 1368.

But besides these long inscriptions, which form part of the architectural ornament of the pillar, there are a few other short records which are worth preserving. On the basement storey is recorded the name of Fazzil, son of Abul Muáli, the *Mutawali* or high priest; and on one side of the third storey is found the name of *Muhammad Amircho*, Architect. On the same storey, also, there is a short Nágari inscription in one line with the name of *Muhammad Sultán* and the date of *Samvat* 1382 or A. D. 1325, which was the first year of Muhammad Tughlak's reign. On the wall of the fourth storey there is another Nágari inscription, in two lines, which is dated in the *Samvat* year 1425 or A. D. 1368, in the reign of *Piruj Sáh*, or Firuz Shah Tughlak. A third Nágari inscription is found on the south jamb of the doorway of the fourth storey, cut partly on the white marble and partly on the red sand-stone. This also gives the name of Firuz Shah, but the date is one year later than the last, or *Samvat* 1426. This is the longest and most important of the Nágari inscriptions, but unfortunately it is not in such a state of preservation, more especially the upper portion on the white marble, as to be easily legible. I can make out the words *Sri Viswakarma prasáde ruchita*, and towards the end I find the title of *Silpi*, or " Architect," applied to the son of *Cháhada Deva Pála*, named *Nana satha*, who repaired the Minar. But in the middle of the inscription I find no less than five numbers given in figures, all of which are preceded by the word *gaj*, as *gaj* 22, *gaj* 3, *gaj* 26, *gaj* 131, and *gaj* 131. I infer from these measurements that the inscription may probably be of some importance in determining the nature and extent of the repairs that were executed by Firuz Shah. As I read one passage of this inscription, the Architect was obliged to pull down *(uipatit)* a considerable portion of the pillar.*

It now only remains to ascertain who was the actual builder of the Kutb Minar. The learned Syad Ahmad assigns the original building of the basement storey to Rai Pithora, and its adaptation by the Musalmans to Kutb-uddin Aibeg. The name and titles of this King were, he thinks, engraved in the lowermost band of inscriptions, as the legible words of this band correspond with a portion of Aibeg's inscription over the inner arch of the eastern gateway of the Great Mosque. The completion of the Minar he assigns to Altamsh. The claim of the Hindus has already been fully discussed and disposed of as altogether baseless. That of Kutb-uddin Aibeg is founded chiefly on the fact that the pillar is called by his name, and partly on the fact that the name of Muhammad Bin Sám is twice recorded on the lower storey of the column. The occurrence of this name makes it highly probable that the name of Kutb-uddin Aibeg was also engraved on this storey, as argued by Syad Ahmad. With these two names engraved on the basement storey it seems only natural to conclude that the building of the pillar was begun by Aibeg during the life-time of his Suzerain, Muhammad Bin Sám, and in full accordance with this conclusion is the statement recorded over the doorway of the second storey, that the *completion* of the pillar was ordered by Altamsh. Under this view the building of the Minar may have been begun by Aibeg in about A. D. 1200, and completed by Altamsh in about 1220.

The other view which attributes the foundation of the pillar to Altamsh is based chiefly, I believe, on the statements of *Abulfeda* and *Shams-i-Siráj*, which are supported by the inscription of Sikandar Lodi over the entrance door of the pillar. Syad Ahmad refers to the inscription

---

* I may mention that the sum of the two numbers 22 + 28 = 58 *guj*, taken at the value of the *guj* obtained from the length of Firuz Shah's Lát, namely, 16.091 inches, amounts to 62 feet 5½ inches, which I would compare with the height of the two upper storeys of 62 feet 8 inches as derived from Lieutenant Blunt's measurement, taken before the pillar was injured by lightning.

over the doorway of the second storey, which records that
Altamsh ordered the *completion* of the Minar, as a proof that
he did not commence it. But another inscription over the
doorway of the fourth storey seems to be equally explicit in
assigning the *beginning* of the Minar to Altamsh. Both
Syad Ahmad and *Nawáb Zia-uddin* give the same translation
of this inscription, namely, that "the erection of this building was ordered during the reign of Shamsuddin Altamsh."
It is possible, however, that the order recorded in this inscription may refer to the fourth storey only, and as this limited
view of its meaning will bring the two otherwise conflicting
inscriptions into strict accord with each other, I think that
it may be accepted as the most probable intention of the
inscriber. The statements of Abulfeda, Shams-Siráj, and
Sikandar Lodi, all of which agree in calling this pillar the
Minar of Altamsh, may, perhaps, be explained as conveying
only the popular opinion, and are certainly not entitled to
the same weight as the two inscriptions on the basement
storey which record the name and titles of Muhammad Bin
Sám, the Suzerain of Kutb-uddin Aibeg, whose name is now
attached to the pillar. The absence of Altamsh's name in
the inscription of the lower storey is, I think, a conclusive
proof that he himself did not claim it as his own work.[*]

According to Syad Ahmad, the Emperor Altamsh erected
five storeys in addition to the basement storey, and another
storey was afterwards added by Firuz Shah; thus making, altogether, seven storeys, of which he says that "two have fallen
down and five remain to this day." But both of these statements I believe to be quite erroneous, for the mention of 360
steps by Abulfeda in about A. D. 1300, makes it certain that
the Minar, as completed by Altamsh, could not have been
higher than the present one, which has 379 steps. The five
stories of Altamsh must, therefore, have included the basement
storey, which, although begun by Aibeg, was most probably
completed by himself. In this state the Minar must have
remained until the reign of Firuz Tughlak, when, having been
struck by lightning, it was repaired by that Emperor in A. H.
770, or A. D. 1368. The nature and extent of his repairs
may, I think, be gathered from the inscriptions; thus, the
inscription of the fifth storey is placed over the doorway, and

---

[*] The Emperor Firuz Shah, who repaired the pillar, calls it "the Minára of Muzz-ud-din Sam."—Dowson's edition of Sir H. M. Elliot's Historians, III., 382.

there is no record of any other Emperor on this storey. I conclude, therefore, that the whole of the fifth storey was re-built by Firuz Shah. But as there are two inscriptions of his reign recorded on the fourth storey, I infer that he must have made some repairs to it also, although these repairs could not have been extensive, as the inscription over the doorway of this storey belongs to the reign of Altamsh.* Under this view the Kutb Minar has always consisted of five storeys, from the time of its completion by Altamsh in about A. D. 1220, down to the present day.

Of the same age as the Kutb Minar is the tomb of the Emperor Altamsh, who died in A. H. 633 or A. D. 1235. It is situated just outside the north-west corner of the Great Mosque, as enlarged by Altamsh himself. The interior is a square of 29½ feet, with walls 7½ feet thick, making the exterior a square of 44 feet. The main entrance is to the east, but there are also openings to the north and south; and to the west there is a niche, such as is usually found in a small mosque. The interior walls are decorated throughout with elaborate and highly finished ornament of great beauty. There is no roof to the building, but there is good reason to believe that it was originally covered by an overlapping Hindu dome. A single stone of one of the overlapping circles, with Arabic letters on it, still remains.

The only other buildings connected with the Great Mosque of Delhi are the beautiful south gateway of the quadrangle, and the gigantic unfinished Minar, both of which were the work of Ala-uddin Khilji, who reigned from A. D. 1296 to 1316. The south gateway is called by Syad Ahmad

---

* New Bengal Asiatic Society's Journal, 1860, p. 206, where Mr. C. J. Campbell, c. e., argues that the whole of the fourth storey was "newly designed" by Firuz Shah. I had already come to this conclusion when I re-visited the Kutb Minar in October 1864, and I am glad to have my views corroborated by Mr. Campbell, whose long residence at Delhi, and early training as a Civil Engineer, give special weight to his opinion on any architectural point. He particularly notices that the arches in the two upper storeys have true voussoirs, whilst in three lower storeys they are all overlapping Hindu arches. I agree, therefore, with Mr. Campbell that "the old tablet of Altamsh has been simply re-built into the new work of Firuz Shah." But the chief glory of the Kutb Minar lies in its deeply fluted shaft, and its exquisite balconies of bold design and delicate tracery. All these, it seems, we owe to a new claimant whose name has not yet been mentioned. Speaking of the new Minar which Ala-uddin Khilji had ordered to be built, Amir Khusru states that he also "directed that a new casing and cupola should be added to the old one."—Tárikh-i-Alái in Dowson's edition of Sir H. M. Elliot's Historians, III., 70. From this I conclude that the whole of the present red stone facing was added by Ala-uddin, and that to his reign we must assign all that is rich and beautiful in its decoration, while the design alone belongs to the time of Kutb-uddin Aibeg.

the *Alai Darwaza*, or " Gate of Ala-uddin ;" but this appellation is not known to the people. The age of the building is, however, quite certain, as the name of Ala-uddin is several times repeated in the Arabic inscriptions over three of the entrances, with the addition of his well known title of *Sikandar Sani*, and the date of A. H. 710 or A. D. 1310. This date had already been anticipated, from the style of the building, by Mr. Fergusson, who considered the gateway as at least a century more modern than the tomb of Altamsh. The building is a square of 34½ feet inside, and 56½ feet outside, the walls being 11 feet thick. On each side there is a lofty doorway, with a pointed horse-shoe arch; the outer edge of the arch being fretted, and the underside panelled. The corners of the square are cut off by bold niches, the head of each niche being formed by a series of five pointed horse-shoe arches, lessening in size as they retire towards the angle. The effect of this arrangement is massive and beautiful, and justly merits the praise which Mr. Fergusson[*] had bestowed upon it, as "more simply elegant than any other Indian example with which he was acquainted." The interior walls are decorated with a chequered pattern of singular beauty. In each corner there are two windows of the same shape and style as the doorways, but only one-third of their size. These are closed by massive screens of marble lattice-work. The exterior walls are panelled and inlaid with broad bands of white marble, the effect of which is certainly pleasing. The walls are crowned by a battlemented parapet and surmounted by a hemispherical dome. For the exterior view of the building this dome is, perhaps, too low, but the interior view is perfect, and, taken altogether, I consider that the gateway of Ala-uddin is the most *beautiful* specimen of Pathán architecture that I have seen.

The unfinished Minar of Ala-uddin stands due north from the Kutb Minar at a distance of 425 feet. This massive pillar as it stands at present is built wholly of the rough shapeless grey stone of the country, and the surface is so uneven that there can be no doubt it was the Architect's intention either to have faced it with red stone, or to have covered it with plaster. The Minar stands upon a plinth 4½

---

[*] Handbook of Architecture, I, 433.

feet in width, and the same in height, which is raised upon a terrace 21 feet in breadth and 7½ in height. The rough mass of the superstructure is 257 feet in circumference, and 82 feet in diameter; but with a facing of red stone, this diameter would have been increased to at least 85 feet, or nearly double that of the Kutb Minar, as is usually stated by the people.* The entrance is on the east side, and on the north, at same height, there is a window intended to light the spiral staircase. But the steps were never commenced, and there is only a circular passage 9 feet 0 inches wide around the central pillar, which is 26 feet in diameter. The thickness of the outer wall is 18 feet 3 inches, the whole pillar being 82 feet in diameter, as noted above. The total height of the column, as it now stands, is about 75 feet above the plinth, or 87 feet about the ground level. The outer face of the wall is divided into 32 sides of 8 feet and ¼ inch each. The form of each face or flute is difficult to describe, but it may be likened to the shape of a crown work in fortification, or to that of an old Roman M with shallow body and long widely-splayed limbs. I think it probable that the central angle of each face, as it now exists in the rough stone, would have been modified in the red stone facing into a shallow curved flute. The flutes would have been 4 feet wide and 4 feet apart, with a deep angle between them. The plinth is also divided into 32 straight faces, or projections, which are separated by the same number of depressions of equal breadth, the whole being exactly like a gigantic cogwheel. Syad Ahmad states that the building of this Minar was commenced in A. H. 711 or A. D. 1311; but as Ala-uddin did not die until A. D. 1316, the work was probably stopped some time before the end of his reign. I suspect, indeed, that the work was actually stopped in the following year, as I find from Ferishta that in A. D. 1312 the King became so extremely ill that his wife and son entirely neglected him, while his Minister exercised all the powers of the State, and even aspired to the throne. As the King never rallied, it seems not improbable that all the expensive works of Ala-uddin then in progress may have been stopped by the Minister, who wished to secure the money for himself.

---

* Amir Khusru, in his Tárikh-i-Alái, distinctly states that he ordered the circumference of the new Minar to be double that of the old one, and to make it higher in the same proportion.

SIRI, OR KILAH ALAI.

The Fort of Siri, with Ala-uddin's celebrated palace of "The Thousand Pillars," has been identified by Messrs. Cope and Lewis, and also by Lieutenant Burgess, the Surveyor of the ruins of Delhi, with the citadel of Rai Pithora's fort, in the midst of which stands the Kutb Minar. But in describing this fort I have already brought forward strong reasons to show that it was the ancient *Lalkot* of Anang Pál, and I now propose to follow up the same argument by proving that the true site of *Siri* was the old ruined fort to the northeast of Rai Pithora's fort, which is at present called Sháhpur. A glance at the Sketch Map of the ruins of Delhi,* which accompanies this account, is all that is necessary to make the following argument quite clear.

Sharaf-uddin, the historian of Timur, describes Delhi as consisting of three cities, and as quite distinct from Firuzabad, near which the conqueror's camp was pitched. These three cities were *Siri*, *Jahán-panáh*, and *old Delhi*. To the north-east was *Siri*, the walls of which formed a circle, and to the south-west was *old Delhi*, similar in form but larger than *Siri*, and the space between the two forts, which was much larger than old Delhi, was *Jahán-panáh*. The relative sizes and positions of the three cities are here so accurately described that it is quite impossible to mistake them. *Siri* answers exactly to *Sháhpur*, not only in size and position, but also in shape; for, though not circular, it is certainly oval. To the south-west of Sháhpur lies the fort of Rai Pithora, which, therefore, corresponds exactly with the old Delhi of Sharaf-uddin, both in its size and in its position, and somewhat also in its form, which may be described as an oblong square with the corners cut off. The name of old Delhi was appropriately applied to the fort of Rai Pithora as by far the most ancient of the three cities. Between Siri and old Delhi was *Jahán-panáh*, a name which is still applied to the old walled city between Sháhpur and Rai Pithora's fort; and as the size of this city is more than double that of Rai Pithora's fort, there can be no doubt whatever of its identity with the Jahán-panáh of former days.

I now turn to Ferishta's account of Turghai Khan's invasion of India during the reign of Ala-uddin, the founder

---
* See Plate No. XXXV.

of Siri. In A. H. 703 or A. D. 1303 the Mogul Chief reached Delhi with 120,000 horse and encamped on the bank of the Jumna, most probably about the spot where Humayun's tomb now stands, as that is the nearest point of the river towards old Delhi. "The King," as Ferishta relates, "was in no condition to face the enemy on equal terms, and, therefore, contented himself with entrenching his infantry on the plain beyond the suburbs till he could collect the forces of the distant districts." But after the lapse of two months the Mogul troops were seized with a panic, and retreated precipitately to their own country. The historian then relates that "Ala-uddin, relieved from the perils of this invasion, caused a palace to be built *on the spot where he had entrenched himself*, and directed the citadel of old Delhi to be pulled down and built anew."* Now the spot where the King entrenched himself may be fixed with some precision, partly from Ferishta's description that it was outside the suburbs, and partly from the strategical consideration that it must have been on the north-east side facing towards the enemy, and covering the city. On this side the suburbs of old Delhi extended for a considerable distance. We know, also, that they were without walls, because the Moguls plundered them during their stay, and because they were afterwards enclosed by Muhammad Tughlak, when they received the separate name of Jahánpanáh. Immediately in front of these suburbs, and facing towards the enemy, is the old ruined fort of Shâhpur, and inside the western half of this fort there still exist the remains of a large palace and other buildings. This should be the site of the celebrated *Kasr-Hazár-Sutún*, or "Palace of One Thousand Pillars," otherwise *Hazár Minár*, or "thousand minarets," which Ala-uddin built on the spot where he had entrenched himself.

There is yet one more evidence which I can bring forward in favour of the identification of *Siri* with Shâhpur. In the Ain Akbari it is related that Shir Shah destroyed the city built by Ala-uddin, which was called *Siri*, and founded another.† Again, in the Amish-i-Mahfil it is recorded that Shir Shah pulled down the *Kushak Sabz*, or the "Green Palace," and

---

* Briggs's translation, I., 354.
† Gladwin's translation, II., 84.

built a *new* city. Syad Ahmad repeats the same story, adding that the materials of the old fort and palace of *Siri* were used in the construction of the new fort of *Shir-Shah-Kot*. From these accounts it is quite certain that *Siri* cannot be identified with the citadel that surrounds the Kutb Minar, for the walls of *Siri* were pulled down and the materials removed by Shir Shah, while the walls of the Kutb Minar Citadel are still standing. And, further, it seems almost certain that Shahpur must be *Siri*, because of its vicinity to the new site of Shir Shah's fort, for it is hardly possible to believe that the King would have brought his building stones from the Kutb Minar, a distance of seven miles, when he could have obtained them from Shahpur, which is only half the distance. That he did obtain his materials from the latter place, and not from the former, may be regarded as almost certain, for the very sufficient reason that the walls of Shahpur have actually been removed, while those of the Kutb Citadel are still standing.

The only evidence in favour of the identification of Siri with the Kutb Citadel is the fact which Ferishta records, that the citadel of old Delhi was re-built by Ala-uddin, and the existence near the Kutb Minar of the remains of an old Palace, which still bears this King's name.[*] As the historian does not mention the new city of Siri, it would seem to have been inferred that the *re-building* of the citadel of old Delhi was only a perverted account of the founding of the new city of *Siri*. I see no reason, however, why Ferishta's statement should not be accepted exactly as it stands, for, on summing up the works of Ala-uddin, he records[†] that, during his reign, "*Palaces*, Mosques, Universities, Baths, Mansoleas, *Forts*, and all kinds of public and private buildings seemed to rise as if by magic." As from this account it would appear that Ala-uddin built more than one fort, and founded more than one palace, I see no difficulty in assigning to him the building of the palace near the Kutb Minar, and the re-building of the citadel of old Delhi, as well as the founding of the new city of Siri and its celebrated Palace of *Kasr-Hazar-sutun*, or "The Thousand Pillars." Much stress has been laid upon another statement made by Ferishta regarding the meeting

[*] According to Lieutenant Burgess' Map of the Ruins of Delhi.
[†] Brigg's translation, I., 351.

of Nusrat Shah and Mullu Khan in the Palace of Siri at the tomb of Khwaja Kutb-uddin Bakhtiár Káki. But this statement, and others connected with the confused history of this period, only shows that Ferishta was not well acquainted with the topography of ancient Delhi. Thus he records that Mahmud Shah occupied *old Delhi*, and Nusrat Shah held *Firuzabad*, while *Siri* was in the possession of Mullû Khan and other Nobles who professed neutrality. He then relates that Mullû made overtures to Nusrat, who came to Siri, when a mutual compact was sworn at the tomb of Khwaja Kutb-uddin in *Siri*. But as this tomb is close to the Kutb Minar, and within the walls of the citadel of old Delhi, which was then held by Mahmud, *it would have been impossible for Nusrat and Mullá to have met there.*[*] I would suggest that the place of meeting may have been the shrine of the famous Saint called *Chirágh Delhi*, or the "Lamp of Delhi," which is just outside the south-east corner of Shâhpur or Siri.

My identification of Siri with Shâhpur has been contested by Mr. C. J. Campbell, c. e.[†] I have now gone over the whole subject again very carefully, and I have found the most ample, complete, and satisfactory evidence of the absolute correctness of my identification. A brief abstract of the principal facts is all that need be given in this place:

1st.—Whenever Siri is mentioned before Ala-uddin built his fort in A. H. 703, it is described as *a plain outside the city of Delhi*, on which armies encamp. Thus Amir Khusru states that the left wing of the army of Kaikubâd in A. H. 687 was encamped at Indrpat, the centre at Siri, and the right wing at Tilpat.[‡] Siri was, therefore, just half way between Indrpat and Tilpat, which corresponds exactly with the position of Shâhpur.

2nd.—In A. H. 695, when Ala-uddin, after the murder of his uncle, advanced against Delhi, he encamped on the *plain of Siri*, while his cousin Rukn-uddin Ibrahim still held Delhi.[§]

---

[*] *Note.*—I would suggest that Ferishta may have substituted the name of Bakhtiár Káki, who was commonly called *Roshan Zamir* for that of *Roshan Chirágh*, whose fame was more local.

[†] Bengal Asiatic Society's Journal, 1866, p. 206.

[‡] Elliot, III., 525.

[§] Zia-uddin Barni in Elliot, III., 160.

DELHI.   211

3rd.—In A. H. 697, when Kutlugh Khwaja advanced against Delhi, great anxiety prevailed because the old fortifications had not been kept in repair. The people crowded into the city; but "the Sultan marched *out of Delhi*, with great display and pitched his tent in Siri."*

4th.—On a second invasion of the Moguls "the Sultan again *left the city* and encamped at Siri, where the superior numbers and strength of the enemy compelled him to entrench his camp."†

5th.—After this, says Barni, he "built a palace at Siri. He took up his residence there, and made it his capital, so that it became a flourishing place. He ordered the *fort of Delhi* to be repaired." Amir Khusru‡ also mentions the building of the *new* fort of Delhi, and the repairs of the old one. From Abul Fazl we learn that "Sultan Ala-uddin built another city and a new fort which they called Siri."§

6th.—Ibn Batuta‖ says, "Dár ul Khiláfat Siri was a totally separate and detached town, situated at such a distance from old Delhi as to necessitate the construction of the walls of Jahán-panáh, to bring them within a defensive circle; and that the Hauz-i-khás intervened, in an indirect line, between the two localities." Ibn Batuta was one of the Magistrates of Delhi about 30 years after Alau-ddin's death; and the Hauz-i-Khás still exists to the west of the direct road between Sháhpur and Kila Rai Pithora, that is, between Siri and old Delhi.

7th.—Barni¶ states that the fort of Siri was *finished* during the life-time of Ala-uddin, and from Amir Khusru** we learn that Mubarák "ordered the completion of the fort and city of Delhi begun by his father (Ala-uddin), that is, Lálkot, and Kila Rai Pithora, which the father had ordered to be repaired."

---
* Barni in Elliot, III., 168.
† Barni in Elliot, III., 190.
‡ Elliot, III., 70.
‖ Thomas' Chronicles of Pathán Kings, p. 285, note.
¶ French translation, Tom., III., 146, 155, quoted by Thomas.
§ Elliot, III., 201.
** Elliot, III., 561.

8th.—Barni describes Siri as a "spacious and extensive plain," and states that his uncle, the Kotwal of Delhi, advised the Emperor to erect a villa at Siri where he would be able "to take his hawks and fly them."*

9th.—It is unnecessary to multiply the proofs that Siri was not the citadel of old Delhi, which now surrounds the Kutb Minar. I will, therefore, close this note with a clear and vivid description of Delhi, taken from the autobiography of Timur.† "When my mind was no longer occupied with the destruction of the people of Delhi, *I took a ride round the cities.* Siri is a round city. Its buildings are lofty; they are surrounded by fortifications built of stone and brick, and they are very strong; old Delhi also has a similar strong fort, but it is larger than that of Siri. From the fort of Siri to that of old Delhi, which is a considerable distance, there runs a strong wall built of stone and cement. The part called Jahán-panáh is situated in the midst of the inhabited city. The fortifications of the three cities have 30 gates, Jahán-panáh has 13 gates, seven on the south side bearing towards the east, and six on the north side bearing towards the west. Siri has seven gates, four towards the outside, and three on the inside towards Jahán-panáh. The fortifications of old Delhi have 10 gates, some opening towards the exterior, and some towards the interior of the city." This extract corroborates the account which I have given in the text from Sharaf-ud-din.

The next monuments in point of time are the grand old fort of Tughlakabad, with the tomb of its founder Tughlak Shah, and the castle of his son Mahammad, called Adilabad, and the city named Jahán-panáh.

The fort of Tughlakábád may be described, with tolerable accuracy, as a half hexagon in shape, with three faces of rather more than three-quarters of a mile in length each, and a base of one mile and-a-half, the whole circuit being only one furlong less than four miles. The fort stands on a rocky height, and is built of massive blocks of stone, so large and heavy that they must have been quarried on the spot. The largest stone which I observed measured 14 feet in length

---

* Major Fuller's translation in Bengal Asiatic Society's Journal, 1860, p. 299.
† Malfuzat-i-Timuri, in Elliot, III., 447.

by two feet two inches and one foot ten inches in breadth and thickness, and must have weighed rather more than six tons. The short faces to the west, north, and east, are protected by a deep ditch, and the long face to the south by a large sheet of water, which is held up by an embankment at the southeast corner. On this side the rock is scarped, and above it the main walls rise to a mean height of 40 feet, with a parapet of seven feet, behind which rises another wall of 15 feet, the whole height above the low ground being upwards of 90 feet. In the south-west angle is the citadel, which occupies about one-sixth of the area of the fort, and contains the ruins of an extensive palace. The ramparts are raised, as usual, on a line of domed-rooms, which rarely communicate with each other, and which, no doubt, formed the quarters of the troops that garrisoned the fort. The walls slope rapidly inwards, even as much as those of Egyptian buildings. The rampart walls are pierced with loop-holes, which serve also to give light and air to the soldiers' quarters. The parapets are pierced with low sloping loop-holes, which command the foot of the wall, and are crowned with a line of rude battlements of solid stone, which are also provided with loop-holes. The walls are built of large plainly dressed stones, and there is no ornament of any kind. But the vast size, the great strength, and the visible solidity of the whole give to Tughlakabad an air of stern and massive grandeur that is both striking and impressive.

The Fort of Tughlakobad has 13 gates, and there are three inner gates to the citadel. It contains seven tanks for water, besides the ruins of several large buildings, as the Jáma Masjid and the Birij Mandir. The upper part of the fort is full of ruined houses, but the lower part appears as if it had never been fully inhabited. Syad Ahmad states that the fort was commenced in A. D. 1321 and finished in 1323, or in the short period of two years. It is admitted by all that the work was completed by Tughlak himself; and as his reign lasted for only four years, from 1321 to 1325, the building of the fort must have been pushed forward with great vigour.

The fine Tomb of Tughlak Shah was built by his son Muhammad, who is not without suspicion of having caused his father's death. In A. D. 1304, during the reign of Ala-uddin, a second army of 4,000 Mogul horse burst into the Panjáb and plundered the country as far as Amroha, in Rohilkhand, but they were defeated with great slaughter by Tughlak Khan, who, as a reward for his services, was appointed Governor of the Panjáb. In the following year a third Mogul Army of 57,000 horse invaded India and ravaged Multán; but this army was also defeated by Tughlak with such tremendous slaughter that it is said only 3,000 prisoners survived the defeat. Towards the end of the same year, a fourth inarsion of Moguls was driven back by the same able commander, whose very name at last inspired such terror amongst the Moguls that the women made use of it to quiet their children; and whenever a man showed any alarm, his companions would ask "why do you start? Have you seen Tughlak?" From A. D. 1305 to 1321 Gházi Beg Tughlak was Governor of the Panjáb, residing some times at Lahor, and some times at Depálpur and Multán. In the Fort of Multán he built a magnificent tomb for himself, which exists to this day under the title of Rokn-i-álam, a name derived from Rukn-uddin, a very holy Saint of those days, the son of Balá-uddin Zakaria, more commonly called Baháwal Hak. The people of Multán say that Muhammad presented the tomb to Rukn-uddin to secure his silence in the matter of his father's death; but agreeably to another version, Tughlak himself had incurred the displeasure of Rukn-uddin by an attempt to carry off one of his women. The angry Saint prophesied that he would never reach Delhi, and accordingly he was killed near Tilpat just as he was about to enter Delhi. There may, perhaps, be some truth in this tradition, as we learn from Ibn Batuta[*] that Rukn-uddin was the most noted Saint in India, and that his fame had extended even to Alexandria. Under any circumstances it was politic to conciliate the good-will of this influential personage, and the worthy Saint himself was no doubt highly gratified with the magnificence of the gift. In Delhi itself the death of Tughlak is attributed to another Saint, the famous Nizám-uddin Auliya, some of whose labourers had been seized to work on the walls of Tughlakábad. The holy man remonstrated angrily, and his words were conveyed to Tughlak then absent in Bengal, who remarked that, on his return to Delhi, he would humble the proud Saint. The threat was told to Nizám-uddin, who merely remarked—"he

---

[*] Travels, pp. i—ivL

will never return to Delhi." When the Emperor left Bengal on his return to the capital the Saint was reminded of his prophecy, to which he replied "Delhi is far off (*Dihli dur ast*, or *Dihli dur hai*). As the Emperor approached nearer and nearer, he made the same remark; and even when he had reached Afghánpur within four miles of Tughlakabad, he repeated his former words "Delhi is far off,"—Tughlak was killed at Afghánpur, and the words of the holy man became a proverb, which is still in common use. Nizam-uddin died a few years afterwards, and his tomb was erected at the expense of Muhammad, out of gratitude, as the people say, for his assistance in placing him on the throne.

I have referred to this earlier tomb of Tughlak, which still exists in the fort of Multán, as it is the oldest building that I have seen with the rapidly sloping walls, which form the most prominent feature of the Delhi tomb. The Rokn-i-Âlam, however, is octagonal, with small towers at the angles, and is, besides, a much larger building, the inside diameter being 50 feet, and the outer diameter 76 feet. But the Multán tomb is built entirely of brick, while the Delhi tomb is built throughout of stone, and is ornamented with white marble.

The tomb of Tughlak Shah is situated outside the southern wall of Tughlakabad, in the midst of the artificial lake already described, and is surrounded by a pentagonal outwork, which is connected with the fortress by a causeway 600 feet in length, supported on 27 arches. The stern beauty and massive strength of this tomb have justly elicited the following warm praises of Mr. Fergusson:[*] "The sloping walls and almost Egyptian solidity of this Mausoleum, combined with the bold and massive towers of the fortification that surround it, form a picture of a warrior's tomb unrivalled anywhere." In this praise I heartily concur, with only one reservation in favour of the situation of the Multán tomb, which, besides being both larger and loftier, is placed on the very top of the fort close to the northern wall.

In plan the Delhi tomb is a square of 38½ feet interior and 61¼ feet exterior dimensions. The outer walls are 38½ feet in height to the top of the battlement, with a slope of

---

[*] Hand-book of Architecture, I.—434.

2·333 inches per foot. At this rate the whole slope is 7½ feet in 38½ feet. The walls at base are 11½ feet thick, and at top only 4 feet, but the projecting mouldings of the interior increase the thickness of wall at the springing of the dome to about 6 or 7 feet, or perhaps more, for I had no means of making measurements so high up. The diameter of the dome is about 34 feet inside and about 44 feet outside, with a height of 20 feet. The whole height of the tomb to the top of the dome is 70 feet, and to the top of the pinnacle about 80 feet.

Each of the four sides has a lofty doorway in the middle, 24 feet in height, with a pointed horse-shoe arch fretted on the outer edge. There is a smaller doorway, only 5 feet 10 inches in width, but of the same form, in the middle of each of the great entrances, the archway being filled with a white marble lattice screen of bold pattern. The decoration of the exterior depends chiefly on difference of colour, which is effected by the free use of bands and borders of white marble, with a few panels of black marble, on the large sloping surfaces of red-stone. The horse-shoe arches are of white marble, and a broad band of the same goes completely round the building at the springing of the arches. Another broad band of white marble in upright slabs, 4 feet in height, goes all round the dome just above its springing. The present effect of this mixture of colours is certainly pleasing, but I believe that much of its beauty is due to the mellowing hand of time, which has softened the crude redness of the sand-stone, as well as the dazzling whiteness of the marble. The building itself is in very good order, but the whole interior of the little fort in which it stands is filled with filthy hovels and dirty people, and the place reeks with ordure of every description. I would strongly recommend that the whole of these hovels should be removed, and the interior of the fort cleaned.* The people might be located in Tughlakabad, only 200 yards to the north, where there are hundreds of domed-rooms under the ramparts, all in good repair and quite unoccupied.

Inside the Mausoleum there are three tombs, which are said to be those of Tughluk Shah and his Queen, and their

---

* This proposal has since been carried into effect by the late able and energetic Commissioner, Colonel G. W. Hamilton.

son Juna-Khan, who took the name of Muhammad when he ascended the throne. This Prince was the most accomplished of all the Pathán Sovereigns of India; but he was also the most inhumanly cruel and most madly tyrannical of them all. His cruelties were witnessed by his cousin and successor Firuz Tughlak, who adopted one of the most curious expedients which the mind of man has ever conceived for obtaining the pardon of his tyrannical predecessor. I quote the words of Firuz himself, as given by Ferishta,* from the inscriptions on the Great Mosque of Firuzabad. "I have also taken pains to discover the surviving relations of all persons who suffered from the wrath of my late Lord and Master *Muhammad Tughlak*, and, having pensioned and provided for them, have caused them to grant their full pardon and forgiveness to that Prince in the presence of the holy and learned men of this age, whose signatures and seals, as witnesses, are affixed to the documents, the whole of which, as far as lay in my power, have been procured and put into a box, and deposited in the vault in which Muhammad Tughlak is entombed."† This strange device of placing the vouchers in the tomb ready for the dead man's hand to pick up at the last day is as bold as it is original. It would be interesting to read some of these documents, which are, in all probability, still quite safe, as all the tombs appear to be in the most perfect order.

Another work attributed to Muhammad Tughlak is the small detached fort of *Adilabad* or *Muhammadabad*, near the south-east corner of Tughlakabad, with which it was once connected by a double wall along the causeway which crosses the intervening low ground. This fort is built in the same style as Tughlakabad, but it is a very small place, as the exterior line of works is not more than half a mile in circuit.

But the greatest work of Muhammad Tughlak was the fortification of the extensive suburbs of Delhi, lying between

---

* Briggs, I—484.

† The same statement is made by Firuz in his autobiography—"Under the guidance of the Almighty, I arranged that the heirs of those persons who had been executed in the reign of my late lord and patron Sultan Muhammad Shah, and those who had been deprived of a limb, nose, eye, hand, or foot, should be reconciled to the late Sultan, and be appeased with gifts, so that they executed deeds declaring their satisfaction, duly attested by witnesses. These deeds were put into a chest, which was placed in the *Jais-ul-duda* at the head of the tomb of the late Sultan in the hope that God, in His great clemency, would show mercy to my late friend and patron, and make those persons [or] reconciled to him.— See Elliot's Muhammadan Historians III., 385.—*Futuhát-i-Firúz Sháhí.*

the Hindu fort of *Rai Pithora* and the Musalmân Citadel of *Siri*. These suburbs had been plundered by the Moguls in the early part of the reign of Ala-uddin, and their unprotected state fully justified the vast outlay which the King must have incurred upon their defences. The north-west wall is 1¾ mile in length, the east wall is 1¼ mile, and the south wall is 2 miles; the whole length of the walls being just 5 miles, or somewhat more than the circuit of the fort of Rai Pithora. A considerable portion of the south wall still exists; but the east and north-west walls have been pulled down, and are now only traceable by their ruins. Sharaf-uddin states that *Jahán-panáh* had 13 gates, 6 being to the north-west and 7 to the south-west.

Having now described the seven forts of old Delhi, I will complete the account with a detail of the number of gates in each of the forts, which together make up the total of "52 gates," as recorded by the old English traveller William Finch, and as preserved by the people down to the present day in their pithy description of *Sát-kila Báwan-Darwáza* or "seven forts and 52 gates."

		Gates.
Lálkot of Anang Pal, towards Rai Pithora	...	4
Fort of *Rai Pithora*, and Lálkot outside	...	10
Total of Hindu Dilli	...	14 gates.
Siri of Ala-uddin ...	...	7
Jahán-panáh of Muhammad	...	13
Total of Musalmán Delhi	...	20 gates.
Total of old Delhi ...	...	34 gates.
Tughlakabad ...	...	13
Citadel of ditto ...	...	3
Adilabad ...	...	2
Total of Tughlakabad	...	18
Total number ...	...	52 gates.

The next remains in point of antiquity are the buildings of Firuz Tughlak, who devoted the greater part of a long reign of nearly 40 years (A. D. 1351 to 1388) to the construction of numerous works, of which all but 20 palaces, 10 monumental pillars, and 6 tombs, may be called works of real public utility. Perhaps the most useful of these works was the canal which he drew from the west bank of the Jumna to supply his new Capital of Firuzabad with water. This canal, having become choked from neglect, was cleared out by Ali Mardán Khan in the reign of Shahjahán to furnish the Mogul's new Capital with water. Having again become choked, it was once more cleared out and improved by the British Government, and it is still flowing through modern Delhi under the name of the Western Jumna Canal.

But the most extensive work of Firuz was the building of the new city of *Firuzabad*, with its two palaces of *Kushak Firuzabad* and *Kushak Shikár*. Major Lewis has published much interesting information regarding this new city from the Persian of *Shams-i-Siráj Afif*, who was contemporary with the latter end of this Emperor's reign. The new city was begun in the year A. H. 755, or A. D. 1354. It extended from the fort of Indrpat to the *Kushak Shikár*, or hunting palace, a length of five *kos*. Now the distance from old Delhi is said to be also five *kos*, which fixes the position of the Kushak Shikár approximately on the low range of hills to the north-west of the modern Shahjahánábád. But the exact position is absolutely determined by the mention that the second stone pillar from Mirat was erected within the precincts of the palace, as the stone pillar is now lying in five pieces on the top of the hill close to Hindu Rao's house. *Shams-i-Siráj* adds that the whole distance from Indrpat to the Kushak Shikár was occupied by stone-houses, mosques, and bazars, but as the limits noted above include the whole of the modern Shahjahánábád, it is very improbable that the entire space was actually occupied. It is certain, however, that some considerable portion of the site of Shahjahánábád was well populated as the *Kúla Masjid*, which was built in Firuz's reign, is situated at some distance within the Turkomán Gate of the present city. But even if thinly inhabited, the population of Firuzabad could not have been less than that of Shahjahánábád, as it was more than double its size. The number of inhabitants would, therefore, have been about 150,000; and if we add 100,000 more for the population of old Delhi, the total number of inhabitants in the Indian Metropolis during the reign of Firuz Shah must have amounted to one quarter of a million.

The palace of Firuzabad, which formed also the citadel of the new city, was strongly fortified with massive stone walls and towers of more than Egyptian slope. One of the gateways, which still exists, between the well known *Lál Darwáza* and Firuz Shah's Pillar, is a fine specimen of this bold, but rude, architecture. I believe, however, that we now see these old buildings under very favourable circumstances, as time has most effectually stripped off all the flaring and gaudily coloured plaster which the taste of those days so much delighted in. I found it impossible to trace the exact size or shape of Firuz Shah's Citadel, as many of the parts in the best preservation appear to me to be of decidedly later date. Thus the Kâbuli Gate or *Lál Darwáza*, as it is now called from its red colour, is of quite a different style of architecture, and belongs, as I believe, to the time of *Shir Shah* of whose city it formed the northern or Kabul Gate. From what I was able to trace, my opinion is that Firuz Shah's palace was much smaller than the palace of Shahjâhân in the modern city.

A characteristic and favourable specimen of the architecture of this age is the *Kála Masjid*, or "Black Mosque," which is situated inside the present city, at a short distance from the Turkoman Gate. A detailed account of this building has been published by Messrs. Lewis and Cope.[*] According to these authors, the original name was most probably the *Kulán Masjid* or "Great Mosque." This is no doubt correct, as, when I first visited this Mosque in February 1838, the people in charge called it by that name. The common name, however, is the *Kála Masjid*. But I am quite satisfied that this could not have been the original name, as the taste of those days would most assuredly have covered the whole building with a coating of coloured plaster. The present name of *Kála Masjid* could not therefore have been given to it until most of the plaster had fallen off, and the bare walls of dark-grey quartzose sand-stone had become visible.

The *Kála Masjid* is a single room 71 feet in length by 41 feet in breadth, with two rows of four pillars each down the centre, and one row of coupled pillars along the front. These columns divide the whole area into 15 squares, each of which

---

[*] Bengal Asiatic Society's Journal, 1847, p. 577.

is covered by a small dome, the central dome being somewhat higher than the others. The walls are six feet thick, with three openings at each end, closed by massive red stone lattice-work. In front of the building there is a small open quadrangle, of the same dimensions as the interior of the Mosque, and on three sides of the quadrangle there are cloisters which are continued round the Mosque itself. The whole is enclosed by an outer wall 5 feet thick, which forms an oblong block of building 140 feet in length by 120 feet in breadth. On the outside the building consists of two storeys, the middle of the lower storey being a solid mass, which forms the floor of the Masjid. The four faces of the lower storey have two rows of small rooms, which are now rented to petty shop-keepers. This is the invariable practice at present, and was, no doubt, the same in the time of Firuz, as the money thus obtained always formed the principal revenue, and eventually became the only income of the attendants of a Mosque. The lower storey is 28 feet in height, and the upper storey to the top of the battlements is 38 feet, making a total height of 66 feet. The four angles are supported by small round towers with sloping walls as plain and bare as the rest of the building. The entrance to the upper storey is reached by a steep flight of steps, at the head of which, but outside the general mass of building, is a domed ante-room of small dimensions. The walls of the upper storey are pierced with a row of arched openings which correspond in number and size with the doorways of the lower storey. These were once filled with bold strong lattice-work, but many of them have been built up. The plain but massive appearance of the walls is highly suggestive of strength and solidity, which is fully borne out by the excellent state of preservation of this old building after a lapse of nearly five centuries.

The small fort of *Indrpat*, or *Purána Kilah*, was repaired by the Emperor Humáyun in A. H. 940, or A. D. 1533, and re-named by him *Din-panáh*; but the new name is never used, except by pedantic or bigotted Muhammadans. Within a few years, or about A. D. 1540 the works were much strengthened by *Shir Shah*, who made *Indrpat* the Citadel of his new city under the name of *Shirgarh*, by which it is now very generally known, although *Purána Kilah*, or "the old Fort," is perhaps the most common appellation. The lofty massive towers and solid walls of this fort were strengthened by a ditch which once communicated with the Jumna. *Shirgarh* is, however, but a small place when compared with the mighty fortresses of *Rai Pithora*, *Siri*, and *Tughlakabad*, the whole circuit of its walls being only one mile and one furlong. In shape it is almost rectangular, being 3 furlongs in length by 1½ furlongs in breadth. The fort had four gates, one in the middle of each face, of which the south-west gate alone is now open. The interior is almost filled with Native huts; but towering above these hovels are two fine remains of former days, a handsome massive Mosque, generally known as the *Kila-Kona Masjid*, and a lofty octagonal building, which is still called *Shir Mandir*, or "Shir's Palace." The front of the Mosque has five horse-shoe arches, and is decorated with blue tiles and marble. The roof is formed of low flattened domes. It was built by Shir Shah in A. H. 948, or A. D. 1541, and is the finest existing specimen of the architecture of the Afghan period.

The new city of Shir Shah called *Delhi Shirshah* extended from the neighbourhood of Humayun's tomb on the south to Firuz Shah's Kotila on the north, near which there still exists a fine massive gateway, which was the *Kábuli Darwáza* of the new city. It is now, however, always called the *Lál Darwáza* or "red gate." William Finch, who entered Delhi from the Agra side on 16th January 1611, describes the city as being two *kos* in length from gate to gate, "surrounded by a wall which has been strong, but is now ruinous." The value of Finch's *kos* is determined at rather more than 1¼ mile, by his mention that the hunting seat or *mole* (that is, *Mahal* of Firuz Shah) was two *kos* from the city. From the *Lál Darwáza* to the ruins of the Kushak Shikár, the distance is 3¼ miles, and from the same point to Humayun's tomb the distance is exactly 3 miles. But as Purchas, on the authority of other English travellers, states that Humayun's tomb was in the city of *Shir Shah Salim*, the south gate of the city must have been somewhere beyond the tomb. The distance, however, could not have been great, as Finch mentions that "a short way from Delhi is a stone bridge of 11 arches," which is clearly the long massive bridge of 11 arches, that is now called *Bara Pul* or the "Great Bridge."* The south gate of Shir Shah's city

---

* Syad Ahmad writes the name *Harah Pulah*, or the "12 arches," and states that the bridge was built in A. H. 1021, which began on 23rd February 1612. But there is probably a mistake of one year in this date, which, I think, should be A. H. 1020, or A. D. 1611. This would agree with Finch's date of 16th January 1611, or properly 1612, according to our present reckoning.

must therefore have been somewhere between the *Bara Pul* and Humáyun's tomb. The east wall of the city is determined by the line of the high bank of the Jumna, which formerly ran due south from Firuz Shah's Kotila towards Humáyun's tomb. On the west the boundary line of the city can be traced along the bank of a torrent bed, which runs southward from the Ajmer Gate of Shahjahánábád, and parallel to the old course of the Jumna, at a distance of rather more than 1 mile. The whole circuit of the city walls was therefore close upon 9 miles, or nearly double that of the modern Shahjahánábád.

The small fort of *Salimgarh* was built by *Salim Shah*, the son of Shir Shah, in A. H. 953, or A. D. 1546. It is situated at the north end of Shahjahán's Palace, after the building of which it was used only as a state prison. It is not quite one quarter of a mile in length, and the whole circuit of its walls is only of three quarters of a mile. It stands on an island close to the west bank of the river, and with its lofty towers and massive walls, forms a most picturesque object from the opposite side of the Jumna. A bridge of five arches was built in front of the South Gate by Jahangir, after whom the name of the place was changed to *Nurgarh* according to Syad Ahmad. But the old name of *Salimgarh* has prevailed, and is the only one that I have ever heard used by the people, either educated or uneducated.

The tomb of Humáyun is too well known to need any detailed description, unless illustrated by pictorial representations, which will more appropriately accompany my proposed account of Mogul architecture. It was built after the Emperor's death in A. H. 962, or A. D. 1554, by his widow *Haji Begam*. It is therefore the earliest specimen of the architecture of the Mogul dynasty. The exterior form of the main body of the tomb is a square with the corners cut off, or an octagon with four long and four short faces, and each of the short faces forms one side of the four octagonal corner towers. The dome is built entirely of white marble, the rest of the building being of red stand-stone, with inlaid ornaments of white marble. In this tomb we first see towers attached to the four angles of the main building. It is true that these towers are very stout and massive, but they form an important innovation in the Muhammadan architecture of Northern India, which was gradually improved and developed, until it culminated in the graceful Minars of the Táj Mahal. The intervening links are, 1st, the one-storeyed towers of Itimád-uddaolah's tomb at Agra; 2nd, the two-storeyed Minars of the gateway of Akbar's tomb at Sikandra; and 3rd, the three-storeyed octagonal Minars of Jahangir's tomb at Lahor. In all these specimens the Minars are attached to the main building, as in the original example of Humáyun's tomb. But in the Táj Mahal the Minars are placed at the four angles of the square terrace or plinth, on which the tomb is raised, an arrangement which was probably copied from the position of the four corner towers of the platform of Shir Shah's tomb at Sasaram. Another innovation observable in this tomb is the narrow-necked dome, which was afterwards adopted in all the Mogul buildings.

The citadel or palace of Shajahánábád was begun by the Emperor Shahjáhán in the year A. H. 1048, or A. D. 1638, but the new city was not commenced until 10 years later. The circuit of the walls of the citadel is 1½ mile, or just the same as that of the old citadel of Tughlakabad; but the new city is considerably larger than either *Tughlakabad* or *Rai Pithora's* Fort, the circuit of its walls being 5½ miles. The citadel has two gates, named the *Lahor* and *Delhi* Gates. The city has twelve gates, which are named as follows, beginning from the north-east gate near Salimgarh, which is now called the Calcutta Gate, because it leads to the bridge-of-boats over the Jumna on the line of the high road to Calcutta:

1. Calcutta Gate to north-east.
2. Nigambad Gate to north-east.
3. Kashmir Gate to north.
4. Mori Gate to north.
5. Kábul Gate to west.
6. Lahor Gate to west.
7. Farash Khana to south-west.
8. Ajmer Gate to south-west.
9. Turkoman Gate to south.
10. Delhi Gate to south.
11. Khyráti Gate to east.
12. Rajghat to east on river face.

The original round towers of the city defences were much enlarged and altered into angular bastions by the British Government early in the present century, and at the same time a regular glacis was formed all round the land faces of the fortress. These new works added considerably to the strength of the fortifications, as we found, to our cost, in the mutiny of 1857. The two principal streets, forming nearly a right angle, ran from the Lahor and Delhi Gates of the Citadel to the Lahor and Delhi Gates of the city. The two principal buildings in the city are the *Jáma Musjid* and the *Zinat Musjid*. The former was built by Shahjáhán in A. D. 1648, and is one of the largest and finest Mosques in India. The later was built by *Zinat-un-nissa*, the daughter of Aurangzib, in A. D. 1710, and is a favorable specimen of the later style of Mogul architecture. Both of these buildings will be described more fully hereafter in my proposed historical account of the Muhammadan architecture of Northern India.

The Citadel of Shahjahánábád, which contained the Emperor's palace, and the two celebrated open halls or courts called the *Dewán-i-ám* and the *Dewán-i-khás*, is too well known to require any description in this place; but it will be duly considered hereafter in my account of the architecture of Shahjáhán's reign. I will, therefore, confine my remarks at present to the short account of the two life-size statues of elephants and their riders that have lately been discovered, and which, as we learn from Thevenot and Bernier, once stood outside the Delhi Gate of the Citadel.

The earliest notice is that by Bernier in his description of Delhi, written on 1st July 1663: "I find nothing remarkable at the entry (of the palace), but two great elephants of stone, which are on the two sides of one of the gates. Upon one of them is the statue of *Jamel*, the famous Raja of Chitor, and upon the other that of *Patta*, his brother. These are those two gallant men that, together with their mother, who was yet braver than they, cut out so much work for *Eckbar*, and who in the sieges of towns, which they maintained against him, gave such extraordinary proofs of their generosity, that at length they would rather be killed in the out-falls with their mother than submit: and for this gallantry it is that even their enemies thought them worthy to have these statues erected for them. Those two great elephants, together with the two resolute men sitting on them, do, at the first entry into this fortress, make an impression of I know not what greatness and awful terror." *Thevenot*, who was at Delhi in 1667, corroborates *Bernier's* account of these statues; but as he knew that Bernier intended to publish a description of Delhi, he merely notices the principal objects, of which the first are, "the two elephants at the entry which carry two *warriors*."

The next reference that I have been able to find is by Lieutenant Franklin, who visited Delhi in 1793. Stimulated by Bernier's account, he made enquiries after the statues, and was informed that "they were removed by order of Aurangzib as savoring too much of idolatry, and he enclosed the place where they stood with a screen of red stone, which has disfigured the entrance of the palace."[*]

The romantic account of Bernier did not escape the notice of the enthusiastic historian of the Rajputs, who, after quoting the passage given above, adds,[†] that "the conqueror of Chitor evinced an exalted sense, not only of the value of his conquest, but of the merits of his foes, in erecting statues to the names of *Jaymal* and *Patta* at the most conspicuous entrance of his palace at Delhi." From Colonel Tod also we learn that Jaymal was a *Mertiya Ráthor* of Bednor, and that Patta was the Chief of the *Jagáwat Sisodigas* of Salûmbra, both being feudatories of Udaypur. Their names, he says, are as household words inseparable in Mewâr, and will be honoured while the Rajput retains a shred of his inheritance, or a spark of his ancient recollections." On Akbar's advance to Chitor, the spiritless Rana Uday Sing retired to the western jungles, and the defence of the capital of the Sisodyas was left to the Rathor Governor Jaymal. But the warlike spirit of the Sisodiyas was roused by the mother of the young Chief of Salûmbra, who "commanded him to put on the saffron robe and to die for Chitor." Patta was then only sixteen years old, and had lately married; but to check any compunctious reluctance which he might feel in leaving his bride, the heroic mother armed the young wife as well as herself, and "with her descended the rock, and the defenders of Chitor saw her fall, fighting by the side of her Amazonian mother." The siege still continued, but without making any progress, when, through some unfortunate delay in the springing of one of their mines, the assailants suffered a severe loss, and fled in disorder to their camp. The operations

---

[*] Asiatic Researches, IV.—414.
[†] Rajasthan, I—378.

of the siege had now to be re-commenced, when a lucky shot deprived the Rajputs of their leader. "Other mines," says Ferishta,* "were directed to be constructed, and as the works were in progress, the King while in the batteries observed *Jaymal*, the Governor of the place, superintending the repairs of the breaches, and giving his orders by torch-light. Akbar, seizing a matchlock from one of his attendants, fired at him, and was so fortunate as to lodge the ball in Jaymal's forehead. The spirit of the besieged fell with their Governor, and, in their dispair, they performed the ceremony of the *Johar*, and putting their wives and children to death, burned them with the corpse of their Chief on a funeral pile." Akbar then entered the fort, and after a slight opposition, the capital of the Sisodiyas, for the third time, was in the hands of the Musalmáns.

It remains now to consider the value of the evidence recorded in the above statements. In the first place, then, with respect to the statues, I feel quite satisfied with the testimony of Bernier. As the physician and companion of *Dánishmand Khan*, a highly respectable nobleman of Aurangzib's Court, he was most in the favorable position for obtaining accurate information regarding the history of Akbar and his successors. I accept, therefore, without any hesitation, the account of Bernier that the statues were those of *Jaymal* and *Patta*, the two Rajput heroes who defended Chitor against Akbar. Both statues as I have already pointed out, are those of Hindus, as their dresses open over the right breast. Admitting this much, I am likewise prepared to allow that the two statues must have been made by Akbar, as is also stated by Bernier. But, as the building of Shahjahánábád was not begun until seventy years after the siege of Chitor, it is absolutely certain that Akbar could not have erected the statues in front of the gate of the Delhi Palace, where they were seen by Bernier and Thevenot. What, then, was their original site? This I believe to have been the fort of Agra in front of the river gate.

In his account of the city of Agra, Abul Fazl,† the Minister of Akbar, states that "His Majesty has erected a fort "of red stone, the like of which no traveller has ever beheld."

* Briggs, II—241.
† Áin Akbari, II—36.

"At the *eastern* gate are carved in stone two elephants with their riders, of exquisite workmanship." The *eastern* gate of the fort of Agra is the *river* gate, in front of which the two statues most probably remained undisturbed until the reign of Shahjahán, who, as I presume, must have removed them to Delhi to adorn his new capital of Shahjahánábád. It is scarcely possible that Jahángir could have removed them to Delhi; but, if he did so, they would have been placed in front of the gate of *Salimgarh*, to which he added a bridge, at the same time changing the name of the place to *Nurgarh*, after his own title of *Nur-uddin*.

I have been disappointed in not finding any mention of these elephant statues in the accounts of our early English travellers. Captain Hawkins and William Finch both visited Agra in the beginning of Jahangir's reign. The former attended the Royal Darbar in the Agra Fort regularly for two years, and describes minutely the King's daily occupations, which, according to William Finch, included the witnessing of animal fights on every day except Sunday and of executions on every Tuesday. Both the fights and the executions took place in a courtyard, or out-work, in front of the river gate. This gate is described by Finch as follows: "The fourth gate is to the river called the *Duraune (Darsan Darwáza*, or "Gate of Sights") leading to a fair court, extending along the river, where the King looks out every morning at sunrising." " Right under this place is a kind of scaffold, on which the Nobles stand." " Here, likewise, the King comes every day at noon to see the *Tamdsha* (shows) or fighting with elephants, lions, and buffaloes, and killing of deer by leopards." " Tuesdays are peculiarly the days of blood, both for fighting beasts and killing men, as on that day the King sits in judgment, and sees it put in execution." I can only account for the silence of Finch and Hawkins by supposing that they had never seen these two remarkable elephants with their warrior riders. This, indeed, is likely enough, for the principal gate near the city, by which they would have entered the fort, is on the western side, and unless they had passed right through the fort, they could not possibly have seen the statues. There was formerly no road along the bank of the river, and no one would think of passing in that direction without some special reason. No doubt the statues might have been seen from the opposite bank of the river, but as our travellers had no call to go there, they probably never went. Both of them came to Agra from Surat, and approached the fort on the south side; and Finch left Agra by the Delhi Road *viâ* Mathura, without crossing the river, while Hawkins returned to Surat. Had Finch seen the statues, I feel satisfied that he would have mentioned them, as he takes notice of the elephant statue in front of the *Háthi Páur*, or "Elephant Gate," of the Gwalior Fort.

With regard to Akbar's object in setting up these statues, I differ altogether from Bernier and Tod. Speaking of the heroes *Jaymal* and *Patta*, the former says that "even their enemies thought them worthy to have these statues erected to them." This is somewhat amplified by Tod, who says that Akbar "evinced an exalted sense, not only of the value of his conquest, but of the merits of his foes in erecting statues to the names of Jaymal and Patta." Here we see that both Bernier and Tod were of opinion that these statues were erected by Akbar in honour of his enemies, the two Rajput heroes of Chitor. But when we remember that Akbar prided himself on having killed Jaymal with his own hand; that he gave the name of *Durust Andáz*, or "true-shooter," to his matchlock, and that both his Minister Abul Fazl and his son Jahangir make much boasting of the Emperor's lucky shot, the more natural conclusion is that the statues were erected in honour of Akbar himself. Had they been set up in honour of his gallant foes, the fact would most assuredly have been commemorated in their loudest voice by the Rajput bards; but so far was this from being the case, that Colonel Tod was entirely indebted to Bernier for his knowledge of their existence.

Again, when I remember that the same Akbar assumed the title of *Ghází* (or warrior for the faith) after putting to death with his own hand in cold blood his able, gallant, and wounded antagonist *Himu*, I cannot believe that he would afterwards erect statues in honour of any infidel Hindus, however noble in blood, or gallant in the field. When I recollect, also, the position that the statues occupied, one on each side of the eastern gateway of the Agra fort, I cannot help feeling that they stood, like the two horsemen at the gate of the Horse Guards in London, as sentinels at the gate of their imperial foe, to do honour to their conqueror. Admitting his view to be correct, I can understand why

Shahjahán removed them to Delhi to occupy the same position at the gate of his new citadel. Under the same view I can also understand why they were spared for a time by the bigotted Aurangzib. On the other hand, if we suppose with Bernier and Tod that the statues were set up in honour of the two Rajput warriors, their re-erection by Shahjáhán is to me quite incomprehensible.

But the question of Akbar's intention, whether it was to do honour to his foes or to himself, is one of comparatively little moment. To us the statues are simply valuable as works of art, as they are, perhaps, the only portrait statues that have been executed in India for many centuries. They are made of red sand-stone, and are of life-size, while the huge elephants on which they sit are of black marble, and the housings are decorated with white and yellow marbles. On these grounds I conclude that the dresses and turbans of the Rajput Chiefs were coloured, while the faces and hands were most probably left of the natural redish brown colour of the sand-stone. When set up again in the Delhi Garden, I have no doubt that they will command as much attention and admiration from our own countrymen as they did two hundred years ago from the enthusiastic Frenchman Bernier.

There are many other remains at Delhi that are both beautiful and interesting, but as their age and origin are well known, they will naturally form a part of my proposed account of the Muhammadan architecture of Northern India. Such are the *Zinat Masjid*, more commonly called the *Kudri Masjid*, or "Maiden's Mosque," because built by *Zinat-un-nissa*, the virgin daughter of Aurangzib;* the *Kashmiri Masjid*, and the *Begam Masjid* in the city, and the tombs of *Jahámirá Begam* and *Zib-un-nissa*, the sister and daughter of Aurangzib, outside the city. I will only notice here a grave mistake made by Mrs. Colin Mackenzie in her account of the epitaph on *Jahánári's* tomb. The marginal inscription records the name of "the perishable Fakir, *Jahánári Begam*, the daughter of Shahjahán, and the disciple of the saints of *Chist* A. H. 1004 (or A. D. 1092)." The holy men here mentioned are the Muhammadan saints of the well known family of *Chisti*, of whom famous shrines exist at Ajmer,

---

* The people have a tradition that Zinat-un-nissa demanded the amount of her dowry from her father, and spent it in building this Mosque, instead of marrying.

Fatehpur—Sikri, Thaneswr, and Kasûr. This notorious
Muhammadan name is changed by Mrs. Mackenzie as follows:
"the humble, the transitory Jahánárá was a disciple of the
holy men of *Christ*, supposed to be Roman Priests."*
Jahánárá was the builder of the Jáma Masjid at Agra, and
has always been considered a most devout follower of
Muhammad. Her name is still held in much veneration
in Delhi for her numerous charities.

II. MATHURA.

In the Brahmanical city of Mathura, in A. D. 634, the
temples of the gods were reckoned by Hwen Thsang at five
only, while the Buddhist monasteries amounted to 20, with
2,000 resident monks. The number of *Stupas* and other
Buddhist monuments was also very great, there being no less
than seven towers, containing relics of the principal disciples
of Buddha. The King and his ministers were zealous Buddhists, and the three great fasts of the year were celebrated
with much pomp and ceremony, at which times the people
flocked eagerly to make their offerings to the holy *Stupas*
containing the relics of Buddha's disciples. Each of them,
says Hwen Thsang, paid a special visit to the statue of the
Bodhisatawa whom he regarded as the founder of his own
school. Thus the followers of the *Abidharma*, or transcen-
dental doctrines made their offerings to *Sáriputra*; they who
practised *Samádhi* or meditation, to *Mudgalaputra*; the
followers of the *Sautrántikas*, or aphorisms, to *Purva Mai-
treyani Putra*; they who adhered to the *Vinaya*, or discipline, to *Upáli*; the *Bhikshunis* or Nuns, to Ananta; the
Anupásampannas, or novices, to *Ráhula* (the son of *Buddha*);
and they who studied the *Maháyána*, or "Greater means of
advancement," to the great Bodhisatwa *Manju Sri* or
Avalokiteswara, who plays such a conspicuous part in later
Buddhism. But notwithstanding this apparently flourishing
condition of Buddhism, it is certain that the zeal of the
people of Mathura must have lessened considerably since
A. D. 400, when Fa Hian reckoned the body of monks in

---

* Delhi, the city of the Great Mogul, 2nd edition, p. 61. I presume that this curious
mistake is due to the English printer's correction of Sir W. Sleeman's translation, Rambles,
II., 270, " where *Christ* is an evident misprint for *Chist*, as Sleeman was a guest at *bodat*. It is
curious that the same insertion of the letter *r* is made in this name in the travels of another
lady. " Tour in Upper Provinces of Hindustan by A. D.," where she speaks, or is made to
speak by the English compositor, of " the Mausoleum of *Christie* at Futteypoor Sicura."

the 20 monasteries to be 3,000, or just one-half more than their number at the time of Hwen Thsang's visit in A. D. 634.*

Fa Hian and his companions halted at Mathura for a whole month, during which time "the clergy held a great assembly and discoursed upon the law." After the meeting they proceeded to the *Stupa* of *Sáriputra,* to which they made an offering of all sorts of perfumes, and before which they kept lamps burning the whole night. Hwen Thsang describes these processions as carrying flying steamers and stately parasols, while the mists of perfumes and the showers of flowers darkened the sun and moon! I can easily realize the pomp and glittering show of these ceremonies from the similar scenes which I have witnessed in Burma. I have seen steamers from 100 to 200 feet in length carried in processions, and afterwards suspended from pillars or holy trees. I have beheld hundreds of gorgeous parasols of gold and silver brocade flashing in the sun; and I have witnessed the burning of thousands of candles day after day before the great *Stupa* of *Shwe-Dagon* at Rangoon, which is devoutly believed to contain eight hairs of Buddha. Before this sacred tower, I have seen flowers and fruits offered by thousands of people, until they formed large heaps around it, while thousands of votaries still came thronging in with their offerings of candles, and gold leaf, and little flags, with plantains and rice, and flowers of all kinds.

From these accounts of the Chinese pilgrims it would appear that the Buddhist establishments at Mathura must have been of considerable importance, and this conclusion is fully borne out by the number and interest of the recent discoveries. Contrary to his usual practice, Hwen Thsang has unfortunately given us but few details regarding the monasteries and temples of Mathura. This is the more to be regretted, as we now know that one of the monasteries was established by the great Indo-Scythian King *Huvishka,* about the beginning of the Christian era, and that one of the stone statues, judging by the size of its hand, could not have been less than 20 feet in height.

The first place described by Hwen Thsang is a monastery situated on a mound, at 5 or 6 *li,* or about one mile, to the

---

* See Beal's "Fa Hian," C. XVI; and Julien's Hwen Thsang, II., p. 207.

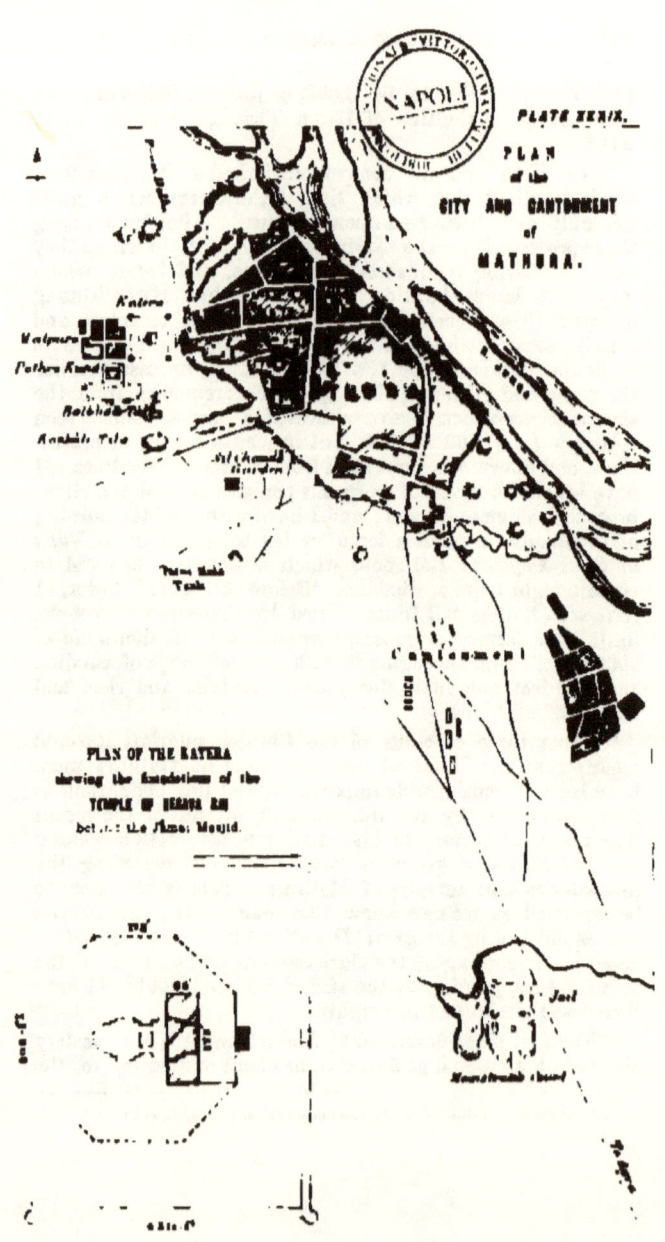

east of the city. Cells were formed in the sides of the mound, which was approached through a hollow, and in the midst was a *Stupa* containing the nails of Buddha. This monastery is said to have been built by the holy *Upagupta*, who, as we learn from one of the legends of *Pátali Putra*, was a contemporary of Asoka. The nails and beard of the holy man were still preserved.

On another mound to the north of this monastery, there was a cave containing a stone chamber, 20 feet high and 30 feet long, which was full of bamboo spikes only four inches in length. These spikes represented the number of husbands and their wives who had been converted by *Upagupta*.

At 24 or 25 *li*, or just four miles to the south-east of the stone chamber, there was a large dry tank, with a *Stupa* on its bank, which marked the spot where Buddha was said to have taken exercise. On this spot also, according to the local legends, a monkey had offered honey to Buddha, which the teacher graciously accepted and directed that it should be mixed with water and given to the monks. The glad monkey made a wild bound, and fell into the tank and died; but owing to the powerful influence of his good act, he became a man in his next birth.

In a forest at a short distance to the north of the tank there was another holy spot, where the four previous Buddhas were said to have taken exercise; and all round it there were numerous *Stupas*, which marked the places where no less than 1,250 *arhats*, or holy men, including *Sáriputra*, *Mudgalaputra*, and others, used to sit in meditation. But besides these, there were several other *Stupas* on the spots where Buddha at different times had explained the law.

The two principal sites described by Hwen Thsang can, I think, be fixed with tolerable certainty, namely, that of the famous *Upagupta* monastery, and that of the monkey's offering. The first is said to be at 5 or 6 *li*, or just one mile, to the east of the city; but as an eastern direction would take us to the low ground, on the opposite bank of the Jumna, where no ruins now exist, I feel quite satisfied that we should read *west* instead of *east*. This change is rendered almost certain by the discovery of numerous Buddhist remains inside the great square of the *Katra*, which is just one mile to the westward of the old fort of Mathura. But it is rendered quite certain by the more recent discovery of very important Buddhist remains and old inscriptions in a mound *beside a tank* which is situated just three miles to the southeast of the *Katra* mound. This tank mound I take to be the place where Buddha was said to have taken exercise, and where the monkey made his offering of honey. The direction is precisely the same, and the distance agrees also as well as can be made out from Hwen Thsang's statements. He gives the distance as four miles from the stone chamber, which was at some unstated, but certainly short, distance to the north of the *Upagupta* monastery. The nearest mounds are about half a mile to the north of the *Katra*, which will make the whole distance 3½ miles, if measured in a direct line by the British road, which passes outside the city, but which will be fully four miles if measured by the old road, which goes through the city. Had the Chinese pilgrim given us the name of the monastery built by *Upagupta*, we might, perhaps, have obtained some absolute proof of its identity with the site of the *Katra*; but I believe that the very strong reasons which I have just before given are amply sufficient to fix the site of the *Upagupta* monastery at the present *Katra*.*

There are a great number of lofty earthen mounds around Mathura which are covered with fragments of stone and brick. Nothing, however, is known about them, although every one of them has a separate name. The numerous fragments of stone which are found upon them show that they are not old brick-kilns, as might have been supposed from their vicinity to the city. Apparently, they are natural mounds such as are found everywhere along the lower course of Jumna, and which have usually been taken advantage of for the sites of forts or temples. Thus the old fort of Mathura is perched upon a similar mound, and so also is the Jáma Masjid in the middle of the *Katra* square. Most of the names of these mounds refer to the Brahmanical divinities; but there are two of them, such as the *Anand Tila* and the *Vindyak Tila*, that are unmistakeably Buddhist, and which may possibly refer to the two *Stupas* of *Ananda* and

* I am indebted to Mr. S. Growse, of the Civil Service, for the important information that numerous ruined mounds exist to the south-west of the Katra, about 1½ miles distant, in one of which, just two years ago, was found a golden casket with the usual Buddhist deposits of the seven precious things. The position of these mounds agrees better with the distance of one mile from the city than the site of the Katra which is only just outside the city.— See Plate No. XXXIX. for a map of Mathura.

Upáli (the *Vinâyak* or teacher of *Vinaya*) as described by Hwen Thsang. Both of these mounds are to the north of the city. To the south there are seven mounds known as the *Sát Tila* which are severally named as follows:—1, *Dhúka-Tila*; 2, *Sapt Rishi*; 3, *Bal*, or *Bul*, *Tila*; 4, *Narad*; 5, *Kans*; 6, *Kal-jug*; 7, *Nágakesha*.* Now, it is remarkable that the number of great *Stupas* of the disciples of Buddha was also seven; but unfortunately as nothing is recorded regarding their relative positions, we are left entirely to conjecture whether these mounds may possibly represent the seven famous *Stupas* of Buddha's principal disciples. I think that it would be worth while to make some excavations in all of these seven mounds to the south, as well as in the two northern mounds which still bear Buddhistical names.

The *Katra* mound has been successively occupied by Buddhists, Brahmans, and Musalmâns. The *Katra*, or market-place, is an oblong enclosure like a *Sarái*, 604 feet in length by 653 feet in breadth. In the midst of this square stands the *Jáma* Masjid, on a large mound from 25 to 30 feet in height. The mosque is 172 feet long and 66 feet broad, with a raised terrace in front of the same length, but with a breadth of 80 feet, the whole being 30 feet in height above the ground. About 5 feet lower, there is another terrace 286 feet in length by 268 feet in breadth, on the eastern edge of which stands the mosque. There is no inscription on the building, but the people ascribe it to Aurungzib, who is said to have pulled down the great Hindu temple of *Kesava Deva*, or *Keso Ray*, that formerly stood on this high mound, a most noble position, which commands a fine view of the whole city. Curiously enough I have been able to verify this charge against Aurungzib by means of some inscriptions on the pavement slabs which were recorded by Hindu pilgrims to the shrine of Kesava Ray. In relaying the pavement, the Muhammadan architect was obliged to cut many of the slabs to make them fit into their new places. This is proved by several of the slabs bearing incomplete portions of Nâgari inscriptions of a late date. One slab has

---

* During a short visit in the present year, 1871, I could not find a single person who knew the *Anand Tila*. The *Dhu-ka-Tila* is also an invention of my informant as it is evidently intended for *Dhúl-ka-tila*, or the "mound of dust," that is, the refuse of a brick kiln, of which the mound in question is actually composed.

"*bat* 1713, *Phálgun*," the initial *Sam* of *Sambat* having been cut off. Another slab has the name of *Keso Ray*, the rest being wanting; while a third bears the late date of S. 1720. These dates are equivalent to A. D. 1656 and 1663; and as the latter is *five* years subsequent to the accession of Aurungzib, it is certain that the Hindu temple was still standing at the beginning of his reign.*

The greater part of the foundations of the Hindu temple of Kesava Ray may still be traced at the back of the Masjid. Indeed, the back wall of the mosque itself is actually built upon the plinth of the temple, one of the *cyma reversa* mouldings being filled up with brick and mortar. I traced the walls for a distance of 163 feet to the westward, but apparently this was not the whole length of the temple, as the mouldings of the Hindu plinth at the back of the Masjid are those of an exterior wall. I think it probable that the temple must have extended at least as far as the front of the mosque, which would give a total length of 250 feet, with an extreme breadth of nearly 72 feet, the floor of the building being no less than 25 feet above the ground. Judging from these dimensions, the temple of *Kesava Deva* must have been one of the largest in India.† I was unable to obtain any information as to the probable date of this magnificent fane. It is usually called Keso Ray, and attributed to Raja Jagn Deva, but some say that the enshrined image was that of *Jaga Deva*, and that the builder's name was Ray or *Raja Kesava Deva*. It is possible that it may have been one of the "innumerable temples" described by Mahmud in his letter to the Governor of Ghazni written in A. D. 1017, as we know that the conqueror spared the temples either through admiration of their beauty, or on account of the difficulty of destroying them. Mahmud remained at Mathura only 20 days, but during that time the city was pillaged and burned, and the temples were rifled of their statues. Amongst these there were "five golden idols whose eyes were of rubies, valued at 50,000 dinars," or £25,000. A sixth golden image

---

* I have since found the most complete and satisfactory confirmation of my opinion in the travels of Tavernier, Part II., b. III., ch. 12, where he describes the Hindu temple as still standing at the time of his visit, apparently about A. D. 1650, and certainly after the accession of Aurungzib.

† This opinion is fully confirmed by Tavernier, who describes the temple as "très magnifique," and states that it ranked next after the temples of Jagannath and Banára.—See Plate No. XL. for a plan of the Masjid and Temple.

weighed 98,300 *mishkals*, or 1,120 lbs., and was decorated with a sapphire weighing 300 *mishkals*, or 3½ lbs. But, "besides these images, there were above one hundred idols of silver, which loaded as many camels." Altogether the value of the idols carried off by Mahmud cannot have been less than three millions of rupees, or £300,000.

The date of Mahmud's invasion was A. D. 1017, or somewhat less than 400 years after the visit of the Chinese pilgrim Hwen Thsang, who in A. D. 634 found only five Brahmanical temples in Mathura. It is during these four centuries, therefore, that we must place, not only the decline and fall of Buddhism, but its total disappearance from this great city, in which it once possessed twenty large monasteries, besides many splendid monuments of its most famous teachers. Of the circumstances which attended the downfall of Buddhism we know almost nothing; but as in the present case we find the remains of a magnificent Brahmanical temple occupying the very site of what must once have been a large Buddhist establishment, we may infer with tolerable certainty that the votaries of *Sakya Muni* were expelled by force, and that their buildings were overthrown to furnish materials for those of their Brahmanical rivals; and now these in their turn have been thrown down by the Musalmáns.

I made the first discovery of Buddhist remains at the temple of *Kesava Ray* in January 1853, when, after a long search, I found a broken pillar of a Buddhist railing sculptured with the figure of *Máyá Devi* standing under the *sál* tree.* At the same time I found the capitals of two large round pillars of an early date, which are most probably Buddhist, along with a fragment of an inscription of the Gupta dynasty, containing the well known genealogy from Gupta, the founder, down to Samudra Gupta, where the stone is broken off. During the present year I have discovered the peculiarly curved architrave of a Buddhist gateway, which is richly sculptured on both sides with buildings, figures, and trees, including a representation of a gateway itself. I found also a very perfect standing figure of Buddha, the Teacher, which had lately been discovered in clearing out a well at the north-west corner of the temple. The figure is 3¼ feet high, with the left hand grasping the drapery, and the right hand

---

* Now in the Lahor Museum.

raised in the act of teaching. On the pedestal there is a dated inscription, in two lines, in characters of an early period. The date is given in figures which I read as S. 281 or A. D. 359. The remainder of the inscription, which is in perfect order, records the gift of a statue of *Sakya Bhikshu* to the *Yasa Vihára*, or, "splendid monastery," which I take to have been the name of the Buddhist establishment that once existed on the spot.

In the same well there were found five other pieces of Buddhist sculpture, of which the only specimens worth mentioning are a colossal arm and hand, and a small figure of Buddha, the Ascetic, with an imperfect inscription on its pedestal in characters of the Gupta dynasty. All these discoveries are sufficient to show that the mound of Kesava Ray must have been the site of a Buddhist establishment of much wealth and of considerable size. The inscribed statue proves that here stood the *Yasa* monastery, and the gateway architrave shows that there must also have been a *Stupa* surrounded with the stone railing which is peculiar to Buddhist architecture, and which on that account I have ventured to call the Buddhist railing. The site is a most promising one for discovery; and as the Masjid has long been disused, owing to many dangerous cracks in both roof and walls, I believe that there would not be any objection whatever to a complete exploration of the mound.

The most extensive discoveries at Mathura have been made in a mound close to the Jail, which, according to the inscriptions, would appear to have been the site of at least two different monasteries, named the *Huvishka Vihára* and the *Kunda-Suka Vihára*. The first of these names I deciphered in 1860 from a circular inscription round the base of a column, and the second name I found early in the present year, 1863, on a large flat slab of stone which had apparently been used as a seat.

In my notice of the first discovery, which was published in the Asiatic Society's Journal for 1860, I identified this *Huvishka* with his namesake of the Wardak inscription, and with the *Hushka* of the Raja Tarangini; and this identification has since been adopted by all who have made any reference to either of these records. The question is one of considerable importance, as it enables us to fix the date of the building of the monastery in the latter half of the century immediately preceding the Christian era, at which period the three Indo-Scythian princes, *Hushka* and his brothers, *Kanishka* and *Jushka*, ruled over Kabul, Kashmir, and the Punjab. The bases of about 30 pillars belonging to this monastery have now been discovered, of which no less than 15 are inscribed with the names of the donors who presented the columns to the monastery. But as one of these gifts consisted of six pillars, a second of 25, and a third of 20 pillars, there still remains 40 columns to be discovered, which will bring up the total number to 70. The diameter of the circular shafts of these pillars varies from 17 to 18 inches, and the side of the square base 23½ to 24 inches. They are all very coarsely worked, the rough marks of the chisel never having been smoothed away.

The name of the second monastery, *Kunda-Suka*, refers, I believe, to the tank which lies immediately to the westward of the mound. *Kunda-Suka* means the "dry tank;" and as the position of the tank agrees with that assigned by Hwen Thsang to the 'dry tank' in which the monkey was killed, I think there can be no doubt of the accuracy of my identification.

The discoveries already made in the Jail mound, amongst the ruins of the *Huvishka* and *Kunda-Suka* monasteries, have been very interesting on account of their variety, as they comprise statues of all sizes, bas-reliefs, pillars, Buddhist railings, votive *Stupas*, stone umbrellas, and many other objects peculiar to Buddhism, of a date as early as the first century of the Christian era.* Amongst the broken statues there is the left hand of a colossal figure of Buddha, the Teacher, which measures exactly one foot across the palm. The statue itself, therefore, could not have been less than from 20 to 24 feet in height, and with its pedestal, halo, and umbrella canopy it must have been fully 30 feet in height. Stone statues of this great size are so extremely difficult to move, that they can be very rarely made. It is true that some of the Jain statues of Gwalior are larger, such as the standing colossus in the *Urwāhi* of the fort, which is 57 feet

---

* Several inscriptions have since been discovered which belong to the first century before Christ. The earliest is of the Satrap Sauddas, and the next of the Great King Kanishka, dated in the year 9.

high, with a foot 9 feet in length, and the great seated figure on the east side of the fort, which is 20 feet high, with a hand 7 feet in length. But these figures are hewn out of the solid rock, to which they are still attached at the back. There are larger statues also in Barma, but they are built up on the spot of brick and mortar, and cannot be moved. I look forward, therefore, with great interest to the discovery of other portions of the Mathura Colossus, and more especially to that of the pedestal, on which we may expect to find the name of the donor of this costly and difficult work.

Most of the statues hitherto discovered at Mathura have been those of Buddha, the Teacher, who is represented either sitting or standing, and with one or both hands raised in the attitude of enforcing his argument. The prevailing number of these statues is satisfactorily illustrated by Hwen Thsang, who records that when Buddha was alive he frequently visited Mathura, and that monuments have been erected "*in all the places where he explained the law.*" Accordingly, on this one spot there have already been found two colossal standing figures of the Teacher, each 7½ feet in height, two life-size seated statues, and one three-quarter size seated statue, besides numerous smaller figures of inferior workmanship.

The most remarkable piece of sculpture is that of a female of rather more than half life-size. The figure is naked, save a girdle of beads round the waist, the same as is seen in the Bhilsa sculptures and Ajanta paintings. The attitude and the positions of the hands are similar to those of the famous statue of Venus of the Capitol. But in the Mathura statue the left hand is brought across the right breast, while the right hand holds up a small portion of drapery. The head is slightly inclined towards the right shoulder, and the hair is dressed in a new and peculiar manner, with long curls on each side of the face, which fall from a large circular ornament on the top of the head. The back of the figure is supported by a thick cluster of lotus stalks covered with buds and flowers, which are very gracefully arranged and boldly executed. The plump face with its broad smile is the least satisfactory part of this work. Altogether this statue is one of the best specimens of unaided Indian art that I have met with. I presume

DANCING GIRL

that it represents a dancing girl, and that it once adorned one of the gateways of the great *Stupa* near the monastery of *Huvishka*.*

Three statues of lions have also been discovered, but they are inferior both in design and in execution to most of the other sculptures. They are all of the same height, 3 feet, and are all in the same attitude, but two of them have the left foot advanced, while the third has the right foot brought forward. The attitudes are stiff, and the workmanship, especially of the legs, is hard, wiry, and unnatural. It is the fore-part only of the animal that is given, as if issuing out of the block of stone in rear, from which I infer that they must originally have occupied the two sides of some large gateway, such as we may suppose to have belonged to the great monastery of *Huvishka*.

The most numerous remains are the stone pillars of the Buddhist railings, of which at least three different sizes have been found. Those of the largest size are 4½ feet in height, with a section of 12¼ by 6 inches. When complete with base and coping, this railing would have been about 7 feet in height. The middle-sized pillars are 3 feet 8 inches high, with a section of 9 by 4¾ inches. The railings formed of these pillars would have been 5¼ feet in height. Those of the smallest size are 2¾ feet high, with a section of 6¼ by 3¼ inches, which would have formed a railing of only 4 feet in height. Of this last size no more than six specimens have yet been found, but two of them are numbered in the ancient Gupta numerals as 118 and 129, so that many more of them still remain to be discovered. If we assume the number of these pillars to have been no more than 120 the length of railing which they formed would have been 144 feet, or with two entrances not less than 160 feet. This might have been disposed either as a square enclosure of 40 feet side, or as a circular enclosure of upwards of 50 feet diameter. The last would have been sufficient for the circular railing of a *Stupa* 40 feet in diameter.

No inscriptions or numbers have been found on any of the large sized pillars, but there can be no doubt that they must have formed parts of the surrounding railings either of

---

* The pedestal of this statue, which has since been discovered, shows that the figure was originally placed on the top of a small column.

Stupas or of holy trees, such as are represented in the Sanchi bas-reliefs, or as we see them in still existing examples at Sanchi and Sonâri. Of the middle-sized railing I found a single broken rail, and also a single specimen of the architraves or coping stones. In the Sanchi and Sonâri examples the coping is quite plain, but this Mathura specimen is ornamented on both faces with semi-circular panels or niches containing figures and flowers.

The sculptures on the Mathura pillars are of two kinds, namely, large single figures on the front, and on the back either small bas-reliefs in compartments one above the other, or else full-blown flowers at regular intervals. Both in the single figures and in the bas-reliefs we find the same mixture of religious and social subjects as in the sculptures of Sanchi and Buddha-Gaya. On one pillar we have a standing figure of Buddha, the Teacher, with a halo and umbrella canopy, and on the back four small bas-reliefs representing, 1*st*, a holy tree with suspended garlands, surrounded by a Buddhist railing; 2*nd*, a pair of figures, male and female; 3*rd*, a kneeling figure presenting an offering to a standing figure; and 4*th*, an elephant with rider. One of the other single figures is a female holding a water vessel to her lips, and no less than four of the others are representations of Mâyâ Devi standing under the *Sâl* tree, and holding one of its branches, in which position she is described as having given birth to Buddha. A specimen of one of the large-sized Mathura pillars may be seen in the Asiatic Society's Museum in Calcutta, where it was deposited by Colonel Stacy.

But, perhaps, the most curious of all the Mathura sculptures is that which was figured and described by James Prinsep in 1836 as a Statue of Silenus. The block is 3 feet 10 inches in height, 3 feet broad, and 1 foot 4 inches thick. On the top there is a circular basin 10 inches in diameter and 8 inches deep. On the front there is a group of three figures about three-fourths of life-size with two smaller figures, and on the back a group of four figures of half life-size. In the front group the principal figure is a stout, half naked man resting on a low seat, with ivy or vine-crowned brow, and outstretched arms, which appear to be supported by the figures, male and female, standing one on each side. The dress of the female is most certainly not Indian, and is almost as certainly

Greek. The dress of the male figure also appears to be Greek. Colonel Stacy describes it as "a kerchief round the neck with a tie in front as worn by sailors;" but as it widens so it approaches the shoulders; I presume that it must be the short cloak of the Greeks which was fastened in front in the very same manner as represented in this sculpture. Prinsep agrees with Stacy in considering the principal figure to be Silenus: "His portly carcass, drunken lassitude, and vine-wreathed forehead, stamp the individual, while the drapery of his attendants pronounces them at least to be foreign to India, whatever may be thought of Silenus's own costume, which is certainly highly orthodox and Brahmanical. If the sculptor were a Greek, his taste had been somewhat tainted by the Indian beau-ideal of female beauty. In other respects his proportions and attitudes are good; nay, superior to any specimen of pure Hindu sculpture we possess; and, considering the object of the group, to support a sacrificial vase (probably of the juice of the grape), it is excellent." Of the group on the back I have but little to say: the two female figures and one of the men are dressed in the same Greek costume as the figures of the other group, but the fourth figure, a male, is dressed in a long tunic, which is certainly not Greek, and cannot well be Indian. The religious Buddhist would have his right shoulder bare, and the layman would have the *dhoti*, or waist-cloth. The Greek clad male figure may possibly be Silenus, but I am unable to offer even a conjecture as to the figure in the tunic.

The question now arises, how is the presence of this piece of Greek sculpture to be accounted for? Perhaps the most reasonable solution is to assume the presence of a small body of Bactrian Greek sculptors who would have found ready employment for their services amongst the wealthy Buddhists, just in the same way as goldsmiths and artillerymen afterwards found service with the Mogul Emperors. It must be remembered that Mathura is close to the great sand-stone quarries which for ages past have furnished materials for the sculptors and architects of Upper India. All the ancient statues that I have met with in Rohilkhund and Oudh are made of this stone, and there can be little doubt that the Buddhist custom of making gifts of statues and pillars to the various monasteries must have created such a steady demand for the sculptor's works as would have ensured the continuous employment of many skilled workmen. Many of the

Bactrian Greeks may thus have found remunerative service amongst the Indian Buddhists. Indeed, this is the only way in which I can account, not only for the very superior execution of many of the earliest specimens of Indian art, but also for many of their ornamental details, such as the fluting of the pillars in the Western Panjab architecture, and the honeysuckle and astragal ornaments of Asoka's monoliths, all of which are of undoubted Greek origin. In the great fort of Narwar there still exists a Roman Catholic Chapel, with a burial-ground attached, containing fifty tombs of all sizes, of which two only are inscribed. One records the death of a German, named Cornelius Oliver, in A. D. 1747; the other of a young girl, named Margarita, the daughter of a *Hakim* or Doctor. The first is recorded in Portuguese, the other in Persian. That the fifty tombs are those of Christians is proved, not only by the presence of the cross on several of the uninscribed head-stones, but by the occurrence of the letters J. H. S. surmounted by a cross on the wall immediately above the altar. I presume that these Christians were gunners who formed the artillery portion of the garrison of the important fortress of Narwar. Here, then, we have the clearest proof of the existence of a small body of foreigners in the very heart of India, who were permitted the open exercise of their religion by the most bigoted of all mankind, the Indian Muhammadans. Such also, I think, may have been the position of a small party of Bactrian Greeks amongst the tolerant Buddhists of the great city of Mathura about the beginning of the Christian era. Their very names are unknown, and their occupations are uncertain, but their foreign religion is attested beyond all doubt by the presence of a Bacchic altar, bearing the well known figure of the wine-bibbing Silenus.

III. KHALSI.

About 15 miles to the westward of Masuri, and on the right bank of the Jumna just above the junction of the Tons River, there stands a huge quartz boulder covered with one of the well known inscriptions of Asoka. The inscribed rock is situated close to the little villages of Byâs and Haripur, and about one mile and a half to the south of the large and well known village of Khâlsi, by which name I propose to distinguish this copy of Asoka's edicts from those of

Kapurdagiri, Junagiri, Rokilás, and *Ganjam.*[*] In speaking of Firuz Shah's Pillar at Delhi, which we know was brought from the foot of the hills on the western bank of the Jumna near Khidrabad, I have already identified the district of Khâlsi with part of the ancient kingdom of Srughna, as described by Hwen Thsang. As my reasons for coming to this conclusion are based entirely upon the statements of the Chinese pilgrim, it is necessary that they should be given in detail.

On leaving *Sthânesvara* or *Thânesar,* Hwen Thsang records that he went 400 *li,* or 66 miles, to the eastward, to the kingdom of Su-lu-kin-na, or Srughna, which he describes as being bounded by the Ganges on the east, and by high mountains on the north, and as being watered by the Jumna, which ran through the midst of it. The capital, which was 20 *li,* or upwards of three miles, in circuit, was situated immediately on the west bank of the Jumna; and, although much ruined, its foundations were still standing. Amongst other monuments it possessed a *Stupa* of King Asoka. The direction given by Hwen Thsang is undoubtedly wrong, as the Jumna is not more than 24 miles distant from Thânesar towards the east. But the mention of the hills shows most clearly that the bearing should be north-east; and as the recorded distance of the Jumna at the foot of the hills agrees with the actual distance, the situation of the capital of Srughna must be looked for along the western bank of the Jumna, somewhere between Khâlsi and Khidrabad. At first I was inclined to fix the position of the capital in the immediate neighbourhood of the inscribed rock of Khâlsi, but I could neither find nor hear of any ruins in its vicinity, and the distance is besides too great, being 71 miles in a direct line, or about 80 miles by the road. If Hwen Thsang's distances is correct, the most probable position of the capital is *Paota,* on the right bank of the Jumna, which is 57 miles distant from *Thânesar* in a direct line, or about 65 miles by the road. I believe also that *Paota* is the very place from whence Firuz Shah removed the Delhi column, for the name of its original site is variously written as *Taopar,* or *Topara,* or *Tooparauk,* any one of which by the mere shifting of the diacritical points might be read as *Paotar.* It is possible

---

[*] See Plate No. II. for a map of North-Western India, showing the position of Khâlsi.

also that the word *Suk* may still preserve a trace of the ancient name of *Sughan*, which is the spoken form of the Sanskrit *Srughna*. I propose to explore this neighbourhood during the ensuing cold season. In the meantime I am satisfied with having shown that the inscribed rock of Khálsi is situated within the territory of Srughna, in whose great monastery the Chinese pilgrim spent upwards of four months, because the monks discussed the most difficult questions so ably that all doubts where cleared up. By the hands of this learned fraternity were most probably engraved the two great copies of the edicts of Asoka which are still extent on the Khálsi rock and on the Delhi pillar of Firuz Shah.

Between Khálsi and the Jumna the land on the western bank of the river is formed in two successive ledges or level steppes, each about 100 feet in height. Near the foot of the upper steppe stands the large quartz boulder which has preserved the edicts of Asoka for upwards of 2,000 years. The block is 10 feet long and 10 feet high, and about 8 feet thick at bottom. The south-eastern face has been smoothed, but rather unevenly, as it follows the undulations of the original surface. The main inscription is engraved on this smoothed surface, which measures 5 feet in height with a breadth of $5\frac{1}{2}$ feet at top, which increases towards the bottom to 7 feet $10\frac{1}{2}$ inches. The deeper hollows and cracks have been left uninscribed, and the lines of letters are undulating and uneven. Towards the bottom the letters increase in size until they become about thrice as large as those of the upper part. Owing either to this enlargement of the letters, or perhaps to the latter part of the inscription being of later date, the prepared surface was too small for the whole record, which was, therefore, completed on the left hand side of the rock.

On the right hand side an elephant is traced in outline, with the words *Gajatame* inscribed between his legs in the same characters as those of the inscription. The exact meaning of these words I do not know; but as the Junagiri rock inscription closes with a paragraph stating that the place is called *Sweta Hasti*, or the "white elephant," I think it probable that *Gajatame* may mean the "dark or black elephant," and may, therefore, be the name of the rock itself. Amongst the people, however, the rock is known by the name of *Chhatr Sila*, or "the canopy stone," which would seem to

KHALSI

Plate XLI

North face of Rock.

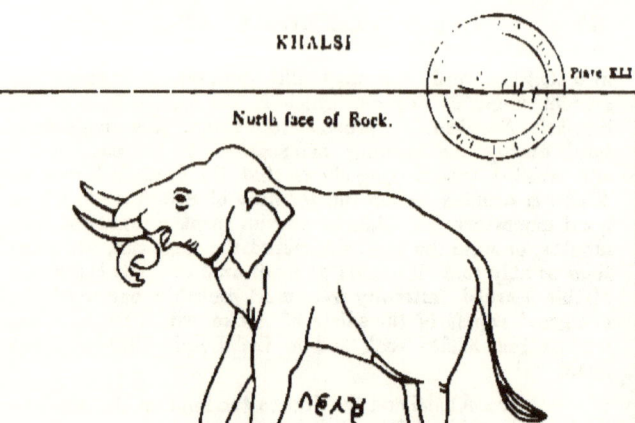

Gajatame

INSCRIPTION ON SOUTH FACE OF ROCK
Edicts of Asoka — mentions Ptolemy, Antigonus, Magas and Alexander.

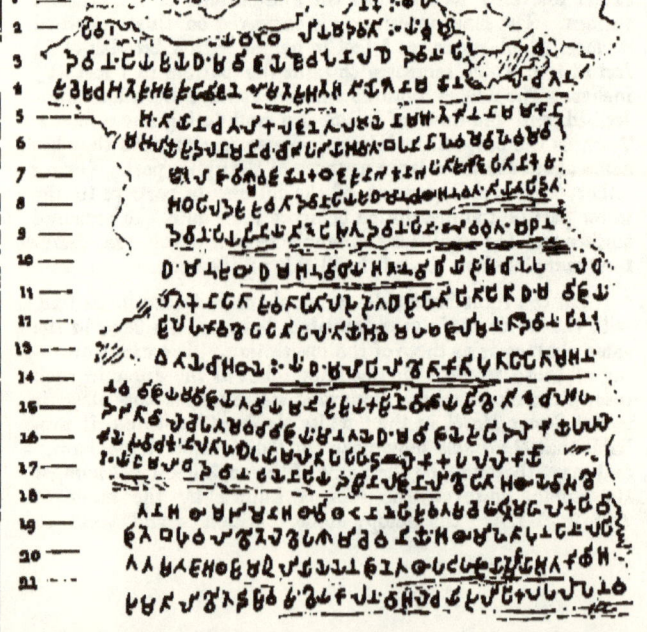

A. Cunningham, del.

show that the inscribed block had formerly been covered over by some kind of canopy, or perhaps only by an umbrella, as the name imports. There are a number of squared stones lying about close to the rock, as well as several fragments of octagonal pillars and half pillars or pilasters, which are hollowed out or fluted on the shorter faces, after the common fashion of the pillars of Buddhist railings. There is also a large carved stone, 7 feet long, 1½ foot broad, and 1 foot in height, which from its upper mouldings I judged to have formed the entrance step to some kind of open porch in front of the inscription stone.

When found by Mr. Forrest early in 1860 the letters of the inscription were hardly visible, the whole surface being encrusted with the dark moss of ages; but on removing this black film the surface becomes nearly as white as marble. At first sight the inscription looks as if it was imperfect in many places, but this is owing to the engraver having purposely left all the cracked and rougher portions uninscribed. On comparing the different edicts with those of the *Kapurdagiri*, *Junagiri*, and *Dhauli* versions, I find the Khálsi text to be in a more perfect state than any one of them, and more specially in that part of the 13th edict which contains the names of the five Greek Kings,—Antiochus, Ptolemy, Antigonus, Magas, and Alexander.[*] The Khálsi text agrees with that Dhauli in rejecting the use of the letter *r*, for which *l* is everywhere substituted. But the greatest variation is in the use of the palatal sibilant *s*, which has not been found in any other inscription of this early date. This letter occurs in the word *Pásanda*, which, curiously enough, is spelt sometimes with one *s*, and sometimes with the other, even in the same edict. As the proper spelling of this word is *Páshanda*, it seems almost certain that the people of India Proper did not possess the letter *sh* in the time of Asoka.

I made a complete impression of the whole of this important inscription. I also copied the whole of the inscription on the left side by eye, as well as most of the more obscure parts in the front inscription. I have since compared the entire text with those of the other rock tablets, and I am now engaged in making a reduced copy of this valuable record for early publication. I propose, however, first,

---

[*] See Plate No. XLI. for this portion of the Khálsi inscription.

to compare it with the *Kapurdagari* version in the Arian characters. With good copies of all the different texts before them, the scholars of Europe will be able to give a more satisfactory interpretation of Asoka's edicts than has hitherto been made, even with the aid of all the learning of Burnouf and Wilson.

IV. MADAWAR, OR MADIPUR.

From Srughna the Chinese pilgrim proceeded to Mo-ti-pu-lo, or *Madipur*, to the east of the Ganges, a distance of 800 *li*, or 133 miles. Madipur has been identified by M. St. Martin with *Mandáwar*, a large old town in Western Rohilkhund near Bijnor. I had made the same identification myself before reading M. St. Martin's remarks, and I am now able to confirm it by a personal examination of the locality. The actual distance from *Paota* on the Jumna to *Mandáwar viâ Haridwár*, is not more than 110 miles by the present roads; but as it would have been considerably more by the old Native tracks leading from village to village, the distance recorded by Hwen Thsang is most probably not far from the truth, more especially when we remember that he paid a visit to Ma-yu-lo, or *Mayurapura*, now *Myapoor*, near Hardwâr at the head of the Ganges Canal. But the identity of the site of *Maddwar* with Madipur is not dependent on this one distance alone, as will be seen from the subsequent course of the pilgrim, which most fully confirms the position already derived from his previous route.

The name of the town is written with the *Maddwar* with the cerebral *d*, and without the nasal. In our maps it is spelt Mundore and Mundâwar. According to *Johari Lal*, Chaodri and Kanungo of the place, *Madáwar* was a deserted site in Samvat 1171, or A. D. 1114, when his ancestor *Dwárka Dás*, an Agarwâla Baniya, accompanied by *Katár Mall*, came from *Morari* in the Mirat District, and occupied the old mound. The present town of *Madáwar* contains 7,000 inhabitants, and is rather more than three-quarters of a mile in length by half a mile in breadth. But the old mound which represents the former town is not more than half a mile square. It has an average height of 10 feet above the rest of the town, and it abounds with large bricks, a certain sign of antiquity. In the middle of the mound there is a ruined fort, 300 feet square, with an elevation of 6 or 7 feet above the rest of the

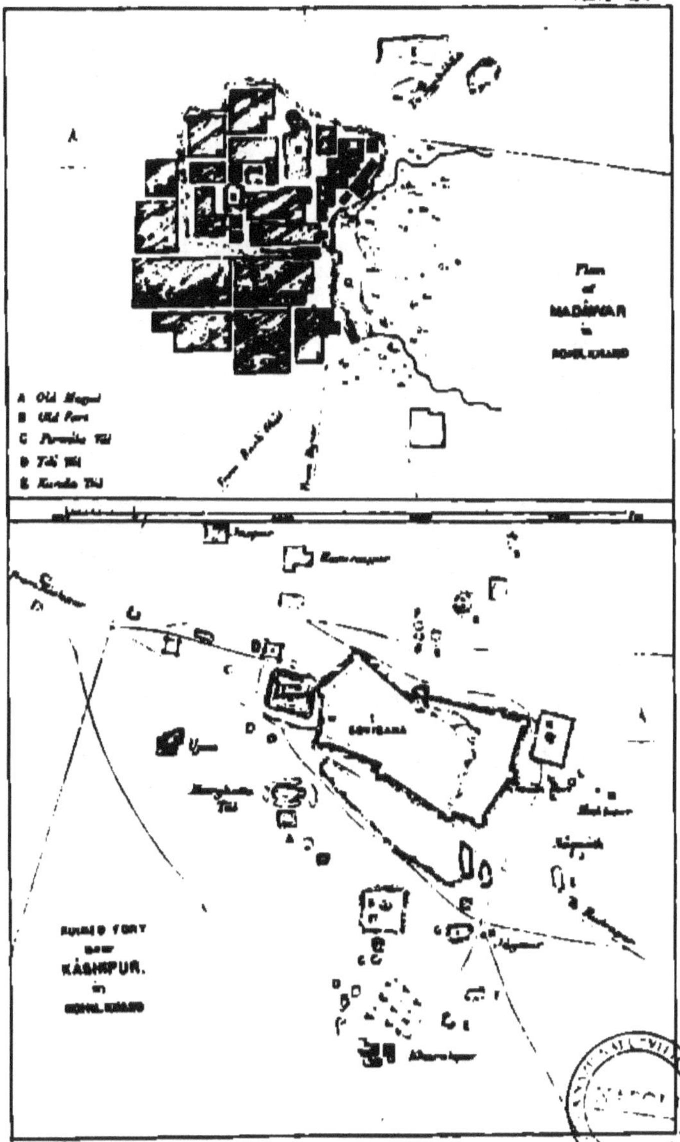

PLATE XLII.

Plan
of
MADANWAR
in
ROHILKHAND

A Old Mogul
B Old Fort
C Parmān Tīl
D Tīlī Tīl
E Kurāla Tīl

RUINED FORT
of
KÁSHIPUR.
in
ROHILKHAND

A Cunningham del.

MADAWAR, OR MADIPUR.

city. To the north-east, distant about one mile from the fort, there is a large village, on another mound, called *Madiya;* and between the two lies a large tank called *Kúnda Tál,* surrounded by numerous small mounds which are said to be the remains of buildings. Originally these two places would appear to have formed one large town about 1¼ mile in length by half a mile in breadth, or 3½ miles in circuit. The Ka- nungo states that *Madáwar* formed part of the dominions of Pithora Raja, and that it possessed a large Hindu temple of stone, which was afterwards destroyed by one of the Ghori Sultans, who built the present Jáma Masjid on its site, and with its materials. The stones of the mosque are squared blocks of soft grey sandstone, and as many of them exhibit cramp-holes on the outside, there can be no doubt that they must originally have belonged to some other building.

To the south-east of the town there is a large, deep, irre- gularly shaped piece of water called *Piradli Tál.* It is near- ly half a mile in length, but not more than 300 feet broad in its widest part. It is filled in the rains by a small chan- nel carrying the drainage of the country from the north-east, and its overflow falls into the *Málini* River, about two miles distant. This pool is only part of a natural channel of drain- age which has been deepened by the excavation of earth for the bricks of the town. But in spite of this evident origin of the *Madáwar* tank, it was gravely asserted by the Bud- dhists to have been produced by an earthquake which accom- panied the death of a celebrated saint, named *Vimala Mitra.*

According to Hwen Thsang, *Madipur* was 20 *li,* or 3⅓ miles, in circuit, which agrees very closely with what would appear to be the most probable size of the old town. The King was a *Sudra,* who cared nothing for Buddhism, but worshipped the *Devas.* There were 12 Buddhist monasteries containing about 800 monks, who were mostly attached to the school of the *Sarvástivádas,* and there were also about 50 Brahmanical temples.* To the south of the town, at 4 or 5 *li,* or ¾ of a mile, there was a small monastery in which *Gunaprabha* was said to have composed 100 works; and at half a mile to the north of this there was a great monastery which was famous as the scene of *Sanghabhadra's* sudden

---

* Julien's Hwen Thsang, II. 219.

death from chagrin, when he was overcome in argument by *Vasubandhu*. His relics were deposited in a *Stupa* in the midst of a mangoe grove only 200 paces to the north-west of the monastery. These two chiefs of Buddhism lived about the beginning of the Christian era, and the *Stupa* was still standing in A. D. 634 at the time of Hwen Thsang's visit. There is no trace now existing either of the monasteries or of the *Stupa*, but their sites can be fixed with tolerable certainty by the aid of Hwen Thsang's descriptions. The village of Lâlpur, which is situated on a mound about three-quarters of a mile to the south-south-east of the Jâma Masjid, and which is built partly of old bricks, represents the site of the small monastery of *Gunaprabha*. To the north of Lâlpur, and just half a mile distant, is the shrine of Hidâyat Shah, with a Masjid attached, both of which are built of old bricks. This spot I believe to be the site of the great monastery of *Sanghabhadra*. Lastly, to the west-north-west of Hidâyat's shrine, at a distance of 200 paces, there is another shrine, or *Fakir's takia*, standing in the midst of a mangoe grove, like the old *Stupa* of *Sanghabhadra*, the site of which it represents almost exactly as described by Hwen Thsang.[*]

Besides the mangoe grove there was a second *Stupa* which contained the relics of *Vimala Mitra*, who, as a disciple of *Sanghabhadra*, must have lived in the first century of the Christian era. The legend relates that, on passing the *Stupa* of his master *Sanghabhadra*, he placed his hand on his heart, and with a sigh expressed a wish that he might live to compose a work which should lead all the students of India to renounce the "Great Vehicle" *(Mahâ Yâna)*, and which should blot out the name of *Vasubandhu* for ever. No sooner had he spoken, than he was seized with frenzy, and five spouts of burning hot blood gushed from his mouth. Then feeling himself dying, he wrote a letter "expressing his repentance for having maligned the *Mahâ Yâna*, and hoping that his fate might serve as an example to all students." At these words the earth quaked, and he expired instantly. Then *the spot where he died suddenly sank and formed a deep ditch*, and a holy man who witnessed his end exclaimed—"To-day this master of the scriptures, by giving way to his passions, and by persisting in erroneous opinions,

---

[*] See Plate No. XLIII. for map of Malabar.

has calumniated the *Mahá Yána*, for which he has now fallen into everlasting hell." But this opinion of the holy man would appear to have been confined to the followers of the *Mahá Yána*, for the brethren of *Vimala Mitra*, who were *Sarrdstivádas* or students of the lesser vehicle, burned his body and raised a *Stupa* over his relics. It must be remembered also that Hwen Thsang, who relates the legend, was a zealous follower of the *Mahá Yána*, and this no doubt led him to overlook the manifest contradiction between the statement of the uncharitable *arhat*, and the fact that his brethren had burned his body in the usual manner. This legend, as well as several others, would seem to show that there was a hostile and even bitter feeling between these two great sects of the Buddhist community.

The site of *Vimala Mitra's Stupa* is described as being at the edge of the mango grove, and from the details of the legend it is clear that it could have been at no great distance from the *Stupa* of *Sanghabhadra*. It would appear also that it must have stood close by the great ditch, or hollow, which his opponents looked upon as the rent in the earth by which he had sunk down to "everlasting hell." Now the mango grove which I have before mentioned extends only 120 paces to the westward to the bank of the deep tank called the *Pirsáli Tál*. I conclude, therefore, that the *Stupa* of *Vimala Mitra* must have stood close to the edge of this tank and on the border of the mango grove which still exists in the same position as described by Hwen Thsang.

It seems probable that the people of *Madawar*, as pointed out by M. St. Martin, may be the *Matka* of Megasthenes who dwelt on the banks of the Erineses. If so, that river must be the Málini. It is true that this is but a small stream, but it was in a sacred grove on the bank of the *Málini* that *Sakuntala* was brought up, and along its course lay her route to the court of *Dushmanta* at *Hastinapur*. While the lotus floats on its waters, and while the *Chakwa* calls its mate on its bank, so long will the little *Málini* live in the verse of *Kálidás*.

V. KASHIPUR, OR GOVISANA.

On leaving *Madipur* the Chinese pilgrim travelled 400 *li*, or 66 miles to the south-east, and arrived in the kingdom of *Kia-pi-shwang-na*, which M. Julien renders by

Govisana.* The capital was 14 or 15 *li*, or 2½ miles in circuit. Its position was strong, being elevated, and of difficult access, and it was surrounded by groves, tanks, and fish ponds. There were two monasteries containing 100 monks, and 30 Brahmanical temples. In the middle of the larger monastery, which was outside the city, there was a *Stupa* of Asoka, 200 feet in height, built over the spot where Buddha was said to have explained the law. There were also two small *Stupas*, only 12 feet high, containing his hair and nails.

According to the bearing and distance from Madipur, as given by Hwen Thsang, we must look for Govisana somewhere to the north of Muradabad. In this direction the only place of any antiquity is the old fort of *Ujain*, which is just one mile to the east of Káshipur. According to the route which I marched, the distance is 44 *kos*, or 66 miles. I estimate the value of the *kos* by the measured distance of 59 miles between the Post Offices of Bareli and Murndabad, which is always called 40 *kos* by the Natives. The true bearing of Káshipur is east-south-east, instead of south-east, but the difference is not great; and as the position of Káshipur is equally clearly indicated by the subsequent route to *Ahichhatra*, I feel quite satisfied that the old fort of *Ujain* represents the ancient city of *Govisana* which was visited by Hwen Thsang.

Bishop Heber describes Káshipur as a " famous place of Hindu pilgrimage which was built by a divinity, named Kashi, 5,000 years ago."† But the good Bishop was grossly deceived by his informant, as it is well known that the town is a modern one,—it having been built about A. D. 1718 by Kashi Náth, a follower of Raja Devi Chandra, or Deb Chand, of Champáwat, in Kumaon. The old fort is now called Ujain; but as that is the name of the nearest village, it seems probable that the true name has been lost. The place itself had been deserted for several hundred years before the occupation of Káshipur; but as the holy tank of *Dron Ságar* had never ceased to be visited by pilgrims, I presume that the name of the tank must have gradually superseded that of the fort. Even at the present day, the name *Dron Ságar* is just as well known as that of Káshipur.

---

* Julien's Hwen Thsang, II, 233.
† Travel. Vol. II, p. 246.

KASHIPUR, OR GOVISANA.

The old fort of Ujain is very peculiar in its form, which may be best compared to the body of a guitar. It is 3,000 feet in length from west to east, and 1,500 feet in breadth, the whole circuit being upwards of 9,000 feet, or rather less than 2 miles. Hwen Thsang describes the circuit of Govisana as about 12,000 feet, or nearly 2½ miles; but in this measurement he must have included the long mound of ruins on the south side, which is evidently the remains of an ancient suburb. By including this mound as an undoubted part of the old city, the circuit of the ruins is upwards of 11,000 feet, or very nearly the same as that given by Hwen Thsang. Numerous groves, tanks, and fish ponds still surround the place. Indeed, the trees are particularly luxuriant, owing to the high level of the water which is within 5 or 6 feet of the surface. For the same reason the tanks are numerous and always full of water. The largest of these is the *Dron Ságar*, which, as well as the fort, is said to have been constructed by the five Pandu brothers for the use of their teacher *Drona*. The tank is only 600 feet square, but it is esteemed very holy, and is much frequented by pilgrims on their way to the source of the Ganges. Its high banks are covered with *sati* monuments of recent date. The walls of the fort are built of large massive bricks, 15 inches by 10 inches by 2½ inches, which are always a certain sign of antiquity. The general height of the walls is 30 feet above the fields; but the whole is now in complete ruin, and covered with dense jungle. Shallow ditches still exist on all sides except the east. The interior is very uneven, but the mass has a mean height of about 20 feet above the country. There are two low openings in the ramparts, one to the north-west and the other to the south-west, which now serve as entrances to the jungle, and which the people say were the old gates of the fort.*

There are some small temples on the western bank of the *Dron Ságar;* but the great place of worship is the modern temple of Jwálá Devi, 600 feet to the eastward of the fort. This goddess is also called *Ujaini Devi*, and a great fair is held in her honour on the 5th day of the waning moon of Chaitra. Other smaller temples contain symbols of Mahádeva under the titles of *Bhutesar*, *Muktesar*, *Náynáth*, and

---

* See Plate No. XLII. for a map of Ujain or Govisana.

Jágesar. But all of these temples are of recent date; the sites of the more ancient fanes being marked by mounds of various dimensions from 10 to upwards of 30 feet in height. The most remarkable of these mounds is situated inside the northern wall of the fort, above which the ruins rise to a height of 52 feet above the country, and 22 feet above the ramparts. This mound is called *Bhimgaja* or *Bhimgada*, that is, Bhim's club, by which I understand a large *lingam* of Mahádeva. Were it not for this name, I should be inclined to look upon this huge mound as the remains of a palace, as I succeeded in tracing the walls of what appeared to have been a large room, 72 feet in length from north to south, by 63 feet in width, the walls being 6 feet thick. About 500 feet beyond the north-east angle of the fort there is another remarkable mound which is rather more than 34 feet in height. It stands in the midst of a quadrangular terrace, 600 in length by 500 feet in breadth, and, as well as I could ascertain from an excavation at the top, it is the remains of a large square temple. Close by on the east, and within the quadrangle, there are the ruins of two small temples. To the eastward of the Jwálá Devi temple, there is a curious circular flat-topped mound of earth, 68 feet in diameter, surrounded by a brick wall from 7 to 11 feet in height. It is called *Rámgir Gosain-ka-tila*, or "the mound of *Rámgir Gosain*," from which I infer that it is the burial place of a modern Gosain. To the south of the fort, near the temple of Jágesar Mahádeva, there is a third large mound, 22 feet in height, which was once crowned by a temple of 20 feet square inside. The bricks have only recently been removed, and the square core of earth still remains perfect. To the westward of this last, there is a fourth mound, on which I traced the ruins of a temple 30 feet square standing in the midst of a raised quadrangle about 500 feet square. Besides these there are ten smaller mounds, which make up altogether 14, or just one-half the number of the Brahmanical temples which are mentioned by Hwen Thsang.

The only ruin which appeared to me to be of undoubted Buddhist origin was a solid brick mound 20 feet in height, to the south-west of Jágesar Mahádeva, and close to the small village of Khargpur. The base of the mound is upwards of 200 feet in diameter. The solid brick-work at the top is still 60 feet thick; but as it is broken all round, its original

diameter must have been much greater, probably not less than
60 feet. But even this larger diameter is too small for a
Stupa of 200 feet in height of the hemispherical form of
Asoka's time; a *Stupa* of that early period, even when provided with both plinth and cupola, would not have exceeded
100 feet in height. Unless, therefore, we may suppose that
there is a mistake of 100 feet in the text of Hwen Thsang, I
feel quite unable to offer any identification whatever of the
Buddhist remains of Govisana as described by the Chinese
pilgrim.

VI. RAMNAGAR, OR AHICHHATRA.

From Govisana Hwen Thsang proceeded to the southeast 400 *li*, or 66 miles, to *Ahi-chi-ta-lo*, or *Ahichhatra*. This
once famous place still preserves its ancient name as
Ahichhatr, although it has been deserted for many centuries.
Its history reaches back to the time of the *Mahábhárata*, at
which date it was the capital of Northern *Panchála*. The
name is written *Ahi-kshetra*, as well as *Ahi-chhatra*, but the
local legend of Adi Raja and the Nága, who formed a canopy
over his head when asleep, shows that the latter is the correct
form. This grand old fort is said to have been built by *Raja
Adi*, an Ahir, whose future elevation to sovereignty was foretold by *Drona* when he found him sleeping under the
guardianship of a serpent with expanded hood. The place is
mentioned by Ptolemy as *Adisadra*, which proves that the
legend attached to the name of *Adi* is at least as old as the
beginning of the Christian era. The fort is also called
Adikot, but the more common name is *Ahichhatr*.

According to the *Mahábhárata* the great kingdom of
Panchála extended from the Himálaya Mountains to the
Chambal River. The capital of North *Panchála*, or Rohilkhand, was *Ahi-chhatra*, and that of South *Panchála*, or the
central Gangetic Doab, was *Kámpilya*, now *Kampil*, on the
old Ganges between Budaon and Farokhabad.* Just before
the great war, or about 1430 B. C., the King of *Panchála*,
named *Drupada*, was conquered by *Drona*, the preceptor of
the five Pándus. *Drona* retained North *Panchála* for himself,
but restored the southern half of the kingdom to *Drupada*.
According to this account the name of *Ahi-chhatra*, and

---

* See Plate No. II. for the positions of the two Panchalas in the map of the North-Western Provinces.

consequently also the legend of *Adi Raja* and the serpent, are many centuries anterior to the rise of Buddhism.

It would appear, however, that the Buddhists must have adopted and altered the legend to do honour to their great teacher, for Hwen Thsang records that outside the town there was a *Nága-hrada*, or ."serpent tank," near which Buddha had preached the law for seven days in favour of the Serpent King, and that the spot was marked by a *Stupa* of King Asoka. Now, as the only existing *Stupa* at this place is called *Chattr*, I infer that the Buddhist legend represented the *Nága* King after his conversion as forming a canopy over Buddha with his expanded hood. I think, also, that the *Stupa* erected on the spot where the conversion took place would naturally have been called *Ahi-chhatra*, or the "serpent canopy." A similar story is told at Buddha-Gaya of the Nága King *Muchalinda*, who with his expanded hood sheltered Buddha from the shower of rain produced by the malignant demon *Mára*.

The account of *Ahi-chhatra* given by Hwen Thsang is unfortunately very meagre, otherwise we might most probably have identified many of the existing ruins with the Buddhist works of an early age.[*] The capital was 17 or 18 *li*, or just three miles, in circuit, and was defended by natural obstacles. It possessed 12 monasteries, containing about 1,000 monks, and nine Brahmanical temples, with about 300 worshippers of *Iswara Deva* (Siva), who smeared their bodies with ashes. The *Stupa* near the serpent tank outside the town has already been mentioned. Close beside it there were four small *Stupas* built on the spots where the four previous Buddhas had either sat or walked. Both the size and the peculiar position of the ruined fortress of *Ahi-chhatra* agree so exactly with Hwen Thsang's description of the ancient *Ahi-chhatra*, that there can be no doubt whatever of their identity. The circuit of the walls, as they stand at present, is 10,400 feet, or upwards of 3¼ miles. The shape may be described as an irregular right-angled triangle, the west side being 5,000 feet in length, the north side 6,400 feet, and the long side to the south-east 7,400 feet. The fort is situated between the *Rám Ganga* and *Gánghan Rivers*, which are both difficult to cross; the former on account of its broad sands, the latter on account of its extensive ravines. Both on

---

[*] Julien's *Hwen Thsang*, II., p. 234.

the north and east the place is rendered almost inaccessible by the *Piria Nala*, a difficult ravine with steep broken banks, and numerous deep pools of water quite impassable by wheeled vehicles. For this reason the cart road to Bareli, distant only 18 miles due east, is not less than 23 miles. Indeed the only accessible side of the position is the north-west, from the direction of *Lakhnor*, the ancient capital of the Katehria Rajputs. It, therefore, fully merits the description of Hwen Thsang as being defended by "natural obstacles."* *Ahi-chhatra* is only seven miles to the north of *Aonla*, but the latter half of the road is rendered difficult by the ravines of the *Gánghan River*. It was in this very position, in the jangals to the north of *Aonla*, that the Katehria Rajputs withstood the Muhammadans under Firuz Tughlak.

The ruins of *Ahi-chhatra* were first visited by Captain Hodgson, the Surveyor, who describes the place as "the ruins of an ancient fortress several miles in circumference, which appears to have had 34 bastions, and is known in the neighbourhood by the name of the 'Pándus Fort.'" According to my survey there are only 32 towers, but it is quite possible that one or two may have escaped my notice, as I found many parts so overgrown with thorny jungle as to be inaccessible. The towers are generally from 28 to 30 feet in height, excepting on the west side, where they rise to 35 feet. A single tower near the south-west corner is 47 feet in height above the road outside. The average height of the interior mass is from 15 to 20 feet. Many of the present towers, however, are not ancient, as an attempt was made by Ali Muhammad Khan, about 200 years ago, to restore the fort with a view of making it his stronghold in case he should be pushed to extremities by the King of Delhi. The new walls are said to have been 1¼ *gaz* thick, which agrees with my measurements of the parapets on the south-eastern side, which vary from 2 feet 0 inches to 3 feet 3 inches in thickness at top. According to popular tradition, Ali Muhammad expended about a *karor* of rupees, or one million pounds sterling, in this attempt, which he was finally obliged to abandon on account of its costliness. I estimate that he may, perhaps, have spent about one lakh of rupees, or

---

* Julien's Hwen Thsang, II., 234.

£10,000, in repairing the ramparts and in re-building the parapets. There is an arched gateway on the south-east side, which must have been built by the Musulmáns, but as no new bricks were made by them, the cost of their work would have been limited to the labour alone. The ramparts are 18 feet thick at the base in some places, and between 14 and 15 feet in others.*

There are three great mounds inside the fort, and outside, both to the north and west, there are number of mounds of all sizes, from 20 feet to 1,000 feet in the diameter. To the north-west, distant one mile, there is a large tank called the *Gandhán Ságar*, which has an area of 125 *bigahs*, and about one-quarter of a mile beyond it there is another tank called the *Adi Ságar*, which has an area of 150 *bigahs*. The latter is said to have been made by *Adi Raja* at the same time as the fort. The waters are collected by an earthen embankment faced on both sides with bricks of large size. The *Gandhán Ságar* is also embanked both to the east and south. The mounds to the south of the tanks are covered with large bricks, both plain and moulded; but judging from their shapes, they must all have belonged to temples, or other straight walled buildings, and not to *Stupas*. There is nothing to show whether these are the remains of Buddhist or of Brahmanical buildings, but from their extent it is probable that they were the former.

According to Hwen Thsang there were only nine Brahmanical temples at *Ahi-chhatra* in A. D. 634, all of which would appear to have been dedicated to Siva. But as Buddhism declined this number must have been increased, for I discovered the ruins of not less than twenty temples of various sizes, of which one is gigantic, four are large, five are of middle size, and twelve of small dimensions. Three of these are inside the fort, and the others are grouped together outside on the west road. I made excavations in most of these mounds, all of which yielded moulded bricks of various patterns, but only two of them afforded sculptures by which their original purpose could be absolutely identified. These two temples are marked as Nos. I. and IV. in my survey of the ruins.

---

* See Plate No. XLIII. for a map of Ahi-chhatra.

AHICHHATRA.

Plate XLIV.

View of the Chhatr, or Great Stupa.

Inscribed Stone at Dewin.

Bhamlaur Ruined Lingam Temple.

Plan of Temple.

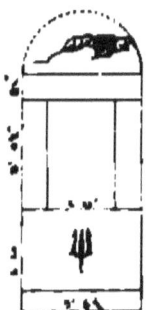

Pillar of Buddhist Railing Kathji-Khera.

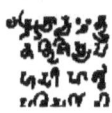

The remains of No. I. temple form a mound 65 feet 9 inches in height above the country, and upwards of 30 feet above the walls of the fortress. This lofty mound stands inside the fort near the middle of the north wall, and forms the most conspicuous object amongst the ruins of the mighty fortress of *Ahi-chhatra*. The floor of the temple is 60 feet above the ground, and at this enormous height stood a colossal *lingam*, 3 feet 6¼ inches in diameter, and upwards of 8 feet in height, which must have been visible from both east and west through the open doors of the temple for a distance of some miles. The interior of the temple is only 14 feet 4 inches by 10¼ feet. The north and south walls are 9 feet 5 inches thick, and the east and west walls only 5 feet 0 inches; but on these two sides there are open porches outside the two entrances which increase the thickness of the walls to 19 feet on the west side, and to 14 feet 11 inches on the east. The exterior dimensions of the temple are 48 feet 3 inches by 29 feet 4 inches. From these dimensions I calculate that the temple must have been about 100 feet in height above its own floor, or 165 feet above the country. The base of the stone *lingam* is square, the middle part octagonal, and the upper part hemispherical. A *trisul*, or trident, is cut upon the base. The upper portion of the *lingam* is broken. The people say that it was struck by lightning, but from the unshattered state of the large block I am more disposed to ascribe the fracture to the hammer of the Muhammadans.

Mound No. II., which is also inside the fort to the west of the large mound, is 35 feet in height, and from 5 to 10 feet above the general line of the ramparts. It shows the remains of a large square building with a long flight of steps on the west side. No. III. mound is only 30 feet in height, and is covered with scrub jungle. There are traces of walls on the surface, but the jungle prevented their immediate excavation. I will take an early opportunity of exploring both of these mounds, as I feel satisfied that they are the remains of large Brahmanical temples.

No. IV. mound stands about 1,000 feet outside the west gate of the fort. It is 300 feet square at base, and 30 feet in height, and has two smaller mounds attached to the northeast corner. On excavating the surface I discovered the foundations of a temple, 11 feet square inside, with walls 3½ feet thick, and a long pedestal or raised platform for the reception of statues. The entrance is on the east side towards the town. Amongst the ruins I found a seated terracotta figure of Siva, 12 inches in height, with four arms and three eyes, and one hand holding a large lotus flower. I found also in red stone a small right hand grasping the hilt of a sword, and a left hand of three-quarter life size, grasping a large conch. As the last must have belonged to a figure of Vishnu, it is possible that the temple was dedicated to that god; but a projecting portion of the pedestal leads me to believe that it must have been occupied by a *lingam*, and if so, the principal figure would have been that of Mahadeva. There was also a large quantity of ashes inside this temple, from which I infer that it was most probably destroyed by the Musulmans in one of their early expeditions against the Katehria Rajputs.

The Buddhist remains at *Ahi-chhatra* are both more extensive and more ancient than those of the Brahmans. In my survey I have marked them by the letters of the alphabet to distinguish them from the Brahmanical ruins, which are numbered. Only three of the Buddhist mounds have been excavated, but as most of the others have furnished materials for the neighbouring villages, it does not seem likely that their excavation would be attended with any success.

The most important of the Buddhist ruins is an irregular shaped mound, about 1,000 feet square, from the centre of which rises a large *Stupa* of solid brick-work, which the people call *Chhatr*. I have already identified this with the great *Stupa* which was built over the spot where Buddha converted the Serpent King. It is surrounded by eight smaller mounds, of which four would appear to be the ruins of *Stupas*, and three of temples, whilst one only is doubtful. Now, Hwen Thsang describes the great *Stupa* as having on one side of it four small *Stupas*, which account agrees exactly with the position of the four small mounds above-mentioned. I have no doubt, therefore, as to the identity of the *Chhatr* mound with the *Stupa* of Hwen Thsang, although I was unable to discover any certain trace of the tank called the *Naga-hrada* or "serpent pond" by the Chinese pilgrim. It is quite possible, however, that a tank may once have existed on the south-west side, where the ground is still very low.

The great ruin called *Chhatr* is a mass of solid brickwork, 40 feet in height above the fields, and 30 feet in diameter at top. The original building was a hemisphere of 50 feet diameter, which was raised upon a base or plinth 15 feet in height. At some later period an outer casing, 12½ feet thick, was added, which increased the diameter to 75 feet, and the height of the crown of the hemisphere to 52½ feet. Allowing two-sevenths of the diameter for the height of the cupola or pinnacle, which is the proportion observed in the Sanchi bas-reliefs, the total height of the original *Stupa* would have been 57 feet, and that of the later *Stupa* 77 feet. I made several superficial excavations around the base in the hope of finding some portions of the stone railings with which the *Stupa* was most probably surrounded, but without success. I still believe, however, that there must have been the usual Buddhist railings around this *Stupa*, and that a further search would probably bring some of the pillars to light. I found, however, a number of curved wedge-shaped bricks that must have belonged to a circle of between 15 and 16 feet in diameter, and which, I presume, are the remains of the cupola.*

If I am right in my identification of this *Stupa* with that which was built near the Serpent Tank, its original construction must be referred to the reign of Asoka, or about 250 B. C. A strong argument in favor of this date is the similarity of its shape to that of the Bhilsa *Topes*, which are undoubtedly of Asoka's age. The date of the enlargement of the *Stupa* can only be fixed approximately by inferring from Hwen Thsang's silence that it must have been in good order at the time of his visit. Admitting this to have been the case, the date of the enlargement cannot be placed earlier than about A. D. 400 to 500.

The great *Stupa* attracted the attention of some British Officer, about 30 years ago, who dug a gallery into it, 21 feet in length, and then sunk a well for some unknown depth, which I found filled with rubbish. I made use of this old gallery, and continued it to the centre of the *Stupa*, where it met a shaft which I had sunk from the top. From this point I carried the shaft downwards, making use of the gallery, for the removal of the bricks. At a depth of 27 feet from the present top, or at 7 feet below the centre of the

---

* See Plate No. XLIV. for a view of this Stupa.

older hemisphere, I found a low pyramidal topped vessel of common red unglazed earthenware, 8 inches in diameter. Inside this vessel there was a small steatite box containing many minute fragments of seed pearls, several pieces of blue glass, one large bead of red amber, and about a tea spoonful of little bits of rock crystal. Mixed with these were ten small cylindrical pierced beads of a dirty white colour like old chalk. They consist chiefly of carbonate of lime with a trace of some other substance, and are most probably only the remains of some artificial beads. The little steatite box is a sphere of 2 inches diameter, but rather pointed at the top and bottom. Its general colour is white with a few purple blotches. The whole is rudely ornamented, the top with flowers, and the bottom with animals of school-boy design. The inside also is rudely ornamented, but with simple lines only. There is no trace of any inscription.

At $6\frac{3}{4}$ feet below the deposit just described, or at $13\frac{3}{4}$ feet below the centre of the hemisphere, a second deposit was found, imbedded in the ground immediately under the last course, of a globular-shaped mottled steatite vase, $6\frac{1}{4}$ inches in diameter and 6 inches in height. This vase has a neck 3 inches in diameter inside and $2\frac{3}{4}$ inches in height, thus making the whole height of the vessel $8\frac{3}{4}$ inches. This is divided into two equal portions, the lower half having an inner lip, which is overlapped by the upper half. The vessel is quite plain, excepting only a few belts of simple lines which encircle it. The open mouth was found closed by the lid of a small dark-colored steatite vase exactly similar to several that were discovered in the Bhilsa *Topes*. Inside there was nothing but a hard cake of earth, 6 inches in diameter, mixed with small stones. A similar earthen cake, but only $2\frac{1}{2}$ inches in diameter, was found in the earthenware jar of the upper deposit. What this cake may be I cannot at present say, but it does not effervesce with acids.

The second Buddhist mound which has yielded important evidence of its former occupation is called *Katári Khera*. It is situated 1,200 feet to the north of the old fort, and 1,000 feet to the east of the small village of Nasratganj. The mound is about 400 feet square and 20 feet in height. Close by there is a small pond called the *Masráse Tál;* but neither this name, nor that of *Katári Khera*, would seem to have any reference to the old Buddhist establishment which formerly stood there. Unfortunately this mound has furnished bricks to the neighbouring village for many generations, so that but little is now left to point out the nature of the original buildings. A surface excavation brought to light a temple 26¼ feet in length by 22 feet in breadth outside, and 11 feet square inside. The plinth is still standing 4½ feet in height, formed of blocks of *kankar*, but the walls have altogether disappeared, excepting some portions of a few courses. The doorway faces the east, from which I infer that the enshrined statue was most probably that of the ascetic Buddha, who is always represented seated in a similar position under the holy Pipal Tree of Buddha-Gaya. I am also led to the same conclusion by the discovery of a broken statue of Buddha with two flying figures over the right shoulder, which are the usual accompaniments of the ascetic figures of Buddha. This statue is broken at the waist, and both arms are lost; but the fragment is still 2 feet high and 2 feet broad, from which I infer that the size of the original statue was not less than 4 feet in height by 3 feet in breadth; and this I believe to have been the principal figure of the temple.

In the same place, five other carved and sculptured stones were discovered, of which one is an inscribed pillar of a Buddhist railing of middle age. The pillar is broken, but the remaining portions of the socket holes are sufficient for the restoration of the original dimensions. The fragment is 1 foot 11 inches in length, with a section of 6½ inches by 4 inches. The socket holes are 8 inches long, and 4¾ inches apart, which in a pillar of two rails would give a height of 3 feet 2½ inches, or of 4 feet 3 inches in a pillar of three rails. The face of the pillar is sculptured with six rows of naked standing figures, there being 5 figures in the lowest row, and only four figures in each of the others. On one of the sides there is the following short inscription in four lines of the age of the Guptas :—

Achárya Indranandi Sishya Mahádari Púrnwamatisya Kottari.

The last word but one might, perhaps, be read as *patisya*; but the remainder of the inscription is quite clear. I understand it to record the gift of "*Mahádari*, the disciple of the teacher *Indranandi*, to the temple *(Kottari)* of *Púrnwamati*." Perhaps the term *Kottari* may be preserved in the name of *Kátári Khera*, by which the mound is now known.

The other sculptured stones are not of much interest. The largest is a broken statue of a standing figure, 3 feet high by 2 feet broad, which appears to be naked. The head, the feet, and the right arm are gone. A second small stone, 1 foot long and 5 inches broad, bears the figures of the *Navagraha*, or "Nine Planets." On the back there is a short inscription of only eight letters, of which two are somewhat doubtful. I read the whole as *Sahada, Bhima, Devindra*, but the word *Bhima* is very doubtful. A third stone, 2½ feet long and 1¼ feet square, is the fragment of a large pillar, with a lion sculptured on each of its four faces. The naked figures of these sculptures belong to a somewhat late period of Buddhism, after the introduction of the *Tantrika* doctrines, which, as we learn from Skanda Gupta's inscription on the Bhitari Pillar, were prevalent during the time of the later Guptas, in the 3rd and 4th centuries A. D.* As the forms of the letters of these inscriptions are also those of the Gupta period, we may conclude with some certainty that the *Kottari*, or temple of *Parswanati*, was erected before the fall of the Gupta dynasty in A. D. 319.

Four hundred feet to the south of the great bastion, and close to the south-west angle of the fort, there is another extensive mound, marked D in the map, upwards of 300 feet square and 35 feet in height above the road. The principal mass of ruin, which is in the middle of the west side, is the remains of a large temple, 40 feet square outside. In the middle of the south side there are the ruins of a small building which may, perhaps, have been the entrance gateway. To the right and left of the entrance there are the ruins of two small temples, each 14 feet square outside, and 9 feet 4½ inches inside, raised upon a plinth 24 feet square. The centre of the square is open, and has evidently never been built upon. My excavations were too limited to ascertain more than I have noted above, but I propose to continue the exploration hereafter. I believe that this mound is the remains of a very large monastery with its lofty enclosed temple, which could not have been less than 80 or even 100 feet in height.

Connected with *Ahi-chhatra* is an inscription of the Gupta period on a square pillar found near the village of

---

* I now (1871) believe these naked figures to be Digambara Jain statues. I possess several as old as the first century before Christ.

Dilwári, 3 *kos*, or 4½ miles, to the south of the fort. The inscription consists of 14 lines of five letters each, the letters of one line being placed exactly under those of the line above, so as to form also five straight perpendicular lines. The stone is 2½ feet long, 1 foot broad, and 9 inches thick in the middle, but the continual sharpening of tools has worn down the edges to a breadth of from 7 to 7½ inches. The inscription, which is on one of the narrow faces, has accordingly suffered in the partial loss of some of the initial and final letters of several lines. The other three faces of the stone are quite plain, and there is nothing whatever to show what the pillar may have been originally intended for.

My account of *Ahi-chhatra* would not be complete without a reference to the gigantic *lingam* near the village of *Gulariya*, 2½ miles to the north of the fort, and to the Priapian name of the village of *Bhim-laur*, one mile to the east of the fort. *Bhim-gaja* and *Bhim-laur* are common names for the *lingam* in all the districts to the north of the Ganges. I have already quoted Hwen Thsang's remark that the nine Brahmanical temples of Ahi-chhatra in A. D. 634 were dedicated to Siva, and I may now add, in illustration, that only in one of the many ruins about the old fort did I find a trace of the worship of any other divinity.

VII. SORON, OR SUKARA-KSHETRA.

From *Ahi-chhatra* the Chinese pilgrim proceeded in a south direction, a distance of from 260 to 270 *li*, from 23 to 25 miles, to the Ganges, which he crossed, and then turning to the south-west he arrived in the kingdom of *Pi-lo-shan-na*. His route to the south would have taken him through Aonla and Budaon to the *Budh Ganga* (or old Ganges) somewhere near Saháwar, a few miles below *Soron*, both of which places stood on the main stream of the Ganges so late as 400 years ago. As his subsequent route is said to have been to the south-west, I believe that he must have crossed the Ganges close to Saháwar, which is 42 miles from Ahi-chhatra in a direct line. From all my early enquiries I was led to believe that *Soron* was the only ancient place in this vicinity; and as Hwen Thsang does not give any distance for his south-west march, I concluded that *Soron* must have been the place to which he gives the name of Pi-lo-shan-na. I accordingly visited *Soron*, which is undoubtedly a place of very great antiquity, but which cannot, I think, be the place visited by the Chinese pilgrim. I will, however, first describe *Soron* before I proceed to discuss the superior claims of the great ruined mound of *Atranji-Khera* to be identified with the Pi-lo-shan-na of the Chinese pilgrim.

Soron is a large town on the right, or western, bank of the Ganges, on the high road between Bareli and Mathura. The place was originally called *Ukala Kshetra* ; but, after the demon *Hiranyáksha* had been killed by the *Varáha Avatár*, or Boar Incarnation of Vishnu, the name was changed to *Sukara Kshetra*, or "the place of the good deed." The ancient town is represented by a ruined mound called the *Kiluh* or "fort," which is one-quarter of a mile in length from north to south, and somewhat less in breadth. It stands on the high bank of the old bed of the Ganges, which is said by some to have flowed immediately under it so late as 200 years ago. The modern town stands at the foot of the old mound on the west and south sides, and probably contains about 5,000 inhabitants. There are no dwellings on the old mound, which is occupied only by the temple of *Sita-Rámji* and the tomb of *Shekh Jamál*. But it is covered with broken bricks of large size, and the foundations of walls can be traced in all directions. The mound is said to be the ruins of a fort built by Raja *Somadatta* of Soron many hundred years ago. But the original settlement of the place is very much older, being attributed to the fabulous *Raja Vena Chakravartti*, who plays such a conspicuous part in all the legends of North Bihár, Oudh, and Rohilkhand.

The temples of Soron are very numerous, and several of them are said to be old. But the only temples of any consequence are those of *Sita-Rámji*, on the top of the mound, and *Varáhaji* to the north-west of the city. A great annual fair is held near the latter temple on the 11th of the waxing moon of *Márgasirsha*, in remembrance of the destruction of the demon by the Boar Incarnation of Vishnu. It contains a statue of *Varáha-Lakshmi*, and is visited by crowds of pilgrims. The temple of *Sita-Rámji*, which is said to have been ruined by Aurang Shah (or Aurangzib) was restored by a wealthy Baniya, only four years ago, by building up the spaces between the pillars with plain white-washed walls. Internally the temple is a square of 27 feet supported on 16 stone pillars; but the people say that the original building was much larger, and that it contained 32 pillars. This account is most probably correct, as the foundations of the walls of the *sanctum*, or shrine, are still standing at the back, or west side, of the temple. There are also 10 superfluous pillars inside the temple, of which two support the broken architraves, and eight are built into the corner spaces of the walls. The style of these columns is similar to that of the set of pillars in the south-east corner of the quadrangle of the Great Kutb Mosque at Delhi, which bear the date of Samvat 1124, or A. D. 1067. That this date is not too early for the Soron temple is proved by the inscriptions of various pilgrims who have visited the shrine. As the oldest legible record bears the date of Samvat 1226, or A. D. 1169, the date of the erection of the temple cannot, therefore, be placed later than A. D. 1000.

These pilgrims' records are generally short and uninteresting, but as there are no less than 38 of them, bearing dates which range from A. D. 1169 to 1511, they become valuable for tracing the history of the temple. The earliest date after the Muhammadan conquest is A. D. 1241, and from that time down to A. D. 1290 there are no less than 15 dated records, showing that Soron continued to be a much frequented place of pilgrimage during the whole period of the *Ghori* dynasty, which ended in A. D. 1289. But during the rule of the next two dynasties, the *Khiljis* and *Tughlaks*, there is only one inscription, dated in A. D. 1375, in the reign of Firuz. Now, as nearly one-half of this period was occupied by the reigns of the cruel despot Ala-ud-din Khilji and the ferocious madman Muhammad Tughlak, it seems only reasonable to conclude that the people were deterred from making their usual pilgrimages by the persecution of their Muhammadan rulers. The next record is dated in A. D. 1429, and from that time down to 1511 there are 16 dated inscriptions; but as no less than 13 of this number belong to the reign of Bahlol Lodi, I infer that the rule of the Syad dynasty was not favourable to Hindu pilgrimages. I infer also that the temple must have been destroyed during the reign of the intolerant Sikandar Lodi, because the series of inscriptions closes with A. D. 1511, or just six years before the end of his reign. Had the temple existed during the happy century when the sceptre of India was swayed by the tolerant Akbar, the indifferent Jahangir, and the politic Shah Jahan, it is almost certain that some records of the pilgrims' visits would have been inscribed on the pillars of the temple. For this reason I feel satisfied that the destruction of the great temple of Soron must be assigned to an earlier period than that of the bigoted Aurang Shah.

VIII. ATRANJI-KHERA, OR PI-LO-SHAN-NA.

The great mound of ruins called *Atranji-Khera* is situated on the right, or west bank, of the *Káli Nadi*, four miles to the south of *Karsána*, and eight miles to the north of *Eyta*, on the Grand Trunk Road. It is also 15 miles to the south of Soron, and 43 miles to the north-west of *Sankisa* in a direct line, the road distance being not less than 48 or 50 miles. In the *Ain Akbari* Atranji is recorded as one of the Parganahs of Kanoj, under the name of *Sikandarpur Atreji*. *Sikandarpur*, which is now called *Sikandrabad*, is a village on the left bank of the *Káli Nadi* opposite Atranji. From this it would appear that Atranji was still occupied in the reign of Akbar. The Parganah was afterwards called *Karsána*, but it is now known by the name of *Sahdwar Karsána*, or of *Sahdwar* only. The name given by the Chinese pilgrim is *Pi-lo-shan-na*, for which M. Julien proposes to read *Virasana*.[*] So far back as 1848 I pointed out that, as both *pil* and *kar* are Sanskrit names for an elephant, it was probable that *Pilosana* might be the same as *Karsána*, the large village which I have already mentioned as being four miles to the north of *Atranji Khera*. The chief objection to this identification is the fact that *Karsána* is apparently not a very old place, although it is sometimes called *Deora Karsána*, a name which implies the possession of a temple of note at some former period. It is, however, possible that the name of *Karsána* may once have been joined to *Atranji*, in the same way that we find *Sikandarpur Atreji* in the *Ain Akbari*. As the identification of *Karsána* with *Pilosana* is purely conjectural, it is useless to hazard any more speculations on this subject. The bearing and distance from *Sankisa*, as recorded by Hwen Thsang, point to the neighbourhood of *Sirpura*, near which there is a small village called *Pilkuni* or *Pilokuni*, which is the *Pilukhoni* of

---

[*] Julien's Hwen Thsang, II., 233.

our maps. It is, however, a very petty place; and, although it boasts of a small *khera*, or mound of ruins, it cannot, I think, have ever been more than one-fourth of the circuit of two miles which Hwen Thsang attributes to *Pi-lo-shan-na*. But there are two strong points in its favour, namely, 1st, its position which agrees both in bearing and distance with the Chinese pilgrim's account; and 2nd, its name, which is almost identical with the old name, *sh* being very commonly pronounced as *kh*, so that Hwen Thsang's *Piloshanna* would usually be pronounced *Pilokhana*.

In proposing *Atranji-Khera* as the site of the ancient *Piloshanna*, I am influenced solely by the fact that this is the only large place besides *Soron* of any antiquity in this part of the country. It is true that the distance from *Sankisa* is somewhat greater than that recorded by the Chinese pilgrim, namely, 45 miles, instead of 33 miles, but the bearing is exact; and as it is quite possible that there may be some mistake in Hwen Thsang's recorded distance, I think that *Atranji-Khera* has a better claim than any other place to be identified with the ancient *Piloshanna*. I have not visited the place myself, as I was not aware of its importance when I was in its neighbourhood. I have had it inspected by a trustworthy servant, whose report shows that *Atranji* must once have been a place of considerable extent and importance. According to him, the great mound of *Atranji* is 3,250 in length, and 2,550 in breadth at the base. Now, these dimensions would give a circuit of about two miles, which is the very size of *Piloshanna* as recorded by Hwen Thsang. Its highest point is 44 feet 9 inches, which, if my identification is correct, should be the ruins of the great *Stupa* of Asoka, upwards of 100 feet in height, as this lofty tower is said to have been situated inside a monastery in the middle of the town. Outside the town there were two other monasteries, inhabited by 300 monks. These may, perhaps, be represented by two small mounds which still exist on the east side of the Great *Khera*. To the south there is a third mound, 105 feet in length by 105 feet in breadth, which may possibly be the remains of one or more of the five Bramanical temples described by Hwen Thsang.

Atranji-Khera had two gates,—one to the east, towards the *Káli Nadi*, and the other to the south. The foundation of the place is attributed to *Raja Vena Chakravartti*.

The mound is covered with broken bricks of large size and fragments of statues, and old coins are said to be frequently found. All the existing fragments of statues are said to be Brahmanical. There is a temple of Mahadeo on the mound, and there are five *lingams* in different places, of which one is 6 feet in height. The principal statue is that of a four-armed female called *Devi*, but which, as she is represented treading upon a prostrate figure, is most probably *Durga*.*

The only objection to the identification of *Atranji* with Piloshanna is the difference between the distance of 200 *li*, or 33 miles, as stated by Hwen Thsang, and the actual distance of 43 miles direct, or about 48 or 50 miles by road. I have already suggested the possibility of there being some mistake in the recorded distance of Hwen Thsang, but perhaps an equally probable explanation may be found in the difference of the length of the *yojana*. Hwen Thsang states that he allowed 40 Chinese *li* to the *yojana*; but if the old *yojana* of Rohilkhand differed from that of the Central Doab as much as the *kos* of these districts now differ, his distances would have varied by half a mile in every *kos*, or by two miles in every *yojana*, as the Rohilkhand *kos* is only 1½ mile, while that of the Doab is two miles—the latter being one-third greater. Now, if we apply this difference to Hwen Thsang's measurement of 200 *li*, or 33 miles, we increase the distance at once to 44 miles, which agrees with the direct measured distance on the map. I confess, however, that I am rather inclined to believe in the possibility of there being a mistake in Hwen Thsang's recorded distance, as I find exactly the same measurement of 200 *li* given as the distance between *Sankisa* and *Kanoj*. Now, the two distances are precisely the same, that is, *Sankisa* is exactly midway between *Atranji* and *Kanoj*; and as the latter distance is just 50 miles by my measurement along the high road, the former must also be the same. I would, therefore, suggest the probability that both of these distances should be 300 *li*, or 50 miles, instead of 200 *li* as recorded in the text. In favor of this proposed correction I may cite the testimony of the earlier Chinese pilgrim Fa Hian, who makes the distance from San-

* At my request Atranji was visited in 1865 by my friend Mr. C. Horne, then Judge of Mainpuri, whose account of the ruined mound will be found in the Bengal Asiatic Society's Journal, 1866, p. 165. The mound has been dug up in all directions for many centuries in search of bricks, and it was with difficulty that an entire brick was found for measurement.

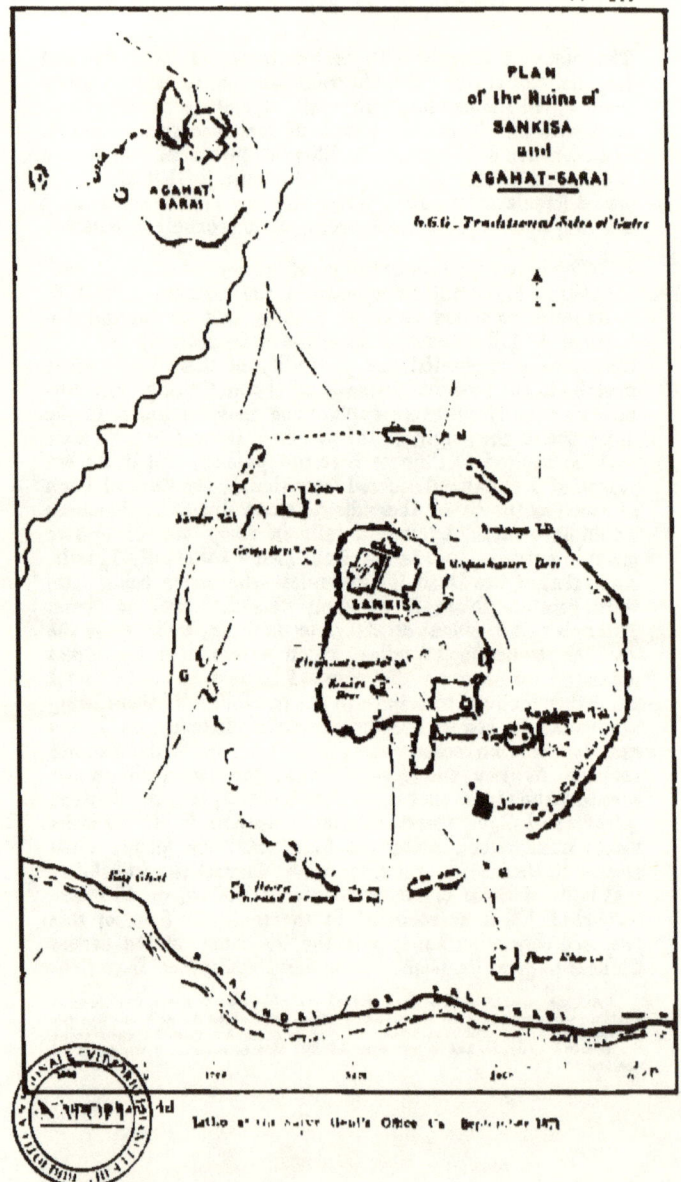

kisa to Kanoj 7 *yojanas*, or 49 miles. At Hwen Thsang's own valuation of 40 *li* to the *yojana*, this measurement would give 280 *li*; and as Fa Hian does not record half *yojanas*, we may increase the distance by half a *yojana*, or 20 *li*, which brings the total up to 300 *li*, or exactly 50 miles.

But whatever may be the true explanation of the difference between the actual distances and those recorded by Hwen Thsang, there still remains the important fact that *Sankisa* was exactly midway between *Kanoj* and *Piloshanna* just as it now is midway between *Kanoj* and *Atranji*. If we couple this absolute identity of position with the fact that *Atranji* is the only old place in the part of the country indicated by Hwen Thsang, we can scarcely arrive at any other conclusion than that the great ruined mound of *Atranji* is the site of the ancient *Piloshanna*.

IX. SANKISA.

The site of *Sankisa* was discovered by me in 1842, but it was not until the end of 1862 that I got an opportunity of exploring the ruins at leisure. The name of the place is written *Seng-kia-she* by the Chinese pilgrims, a spelling which is well preserved in the *Sankisa* of the present day, and which represents, with considerable faithfulness, the *Sankāsya* of Sanskrit. Hwen Thsang calls it also by the name of *Kie-pi-tha*, or *Kapitha*, of which I was unable to discover any trace.[*] *Sankisa* was one of the most famous places of Buddhist pilgrimage, as it was there that Buddha was believed to have descended from the *Trayastrinsa* heaven by the ladder of gold or gems, accompanied by the gods Indra and Brahma. According to this curious legend, *Māyā*, the mother of Buddha, died seven days after his birth, and ascended at once to the *Trayastrinsa* heaven, the abode of the 33 gods, of whom Indra was the chief. But as she had no opportunity in this abode of the gods of hearing the law of Buddha, her pious son ascended to the *Trayastrinsa* heaven and preached for three months in her behalf. He then descended to the earth with the gods Brahma and Indra by three staircases, one of which was formed either of crystal or precious stones, another of gold, and the third of silver. According

---
[*] Julien's Hwen Thsang, II., 237.—In the *Brihaj-Jâtaka* it is said that the famous astronomer, Varâha Mihira, "obtained the precious favour of the sun at Kâpitthaka." I presume that this is the *Kie-pi-tha* of the Chinese pilgrim. Dr. Kern thinks that Varâha Mihira was very probably educated there. Sankisa must at any rate have been a place of considerable importance in the 6th century.

to Fa Hian,* Buddha descended by a staircase formed of the "seven precious things," that is, the precious metals and precious gems; whilst Brahma accompanied him on his right side by a silver ladder, and Indra on his left by a golden one. But Hwen Thsang† assigns the golden staircase to Buddha himself, the silver staircase on the right to Brahma, and the crystal staircase on the left to Indra. The descent was accompanied by a multitude of *Devas*, who scattered showers of flowers on all sides as they sang the praises of Buddha.

Such are the main points of this curious legend, which is believed as firmly in Burma at the present day, as it was by Asoka 2,100 years ago, or by the Chinese pilgrims of the 5th, 6th, and 7th centuries of our era. According to Fa Hian, the three staircases disappeared under ground immediately after the descent, leaving only seven steps visible. Apparently these seven steps must have existed in the time of Asoka, as he is reported to have been anxious to behold their foundations, and accordingly sent men to dig down to their base. But the diggers "reached a yellow spring without being able to penetrate to the foundation." The King, however, "felt sensible of a great increase of his faith and veneration," and therefore built a chapel over the three staircases, and upon the middle one erected a full length statue of Buddha 60 feet high. According to Hwen Thsang's account, the three staircases still existed in his time (A. D. 630), but were completely sunk in the earth. On their foundations, however, the pious Kings of different countries had erected three staircases, similar to the first, of bricks and stones, ornamented with many precious things. The height of these staircases was about 70 feet. Over them there was a *Vihár* containing statues of Buddha, Brahma, and Indra, who were represented leaning forward as if about to descend. The Barmese say that the descent took place at the full moon of *Thadingkyut* (October), and that the foot of the steps were at the gate of the city of *Thing-ka-tha-na-go*, or *Singkasanagara*.‡ Hwen Thsang adds that the three staircases were placed in a line from north to south, with the descent facing the east, and that they stood within the walls of a great monastery.

---

* Beal's translation, C. XVII.
† Julien's translation, II., 237.
‡ Bishop Bigandet's Life of the Barmese Buddha, p. 140.

Close to the staircases there was a stone pillar, 70 feet in height, which had been erected by King Asoka. It was formed of a hard, fine-grained reddish stone, and had a brilliant polish. On its summit was a lion, who was seated facing the steps. There were figures also sculptured *inside the pillar* with marvellous art, which were visible only to the virtuous. This is Hwen Thsang's account, with which Fa Hian's agrees in almost every particular; but he adds a curious legend about a dispute between the *Srámanas* and heretics. "If," said the former, "this place ought to be the abode of the Srámanas, let a supernatural testimony proclaim it. They had no sooner finished this speech than the lion on the summit uttered a loud roar."

There were several *Stupas* at *Sankisa*, of which the most famous were the following:

1st.—On the spot where Buddha descended from the *Trayastrinsa* heaven, accompanied by Indra and Brahma. This *Stupa* is not mentioned by Hwen Thsang, but it is noticed by Fa Hian, and in the Barmese life of Buddha.

2nd.—On the spot where the four Buddhas had formerly sat and taken exercise.

3rd—At the place where Buddha bathed.

4th and *5th.*—Two small *Stupas* of Indra and Brahma.

6th.—On the spot where the female mendicant *Pundarikavarná* obtained the first sight of Buddha on his descent.

7th.—On the spot where Buddha cut his hair and nails.

The only other place of note at *Sankisa* was the tank of a *Nága*, or serpent, which was situated to the south-east of the great *Stupa*. Fa Hian says that this *Nága* had white ears; that he lived in the dwelling-place of the "ecclesiastics," and that he conferred fertility and abundance on the "country by causing gentle showers to fall upon the fields, and securing them from all calamities." A chapel was erected for his use, and he was said to make his appearance once a year. "When the ecclesiastics perceive him, they present him with cream in a copper vessel."

Hwen Thsang's account of *Sankisa* is unfortunately so meagre that we have but little to guide us in our attempt to identify the holy places of his time with any of the ruins of the present day. The only spot that can be identified with any certainty is the tank of the *Nága*, which still exists to the south-east of the ruins, in the very position described by Hwen Thsang. The name of the *Nága* is *Kárewar*, and that of the tank *Kándaiya Tál*. Milk is offered to him during every day of *Vaisákh*, and on the *Nág-panchami* of *Srávana*, and "at any other time when rain is wanted." In a note on the word *Chaurási* Sir Henry Elliot* has given an account of *Sankisa*, in which he asserts that this *Nága* is the common *Nág* of the Hindu worship to whom the *Nágpanchami* is specially dedicated. But this opinion is certainly wrong, as the above account shows that the *Sankisa Nága* of the present day is propitiated with offerings of milk whenever rain is wanted, just as he was in A. D. 400, when Fa Hian visited the place. This, therefore, is not the common *Nága* of Hindu worship, but the local *Nága* of *Sankisa*, who is commonly invoked as *Kárewar Nág Devata*.

Before attempting to indentify the site of the great monastery with its three famous staircases, its lion pillar and attendant *Stupas*, it will be better to describe the place as it is at present, although but little is now left of the great city of *Sankisa* with all its magnificent monuments. The small village which still preserves the name of *Sankisa* is perched upon a lofty mound of ruins 41 feet in height above the fields. This mound, which is called the *Kilah*, or "fort," is 1,500 feet in length from west to east, and 1,000 feet in breadth.† On the north and west faces the sides are steep, but on the other faces the slope is much more easy. Due south from the centre of the *Kilah*, at a distance of 1,600 feet, there is a mound of solid brick-work which is crowned by a modern temple dedicated to *Bisári Devi*, who is described as a goddess of great power. At 400 feet to the north of the temple mound there is a capital of an ancient pillar bearing the figure of an elephant, standing, but both his trunk and tail are wanting. The capital itself is of the well known bell-shape, corded or reeded perpendicularly, with an abacus of honeysuckle similar to that of the Allahabad pillar. The figure of the elephant is by far the best representation of that animal that I have seen in any Indian sculpture. The veins of the legs are carefully chiselled, and the toes of the feet

---

* Glossary, p. 154.
† See Plate XLV. for a map of Sankisa.

SANKISA.

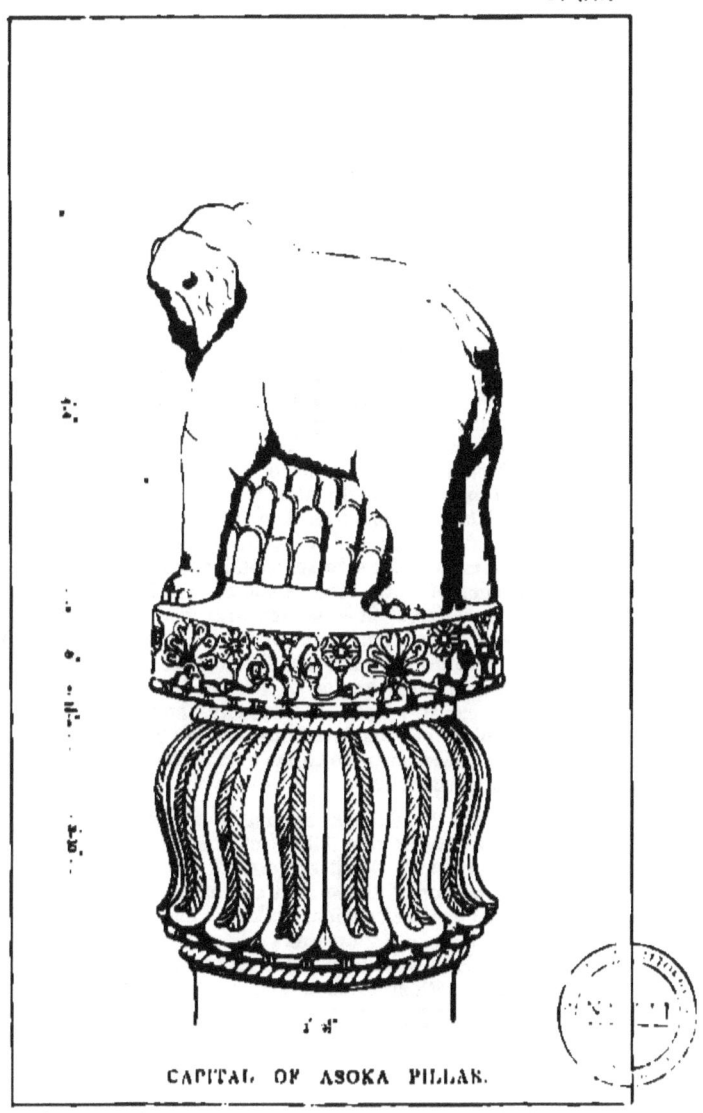

CAPITAL OF ASOKA PILLAR.

are well and faithfully represented, but the loss of the trunk prevents us from forming a decided opinion as to its excellence as a work of art. If we may judge from the position of the legs, the animal was most probably represented as standing still with his trunk hanging down.[*] The stone is a fine-grained sandstone of reddish hue, and has been very highly polished. The bell-capital is low, its breadth being greater than its height, in which particular it resembles the Asoka Pillar of *Navandgarh Lauriya*, to the north of Bettiah. Taking all these circumstances into consideration along with the superior execution of the work, I feel satisfied that this capital is of the same age as the well known Asoka Pillars of Allahabad and Navandgarh.

Due south from the temple of Bisári Devi, at a distance of 200 feet, there is a small mound of ruins which appears to be the remains of a *Stupa*. Due east from the temple 600 feet, there is an oblong mound 600 feet in length by 500 feet in breadth, which is known by the name of *Nivi-ka-kot*. *Nivi* I believe to have been the name of the man who formerly brought this piece of ground into cultivation; and *Kot*, in the phraseology of *Sankisa*, means simply any mound of ruins, and is applied to all the isolated portions of the ramparts. *Nivi-ka-kot* would, however, appear to be the remains of some large enclosed building, such as a Buddhist monastery. It is covered with broken bricks of large size, and a few fragments of stone; but I could not trace any remains of walls on the surface. At the south-east and north-east angles of *Nivi-ka-kot* there are large circular mounds which are probably the remains of *Stupas* from which all the available bricks have been removed; and at a short distance to the north there is a third mound of the same character.

The *Kilah* and the different mounds of all sizes around the temple form a mass of ruin 3,000 feet in length by 2,000 feet in breadth, or nearly 2 miles in circuit. But this was only the central portion of the ancient city of *Sankisa*, comprising the citadel and the religious buildings that were clustered around the three holy staircases. The city itself, which would appear to have surrounded this central mound on all sides, was enclosed with an earthen rampart, 18,900 feet, or

---

[*] See Plate No. XLVI. for a side view of this capital.—See also Fergusson's History of Architecture, II., 459, No. 970, for a front view.

upwards of 3½ miles in circuit. The greater part of this rampart still remains, the shape being a tolerably regular dodecagon. On three sides, to the east, the north-east, and the south-east, there are breaks or openings in the line of rampart which are traditionally said to be the positions of the three gates of the city. In proof of the tradition, the people refer to the village of *Paor-Kheria*, or " *Gate-village*," which is just outside the south-east gap in the ramparts. But the name is pronounced *Paor*, and not *Paur*, and may, therefore, refer to the staircases or steps *(Paori)*, and not to the gate. The Káli or *Kálindri Nadi* flows past the south-west corner of the ramparts from the *Rájghát*, which is half a mile distant, to the *Kakra Ghát*, which is rather more than one mile to the south of the line of ramparts.

To the north-west, three-quarters of a mile distant, stands the large mound of *Agahat*, which is 40 feet in height, and rather more than half a mile in diameter at base. The name of the old town is said to have been *Agahat*, but the place is now called *Agahat Sarai* (Agahat of the maps) from a modern *Sarai*, which was built in A. H. 1080, or A. D. 1069, on the north-east corner of the mound, by the ancestor of the present Pathán Zamindar. The people say that before this the place had been deserted for several centuries; but as I obtained a tolerably complete series of the copper coins of the Muhammadan Kings of Delhi and Jonpur, I presume that it could not have been deserted for any very long time. The mound is covered with broken bricks of large size, which alone is a sure test of antiquity: and as it is of the same height as that of *Sankisa*, the people are most probably right in their assertion that the two places are of the same age. In both mounds are found the same old coins without any inscriptions, the more ancient being square pieces of silver covered with various punch marks, and the others square pieces of copper that have been cast in a mould,—all of which are, in my opinion, anterior to the invasion of Alexander the Great.

In identifying *Sankisa* with the *Sangkasya* of the *Rámáyana* and the *Seng-kia-she* of the Chinese, we are supported, not only by its absolute identity of name, but likewise by its relative position with regard to three such well known places as *Mathura*, *Kanoj*, and *Ahichhatra*. In size, also, it agrees very closely with the measurement given by

Hwon Thsang; his circuit of 20 *li*, or 3⅓ miles, being only a little less than my measurement of 18,000 feet, or 3⅖ miles. There can be no doubt, therefore, that the place is actually the same; but in attempting to identify the sites of any of the holy spots mentioned by Hwen Thsang, I find myself baffled at the outset by the indefiniteness as well as the meagreness of the pilgrim's descriptions. It is his usual practice to state the relative bearings and distances of most of the chief places of Buddhist veneration, but in describing *Sankisa* he has given only one bearing and not a single distance. The tank of the *Nága* is the one solitary spot that can be identified with certainty, the sites of all the rest being only guesses of more or less probability.

But the difficulty regarding the identification of the Asoka Pillar is of a different kind. Both of the Chinese pilgrims make mention of only one pillar at *Sankisa*, which was crowned with the figure of a *lion*, and Fa Hian records a silly legend which refers to the miraculous roar of this lion statue. Now, the only piece of an Asoka Pillar at present existing is the *elephant* capital, which I have already described, and which, however absurd it may seem, I think may possibly be the *lion* pillar of the Chinese pilgrims. The reasons which induce me to think so are the following: First, the *elephant* capital is undoubtedly much older than the date of either of the pilgrims, and yet, if it is not the same as the lion capital, it has been left altogether undescribed by them, although its great size could scarcely have allowed it to remain unnoticed; second, the height of the elephant pillar would seem to correspond very closely with that of the lion pillar, as recorded by Fa Hian, who calls it 30 cubits, or from 45 to 60 feet according to the value of the Chinese *chhi*. Now, the diameter of the neck of the elephant pillar is 2 feet 9½ inches, which, compared with the dimensions of the Allahabad pillar, 2 feet 2 inches neck diameter, to 35 feet of height, gives a total for the shaft of the *Sankisa* Pillar of 44 feet 3 inches. By adding to this the height of the capital, we obtain 52½ feet as the probable height of the *Sankisa* Pillar.* Third, as the trunk of the elephant has long been lost, it is possible that it was missing before the time of the Chinese pilgrims, and if so, the nature of the animal might

---

* The bell-capital with its honey-suckle ornamentation is 2 feet 10 inches high, and the same in diameter. The elephant is 4 feet 4 inches in height, making the total height of capital 8 feet 2 inches.

easily have been mistaken at a height of 50 feet above the ground. Indeed, supposing the pillar to be the same, this is the only way in which I can account for the mistake about the animal. But, if the pillar is not the same, the silence of both pilgrims regarding this magnificent elephant pillar seems to me quite unaccountable. On the whole, therefore, I am inclined to believe that the elephant's trunk having been long lost, the nature of the animal was mistaken when viewed from a distance of 50 feet beneath. This is confirmed by the discrepancy in the statements of the two pilgrims regarding the capital of one of the *Srávasti* pillars, which Fa Hian calls an ox, and Hwen Thsang an elephant.*

Admitting, then, that this elephant capital is not improbably the same as the lion pillar described by the Chinese pilgrims, we have a clue to the site of the great monastery which would seem to have enclosed within its walls the great stone pillar as well as the three holy staircases. I infer, therefore, that the temple of *Bisári Devi* most probably occupies the site of the three staircases, and that the three mounds which stand to the east of the *Nivi-ka-kot* may be the remains of the three *Stupas* which were erected on the three other holy spots of *Sankisa*, which have already been described. I made several excavations about the different mounds just noticed, but without any success.

I made also a careful but an unsuccessful search for some trace of the base of the stone pillar. The people were unanimous that the elephant capital had been in its present position beyond the memory of any one now living, and most of them added that it now stands in its original position. But there were a few men who pointed to a spot on the west of the village, or *Kilah* mound, as the original site of the capital. Here, indeed, there is an octagonal hole in a small mound, from which the bricks of a solid foundation have been removed. If any dependence could be placed upon this statement, the mound on which the village now stands would almost certainly be the site of the great monastery with its three holy staircases, and the three mounds to the east of *Nivi-ka-kot* would still represent the three *Stupas*. The main objection to our accepting this statement as correct is the apparent want of all object in the removal of the

---

* Beal's Fa Hian, C. XVII, p. 65 ; and Julien's Hwen Thsang, II., p. 239.

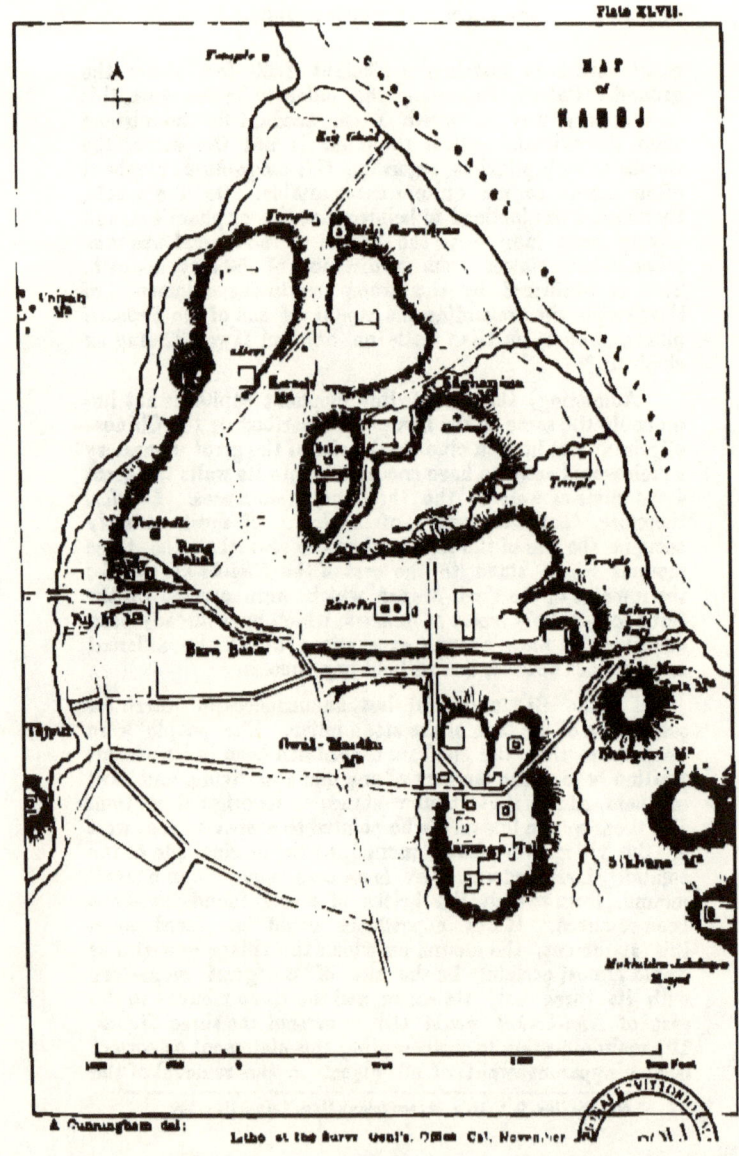

elephant capital to any other site. It is, however, quite possible that the capital may have been stopped on its way to the temple of *Mahâdeva*, near the *Nága* mound and tank. The temple of *Bisári Devi* would then be the site of one of the ten ancient Brahmanical fanes which are described by Hwen Thsang. Altogether, this is, perhaps, a more probable solution of the difficulties of the case than that first described.*

In his description of *Sankisa*, Hwen Thsang mentions a curious fact, that the Brahmans who dwelt near the great monastery were "many tens-of-thousands" in number. As an illustration of this statement, I may mention that the people have a tradition that *Sankisa* was deserted from 1800 to 1000 years ago, and that 1300 years ago, or about A. D. 500, it was given by a *Kayath* to a body of Brahmans. They add also that the population of the village of *Paor-Kheria* is known to have been wholly Brahman until a very recent period.

X. KANOJ.

Of the great city of Kanoj, which for many hundred years was the Hindu Capital of Northern India, the existing remains are few and unimportant. In A. D. 1010, when Mahmud of Ghazni approached Kanoj, the historian relates that "he there saw a city which raised its head to the skies, and which in strength and structure might justly boast to have no equal."† Just one century earlier, or in A. D. 915, Kanoj is mentioned by Masudi as the capital of one of the Kings of India, and about A. D. 900 Abu Zaid, on the authority of Ibn Wahab, calls "*Kaduge*, a great city in the kingdom of *Gozar*." At a still earlier date, in A. D. 634, we have the account of the Chinese pilgrim Hwen Thsang, who describes Kanoj as being 20 *li*, or 3½ miles, in length, and 4 or 5 *li*, or three-quarter of a mile, in breadth. The city was surrounded by strong walls and deep ditches, and was washed by the Ganges along its eastern face.‡ The last fact is corroborated by Fa Hian, who states that the city touched the River *Heng* (Ganges) when he visited it in A. D. 400.§

---
* I have already noticed, p. 272, that the Burmese Life of Buddha fixes the point of descent at the "gate of the city," and this position seems also to be indicated by the still existing name of *Paor-Kheria*, or "Hairmen Village," which is situated just outside the south-east opening, or gate, in the earthen ramparts.—See Plate No. XLV.
† Briggs's Ferishta, I., p. 57.
‡ Julien's Hwen Thsang, II., p. 242.
§ Beal's Fa Hian, C. XVIII, p. 70.

Kanoj is also mentioned by Ptolomy, about A. D. 140, as *Kanogiza*. But the earliest notice of the place is undoubtedly the old familiar legend of the Puránas, which refers the Sanskrit name of *Kanya-Kubja*, or the "hump-backed maiden" to the curse of the sage *Vayu* on the hundred daughters of *Kusandbha*.

At the time of Hwen Thsang's visit, Kanoj was the capital of Raja *Harsha Vardhana*, the most powerful sovereign in Northern India. The Chinese pilgrim calls him a *Fei-she*, or *Vaisya*, but it seems probable that he must have mistaken the *Vaisa*, or *Bais*, Rajput, for the *Vaisya*, or *Bais*, which is the name of the mercantile class of the Hindus; otherwise Harsha Vardhana's connexion by marriage with the Rajput families of Malwa and Balabhi would have been quite impossible.* Baiswára, the country of the Bais Rajputs, extends from the neighbourhood of Lucknow to Khara Mánikpur, and thus comprizes nearly the whole of Southern Oudh. The Bais Rajputs claim descent from the famous *Sálivdhan*, whose capital is said to have been *Daundia-Khera*, on the north bank of the Ganges. Their close proximity to Kanoj is in favour of the sovereignty which they claim for their ancestors over the whole of the Gangetic Doab from Delhi to Allahabad. But their genealogical lists are too imperfect, and most probably also too incorrect, to enable us to identify any of their recorded ancestors with the Princes of Harsha Vardhana's family.

The vast empire which Harsha Vardhana raised during his long reign of 42 years, between A. D. 607 and 648, is described by Hwen Thsang as extending from the foot of the Kashmir Hills to Assam, and from Nepal to the Narbada River. He intimidated the Raja of Kashmir into surrendering the tooth of Buddha, and his triumphal procession from Pátaliputra to Kanoj was attended by no less than 20 tributary Rajas from Assam and Magadha on the east, to Jálandhar on the west. In the plenitude of his power, Harsha Vardhana invaded the countries to the south of the Narbada, where he was successfully opposed by Raja *Pulakesi*, and after many repulses was obliged to retire to his own kingdom. This account of Hwen Thsang is most singularly

---

* I have no doubt on this subject now (1871), as there is Indian Sanskrit authority for the intermarriage with the Malwa family.

corroborated in every particular by several ancient inscriptions of the *Chálukya* Rajas of *Kalyán*. According to these inscriptions, Raja Vikramáditya, the grandson of *Pulakesi Tallabha*, gained the title of *Parameswara*, "by the defeat of Sri Harsha Vardhana, famous in the north countries."* Now Vikramáditya's reign is known to have commenced in *Sake* 514, or A. D. 592, as one of his inscriptions is dated in Sake 530, or A. D. 608, which is called the 16th year of his reign;† and as his grandson did not succeed to the throne until the *Sake* year 618, or A. D. 696, it is certain that Vikramáditya must have been a contemporary of Harsha Vardhana throughout the greater part, if not the whole, of his reign. The unusually long reigns of the earlier *Chálukya* Princes have led Mr. Walter Elliot to suspect the accuracy of the dates, although, as he points out, "the succeeding dates tally with each other in a way that affords the strongest presumption of their freedom from any material error." The question of the accuracy of these dates is now most satisfactorily confirmed by the unimpeachable testimony of the contemporary record of Hwen Thsang, which I have quoted above.

In determining the period of Harsha's reign, between the years 607 and 648 A. D., I have been guided by the following evidence: 1st, the date of his death is fixed by the curious reported fulfilment of Hwen Thsang's dream,‡ and by the report of the Chinese embassy§. 2nd, in speaking of Harsha's career, the pilgrim records that from the time of his accession Harsha was engaged in continual war for 5½ years, and that afterwards for about 30 years he reigned in peace. This statement is repeated by Hwen Thsang, when on his return to China, on the authority of the King himself, who informed him that he had then reigned for *upwards* of 30 years, and that the quinquennial assembly then collected was the *sixth* which he had convoked. From these different statements it is certain that at the date of Hwen Thsang's return to China, in A. D. 640, Harsha had

---

* Bombay Asiatic Society's Journal, III., 206.
† Royal Asiatic Society's Journal, IV., 10.
‡ See the discussion on this date in my "Ancient Geography of India," Appendix, p. 569.
§ Journal, "Asiatic Society," Bengal, 1837, p. 69,—anonymous translation. See also Journal Asiatique, 1839, p. 398, French translation by M. Pauthier.

reigned *upwards of* 30 *years*, and somewhat *less than* 35 *years*. His accession must, therefore, be placed between A. D. 605 and 610. 3rd, now, in the middle of this very period, in A. D. 607, as we learn from Abu Rihan, was established the Sri *Harsha* era, which was still prevalent in Mathura and Kanoj in the beginning of the 11th century. Considering the exact agreement of the names and dates, it is impossible to avoid coming to the conclusion that the *Harsha*, who established an era in *Kanoj* in A. D. 607, was the great King *Harsha Vardhana* who reigned at Kanoj during the first half of the seventh century.

Hwen Thsang adds some particulars regarding the family of Harsha Vardhana, which induce me to think it probable that it may be identified with one of the dynasties whose names have been preserved in the genealogies of the Rájavali. The names differ in the various copies, but they agree generally in making *Rāj Sing*, who reigned only nine years, the predecessor of *Hara* or *Hari Sing*, who is recorded to have reigned for 44 or 45 years. Now, according to Hwen Thsang, the predecessor and elder brother of *Harsha Vardhana* was *Rájya Vardhana*, who was assassinated shortly after his accession. Here both the names of these two Kings and the lengths of their reigns agree so well together as to suggest the probability of their identity. In most copies of the Rájavali, this dynasty of six Kings, of which *Raja* and *Hara* are the 3rd and 4th names, is made the immediate predecessor of the Great Tomar dynasty, whose accession has already been assigned in my account of the Kings of Delhi to the year 736 A. D. The following lists give the names of all the Kings of this dynasty according to the various authorities in my possession:

Mritunjaya and Ward.		Punjib, MS.		Chanderi, MS.		Sayid Ahmad.		Hwen Thsang.
	Yrs.		Yrs.		Yrs.		Yrs.	
Inga Sinha	27	Düp R.	17	Düp R.	17	Düp Sing	17	
Ráin N.	32	Rái N.	11	Ram N.	11	Ram Sing	16	Prakára Vardhana
Skija s.	9	Ráj S.	9	Rain M.	9	Ráj Sing	9	Rájya ditto.
Varn R.	46	Hari R.	45	Mir R.	45	Shir Sing	45	Harsha ditto.
Nara N.	25	Nar K.	44	Bir K.	15	Hara Sing	11	
Jawana	24	Jiwan	8	Jiwan	8	Jiwan Sing	7	
Total	154		137		107		105	

According to Sayid Ahmad the accession of *Shir Sing*, who is the *Hara* or *Hari* of the other lists, took place in A. D. 611, or within four years of the date already obtained for Harsha Vardhana.

In my account of Delhi I have given my reasons for believing that Kanoj was the capital of the *Tomars* down to the invasion of Mahmud in A. D. 1021, immediately after the defeat and death of *Rája Jay Pál*. Shortly after that date, the small town of Bári to the north of Lucknow became the capital, until about A. D. 1050, when the *Tomars* retired to Delhi before the growing power of the *Ráhtors*. Once more Kanoj became the capital of a powerful kingdom, and the rival of Delhi, both in extent and in magnificence. Here Jaya Chandra, the last of the *Ráhtors*, celebrated the *Aswamedha*, or "Horse-sacrifice;" and here in open day did Prithi Raja, the daring Chief of the Choháns, carry off the willing daughter of the *Ráhtor* King, in spite of the gallant resistance of the two *Banáfar* heroes, *Alha* and *Udal*. The fame of these two brothers, which is fully equal to that of Prithi Raja himself, is still preserved in the songs and traditions of the people amongst the Chandels of *Mahoba* and the Ráhtors and Chandels of the Doab. After the fall of Delhi in January 1101 A. D., Muhammad Ghori marched against Kanoj. Raja Jaya Chandra retired before him as far as Banáras, where he made his last stand, but was defeated with great slaughter. The Raja escaped from the field, but was drowned in attempting to cross the Ganges. When his body was recovered by the conquerors, it was found that he had false teeth fixed with wires of gold. With Jaya Chandra ended the dynasty of the *Ráhtors* of the Doab, and the wealth and importance of the far-famed capital of Kanoj. Only one hundred and fifty years later it is described by Ibn Batuta as a "small town," and from that time down to the present this ancient city has gradually lessened in consequence; but as it was close to the high road of the Doab, it still continued to be visited by numerous travellers who where attracted by its ancient fame. The final blow to its prosperity has now been given by the diversion of the railroad to Etáwa, which leaves Kanoj far away to the east, to be visited for the future only by the curious antiquary and the civil officials of the district.

In comparing Hwen Thsang's description of ancient Kanoj with the existing remains of the city, I am obliged to confess with regret that I have not been able to identify even one solitary site with any certainty; so completely has almost every trace of Hindu occupation been obliterated by the Musalmáns. According to the traditions of the people, the ancient city extended from the shrine of *Háji Harmáyan* on the north near the Raj Ghát, to the neighbourhood of *Miranka-Sara* on the south, a distance of exactly three miles. Towards the west, it is said to have reached to *Kapatya* and *Makarandnagar*, two villages on the high road, about three miles from *Háji Harmáyan*. On the east the boundary was the old bed of the Ganges, or *Chota Gangá* as the people call it, although it is recorded in our maps as the *Káli Nadi*. Their account is, that the *Káli*, or *Kálindri Nadi*, formerly joined the Ganges near *Sangirámpur* or *Sangrámpur*; but that several hundred years ago the great river took a more northerly course from that point, while the waters of the *Káli Nadi* continued to flow down the deserted channel. As an open channel still exists between *Sangrámpur* and the *Káli Nadi*, I am satisfied that the popular account is correct, and that the stream which flows under Kanoj, from *Sangrámpur* to *Mhendi Ghát*, although now chiefly filled with the waters of the *Káli Nadi*, was originally the main channel of the Ganges. The accounts of Fa Hian and Hwen Thsang, who place Kanoj on the Ganges, are therefore confirmed, not only by the traditions of the people, but also by the fact that the old channel still exists under the name of the *Chota Gangá*, or little Ganges.*

The modern town of Kanoj occupies only the north end of the site of the old city, including the whole of what is now called the *Kílah* or citadel. The boundaries are well defined by the shrine of *Háji Harmáyan* on the north, the tomb of *Táj Báj* on the south-west, and the Masjid and tomb of *Makhdúm Jaháníya* on the south-east. The houses are much scattered, especially inside the citadel, so that though the city still covers nearly one square mile, yet the population barely exceeds 16,000 in number. The citadel, which occupies all the highest ground, is triangular in shape, its northern point being the shrine of *Háji Harmáyan*, its south-west point the temple of *Ajay Pál*, and its south-east point the large bastion called *Kshem Kali Búrj*. Each of the faces is about 4,000 feet in length, that to the north-

---

* See Plate No. II. for the situation of Kanoj in the Map of North-Western India.

west being protected by the bed of the nameless dry Nala; that to the north-east by the *Chota Gangá*; while that to the south must have been covered by a ditch, which is now one of the main roads of the city, running along the foot of the mound from the bridge below Ajay Pál's temple to the Kshem Kali bastion. On the north-east face the mound rises to 60 or 70 feet in height above the low ground on the bank of the river; and towards the Nala on the north-west, it still maintains a height of from 40 to 50 feet. On the southern side, however, it is not more than 30 feet immediately below the temple of *Ajay Pál*, but it increases to 40 feet below the tomb of *Bála Pir*. The situation is a commanding one; and before the use of cannon the height alone must have made Kanoj a strong and important position. The people point out the sites of two gates,—the first to the north, near the shrine of *Háji Harmdyan*, and the second to the south-east, close to the *Kshem Kali Bárj*. But as both of these gates lead to the river it is certain that there must have been a third gate on the land side towards the south-west, and the most probable position seems to be immediately under the walls of the *Rang Mahal*, and close to the temple of *Ajay Pál*.

According to tradition, the ancient city contained 84 wards, or *Mahalas*, of which 25 are still existing within the limits of the present town. If we take the area of these 25 wards at three-quarters of a square mile, the 84 wards of the ancient city would have covered just 2¼ square miles. Now, this is the very size that is assigned to the old city by Hwen Thsang, who makes its length 20 *li*, or 3⅓ miles, and its breadth 4 or 5 *li*, or just three-quarters of a mile, which multiplied together give just 2¼ square miles. Almost the same limits may be determined from the sites of the existing ruins, which are also the chief *find-spots* of the old coins with which Kanoj abounds. According to the dealers, the old coins are found at *Bála Pir* and *Rang Mahal*, inside the Fort; at *Makhdúm Jaháuia*, to the south-east of the Fort; at *Makarandnagar* on the high road; and intermediately at the small villages of *Singh Bhawáni* and *Kátlápur*. The only other productive site is said to be *Rájgir*, an ancient mound covered with brick ruins on the bank of the *Chota Gangá*, three miles to the south-east of Kanoj. Taking all these evidences into consideration, it appears to me almost certain that the ancient city of Hwen Thsang's time must have extended from *Háji Harmáyan* and the *Kshem Kali Bárj*, on the bank of the Ganges (now the *Chota Ganga*), in a south-west direction, to *Makarandnagar*, on the Grand Trunk Road, a length of just three miles, with a general breadth of about one mile or somewhat less. Within these limits are found all the ruins that still exist to point out the position of the once famous city of Kanoj.*

The only remains of any interest are, 1st, the ruins of the old palace, now called the *Rang Mahal*; 2nd, the Hindu pillars of the *Jáma Musjid*; 3rd, the Hindu pillars of the Mosjid of *Makhdúm Jahániya*; and 4th, the Hindu statues in the village of *Singh Bhawáni*. The other remains are simple mounds of all sizes, covered with broken bricks, traces of brick walls, and broken figures. These are found in several places inside the citadel, but more particularly at the temple of *Ajay Pál*, a modern building on an ancient site. Outside the citadel they are found chiefly about the shrine of *Makhdúm Jahániya* on the south-east, and about *Makrandnagar* on the south-west.

The ruins of the *Rang Mahal*, which are situated in the south-west angle of the citadel, consist of a strong brick wall faced with blocks of *kankar*, 240 feet in length, and 25 feet in height above the sloping ruins, but more than 40 feet above the level of the bazar. It is strengthened in front by four towers or buttresses, 14 feet broad and 61 feet apart. The wall itself is 7 feet thick at top, and behind it, at 10 feet distance, there is a second wall 5 feet thick, and at 9½ feet farther back a third wall 3½ feet thick, and a fourth wall at 21 feet. The distances between the walls most probably represent the width of some of the rooms of the old Hindu palace, which would thus have a breadth of 56 feet. But the block *kankar* walls can be traced for a distance of 180 feet back from the south-east buttress to a wicket or small door which would appear to have formed a side entrance to the courtyard of the palace. As far as it can be now traced, the palace covered an area of 240 feet in length by 180 feet in breadth. It is said to have been built by *Ajay Pál*, to whom also is attributed a temple which once stood close by. *Ajay Pál* and *Mahi Pál* are said to

---

* See Plate No. XLVII. for a plan of the ruins of Kanoj.

have reigned a short time before *Jay Chand*, but the names of the intervening Princes are not known. I think it highly probable that *Ajay Pál* is the Tomar Prince *Jay Pál*, who was conquered by Mahmud of Ghazni, and afterwards defeated and killed, in A. D. 1021, by a confederate army under the leadership of the Chandel Raja of *Kálanjar*. Just outside the south-east buttress of the palace, the people point out a spot where they affirm that 20 golden ingots were discovered in 1834, of which 9 were made over to Mr. Wemyss, the Collector of Cawnpoor, and the remainder were secreted by the finders. Accounts differ as to the weight of the ingots, but the general belief is that they weighed about 1 *ser*, or 2 lbs. each. The coin dealers, however, affirm that the 9 ingots which were taken to the Cawnpoor Treasury weighed Rs. 13,500, that is Rs. 1,500, or 18¾ *sers* each.

The *Jáma*, or *Dina*, *Masjid* of Kanoj is cited by Mr. Fergusson as a specimen of Hindu cloisters, which has been re-arranged to suit the purposes of Muhammadan worship; and in this opinion I most fully concur. The inscription over the entrance doorway is now much decayed, and several portions are quite obliterated, but a copy has been fortunately preserved by Rajab Ali, a teacher of children, in the court of the Masjid. According to this copy, the Masjid was built in the Hijira year 809, or A. D. 1406, in the reign of Ibrahim Shah (of Jonpur). It is situated on a lofty mound in the very middle of the old fort, and this commanding position alone would be sufficient to show that it must originally have been the site of some Hindu building of considerable importance. This conclusion is partly confirmed by the traditions of the temple, who, however, most absurdly call the place *Sita-ka Rasúi*, or "Sita's kitchen." We know also that it was the usual practice of the Muhammadan Kings of Jonpur to raise their Masjids on the sites, and with the materials, of the Hindu temples which they demolished. On comparing, therefore, this cloistered Masjid with those of Jonpur, which are acknowledged re-arrangements of Hindu materials, we see at once that the pillars are all Hindu, and that the domes formed of courses of overlapping stones, and decorated with Hindu symbols are certainly not Muhammadan. When I first visited Kanoj in January 1838 the arrangement of the pillars was somewhat different from what I found it in November 1862. The cloisters which originally extended all round the square, are now confined to the Masjid itself, that is, to the west side only. This change is said to have been made by a Muhammadan Tahsildar shortly before 1857. The same individual is also accused of having destroyed all the remains of figures that had been built into the walls of the *Jáma* and *Makhdúm Jahániya* Masjids. It is certain that there are none visible now, although in January 1838, as recorded in my journal, I saw "several Hindu figures placed sideways and upside down" in the walls of the *Jáma* Masjid, and three broken figures lying outside the doorway of the Masjid of *Makhdúm Jahániya*. The inscription over the doorway of the last, which I saw in its place in 1838, is said to have been removed at the same time for the purpose of cutting off a Hindu figure on the back of it. I recovered this inscription by sending to the present Tahsildar for it.

The *Jáma* Masjid, as it stands now, is a pillared room, 108 feet in length by 26 feet in width, supported on four rows of columns. The roof is flat, excepting the centre and ends, which are covered with domes formed by circles of stones gradually lessening until they meet. In front of the Masjid there is a court-yard 95 feet in width, the whole being surrounded by a stone wall 6 feet in thickness. The exterior dimensions are 133 feet from west to east, by 120½ feet. In 1838 there were still standing on the three sides of the court-yard portions of the original cloisters formed of two rows of pillars. The Masjid itself was then confined to the five openings in the middle of the west side, the seven openings on each flank of it being formed of only two rows of pillars the same as on the other three sides. The Masjid now consists of a single room supported on 60 pillars without any cloisters; but originally the Masjid itself was supported on 20 pillars, with cloisters on each flank, and also on the other three sides of the court-yard. The whole number of pillars was then 128. To make up this number we have the 60 pillars of the present Masjid, and no less than 58 spare capitals still lying in the court-yard, which together make up 118, or within 10 of the actual number required to complete the original design.

The pillars of the *Jáma* Masjid may, I think, be seen in their original Hindu form at the sides of the small door ways in the north and south walls of the court. Each pillar is formed of five pieces, *viz.*, a base and capital, with a middle piece which divides the shafts into two equal portions, and may be called the upper and lower shafts. The shafts are 10 inches square and 3 feet 9 inches in height. The base is 1 foot high, and the middle piece and capital are each 3 inches, thus making the whole height 9 feet 10 inches. But the pillars, as re-arranged by the Muhammadans, are 11 feet 2 inches high, the extra height having been gained by adding a piece to each portion of the shaft. These shorter pieces, which are 2 feet 1 inch in height, are always placed above the original shafts of 3 feet 8 inches. As there could have been no *difficulty* in purchasing a single shaft of the required length of 5 feet 10 inches, it seems certain that the whole of these made-up pillars must have been obtained after the usual cheap Muhammadan manner—by the demolition of some Hindu buildings, either Buddhist or Brahmanical.

The Masjid and tomb of *Makhdúm Jahániya* are situated on a lofty mound in the *Sikhdna Mahalla* to the south-east of the citadel, overlooking the *Chota Gangá*. The mound is 40 feet in height above the fields, and is partly occupied by weavers' houses. The tomb of the *Makhdúm* is a common-looking building, 35 feet square. Beside it there are two other plain square tombs holding the remains of his descendants, both male and female. The tomb itself, as recorded in the mutilated inscription which formerly existed over the doorway, was erected over *Sayid Jalil Makhdúm Jahániya* by his son *Ráju* in the Hijra year 881, or A. D. 1476. The Masjid was built in the same year, in the reign of Husen Shah, of Jonpur, to whom Kanoj still belonged, although some writers place his final defeat by Bahlol Lodi, of Delhi, in this very year, A. H. 881, and others in A. H. 883. The central dome of the Masjid has long ago fallen in, and all the pointed arches are seriously cracked and propped up by unsightly masses of masonry. There is nothing peculiar about the building, save the decoration of the panels of the back wall, which have the name of Allah inscribed on a tablet suspended by a rope. The appearance of the tablet and rope is so like that of the Hindu bell and chain that one is almost tempted to believe that the Muhammadan architect must have simply chiselled away the bolder points of the Hindu ornament to suit his own design. But whether this may have been the case or not, it is impossible to miss seeing that the Hindu bell and chain must have been directly suggestive of the Muhammadan tablet and cord. The Masjid and tombs are surrounded by a wall with four small towers at the corners, and an entrance gate on the south side. In the steps leading up to this entrance I found in 1838 a broken figure of *Shasti*, the goddess of fecundity, and a pedestal with a short inscription, dated in *Samvat* 1193, or A. D. 1136. The people also affirm that a large statue formerly stood under a tree close by. All of these are now gone, but the fact that two of them were built into the entrance steps is sufficient to show that the mound on which the Masjid stands must once have been the site of some important Hindu building.

The two statues in the village of *Singh Bhawáni* were discovered about 100 years ago in a field close by the brick hovel in which they are now placed. The people call them *Rám* and *Lakshman*, and the attendant Brahman does so too, although the figures have eight arms each, and although the Fish, Tortoise, Boar and Lion Incarnations of Vishnu are represented round the head of one of them. Each of the figures is 3 feet in height, but the whole sculpture is 6 feet. Vishnu is also known by the *discus (chakra)*, and club *(gadá)*, from which he derives his well-known titles of *chakradhar* and *gadádhar*. Along with these sculptures there are some other figures, of which the most important is a statue of the Tántrika Buddhist goddess, *Vajrá Varáhi*. The figure is 2½ feet in height, and has three heads, of which one is porcine, and the usual number of seven hogs is represented on the pedestal. Outside the building there are figures of *Durgá* slaying the *Maheshásur*, or buffalo demon, and of *Siva* and *Párbati* sitting on the bull *Nandi*. In the neighbouring village of *Kutlupur* I found the lintel of a temple door-way with a figure of Vishnu in the middle, showing that the temple had been dedicated to that god. He is represented sitting on the *Garuda*, or eagle, and holding the club and *discus*.

The only remaining place of any note is the *Suraj-kund* or "Tank of the Sun," to the south-east of *Makarandnagar*. It is now nearly dried up, and at the time of my visit its bed was planted with potatoes. But it is one of the oldest places of worship in Kanoj, and an annual fair is still held on its bank in the month of *Bhádon* (August—September). Close beside it there is a modern templo of *Mahádeva*, which is said to have replaced a ruined one of some antiquity. To the south-west of *Makaranduagar* there are three mounds covered with broken bricks and pottery; and under a tree on the south mound, are collected a number of fragments, of sculpture at a spot dedicated to *Maorári* Devi.

Most of the ancient monuments of Kanoj that are noticed by the Chinese pilgrims are of course Buddhist; but numerous as they were, I am unable to do more than offer conjectures more or less probable regarding their sites, as Muhammadan spoliation has not left a single place standing to give even a faint clue towards identification. The position of one of the most remarkable of the monuments is rendered more than usually doubtful by the conflicting evidence of the two pilgrims. According to Fa Hian, the great *Stupa* of *Asoka*, 200 feet in height, which was built on the spot where Buddha had preached on the instability of human existence, was situated at 6 or 7 *li* to the west of the town, and on the north bank of the Ganges. But according to Hwen Thsang, this great Stupa was situated at 6 or 7 *li* to the south-east of the capital, and on the south bank of the Ganges. Now, as the ground to the north of the Ganges, as it existed during the first centuries of the Christian era, was very low, and therefore liable to inundation, it seems highly improbable that any monument would have been erected in such an insecure position. I conclude, therefore, that Hwen Thsang's account is most likely right, but I failed in my search for any remains of this vast monument in the position indicated, that is, at rather more than one mile to the south-east of the capital, and on the south bank of the *Chota Gangá*.

To the north-west of the town Hwen Thsang places another *Stupa* of Asoka; but as he gives no distance, the mere bearing is too vague to enable us to fix upon the site with any probability. Perhaps the small village of *Kapatya*, or *Kaptcswari*, nearly opposite the burnt dâk bungalow, is the most probable site; but, although there are the remains of brick buildings in its vicinity, there is nothing to indicate the previous existence of any large *Stupa*. A smaller *Stupa* containing the hair and nails of Buddha has also disappeared, as well as the memorial monument to the four Buddhas.

To the south of the town, and close to the Ganges, there were three monasteries, with similar looking walls, but differing gateways. In one of these monasteries there was a *Vihára* or chapel which possessed a tooth of Buddha preserved in a casket adorned with precious stones raised on a high pedestal. This tooth was shown daily to crowds of people, although the tax charged for its exhibition was "a large piece of gold." Perfumes were burned before it by thousands of votaries, and the flowers which were strewn in profusion over it were devoutly believed never to conceal the casket. Right and left in front of the monasteries there were two *Viháras*, each about 100 feet in height. Their foundations were of stone, but their walls of brick. In front of each *Vihára* there was a small monastery. The most probable site of the three monasteries and the *Vihára* with the tooth of Buddha seems to me to be the large mound immediately to the south of the *Kshen Kali Bárj*, to the south-east of the town, and on the the immediate bank of the river. This is now called the *Mahalla* of *Lála Misr Tola*. The mound is covered with broken bricks, but no remains of any extensive buildings are now visible.

At a short distance to the south-east of the three monasteries there was a lofty *Vihára*, 200 feet in height, which enshrined a statue of Buddha 30 feet high. The foundations of the building were of stone, but the walls of brick. On the surrounding walls of the *Vihára*, which were of stone, were sculptured all the acts of Buddha's life until he became a *Bodhisatwa*. The position of this lofty *Vihára* was most probably on the large mound in the midst of the present *Bhatpuri Mahalla*, which stands about 800 feet to the south-east of the mound in the *Mahalla* of *Lála Misr Tola*. There are no remains now to be seen on this mound, but it is probable that excavations would be attended with success, as there can be little doubt that this was once the site of some important buildings. At a little distance from the *Vihára* towards the south there was a temple, and a little further to the south there was a second temple dedicated to *Siva*. Both of these temples were of the same form and size as the *Viháras* of Buddha. They were built of a blue stone which was highly polished, and adorned with admirable sculptures. The probable position of these Brahmanical temples was on the high mound of *Makhdúm Jahániya*, in the *Sikhána*

Mahalla, which is about 700 feet to the south of the last mentioned mound in the *Bhatpuri* Mahalla. That this mound was the site of one or more Brahmanical temples seems almost certain from my discovery of a figure of *Shasti*, the goddess of fecundity, and of a pedestal bearing the date of *Samvat* 1193, or A. D. 1136, which is posterior to the extinction of Buddhism in Kanoj. I think it probable that excavations in this mound would be attended with success, as the two temples are said to have been built of stone, which no doubt furnished the whole of the materials for the Masjid and tomb of *Makhdûm Jahániya*.

XI. A-YU-TO, OR AYODHYA.

From Kanoj the two Chinese pilgrims followed different routes, Fa Hian having proceeded direct to *Sha-chi* (the modern Ajudhya, near Fyzabad on the Ghâghra), while Hwen Thsang followed the course of the Ganges to Prayâg, or Allahabad. The first stage of both pilgrims would, however, appear to be the same. Fa Hian states that he crossed the Ganges and proceeded 3 *yojans*, or 21 miles, to the forest of *Holi*, where there were several *Stupas* erected on spots where Buddha had "passed, or walked, or sat."[*] Hwen Thsang records that he marched 100 *li*, nearly 17 miles, to the town of *Nava-deva-kula*, which was on the eastern bank of the Ganges, and that at 5 *li*, or nearly 1 mile, to the south-east of the town there was a *Stupa* of Asoka, which was still 100 feet in height, besides some other monuments dedicated to the four previous Buddhas.[†] I think it probable that the two places are the same, and that the site was somewhere near Nobatganj, just above the junction of the *Isan River* and opposite *Nanamow Ghât*. But as there are no existing remains anywhere in that neighbourhood, the place has been most likely swept away by the river. This is rendered almost certain by an examination of the Ganges below the junction of the *Isan*. Formerly the river continued its course almost due south from Nanamow for many miles, but some centuries ago it changed its course first to the south-east for 4 or 5 miles, and then to the south-west for about the same distance, where it rejoined its old bed, leaving an island, some 6 miles in length by 4 in breadth, between the two channels. As Hwen Thsang's account places *Nava-deva-kula* on the very

---

[*] Beal's Fa Hian, C. XVIII.
[†] Julien's Hwen Thsang, II, 265.

site of this island, I conclude that the town as well as the Buddhist monuments must all have been swept away by the change in the river's course.*

On leaving *Nava-deva-kula*, Hwen Thsang proceeded 600 *li*, or 100 miles, to the south-east, and re-crossing the Ganges he reached the capital city of *A-yu-to*, which was 20 *li*, or upwards of 3 miles, in circuit. Both M. Julien and M. St. Martin have identified this place with *Ayodhya*, the once celebrated capital of Rama. But though I agree with them as to the probable identification of the name as that of the country, I differ with them altogether in looking for the capital along the line of the *Ghâghra River*, which is due east from Kanoj, whereas Hwen Thsang states that his route was to the south-east. It is, of course, quite possible that the pilgrim may occasionally use the generic name of Ganges as the appellation of any large river, such, for instance, as the *Ghâghra*; but in the present case, where the recorded bearing of south-east agrees with the course of the Ganges, I think it is almost certain that the Ganges itself was the river intended by the pilgrim. But by adopting the line of the Ganges we encounter a difficulty of a different kind in the great excess of the distance between two such well known places as Kanoj and Prayâg. According to Hwen Thsang's route, he first made 100 *li* to *Nava-deva-kula*, then 600 *li* to *Ayutho*, then 300 *li* by water to *Hayamukha*, and lastly 700 *li* to *Prayâga*. All these distances added together make a total of 1,700 *li*, or 283 miles, which is just 100 miles, or 600 *li*, in excess of the true distance. But as a part of the journey, viz., 300 *li*, or 50 miles, was performed by water, the actual excess may, perhaps, not be more than 85 or 90 miles; although it is doubtful whether the distance of 300 *li* may not have been the road measurement and not the river distance. It is sufficient for our purpose to know that Hwen Thsang's recorded measurement is somewhere about 100 miles in excess of the truth. The only explanation of this error that suggests itself to me is, that there may have been an accidental alteration of one set of figures, such as 600 *li* for 60 *li*, or 700 *li* for 70 *li*. Supposing that the former

---

* If we might read 10 li instead of 100 li, this place might be identified with *Jhuball*, which is situated on the Choia Gungi about 2 miles below Kanoj. The two names are precisely the same, excepting that the modern one has dropped the two initial syllables *nava*, or "new," which, however appropriate in the time of the Chinese pilgrim, would almost certainly have been dropped in the course of a few centuries.—See Julien's Hwen Thsang, II. 266.

was the case, the distance would be shortened by 540 *li*, or 90 miles, and if the latter, by 630 *li*, or 105 miles. This mode of correction brings the pilgrim's account into fair accordance with the actual distance of 160 miles between Kanoj and Prayág.

By adopting the first supposition, Hwen Thsang's distance from *Nava-deva-kula* to the capital of *Ayutho* will be only 60 *li*, or 10 miles, to the south-east, which would bring him to the site of an ancient city named *Kákúpur*, just 1 mile to the north of Seorájpoor, and 20 miles to the north-west of Cawnpoor. If we adopt the latter correction, the pilgrim's distance to *Ayutho* of 600 *li*, or 100 miles, will remain unchanged, and this would bring him *via Mánikpur*, which is also an ancient place. By the first supposition the subsequent route would have been from *Kákúpur* to *Daundiakhera* by boat, a distance of exactly 50 miles, or 300 *li*, and from thence to *Prayág*, a distance of more than 100 miles, which agrees with the 700 *li*, or 116 miles, of the pilgrim. By the second supposition the subsequent route would have been from *Khara* to *Papamow* by water, about 50 miles, and thence to Prayág, about 8 miles of land, which agrees with the 70 *li* of the proposed correction. In favour of this last supposition is the fact that the bearing from *Khara* to *Papamow* of east by south is more in accordance with Hwen Thsang's recorded east direction than the south-east bearing of Daundiakhera from Kákúpur. I confess, however, that I am more inclined to adopt the former correction, which places the chief city of *Ayutho* at Kákúpur, and the town of *Hayamukha* at Daundiakhera, as we know that the last was the capital of the *Bais Rajputs* for a considerable period. I am partly inclined to this opinion by a suspicion that the name of *Kákúpur* may be connected with that *Bágud*, or *Vágud*, of the Tibetan books. According to this authority a *Sákya*, named *Shámpaka*, on being banished from Kapiln retired to *Bágud*, carrying with him some of Buddha's hairs and nail-parings, over which he built a *chaitya*. He was made King of *Bágud*, and the monument was named after himself *(? Shámpaká Stupa)*.* No clue is given as to the position of *Bágud*; but as I know of no other name that resembles it, I am induced to think that it is

---

* Csoma de Körös in Asiatic Researches, XX, p. 88.

probably the same place as the *Ayutho* of Hwen Thsang, which was also possessed of a *Stupa* containing some hairs and nail-parings of Buddha. *Kákúpur* is well-known to the people of Kanoj, who affirm that it was once a large city with a Raja of its own. The existing remains of *Kákúpur* consist of numerous foundations formed of large bricks, and more particularly of a connected set of walls of some large building which the people call "the palace." I have not yet visited this place, which lay out of my line of route, but I hope to have an opportunity of examining it hereafter.

XII. HAYAMUKHA OR AYOMUKHA.

From *Ayutho* the Chinese pilgrim proceeded a distance of 300 *li*, or 50 miles, down the Ganges by boat to *O-ye-mu-khi*, which was situated on the north bank of the river. M. Julien reads this name as *Hayamukha*, equivalent to "Horse face," or "Iron face," which was the name of one of the *Dánavas* or Titans.[*] Neither of these names, however, gives any clue to the site of the old city; but if I am right in my identification of *Ayutho* with *Kákúpur*, it is almost certain that *Ayomukha* must be the same as Daundiakhera. Hwen Thsang makes the circuit of the town 20 *li*, or upwards of 3 miles, but *Daundikhera* presents no appearance of having ever been so large. There still exist the ruins of an old fort or citadel, 385 feet square, with the walls of two buildings which are called the Raja's and Rani's palaces. The foundation of this citadel is attributed to Raja Raghunâth Sinh, but he was apparently some comparatively modern *Thákur*, or petty Chief, as Daundiakhera is universally allowed to have been the capital of the *Bais* Rajputs, who claim descent from the famous Sálivâhan. As there are no remains of any buildings which can be identified with the monuments described by Hwen Thsang, the actual site of Ayomukha must still remain doubtful.

XIII. PRAYAGA, OR ALLAHABAD.

From Ayomukha the pilgrim proceeded 700 *li*, or 110 miles, to the south-east, to *Prayága*, the well known place of pilgrimage at the junction of the Ganges and Jumna, where

---

[*] Julien's Hwen Thsang, II., p. 274.—See my "Ancient Geography of India," p. 387. "*Daundia* means simply a "drum-beater," and was probably applied to some unimportant, who took up his abode on the *kera*, or mound; and as this name is not likely to have been imposed on the place until it was in ruins, the difference of name offers no impediment to the identification of Daundiakhera with Hayamukha.

PRAYAGA, OR ALLAHABAD

Akbar some centuries later built his fort of *Ilâhabâs*, or *Allâhâbâd*, as it was afterwards called by Shahjahan. The distance and bearing given by Hwen Thsang agree almost exactly with those of Prayâga from Daundiakhera. The distance is 104 miles by the nearest road to the south of the Ganges; but as the pilgrim followed the north road, the distance must have been increased to about 115 or 120 miles. According to him the city was situated at the confluence of the two rivers, but to the west of a large sandy plain. In the midst of the city there was a Brahmanical temple, to which the presentation of a single piece of money procured as much merit as that of one thousand pieces elsewhere. Before the principal room of the temple there was a large tree with wide-spreading branches, which was said to be the dwelling of an anthropophagous demon. The tree was surrounded with human bones, the remains of pilgrims who had sacrificed their lives before the temple—a custom which had been observed from time immemorial.*

I think there can be little doubt that the famous tree here described by the Chinese pilgrim is the well known *Akshay Bat*, or "undecaying Banian tree," which is still an object of worship at Allahabad. This tree is now situated underground at one side of a pillared court, which would appear to have been open formerly, and which is, I believe, the remains of the temple described by Hwen Thsang. The temple is situated inside the fort of Allahabad to the east of the Ellenborough Barracks, and due north from the stone pillar of Asoka and Samudra Gupta. Originally both tree and temple must have been on the natural ground level; but from the constant accumulation of rubbish they have been gradually earthed up until the whole of the lower portion of the temple has disappeared underground. The upper portion has long ago been removed, and the only access to the *Akshay Bat* now available is by a flight of steps which leads down to a square pillared court-yard. This court has apparently once been open to the sky, but it is now closed in to secure darkness and mystery for the holy Fig tree.

The *Akshay Bat* is next mentioned by Rashid-ud-din in the *Jámiut-tawárikh*, in which he states that the "tree of *Prág*" is situated at the confluence of the Jumna and

---
* Julien's Hwen Thsang, II., p. 276.

Ganges. As most of his information was derived from *Abu Rihán*, the date of this notice may with great probability be referred to the time of Mahmud of Ghazni. In the 7th century a great sandy plain, 2 miles in circuit, lay between the city and the confluence of the rivers, and as the tree was in the midst of the city, it must have been at least one mile from the confluence. But nine centuries later, in the beginning of Akbar's reign, Abdul Kádir speaks of the "tree from which people cast themselves into the river."* From this statement I infer that, during the long period that intervened between the time of Hwen Thsang and that of Akbar, the two rivers had gradually carried away the whole of the great sandy plain, and had so far encroached upon the city as to place the holy tree on the very brink of the water. Long before this time the old city had no doubt been deserted, for we know that the fort of *Iláhábád* was founded on its site in the 21st year of Akbar's reign, that is, in A. H. 982, or A. D. 1572. Indeed, the way in which Abu Rihán speaks of the "tree" instead of the city of Prág, leads me to believe that the city itself had already been deserted before his time. As far as I am aware, it is not once mentioned in any Muhammadan history until it was refounded by Akbar.†

As the old city of *Prayág* has totally disappeared, we can scarcely expect to find any traces of the various Buddhist monuments which were seen and described by the Chinese pilgrim in the 7th century. Indeed, from their position to the south-west of the city, it seems very probable that they may have been washed away by the Jumna even before the final abandonment of the city, as the course of that river for three miles above the confluence has been due west and east of many centuries past. At any rate, it is quite certain that no remains of those buildings are now to be seen; the only existing Hindu monument being the well known stone pillar which bears the inscriptions of Asoka, Samudra Gupta, and Jahángir. As Hwen Thsang makes no mention of this pillar, it is probable that it was not standing in his day. Even its original position is not exactly known, but it was probably not far from its present site. It was first erected by King Asoka about B. C. 240 for the purpose of inscribing

---

* Elliot's Muhammadan Historians of India, p. 249.
† Reinaud, Fragments Arabs, etc., p. 103, and Dowson's Elliot, I., 55.

his edicts regarding the propagation of Buddhism. It was next made use of by Samudra Gupta, about the second century of the Christian era, for the record of his extensive sovereignty over the various nations of India—from Nepâl to the Dakhan, and from Gujarât to Assam. Lastly, it was re-erected by the Mogul Emperor Jahângir to commemorate his accession to the throne in the year 1605 A. D. These are the three principal inscriptions on the Allahabad Pillar, but there are also a number of minor records of the names of travellers and pilgrims of various dates, from about the beginning of the Christian era down to the present century. Regarding these minor inscriptions, James Prinsep remarks that "it is a singular fact that the periods at which the pillar has been overthrown can be thus determined with nearly as much certainty from this desultory writing, as can the epochs of its being re-erected from the more formal inscriptions recording the latter event. Thus that it was overthrown some time after its first erection by the great Asoka in the middle of the third century before Christ, is proved by the longitudinal or random insertion of several names in a character intermediate between No. 1 and No. 2, in which the *m, b*, &c., retain the old form." Of one of these names he remarks—"Now it would have been exceedingly difficult, if not impossible, to have cut the name No. 10 up and down at right angles to the other writing, *while the pillar was erect*, to say nothing of the place being out of reach, unless a scaffold were erected on purpose, which would hardly be the case, since the object of an ambitious visitor would be defeated by placing his name out of sight and in an unreadable position." The pillar "was erected as Samudra Gupta's arm, and there it probably remained until overthrown again by the idol-breaking zeal of the Musulmâns; for we find no writings on it of the *Pâla*, or Sârnâth type (*i. e.*, of the tenth century), but a quantity appears with plain legible dates from the *Samvat* year 1420, or A. D. 1363, down to 1660 odd, and it is remarkable that these occupy one side of the shaft, or that which was uppermost when the pillar was in a prostrate position. A few detached and ill executed Nâgari names with *Samvat* dates of 1800 odd, "show that ever since it was laid on the ground again by General Garstin, the passion for recording visits of piety or curiosity has been at work."* In this last passage James Prinsep has,

---

* Bengal Asiatic Society's Journal, 1837, p. 967.

I believe, made a mistake in the name of the Vandal Engineer who overthrew the stone pillar because it stood in the way of his new line of rampart near the gateway. It was General Kyd, and not General Garstin, who was employed to stengthen the Fort of Allahabad, and his name is still preserved in the suburb of Kydganj, on the Jumna, immediately below the city.

The pillar was again set up in 1838 by Captan Edward Smith, of the Engineers, to whom the design of the present capital is entirely due. At first it was intended to have placed a fancy flower as an appropriate finish to the pillar, but as the people had a tradition that the column was originally surmounted by the figure of a lion, it was suggested by a committee of the Asiatic Society that the design of the new capital should be made as nearly as possible the same as the original, of which the Bakra and Lauriya pillars were cited as examples. The lion statues which crown the bell capitals of these two pillars I have seen and admired, and I can affirm that they are the figures of veritable lions. Both of them are represented half couchant, with the head raised and the mouth open. The bell capital swells out boldly towards the top to receive a massive abacus, which forms the plinth of the statue. In these examples the broad swelling capital is in harmony with the stout and massive column. But the new capital designed by Captain Smith is, in my opinion, a signal failure. The capital lessens towards the top, and is surmounted by an abacus of less diameter than that of the pillar itself. The animal on the top is small and recumbent, and altogether the design is insignificant. Indeed, it looks to me not unlike a stuffed poodle stuck on the top of an inverted flower pot.

According to the common tradition of the people, the name of Prayága was derived from a Brahman, who lived during the reign of Akbar. The story is that when the Emperor was building the fort, the walls on the river face repeatedly fell down in spite of all the precautions taken by the architect. On consulting some wise men, Akbar was informed that the foundations could only be secured by being laid in human blood. A proclamation was then made, when a Brahman, called Prayága, voluntarily offered his life on the condition that the fort should bear his name. This idle story, which is diligently related to the pilgrims who visit

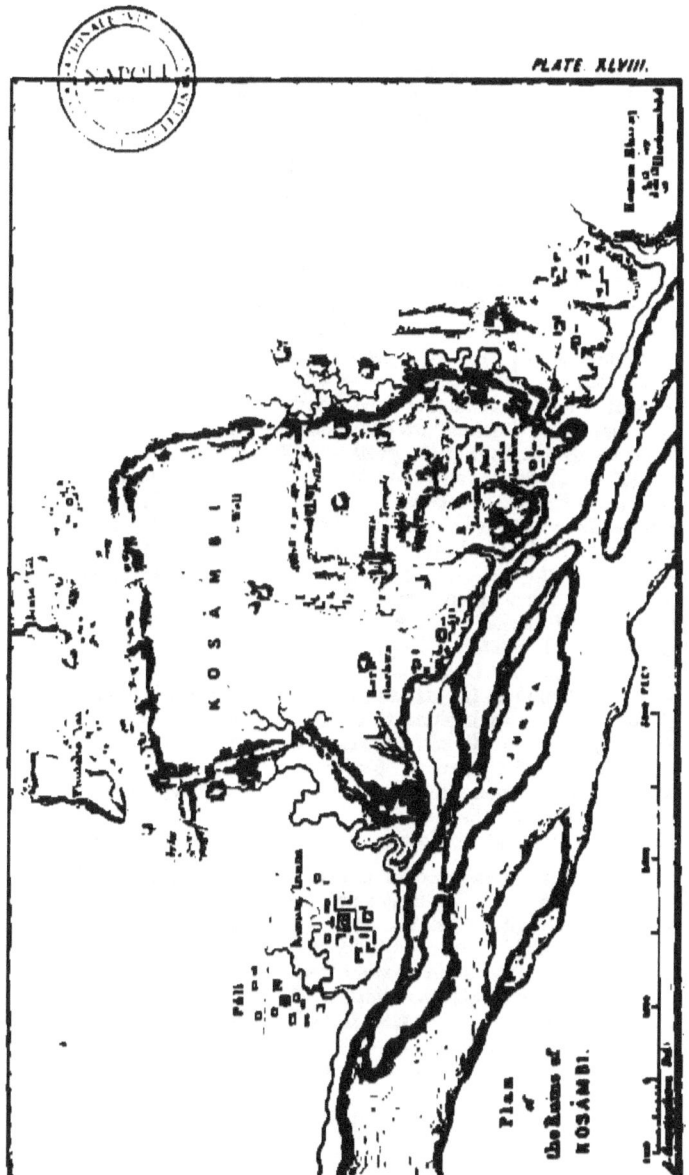

PLATE XLVIII.

Plan of the Ruins of KOSÁMBI.

the *Akshay Bat*, may at least serve one useful purpose in warning us not to place too much faith in these local traditions. The name of *Prayága* is recorded by Hwen Thsang in the 7th century, and is, in all probability, as old as the reign of Asoka, who set up the stone pillar about B. C. 240, while the fort was not built until the end of the 16th century.

XIV. KOSAM, OR KOSAMBI.

The city of *Kosámbi* was one of the most celebrated places in ancient India, and its name was famous amongst Brahmans as well as Buddhists. The city is said to have been founded by *Kusamba*, the tenth in descent from Pururavas; but its fame begins only with the reign of *Chakra*, the eighth in descent from *Arjuna Pándu*, who made Kosámbi his capital after Hastinapura had been swept away by the Ganges. If the date of the great war *(Mahábhárata)* be fixed at 1426 B. C., which, as I have already shown in my account of Delhi, is the most probable period, then the date of Chakra will be about 1200 or 1150 B. C. Twenty-two of his descendants are said to have reigned in Kosámbi down to Kshemaka, the last of the dynasty; but it seems almost certain that some names must have been omitted, as the very longest period of 30 years which can be assigned to a generation of Eastern Kings will place the close of the dynasty about B. C. 500, and make the period of *Udáyana* about 630 to 600 B. C. If we take all the recorded names of the different authorities, then the number of generations will be 24, which will place the close of the dynasty in B. C. 440, and fix the reign of *Udáyana* in 570 to 540 B. C. As Udáyana is represented by the Buddhists to have been a contemporary of Buddha, this date may be accepted as wonderfully accurate for so remote a period of Indian History.

Kosámbi is mentioned in the Rámáyana, the earliest of the Hindu Poems, which is generally allowed to have been composed before the Christian era. The story of *Udáyana*, King of Kosámbi, is referred to by the Poet Káli Dása in his *Megha-duta*, or "Cloud Messenger," when he says that *Avanti* (or Ujain) is great with the number of those versed in the tale of Udáyana."[*] Now Káli Dása flourished shortly after

---
[*] H. H. Wilson, "Megha-duta," note 64.

A. D. 500. In the Vrihat Katha, of Somadeva, the story of Udáyana is given at full length, but the author has made a mistake in the genealogy between the two *Satánikas*. Lastly, the kingdom of *Kosámbi*, or *Kosámba Mandala*, is mentioned in an inscription taken from the gateway of the fort of *Khara*, which is dated in *Samvat* 1092, or A. D. 1035, at which period it would appear to have been independent of Kanoj.* Kosámbi, the capital of Vatsa Raja, is the scene of the pleasing drama of *Ratnávali*, or the "necklace," which was composed in the reign of King Harsha Deva, who is most probably the same as Harsha Vardhana of Kanoj, as the opening prelude describes amongst the assembled audiences "princes from various realms recumbent at his feet."† This we know from Hwen Thsang to have been true of the Kanoj prince, but which even a Brahman could scarcely have asserted of Harsha Deva of Kashmir. The date of this notice will, therefore, lie between 607 and 648 A. D.

But the name of *Udáyana*, King of Kosámbi, was perhaps even more famous among the Buddhists. In the Mahá-wanso, which was composed in the 5th century A. D., the venerable Yasa is said to have fled from "*Vaisdli* to Kosámbi, just before the assembly of the second Buddhist Synod.‡ In the Lalita Vistára, which was translated into Chinese, between 70 and 76 A. D., and which must, therefore, have been composed not later than the beginning of the Christian era, Udáyana Vatsa, son of Satánika, King of Kosámbi, is said to have been born on the same day as Buddha. In other Coylonese books, Kosámbi is named as one of the 19 capital cities of ancient India. Udáyana Vatsa, the son of Satánika, is also known to the Tibetans as the King of Kosámbi. In the Ratnaváli he is called Vatsa Raja, or King of the Vatsas, and his capital *Vatsa-pattana*, which is, therefore, only another name for Kosámbi. In this celebrated city Buddha is said have spent the 6th and 9th years of his Buddhahood. Lastly, Hwen Thsang relates that the famous statue of Buddha in red sandal wood, which was made by King Udáyana during the life time of the teacher, still existed under a stone dome in the ancient palace of King Udáyana.

* Asiatic Researches, IX., 123, and Journal, Asiatic Society's, of Bengal, V., 731.
† Wilson's Hindu Theatre, "Ratnavali," prelude, II., 261.
‡ Turnour's translation, p. 16.

The site of this great city, the capital of the later Pandu Princes, and the shrine of the most sacred of all the statues of Buddha, has long been sought in vain. The Brahmans generally asserted that it stood either on the Ganges, or close to it, and the discovery of the name of *Kosâmbi mandala*, or "Kingdom of Kosâmbi," in an inscription over the gateway of the fort of *Khara*, seemed to confirm the general belief, although the south-west bearing from Prayâga or Allahabad, as recorded by Hwen Thsang, points unmistakably to the line of the Jumna. In January 1861 Mr. E. C. Bayley informed me that he believed the ancient Kosâmbi would be found in the old village of Kosam, on the Jumna, about 30 miles above Allahabad. In the following month I met Babu Siva Prasâd, of the Educational Department, who takes a deep and intelligent interest in all archæological subjects, and from him I learned that *Kosam* is still known as *Kosâmbi-nagar*, that it is even now a great resort of the Jains, and that only one century ago it was a large and flourishing town. This information was quite sufficient to satisfy me that *Kosam* was the actual site of the once famous Kosâmbi. Still, however, there was no direct evidence to show that the city was situated on the Jumna; but this missing link in the chain of evidence I shortly afterwards found in the curious legend of Bakkula.* The infant Bakkula was born at Kosâmbi; and while his mother was bathing in the *Jumna*, he accidentally fell into the river, and being swallowed by a fish was carried to Banâras. There the fish was caught and sold to the wife of a nobleman, who, on opening it, found the young child still alive inside, and at once adopted it as her own. The true mother hearing of this wonderful escape of the infant, proceeded to Banâras, and demanded the return of the child, which was of course refused. The matter was then referred to the King, who decided that both of the claimants were mothers of the child —the one by *maternity*, the other by *purchase*. The child was accordingly named *Bakula*; that is, of "two *kulas*, or races." He reached the age of 90 years without once having been ill, when he was converted by the preaching of Buddha, who declared him to be "the chief of that class of his disciples who were free from disease." After this

---

* Hardy, "Manual of Buddhism," p. 501.

he is said to have lived 90 years more, when he became an *arhat*, or Buddhist saint.

But the negative kind of merit which Bakkula acquired by his freedom from disease was not appreciated by Asoka, as we learn from a very curious legend which is preserved in the Divya Avadâna.* In the first ardour of his conversion to Buddhism the zealous Asoka wished to do honour to all the places which the life and teaching of Buddha had rendered famous, by the erection of *Stupas*, and the holy Upagupta volunteered to point out the sacred spots. Accordingly the goddess of the Sâl tree, who witnessed Buddha's birth, appeared to Asoka and vouched for the authenticity of the venerated tree, which had given support to Mâyâ-Devi, at the birth of the infant Sâkya. Other holy sites are also indicated, such as the *Bodhi-drûm*, or sacred Pipal tree at Buddha-Gaya, under which Buddha sat for six years in meditation; and the Sâl trees at Kusinagura, beneath which he obtained *Nirvâna*, besides various spots rendered famous by the acts of his principal disciples, Sâriputra, Maudgalyâyana, Kâsyapa, and Ananda. To all these holy places the pious King allotted large sums of money for the erection of *Stupas*. Upagupta then pointed out the holy place of Bakkula at Kosâmbi. "And what was the merit of this sage?" asked Asoka. "He lived," answered Upagupta, "to a great age without once having known disease." "On him," said the King, "I bestow one farthing *(K'dkani)*."† In Burnouf's version of this story Bakkula is said to be the disciple who had encountered the fewest obstacles, from which Asoka rightly argued that the fewer the obstacles the less the merit. The same idea is even more tersely expressed by the old author of the "Land of Cockaigne" in describing the sinlessness of its inhabitants:

"Very virtuous may they be
"Who temptation never see."

As this legend of Bakkula is sufficient to prove that the famous city of Kausâmbi was situated on the Jumna, it now only remains to show that the distance of Kosam from Allahabad corresponds with that between Prayâga and

---

* Burnouf, "Buddhisme Indien," p. 391.
† The *K'ckani* was the fourth part of the copper *pana*, and was, therefore, worth only 20 cowries. Its weight was 80 ratikas, or *ratis* of copper, or 1¾ x 20 = 36 grains.

Kosámbi, as recorded by Hwen Thsang. Unfortunately this distance is differently stated in the life and in the travels of of the Chinese pilgrim.* In the former, the distance is given as 50 *li*, and in the latter as 500 *li*, whilst in the return journey to China the pilgrim states that, between Prayág and Kosámbi, he travelled for *seven* days through a vast forest and over bare plains. Now, as the village of Kosam is only 31 miles from the fort of Allahabad, the last statement would seem to preclude all possibility of its identification with the ancient Kosámbi. But, strange to say, it affords the most satisfactory proof of their identity; for the subsequent route of the pilgrim to Sankissa is said to have occupied one month; and as the whole distance from Prayág to Sankissa is only 200 miles, the average length of the pilgrim's daily march was not more than 6½ miles. This slow progress is most satisfactorily accounted for, by the fact that the march from Prayág to Sankissa was a religious procession, headed by the great King Harsha Vardhana of Kanoj, with a train of no less than 18 tributary Kings, besides many thousands of Buddhist monks, and all the crowd of an Indian camp. According to this reckoning, the distance from Prayág to Kosámbi would be 38 miles, which corresponds very closely with the actual road distance as I found it. By one route on going to Kosam, I made the distance 37 miles, and by the return route 35 miles. The only probable explanation of Hwen Thsang's varying distance of 50 *li* and 500 *li* that occurs to me is, that as he converted the Indian *yojanas* into Chinese *li* at the rate of 40 *li* per *yojana*, or of 10 *li* per *kos*, he must have written 150 *li*, the equivalent to 15 *kos*, which is the actual distance across the fields for foot passengers from Kosam to the fort of Allahabad, according to the reckoning of the people of Kosam itself. But whether this explanation be correct or not, it is quite certain that the present Kosam stands on the actual site of the ancient *Kosámbi*; for not only do the people themselves put forward this claim, but it is also distinctly stated in an inscription of the time of Akbar, which is recorded on the great stone pillar, still standing in the midst of the ruins, that this is *Kausámbi pura*.

The present ruins of Kosámbi consist of an immense fortress formed of earthen ramparts and bastions, with a

* See Julien's Hwen Thsang, I., 121, 300 (?, and II., 283.

circuit of 23,100 feet, or exactly 4 miles and 3 furlongs.*
The ramparts have a general height of from 30 to 35 feet
above the fields, but the bastions are considerably higher;
those on the north face risings to upwards of 50 feet, while
those at the south-west and south-east angles are more than
60 feet. Originally there were ditches all round the fortress,
but at present there are only a few shallow hollows at the
foot of the rampart. The parapets were of brick and stone;
but, although the remains of these defences can be traced
nearly all round, I could not find any portion of the old
wall with a facing sufficiently perfect to enable me to determine its thickness. The large size of the bricks, which are
19 inches long by 12½ by 2⅜, shows that these are the ruins
of very old walls. In shape the fortress may be described
as an irregular rectangle, with its longer sides running
almost due north and south. The length of the different
faces is as follows:—

North front	...	4,500 feet.
South	...	6,000 ,,
East	...	7,500 ,,
West	...	5,100 ,,
Total	...	23,100 feet.

The difference in length between the north and south
fronts is due to the original extension of the fortress on the
river face; but the difference between the east and west
fronts is, I believe, chiefly, if not wholly, due to the loss of
the south-west angle of the ramparts by the gradual en-
croachments of the Jumna. There are no traces now left
of the western half of the ramparts on the southern face,
and the houses of the village of *Garhawá* are standing on the
very edge of the cliff overhanging the river. The reach of
the river also from the *Pakka Burj* at the south-west angle
of the fortress up to the hill of *Prabhása*, a clear straight
run of four miles, bears 12 degrees to the north of east,
whereas in the time of Hwen Thsang there were two *Stupas*
and a cave at a distance of 1¼ miles to the south-west of
Kosámbi. From all these concurring circumstances, I conclude that the west front of the fortress was originally as

---

* See Plate XLVIII, for a map of the ruins of Kosam.

nearly as possible of the same length as the east front. This would add 2,400 feet, or nearly half a mile to the length of the west front, and would increase the whole circuit of the ramparts to 4 miles and 7 furlongs, which is within one furlong of the measurement of 5 miles, or 30 *li* recorded by Hwen Thsang. In three main points therefore of name, size, and position, the present Kosam corresponds most exactly with the ancient Kosâmbí, as it is described by the Chinese pilgrim in the 7th century.

Viewed from the outside, the ruins of Kosâmbí present a most striking appearance. My previous enquiries had led me to except only a ruined mound some 20 or 30 feet in height covered with broken bricks. What was my surprise, therefore, when still at some distance from the place on the north-east side, to behold extending for about 2 miles a long line of lofty earthen mounds as high as most of the trees. I felt at once that this was the celebrated Kosâmbí, the capital of the far-famed Raja Udâyana. On reaching the place I mounted one of the huge earthen bastions, from whence I had a clear view of the interior. This was very uneven but free from jangal, the whole surface being thickly covered with broken bricks. In many places the bricks were partially cleared away to form fields, but in others the broken bricks were so thickly strown that the earth beneath was scarcely discernible. But I was disappointed to find that there were no prominent masses of ruin,—the only object that caught the eye being a modern Jain temple. I recognized the positions of six gates by the deep depressions in the lines of rampart. There are two of these openings on each of the three land faces of the fortress.

The present village of Kosam consists of two distinct portions, named *Kosam Inâm* and *Kosam Khirâj*, or "Rent-free" and "Rent-paying" Kosm, the former being on the west, and the latter on the east side of the old fortress. Inside the ramparts, and on the bank of the Jumna, there are two small villages called *Garhawâ Barâ* and *Garhawâ Chota*, their names being no doubt derived from their position within the fort or *garh*. Beyond Kosam Inâm is the large village of Pâli, containing 100 houses, and beyond Kosam Khirâj on the bank of the Jumna stands the hamlet of *Gop-Sahawa*. To the north there is another hamlet called *Ambâ-Kua*, because it possesses a large old well surrounded by a grove of mango trees. All these villages together do not contain more than 350 or 400 houses, with about 2,000 inhabitants.

The great object of veneration at Kosâmbi was the celebrated statue of Buddha in red sandal wood, which was devoutly believed to have been made during the life time of Buddha by a sculptor whom King Udâyana was permitted to send up to the *Trayastrinsa* heaven, while the great Teacher was explaining his law to his mother Mâyâ. The statue was placed under a stone dome, within the precincts of the palace of Udâyana, which is described by Hwen Thsang as being situated in the very middle of Kosâmbi. This description shows that the place must have occupied the position of the great central mass of ruin, which is now covered by a small Jain temple. The temple is said to have been built in 1834, and is dedicated to *Pârasnâth*. By the people, however, it is generally called *Deora* or the Temple, which was the old name of the mound, and which, therefore, points unmistakably to the position of the ancient temple that once held the famous statue of Buddha. The foundations of a large building are still traceable both to the east and west of the temple; but there are no remains either of sculpture or of architectural ornament. But in the village of Bara Garhawâ, distant 1,500 feet to the south-west, I found two sculptured pillars of a Buddhist railing, and the pedestal of a statue inscribed with the well-known Buddhist profession of faith, beginning with *Ye dharmma hetu prabhaoâ*, &c., in characters of the 8th or 9th century. In the village of Chota Garhawâ, distant half a mile to the south-east, I found a small square pillar sculptured on three faces with representations of *Stupas*. The discovery of these undoubted Buddhist remains is alone sufficient to prove that some large Buddhist establishment must once have existed inside the walls of Kosâmbi. I would, therefore, assign the two pillars of the Buddhist railing and the inscribed statue to the great *Vihar* in the palace, which contained the famous sandal wood statue of Buddha. The third pillar I would assign to the *Stupa* which contained the hair and nails of Buddha, as it was situated inside the south-east corner of the city, on the very site of Chota Garhawâ, where the pillar itself was found. The two railing pillars found at Barâ Garhawâ are sculptured with figures of a male and female; and as both of these figures exhibit the very same scanty clothing as is seen in those of the bas-reliefs of the Sánchi Tope, near Bhilsa, I would refer the Kosámbi pillars to the same age, or somewhere about the beginning of the Christian era.

The only other existing relic of Buddhism inside the fort is a large stone monolith similar to those of Allahabad and Delhi, excepting only that it bears no ancient inscription. This column is now standing at an angle of 5°, about one-half of the shaft being buried in a mound of brick ruins. The portion of the shaft above ground is 14 feet in length, and close by there are two broken pieces, measuring respectively 4 feet 6 inches and 2 feet 3 inches. I made an excavation completely round the pillar to a depth of 7 feet 4 inches, without reaching the end of the polished portion of the shaft. All these figures added together give a total length of 28 feet; but the pillar was no doubt several feet longer, as the shafts of all the five known monoliths exceed 30 feet. The smallest diameter is 20¼ inches, or nearly the same as that of the *Lauriya-Ara-Raj* pillar, and as the diameter increases in nearly the same proportion, I presume that the Kosámbi pillar most probably had about the same height of 36 feet. According to the villagers, this pillar was in one piece as late as 50 years ago; but it was leaning against a large *Nimb* tree. The tree was old and hollow, and some cowherds having accidentally set fire to it, the top of the pillar was broken by the heat. Several different persons affirmed that the shaft was originally nearly double its present height. This would make the height above ground somewhat less than twice 14 feet, or say about 27 feet, which, added to the ascertained smooth portion of 7 feet 4 inches under ground, would make the original height of the smooth shaft upwards of 34 feet.* I found numerous roots of the old tree in my excavation round the pillar. The statement of the people that the Kosámbi pillar has been leaning in its present position as long as they can remember, is curiously corroborated by the fact that an inscription dated in the reign of Akbar is cut across the face of the shaft at an angle of about 50° but parallel to the horizon. It seems

* An excavation was made in 1850 by Mr. Nesbitt, District Engineer, which exposed a total length of 31 feet, when the work was suspended. Mr. Nesbitt suggests the length to exceed 40 feet.

certain, therefore, that the pillar was in its present leaning position as early as the reign of Akbar; and further, as this inscription is within reach of the hand, and as there are also others engraved beneath the present surface of the soil, I conclude that the pillar must have been buried as we now see it for a long time previous to the reign of Akbar.

The inscriptions recorded on the Kosâmbî pillar range from the age of the Guptas down to the present day. The only record of the earliest period is the name of a pilgrim in six letters, which I have not succeeded in reading. At the top of the broken shaft there is an incomplete record of three letters ending in *prabhâra*, which I would ascribe to the 4th or 5th century. The letters, which are three inches in length, are boldly cut, but the line which they form is not parallel to the sides of the pillar. The next inscription in point of time consists of six lines in characters of the 6th or 7th century. As this record is placed on the lower part of the shaft, from 3 to 4 feet beneath the present ground level, and as the lines are perpendicular to the sides of the shaft, I infer that at the time when it was inscribed, the pillar was still standing upright in its original position, and that the surrounding buildings were still in perfect order. This inference is fully borne out by Hwen Thsang's account of the ancient palace of Udâyana with its great Vihâra, 60 feet in height, and its stone dome forming a canopy over the statue of Buddha, all of which would seem to have been in good order at the date of his visit, as he carefully mentions that the two different bath-houses of Buddha, as well as the dwelling-house of Asanga Bodhisatwa were in ruins. Just above this inscription there are several records in the peculiar shell-shaped letters which James Prinsep noticed on the Allahabad pillar, and which I have found on most of the other pillars throughout Northern India. The remaining inscriptions, which are comparatively modern, are all recorded on the upper part of the shaft. That of Akbar's time, which has already been referred to, is in Nâgari as follows:—

Mogal Pâtisâh Akbar Patisâh Gaji; for
Mogal Pâdshâh Akbar Pâdshâh Ghâzi.

This is followed by a short record of a *soni*, or goldsmith, in three lines, below which is a long inscription dated in Samvat

1621, or A. D. 1564, in the early part of Akbar's reign, detailing the genealogy of a whole family of goldsmiths. It is in this inscription that the name of *Kosâmbipura* occurs, the founder of the family, named Anand Râm Dâs, having died at Kosam. The monolith is called *Râm-ka-charri*, "Ram's walking stick," by some, and by others *Bhim-sen-ka-Gadá*, or "Bhim-sen's club." Inside the fort also, about midway between the two villages of *Garhaiwá*, I found a large *lingam*, bearing four heads, with three eyes each, and with the hair massed on the top of each head. The discovery of this costly symbol of Mahadeva shows that the worship of *Siva* must have been firmly established at Kosâmbi at some former period; and as Hwen Thsang mentions the existence of no less than 50 heretical (that is Brahmanical) temples at the time of his visit, I think it probable that the large *lingams* may have belonged to one of those early temples.

To the south-west of *Kosâmbi*, distant 8 or 9 *li*, or 1½ miles, Hwen Thsang describes a lofty *Stupa* of Asoka, 200 feet in height, and a stone cavern of a venomous dragon, in which it was devoutly believed that Buddha had left his shadow. But the truthful pilgrim candidly says that this shadow was not to be seen in his time. If Hwen Thsang's south-west bearing is correct, the holy cave must have been carried away long ago by the encroachment of the Jumna, as the clear reach of the river above Kosâmbi, as far as the hill of Prabhâsa, a distance of 4 miles, now bears 282° from the south-west, of the old city, or 12° to the north of west. The hill of Prabhâsa, which is on the left bank of the Jumna, is the only rock in the *Antarved* or Doab of the Ganges and Jumna. In a hollow between its two peaks stands a modern Jain temple, but there is no cavern, and no trace of any ancient buildings.

At a short distance to the south-east of *Kosâmbi*, there was an ancient monastery containing a *Stupa* of Asoka, 200 feet in height, which was built on the spot where Buddha had explained the law for many years. Beside the monastery, a householder named *Kiu-shi-lo*, formerly had a garden. Fa Hian calls it the garden of *Kiu-sse-lo*; but by the Buddhists of Ceylon it is called the *Ghosika* garden. M. Julien renders the name doubtfully by *Goshira*, but it appears to me that the true name was most probably the Sanskrit

Gosirshn, and the Pali *Gosisa*, which I believe to be still preserved in *Gopahsa*, the name of a small village close to *Chota Garhawa*. This name is now written *Gopshasa*, but as the well known name of Janamejaya is written *Jugmedau*, and also *Jalmedar*, by the half educated people of Kosam, I do not think that the slight difference of spelling between the ancient *Gosisa* and the present Gopshasa, forms any very strong objection to their identification, more especially as the position of the Gosisa garden must have been as nearly as possible on the site of the *Gopshasa* village. There are no ancient remains about this village; nor, indeed, could we expect to find any traces of the garden. But in the neighbouring village of Kosam *Khiráj* or *Hisámábád*, the vestiges of ancient occupation are found everywhere, and this village I believe to have been the site of the monastery with its lofty *Stupa* of 200 feet, built by *Asoka*, and its similar *Stupa* containing the hair and nails of Buddha. The position of this village, within one-quarter of a mile of the south-east corner of the ancient fort, agrees precisely with the site of the monastery as described by Hwen Thsang, "*à une petite distance au sud-est de la ville.*" In this village squared stones of all sizes may be seen in the walls of most of the houses, and after a little search I succeeded in finding four plain pillars of two different sizes which had once belonged to two different Buddhist railings. Two of these pillars are 4 feet 0 inches in height, with a section of 12½ by 7 inches, which are also the exact dimensions of the largest railing pillars that have been found at Mathura. The other two pillars are 2 feet 0 inches in height with a section of 7 by 3¼ inches, which are the exact dimensions of the smallest sized railing pillars that have been found at Mathura. The larger pillars I would assign to the Buddhist railing, which in all probability once surrounded the lofty *Stupa* of Asoka, and the smaller pillars I would assign to the smaller *Stupa*, which contained the hair and nails of Buddha.

I found also the fragment of a corner pillar with the mortice holes for the reception of the rails on two adjacent sides at right angles to each other. I conclude, therefore, that this pillar must have belonged to the entrance doorway of one of the railings, although its face of 9 inches does not agree with the dimensions of either of the other pillars.

XV. KUSAPURA.

From Kosâmbi the Chinese pilgrim travelled to the north-east, through a vast forest as far as the Ganges, after crossing which his route lay to the north for a distance of 700 *li*, or 117 miles, to the town of *Kia-she-pu-lo*, which M. Julien correctly renders by *Kasapura*. In searching for the site of this place the subsequent route of the pilgrim to *Visâkhâ*, a distance of 170 to 180 *li*, or from 28 to 30 miles, to the north is of equal importance with the bearing and distance from Kosâmbi. For as the Visâkhâ, of Hwen Thsang, as I will presently show, is the same place as the *Sha-chi* of Fa Hian, and the *Sâketa* or Ayodhya of the Hindus, we thus obtain two such well fixed points as Kosâmbi and Ayodhya to guide us in our search. A single glance at the map will be sufficient to show that the old town of *Sultânpur* on the *Gomati* (or Gumti) River is as nearly as possible in the position indicated. Now the Hindu name of this town was *Kusabhavanapura*, or simply *Kusapura*, which is almost the same name as that of Hwen Thsang. Remembering Mr. Bayley's note of information derived from Raja Mân Sinh that there was "a *tope* near Sultânpur," I pitched my tent on one side of the now utterly desolate city, and searched the whole place through most carefully, but all in vain: I could neither find the trace of any tope, nor could I even hear of ancient remains of any kind. On the following day, however, after I had left Sultânpur, I heard that the village of Mahmûdpur, about 5 miles to the north-west, was situated on an ancient mound of somewhat larger size than that of Sultânpur, and on my arrival at Faizabad, I learned from Lieutenant Swetonham, of the Royal Engineers, that there is an old tope to the north-west of Sultânpur, not far from this village. I conclude, therefore, that Sultânpur, the ancient Kusapura, is the same place as the Kasapura of Hwen Thsang, and this identification will be made even more certain on examination of the recorded distances.

On leaving Kosâmbi, the pilgrim proceeded first in a north-east direction to the Ganges, after crossing which he turned to the north to Kasapura, the whole distance being 117 miles. Now, the two great ghâts on the Ganges to the north-east of Kosam are at Mau-Saraya and Pâpamau, the former being 40 miles, and the latter 43 miles distant. But as these two ghâts are close together, and almost immediately to the north of Allahabad, the total distance to Kasapura will be the same whichever place of crossing be taken. From Pāpamau to Sultânpur the direction is due north, and the distance 66 miles, the whole line from Kosam to Sultânpur being 109 miles, which is within 8 miles of the round number of 700 li, or 116⅔ miles as given by Hwen Thsang, while both of the bearings are in exact accordance with his statements.* From Kasapura to *Visākha* the direction followed by the pilgrim was to the north, and the distance was from 170 to 180 li, or from 28 to 38 miles. Now the present city of *Ajudhya*, the ancient *Ayodhya* or Sâketa, is almost due north from *Sultânpur*, the distance being 30 miles to the nearest point, or just six miles in excess of the distance given by Hwen Thsang. As the former of these distances is in default, while the latter is in excess, I would suggest, as a possible alternative, that our measurements should be taken from the village of *Mahmūdpur*, which would make the route from Kosam to the Buddhist establishment near Kasapura up to 114 miles, or within three miles of the number stated by Hwen Thsang, and lessen the subsequent route to Ayodhya from 36 to 31 miles, which is within one mile of the number given by the Chinese pilgrim. As all these bearings are in perfect accordance, and as the names of the two places agree almost exactly, I think that there can be little hesitation in accepting the identification of *Sultânpur* to *Kusapura*, with the Kasapura of Hwen Thsang.

Kusapura or *Kusa-bhavana-pura* is said to have been named after Râma's son Kusa. Shortly after the Muhammadan invasion it belonged to a *Bhar* Raja Nand Kunwar, who was expelled by Sultan Alauddin *Ghori* (read Khilji). The defences of the town were strengthened by the conqueror, who built a mosque and changed the name of the place to Sultânpur. The site of *Kusapura* was, no doubt, selected by its founder as a good military position on account of its being surrounded on three sides by the River Gomati or Gomtī. The place is now utterly desolate; the whole population having been removed to the new civil station on the opposite or south bank of the river. The ruined fort of Sultânpur now forms a large mound, 750 feet square,

---

* Julien. Hwen Thsang, II., 290.

with brick towers at the four corners. On all sides it is surrounded by the huts of the ruined town, the whole together covering a space of about half a mile square, or about two miles in circuit. This estimate of the size of Sultánpur agrees very closely with that of Kusapura given by Hwen Thsang, who describes the place as being 10 *li*, or 1⅔ miles, in circuit.

XVI. DHOPAPAPURA.

Before accompanying the pilgrim to the ancient city of *Sáketa* or *Ayodhya*, I will take the opportunity of describing the famous place of Hindu pilgrimage called *Dhopápapura*, which is situated on the right or west bank of the Gomati River, 18 miles to'the south-east of Sultánpur, and immediately under the walls of the fort of *Garhá*, or *Shirka-Garhi*. The legend of the place is as follows:—After Rama Chandra had killed the giant Rávana he wandered about trying to obtain purification for his guilt in having thus extinguished a portion of the spirit of Brahmá *(Brahmá-ka-ans)*; but all his efforts were ineffectual, until he met with a white crow, when he was informed by the Muni Vasishtha that the crow had become white from having bathed in the Gomati River at a particular spot. Ráma proceeded to bathe at the same spot, and was immediately purified, or "cleansed" from his sin. The place was accordingly named *Dho-pápa*, or "cleanser of sins" and the town which soon sprang up beside it was called *Dhopápapura*. In Sánskrit the form is *Dhútapápa*, which is given in the list of the Vishnu Purána as the name of a river distinct from the Gomati; but as the name immediately follows that of the Gomati, I think it probable that the term may have been intended only as an epithet of the *Gomati*, as the *Dhútapápa*, or "Sin-cleanser," in allusion to the legend of Ráma's purification. An annual fair is held here on the 10th day on the waning moon of *Jyesth*, at which time it is said that about fifty thousand people assemble to bathe in the far-renowned pool of *Dhopápa*.

The site of *Dhopáp* is evidently one of very considerable antiquity, as the whole country for more than half a mile around it is covered with broken bricks and pottery. The place is said to have belonged to the *Bhar* Rajas of *Kusabhavanapura* or Sultánpur, but the only name that I could hear of as specially connected with *Dhopáp*, was that of Raja *Hel* or *Hela*. The village of *Dhopáp-pur* is now a very small one, containing less than 200 houses; but they are all built of burnt brick, and numerous foundations are visible on all sides near the Gomati River. Several carved stones have been collected by the people from the ruined walls of the fort of *Garhá*. Amongst them I observed the following:—1*st*, a broken pilaster with two human figures; 2*nd*, a stone bracket; 3*rd*, a square capital of pillar; 4*th*, a four-bracket capital of a pillar; 5*th*, two stones with socket holes for iron cramps. All of these stones point unmistakably to the existence at some former period of a large temple at Dhopáp, which was probably situated immediately above the bathing ghát. It seems almost certain, however, that there must once have been a considerable number of temples at this place, for the whole of the eastern wall or river front of the fort of *Garhá* has been built or faced with square stones, which, by their carvings and cramp-holes, show that they belonged to Hindu temples.

The fort of *Garhá* is situated to the north of the village on a lofty natural mound overhanging the River Gomati on the east. To the north and south the place is defended by two deep ravines supplied with running water, and to the west by a deep dry ravine. The position is, therefore, a strong one; for, although the neighbouring mounds to the north and west rise to nearly the same height, yet they once formed part of the city, which can only be approached over much low and broken ground. The strength of the position would seem to have early attracted the notice of the Muhammadan Kings of Delhi, as the fort is stated to have been *repaired* by Salim Shah, whilst a very old ruinous masjid stands on the west mound. The fort itself is a small place, its northern face being only 550 feet long, its eastern and western faces 550 feet each, whilst its south face is but 250 feet. The greater part of the stone work of the south-east tower has fallen into the river, where many of the stones are now lying, and much of the eastern wall has also disappeared, the stones being very valuable in a stoneless country for the sharpening of tools of all kinds. The entrance gate was on the south side, near the river bastion just mentioned. I obtained coins of many of the early Muhammadan Kings, from Naseruddin Mahmud Ghori down to Akbar, but not a single

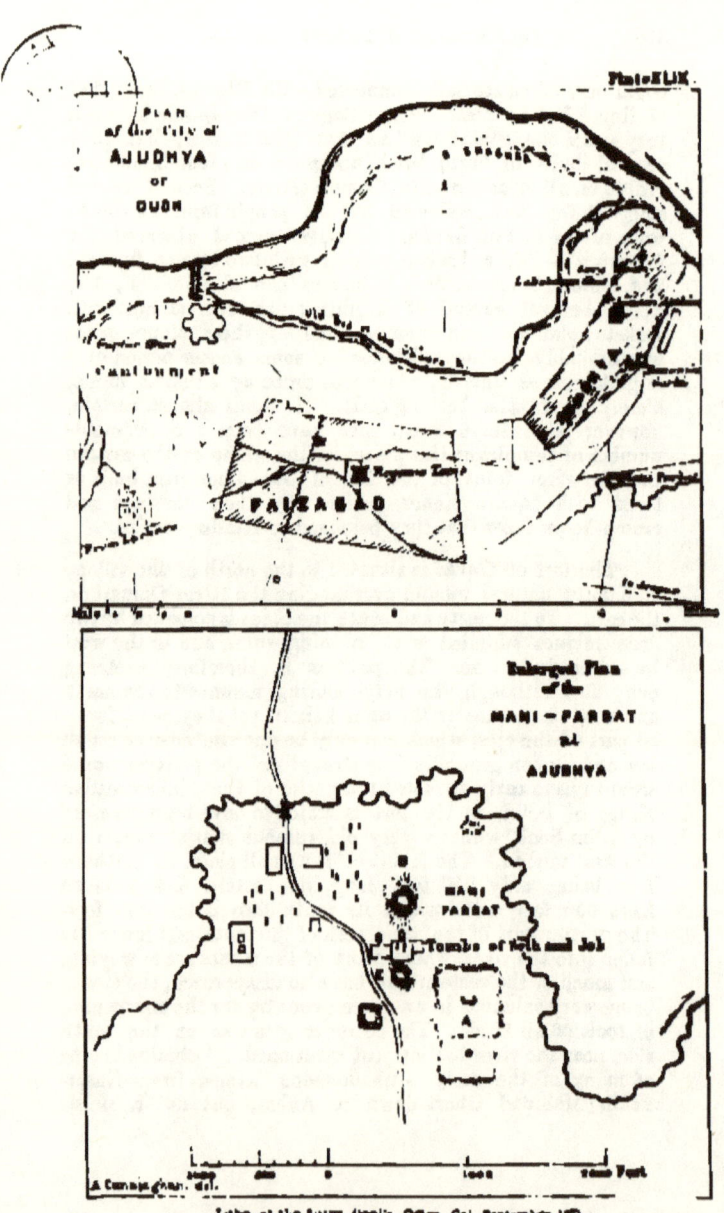

DHOPAPAPURA — SAKETA, OR AJUDHYA. 317

specimen of any Hindu coinage, although I was informed that coins bearing figures are found every year during the rainy season.

I may here mention that I heard of another place of Hindu pilgrimage on the north bank of the Gomati River, at a spot called *Set-Barâh*, that is *Sweta-Varâha*, or "the white Boar," 15 *kos*, or 30 miles, from Sultânpur towards Lucknow. Two annual fairs are held there,—1*st*, on the ninth day of the waxing moon of Chaitra, and the 2*nd*, on the fifteenth day of the waxing moon of Kartik, when it is said that about fifty thousand people assemble to bathe. The former period is connected with the history of Râma Chandra, as it is commonly known as the *Râm-navami Tirath* or "Râma's ninth (day) place of pilgrimage." I could not learn anything regarding the origin of the name of *Set Barâh*.

XVII. SAKETA, OR AJUDHYA.

Much difficulty has been felt regarding the position of Fa-Hian's "great kingdom of *Sha-chi*, and of Hwen Thsang's *Visâkhá*, with its enormous number of heretics," or Brahmanists; but I hope to show in the most satisfactory manner that these two places are identical, and that they are also the same as the *Sâketa* and *Ajudhya* of the Hindus. The difficulty has arisen chiefly from an erroneous bearing recorded by Fa Hian, who places *Shewei*, or *Srâvasti*, to the south of *Sha-chi*, while Hwen Thsang locates it to the north-east, and partly from his erroneous distance of $7 + 3 + 10 = 20$ *yojans*, instead of 30, from the well-known city of Sankisa. The bearing is shown to be erroneous by the route of a Hindu pilgrim from the banks of the Godavery to *Sewet*, or *Srávasti*, as recorded in the Ceylonese Buddhist works.* This pilgrim, after passing through Mahissati and Ujani, or Maheshmati and Ujain, reaches Kosâmbi, and from thence passes through *Sâketa* to *Sewet*, that is, along the very route followed by Hwen Thsang. We have, therefore, two authorities in favour of *Sewet* being to the north of Sâket. With regard to the distance, I refer again to the Buddhist books of Ceylon, in which it is recorded that from *Sakespura* (or *Sangkasyapura*, now Sankisa) to *Sewet* was a journey of

---

* Hardy, "Manual of Buddhism," p. 334.

30 *yojans*. Now, Fa Hian makes the distance from Sankisa to Kanoj 7 *yojans*, thence to the forest of *Holi*, on the Ganges, 3 *yojans*, and thence to *Shachi* 10 *yojans*, or altogether only 20 *yojans*, or 10 less than the Ceylonese books.* That Fa Hian's statement is erroneous is quite clear from the fact that his distance would place Shachi in the neighbourhood of Lucknow; whereas the other distance would place it close to Ajudhya, or Faizabad, or in the very position indicated by Hwen Thsang's itinerary. Here, again, we have two authorities in favour of the longer distance. I have no hesitation, therefore, in declaring that Fa Hian's recorded bearing of *Sho-wei* from *Sha-chi* is wrong, and that "north" should be read instead of "south."

I have now to show that Fa Hian's *Sha-chi* is the same as Hwen Thsang's *Visákha*, and that both are identical with *Sáketa* or *Ajudhya*. With respect to *Sha-chi*, Fa Hian relates that, on "leaving the town by the *southern gate*, you find to the *east* of the road the place where Buddha bit off a piece of his tooth brush, and planted it in the ground, where it grew to the height of seven feet, and never increased or diminished in size." Now this is precisely the same legend that is related of *Visákha* by Hwen Thsang, who says that "to the *south* of the capital, and to the left of the road (that is, to the east as stated by Fa Hian), there was, amongst other holy objects, an extraordinary tree 6 or 7 feet high, which always remained the same, neither growing nor decreasing.† This is the celebrated tooth-brush tree of Buddha, to which I shall have occasion to refer presently. Here I need only notice the very precise agreement in the two descriptions of this famous tree, as to its origin, its height, and its position. The perfect correspondence of these details appears to me to leave no doubt of the identity of Fa Hian's *Shachi* with the Visákha of Hwen Thsang.

With respect to the identification of Visákha with the Sáketa of the Hindus, I rest my proofs chiefly on the following points:—1*st*, that *Visákha*, the most celebrated of all females in Buddhist history, was a resident of Sáketa before her marriage with *Purana Varddhana*, son of *Mrigára*, the

---

* Beal's "Fa Hian," pp. 71-72; and Hardy, Manual of Buddhism, p. 301.
† Beal's Fa Hian, c. XIX; and Julien's Hwen Thsang, II., 291.

rich merchant of *Srávasti*; and 2nd, that Buddha is recorded by Hwen Thsang to have spent six years at *Visákha*, while by the Pali annals of Turnour he is stated to have lived 16 years at *Sáketa*.

The story of the noble maiden Visákha is related at great length in the Ceylonese books. According to Hardy, she erected a *Purvárdma* at *Srávasti*, which is also mentioned by Hwen Thsang. Now there was also a *Purvárdma* at Sáketa, and it can hardly be doubted that this monastery was likewise built by her.[*] She was the daughter of *Dhananja*, a rich merchant, who had emigrated from *Rajagriha* to *Sáketa*. Now, amongst the oldest inscribed coins which have been discovered only at Ajudhya, we find some bearing the names of *Dhana Deva* and *Visákha-Datta*. I mention this because it seems to me to show the probability that the family of *Dhananja* and *Visákhá* was of great eminence in Sáketa or Ayodhya; and I infer from the recurrence of their names, as well as from the great celebrity of the lady, that the city may possibly have been called *Visákha* after her name.

The other proof which I derive from the years of Buddha's residence is direct and convincing. According to the Ceylonese annals, Buddha was 35 years of age when he attained Buddhahood; he then led a houseless life for 20 years, preaching in various places in Northern India, all of which are detailed; and of the remaining 25 years of his life he spent 9 in the *Jetavana* monastery at Srávasti, and 16 in the *Pubhárámo* monastery at Sáketapura. Now, in the Burmese annals, these numbers are given as 19 years and 6 years, and in the last figure we have the exact number recorded by Hwen Thsang. Nothing can be more complete than this proof. There were only two places at which Buddha resided for any length of time, namely, *Srávasti*, at which he lived either 9 or 19 years, and *Sáketa*, at which he lived either 6 or 16 years; and as according to Hwen Thsang he lived for 6 years at Visákha, which is described as being at some distance to the south of Srávasti, it follows of necessity that Visákha and Sáketa were one and the same place.

---

[*] Hardy, Manual of Buddhism, p. 227; and Julien's Hwen Thsang, I., 305. See also Publication translated by Turnour in Bengal Asiatic Society's Journal, VII., 790.

The identity of *Sáketa* and *Ayodhya* has, I believe, always been admitted; but I am not aware that any proof has yet been offered to establish the fact. Csoma-de-koros, in speaking of the place, merely says "*Saketana* or Ayodhya," and H. H. Wilson, in his Sanskrit Dictionary, calls *Sáketa* "the city Ayodhya." But the question would appear to be set at rest by several passages of the Rámáyana and and Raghuvansa, in which *Sáketnagara* is distinctly called the capital of Raja *Dasaratha* and his sons. But the following verse of the Rámáyana, which was pointed out to me by a Brahman of Lucknow, will be sufficient to establish the identity. *Anonjita*, father of *Kaikeyi*, offers to give his daughter to Dasaratha, Rajah of *Sáketanagara* :—

Sáketam nagaram Raja námna Dasaratho bali,
Túsmai deyá mayá Kanyá Kaikeyi náma to janá.

The ancient city of Ayodhya or Sáketa is described in the Rámáyana as situated on the bank of the *Sarayu* or *Sarju* River. It is said to have been 12 *yojans*, or nearly 100 miles in circumference, for which we should probably read 12 *kos*, or 24 miles—an extent which the old city, with all its gardens, might once possibly have covered. The distance from the *Guptár* Ghát on the west, to the Rám Ghát on the east, is just 6 miles in a direct line; and if we suppose that the city with its suburbs and gardens formerly occupied the whole intervening space to a depth of two miles, its circuit would have agreed exactly with the smaller measurement of 12 *kos*. At the present day the people point to Rám Ghát and Guptár Ghát as the eastern and western boundaries of the old city, and the southern boundary they extend to *Bharat-Kund* near *Bhadaraá*, a distance of 6 *kos*. But as these limits include all the places of pilgrimage, it would seem that the people consider them to have been formerly inside the city, which was certainly not the case. In the Ain Akbari, the old city is said to have measured 148 *kos* in length by 36 *kos* in breadth, or in other words it covered the whole of the Province of Oudh to the south of the Ghághra River.[*] The origin of the larger number is obvious. The 12 *yojans* of the Rámáyana, which are equal to 48 *kos*, being considered too small for the great city of Rama, the Brahmans simply added 100 *kos* to make the size tally with

---

[*] Gladwin's translation, II., 32.

their own extravagant notions. The present city of Ajudhya, which is confined to the north-east corner of the old site, is just two miles in length by about three-quarters of a mile in breadth; but not one-half of this extent is occupied by buildings, and the whole place wears a look of decay. There are no high mounds of ruins, covered with broken statues and sculptured pillars, such as mark the sites of other ancient cities, but only a low irregular mass of rubbish heaps, from which all the bricks have been excavated for the houses of the neighbouring city of Faizabad. This Muhammadan city, which is two miles and-a-half in length, by one mile in breadth, is built chiefly of materials extracted from the ruins of Ajudhya. The two cities together occupy an area of nearly six square miles, or just about one-half of the probable size of the ancient Capital of Ráma. In Faizabad the only building of any consequence is the stuccoed brick tomb of the old Bhao Begam, whose story was dragged before the public during the famous trial of Warren Hastings. Faizabad was the capital of the first Nawabs of Oudh, but it was deserted by Asaf-ud-daolah in A. D. 1775.

According to the Rámáyana, the city of Ayodhya was founded by Manu, the progenitor of all mankind. In the time of Dasaratha, the father of Ráma, it was fortified with towers and gates, and surrounded by a deep ditch. No traces of these works now remain, nor is it likely, indeed, that any portion of the old city should still exist, as the *Ayodhya* of Ráma is said to have been destroyed after the death of *Vrihadbala* in the great war about B. C. 1426, after which it lay deserted until the time of Vikramáditya. According to popular tradition this Vikramáditya was the famous Sákári Prince of Ujain, but as the Hindus of the present day attribute the acts of all Vikramas to this one only, their opinion on the subject is utterly worthless. We learn, however, from Hwen Thsang that a powerful Prince of this name was reigning in the neighbouring city of Srávasti, just one hundred years after Kanishka, or close to 78 A. D., which was the initial year of the *Sáke era* of *Sálivahana*. As this Vikramáditya is represented as hostile to the Buddhists, he must have been a zealous Brahmanist, and to him therefore I would ascribe the re-building of Ayodhya and the restoration of all the holy places referring to the history of Ráma. Tradition says that when Vikramáditya came to Ayodhya, he found it utterly desolate and overgrown with *jangal*, but he was able to discover all the famous spots of Ráma's history by measurements made from Lakshman Ghát on the *Sarju*, according to the statements of ancient records. He is said to have erected 360 temples, on as many different spots, sacred to *Rāma*, and *Sitá* his wife, to his brothers *Lakshmana*, *Bharata*, and *Satrughna*, and to the monkey god *Hanumána*. The number of 360 is also connected with *Sálivāhana*, as his clansmen the *Bais Rajputs* assert that he had 360 wives.

There are several very holy Brahmanical temples about Ajudhya, but they are all of modern date, and without any architectural pretensions whatever. But there can be no doubt that most of them occupy the sites of more ancient temples that were destroyed by the Musulmáns. Thus *Rámkot*, or *Hanumán Garhi*, on the east side of the city, is a small walled fort surrounding a modern temple on the top of an ancient mound. The name Rámkot is certainly old, as it is connected with the traditions of the *Mani Parbat*, which will be hereafter mentioned; but the temple of Hanumán is not older than the time of Aurangzib. Rám Ghát, at the north-east corner of the city, is said to be the spot where Ráma bathed, and *Sargdwári or Swargadwári*, the " Gate of Paradise." On the north-west is believed to be the place where his body was burned. Within a few years ago there was still standing a very holy Banyan tree called *Asok Bat*, or the " Griefless Banyan," a name which was probably connected with that of *Swargadwári*, in the belief that people who died or were burned at this spot were at once relieved from the necessity of future births. Close by is the *Lakshman* Ghát, where his brother Lakshman bathed, and about one-quarter of a mile distant, in the very heart of the city, stands the *Janam Asthán*, or " Birth-place temple" of Ráma. Almost due west, and upwards of five miles distant, is the *Guptár* Ghát, with its group of modern white-washed temples. This is the place where Lakshman is said to have disappeared, and hence its name of *Guptár* from *Gupta*, which means " hidden or concealed." Some say that it was Ráma who disappeared at this place, but this is at variance with the story of his cremation at *Swargadwári*.

The only remains at Ajudhya that appear to be of any antiquity, are three earthen mounds to the south of the city, and about a quarter of a mile distant. These are called

Mani-Parbat, Kuber-Parbat, and *Sugrib-Parbat*.[1] The first, which is nearest to the city, is an artificial mound, 65 feet in height, covered with broken bricks and blocks of *kankar*. The old bricks are eleven inches square and three inches thick. At 46 feet above the ground on the west side, there are the remains of a curved wall faced with *kankar* blocks. The mass at this point is about 40 feet thick, and this was probably somewhat less than the size of the building which once crowned this lofty mound. According to the Brahmans the *Mani-Parbat* is one of the hills which the monkeys made use of when assisting Ráma. It was accidentally dropped here by Sugriva, the monkey-king of *Kishkindhya*. But the common people, who know nothing of this story, say that the mound was formed by the labourers shaking their baskets on this spot every evening on their return home from the building of Ramkot. It is therefore best known by the name of *Jhnoa-Jhár* or *Ora Jhár,* both of which mean "basket-shakings." A similar story is told of the large mounds near Banáras, Nimsár, and other places.

Five hundred feet due south from the large mound stands the second mound called *Kuber-Parbat,* which is only 28 feet in height. The surface is an irregular heap of brick rubbish, with numerous holes made by the people in digging for bricks, which are of large size, 11 inches by 7½ by 2. It is crowned by two old tamarind trees, and is covered with *jangal*. Close by on the south-west there is a small tank, called *Ganes-Kund* by the Hindus, and *Husen Kund* or *Imám Talao* by the Musulmáns, because their *Táziás* are annually deposited in it. Still nearer on the south-east there is a large oblong mound called *Sugrib-Parbat,* which is not more than 8 or 10 feet above the ground level. It is divided into two distinct portions; that to the north being upwards of 300 feet square at top, and the other to the south upwards of 200 feet. In the centre of the larger enclosure there is a ruined mound containing bricks 8½ inches square, and in the centre of the smaller mound there is a well.

Between the *Mani* and *Kuber* mounds there is a small Muhammadan enclosure, 64 feet long from east to west and 47 feet broad, containing two brick tombs, which are attributed to *Sis Paighambar* and *Ayub Paighambar,* or the "prophets Seth and Job." The

[1] See Plate No. XLIX. for a map of the ruins of Ajudhya.

first is 17 feet long and the other 12 feet. These tombs are mentioned by Abul Fazl, who says—"Near this city are two sepulchral monuments, one seven and the other six cubits in length. The vulgar pretend that they are the tombs of Seth and Job, and they relate wonderful stories of them."* This account shows that since the time of Akbar, the tomb of Seth must have increased in length from 7 cubits, or 10½ feet, to 17 feet through the frequent repairs of pious Musulmáns.

The mounds are surrounded by Musulmán tombs, and as it is the Muhammadan practice to bury the dead along the sides of the high roads close to their cities, I infer that the road which now runs close to the westward of the mounds, is one of the ancient high ways of the district. This is confirmed by the existence of an old masonry bridge of three arches over the *Tiláhi nala*, to the north-west of the Mani-Parbat, as well as by the direction of the road itself, which leads from the south-end of the city straight to the Dharat-kund, and onwards to Sultánpur or *Kusapura*, and Allahabad or *Práyága*. I notice this road thus minutely, because the identifications which I am about to propose are based partly on its position and direction, as well as on the general agreement of the existing remains with the holy places described by the Chinese pilgrims.

According to Fa Hian the place where Buddha planted the holy trees was to the *east* of the road, on issuing from the town by the southern gate. Hwen Thsang's account agrees with this exactly in placing the "extraordinary tree" to the south of the capital and to the *left* of the route. This tree was the celebrated "tooth brush," or twig used in cleaning the teeth, which having been cast away by Buddha, took root and grew to between 6 and 7 feet in height. Now, it will be observed that the ruined mounds that still exist, as well as the tombs of Seth and Job, are to the south of the city and to the east or left of the road. The position, therefore, is unmistakably the same as that described by the Chinese pilgrims, and as the actual state of the ruins agrees well with the details given by Hwen Thsang, I think that there can be no reasonable doubt of their identity.

Hwen Thsang describes the city of *Visákha* as being 16 *li*, or 2⅔ miles in circuit. In his time, therefore, the capital of

---

* Gladwin's "Ain Akbari," II, 33.

Râma was not more than half of its present size, although it probably contained a greater population, as not above one-third, or even perhaps less, of the present town is inhabited. The old city then possessed no less than twenty monasteries with three thousand monks and about fifty Brahmanical temples, with a very large Brahmanical population. From this account we learn that so early as the seventh century more than three hundred of the original temples of Vikramáditya had already disappeared, and we may therefore reasonably infer that the city had been gradually declining for some time previously. The Buddhist monuments, however, would appear to have been in good order, and the monks were just as numerous as in the eminently Buddhist city of Banáras.

The first monument described by Hwen Thsang is a great monastery without name, but as it was the only notable monastery, it was most probably either the *Kâlakârâma* of Sâketa, or the *l'srovârâma*, both of which are mentioned in the Ceylonese Maháwanso. The monks were of the school of the *Samattiyas*, and their monastery was famous for having produced three of the most eminent Buddhist controversialists. This monastery I would identify with the *Sugrib Parbat* which I have already described as being about 600 feet long by 300 feet broad. The great size and rectangular form of this ruin are sufficient to show that it must have been a monastery, but this is placed beyond all doubt by the existence of an interior well and by the remains of cloistered rooms forming the four sides of the enclosure. Its position to the south of the city, and to the east or left of the road, has already been specially noticed as agreeing with the recorded position of the monastery.

Beside the monastery there was a *Stupa* of Asoka, 200 feet in height, built on the spot where Buddha preached the law during his six years' residence at Sâketa. This monument I would identify with the *Mani-Parbat*, which is still 65 feet in height, and which with its masonry facing must once have been at least as high again, and with the usual lofty pinnacle of metal may easily have reached a height of 200 feet. Hwen Thsang ascribes the erection of this monument to Asoka, and I see no reason to question the accuracy of his statement, as the mixed structure of half earth and half masonry must undoubtedly be very ancient. The earliest *Stupas*, or topes, were simple earthen mounds or barrows,

similar to those that still exist in England. There are many
of these barrows still standing at *Lauriya-Navandgarh* to
the north of Bettiya, but this is the only place where I have
yet seen them. They are undoubtedly the most ancient
monuments of the Indian population, and I firmly believe
that even the very latest of them cannot be assigned to a
lower date than the fifth century before Christ. I base this
belief on the known fact that all the monuments of Asoka's
age, whether described by Hwen Thsang, or actually opened
by myself near Bhilsa, are either of stone or brick. The earthen
barrows are therefore of an earlier age; but such as are
Buddhist cannot possibly be earlier than the beginning of
the fifth century before Christ. In the case of the *Mani-
Parbat* at Ajudhya I infer that the earthen barrow, or lower
portion, may belong to the earlier ages of Buddhism, and
that the masonry or upper portion was added by Asoka.
At the foot of the mound I picked up a broken brick with
the letter *sh*, of the oldest form, stamped upon it; but as this
is almost certainly of later date than Asoka, it most probably did not belong to the *Mani-Parbat* building.

Hwen Thsang next describes the sites of the tooth-
brush tree and of the monument where the four previous
Buddhas used to sit and to take exercise, as being close to
the great *Stupa*. These places I would identify with the
court-yard containing the tombs of Seth and Job, which
touches the south side of the *Mani-Parbat*. The two tombs
I take to be the remains of the seats of the four previous
Buddhas, and the paved court-yard to be the scene of their
daily walks, although I was unable to trace their foot-marks,
which were seen by the Chinese pilgrim.

The last monument described by Hwen Thsang is a
Stupa containing the hair and nails of Buddha. This was
surrounded by a number of smaller monuments which seemed
to touch one another, and by several tanks which reflected
the sacred buildings in their limpid waters. The *Stupa* I
would identify with the *Kuber-Parbat*, which touches the
south side of the enclosure round the tombs of Seth and
Job, and is close to the west side of the ruined monastery.
One of the tanks described by the pilgrim may be the *Ganes-
Kund*, which has already been noticed; but all the smaller
monuments have disappeared long ago, as they afforded

cheap and ready materials for the construction of the numerous Muhammadan tombs, as well as of the neighbouring bridge and mosque. If I am right in my identification of this mound as the remains of the *Stupa* containing the hair and nails of Buddha, I think that an excavation in the centre of the mound might, perhaps, verify the accuracy of my conclusions.

The people are unanimous in their assertion that the old city to the north of these mounds was called *Barcla*. Ayodhya or Ajudhya, they say, was the capital of Rama, but the later city was called *Barcla*. As this name has no similarity either to *Sáketa* or *Visákha*, I can only set it down as another appellation of the old town, for which we have no authority but tradition. I was disappointed when at Ajudhya in not hearing even the most distant allusion to the legend of the tooth-brush tree of Buddha, but the tradition still exists, as I heard of it quite unexpectedly at two different places immediately afterwards, first at *Hátila*, distant 15 miles, and next at Gonda, 29 miles to the north of Ajudhya.

XVIII. HATILA, OR ASOKPUR.

The ancient territory of Ayodhya was divided by the Sarju or *Ghághra* River into two great provinces,—that to the north being called *Uttara Kosala*, and that to the south *Banaodha*. Each of these was again sub-divided into two districts. In Banaodha these are called *Pachham-rát* and *Purab-rát*, or the western and eastern districts, with reference to their bearing from Ajudhya; and in Uttara Kosala they are *Gauda* (vulgarly Gonda) to the south of the Rapti, and Kosala to the north of the Rapti, or Ráwati, as it is universally called in Oudh. Some of these names are found in the Puránas; thus in the Vayu Purana, Lava, the son of Rama, is said to have reigned in Uttara Kosala; but in the Matsya, Linga, and Kurma Puráns, Srávasti is stated to be in *Gauda*. These apparent descrepancies are satisfactorily explained when we learn that *Gauda* is only a sub-division of Uttara Kosala, and that the ruins of Srávasti have actually been discovered in the district of *Gauda*, which is the Gonda of the maps.[*] The extent of *Gauda* is also proved by the old

---

[*] See Plate No. 1, map of the Gangetic Provinces.

name of *Balrámpur* on the Rapti, which was formerly *Rámgarh Gauda*. I presume therefore that both the *Gauda Brahmans* and the *Gauda Tagas* must have belonged to this district originally, and not to the mediæval city of *Gauda* in Bengal. Brahmans of this name are still numerous in Ajudhya and Jahangirabad on the right bank of the Ghághra River in Gonda, Pákbapur, and Jaisni of the Gonda District, and in many parts of the neighbouring Province of Gorakhpur.

The small village of *Hátila* derives its name from the sister's son of Sayid Sálár. The old Hindu name was *Asokpur*, so called from a large temple of *Asoknáth Mahadeo*. Hátila was killed in an assault on the temple, and his tomb, a low-domed building only 20 feet square, is still much frequented as the shrine of a *Gházi* or martyr for the faith. It is built entirely of large bricks from the ruins of the old temple of *Asoknáth*. The remains consist of a low mound, 700 feet long by 500 feet broad, with three prominent masses of ruin on the north side. I made an excavation in the north-west ruin near the base of a large *Mahwa* tree, but without any result, as a small Muhammadan tomb on the top prevented me from digging in the centre. But the coolies employed on the work voluntarily informed me that the *Mahwa* tree had been the "tooth-brush" of a Raja who stuck it in the ground and it grew to be a tree. From this tradition, which also exists at Gonda, I infer that it was usual to make cuttings and to take seeds from the famous *danta-dháwan* or "tooth-brush tree" of *Sáketa* for distribution to religious establishments, just as cuttings from the Bodhi tree at Gaya were made for the same purpose. Both Fa Hian and Hwen Thsang agree in stating that the *Danta-dháwan* of Sáketa was only seven feet high, and that it never grew any higher, which would seem to show that it was only a small tree or shrub; and this, indeed, is actually the case with the *Datton*, or "tooth-brush tree" of Gonda, which is a *Chilbil*, or shrub eaten by goats, that never exceeds 8 or 10 feet. I conclude therefore that the original toothbrush tree of Hátila has disappeared, and that the name has been applied to the *Mahwa*, which is the only tree now remaining on the mound.

The north-east mound is a mere undistinguishable mass of broken bricks, but the central mound is still covered

HATILA, OR ASOKPUR.   329

with the ruins of the temple of Asoknáth Mahadeo containing a large broken *lingam*. Portions of the brick walls, which still remain, show that the temple was only 12 feet square; but the whole has been lifted up by the roots of a gigantic Pipal tree, which still hold the bricks together by their interlacings. These remains attracted the attention of Buchanan Hamilton during his survey of Gorakhpur, who remarks that "a wild fig tree having taken root on the *linga* will soon cover it."[*] This actually took place, and the *linga* was almost completely hidden by the matted roots of the Pipal, until the tree was cut down by the Tahsildar of the neighbouring village of Vazirganj in A. D. 1802. As the cut stem of the Pipal shows 849 annual rings, the tree must have been planted in A. D. 1013, during the reign of Mahmud of Ghazni. This, indeed, is about the date of the temple itself, which is said to have been built by *Suhri-dal*, Raja of Asokpur, and the antagonist of Sayid Sálár. The Raja is also called *Sukal-dhar*, *Sohil-dal*, and *Sohil Deo*, and is variously said to have been a *Thárn*, a *Bhar*, a *Kálahansa*, or a *Bais Rajput*. The majority, however, is in favor of his having been a *Thárn*. The mound with the *Mahwa* tree is called *Raja Sohil-dal-ka-khalanga*, or Sohil-dal's seat." His city of Asokpur is said to have extended to *Domariya-Dih*, 2 *kos* to the north, and to *Sareya Dih*, half a *kos* to the south of the temple. At both of these places there are old brick-covered mounds, in which several hundreds of coins have been lately found. Most of the coins belong to the early Musulmán Kings of Delhi, the Ghoris and Khiljis; but there were also a few Hindu coins, in base silver and copper, with the Boar incarnation of Vishnu on one side, and the legend of *Sri-mad-Adi-Varáha* on the reverse in mediæval characters. As these coins are referred to by name, in an inscription of A. D. 920, as *Sri-mad-Adi-Varaha drammas*, or "Boar incarnation drachmas," the mounds in which they have been discovered must be of still earlier date. Tradition gives the genealogy of the Rajas of *Gauda* as follows :

    A. D. 900 1 Mora-dhaj, or Mayura-dhwaja.
            925 2 Hans-dhaj, or Hansa-dhwaja.
            950 3 Makar-dhaj, or Makara-dhwaja.
            975 4 Sudhanwa-dhaj.
      1000 5 Suhridal-dhaj, contemporary of Mahmud.

I give this genealogy with the probable dates, as it may, perhaps, be of use hereafter in fixing the age of other Princes and their works.*

XIX. SAHET-MAHET, OR SRAVASTI.

The position of the famous city of *Srâvasti*, one of the most celebrated places in the annals of Buddhism, has long puzzled our best scholars. This was owing partly to the contradictory statements of the Chinese pilgrims themselves, and partly to the want of a good map of the Province of Oudh. In page 317 I have compared the bearings and distances recorded by Fa Hian and Hwen Thsang with those preserved in the Buddhist annals of Ceylon, and I have shewn conclusively that Fa Hian's distance from Sankisa and his bearing from *Shachi* or *Sâket* are both erroneous. We know from Hwen Thsang and the Buddhist books in Ceylon that *Srâvasti* was to the north of Sâhet or Ayodhya, or in other words, that it was in the District of *Gauda* or *Uttara Kosala*, which is confirmed by the statements of no less than four of the Brahmanical Purânas. As Fa Hian also says that *Shewei* or *Sewet* was in Kosala, there can be no doubt whatever that Srâvasti must be looked for within a few days' journey to the northward of *Saket* or *Ayodhya*. According to Fa Hian the distance was 8 *yojanas*, or 56 miles, which is increased by Hwen Thsang to 500 *li*, or 83 miles. But as the latter pilgrim reduced the Indian yojana to Chinese measure at the rate of 40 *li* per *yojana*, I would correct his distance by the nearest round number of 350 *li* or 58 miles to bring it into accordance with the other. Now, as this is the exact distance from Ajudhya of the great ruined city on

---

* Since this account was written, I have found the name of Moruadhaj attached to several other places, especially to an old ruined fort in Bhabilkhand, which is still named Moruadhaj, and which will be described in Volume II. In Sir Henry Elliot's Muhammadan Historians, Volume II., p. 513, will be found a detailed account of the mad expedition of Kálár Musaud, which, although a late compilation of the traditions current in the reign of Jahangir, is probably correct in its general outlines. According to this account Sálár Musaud, after an engagement with the Hindus, rested under the shade of a *Madâra* tree, on the bank of the Suraj-kund, close to the idol temple of Bálárukh. The place was several marches distant from Bahraich, as he returned to Bahraich from the Suraj-kund "by regular stages." As he had taken a great fancy to the spot, he ordered a platform of masonry to be built under the shade of the *Madâra* tree to serve him for a seat. Apparently, this was the scene of his death, as, during the battle, he directed his followers to throw the bodies of the dead believers into the Suraj-kund, while the few troops that remained stood round him in the garden. His chief opponent in this last battle was Hal Sahar Deo, who is clearly the same as Sakri Dal or Sahil Deo, of my informants. Musaud's tomb is at Bahraich, but this was not built until two centuries later. The tomb at Amkpur, may, I think, be that of his relative Sálár Saifuddin, who was killed in the same battle.

† Beal's Fa Hian, c. XIX., XX.; and Jullou's Hwen Thsang, II., 292.

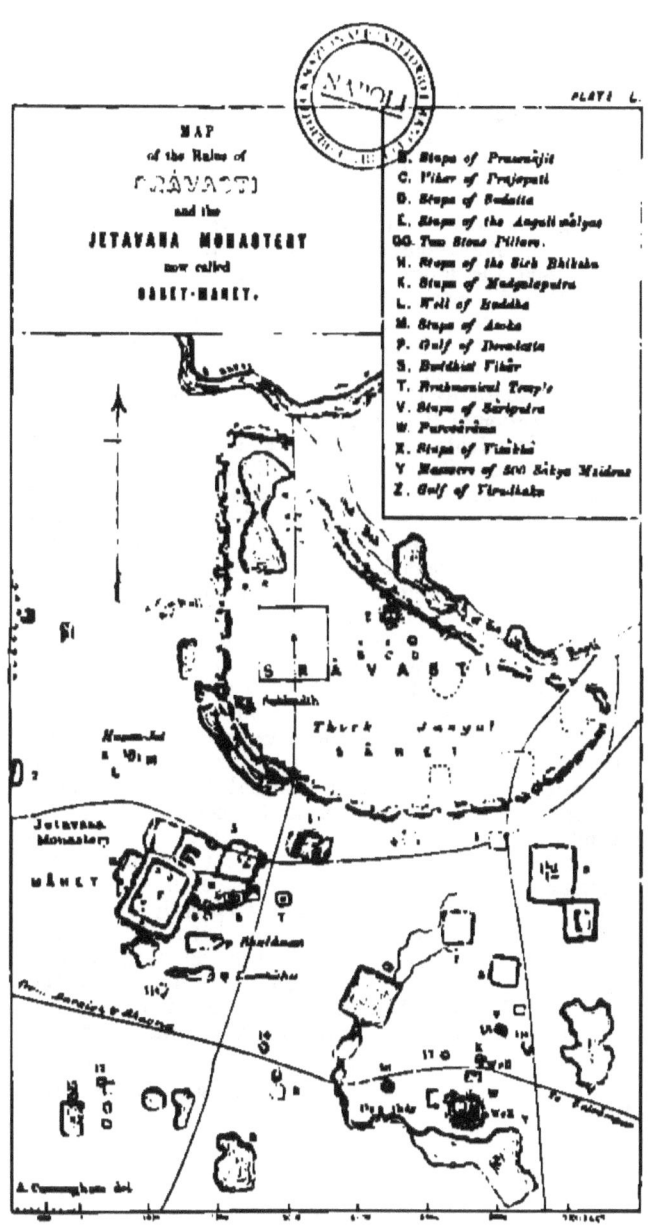

the south bank of the Rapti, called *Sáhet Máhet*, in which I discovered a colossal statue of Buddha with an inscription containing the name of Srávasti itself, I have no hesitation in correcting Hwen Thsang's distance from 500 *li* to 350 *li* as proposed above.

The ruined city of Sáhet Máhet is situated between Akaona and Balrámpur, at 5 miles from the former and 12 miles from the latter, and at nearly equi-distances from Bahraich and Gonda. In shape it is an almost semi-circular cresent, with its diameter of one mile and a third in length curved inwards and facing the north-east, along the old bank of the Rapti River. The western front, which runs due north and south, for three-quarters of a mile, is the only straight portion of the enclosure. The ramparts vary considerably in height; those to the west being from 35 to 40 feet in height, while those on the south and east are not more than 25 or 30 feet. The highest point is the great north-west bastion, which is 50 feet above the fields. The north-east face, or shorter curve of the cresent, was defended by the Rapti, which still flows down its old bed during the annual floods. The land ramparts on the longer curve of the cresent must once have been defended by a ditch, the remains of which yet exist as a swamp, nearly half a mile in length, at the south-west corner. Everywhere the ramparts are covered with fragments of brick, of the large size peculiar to very ancient cities; and, though I was unable to trace any remains of walls except in one place, yet the very presence of the bricks is quite sufficient to show that the earthen ramparts must once have been crowned by brick parapets and battlements. The portion of the parapet wall, which I discovered still standing in the middle of the river face, was 10 feet thick. The whole circuit of the old earthen ramparts, according to my survey, is 17,300 feet, or upwards of 3¼ miles. Now, this is the exact size of 20 *li* or 3⅓ miles which Hwen Thsang gives to the palace alone; but as the city was then deserted and in ruins, he must have mistaken the city itself for the palace.[*] It is certain at least that the suburbs outside the walls must have been very limited, indeed —as the place is almost entirely surrounded with the remains

---

[*] See plate No L. for a map of the ruins of Sravasti, and compare Julien's Hwen Thsang, II., 93.

of large religious buildings, which would have left but little room for any private dwellings. I am therefore quite satisfied that the city has been mistaken for the palace; and this mistake is sufficient to show how utterly ruined this once famous city must have been at so distant a period as the 7th century, when the place was visited by Hwen Thsang. As Fa Hian describes the population as already very inconsiderable in A. D. 400, while the Ceylonese annals* speak of *Khirádhára*, King of *Sawatthipura*, between A. D. 275 and 302, the great decline of Srávasti must have taken place during the fourth century, and we may, perhaps, not be far wrong in connecting it with the fall of the Gupta Dynasty in A. D. 319.

Srávasti is said to have been built by Raja *Srávasta*, the son of *Yuvandswa* of the Solar race, and the tenth in descent from Surya himself. Its foundation therefore reaches to the fabulous ages of Indian History, long anterior to Rama. During this early period it most probably formed part of the kingdom of Ayodhya, as the Vayu Purána assigns it to Lava, the son of Rama. When Srávasti next appears in history, in the time of Buddha it was the capital of King Prasenajit, the son of Maha Kosala. The King became a convert to the new faith, and during the rest of his life he was the firm friend and protector of Buddha. But his son Virudhaka hated the race of Sákyas, and his invasion of their country and subsequent massacre of 500 Sákya maidens, who had been selected for his harem, brought forth the famous prediction of Buddha, that within seven days the King would be consumed by fire. As the story has been preserved by Buddhists, the prediction was of course fulfilled, and upwards of eleven centuries afterwards the tank in which the King had sought to avoid the flames was pointed out to the credulous Hwen Thsang.

We hear nothing more of Srávasti until one century after Kanishka, or five centuries after Buddha, when, according to Hwen Thsang, Vikramaditya, King of Srávasti, became a persecutor of Buddhists, and the famous Manorhita, author of the *Vibháshá Sástra*, being worsted in argument by the Brahmans, put himself to death.† During the reign

---

* Bengal Asiatic Society's Journal, 1838, p. 865
† Julien's Hwen Thsang, II., 115.

of his successor, whose name is not given, the Brahmans, were overcome by *Vasubandhu*, the eminent disciple of *Manorhita*. The probable date of these two Kings may be set down as ranging from A. D. 79 to 120. For the next two centuries *Srávasti* would seem to have been under the rule of its own Kings, as we find *Khirádhára* and his nephews mentioned as Rajas between A. D. 275 and 319. But there can be little doubt that during the whole of this time Srávasti was only a dependency of the powerful Gupta Dynasty of Magadha, as the neighbouring city of Sáketa is specially said to have belonged to them. "Princes of the Gupta race," says the Vayu Puráña, "will possess all those countries,— the banks of the Ganges to Prayága, and Sáketa, and Magadha."* From this time Srávasti gradually declined. In A. D. 400 it contained only 200 families, in A. D. 632 it was completely deserted, and at the present day the whole area of the city, excepting only a few clearances near the gateways, is a mass of almost impenetrable jangal.

Before attempting to identify the existing remains of *Sáhet-Máhet* with the famous monuments of Srávasti, it will be as well to compare and reconcile the few discrepant statements of the Chinese pilgrims, so that the description of the holy places may not be interrupted by discussion. Of these discrepancies, perhaps the most notable is the difference in the name of the city itself, which Fa Hian gives as *She-wei*, while Hwen Thsang writes it, as correctly as it is possible to do in Chinese syllables, *She-lo-fa-si-ti*, or Srávasti. But this difference is more apparent than real, as there can be little doubt that *She-wei* is only a slight alteration of the abbreviated Pali form of *Sewet* for *Sáwatthi*, which is found in most of the Ceylonese books. Similarly the modern name of *Sáhet* is evidently only a variation of the Pali *Sáwet*. The other name of *Máhet* I am unable to explain, but it is perhaps only the usual rhyming addition of which the Hindus are so fond, as in *ulta-pulta*, or "topsy-turvey," which many of the people say is the true meaning of *Sáhet-Máhet*, in allusion to the utter ruin of the whole place. But some say that the name was originally *Set-met*, and as this form seems to be only a corruption of *Sewet*, it is probable that *Saket-Mahet*, or *Sáhet-Máhet* is simply a

---

* H. H. Wilson's Vishnu Puráña, p. 479, note.

lengthened pronunciation of *Set-met*. One man alone, and he, strange to say, was the Musulmán in charge of the tomb of Pir-Barína close to the ruined city, affirmed that the true name was *Sávitri*, which is so close to the correct Páli form of *Sawatthi* as to leave but little doubt that it preserves the original name of the place.

The next point of difference is the distance of the celebrated monastery of *Jetavana* from the south gate of the city. According to Fa Hian this was 1,200 paces, or about half a mile, which is increased by Hwen Thsang to 5 or 6 *li*, or nearly one mile. But as the only mass of ruins which can possibly be identified with the *Jetavana* is exactly half a mile from the nearest opening in the south rampart of the old city, there is clearly some mistake in the distance given by Hwen Thsang, unless we may suppose him to have approached the monastery by a somewhat longer route through the multitude of holy places, of which the remains still exist to the east of the *Jetavana* ruins. By this route the distance would be increased to three-quarters of a mile, or 4½ *li*, which is sufficiently close to the number given by Hwen Thsang.

Both pilgrims begin their account of *Srávasti* at the old palace of King *Prasenajita*, and as both, after describing the surrounding buildings leave the city by the south gate, it is certain that the palace was inside the city. Its exact position I was unable to determine, as the greater part of the interior is covered with dense jangal; but as the east half is comparatively clear, and the jangal low, I was able to satisfy myself that no large building had ever existed in this part, and consequently that the place must have been in the west half of the city. This conclusion is confirmed by the position of the two *stupas* of Sudatta and the Anguli-mályas, which Hwen Thsang places to the east of the palace; for as the only existing mounds that can be identified with these *stupas* are near the middle of the river face of the city, the palace must have been to the west of them, and therefore in the west half of the city.

The two principal places inside the city, which are mentioned by both pilgrims as being to the east of the palace, were the dwelling-house and *stupa* of Sudatta, the builder of the *Jetavana*, and the great *stupa* of the *Anguli-mályas*. These *stupas* I have already identified with the two existing mounds near the middle of the river face of the ramparts. The smaller one, which is about 25 feet in height, corresponds with the *stupa* of Sudatta, and the larger one, which is 35 feet in height, with the other *stupa*, which is particularly stated to have been a larger one. The *Anguli-mályas* were the followers of a particular sect which was established by a converted brigand who had received the name of *Anguli-mála* or "finger garland," from his practice of cutting off the fingers of his victims to form a garland which he wore round his neck.

On leaving the city by the south gate, both pilgrims went at once to the eastern gate of the great monastery of *Jetavana*, which was one of the eight most celebrated Buddhist buildings in India.* It was erected during the life-time of Buddha by *Sudatta*, the minister of King Prasenajita, and it received its name of *Jetavana*, or "Jeta's garden," because the garden in which it was built had been purchased from Prince Jeta. The story of the building is given by Hardy from the Ceylonese annals.† According to them the Prince, who was unwilling to part with his garden, demanded as its price as many gold *masurans* as would cover it, which Sudatta at once promised. When the garden was cleared, and all the trees, except Sandal and Mango, were cut down, the money was brought and spread out over the ground until the whole was covered, when the sum was found to be 18 *kotis*, or 180 millions of *masurans*. The garden is said to have been 1,000 cubits in length and the same in breadth, or 4,000 cubits in circuit. Extravagant as the sum may seem, it is still too small to have covered the garden, if we are to take Mr. Hardy's cubits at 18 inches, as each *masuran* would be one inch and eight-tenths in length and breadth, which is about three times the size of the old Indian silver coins. Unfortunately the dimensions of the Jetavana are not stated either by Fa Hian or Hwen Thsang; but the ruined mound of the monastery still exists, and its dimensions do not exceed 1,000 feet in length by 700 feet in breadth. Now, it is curious

---

* In Remusat's translation of Fa Hian's travels, it is stated that "the town has two gates,— one facing the east, and the other the north." As the south gate is mentioned by both pilgrims, it was certain that this statement was erroneous. Mr. Beal's more accurate translation shows that the two gates thus described belong to the Vihara and not to the city. The position of the north gate is distinctly indicated by a depression in the centre of that side.

† Hardy, "Manual of Buddhism," p. 216.

that these numbers give an area which is only one-third of the size of that recorded in the Ceylonese annals, and which therefore would be exactly covered by 180 millions of old Indian silver coins, allowing rather more than half an inch for the length and breadth of each coin. The amount said to have been paid for the garden is of course only the usual extravagant style of Indian exaggeration, for the sum of 18 *kotis*, even if taken at the lowest value of gold as ten times that of silver, would be equal to 45 krors of rupees, or 45 millions sterling.

The *Jetavana* is described in the Ceylonese annals as consisting of a central *vihár*, or temple, with surrounding houses for priests, rooms for day and night, an ambulatory, tanks, and gardens of fruit and flower trees, and around the whole a wall 18 cubits in height. According to this description the *Jetavana* must have included not only the great ruined mound now called *Jogini-baria*, but all the ruins to the east and north of it, unless it extended to the westward, where there are no remains at present existing. But as I can show that most of the ruins to the east correspond with the descriptions which Fa Hian and Hwen Thsang have given of many of the holy places outside the *Jetavana*, it is certain that the original monastery must have been confined to the *Jogini-baria* only, and that the other buildings, with the tanks and gardens, were outside the walls of the *Jetavana* itself, although it is most probable that many of them were connected together by different enclosing walls. When the Jetavana was completed by Sudatta, the Prince Jeta expended the whole of his purchase-money in adding a palace, seven storeys in height, to each of the four sides of the garden. It is probably to these palaces that Fa Hian refers when he states that "the temple of *Shi-hwan*" (read *Shi-to-hwan*, or Jetavana) "had originally seven storeys. Canopies and streamers were hung up, flowers were scattered, perfumes burned, lanterns supplied the place of day, and even in day time were never extinguished. A rat having taken into its mouth the wick of one of these lanterns, set fire to the flags and to the drapery of the pavilions, and the seven storeys of the temple were utterly consumed." This occurred some time before A. D. 400, as Fa Hian adds that "they re-constructed the temple, and when they had completed the second storey, they installed the statue in its former place."

From this account I infer, though somewhat doubtfully, that the new temple was not more than two storeys in height. I conclude also that the place was already on the decline, as a little more than two centuries later, when visited by Hwen Thsang, it was found utterly ruined and deserted.

The great mound of ruins, which I propose to identify with the Jetavana, is situated just half a mile distant from the south-west corner of the old city. It is rectangular in form, being 1,000 feet long from north-east to south-west, and 700 feet broad. It is worth noting, as it is most probably not accidental, that the central line of the rectangle falls upon a lofty mound, inside the south-west angle of the city called *Sobhnáth*, which is the name of one of the Jain hierarchs. The shape of the monastery is defined by a gentle rise all round the edge of the mound, which I take to represent the ruins of the monks' cells that once formed the surrounding walls of the enclosure. The highest part, which is the south side, is not more than 12 feet above the neighbouring ground, while the other sides are not more than eight or ten feet. But the whole area was so thickly covered with jangal, that I found it difficult to take even a few measurements. During my stay at Sáhet I cut pathways to all the ruined eminences within the enclosure, and after clearing the jangal around them, I began an excavation in each to ascertain the nature of the original building. With the largest mound, which was near the south end of the central line of the enclosure, I was unsuccessful. It was 15 feet in height, and looked the most promising of all; but I found nothing but earth and broken bricks, although I was assured by the people that numbers of large bricks had been carried away from it at different times. Both from its size and position, I am inclined to look upon this mound as the remains of the original temple of the *Jetavana*. In a lower mound, close by to the west, my excavations disclosed the walls of a small temple, not quite 6½ feet square inside, with a doorway to the north, and the remains of a semi-circular brick pedestal against the south wall. The walls were upwards of three feet thick, but the whole building was only a little more than 13 feet square, from which, taking the altitude at three and a half times the side, I conclude that the temple could not have exceeded 46 feet in height.

Near this temple there are three brick wells: the largest to the north is octagonal, above with a side of 4½ feet, and circular below at a depth of 12 feet. The second, to the south which is circular, is only 3½ feet in diameter; and the third, still farther to the south, is also circular, with a diameter of 6¾ feet. It is curious that all these wells, which are the only ones known to the people, are in the south-west corner of the enclosure.

A third mound near the north end of the central line[*] of the enclosure gave promise of a better result than the others, as a previous excavation had disclosed the head and shoulders of a colossal figure, which from its curly hair and long split ears I knew to be that of Buddha. I was assured, however, that the Jains, who come annually to Sáhet in great numbers during the months of Mâgh and Baisákh, look upon the statue as belonging to themselves. But my experience having taught me that Jains are no more particular than Brahmans as to the figures that they worship, I began to dig in the certain expectation of finding a very old Buddhist statue, and with a strong hope of discovering some inscription on its pedestal that might, perhaps, be of value in determining the name and probable date of these long deserted ruins. After a few hours' work the four walls of the temple were brought to light, and the figure was seen to be leaning against the back wall. The interior was only 7¼ feet square, but the walls were upwards of 4 feet thick, with a projection of 6 inches in the middle of each face. The front wall to the east was thicker than the rest by one foot, which was the breadth of the jamb of the doorway. The extreme outside dimensions were 19 feet by 18 feet, which would give a probable height of between 60 and 70 feet. As the excavation proceeded it was seen that the statue was a standing figure which had been broken off a few inches above the ankles by the fall of the temple. After the figure was removed with much difficulty on account of its great weight, and the floor of the temple had been cleared, it was seen that the pedestal of the statue was still standing erect in its original position. The floor was paved with large stones, and immediately in front of the pedestal there was a

---

[*] Beal's Fa Hian, c. XX, p. 79.—As the "chapel" of the Jetavana is said to have been placed "in the exact centre of it," I think that this temple must be the famous Vihára of Sudatta. In the plan of the ruins the Jetavana is marked with the letter F.

long flat slab 3½ feet by 1½ foot, with a pair of hollow foot-marks in the centre and two sunken panels on each side. At the back of the incised foot towards the pedestal there was a rough hollow, 3½ feet long by 4 inches broad, which, judging from what I have seen in Burma, must once have held a long stone or metal frame for the reception of lights in front of the statue. But all this arrangement was certainly of later date than the statue itself, for on opening up the floor it was found that the *Buddha-pad* slab concealed the lower two lines of an inscription, which fortunately had been thus preserved from injury, while the third or uppermost line had been almost entirely destroyed.

The statue is a colossal standing figure of Buddha the Teacher, 7 feet 4 inches in height. His left hand rests on his hip, and his right hand is raised in the act of teaching. The right shoulder is bare as in all Buddhist figures, and there is the usual aureole or nimbus round the head; close to the neck there are two small holes cut through the nimbus which, being larger in front than behind, were evidently intended for metal cramps to fix the statue to the wall. Unfortunately the head is broken, as well as both arms, but the body of the figure is uninjured. The attitude is stiff and restrained, the two feet being exactly in the same position and somewhat too far apart. The statue is of spotted red sandstone, such as is found in the quarries near Mathura and Fatehpur Sikri; and as we know from recent discoveries that the sculptor's art was in a very flourishing state at Mathura during the first centuries of the Christian era, I feel satisfied that the *Srâvasti* colossus must have been brought from that city. The inscription is imperfect at the beginning just where it must have contained the date. It now opens with the figure 10 and some unit of the Gupta numerals, which must be the day of the month, and then follow the words *etaye purvvaye*, which Professor Dowson thinks must mean "on this notable occasion," or some equivalent expression.[*] Then come the names of the donors of the statue, three mendicant monks, named *Pushpa, Siddhya-Mihira*, and *Bala-Trepitaka*; next follow the title of *Boddhisatwa*, the name of the place, *Srâvasti*, and the name of Buddha as *Bhagavata*. The inscription closes with the

[*] Bengal Asiatic Society's Journal, 1863, p. 437.

statement that the statue is the "accepted gift of the Sarvas-
tivadina teachers of the Kosamba hall."* Judging from the
old shapes of some of the letters in this record, the age of
the statue may be fixed with some certainty as not later
than the first century of the Christian era. The characters are
exactly the same as those of the Mathura inscriptions, which,
without doubt, belong to the very beginning of the Christian
era, and as the Srâvasti statue was in all probability executed
at Mathura, the correspondence of the lapidary characters shows
that the inscriptions must belong to the same period. As there
is no mention of this statue in Fa Hian's narrative, I conclude that the temple in which it stood must have fallen
down in the great conflagration which destroyed the seven-
storyed pavilions. But the account of Fa Hian is not very
intelligible. He states that the original image of Buddha
was "the head of an ox carved in sandal-wood;" that on
Buddha's approach the statue "rose and went to meet him,"
and that when Buddha said "return and be seated," the
statue "returned and sat down." The origin of this rather
puzzling account must, I believe, be traced to a mistake,
either of Fa Hian himself, or of his translator. In Sanskrit
Gosirsha or "Bull's head" is the name of the most fragrant
kind of sandal-wood, and as we know that the famous early
statue of Buddha at Kosambi was made of this very wood,
it is natural to conclude that the earliest statue at Srâvasti
may have been made of the same material. As this is the
only figure of Buddha noticed by Fa Hian, I infer that the
colossal stone figure which I discovered must have been
buried beneath the ruins of its own temple some time before
A. D. 400, and most probably, therefore, during the great
fire which destroyed the whole monastery. It was concealed
also at the time of Hwen Thsang's visit in A. D. 632, as
he specially mentions that the only temple then standing
amidst the ruins of the monastery was a small brick house
containing a statue of Buddha in sandal-wood. The statue
now discovered was therefore not visible in his time.

Both pilgrims entered the garden of the monastery
by the east side, and although I was unable to find any certain trace of an opening, I am quite satisfied that there must

---

* This inscription has been translated by Professor Dowson in the Royal Asiatic Society's Journal for 1870.

have been a gate to the east, as all the existing ruins are on that side. On issuing from the gate the first monuments noticed by both pilgrims are two lofty stone pillars, one on each side of the road. Hwen Thsang says that they had been erected by Asoka, that they were 70 feet high, and that the left column was crowned by a cupola or dome, and the other by an elephant. But Fa Hian, on the contrary, describes these figures as a wheel and an ox. I feel satisfied that Fa Hian is right as to the first, as the wheel is frequently represented in the Sanchi sculptures as crowning the capitals of columns, and we know that it was also used as a type of Buddha himself as the *Chakravartti* Raja, or King who "turned the wheel" of the law, or, in other words, who made religion advance. With regard to the animal that crowned the other pillar I am unable to offer any remark, except the obvious explanation that the trunk of the elephant must have been broken off before the time of Fa Hian, otherwise it is impossible to conceive how he could have mistaken the figure for that of an ox. But this discrepancy in the accounts of the two pilgrims is the best argument that I can offer for the mistake which I believe them both to have made regarding the animal that crowned the Sankisa pillar.* There are no remains of these pillars, but there are two slight eminences only 300 feet distant from the monastery which may have been the basements on which the pillars stood, as the pathway leading to the ruined mound on the east side runs between them.

To the north-east of the monastery of Jetavana, and therefore to the north of the pillars, there was a *stupa* built on the spot where Buddha had washed the hands and feet of a sick monk and had cured his sickness. The remains of this *stupa* still exist in a mass of solid brick-work, to the north of the presumed pillar basements, and at a distance of 550 feet from the Jetavana monastery. This ruined mass, which is 24½ feet in height, is built entirely of large bricks, 21 by 10 by 3¼ inches, which is a sufficient proof of its antiquity. I made an excavation from the top, to a depth of 20 feet, without any result save the verification of the fact that the ruin was a mass of solid brick-work.†

---

* See ante pp. 276-277. The supposed sites of these pillars are marked GG. in the plan.

† The site of this stupa is marked H. in the plan.

To the east of the monastery, at a distance of 100 paces, or 250 feet, there was a large deep trench, which was said to be the spot where the earth had opened and engulfed *Devadatta*, the cousin and implacable enemy of Buddha. Fa Hian calls the distance only 70 paces, or less than 200 feet, in a northerly direction from the east gate of the monastery. But as the two pillars and the *stupa*, which have just been described, stood in the very position here indicated by Fa Hian, it is certain that we must read "southerly." The accuracy of this correction is confirmed by the existence of a large deep tank within 200 feet of the south-east corner of the ruined monastery, called *Bhulánan*. This tank is 600 feet long and 250 feet broad, and is now filled with water. Close by, on the south side, there was another great hollow, in which it was said that the mendicant monk *Kukáli*, a disciple of Devadatta, had been swallowed up alive for calumniating Buddha. This is represented by the *Lambtha Tál*, a long narrow tank only 200 feet to the south of the Devadatta gulf. The third great fissure or hollow is described by Hwen Thsang as being at 800 paces, or 2,000 feet, to the south of the second. According to the legend this was the spot in which a Brahmani girl, named *Chanchá*, had been engulfed alive for falsely accusing Buddha of incontinence. This *Chanchá* gulf is represented by a nameless deep tank, 600 feet long by 400 feet broad, which lies 2,200 feet to the south of the Kukáli gulf. The exact correspondence of position of these three tanks with the three great fissures or gulfs of the Buddhist legends offers a very strong confirmation of the correctness of identification of the *Jogini-baria* mound with the great Jetavana monastery.*

The pilgrims next describe a pair of temples of the same dimensions, of which one was situated to the east and the other to the west of the road, which should therefore be the main road that led from the city towards the south. Hwen Thsang says that the first temple was only 70 paces to the east of the monastery, while Fa Hian places it at the same distance from the eastern gate, but towards the north. The position of these temples is doubtful, as I was unable to discover any remains in the immediate vicinity of the monastery that corresponded with the

---

* These tanks are marked P, Q, and R in the plan.

description. There are, however, in another position the remains of two temples which answer the description so accurately as to leave but little doubt that they must be the buildings in question. The first, or west temple is described by both pilgrims as containing a seated figure of Buddha, while the second or east temple belonged to the Brahmans. Both were 60 feet in height, and the Brahminical temple was called the "shadow-covered," because, as the credulous Buddhists asserted, it was covered by the shadow of the Buddhist temple when the sun was in the west, while its own shadow, when the sun was in the east, never covered the Buddhist temple, but was always "deflected to the north." Now, the two ruins which I would identify with these temples are situated to the east and west of the road leading from the city, and due east and west from each other.* They correspond, therefore, exactly as to the relative position with each other; but instead of being only 70 paces, or 175 feet, from the monastery, the nearest is nearly 700 feet from the great mound of ruins. It is highly probable, however, that the surrounding walls of the monastery may have extended as far as the two stone pillars on the east, in which case the nearest temple mound would be within 250 feet of the walls, and the whole enclosure would then very nearly correspond in size with the dimensions recorded in the Ceylonese annals. As this increased size would also bring two tanks within the limits of the monastery, which, according to the *Cingalese*, were actually included within the walls, I feel inclined to adopt the larger measurement of 1,000 cubits side, or 4,000 cubits circuit, as the true size of the Great Jetavana Monastery.

To the north-west of the monastery Hwen Thsang places a well and a small *stupa*, which marked the spot where *Maudgala-putra* tried in vain to unloose the girdle of *Sariputra*. As the distance is not mentioned it may be inferred that the *stupa* was close by, and therefore I would identify the site with that of the shrine of *Pir-Bardan* in the small village of Husen Jot, which is within 700 feet of the north-west corner of the monastery.† Near the same place there was also a *stupa* of Asoka, and a stone

---
* These sites are marked S and T in the plan.
† Marked K in the plan.

pillar, which the King had raised to note the spot where Buddha and his right-hand disciple Sâriputra had taken exercise and explained the law. I could find no trace of any of these monuments, and I conclude that the *stupas*, as usual, must have furnished materials for the erection of *Pir-Baráṇa's* shrine.

The situation of the next holy place, which both pilgrims call the "Wood of the Recovered Eyes," is fixed at 4 *li*, or two-thirds of a mile, to the north-west of the monastery.* This position is now represented exactly by the village of *Rájgarh Gulariya*, which is situated in the midst of a very large grove of trees. The present grove is said to have been planted only two generations back, but the trees about the village itself are of great age, and the name of *Gulariya* points to some remarkable *Gular* tree as more ancient than the village itself. The legend attached to this spot is sufficiently marvellous. Five hundred brigands having been blinded by order of King Prasenajita, attracted the commiseration of Buddha, who restored their sight. The five hundred men who had thus recovered their eye-sight, threw away their staves, or, according to Fa Hian, planted them in the ground, when they immediately took root, and grew to be a large grove, which was called the "Wood of the Recovered Eyes." The monks of *Jetavana* were in the habit of repairing to this grove for exercise and meditation, and all the spots which holy Buddhists had made famous by their meditations were marked by inscriptions or by *stupas*. There is one small brick mound to the east of the grove, but I could find no trace of any inscriptions, although rewards were offered for even a single letter.

We now come to the second great monument of *Srávastí*, the celebrated *Purvárâma*, or "Eastern Monastery," which was built by the lady *Visâkhâ*, who has already been mentioned in my account of Sâket, or Ayodhya. Fa Hian places this monument at 6 or 7 *li*, or rather more than a mile, to the north-east of the Jetavana. But this bearing is certainly wrong, as it would carry us right into the middle of the old city. I would therefore read "south-east," which

---

* Beal's Fa Hian, p. 78, and Julien's Hwen Thsang, II., 308.—In this instance, the latter pilgrim has omitted to give his usual transliteration of the name in Chinese syllables. M. Julien proposes *Ápanctvarana*; but I prefer *Ajitabhavana*, or *Ajatabhavana*, which I think may be the original name of the neighbouring town of *Akauna* or *Andhava*, which is only three miles distant.

is the direction of a very large mound, called *Ora-jhár* or "Basket-shakings," that is upwards of a mile from the *Jetavana*.* Hwen Thsang places the *Vihára* and *stupa* of Visákhá at more than 4 *li*, or upwards of 3,500 feet, to the east of the "shadow-covered temple" of the Brahmans. Now, the *Ora-jhár* mound is just 4,000 feet to the south-east of the ruined mound, which I have already identified with the Brahminical temple. I am therefore quite satisfied that it is the remains of the great *Vihára* of the *Purvárâma*, or Eastern Monastery. Hwen Thsang's account of this famous monastery is meagre; his whole description being limited to the fact that " in this place Buddha overcame the Brahmans and received an invitation from a lady named Visákhá." Fa Hian's notice is equally brief. We must therefore turn to the Ceylonese annals for an account of the lady and her works.† According to them Visákhá was the daughter of Dhananja, a wealthy merchant of *Sáhet*. At 15 years of age she was married to Purnna-Vardhana, the son of *Migára*, a rich merchant of *Srávasti*, and from that time her whole life was spent in the observance of the religious rites of Buddhism. She was the means of converting her father-in-law Migára, and " she was called in consequence" *Migára-Mátáwi*, and became the mother or chief of the *Upásekawas*, or female lay-disciples of Buddha. Towards the end of her career she determined to sell her wedding ornaments to obtain funds for the erection of a *Vihára*, " but there was no one in *Sewet* who had wealth enough to purchase them." She therefore bought a garden at the east side of the city, and expended immense treasures in the erection of a *Vihára*, which was called *Purvárâma*, or the Eastern Monastery, from the place in which it stood."

The great mound, now called *Ora-jhár*, is a solid mass of earth 70 feet in height, which was formerly crowned by a

---

* Mr. Beal thinks that Fa Hian is probably correct, as the name of *Purvárâma* "would indicate east from the city."—Fa Hian, page 75. I have surveyed these ruins, and have the plan now before me, and I can only repeat that Fa Hian's bearing of N. E. is undoubtedly wrong, as 6 or 7 *li* to the north-east would place the *Purvárâma* in the midst of the Rapti River due north of the city. I take the name of *Purvárâma*, or Eastern Monastery, to refer to its position, with regard to the Jetavana Monastery, from which the *Ora-jhár* mound lies south-east by east. There are no ruins to the east of the old city, and the *Purvárâma* can only be looked for somewhere between east and south-east of the Jetavana.—See Plate No. L. I have now considered the whole subject over again, and I adhere to my first identification. The mound marked No. 6 would answer the requirements of both pilgrims; but it is very low, while the great *Ora-jhár* mound seems much more likely to be the remains of the great monastery built by the wealthiest lady in the land.—See W in the plan.

† Hardy " Manual of Buddhism," p. 227.

brick temple. Within the last century a Musalmán fakir, who had lived under the trees at the foot of the mound, was buried in a tomb on the very top of it, which was built with the bricks of the ruin. Some years later his successor was buried beside him, and their two tombs at present preclude all hope of making any excavation from the top of the mound. I cleared the north face completely, and the other three faces partially, until I reached the paved brick flooring which surrounded the original Buddhist temple, at a height of 55 feet above the ground. The wall of the temple on the north face is only 20 feet long, and, although I failed to reach the other two corners of the building, I was satisfied that it must have been square. Its height, at 3½ times its side, would not therefore have been more than 70 feet, but as its floor is 55 feet above the ground, the total height of the temple would have been 125 feet. The wall of the north face is divided into four panels by pilasters six inches thick. The bases of these pilasters, which are still very perfect, are of the same style as those at Gaya and Baragaon in Bihár, and of Mánikyála and Sháh Dheri in the Panjab. The style would therefore seem to be one that was peculiar to early Buddhism. The other faces of the temple I was unable to examine, as the foundations of the Muhammadan tomb, which are only 2½ feet above the broken walls of the temple, project 16 feet beyond its east and west faces. Unfortunately the doorway of the temple must have been towards the east, as there are traces of steps at several places down the slope of that side. There is an old well also amongst the trees on the east side of the mound, but I could find no traces of cloisters for the resident monks who ministered at the temple. The mound, however, is still surrounded by fine trees, and there are two small tanks at the very foot of it, which would of course have been included within the limits of the monastery.

The *stupa* mentioned by Hwen Thsang as belonging to the *Pureedráma* may perhaps be represented by a small ruined mound close to the north-east corner of the *Ora-jhár*. The mound is only 8 feet high, but an excavation which I made to the depth of 11 feet, showed it to be made of solid bricks of large size, 12 by 9 by 3 inches. It is 40 feet in diameter, and when complete with its pinnacle it must have been about 50 or 60 feet in height. From its vicinity to the Purvvârâma I have little doubt that this is the *stupa* which *Visâkhá* built on the spot where Buddha had overcome the Brahmans in argument.*

The last place mentioned by the pilgrims is the spot where King *Virudhaka* halted with his army to converse with Buddha, and out of respect for the teacher gave up his expedition against the *Sâkyas*, and returned to his capital. Hwen Thsang states that this famous spot was close to the monastery of Visâkha on the south side, while Fa Hian says that it was 4 *li*, or two-thirds of a mile, to the south-west of the city. The former is the more probable position, as it is to the south-east and on the high road to *Kapilanagara*, the capital of the Sâkyas. Close by there was a *stupa* to mark the spot where 500 Sâkya maidens were afterwards massacred by Virudhaka for refusing to enter his harem. Near the *stupa* there was a dry tank, or gulf, in which Virudhaka had been swallowed up.† According to the legend, Buddha had predicted that Virudhaka would be destroyed by fire within seven days after the massacre. When the seventh day arrived, the King, accompanied by his women, proceed gaily to a large tank where he entered a boat, and was rowed to the middle of the water. But flames burst forth from the waters and consumed the boat, and the earth opened beneath the tank, and Virudhaka "fell alive into hell." The only large piece of water that I could find is a nameless tank close to the south side of Visâkha's temple, and therefore in the very position indicated by Hwen Thsang; but there are no existing remains near it that could be indentified with the *stupa* of the 500 Sakya maidens.

The monuments of *Srâvasti* hitherto described by the pilgrims are directly connected with the personal history of Buddha. The places where he sat and walked, where he taught his law, and where he worsted the Brahmans in argument, were all specially holy in the eyes of devout Buddhists. But these sacred monuments formed only a small portion of the Buddhist buildings of the great city of Srâvasti, where, according to Hwen Thsang, the monuments were counted by hundreds. Fa Hian, however, quotes a tradition which

---

* Marked X in the plan.
† Marked Y and Z in the plan.

limited their number to ninety-eight, at a period not remote from his own time, and as he visited the place nearly two centuries and a half earlier than Hwen Thsang, when most of the monasteries were in ruins, we may be satisfied that their number never reached one hundred even at the most flourishing period of Buddhism. I traced the ruins of nine monasteries in the immediate neighbourhood of the old city, and there are probably as many more within a range of two miles. I found also the foundations of at least ten temples of various sizes, but they were all in too ruinous a state to be of any interest. But when I remember that the Jetavana itself, as well as nearly the whole of the ninety-eight monasteries of Srávasti, were in complete ruins upwards of twelve centuries ago, I think it is more wonderful that so much should still be left for the use of the archæologist than that so little should remain of all the magnificent buildings of this one famous city. Sáhet is said to have been the capital of Raja Suhir-dal, whose ancestor Hansa Dhwaja was reigning in the time of the Pándus, when the city was called *Chandriká-puri.*

XX. TANDA, OR TADWA.

From *Srávasti* both pilgrims proceeded to visit the birth-place of Kásyapa Buddha, at *To-wai,* which Fa Hian places at 50 *li,* or 8⅓ miles to the west. Hwen Thsang does not name the town, but he states that it was about 60 *li*, or 10 miles, to the north-west of Srávasti.[*] The bearing and distance point to the village of *Tadwa,* which is just 9 miles to the west of *Sáhet-Máhet.* Some people refer this name to *Tanda,* because for the last hundred years the Banjáras have been in the habit of halting, or of making their *Tanda,* at this place. But the people themselves spell the name of their village *Tadwa,* and not *Tanda,* which properly means the whole venture of goods belonging to a party of Banjáras, but which is also applied to the places at which they halt. I think, therefore, that the name of *Tadwa* may possibly refer to the old name of *To-woi* as it is written by Fa Hian. There can, however, be no doubt as to the identity of the two places, as Tadwa is a very old site, which is still covered

---

[*] Beal's Fa Hian, c. XX, p. 53 ; and Julien's Hwen Thsang, II., 309.

with brick ruins. According to tradition, the town belonged to Raja *Suhir-dal*, after whose death it was destroyed by the Muhammadans, and remained uninhabited until about one hundred years ago, when a *Bairágí*, named *Ajudhya Dás*, established himself under the Banyan tree and discovered the female figure which is now worshipped as *Sita Mái*. The present village is situated amongst brick ruins one-quarter of a mile to the north of the road leading from Akaona to Bahraich. All the fields around are strewn with broken bricks, and within 1,000 feet of the village to the north-west there is a mound of brick ruins 800 feet long from east to west, and 300 feet board. Beyond the mound, and to the north of the village, there is a large irregular shaped sheet of water, nearly half a mile in length, called Sita-Deva Tál. But this name cannot be older than the discovery of the statue which is attributed to Sitá.

The west end of the mass of ruins is very low, but it is covered with broken walls and fine trees, and was therefore most probably the site of the monastic establishment. The general height of the east end is 10 feet above the fields, but rises to 20 feet at the south-west corner. At this point the mound is formed of solid brick-work, which, after close examination, I discovered to be the remains of a large *stupa*. As two different measurements gave a diameter of not less than 70 feet, this *stupa* must have been one of the largest and most important in the famous Province of *Uttara Kosala*. Hwen Thsang mentions only two *stupas* at this place,—one to the south of the town being built on the spot where *Kásyapa Buddha* had performed his meditations under a Banyan tree, and the other to the north of the town, containing the complete body of Kásyapa. This is also confirmed by its size, as Fa Hian calls this *stupa* a great one. The *stupa* on the mound must certainly represent the latter monument, because the tank precludes the possibility of any other having existed to the northward of it. I wished very much to have made an excavation in this mound, but the presence of a *lingam* of Mahadeo on the top of it, which with *Sita-Máí* shares the devotions of the villagers, was an effectual check against any excavations. This is the more to be regretted, as the *stupa* is said to have been built by Asoka, an attribution which might have been verified by an exploration of its interior.

350   ARCHÆOLOGICAL REPORT, 1862-63.

The figure which the ignorant villagers worship as *Sítá* is in reality a statue of *Máyá Deví*, the mother of *Sakya Buddha*. She is represented standing under the *Sál* tree, with her right hand raised and holding one of the branches, which is the well known position in which she is said to have given birth to Sákya. Her left hand is placed on her hip, and there is a parrot perched on her shoulder. The statue is 3 feet 4 inches in height.

XXI. NIMSAR, OR NIMKAR.

Nimsar is a famous place of pilgrimage on the left bank of the *Gumti* (or Gomati) River, 45 miles to the north-west of Lucknow. The Brahmans derive the name from *Nimisha*, a "twinkling of the eye;" hence *Naimisha-saras* or *Nimsar* means the pool where in the twinkling of an eye the sage *Gaura-Mukha* destroyed the *Asuras*. The place is also called *Nimkhár*, which is formed from *Naimisha*, pronounced *Naimikha*, and *aranya* a forest, which becomes *Naimikharan* and *Nimkhár*. The Vishnu Purâna declares that "he who bathes in the Gomati at *Naimisha* expiates all his sins."* Its popularity is therefore very great. It is noticed in the Ain Akbari as "a famous large fort, with a great number of idolatrous temples, and a reservoir."† This reservoir is called the *Chakra-tírtha*, and is said to be the place where the *Chakra*, or "discus," of Vishnu fell during the contest with the Asuras. The shape of the pool is nearly hexagonal with a diameter of 120 feet. The water springs up from below and flows out by the south side into a swampy rill about 20 feet broad called the Godáveri Nala. The pool is surrounded with a number of shabby brick temples and *dharmsálas*, and though the water is clear, yet the place looks dirty and uninviting.

The fort of *Nimsar* is situated on a precipitous mound to the north of the holy pool, about 1,100 feet long, from east to west, between 300 and 400 feet broad, and 50 feet high. The west end is a high cliff called the *Shah Búrj*, or King's Tower, which overhangs the Gumti. The gate of the fort, which is at the east end, is arched and therefore of Muhammadan construction. But it is built of Hindu materials,

---

* H. H. Wilson's Translation, p. 325.
† Gladwin's Translation, II., 31 & 210.

partly brick and partly *kankar* blocks, which betray their origin by their carvings and by the presence of the *Swastika* symbol, or mystic cross. The walls were originally of brick, but they have long ago disappeared, and the only parts of the old fort now standing are the gateway and the *Shah Bárj*. The foundation of the latter is, however, of Hindu construction, and as there are many carved bricks lying about, I presume that it was a temple. The fort is provided with a well 8½ feet broad and 61½ feet deep to the water level.

The tradition of the place is, that the building of the fort was finished on Friday, the 9th of the waxing moon of *Chaitra*, in the *Samvat* year 1362, or A. D. 1305, by *Háhájál*, a renegade Hindu, who is said to have been the Vazir of *Ala-ud-din Ghori*. For Ghori we must read *Khilji* to bring the King's name into agreement with the date, and as the people are in the habit of styling all the Pathans as Ghoris, the alteration is perfectly allowable. But who was *Háhájál*? As a renegade Hindu and the Vazir of Ala-ud-din, he might perhaps be the same person as *Kafur*, who in A. D. 1305 was appointed as Malik Naib to the command of the army for the conquest of the Dakhan. I procured several of Ala-ud-din's coins at Nimsar, and in his reign I conclude that the fort passed from the hands of the Hindus into those of the Musulmáns. The original fort is said to have been as old as the Pándus; and if the derivation of the name of the place has been truly handed down, it must have been occupied even earlier than the time of the Pándus.*

XXII. BARIKHAR, OR VAIRATKHERA.

Barikhar is the name of a village on the top of an extensive old mound called *Vairátkhera*, which is situated on the high road between Nimsar and Pilibhit, at 42 miles from the former, and 68 miles from the latter place. *Barikhar* is said to be a corruption of *Bariyakhera*, or *Vairát-khera*, and its foundation is attributed to *Vairát* Rája in the time of the Pándus. The ruined mound is 1,000 feet in length at top from east to west by 600 feet in breadth, and from 10 to 20 feet in height. But the dimensions at the base are much more, as the slope is very gentle, being 200 feet in length on

---

* On the opposite bank of the Gumti there is an old mound called Orajhar, and Orajik, as well as Benasagar, which is said to have been the residence of Benu Raja.

the north side, where I measured it. This would make the base of the mound about 1,400 feet by 1,000 feet, which agrees with the size of 50 *bigahs*, or 1,400,000 square feet, which is popularly attributed to it by the villagers themselves. But the fields are strewn with broken bricks for upwards of 1,000 feet to the northward, and for 500 or 600 feet to the eastward, where there are the remains of several temples. The area actually covered by ruins is not less than 2,000 feet square or upwards of 1½ miles in circuit, which shows that Barikhar must once have been a good sized town, but I strongly doubt the story of the Brahmans which attributes its foundation to Vairât Raja. The name is written by the people themselves *Badiskar*, although it is pronounced *Barikhar*, and I believe that similarity of sound alone has led to the identification of Barikhar with Bariyakhera and Vairât Raja.

XXIII. DEORYIA AND DEWAL.

I couple these two places together because they actually form parts of the old nameless capital of the *Báchhal* Rajas, who ruled over Eastern Rohilkhand and Western Oudh before the time of the *Katehriyas*. Dewal itself is a small village which has received its name from a temple in which is deposited a very perfect inscription dated in *Samvat* 1049, or A. D. 992. The opposite village is called *Ilâhábás* by the Muhammadans, but this name is scarcely known to the people, who usually call it *Garh-Gájana*. The inscription is chiefly remarkable for the clean and beautiful manner in which the letters have been engraved; and its perfect state makes it the more valuable, as it furnishes us with a complete specimen of the alphabet of the *Kutila* character in which it is said to be engraved. James Prinsep gave a specimen of the characters along with a translation of the inscription in the Asiatic Society's Journal for 1837, page 777. But the copy from which he framed his alphabet was made by hand, and although it is wonderfully accurate as a mere transcript of the words, yet it is very faulty as a copy of the individual letters. This is the more to be regretted as the alphabet thus framed from an inaccurate copy has become the standard specimen of the *Kutila* characters. Now the term *Kutila* means "bent," and as all the letters of the inscription have a bottom stroke or tail, which is turned, or "bent," to the right, I infer that the alphabet was named *Kutila* from this peculiarity in the formation of its letters. But this peculiarity was unnoticed by the original transcriber, and consequently the print types of the Kutila characters, which have been prepared both in Germany and in England, are entirely wanting in this special characteristic which gives its name to the alphabet. The letter *l* and the attached vowels are perhaps the most faulty.*

The village of Dewal is situated 16 miles to the south south-east of Pilibhit, on the west bank of the *Kau*, or *Katni* Nala. There are two or three plain brick rooms which are called temples, and in one of these the inscription is deposited; but it is said to have been found amongst the ruins of *Garh-Gájana*, or Iláhábás, on the opposite bank of the stream. Garh-Gájana is a large ruined mound, about 800 feet square, which includes two small tanks on the east side; but although it is called a *Garh*, or fort, it was most probably only the country residence of Raja Lalla, who founded it. The small modern village of Iláhábás is situated close to the south-east corner or Garh-Gájana, and near it on the the south side are the ruins of a very large temple, amongst which the inscription is said to have been discovered. The figure of the Varáha Avatar of Vishnu, which is now in the *Dewal* temple, was found in the same place. The mound of ruins is 200 feet square at base, but the walls of the temple are no longer traceable, as the bricks and kankar blocks have been carried away by the villagers. I traced the remains of at least six other temples around the principal mass of ruin, but there was nothing about them worth noting. To the south there are two larger mounds, which appear to be the remains of an old village.

The *Kau* or *Katni* Nala continues its course to the south for three miles, until opposite the large village of Deoriya, when it turns sharply to the east for two miles to the south end of a large ruined fort with is now called *Garha-Khera*, or the "fort mound." The Katni Nala here turns to the north, and after running round the three other sides of the ruined fort returns to within a few hundred yards of the point from whence it took its northerly course. It thus forms

---

* See Plate No. LI. for a photograph fac-simile of this inscription. The translation by Prinsep was published in the Bengal Asiatic Society's Journal, 1837, page 777.

a natural ditch to the old stronghold of the Ikchhal Rajas, which is only approachable on the southern side. The fort has been deserted for many centuries, and is covered with dense jungle, in which several tigers have been killed within the last few years. A single cart tract leads to the nearest portions of the ruins which have afforded materials for all the buildings in the large village of Deoriya. The exact extent of the fort is not known, but the position enclosed by the Katni Nala is about 6,000 feet in length from north to south and 4,000 feet in breadth, and the fort is said to be somewhat less than half a *kos*, or just about half a mile in length. The bricks are of large size, 13 by 9 by 2 inches, which shows considerable antiquity, but the statues of kankar are all Brahmanical, such as the goddess *Devi*, *Siva* and his wife, as *Gauri-Sankar*, and two *arghas* of *lingams*. These figures are said to be discovered only in the foundations of the buildings, which, if true, would seem to show that the existing remains are the ruins of Muhammadan works constructed of Hindu materials.

The Katni Nala is an artificial canal drawn from the *Mála* River near *Sohás*, 10 miles to the south-east of Pilibhit, and 6 miles to the north of Dewal. Its general course is from north to south, excepting where it winds round the old fort of *Garha-Khera*, after which it resumes its southerly course and falls into the *Kaukant* Nala, about 3 miles to the south of the ruins. Its whole course is just 20 miles in length. All the maps are wrong in giving the name of Katni Nala to the *Mála* River, instead of to the artificial canal which joins the *Mála* and *Kankaut* Rivers. The canal varies in width from 30 and 40 feet to 100 feet, and even more at the places where it is usually forded. Its very name of *Katni* Nala, or the "cut stream," is sufficient to prove that it is artificial. But this fact is distinctly stated in the inscription, which records that Raja Lalla "made a beautiful and holy *Katha-Nadi*." That this was the *Katni Nala*, which is drawn from the Mála River, is proved by the previous verse, which records that the Raja presented to the Brahmans certain villages "shaded by pleasant trees, and watered by the *Nirmala Nadi*." This name is correctly translated by James Prinsep as "pellucid stream," which, though perfectly applicable to the limpid waters of the *Mála* River, is evidently the name of the stream itself, and not a

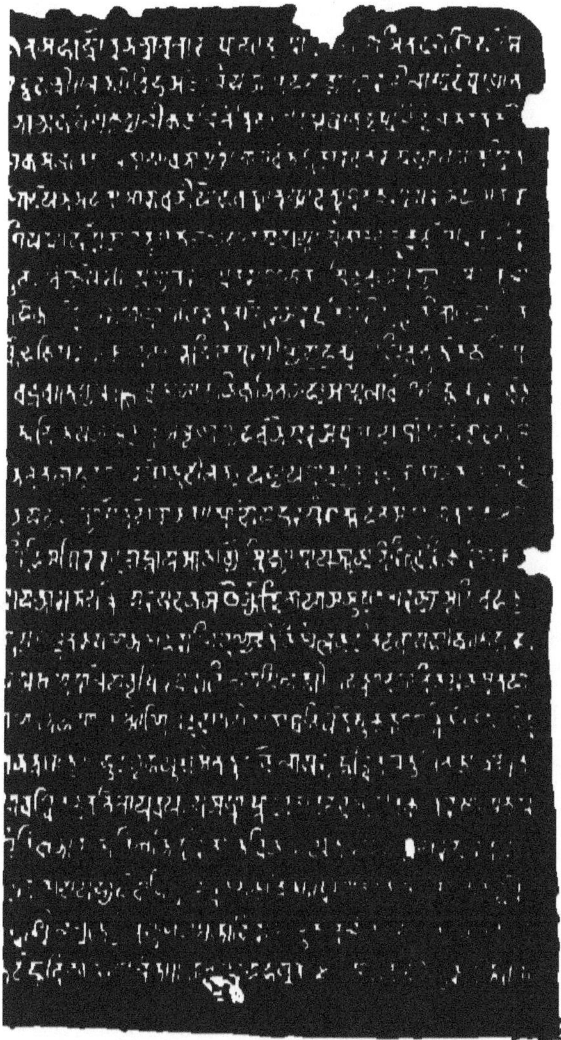

mere epithet descriptive of the clearness of its waters. And as the canal was drawn from the Nirmala River, so the villages on its banks are correctly described as being watered by it.

The inscription goes on to say that Raja Lalla and his wife Lakshmi "made many groves, gardens, lakes, and temples." Prinsep has given the last as "many other extensive works," but the term in the original is *devalayataneshu cha*, "and temples," *devalaya* being one of the commonest names for a temple of any kind. In the 27th verse the great temple to which the inscription was attached is said to have been dedicated to *Siva* by the Raja, while the queen built another fano to Pârvati. In the next verse they are described as "two divine temples" *(sura-griha)*; and in the 32nd verse it is stated that the god and goddess were worshipped together under the title of *Devapalli*. This then must be the origin of the name of *Dewal*, and the great temple mound to the south of *Garh-Gájana* must be the remains of the two temples dedicated to *Devapalli*.

In the inscription Raja Lalla calls himself the nephew of *Mâns Chandra Pratâpa*, and the grandson of *Vira Varmma*, who is said to be of the race of *Chhindu* and descended from the great Rishi *Chyavana*. This holy sage is mentioned in the Vishnu Purâna as having married Sukanyâ, the daughter of Saryâti, the son of Manu. He is also noticed in the Bhâgavata and Padma Purânas, as appropriating a share of the marriage offerings to the Aswini Kumâras, which entailed the quarrel with Indra, that is alluded to in verse 4 of the inscription. The family therefore was reputed to be of ancient descent; but if Vira Varmma, the grandfather of Lalla was the first Raja, the establishment of the dynasty cannot be dated earlier than A. D. 900. Now the *Bâchhal* Rajputs claim descent from Raja *Vena*, whose son was *Virát*, the reputed founder of Barikhar or *Virát Khera*, and whom I believe to be the same as Vira Varmma of the inscription. To Raja *Vena*, or *Ben*, is attributed the erection of the great forts of *Garha-khera*, and *Sâhgarh*, and to his queen, *Ketaki Râni*, is assigned the excavation of the *Râni Tál* at the old town of *Kâbar*. Garh Gájana and the temples of Dewal were built by Raja Lalla. The town and fort of *Maraori* are attributed to *Muradhwaj*, and *Barkhera* to *Harual* Raja; but neither of these names appears in the very imperfect and scanty list of their family which the *Báchhals* now possess.

It is admitted by every one that the *Katehriyas* succeeded the *Báchhals*, but the *Katehriyas* themselves state that they did not settle in *Katehar* until *Samvat* 1231, or A. D. 1174. Up to this date, therefore, the *Báchhal* Rajas may be supposed to have possessed the dominant power in Eastern Rohilkhand beyond the Rámganga, while western Rohilkhand was held by the *Bhiddr*, *Gwála*, and other tribes, from whom the Katehriyas profess to have wrested it. Gradually the *Báchhals* must have retired before the *Katehriyas* until they had lost all their territory to the west of the Deoha or Pilibhit River. Here they made a successful stand, and though frequently afterwards harried by the Muhammadans, they still managed to hold their small territory between the Deoha River and the primœval forests of Pilibhit. When hard pressed they escaped to the jangal, which still skirts their ancient possessions of *Garh Gájana* and *Garha Khera*. But their resistance was not always successful, as their descendants confess that about 300 or 400 years ago, when their capital *Nigohi* was taken by the King of Delhi, the twelve sons of Raja *Udarana*, or *Aorana*, were all put to death. The twelve cenotaphs of these Princes are still shown at *Nigohi*. Shortly after this catastrophe *Chhavi Rána*, the grandson of one of the murdered Princes fled to the *Lakhi* jangal, where he supported himself by plundering, but when orders were given to exterminate his band, he presented himself before the King of Delhi, and obtained the District of *Nigohi* as a *jághir*. This place his descendant Tarsam Sing still holds, but the *jághir* is reduced to the town of Nigohi with a few of the surrounding villages.

The *Gotrácharya* of the *Báchhal* Rajputs declares them to be *Chandravansis*, and their high social position is attested by their daughters being taken in marriage by Chohans, Ráhtors, and Kachwáhas. According to Sir H. Elliot, *Báchhal* Zamindars are found in the Districts of Aligarh and Mathura, as well as in Budaon and Shahjahánpur of Rohilkband. But the race is even more widely spread than the Gangetic Báchhals are aware of, as Abul Fazl records that "the port of Aramray (in the peninsula of Gujarát)

is a very strong place inhabited by the tribe of Bâchhal."*
Of the origin of the name nothing is known, but it is probably connected with *báchhna*, to select or choose. The title of *Chhindu*, which is given in the inscription, is also utterly unknown to the people, and I can only guess that it may be the name of one of the early ancestors of the race.

XXIV. PARASUA-KOT.

Four miles to the westward of Balai-Khera there is a long lofty mound lying east and west called *Parasua-kot*, which is said to be the ruins of a temple and other edifices that Bali Raja built for his *Ahír* servant, named Parasua. The mound is about 1,400 feet long, and 300 feet broad at base, with a height of 35 feet at its loftiest point near the eastern end. On this point there are the brick foundations of a large temple, 42 feet square, with the remains of steps on the east face, and a stone lintel or door step, on the west face. I conclude therefore that the temple had two doors,—one to the east and other to the west,—and as this is the common arrangement of *lingam* temples, it is almost certain that the building must have been dedicated to Siva. Towards the west, the mound gradually declines in height until it is lost in the fields. Forty feet to the west of the temple there are some remains of a thick wall which would seem to have formed part of the enclosure of the temple, which must have been not less than 130 feet square. Five hundred feet further west there are the remains of another enclosure, 100 feet square, which most probably once surrounded a second temple, but the height of the ruins at this point is more than 16 feet above the ground. Although the *Parasua* mound is well known to the people for many miles around, yet there are no traditions attached to the place save the story of *Parasua*, the Ahír, which has already been noticed. When we consider that a temple 24 feet square could not have been less than 3½ times its base, or 147 feet in height, and that its floor being 35 feet above the ground the whole height of the building would have been 182 feet, it is strange that no more detailed traditions should exist regarding the builders of so magnificent an edifice. I am of opinion that the temple must have been

---

* Gladwin's Translation, II., 69.

the work of one of the earlier *Báchhal* Rajas, but unfortunately the records of this race are too imperfect to afford any clue to the ancient history of the country.

XXV. BALAI-KHERA.

Baliya, or *Balai Khera*, is a large ruined mound about 1,200 feet square, or nearly one mile in circuit, and not less than 20 feet in height at the southern end. The mound is situated close to the Muhammadan town of *Jahánábád*, which is just 6 miles to the westward of Pilibhit. It is covered with broken bricks of large size, and from its square form I infer that it must once have been fortified, or at least walled round. Near the south-east corner there is a very old Banyan tree, and the ruins of a brick temple. To the west there are two tanks and six ruined heaps which are said to be the remains of temples. There is nothing now standing that can give any clue to the probable age of the town, as the bricks are moved to *Jahánábád* as soon as they are discovered. But the large size of the bricks is a proof of antiquity which is supported by the traditions of the people, who ascribe the foundation of *Balpur* or *Baliya* to the well known Daitya or demon, named *Bali*.

XXVI. KABAR, OR SHIRGARH.

The old town, *Kábar* is situated on a lofty mound, 20 miles to the north of Bareli, and 20 miles to the west of Pilibhit. The ruins consist of a circular mound, 900 feet in diameter and 25 feet in height, which is still surrounded by a deep ditch from 50 to 100 feet in width. This was the old fort of *Kábar* in the time of the Hindus, and there are still some remains of the walls of a large oblong building on the top of the mound, which the people say was a temple. The old city, which surrounded the fort on all sides, is now divided into four separate villages, called *Kábar, Islámpur, Dongarpur*, and *Shirgarh*. All these are situated on old mounds, which are nearly as lofty as the fort mound itself. The place is usually called *Kábar* by the Hindus, and *Shirgarh* by the Musulmáns. It is said to have been taken from the Hindu Rajas 550 years ago, or in A. D. 1313, during the reign of Ala-ud-din Khilji.* Falling again into the

---

* Sir Henry Elliot in his Glossary, article *Dee*, p. 115, states that *Kábar* was the northern boundary of cultivation in the reign of Jalaluddin Firuz, who was the predecessor of Ala-ud-din.

hands of the Hindus after the death of Firuz Tughlak, it was again captured by Shir Shah, who built the fort of *Shirgarh* to the south of the old fort, for the purpose of keeping the townspeople in check. To the south of Shirgarh there is a fine tank called *Khawâs-Tâl*, which no doubt belongs to the same period, as Khawâs Khan was the name of Shir Shah's most trusted general. That portion of the town called Islâmpur is said to have been built by Islâm Shah, the son of Shir Shah, but it was more probably only re-named by Khawâs Khan in honour of his master's son, during the life time of Shir Shah himself. On the north side there is a shallow sheet of water called the Râm Sâgar, and on the north-west there is an old tank called Râni Tâl, which is attributed to Ketakhi Râni, the queen of Raja Ben, the founder of the dynasty of *Báchhal* Rajputs. The extreme length of the whole mass of ruins from east to west is 3,500 feet, and the breadth 2,500 feet, the complete circuit being 9,600 feet, or nearly 2 miles. The long continued Muhammadan occupation of five centuries has most effectually swept away all traces of Hinduism; but old coins are occasionally found, of which a few belong to the later Hindu dynasties of the ninth and tenth centuries. From the great size of the place, as well as from its evident antiquity, I should have expected that very old Hindu coins would occasionally be found; but all my enquiries were fruitless, and the only actual traces of Hindu occupation that I could hear of were two small stone figures, of which one was a representation of Durgâ slaying the Mahesâsur, or "Buffalo-Demon," and the other a broken statue of some god which was too much injured to be recognized.

END OF VOLUME I.

INDEX.

ARCHÆOLOGICAL SURVEY OF INDIA.

Subject.	Page.
A	
Abu Rihan. Silence of — as to Dilli	145
—— Zaid, on the authority of Ibn Wahab, calls "Kadage a great city in the Kingdom of Gozar"	272
Account given in the Mirat-i-Asrar as to later Kings of Delhi	147
Accounts given by Shams-i-Siraz of the removal of two stone pillars from their original sites to Delhi	161
Acharya Sri Yogananda, an Inscription on the door of the great cave in the Nagarjuni Hill	49 & 50
Actual builder of the Kutb Minar	212
Adi Rajah. The legend of —	255
Adilabad, or Mohammadabad. The fort of —	217
Adina Masjid. The great mosque of Kutbuddin called —	185
Adisadra, the name given to Ahichhatra by Ptolemy	255
Ahalya Bai. Temple on the Pretsila Hill at Gaya erected by —	4
Ahichhatra, or Ramnagar. An account of the city of —	255
—————— The name of — written as Ahi-kshetra	ib.
—————— mentioned by Ptolemy as Adisadra	ib.
—————— the capital of North Panchala	ib.
—————— Description of — given by Hwen Thsang	256

INDEX.

SUBJECT.	PAGE.
Ahichhatra. Ruins of — first visited by Captain Hodgson	246
——— Brahmanical temples at —	249
——— Buddhist remains at —	260
Ahi-kshetra. The name of Ahichhatra written as —	255
Ain Akbari. Date of Anang Pal in the —	143
Ajatasatru, the contemporary of Buddha	23
Ajayapura, the ancient name of Bairor	13
Ajudhya. Fa Hian's route to —	296
——— or Sakets. An account of the city of —	317
——— identified with Sakets	323
——— Remains of antiquity at —	ib.
——— Uttara Kosala, the Northern part of —	327
——— Banaodha, the Southern part of —	ib.
Akshay Bat, or "undecaying Banian tree" at Prayaga	297
Alai Darwaza, or Gate of Alauddin	205
Alauddin Khiliji. Mosque of Kutbuddin enlarged by — ...	184
——— Unfinished minar of — stands North from the Kutb Minar	205
Alha, a Banafar hero...	283
Allahabad, or Prayaga. An account of the city of —	296
Altamsh. Mosque of Kutbuddin enlarged in the reign of — ...	187
——— An account of the tomb of —	214
Amara Sinha. Temple near the Pipal tree at Buddha Gaya supposed to have been built by —	6
——— identified with Amara Deva	7
——— Deva identified with Amara Sinha	ib.
Amir Khusru's description of the work carried on by Alauddin Khiliji in the great mosque of Kutbuddin	189
Anand Tila. A mound at Mathura called —	231
Anang Pal. Re-building of Dilli by —	141

INDEX.

SUBJECT.	PAGE.
Anang Pal Date of — in the Ain Akbari ...	143
———— Date of — in the Kumaon and Garhwal manuscripts ...	143
———— Date of — ...	144
———— An anecdote of — given by Mir Khasru ...	ib.
———— Dilli re-built by — owing to the loss of Kanoj ...	151
———— An account of the tank called — to the North-West of Kutb Minar ...	152
———— Anekpur, a village supposed to have been built by — ...	ib.
———— Erection of a certain temple close to the iron pillar of Dilli attributed to — ...	152
———— Accounts of the sons of — ...	ib.
———— Extent of the dominions of — ...	ib.
———— (or Dilao Deo). Iron pillar of Delhi supposed to have been erected by — ...	171
Anant Bhkhi. A hot spring at Rajgir called — ...	27
Anecdote of Anang Pal given by Mir Khasru ...	144
Anekpur, a village in the Balamgarh District supposed to have been built by Anang Pal ...	152
Aniruddha, the cousin of Buddha ...	24
Anuradhwa. The village called — received its name from Aniruddha, the cousin of Buddha ...	ib.
Aphsar. An account of the village of — ...	40
Ara Raj Pillar. The description of — ...	62 & 68
Arguments in support of the Hindu origin of Kutb Minar ...	120
Ariana Antiqua, a work by Horace Hayman Wilson ...	v
Arjuna Pandu. Chakra, eighth in descent from — made Kosambi his capital ...	201
Aunagar. A village near Ghasrawa called — ...	39
Ashta Sakti. A sculpture representing — in a temple at Benarh ...	85
Asiatic Society of Bengal founded by Sir William Jones ...	i

Subject.	Page.
Asoka. Erection of the original temple at Buddha Gaya ascribed to —	8
——— The edicts of — on two stone pillars at Delhi	161
——— Stupa of — at Kanoj	301
Asoknath. Temple of — at Asokpur	329
Asokpur, the ancient name of Hutila	ib.
Aswamedha. Celebration of — by Jaya Chandra	283
Atranji-khera. An account of a ruined mound called — ...	268
——————— the site of the ancient Pikashanna	269
——————— The foundation of — attributed to Rajah Vena Chakervartti	ib.
Aurang Shah. Destruction of the statue of Sakti at Gaya attributed to —	3
Aurangzib said to have pulled down the temple of Kesava Deva at Mathura	235
Avalokiteswara. Statue of — at Nalanda	31
Ayodhya, or A-yu-to. An account of the city of — ...	293
A-yu-to, or Ayodhya. An account of the city of — ...	ib.
Ayutho identified with Kakupur	295

B

Bachhal Rajputs. An account of —	356
Bagheswari Devi. A temple at Kurkihar dedicated to — ...	15
Bagud, or Vagud. An account of the place called —	205
Baibbar (Mount). An account of the —	
Baiswara, the country of the Bais Rajputs	280
Bais Rajputs. Baiswara the country of the —	ib.
——————— claim descent from Salivahan	ib.
Baithak Bhairav. Statue of Buddha in a court-yard called — ...	34
Bakhra, a part of the ancient Vaisali	56
——— Remains at —	58

Subject.	Page.
Bakhra. The lion pillar of —	52
Bakror. An account of the village of —	12
Baladitya. A vihar at Nalanda built by —	34
Dalai-khera. A raised mound called — close to the Muhammadan Town of Jahanabad	349
Balamgarh. Anekpur, a village built by Anang Pal in the District of —	162
Baira Tank at Nalanda	32
Banaphr Heroes, Alha and Udal	283
Banaudha. The Southern part of Ajudhya called —	327
———— Pachham-rat, the Western District of —	id.
———— Purab-rat, the Southern District of —	id.
Banaras Sarnath. An account of the city of — ... —	103 & 104
———— Jaya Chandra defeated by Muhammad Ghori at — ...	283
Barabar Hills. An account of the —	40—49
———— Caves of —	40
———— Resin. An account of the —	43
Baragaon, or Nalanda. An account of the village of — ...	28
Bara Pal, a bridge near Delhi	225
Barikhar, or Vairatkhera. An account of the village of — ...	351
———— said to be a corruption of Vairatkhera	id.
———— The foundation of — attributed to Vairat Rajah ...	id.
Ben Chakravartti (Rajah). Traditions regarding —	65
Bernier's account of two life-size statues of elephants and their riders at Shajahanabad	225
Besadh, or Besarh. An account of the village of —	55
Besarh, or Besadh. An account of the village of —	id.
———— Identified with Vaisali —	id.
———— Remains at —	56
Bhairav. A statue of ascetic Buddha called — at Titarawa ...	39

Subject.	Page.
Bhau Daji, Dr. A short account of his archæological investigations	xxxiii
Bhaipuri Mahalla. Mound in the — of Kanoj	292
Bharatband. Uttanpada, King of —	69
Bhim-lauv. An account of the village of —	263
Bhim-sen-ka-lat. The lion pillar of Bakhra called —	81
Bhitari. An account of the village of —	96
———— An inscribed stone pillar at —	ib.
———— Pillar described	97
———— Excavations by Mr. C. Horn at —	100
Bhuddhistical establishment near Banaras, as described by Hwen Thsang	104
Dhun Mari (Rajah). Erection of the Narandgarh Pillar ascribed to —	74
Biss-kund. A hot spring at Rajgir called —	27
Bihar. An account of the city of —	26 & 27
———— The fort of —	27
Bijoli. Inscription discovered at —	157
Bilan Deo (or Anang Pal). Iron Pillar of Delhi supposed to have been erected by —...	171
Bimbisara, otherwise called Srenika, said to have built the new town of Rajagriha	23
Bodhidram. The celebrated Pipal tree at Buddha known by the name of —	6
———— Renewal of — by Purna Varmma	ib.
———— Destruction of — by Sasangka	ib.
Boulder (quartz) covered with inscriptions of Asoka at Khalsi ...	244
Brahmanical temples at Abichhatra	259
———————— temples on the mound of Makhdam Jahaniya in the Sikhana Mahalla of Kanoj	292
Brahmavarta, or Dharatkhand. Uttampada, King of — ...	69
Brahmjain. A holy hill at Gaya called —	9
Brahm-kand. A hot spring at Rajgir called —	27

Subject.	Page
Buchanan, Dr. Deputation of — to make an agricultural survey of Mysore. His appointment as Statistical Surveyor of the Bengal Presidency. Publication of his work by Mr. Montgomery. Remark on his archæological researches.	iii & iv
Buddha. Gaya. An account of —	4
—— the ascetic. A life-size statue of — at Besarh	81
—— died on a spot at a little distance from the Western bank of the Ajitavati River	82
—— Maya, the mother of —	271
—— Site of a Vihara with the tooth of — near Kanoj	292
—— A statue of — at Kosambi	318
Buddha-kund. A sacred tank at Dakror called —	
—— Supposed to be identical with Maritand Pokhar, or Sujaj-kund	13
Buddha-pad. A temple at Buddha Gaya called —	8
Buddhism. Decline and fall of —	237
Buddhist railing at Buddha Gaya	10
—— Synod (second). Vaisali, the scene of the —	63
—— Monasteries in Mathura amounted to 20	231
—— remains at Abichhatra	260
Buddhistical Inscription found at Ghosrawa	3d
Budhokar Tal. A tank called — to the South-East of the great temple at Buddha Gaya	11
Builder of the Kutb Minar	202
Bukala. Legend of —	303
Burmese inscription discovered at Buddha Gaya	8
C	
Cupola of Firuz Shah on the Kutb Minar	196
—— the Kutb Minar thrown down by an earthquake	199
Cave called Gidhadwar, near Giryek	16

SUBJECT.	PAGE.
Cave described by Hwen Thsang as Vulture's Cave ...	20
—— called Satiapanai Cave at Rajghir	21
—— called Son-bhandar Cave at Rajghir	23—24
—— called Sudama, found in the Barabar Hills ...	43—45
—— called Lomas Rishi, found in the Barabar Hills ...	ib.
—— called Karna Chopar Cave, in the Barabar Hills ...	ib.
—— called Nigoba Cave, in the Barabar Hills ...	46
—— called Viswa Mittra, in the Barabar Hills ...	47
—— in the Nagarjuni Hills	48
—— called Gopi-ka-Kubha, in the Nagarjuni Hills	49
—— called Vapiya-ka-Kubha, in the Nagarjuni Hills	49 & 50
—— called Vadathi-ka-Kubha, in the Nagarjuni Hills ...	50 & 51
Chahara Deva, the tributary Rajah of Dilli under Prithoi Raj ...	167
Chakra, eighth in descent from Arjuna Pandu, made Kosambi his capital	301
Chalukya Rajahs of Kalyan. Inscriptions of the —, corroborates the account given by Hwen Thsang of Harsha Vardhana ...	280 & 281
Chandokhar Tal. A tank called — to the North of the Ratan Hill...	54
Chand. Prithoi Raj Rasa, a work written by — ...	159
Chandra Deva. Kingdom of Kanoj conquered by —	160
—————— the founder of the Rahtor dynasty	ib.
Chandrama-kund. A hot spring at Rajghir called —	27
Chankandi. A ruined mound called — to the South of the great tower of Dhamek at Sarnath	116 & 117
—————— Lorika-ko-dan, the present name of —	117
Chhatr. A stupa at Ahichhatra called —	260
Chohan princes of Ajmere, who were at the same time actual Kings of Dilli	167
—————— dynasty. Lists of the —	168
Chohans under Vasala Deva captured Dilli	156

Subject.	Page.
Chohans. Date of capture of Dilli by the —	150
Christian tomb found at Nalanda...	38
Citadel of Shajahanabad. An account of the —	225
City of Shir Shah called Delhi-Shir-Shah	272
Close of the Tomar dynasty	156
Colebrooke, Henry. Scholarship in Sanskrit...	iii
Colonades of the Court of the Great Musjid ...	175
Coryat, Tom. Accounts of an inscription given by — ...	103
Cunningham, A., Colonel. A list of his writings on Indian Antiquities, as follows:	xxxv
Description of some new Bactrian coins.	
Second notice of some new Bactrian coins.	
Account of the discovery of the ruins of the Buddhist city of Sankisa.	
The ancient coinage of Kashmir.	
Attempt to explain some of the monograms on the Greek coins of Ariana and India.	
Notice of some unpublished coins of the Indo-Scythians.	
The Bhilsa Topes.	
Coins of Indian Buddhist satraps with Greek inscriptions.	
Translation of the Bactro-Pali inscription from Taxila.	
Coins of the nine Nagas and of two other dynasties of Narwar and Gwalior.	
Coin of the Indian Prince Sophytes.	
Coins of Alexander's successors in the East.	
The Ancient Geography of India.	
D	
Daidala, the name given to Dilli by Ptolemy	140
Daniel, Thomas, gave earliest illustrations of Southern India, and made drawings of the seven Pagodas at Mahamallaipur	vi

Subject.	Page.
Daoodia Khera, the capital of Salivahan	220
Dasaratha. Nagarjuni Caves supposed to have been excavated in the reign of —	51
Date of Samaka	10
—— of occupation of Indraprastha by Yudhisthra	138
—— of foundation of Dilli	140
—— of re-founding of Dilli in the Gwalior manuscript of Kharg Rai	141
—— of Anang Pal in the Ain Akbari	142
—— of Anang Pal in the Kumaon and Garhwal manuscripts ...	143
—— of Anang Pal	144
—— of Vasala's inscription on the Firuz Shah's Pillar	156
—— of the capture of Dilli by the Chohans	ib.
—— of abduction of Kanoj Princess	159
—— of the great war with Mahaba	ib.
—— of the final conquest of Dilli by the Musalmans	ib.
—— of Iron Pillar of Delhi	171
—— of Hwen Thsang's return to China, A. D. 640	281
—— of Udayana, King of Komambi	201
Daoodiakhera. Town of Hayamukha identified with — ...	294 & 295
Davis, Samuel. A paper on Hindu Astronomy by—	li
Death of Jaypal about December 1021	147
Decline and fall of Buddhism	237
Decorated pillars around the Iron Pillar of Delhi	171
Deduction from the silence of Abu Rihan as to Dilli	145
Defeat of Dilu by Thar, exactly the same as that of Rajah Pal by Sukwanti	138
—— of Jaya Chandra at Benares by Muhammad Ghori ...	263
Delhi. An account of the city of —	133
—— An account of the seven Forts of —	134

Subject.	Page
Delhi. Early Hindu dynasties of —	136 & 137
—— Hindu remains of —	161
—— Description of the Iron Pillar of —	169
—— Description of — taken from the autobiography of Timur	ib.
—— Jahanpanah, a part of —	212
Delhi-Shir-Shah. The city of Shirshah called —	222
Deoriya, a common village name in the Districts of Tirhoot, Champaran, and Gorakpur, is applied to places possessing either a temple or other holy buildings	66
—————— An account of the village of —	252
Description of Delhi taken from the autobiography of Timur ...	212
—————— of Satkila Bawna Darwaza, of Delhi	218
Devisthan. A mound at Kasia called —	77
Dewal. An account of the village of —	252
Dewan-i-am, the name of a hall in the citadel of Shajahanabad ...	225
Dewan-i-khas, the name of a hall in the citadel of Shajahanabad ...	ib.
Dhamek. The great tower at Sarnath called —	105—107
—————— An account of the Buddhist stupa called —	107
—————— an abbreviation of Dharmmopadesaka	113
Dhaoli. A peak of the Dharawat Hills called —	54
Dharawat Hills. An account of the —	53
Dharmma A statue of — on the Ghosrawa mound	89
Dharmmopadesaka. Dhamek, an abbreviation of —	113
Dhopapapura. An account of the place called —	215
—————— situated on the right bank of the Gomati River ...	ib.
—————— Legend of —	ib.
Dihli dur ast, or Dihli dur hai—prophetic words of Nizam-uddin Auliya	215

Subject.	Page
Dilli. Traditions as to the name of —	137
—— Traditions regarding —	ib.
—— Date of the capture of — by the Chohans	136
—— Date of foundation of —	140
—— possibly Ptolemy's Daidala	ib.
—— Re-building of — by Anang Pal	141
—— Date of re-founding of — in the Gwalior manuscript of Kharg Rai	ib.
—— Lists of the Tomar dynasty of —	143
—— re-built by Anang Pal owing to the loss of Kanoj	151
—— captured by the Chohans under Vasala Deva	155
—— Date of the final conquest of — by the Musulmans ...	159
Dilu. The story of — exactly the same as of Rajah Pal in Rajavali	139
Dilwari. Inscription connected with Abichhatra, found near the village of —	265
Dinapanah. Indrapat, or Purana Kila, re-named — by Humayun ...	221
Discovery of two urns at Sarnath, by Babu Jagat Singh, in the year 1794	105
———— of flat tiles in the ruins near Sarnath	119
Distances from Sankisa to Kanoj, seven yojanas according to Fa Hian	270 & 271
———— of Kosam from Allahabad	301
Drona Sagar. A tank at Kashipur called —	253

E

Early Hindu dynasties of Delhi	136 & 137
Edicts of Asoka on two stone pillars at Delhi	161
Elliot, Walter, collected large number of inscriptions and contributed an interesting historical sketch, founded solely on the inscriptions of the principal dynasties that ruled over the countries between the Narbada and the Krishna ...	xxix
Empire raised by Harsha Vardhana	280

Subject.	Page.
Era of Vikramaditya	139
— of Harsha Vardhana	283
Erection of a certain temple close to the Iron Pillar of Dilli attributed to Anang Pal	153
Erroneous opinion regarding the inscription on Firuz Shah's Pillar adopted by the early English travellers	164
Erskine's account of the Elephanta Caves	vi
Essay on the comparative geography of India, by F. Wilford	ii
Excavations at Dhitari, by Mr. C. Horn	120
———— at Sarnath in 1835-36	121
———— at Sarnath, by Major Kittoe, in 1853	124
Extent of Anang Pal's dominions	153

F

Fa Hian visiting Buddha Gaya	7
———— visiting the great tower at Sarnath	112
———— at Mathura	237
———— makes the distance from Sankisa to Kanoj seven yojanas	270 & 271
———— An account of Kanoj given by —	279
———— places a great stupa of Asoka to the West of Kanoj	291
Fa Hian's description of the old city of Rajgir	29
———— account of the Vaisali	69
———— route to Ajudhya	293
Facts in support of the identification of Siri with Shahpur	210
Fall of Boddhism	237
Fergusson, James, a foremost and successful archæologist	xix
Fergusson's account of the "Rock-cut Temples of India"	ib.
———— dates of Kanhari Caves	xx
———— "Picturesque Illustrations of Ancient Architecture in India"	xxii

Subject.	Page.
Fergusson's " Handbook of Architecture"	xxii
———— " Tree and Serpent Worship"	xxiii
Ferishta's account of Turghai Khan's invasion of India during the reign of Ala-uddin, the founder of Siri	217
Figures on the Kanwa Dol Hill	41
Figure of elephant on an ancient pillar at Sankisa	274
Finch, Wm. An account of Delhi by —	132
Firuz Shah's Pillar. Date of Vasala's inscription on the — ...	155
———————— Inscriptions on the —	165
Firuz Shah. Kushak Shikar, a hunting place of —	168
———— Old cupola of — on the Kutb Minar	126
Firuzabad. An account of the city of —	210
Forest of Holi	253
Fort of Bihar. An account of the —	37
—— of Disarh. An account of the —	56
—— of Matha-kuar at Kasia	77 & 79
—— of Lalkot. An account of the —	180
—— of Rai Pithora. An account of the —	183
—— of Tughlakabad described	213
—— of Adilabad, or Mahammadabad. An account of the —	217
—— of Salimgarh. An account of the —	223
—— (ruined) on a mound at Madawar	249
—— of Ujain to the East of Kashipur	259
—— of Garha, near Dhopapapara	316
—— of Nimar. An account of the —	350
Forts of old Delhi	134
Fortress (ruined) at Buddha Gaya attributed to Rajah Amara Sinha Suvira	11

Subject.	Page
Foundation of Dilli	140
———— of Atranjil-khera attributed to Rajah Vena Chakravartti...	200
Fu-she, or Vaisya. Harsha Vardhana called a — by Hwen Thsang...	280

G

Gadadhar. The temple of — at Gaya	2
Ganda, a District of Uttara Kosala to the South of the Rapti ...	327
———— Genealogy of the Rajahs of —	329
Ganeshnad. A hot spring at Rajgir called —	27
Ganga-Jumna. A hot spring at Rajgir called —	ib.
Ganggapa. A statue of Buddha at Nalanda said to be the gift of —	36
Garha. The fort of —, near Dhopapapara	316
Gates of Shajahanabad. An account of the —	224
Gaya. An account of the city of —	1
Gayeswari Devi. The temple of — at Gaya	2
Ghosrawa. An account of the village of —	38
Genealogy of the Rajahs of Ganda	329
Gidhadwar. A cave near Giryek called —	18
Gidi Pokhar. A tank at Nalanda called —	36
Giri-vraja, the old name of the capital of Jarasandha	21
Giryek. An account of the village of —	16
Goom's Monastery, or Hansa Sangharama. A monastery at Giryek called —	18
Gopi Cave. A cave in the Nagarjuni Hills called —	44—49
Govisana, or Kashipur. An account of the city of — ...	251
———— identified with Kiu-pi-shwangna by M. Julien ...	ib.
———— Ujaln represents the ancient city of —	252
Goram. Kaduga, a great city in the kingdom of —	279
Great Masjid. Colonades of the Court of —	175

Subject.	Page.
Great Mosque of Kutbuddin. An account of the —	184
Gridhrakuta-parvata. The hill called — at Giryek	20
Grounds for identifying Kuran Pal with the father Vacha Deva ...	151
Gulariya. Lingam near the village of —	266
Gupta Dynasty. Inscription of the — found at Mathura ...	237
Gureya. A peak of the Dharawat Hill, called —	54
Gwallor manuscript of Kharg Rai giving the date of re-founding of Dilli	141

H

Halls called Dewan-i-am and Dewan-i-khas in the Citadel of Shajahanabad	225
Hand-book of Architecture, by James Fergusson	xxii
Hansa Sangbrama, or Goose's Monastery at Giryek	19
Harsha Vardhana. Kanoj, the capital of —	280
——————— called a Pu-che, or Vaisya by Hwen Thsang ...	ib.
——————— Vast empire raised by —	ib.
——————— Successfully opposed by Rajah Pulakesi ...	ib.
——————— Hwen Thsang's account of — corroborated by inscriptions of the Chalukya Rajahs of Kalyan	280 & 281
——————— a contemporary of Vikramaditya	281
——————— Rajya Vardhana, the elder brother of — ...	282
Hathiya-dah. An account of an old dry tank called — ...	95
Hathiya-dah-ka-lat. The pillar in the Hathiya-dah Tank called ...	ib.
Hatila, or Asokpur. An account of the village of —	327
Hayamukha identified with Daundiakhera	295 & 296
——— or Ayomukha. An account of the place called — ...	296
Height of Kutb Minar	196
Hill of the Isolated Rock. Accounts of the — at Giryek, given by Fa Hian	18
—— of Prabhasa, near Kosambi	311

INDEX. xvii

Subject.	Page.
Hindu dynasties of Delhi. An account of the —	136 & 147
—— remains of Delhi	161
—— Theatre, a work by Horace Hayman Wilson	v
—— origin of Kutb Minar supported by arguments	190
History of Kutb Minar written on its inscriptions	200
Hodgson, Captain. The ruins of Ahichhatra first visited by —	237
Holl. The forest of —	203
Horne, Mr. Excavations at Bhitari by —	100
Humayon. Description of the tomb of —	223
Huvishka Vihara. A monastery called — at Mathura	234
Hwen Thsang's account of renewal and destruction of the celebrated Bodhi Tree at Buddha Gaya...	6
—— description of a vihar at Buddha Gaya	ib.
—— description of a stupa to the South-West of the great temple at Buddha Gaya	11
—— description of the Vulture's Cave at Giryek	20
—— description of Rajgir	22
—— account of Sariputra	28
—— account of Maha Mogalana	ib.
—— account of a vihar at Nalanda	31
—— account of the grand vihar built by Baladitya at Nalanda	34
—— description of four other buildings and statues at Nalanda	ib.
—— mention of a well at Nalanda	36
—— silence regarding the caves in the Barabar and Nagarjuni Hills	43
—— description of a King's palace in Vaisali	55
—— description of six stupas at Vaisali	57
—— description of two stupas at Vaisali erected on ancient foundations	66

c

Subject.	Page.
Hwen Thsang's account of a stupa at Kesariya	56
———— account of Kusinagara	80
———— account of the spot where Buddha died	82
———— description of the great Buddhistical establishment near Banaras	104
———— story of Mrigadava, or Deer Park, at Sarnath	106
———— account of a stupa at Sarnath	117
———— account of Madipur	249
———— account of Ahichhatra	255
———— account of Harsha Vardhana corroborated by inscriptions of the Chalukya Rajahs of Kalyan	280 & 281
———— return to China, A. D. 640	281
———— description of ancient Kanoj	282
———— route to Prayaga, or Allahabad	293
———— description of a temple at Prayaga	297
Hwen Thsang describes Srughana, and places it at a distance of 66 miles from Thanesar	163
———— Temples in Mathura reckoned by — at five	231
———— allowed 40 Chinese li to the yojana	270
———— Kanoj described by —	279
———— calls Harsha Vardhana a Fo-she, or Vaisya	280
———— places a great stupa of Asoka to the South-East of Kanoj	291
———— visiting Nava-deva-kula	293

I

Ibn Batuta. Mosque of Kutb-uddin visited by —	185
— Wahab. Abu Zaid, on the authority of —, calls "Kadugo a great city in the Kingdom of Gozar"	279
Identification of Siri with Shahpur supported by facts	210

INDEX. xix

Subject.	Page.
Indra Sila Guha. Hwen Thsang's account of the hill of — at Giryek	18
——— Pokhar. A tank called — at Nalanda	36
Indrapal, a small fort at Delhi known by the name of Purana Kila	126
——— or Puranah Kila, repaired by Humayon and re-named Dinpanah	221
Indraprastha. The site of —	131
——— Date of occupation of — by Yudhisthira ...	135
——— or Indrapat. An account of the ancient place called —	135 & 136
Inscribed stone pillar at Bhitari	27 & 88
——— pedestal found at Benares in 1704 ...	104
——— rock at Khalsi	244
Inscriptions dated in the era of the Narvan	1
——— found in the temple dedicated to Surya, or the Sun, at Gaya	3
——— of Sri Mohendra Pala Deva at Rama Gaya ...	4
——— found at Buddha Gaya, ascribing the building of a temple and image of Buddha to Amara Deva ...	6 & 7
——— (Burmese) discovered at Buddha Gaya	8
——— found in the temple called Tara Devi at Buddha Gaya ...	11
——— at Buddha Gaya	19
——— in the Son Dhandar Cave	25
——— found in a temple at Kapatiya giving the date of the reign of Sri Gopala Deva	36
——— of the Gupta dynasty on a pillar in the old fort of Bihar	37
——— obtained from Ghosrawa	38
——— in three lines of small letters at Titarawa	39
——— of the second Gupta dynasty, discovered by Major Kittoe at Aphsar	40
——— of five lines in the Karna Chopar Cave ...	43
——— of two lines in the Sudama Cave	ib.

Subject.	Page.
Inscription found over the doorway of the Lomas Rishi Cave ...	47
———— found in the Viswa Mittra Cave	48
———— of ten lines in the Great Cave in the Nagarjuni Hill ...	ib.
———— on a tablet over the doorway of the Gopi-ka-kubha Cave	49
———— of four lines found in the cave called Vadathi-ka-kubha, in the Nagarjuni Hill	51
———— on the Kahaon Pillar	92
———— on the Hathiya-dah Pillar	96
———— discovered at Bijoli	157
———— of Asoka on the Firuz Shah's Pillar. An account of the — given by Tom Coryat	163
———— (principal) on the Firuz Shah's Pillar	168
———— of Rajahs of Kalyan corroborate Hwen Thsang's account of Harshavardham...	230 & 231
———— of Asoka, Samudra Gupta, and Jahangir on a stone pillar at Prayaga	298
———— on the Kosambi Pillar	310
———— on the Iron Pillar of Dilli giving the date of Anang Pal	149—151
———— (Sanskrit) of six lines on the Iron Pillar of Delhi ...	170
———— giving the history of the Kutb Minar	210
———— of the Gupta dynasty found at Mathura	237
———— of Asoka on a quartz boulder at Khalsi	244
———— connected with Abichhatra found near Dilwari ...	264
———— at Khara mentioning the Kingdom of Kosambi, or Kosamba Mandala	312
———— in a temple at Dewal	352
Iron Pillar of Dili. Inscriptions on the — giving the date of Anang Pal	149—151
———— of Delhi described	169
———— at Delhi bearing a Sanskrit inscription of six lines ...	170
———— not formed of mixed metal	ib.

Subject.	Page.
Iron Pillar. Approximate date of —	171
———— supposed to have been erected by Belan Deo (or Anang Pál)	ib.
J	
Jagadispur. Description of the mound of —	29
Jagat Singh. Discovery of two urns at by — in the year 1794	106
Jahanara Begum. The tomb of —, outside the city of Delhi	230
Jahanpanah. A part of Delhi called —	212
Jama Masjid, of Kanoj. An account of the —	262
Jarasandha-ka-baithak. A tower at Girjek called —	18
Jarasandha. Giri-vraja, the capital of —	21
Jaya Chandra, the last of the Rahtors, celebrated Aswamedha	283
———— retired as far as Banaras	ib.
———— Defeat of — by Muhammad Ghori at Banaras	ib.
———— drowned in attempting to cross the Ganges	ib.
Jaymal, the Rajput hero who defended Chitor	226
Jaypal. Death of — about December 1021	147
Jetavana. Monastery of — near Sravasti	335
———— identified with a mound of ruins near Sravasti	337
Jones, William, Sir, founded the Asiatic Society of Bengal and gave the first impulse to the study of Indian antiquities	ib
K	
Kabar, or Shirgarh. An account of the place called	354
———— situated on a lofty mound 20 miles to the North of Mareli	ib.
Kaboli Durwaza. A gate of the city of Shir Shah called —	229
———— called Lal Durwaza	ib.
Kadugu, mentioned by Abu Zaid, on the authority of Ibu Wahab, as a great city in the Kingdom of Umar	279

Subject.	Page.
Kahaon. An account of the village of —	91
—— Remains at —	92
—— Pillar described	92 & 93
Kakupur. Identification of Ayothe with —	295
Kala Masjid of Delhi. An account of the —	220
Kalapainka supposed by Hwen Thsang to be the birth-place of Sariputra	29
Kalyan. Inscriptions of the Rajahs of — corroborates the account of Harsha Vardhana given by Hwen Thsang	230 & 241
Kampilya (now Kampil), the capital of South Panchala	255
Kandaiya Tal. A tank at Sankisa called —	274
Kanhari Caves described and illustrated by Salt	vi
Kanishka Monastery. Monastery called — in the city of Nagarahara	38
Kanogisa. Kanoj mentioned by Ptolemy as —	280
Kanoj. An account of — given by Masudi	145
—— Name of the Rajah of — at the time of Mahmud's invasion	146
—— Tomar dynasty as Rajahs of —	150
—— The Kingdom of — conquered by Chandra Deva, the founder of the Rahtor dynasty	ib.
—— Dilli re-built by Anang Pal owing to the loss of —	151
—— Khand, a part of Prithvi-Raja-Rasa, giving an account of abduction of a Kanoj Princess	159
—— Princess. Date of abduction of —	ib.
—— An account of the city of —	279
—— mentioned by Masudi as the capital of one of the Rajahs of India in 915 A. D.	ib.
—— called "Kaduge" by Abu Zaid	ib.
—— described by Hwen Thsang	ib.
—— An account of — given by Fa Hian	ib.
—— mentioned by Ptolemy as Kanogiza	280

INDEX. xxiii

Subject.	Page.
Kanoj. The earliest notice of —	230
—— the capital of Harsha Vardhana	ib.
—— Mahammad Ghori marched against — in January 1191 A. D.	283
—— (ancient). Hwen Thsang's description of —	ib.
—— An account of the modern town of —	284
—— Remains of interest at —	286
—— Ruins of the Rang Mahal of —	ib.
—— An account of the Jama Masjid of —	287
Kanya Kubja, the Sanskrit name of Kanoj	280
—— Legend referring the name of — to the curse of the Naga Vayu on the daughters of Kananabha	ib.
Kapatiya. Temple in the hamlet of —	36
Karamar Tal. A tank called — at Punawa	13
Karewar Nag Devata. Naga Senkina commonly invoked as —	274
Kargidya Pokhar. A tank called — at Nalanda	20
Karan Chopar Cave. An account of the —	43—45
Karmar Pal. Traditions regarding the sons of —	154
—— Identification of — with the father of Vacha Deva	ib.
Kashipur, or Govisana. An account of the city of —	251
Kashmiri Masjid at Delhi	330
Kasia. An account of the village of —	76
—— identified with Kusinagara	ib.
Kesawapa Rikhi. A hot spring called — at Rajgir	27
Katagora Hall, the famous edifice in Maharo Vihare at Vaisali	63
Katsal. A ruined mound called — at Bakror	12
Katahria Rajputs. Lakhnor, the capital of the —	257
Kumriya. An account of the village of —	64
—— The mound of — described	ib.

Subject.	Page.
Kesava Deva. The temple of — said to have been pulled down by Aurangzib	235
Khalsi. An account of the village of —	241
——— Inscribed rock at —	ib.
——— identified with part of the ancient Kingdom of Sraghna ...	244
Khara. Inscription found at — mentioning the Kingdom of Kasambi or Kosamba Mandala	302
Kharg Rai's account of old Hindu dynasties of Dilli	135
Khukhuda. An account of the ancient town of —	85 & 86
——— called Kishkindapara by the Agarwal Srawaks ...	86
——— a Brahminical town...	ib.
——— Remains at —	ib.
——— Mounds of — described	87 & 88
Kie-pi-tha, or Kapitha, the name given to Sankisa by Hwen Thsang...	271
Kilughari. An account of the place called —	133
Kila-Kona-Masjid. A mosque called — in the City of Shir Shah ...	222
Kingdom of Panchala. An account of the —	255
Kin-pi-shwang-na. The Kingdom of — identified with Govisana by M. Julien	251
Kittoe, Major. A brief sketch of his Indian life founded chiefly on his archæological investigations	xxiv
——— Excavations at Sarnath by — in the year 1853 ...	121
Konwa Dol Hills. An account of the —	40 & 41
Kosala, a District of Uttara Kosala to the North of the Rapti ...	327
Kosam, or Kosambi. An account of the city of —	301
——— Distance of — from Allahabad	304
Kosambi made capital of Chakra, the eighth in descent from Arjuna Pandu	301
——— or Kosamba Mandala mentioned in an inscription at Khara	302
——— the scene of the Ratnavali or the "Necklace"	ib.

Subject.	Page.
Kosambi. Vasta-pattana, another name for —	312
———— Identified with Kosam	303
———— The ruins of —	305 & 306
———— A statue of Buddha at —	308
Kuari Masjid, the name given to the Zinat Masjid at Delhi	230
Kuber Parbat. A mound at Ajudhya called —	323
———— the site of an ancient stupa	326
Kukkuta-pada-Vihara, or temple of the Cock's Foot connected with the Kukkuta-pada-giri, near Kurkihar	15
Kukkuta-pada-giri, or Cock's Foot Hill, near Kurkihar	15 & 18
Kulika, supposed by Hwen Thsang to be the birth-place of Maha Mogalana	20
Kumaon and Garhwal manuscripts giving the date of Anang Pal	143
Kumara Gupta. Inscription relating to — on a pillar at Bihar	37
Kunda-Suka-Vihara. A monastery at Mathura called —	218
Kunda Tal. A tank at Madawar called —	248
Kundilpur. An account of the ruins of —	28
Kurak-Vihar, the true name of Kurkihar	13
———— believed to be the contracted form of Kukkutapada-Vihara	ib.
Kurkihar. An account of the village of —	14
———— Kurak Vihar, the true name of —	15
Kusanagarapura. The old city of Rajagriha called — by Hwen Thsang	21
Kusapura. An account of the town of —	313
———— identified with Sultanpur on the Gumati	id.
———— said to have been named after Rama's son Kusa	314
Kushak Shikar, or hunting palace of Firuz Shah	188—319
———— Firuzabad. A palace of Firuz Shah called —	219
Kusinagara, identified with Kasia	70

Subject.	Page.
Kusinagara. An account of the place called — given by Hwen Thsang	50
———— Vihar at — containing a statue of Buddha	51
Kuth-uddin. An account of the great mosque of —	184
———— The mosque of — enlarged during the reign of Altamsh	187
———— The mosque of — enlarged by Ala-uddin Khiliji	188
Kutb Minar, whether a Muhammadan building, or a Hindu building, altered by the conquerors	189
———— Arguments in support of the Hindu origin of —	190
———— used as Mazinah	194
———— The height of —	195
———— Old cupola of Firuz Shah on the —	198
———— Old cupola of the — thrown down by an earthquake	199
———— Repairs of the — entrusted to Major Robert Smith	ib.
———— History of — written in its inscriptions	200
———— Actual builder of the —	202

L

Lake called Sarang Tal at Sarnath	106
Lakhnor, the ancient capital of the Katehria Rajpots	247
Lalkot. An account of the Fort of —	180
Lal Darwaza, the present name of Kabuli Darwaza of the city of Shirshah	212
Lassen, Professor, deciphered many of the unknown characters of India, and read the Pali legends on the copper coins of Agathokles	xii
Lauriya-Ara-Raj. An account of the pillar of —	67 & 68
Lauriya Navandgarh. An account of the place called —	68
———— Remains at —	69
———— An account of the pillar of —	79
Legend relating to Vimala Mittra	250

SUBJECT.	PAGE.
Legend of Adi Rajah...	253
——— of Maya, the mother of Buddha	271
——— referring the name of Kanya Kubja to the curse of the sage Vayo on the hundred daughters of Kusanabha ...	280
——— of Dakula	313
——— of Dhapapapara	315
Letters of James Prinsep	ix
Lingam, called Pataleswara, in a temple on the Ramsila Hill at Gaya	4
——— near the village of Gulariya	255
Lion Pillar of Bakhra described	59
Lists of the Tomar dynasty of Dilli	148
List of the Chohan dynasty	158
Lomas Rishi Cave. An account of a cave called —	43—46
Luri-ka-kodan, the present name of the ruined mound to the South of Dhamek at Sarnath	117

M

Mackenzie, Colin, a successful collector of archæological materials ...	vii
——— Mrs. Colin. Mistake made by — in her account of the epitaph on Jahanara's tomb	230
Madawar, or Madipur. An account of the city of —	249
——— People of — supposed to be the Mather of Megasthenes who dwelt on the banks of the Erinesos	251
Madipur, or Madawar. An account of the city of —	249
——— Identified with Mandawar	ib.
——— Description of — given by Hwen Thsang	249
——— Monastery at — famous as the scene of Sanghabhadra's sudden death when overcome by Vasubandhu ...	ib.
Maha Mogala. Regarding the birth-place of —	29
Mahalla of Lala Mier Tola. A mound at Kanoj called — ...	292
Mahammadabad, or Adilabad. The fort of —	317

Subject.	Page.
Mahapala. The name of — found in the Inscription on a statue of Buddha at Tilarawa	39
Maharano Viharo means the Chapel Monastery of the great forest at Vaisali	62
Mahipalpur. An account of the village of —	154
Mahmud's invasion. Name of the Rajah of Kanoj at the time of —	146
Makaranduagar. An account of the mounds to the South-East of —...	291
Makhdumkund. Sringgi Rikhi called —by the Musalmans ...	27
Makhdum Jahaniya. Masjid of — at Kanoj	259
——————— Mound of — in the Sikhana Mahalla at Kanoj	262 & 263
Malini River about two miles distant from Madawar	249
Maniar Math. A Jain temple at Rajgir called —	26
Mani Parvat. A mound at Ajudhya called —	323
——————— the site of a stupa of Asoka	325
Marat-i-Asrar.' Account of the — as to later Kings of Delhi ...	147
Markata-hrada. A small tank at Benarh called—	62
Markundkund. A hot spring at Rajgir called —	27
Martland, or Suraj-kund. Tank called — at Bakror	13
Masjid-Kutbul-Islam. The great mosque of Kutb-addin now known as —	181
——— (Great). Colonades of the Court of —	182
——— of Makhdum Jahaniya at Kanoj	260
Masudi's account of Kanoj	145
Masudi. Kanoj mentioned by — as the capital of one of the Rajahs of India in A. D. 915	270
Matha-kuar-ka-kot. A mound at Kasia called —	27
Matha-kuar. Statue of — at Kasia	28 & 29
Matho. People of Madawar called — by Megasthenes	251
Mathura. An account of the city of —	231

Subject.	Page.
Mathura visited by Fa Hian	229
———— A stupa built by Upagupta at —	231
Manu Swayambhuva. Uttanapada, King of Bharatkhand, the son of —	69
Mausoleum containing tombs of Tughlak Shah and his queen	216
Maya, the mother of Buddha. The legend of —	271
Mazinah. Kutb Minar used as —	194
Megasthenes. People of Madawar called Mathæ by —	251
Meghaduta, a work by Kali Dasa, refers to the story of Udayana, King of Kosambi	301
Mill, Dr., translated certain important Inscriptions —	vii
Minar (unfinished) of Ala-uddin stands North from the Kutb Minar	205
Mir Khusru's anecdote of Anang Pal	141
Mistake made by Mrs. Colin Mackenzie in her account of the epitaph on Jahanara's tomb	230
Modern town of Kanoj. An account of the —	284
Mohabakhand, a part of Prithvi-Raj-Rasa, describing the great war with Mohaba	160
Monasteries (Buddhist) in Mathura amounted to 20	221
Monastery of Nalanda	29
———— called Kanishka Monastery in the city of Nagarahara	38
———— called Huvishka Vihara at Mathura	236
———— called Kunda-Suka Vihara at Mathura	ib.
———— at Madipur famous as the scene of Sanghabhadra's sudden death when overcome by Vasubandhu	240
———— containing a stupa of Asoka near Kosambi	311
———— of Jetavana near Sravasti	335
———— identified with a mound of ruins near Sravasti	337
———— called Purvarama near Sravasti	341
Mosque of Kutb-uddin now known as Masjid Kutbul-Islam	184

Subject.	Page.
Mosque of Kutb-uddin An account of the —	181
———— called Adina Masjid	185
———— visited by Ibn Batata	ib.
———— begun in A. H. 587, or A. D. 1191	ib.
———— enlarged during the reign of Altamsh	187
———— enlarged by Ala-uddin Khilji	188
———— called Kila-Kona-Masjid in the City of Shir Shah	222
Mosques called Zama Masjid and Zinat Masjid at Shajahanabad	225
Mound (ruined) called Katani at Bakror	12
———— bearing a broken statue of the three-handed goddess Vajra Virahi at Punawa	14
———— called Sugatgarh at Kurkihar	ib.
———— of Jagadispur described	20
———— of Kesariya described	64
———— to the North-East of the Kesariya stupa called Rainwas	67
———— called Deviathan and Ramabhar Tila at Kasia	77
———— called Matha-kuar-ka-kot, or Fort of Matha-Kuar, at Kasia	ib.
———— called Siva-ka-tila at Khukhundo	87
———— called Savari-ka-tila to the West of the Hathiyadah Pillar	95
———— (ruined) to the South of Dhamek called Chaukandi	116
———— called Anand Tila at Mathura	234
———— called Vinayak Tila at Mathura	ib.
———— called Nivi-ka-kot at Sankisa	276
———— called Mahalla of Lala Misr Tola at Kanoj	292
———— in Bhatpuri Mahalla at Kanoj	ib.
———— of Makhdum Jahaniya at Kanoj	292 & 293
———— called Mani Parvat at Ajodhya	323
———— called Kuber Parvat at Ajudhya	ib.

SUBJECT.	PAGE.
Mound called Sugrib Parvat at Ajudhya	323
—— of ruins near Sravasti identified with the Jetavana Monastery	337
—— called Ora-jhar near Sravasti	345
—— called Vairatkhera	351
—— called Pars-ens-kot	357
—— called Balai-khera close to the Muhammadan town of Jahanabad	358
Mounds of Khakhundo described	87—89
—— called Sat-Tila at Mathura	235
—— to the South-East of Makarandnagar	291
Mrigadava, or Deer Park. The story of — given by Hwen Thsang...	100
Muchalinda (Dragon). Tank of — at Buddha Gaya	11
Muhammad Ghori marched against Kanoj in 1191 A. D.	283
—— Defeat of Jaya Chandra by — at Banaras	ib.
Murali. A peak of the Barabar Hills called —	43
Musalmans Date of the final conquest of Dilli by the —	149

N

Naga Nalanda. Tank of — at Nalanda	30
—— Deva (or Jaga Deva), the tributary Rajah of Dilli under Prithvi Raj	152
—— Tank at Sankisa	273
—— of Sankisa commonly invoked as Karewar Nag Devta	274
Nagarahara. The Kanishka Monastery in the city of —	39
Nagarjuni Hills. An account of the —	44
—— Caves supposed to have been excavated in the reign of Dasaratha	61
Nalanda, or Baragaon. An account of the village of —	28
—— supposed by Fa Hian to be the birth-place of Saripatra	29
—— said to be the city of Yaso Varmma	31

Subject.	Page.
Name of Dilli. Traditions about the —	137
—— of the Rajah of Kanoj at the time of Mahmud's invasion ...	140
—— of Prayaga. Traditions about the —	300
Narting. The ruined temple on Punnwa Mound called — ...	14
Nava-deva-kula. An account of the town of —	293
Nigambhod Ghát, a place where Yudhisthira celebrated the Hom ...	136
Nigoha Cave. An account of the —	46
Nimsar, or Nimkar, a place of pilgrimage on the left bank of the Gumti...	250
—— Fort of —	ib.
Nirvan. Inscriptions dated in the era of the —	1
Nirvana. Announcement of — at Vaisali	63
Nivi-ka-kot. A mound at Sankisa called — ...	275
Nizam-uddin Auliya. Traditions regarding — ...	214
Nurgarh, the name given to Salimgarh — ...	223

O

Opening of the Great Tower at Sarnath	119
Ora-jhar. A mound near Sravasti called —	345
Otbi. Name of the Rajah of Kanoj, according to — at the time of Mahmud's invasion	140

P

Pachham-rai. The Western District of Banauda called — ...	327
Padaraona. An account of the village of —	74
—— identified with Pawa	ib.
—— Remains at —	74 & 75
Palace of a King at Vaisali described by Hwen Thsang ...	54
—— called Kushak Shikar — ...	104—210
—— Firuzabad	210

Subject.	Page.
Pal (Rajah). The story of — exactly the same as of Dilu ...	138
Panchala. An account of the Kingdom of —	245
Panas Pokhar. A tank at Nalanda called —	36
Para-sna-kot. An account of a mound called —	362
Pataleswara. A lingam called — in a temple on the Ramsila Hill at Gaya	1
Patal Ganga. A sacred spring called — near Barabar	49
Pals demanded by Yudhisthira from Duryodhan	135
Patta, the Rajput hero who defended Chitor	229
Pawn supposed to be a corruption of Padmavana	74
Pedestal (inscribed) found at Banaras in 1794	104
People of Madawar supposed to be the Mathœ of Megasthenes, who dwelt on the banks of Erinasus	251
Phur. Defeat of Dilu by — exactly the same as that of Rajah Pal by Sakwanti	138
"Picturesque Illustrations of Ancient Architecture in India" — a work by James Fergusson	xii
Pillar bearing two separate inscriptions of the Gupta dynasty at Bihar	37
—— of Bakhra described	89
—————— called Bhim-sen-ka-lat	61
—— of Lauriya Ara-Raj described	67 & 68
—————— Navandgarh described	68 & 69
——————————— Erection of the — ascribed to Rajah Bhim Mari	71
—— of Kahaon described	92 & 93
—— called Hathiya-dah-ka-lat in the middle of the Hathiya-dah Tank	95
—— of Bhitari described	97
—— (iron) of Dilli. Date of Anang Pal on the —	149—151
——————— of Delhi described	169
——————— not formed of mixed metal	170

INDEX.

SUBJECT.	PAGE.
Pillar supposed to have been erected by Bilan Deo (or Anang Pal)	171
—— (ancient) bearing the figure of an elephant at Sankim	274
—— (stone) bearing the inscriptions of Asoka, Samudra Gupta, and Jahangir	298
—— at Kosambi bearing certain inscriptions	310
Pillars (stone) at Delhi bearing the edicts of Asoka	141
—————— An account given by Shams-i-Siraz of the removal of — to Delhi	ib.
—— (decorated) around the Iron Pillar of Delhi	172
Piloshanna. The Kingdom of —	205
—————— Identified with Atranji-Khera	209
Pipal Tree known by the name of Bodhidruma at Buddha Gaya	5
Pirwali Tal. A tank at Madawar called —	219
Places visited during tour	131
Popular traditions regarding Dilli	137
Prabhasa. Hill of — near Kosambi	311
Prastha. Different significations of —	
Prayaga, or Allahabad. Hwen Thsang's route to —	293
—————— An account of the city of —	296
—————— Traditions as to the name of —	310
Pretsila. A hill at Gaya called — bearing a temple erected by Ahalya Bai	4
Prinsep, James, brought to light the characters and languages of the earliest Indian inscriptions	vii
—————— Letters of —	ix
—————— His bold appeal to Lord Auckland	xv
—————— The successors of —	xviii
Prithu, son of Rajah Vena Chakervartti	65
Prithvi Raja, the last of the Tuwar Kings	156
—— — a Chohan Prince of Ajmere, as well as a King of Dilli	157

Subject.	Page.
Prithvi Raja. Someswara, the name given to —	159
—————— An account of the reign of —	159
—————— Erection of the Fort of Rai Pethora attributed to —	160
—————— Raj-Rasa, a poem written by Chand	160
—————————— Mohaba Khand, a part of the —	ib.
—————————— Kanojkhund, a part of the —	ib.
Ptolemy. Dilli called Daidala by —	140
———— Ahichhatra mentioned as Adisadra by —	225
———— Kanoj mentioned by — as Kanogiza	280
Pundlal (or Asoka). Satgharn Caves in the Barabar Hills supposed to have been excavated in the reign of —	45—51
Pulakesa. Huraha Vardhana successfully opposed by —	id.
Punwa Mound. A mound to the East of Punwa Tank called —	31
———— Tank. Mound to the East of — at Nalanda called Punwa Mound	ib.
Purab-rat. The Eastern District of Banaoda called —	327
Purana Kila. Indrapat, a small fort at Delhi known by the name of —	136
Purna Varmma (King). Renewal of Bodhi Tree by —	5
Purvvarama. A monastery at Sravasti called —	344
———— identified with the Ora-jhar mound	345

R

Rabela Tank. Mound to the East of — corresponds with the stupa containing hair and nails of Buddha at Nalanda	81
Rahtor dynasty of Kanoj. Chandra Deva, the founder of the —	160
Railing (Buddhist) at Buddha Gaya	10
Rai Pithora. Erection of the fort of — attributed to Prithvi Raja	160
—————— An account of the fort of —	132
Rajagriha called Kusanagara by Hwen Thsang	21

INDEX.

SUBJECT.	PAGE.
Rajagriha. The new town of — said to have been built by King Srenika	23
Rajah Bisal-ka-garh, the present name of a ruined fort at Besarh	85
—— Den-ka-Deora. The stupa on the Kesariya mound called —	65
—— Ben-ka-Dighi. A tank called — at Kesariya	ib.
—— Ben Chakravartti identified with Vena Chakravartti, the father of Prithu	ib.
—— of Kanoj. Name of the — at the time of Mahmud's invasion	116
Rajahs of Ganda. Genealogy of the —	329
Rajgir. An account of the city of —	20
—— Description of — given by Hwen Thsang	23
Rajya Vardhana, the elder brother of Harsha Vardhana	283
Ram Gaya. A hill at Gaya called —	4
Ram Kund. A hot spring at Rajgir called —	27
Ramabhar Tila and Devisthan. A mound at Kasia called —	77
—— Jhil. A large sheet of water called — at Kasia	77—84
Ramnagar, or Ahichhatra. An account of the city of —	255
Ramsila. The hill of — at Gaya	4
Rang Mahal of Kanoj	296
Rasiwas. Mound called — to the North-East of Kesariya Stupa	62
Ranta Pala, the Pali scholar, assisted J. Prinsep in reading certain inscriptions	xiii
Ratani, the name of the Western ridge of the Dharawat Hills	35
Re-building of Dilli by Anang Pal	141
—————————————— owing to the loss of Kanoj	151
Reign of Prithvi Raj. An account of the —	149
Remains at Bakhra	58 & 59
—— at Lauriya Navandgarh	62
—— at Padaraona	74
—— at Khukhundo	86

Subject.	Page
Remains at Kahaon	68
——— at Bhitari	96
——— Sarnath	108
——— (Hindu) of Delhi	161
——— (Buddhist) at Ahichhatra	200
——— of interest at Kanoj	288
——— of antiquity at Ajudhya	322
Repairs of the Kutb Minar entrusted to Major Robert Smith ...	199
Rock (inscribed) at Khalsi	244
Ruined fortress at Buddha Gaya	11
——— fort on a mound at Madawar	848
Ruins of Kundilpur	28
——— of Samanpur at the foot of the Kanwa Dol Hill	41
——— to the North-East of Chandokhar Tal	54
——— of Ahichhatra first visited by Captain Hodgson	257
——— of Kosambi	305 & 308
Ruhn-uddin. Traditions regarding —	214

S

Sahet Mahet, or Sravasti. An account of the city of — ...	330
Saka Vikramaditya era	139
Sakas. Defeat of — stigmatised to Vikramaditya	ib.
Sakota, or Ajudhya. An account of the city of —	317
——— identified with Ajudhya	320
Sahti. Temple dedicated to — on the Brahmjuin Hill at Gaya ...	3
Saleya. A peak of the Dharawat Hills called —	54
Salimgarh. An account of the fort of —	223
——— The name of — changed to Nurgarh	ib.

XXXVIII   INDEX.

SUBJECT.	PAGE.
Salivahan. Bais Rajputs claim descent from —	280
Salt described and illustrated the Kanhari Caves in Salset.	vi
Samanpur. The ruins of — at the foot of the Kauwa Dol Hill	41
Samda Giri. A peak of the Barabar Hills called —	42
Sanghabhadra. Monastery at Madipur famous as the scene of the death of — when overcome by Vasubandhu	249 & 250
Sankasya, the Sanskrit name of Sankisa	271
Sankisa. An account of the place called —	ib.
———— called Seng-kia-she by the Chinese pilgrims	ib.
———— called Sankasya in Sanskrit	ib.
———— called Kie-pi-tha, or Kapitha, by Hwen Thsang	ib.
———— Tank of Naga at —	273
———— Stupas at —	ib.
Sanskrit inscription of six lines on the Iron Pillar of Delhi	170
Sapt Rikhi. A hot spring at Rajgir called —	27
Sarangganatha. Sarnath, an abbreviation of —	105
Sarang Tal. A lake at Sarnath called —	ib.
Sarian, a name given to the eastern portion of the ruins at the foot of the Kauwa Dol Hill	41
Sariputra. Nalanda, the birth-place of —	29
Sarnath. An account of the place called —	103—105
———— An abbreviation of Sarangganatha	105
———— Remains at —	106
———— Excavations at — in 1835-36	121
———— Excavation at — by Major Kittoe in 1853	124
Sasangka (King). Destruction of Bodhi Tree by —	5
———— Date of —	10
Sat Tila. Seven mounds called — at Mathura	235
Satghara. The caves in the Barabar Hills called —	44

INDEX.   XXXIX

SUBJECT.	PAGE.
Satghara supposed to have been excavated in the reign of Rajah Piyadisi	61
Satkila Dawan Darwaza of Delhi. Description of the — ...	218
Sattapanni Cave. A cave called — at Rajgir	21 & 22
Scene of Sanghabhadra's sudden death when overcome by Vasubandhu at Madipur	249 & 250
Sculpture representing Ashta Sakti in a temple at Benarh ...	68
Sculptures at Dhitari	97
Seng-kia-she. The name of Sankisa written as — by the Chinese pilgrims	271
Sewet to the north of Saketa	317
Sha-chi of Fa Hian identified with Visakha of Hwen Thsang ...	319
——— identified with Saketa, or Ajudhya	ib.
Shahpur. Site of Siri at —	207
Shajahanabad. An account of the city of	221
——— Gates of —	ib.
——— An account of the citadel of —	225
——— Statues of two elephants and their riders discovered at —	ib.
Shampaka made King of Bagad, or Vagad	205
Shams-i-Siraj. Account given by — of the removal of two stone pillars	116
Shir Shah made Indrapat the citadel of his city under the name of Shirgarh	221
——— The city of — called Delhi Shir Shah	223
——— Mandir. A lofty building called — in the city of Shir Shah ...	ib.
Shirgarh. Shir Shah made Indrapat the citadel of his city under the name of —	221
——— or Kabur. An account of the place called —	358
Sikhana Mahalla. Mound of Makhdum Jahaniya in the — of Kanoj	293
Silence of Hwen Thsang regarding the caves in the Barabar Hills...	63
Silenus. A statue of — found at Mathura	249

Subject.	Page.
Singh Bhawani. Two statues discovered in the village of — ...	280
Siri, or Kila Alai. An account of the Fort of —	207
———— Site of — at Shahpur	ib.
———— Identification of — with Shahpur supported by facts ...	210
Sita Ramji. Temple of — at Soron	206
Sitakund. A hot spring at Rajgir called —	27
Site of Indraprastha	134
———— of Siri at Shahpur	207
———— of a vihara with the tooth of Buddha at Kanoj	202
Siva-ka-Tila. A mound at Khukhundo called —	87
Siwari-ka-Tila. The mound called — to the West of the Hathiya-dah Pillar	95
Skanda Gupta. Inscription relating to — on a pillar at Bihar ...	37 & 38
Smith, Major Robert. Repairs of Kutb Minar entrusted to — ...	109
Someswara originally called Prithvi Raja	168
Son Bhandar Cave. A cave called — at Rajgir	21—25
Sons of Anang Pal. An account of the —	183
———— of Kuras Pal. Traditions about the —	164
Soron, or Sukara-kshetra. An account of the ancient town called — ...	205
———— originally called Ukula-kshetra	206
Springs (hot) of Rajagriha. An account of the — ...	27
Spring called Patal Ganga near Darabar	42
Sravasti, or Sahet Mahet. An account of the city of — ...	330
———— said to have been built by Rajah Sravasta	332
———— (Rajah) said to have built the city of Sravasti	ib.
Srenika (otherwise called Bimbisara), the father of Ajatasatru, said to have built the new town of Rajagriha	23
Sri Mahendra Pala Deva. Inscription of — at Gaya	4
———— Buddha Damaya, an inscription in the temple called Tara Devi ...	11

Subject.	Page.
Sri Gopala Deva. Inscription on a temple at Nalanda giving the date of the reign of —	28
—— Harsha era	282
Sringgi-Rikhi-kund. A hot spring at Rajgir called —	27
—————— called Makhdum-kund by the Musalmans ...	ib.
Srughana described by Hwen Thsang	162
—————— placed by Hwen Thsang at a distance of 66 miles from Thaneswar	ib.
Statue of Avalokiteswara at Nalanda	31
—— of Tara Bodhisatwa in a vihar at Nalanda	34
—— of Dharmma on the Ghosrawa mound	39
—— of ascetic Buddha at Titarawa	ib.
—— of ascetic Buddha at Benarh	61
—— of Matha Kuar at Kasia	76 & 79
—— representing Buddha on his death bed in a vihar at Kusinagara	81 & 82
—— of Silenus found at Mathura	242
—— of Buddha at Kosambi	309
Statues mentioned by Hwen Thsang at Nalanda	34
—— of two elephants and their riders discovered at Shajahanabad	225
—— discovered in the village of Singh Bhawani	230
Stevenson, J., Reverend, translated numerous Inscriptions discovered in the caves of Western India ...	xxxi
Stone found in the temple of Vegeswari Devi at Buddha Gaya ...	7
—— pillars at Delhi bearing the edicts of Asoka	161
Story of Mrigadava of Sarnath by Hwen Thsang	106
—— of Dilu exactly the same as of Rajah Pal in Rajavali ...	139
—— of Udayana, King of Kosambi, in Meghaduta	301
—— of Visakha	319
Stupa to the South-West of the great temple at Buddha Gaya ...	11

Subject.	Page.
Stupa containing hair and nails of Buddha at Nalanda ...	31
——— (ruined) of solid brick at Benarh	61
——— called Rajah Ben-ka-Deora at Kesariya	65
——— described by Hwen Thsang	ib.
——— means "a mound of earth" in Amara Kosha	69
——— on the Ramabhar Jhíl at Kasia	79
——— called Dhamek at Sarnath	107
——— to the West of Dhamek excavated by Jagat Singh ...	113
——— An account of the — at Sarnath, by Hwen Thsang ...	117
——— built by Upagupta at Mathura	233
——— of Vimala Mitra at Madipur	240
——— called Chhair at Ahichhatra	260
——— of Asoka, according to Fa Hian, situated to the West of Kanoj	281
——————— according to Hwen Thsang, to the South-East of Kanoj	ib.
——————— in a monastery near Kosambi	311
Stupas. Hwen Thsang's description of the — at Vaisali ...	67
——— at Sankisa	273
Sudama. A cave in the Barabar Hills called —	43—46
Sugaigarh (or bones of Sugata). A mound at Kurkihar called — ...	14
Sugrib Parvat. A mound at Ajudhya called —	323
——— the site of an ancient monastery	325
Sukara-kshetra, or Soron. An account of the ancient town called —	205
——————— Chala-kshetra, or Soron, received the name of — ...	200
Saltasper, on the Gomati, identified with Kusapur	313
Suraj-kund. A tank called — at Gaya	3
——— or Martand Pokhar. Tank called — at Bakror ...	13
——— Identified with Buddha-kund	ib.

Subject	Page
Suraj-kund. A hot spring at Rajgir called —	27
———— A tank called — near Anahpur	152
———— A tank at Kanoj called —	290
Surya, or Sun. Temple dedicated to — at Gaya	1

T

Subject	Page
Tanda, or Tadwa. An account of the place called —	318
———— identified with To-wai of Fa Hian	ib.
Tank called Suraj-kund at Gaya	3
—— called Bodhokar Tal at Buddha Gaya	11
—— of the Dragon Muchalinda at Buddha Gaya	ib.
—— called Buddha-kund at Bakror	13
—— called Bodhokar Tal at Punawa	ib.
—— called Karamar Tal at Punawa	ib.
—— of Naga Nalanda at Nalanda	30
—— called Kargidya Pokhar at Nalanda	ib.
—— of Ponwa. Mound to the East of the — called Punwa Mound at Nalanda	31
—— of Rabeh. Mound to the East of the — corresponds with the stupa containing hair and nails of Buddha at Nalanda	ib.
—— called Balen Tank at Nalanda	32
—— called Gidi Pokhar at Nalanda	ib.
—— called Indra Pokhar at Nalanda	ib.
—— called Panso Pokhar at Nalanda	ib.
—— called Chandokbar Tal to the North of the Ratani Hill	54
—— called Markata-hrada to the South of the lion pillar of Bakhra	62
—— called Rajah Ben-ka-Dighi at Kesariya	65
—— called Rathiya-dah	94
—— called Anang Tal to the North-West of Kutb Minar at Dilli	152

SUBJECT.				PAGE.
Tank called Suraj-kund near Anekpur	...	...	...	182
—— called Kunda Tal at Madawar	...	...	...	240
—— called Firwali Tal at Madawar	...	...	...	ib.
—— of Dron Sagar at Kashipur	...	...	...	252
—— of Naga, or serpent, at Sankisa	...	...	...	273
—— called Kandaiya Tal at Sankisa	...	...	...	274
—— called Suraj-kund at Kanoj	...	...	...	290
Tara Devi. A ruined temple called — at Buddha Gaya...			...	11
—— Bodhisatwa. A statue of — in a vihar at Nalanda			...	34
Taylor, Meadows, discovered certain mysterious cromlechs, cairns, and stone circles in the Shorapur District, and attributed them to the Turanian or Scythian race	...	...	...	131
Temple of Vishnupad at Gaya	...	...	...	2
—— of Gadadhar at Gaya	...	...	...	ib.
—— of Gayeswari Devi at Gaya	...	...	...	ib.
—— dedicated to Surya, or Sun, at Gaya	...	...	...	3
—— dedicated to Sakti on the Brahmjuni Hill at Gaya			...	ib.
—— containing a lingam called Pataleswara Mahadeva at Gaya			...	ib.
—— erected by Ahalya Bai on the Pretsila Hill at Gaya			...	4
—— supposed to have been built by Amara Sinha at Buddha Gaya				5
—— of Vageswari Devi at Buddha Gaya, contains a circular stone	...	...	...	7
—— called Tara Devi at Buddha Gaya	...	...	...	11
—— called Vageswari Devi at Buddha Gaya		...	...	ib.
—— of Trilokanath at Punawa	...	...	...	13
—— called Narting on a mound at Punawa	...	...	...	14
—— dedicated to Bhageswari Devi at Kurkihar	...	...	...	15
—— called Maniar Math at Bajgir	...	...	...	20
—— at Nalanda erected on a spot where Buddha had dwelt for three months	...	...	...	31

INDEX. XLV

SUBJECT.	PAGE.
Temple built by Baladitya at Nalanda	24
—— containing a statue of Buddha in the Barabar Hills ...	41
—— close to the Iron Pillar of Dilli supposed to have been built by Anang Pal	153
—— of Kesava Deva at Mathura said to have been pulled down by Aurangzib	235
—— of Sita Ramji at Soron	260
—— at Prayaga described by Hwen Thsang	297
—— of Asoknath at Asokpur	328
—— bearing an inscription at Dewal	352
Temples reckoned by Hwen Thsang at five in Mathura	231
—— (Brahmanical) at Abichhatra	268
—— on the mound of Makhdum Jahaniya in the Sikhana Mahalla of Kanoj	292
Thomas, Edward, noted for his History of India, illustrative of its coins, inscriptions, and other monuments	xxvii
A list of his writings as follows:	
Coins of the Hindu Kings of Cabul.	
Coins of the Kings of Ghazni.	
Coins of the Sah Kings of Saurashtra.	
On the epoch of the Gupta Dynasty.	
On the coins of the Gupta Dynasty.	
On ancient Indian Numerals.	
On Prinsep's Indian Antiquities.	
Supplementary Notice of the coins of the Kings of Ghazni.	
On ancient Indian Weights.	
On the identity of Hendrames and Krananda.	
The initial coinage of Bengal.	
Chronicles of the Pathan Kings of Delhi.	
Titarawa. An account of the village of —	30

Subject.	Page.
Tiles discovered in the ruins near Sarnath	119
Tomar Dynasty of Dilli. Lists of the —	148
———————— as Rajahs of Kanoj	150
———————— Close of the —	156
Tomaravali between Alwar and Shekhavati	158
Tomargbar between Dholpur and Gwalior	ib.
Tomb (Christian) found at Bihar	26
—— of the Emperor Altamsh. An account of the —	204
—— of Tughlak Shah	213—215
———————————— and his Queen inside the Mausoleum ...	216
—— of Humayun described	222
—— of Jaharara Begum	230
—— of Zibun-nissa, the daughter of Aurangzib	ib.
To-wai of Fa Hian identified with Tanda, or Tadwa	118
Tower called Jarasandha-ka-baithak at Giryek	16
—— called Dhamek at Sarnath	105
———————— visited by Fa Hian	118
Traditions as to the name of Dilli	137
———————— as to Dilli	ib.
———————— regarding the sons of Karsar Pal	154
———————— regarding Roko-uddin	214
———————— regarding Nizam-uddin Auliya	ib.
———————— as to the name of Prayaga	300
Tradition regarding the erection of Iron Pillar by Bilan Deo (or Anang Pal)...	171
"Tree and Serpent Worship"—a work by J. Fergusson	xlii
Trilokanath. The temple of — at Punawa	13
Tughlakabad. Fort of — described	212
Tughlak Shah. An account of the tomb of — ... —	213—215

Subject.	Page.
U	
Udal, a Bausfar hero	283
Udayana. Date of —	301
——— Story of — in Megha-duta	ib.
Ujain. The old fort of — to the East of Kashipur	252
——— represents the ancient city of Govisana	ib.
Ukala-kshetra, the original name of Soron, received the name of Sukara-kshetra	266
Upagupta. A stupa said to have been built by — at Mathura ...	232
Urns discovered by Jagat Singh at Sarnath in 1794	105
Uttanapada, King of Brahmavarta, or Bharatkhand ...	62
——— son of Manu Swayambhuva	ib.
Uttara Kosala. The Northern part of Ajudhya called — ...	327
——— Ganda, a District of — to the South of the Rapti ...	ib.
——— Kosala, a District of — to the North of the Rapti ...	ib.
V	
Vacha Deva. The father of — identified with Karusr Pal ...	154
Vadathi-ka-kubha. A cave in the Nagarjuni Hills called — ...	51
Vageswari Devi. Temple of — at Buddha Gaya	7
Vairatkhera. Barikhar, a village on the top of a mound called — ...	351
Vaisa, or Bais, Rajput, mistaken for Vaisya, or Bais, the name of the merchant class of the Hindus	280
Vaisali, supposed to be the ancient name of Besarh	55
——— An account of the stupas at —	57
——— the scene of the second Buddhist synod	62
——— Buddha announced his Nirvana at —	ib.
Vajra Varahi. A broken statue of the three-headed goddess called — at Punawa	16
Vajrasan, or the diamond throne of Buddha, at Buddha Gaya ...	89

SUBJECT.	PAGE.
Vapiya-ka-kubba. A cave in the Nagarjuni Hills called —	49
Vamla's Inscription. Date of — on the Firuz Shah's Pillar	155
Vamla Deva captured Dilli	ib.
———— a Chohan Prince of Ajmere, as well as a King of Dilli...	157
Vasubandhu. Madipur, the scene of Sanghabhadra's death when overcome by —	250
Vatsa-pattana, another name for Kosambi	302
Vena Chakervartti, identified with Rajah Ben	65
———————— The story of —	ib.
———————— (Rajah). The foundation of Atranji Khera attributed to —	269
Vihar at Buddha Gaya described by Hwen Thsang	5
——— An account of a — at Nalanda as given by Hwen Thsang	21
——— built by Baladitya at Nalanda	21
——— containing a copper statue of Tara Bodhisatwa	ib.
——— at Kasinagara containing a statue of Buddha	81 & 82
Vihara with the tooth of Buddha to the South of the town of Kanoj	232
——— 200 feet in height on a mound in Dhatpuri Mahalla of Kanoj	ib.
Vikramaditya. Defeat of Sakas attributed to —	139
——————— era	ib.
——————— being a cotemporary of Harsha Vardhana	221
Vimala Mittra. Stupa of — at Madipur	250
——————— Legend relating to —	ib.
Vinayak Tila. A mound at Mathura called —	231
Vipula (mount), supposed to be identical with Wepollo of Pali annals	22
Virasena, the name given to Pilushanna by M. Julien	208
Visakha identified with Sla-chi	318
——— identified with Saketa, or Ajudhya	ib.

Subject.	Page.
Visakha. The story of —	319
Vishnupad. Temple of — at Gaya	2
Vulture's Cave. A cave at Giryek described by Hwen Thsang as —	20
W	
Webharo Mountain supposed to be identical with Mount Daibhar at Rajgir	21
Well at Nalanda mentioned by Hwen Thsang	86
Wepulla supposed to be identical with Mount Vipula at Rajgir	23
Wilford, Francis, distinguished himself by his essay on the Comparative Geography of India	li
Wilkins, Charles, translated several Inscriptions	ib.
Wilson, Horace Hayman. A short account of his literary career	v
Wilson's "Ariana Antiqua"	ib.
—— "Hindu Theatre"	ib.
Y	
Yojana considered by Hwen Thsang as 40 Chinese li	270
Yudhisthira. Pots demanded from Duryodhan by —	135
—— Date of occupation of Indraprastha by —	ib.
—— celebrated the Hom at Nagambhot Ghát	136
Z	
Zama Masjid. An account of the —	225
Zibun-nissa. The tomb of — outside the city of Delhi	230
Zinat Masjid. An account of the —	225
—— commonly called Kumri Masjid	230

www.ingramcontent.com/pod-product-compliance
Lightning Source LLC
Chambersburg PA
CBHW031946290426
44108CB00011B/697